Dale and Appelbe's Pharmacy and Medicines Law, 10th edition

Edited by Gordon E Appelbe and Joy Wingfield, 2013. ISBN 978 0 85369 989 7

Erratum

On the following page numbers page cross-references listed as '000' should have been replaced as follows:

Page numbers with '000'	Replacement cross-references
p. 90	see p. 112
p. 224	p. 226, see p. 226 in empty columns
p. 240	All references '000' to be replaced with '222'
p. 242	All references '000' to be replaced with '238'
p. 474	see p. 256
p. 478	see pages 251 and 255–258
p. 479	see p. 251
p. 481	see p. 256
p. 482	see p. 256

Pharmaceutical Press would like to apologise for these errors.

Dale and Appelbe's
Pharmacy and Medicines Law

Dale and Appelbe's Pharmacy and Medicines Law

TENTH EDITION

Edited by

Gordon E Appelbe   LL B, PhD, MSc, BSc(Pharm), BA, FRPharmS,
Hon MPS(Aus), FCPP, FCPP (Hons)
Independent Pharmaceutical and Legal Consultant, London, UK

Joy Wingfield   LL M, MPhil, BPharm, FRPharmS, Dip Ag Vet Pharm, FCPP
Honorary Professor of Pharmacy Law and Ethics, University of Nottingham, UK

Pharmaceutical Press

Published by the Pharmaceutical Press

1 Lambeth High Street, London SE1 7JN, UK

© Pharmaceutical Press 2013

 is a trade mark of Pharmaceutical Press

Pharmaceutical Press is the publishing division of the Royal Pharmaceutical Society

First published 1976
Second edition 1979
Third edition 1983
Fourth edition 1989
Fifth edition 1993
Sixth edition 1997
Seventh edition 2001
Eighth edition 2005
Ninth edition 2009

Typeset by Laserwords Private Limited, Chennai, India
Printed in Great Britain by TJ International, Padstow, Cornwall

ISBN 978 0 85369 989 7

A catalogue record for this book is available from the British Library.

Front cover image: © DNY 59/iStockphoto.com

Contents

Appendices 429

Preface to the Tenth Edition

This book again seeks to provide in one volume an outline of the law that affects the practice of pharmacy in Great Britain. The editors hope that the book will prove useful not only to pharmacy undergraduates, pre-registration students and pharmacists in all branches of the profession, but also to others in Britain and overseas who may need some knowledge of contemporary British law relating to medicines and poisons and pharmacy professional regulation. The wide scope means we have invited and incorporated new and revised material from well-known individuals in academia, professional and legal practice to bring the text up to date at the time of going to press (October 2012).

As ever, the period between the 9th and 10th editions has seen yet more changes in almost all the areas of law and regulation addressed by this book. Although all the chapters needed some revision, the principal changes are:

- consolidation and review of medicines regulations and re-enactment in a single consolidated form, the Human Medicines Regulations 2012;
- implementation of legislation to set up the General Pharmaceutical Council and discussion of its new powers regarding education, standard setting and fitness to practice procedures;
- ongoing implementation of law to secure a radically changed NHS operation in England, expected to be fully in place from April 2013.

The first of these changes came rather later than, and has not been as simple as, expected. We are grateful for some assistance from the Medicines and Healthcare products Regulatory Agency in identifying which Statutory Instruments have been repealed totally, which in part and which re-enacted within the consolidated regulations. However, we acknowledge some uncertainties which we had to accept to meet publication deadlines. We have slightly re-ordered the legislation concerning human medicines so that it appears in chapters 2–15 with the law on veterinary medicines in chapter 16.

The General Pharmaceutical Council is some 3 years into its work and we have sought fresh insight into its powers and operation from our new contributors to chapters 22 to 24. The NHS in England is on the brink of major reorganisation from April 2013 and new regulations for pharmaceutical services in the community are discussed in an almost completely revised chapter 26.

We decided to remove all the material relating to the regulatory powers of the former Royal Pharmaceutical Society of Great Britain. This means that chapter 22 concerns solely the powers of the General Pharmaceutical Council. However, the re-born Royal Pharmaceutical Society continues to provide a valuable and comprehensive support and leadership function for pharmacists and others and we have made reference to its resources, and those of other pharmacy bodies, where appropriate. We have dropped most of the fitness to practise (formerly disciplinary, formerly statutory committee) cases from chapter 24. The reasons were twofold. First, the types of case are now very different from those considered in previous decades and the cultural climate as to what is or is not appropriate behaviour has similarly changed considerably. Second, the sanctions available to the General Pharmaceutical Council, and their fitness to practise 'test' and decision-making processes, are significantly different from those of the former Royal Pharmaceutical Society of Great Britain and the precedent value of decisions in earlier cases has become rather tenuous.

The law is that of Great Britain except where otherwise stated in the text. The aim has been to state the law as concisely as accuracy permits, but it should be borne in mind that only the courts can give a legally binding decision on any question of interpretation. The responsibility for the text and any views expressed therein lies with the editors and authors.

It is right to mark that with this edition Dr Gordon Appelbe has relinquished his involvement in the text but has supported and encouraged me in the editing processes. Gordon has been a pioneer in devising and publishing this standard textbook since the first edition in 1976 and has spent more than three decades in this endeavour. I can only claim 20 years commencing my input in the 5th edition in 1993. We have retained and shall continue to retain the names of Dale and Appelbe for the foreseeable future.

With this edition too we have changed the name to *Pharmacy and Medicines Law* to reflect our focus principally on the law and regulation of pharmacy and medicines. The topic of ethics and professionalism warrants separate examination and one which is attempted in a sister publication, *Pharmacy Ethics and Decision Making*.

Finally, we could not have completed this edition without the insight and fresh approaches taken by our team of contributors. Some chapters needed only a little amendment; some have been rewritten. Some contributors had many chapters to cover; some only part of a chapter but all have been invaluable in refreshing and revitalising the contents. So please read our list of contributors – they represent a wealth of expertise and experience in the field of pharmacy law and regulation. Thanks also go to our publishers, in particular Kristina Oberle, Christina DeBono, Linda Paulus and Erasmis Kidd, for their forbearance in accommodating (again) an uncertain legislative programme that takes no account of publication dates!

Joy Wingfield
Gordon E Appelbe
November 2012

Foreword

The practice of pharmacy is changing at a fast pace, making a contribution to health and wellbeing that goes far beyond dispensing medicines on prescription.

And there have been some key changes in pharmacy since the last edition of *Pharmacy and Medicines Law*, not the least of which is the creation of the independent pharmacy regulator for Great Britain, the General Pharmaceutical Council. We are committed to fair and proportionate regulation and an approach which focuses on what is being achieved with and for patients.

From day one, the General Pharmaceutical Council has made clear its belief that professionalism offers the best protection for the public, and that a key part of our role is to support and encourage professionalism and professional practice. This approach to regulation has important implications. It is as much as anything about empowering professionals to practise and behave as such. This should be, and is for many in pharmacy, an exciting and motivating prospect. It is a regulatory approach which respects and acknowledges the expertise and contribution of pharmacists and pharmacy technicians, and the bodies which represent and lead them. It is a way of regulating which purposefully seeks to enable pharmacy, and pharmacy professionals themselves, to maximise the health benefits they can offer to the individuals and communities they serve.

Alongside that professional empowerment agenda goes a clear set of expectations about professional accountability. This is not about blame. It is about expecting pharmacy professionals to be willing and able to give an account of the decisions they have made as they engage with their professional responsibilities.

Having access to and making good use of information and guidance about ethical and legal norms affecting someone's practice is a key aspect of modern professionalism, for which authoritative reference sources such as *Pharmacy and Medicines Law* provide essential underpinning.

Duncan Rudkin
Chief Executive and Registrar
General Pharmaceutical Council
February 2013

About the contributors

Editors

Joy Wingfield, LL M, MPhil, BPharm, FRPharmS, DipAgVetPharm, FCPP, is Honorary Professor of Pharmacy Law and Ethics at the University of Nottingham and an independent pharmacy practice consultant. She qualified as a pharmacist in 1971 and then worked for 5 years in community pharmacy. She joined the staff of the Pharmaceutical Society in 1976 as an inspector under the Pharmacy Acts. From 1986 to 1991, she was the senior administrator in, and later head of, the Ethics Division in the Law Department, responsible for professional and registration matters. This was followed by 9 years as the assistant pharmacy superintendent for Boots before moving into academia.

Gordon E Appelbe, LL B, PhD, MSc, BSc(Pharm), BA, FRPharmS, Hon MPS (Aus), FCPP, FPP (Hons), is a former independent pharmaceutical/legal consultant. He qualified as a pharmacist in 1956 and then worked for 9 years in community pharmacy. He joined the staff of the Pharmaceutical Society in 1965, first as an inspector under the Pharmacy Acts and then, in 1971, as secretary to the Statutory Committee. He was appointed Deputy Head of the Law Department in 1974 and was Head of the Law Department and Chief Inspector from 1978 to 1991.

Contributors

Sarah M E Cockbill, PhD, LL M, BPharm, MPharm, DipAgVetPharm, MIPharmM, FCPP, FRPharmS
Lecturer, Cardiff School of Pharmacy & Pharmaceutical Sciences

Cathal Gallagher, MA, LL M, PhD, BSc(Pharm)
Principal Lecturer, Department of Pharmacy, University of Hertfordshire

Gordon Hockey, BSc MRPharmS
Pharmacist and Barrister, Head of Legal Services / Registrar, Royal College of Veterinary Surgeons

Dai John, BPharm LL M, PhD, FHEA, FRPharmS
   Reader in Pharmacy Education and Practice, Cardiff University

Thomas H John, BPharm (Lond.) LL B MRPharmS
   Barrister-at-Law (called 1997 by the Honourable Society of the Middle Temple)
   Head, Goresbrook Chambers, Essex and self-employed barrister in independent practice

Stephen Lutener, LL B, FRPharmS
   Head of Regulation, Pharmaceutical Services Negotiating Committee

Edward Mallinson, LL M, MPharm, FRPharmS, Hon MFPH, FRSPH
   Retired Consultant in Pharmaceutical Public Health

Susan Melvin, LL M, BSc, MRPharmS
   Inspector of the General Pharmaceutical Council

Karen Pitchford, BSc(Hons), PGDip, MRPharmS
   Principal Lecturer in Pharmacy Practice, De Montfort University

David H Reissner, LL B(Hons)
   Solicitor of the Senior Courts, Partner, Head of Healthcare at Charles Russell LLP

Introduction

Development of the law in relation to pharmacy, medicines and poisons

Before the middle of the 19th century, there were no legal restrictions in England on the sale of poisons or drugs, and anyone could describe themselves as a pharmaceutical chemist. Statutory control over sales was first applied to arsenic because, as the preamble to the Arsenic Act 1851 stated, the unrestricted sale of arsenic facilitates the commission of crime. The first statute relating to pharmacy followed the next year. The Pharmacy Act 1852 confirmed the charter of incorporation of the Pharmaceutical Society of Great Britain, which had been granted in 1843. The 1852 Act established the framework of the Society and gave it power to hold examinations and to issue certificates. It also restricted the use of the title pharmaceutical chemist to members of the Society, although it did not restrict the use of the titles chemist or druggist. The Society received its Royal prefix in 1988. In 2010, the Society was wound up to be replaced by two bodies: the regulator, the General Pharmaceutical Council, and a new professional leadership body, the Royal Pharmaceutical Society. This book focuses only on the first of these bodies.

The Pharmacy Act 1868 brought new developments. It introduced a Poisons List (with 15 entries) and empowered the Society to add other substances to it, subject to the approval of the Privy Council. A poison was defined as any substance included in the Poisons List. Articles and preparations containing poisons could be sold by retail only by pharmaceutical chemists or by a new legal class of chemists and druggists. Both titles were protected by the Act. The class of chemists and druggists comprised (a) all those who before the passing of the Act had been engaged in the keeping of open shop for the compounding of the prescriptions of duly qualified medical practitioners, and (b) all those persons who had been registered as assistants under the provisions of the Pharmacy Act 1852.

The Registrar of the Society was thereafter required to keep registers of pharmaceutical chemists, of chemists and druggists, and of apprentices or students. The qualification of chemist and druggist (the Minor examination) became the statutory minimum for persons carrying on a business comprising the sale of poisons. Chemists and druggists were eligible to be elected members or associates of the Pharmaceutical Society but did not have all the privileges of a member who had qualified as a pharmaceutical chemist (by passing the Major examination). That state of affairs continued – slightly modified by a statute of 1898 – until the Pharmacy Act 1953 combined the two qualifications in one Register of Pharmaceutical Chemists. The profession of pharmacy was now regulated by the Pharmacy Act 1954, which absorbed the 1953 Act. The 1954 Act was subsequently repealed by a section 60 Order under the Health Act 1999, which paved the way for specific legislation establishing the General Pharmaceutical Council.

The 1868 Act not only introduced the first list of poisons but also regulated the manner in which they could be sold, specifying more stringent restrictions on sale for the more dangerous poisons. Fixed penalties, recoverable in the civil courts, were prescribed for breaches of the Act. The list of poisons was extended by the Poisons and Pharmacy Act 1908, which also stipulated that poisons for agricultural and horticultural purposes could be sold by licensed dealers as well as by pharmacists. This Act also prescribed conditions under which corporate bodies could carry on the business of a chemist and druggist. This had become necessary because it had been held in the High Court in 1880 that an incorporated company was not covered by the word person as used in the 1868 Act and was, therefore, not liable for penalties under the Act (*Pharmaceutical Society v London and Provincial Supply Association Ltd*, see earlier editions of this book).

Under the Pharmacy and Poisons Act 1933, a Poisons Board was established to advise the Secretary of State on what should be included in the Poisons List. Poisons in Part I of the list could be sold by retail only at pharmacies; poisons in Part II could be sold also by traders on a local authority list. Poisons were further classified by means of the Schedules to the Poisons Rules made under the Act. Schedule 4, for example, comprised a class of poisons which could be supplied to the public only on the authority of a prescription written by a practitioner. A Register of Premises was set up under the Act, and all registered pharmacists were required to be members of the Pharmaceutical Society.

One of the main features of the 1933 Act was the establishment of a disciplinary body (the Statutory Committee), which had authority not only over pharmacists who committed misconduct but also over pharmacists and corporate bodies convicted of offences under the Pharmacy Act. The Society was placed under a duty to enforce the Act and was authorised to appoint inspectors for the purpose. Proceedings under the Act were to be taken in courts of summary jurisdiction and not, as previously, in the civil courts. The Pharmacy and Poisons Act 1933 was repealed by the Medicines Act

1968. The Poisons Act 1972 dealt only with non-medicinal poisons. The Statutory Committee and its cases was replaced by a Disciplinary Committee in 2007 and then by the current Fitness to Practise processes of the General Pharmaceutical Council in 2010.

Pharmacy and poisons were firmly linked together by statute, but the sale and manufacture of medicines was not regulated in any way except for medicines containing poisons. Some control over quality was provided by a series of Food and Drugs Acts, culminating in the Food and Drugs Act 1955. Under those Acts, it was an offence to sell adulterated drugs, or to sell, to the prejudice of the purchaser, any drug not of the nature, substance or quality demanded. The effectiveness of those provisions was limited by the fact that most drugs were of vegetable origin and there were no precise standards for many of them. Furthermore, a manufacturer of a proprietary medicine did not have to disclose its composition, provided that s/he paid the appropriate duty by way of fixing the appropriate excise stamps to each bottle or packet as required by the Medicine Stamp Acts. That state of affairs was changed by the Pharmacy and Medicines Act 1941, which abolished medicines stamp duty and required, instead, a disclosure of composition of each container. It also restricted the sale of medicines to shops (as distinct from market stalls etc.) and made it unlawful to advertise any article for the treatment of eight named diseases, including diabetes, epilepsy and tuberculosis. This was the first statute in which pharmacy and medicines were directly linked. The 1941 Act, however, did not apply to animal medicines.

The Therapeutic Substances Act 1925 controlled by licence the manufacture (but not the sale or supply) of a limited number of products the purity or potency of which could not be tested by chemical means, for example vaccines, sera, toxins, antitoxins and certain other substances. The list was greatly extended when antibiotics came into use. It had not been held necessary to restrict the retail sale or supply of vaccines, sera and antitoxins, but penicillin and most other antibiotics were found to be substances which were capable of causing danger to the health of the community if used without proper safeguards. Consequently, the Penicillin Act 1947 and the Therapeutic Substances (Prevention of Misuse) Act 1953 permitted the supply of antibiotics to the public only by practitioners, or from pharmacies on the authority of practitioners' prescriptions. The Therapeutic Substances Act 1956 replaced the earlier Acts, so bringing under the control of one statute both the manufacture and the supply of therapeutic substances. It could be regarded as the precursor to the Medicines Act 1968, which replaced it.

Legislation relating to medicines developed in a piecemeal manner, each problem being dealt with as it arose, and the law was scattered throughout a number of statutes. However, rapid developments in pharmaceutical research after the Second World War made available an increasing number of potent substances for use in medicine, and a working party was set up by the government in 1959 to examine the need for new controls. The thalidomide tragedy in 1961 almost certainly precipitated proposals for new legislation, which was published in 1967 in a White Paper entitled Forthcoming Legislation on the Safety, Quality and Description of Drugs and Medicines (Cmnd.3395). The Medicines Act 1968, which was designed to replace all earlier legislation relating to medicines, was based on the proposals in the White Paper.

European Community legislation has had, and still has, a large impact on UK law. The Treaty of Rome and the issue of regulations, directives, decisions and recommendations by the Council of Ministers in Brussels has led to amendments of pharmacy and medicines law in Great Britain, particularly with regard to the mutual recognition of pharmaceutical qualifications and the manufacture and distribution of medicines. In 2005, veterinary (animal) medicines were removed from the 1968 Medicines Act and consolidated under the European Communities Act 1972, with a view to annual updating. By 2012, the need to maintain compliance with European directives precipitated a consolidation and review of all the human medicines (but not pharmacy) regulations issued under the Medicines Act and to issue a single consolidated set of regulations, again under the European Communities Act 1972. The Medicines Act 1968 currently still contains the substantive provisions covering registered pharmacy businesses.

International agreement about the control of narcotics began with the International Opium Convention signed at The Hague in 1912, although the Convention was not implemented until after the First World War. A series of Dangerous Drugs Acts, beginning with the Dangerous Drugs Act 1920, brought the various international agreements into force in Great Britain. The Single Convention on Narcotic Drugs 1961 replaced all the earlier international agreements and was reflected in the Dangerous Drugs Act 1965.

The misuse of amphetamines and other psychotropic drugs widened the problems of abuse, and an International Convention on Psychotropic Substances was signed in 1971. In Great Britain, however, the Drugs (Prevention of Misuse) Act 1964 had provided a measure of control by making the unlawful possession of amphetamines, and certain other drugs, an offence. As problems of drug abuse continued to increase, the law was extended and recast in the Misuse of Drugs Act 1971, which repealed the various Dangerous Drugs Acts and the 1964 Act. The provisions of the 1971 Act and a series of regulations continue to apply to all aspects of dealings in Controlled Drugs.

The National Health Service Act 1946 and the National Health Service (Scotland) Act 1947 provided for a comprehensive health service across Great Britain, including the provision of pharmaceutical services. By 1999, both Scotland and Wales secured devolution of power in matters of health, and their legislation, organisation and practice within the NHS now differs considerably from that of England. Also in 1991, Crown immunity was removed from NHS services provided in hospitals and elsewhere such that medicines licensing legislation applies equally to services within the managed sector and the private sector (however, supply of medicines within hospitals remains exempted from the legislation).

List of legislation

European law

Reference	Title	Chapter
65/65/EEC	Directive on the approximation of provisions laid down by Law, Regulation or Administrative Action relating to proprietary medicinal products (now superseded)	2
78/25/EEC	Directive on the colouring matters which may be added to medicinal products	1
85/432/EEC	Directive concerning the coordination of provisions laid down by Law, Regulation or Administrative Action in respect of certain activities in the field of pharmacy	1
85/433/EEC	Directive concerning the mutual recognition of diplomas, certificates and other evidence of formal qualifications in pharmacy, including measures to facilitate the effective exercise of the right of establishment relating to certain activities in the field of pharmacy	1
89/105/EEC	Directive relating to the transparency of measures regulating the pricing of medicinal products for human use and their inclusion in the scope of national health insurance systems	26
90/2377/EEC	Regulation laying down a Community procedure for the establishment of maximum residue limits of veterinary medicinal products in foodstuffs of animal origin	1
90/3677/EEC	Regulation laying down measures to be taken to discourage the diversion of certain substances to the illicit manufacture of narcotic drugs and psychotropic substances	1, 17
91/412/EEC	Directive laying down the principles and guidelines of good manufacturing practice for veterinary medicinal products	1

Reference	Title	Chapter
92/29/EEC	Directive on the minimum safety and health requirements for improved medical treatment on board vessels	21
92/74/EEC	Directive laying down additional provisions on homoeopathic veterinary medicinal products	1
92/109/EEC	Directive on the manufacture and the placing on the market of certain substances used in the illicit manufacture of narcotic drugs and psychotropic substances	1
2309/93/EEC	Regulation laying down Community procedures for the authorization and supervision of medicinal products for human and veterinary use and establishing a European Agency for the Evaluation of Medicinal Products	1
93/41/EEC	Directive on the approximation of national measures relating to the placing on the market of high- technology medicinal products, particularly those derived from biotechnology	1
95/46/EEC	Directive on the protection of individuals with regard to the processing of personal data and on the free movement of such data	1
2001/20/EC	Directive on the approximation of the laws, regulations and administrative provisions of the Member States relating to the implementation of good clinical practice in the conduct of clinical trials on medicinal products for human use	1
2001/82/EC	Directive on the Community code relating to veterinary medicinal products	1, 16
2001/83/EC	Directive on the Community code relating to medicinal products for human use	1, 3
2003/63/EC	Directive amending Directive 2001/83/EC on the Community code relating to medicinal products for human use	1
2003/94/EC	Directive laying down the principles and guidelines of good manufacturing practice in respect of medicinal products for human use and investigational medicinal products for human use (includes labelling and good manufacturing practice)	1
EC/727/2004	Directive amending Directive 2001/82/EC on the Community code relating to veterinary medicinal products	1
2004/24/EC	Directive amending, as regards traditional herbal medicinal products, Directive 2001/83/EC on the Community code relating to medicinal products for human use	1, 14
2004/28/EC	Directive amending Directive 2001/82/EC on the Community code relating to veterinary medicinal products	1, 16

Reference	Title	Chapter
2004/27/EC	Directive amending Directive 2001/83/EC on the Community code relating to medicinal products for human use	1, 2
2004/726/EC	Regulation laying down Community procedures for the authorisation and supervision of medicinal products for human and veterinary use and establishing a European Medicines Agency	1, 3, 16
2005/36/EC	Directive on the recognition of professional qualifications	1, 22
EC/2008/689	Regulation concerning the export and import of dangerous chemicals	20
EU/1272/2008	Regulation on classification, labelling and packaging of substances and mixtures, amending and repealing Directives 67/548/EEC and 1999/45/EC, and amending Regulation (EC) 1907/2006	18, 20
2010/32/EU	Directive implementing the Framework Agreement on prevention from sharp injuries in the hospital and healthcare sector concluded by HOSPEEM (European Hospital and Healthcare Employers Association) and EPSU (European Public Services Union)	21
2011/62/EU	Directive amending Directive 2001/83/EC on the Community code relating to medicinal products for human use, as regards the prevention of the entry into the legal supply chain of falsified medicinal products	3

UK law

Laws	Statutory Instruments	Chapter
Access to Health Records Act 1990		21, 26
AIDS (Control) Act 1987 (repealed)		26
Alcoholic Liquor Duties Act 1979 and Customs and Excise Management Act 1979		19
	SI 2005 No. 1524 Denatured Alcohol Regulations 2005	19
Animal (Cruel Poisons) Act 1962		21
	SI 1963 No. 1278 Animal (Cruel Poisons) Regulations 1963	21

Laws	Statutory Instruments	Chapter
Animal (Scientific Procedures) Act 1986		21
Bribery Act 2010		21
Business Names Act 1985		21
Care Homes Registration (Scotland) Act 1938		17
Care Standards Act 2000		9
	SI 2008 No. 1976 Private Dentistry (Wales) Regulations 2008	9
Children Act 2004		26
Chiropractors Act 1994		3
Companies Act 2006		26
Competition Act 1998		21
Computer Misuse Act 1990		26
Consumer Protection Act 1987		21
Corporate Manslaughter and Corporate Homicide Act 2007		26
Criminal Justice Act 2003		21
Data Protection Act 1998		21, 26
	SI 2000 No. 191 Data Protection (Subject Access) (Fees and Miscellaneous Provisions) Regulations 2000	21
	SI 2000 No. 413 Data Protection (Subject Access Modification) (Health) Order 2000	21
	SI 2000 No. 417 Data Protection (Processing of Sensitive Personal data) Order 2000	21
Dentists Act 1984		3, 25
	SI 2006 No. 1440 General Dental Council (Professions Complementary to Dentistry) Regulations Order of Council 2006	25

Laws	Statutory Instruments	Chapter
	SI 2000 No. 1059 Ionising Radiation (Medical Exposure) Regulations 2000	8
	SI 2000 No. 2381 Chemicals (Hazard Information and Packaging for Supply (Amendment) Regulations 2000	20
	SI 2002 No. 236 Medicines (Codification Amendments, Etc.) Regulations 2002 (repealed)	3
	SI 2002 No. 618 Medical Devices Regulations 2002	2
	SI 2002 No. 2677 Control of Substances Hazardous to Health Regulations 2002	20
	SI 2003 No. 697 Medical Devices (Amendment) Regulations 2003	2
	SI 2003 No. 2426 Privacy and Electronic Communications (EC Directive) Regulations 2003	21
	SI 2003 No. 3148 European Qualifications (Health Care Professions) Regulations 2003	25
	SI 2004 No. 1031 Medicines for Human Use (Clinical Trials) Regulations 2004	3
	SI 2004 No. 1947 European Qualifications (Health and Social Care Professions and Accession of New Member States) Regulations 2004	25
	SI 2005 No. 2754 Medicines (Advisory Bodies) (No. 2) Regulations 2005 (partly consolidated in HMRs, remaining provisions amend SI 2004 No. 1031	3
	SI 2005 No. 2759 Medicines (Marketing Authorisations, etc.) (Amendments) Regulations 2005 (repealed)	3
	SI 2006 No. 1928 Medicines for Human Use (Clinical Trials) Amendment Regulations 2006	3
	SI 2007 No. 400 Medical Devices (Amendment) Regulations 2007	2
	SI 2007 No. 3101 European Qualifications (Health and Social Care Professions) Regulations 2007	25

Laws	Statutory Instruments	Chapter
	SI 2008 No. 296 Controlled Drugs (Drug Precursors) (Community External Trade) Regulations 2008	17
	SI 2008 No. 2852 REACH Enforcement Regulations 2008	20
	SI 2008 No. 2936 Medical Devices (Amendment) Regulations 2008	2
	SI 2009 No. 716 Chemicals (Hazard Information and Packaging for Supply) Regulations 2009	18
	SI 2010 No. 2785 Medicines for Human Use (Prescribing by EEA Practitioners) (Amendment) (No. 2) Regulations 2010	17
	SI 2011 No. 2159 Veterinary Medicines Regulations 2011 (VMRs)	16, 18
	SI 2012 No. 1426 Medical Devices (Amendment) Regulations 2012	2
	SI 2012 No. 1916 Human Medicines Regulations 2012 (HMRs)	2-18
Fair Trading Act 1973		16
	SI 2005 No. 2751 Supply of Relevant Medicinal Products Order 2005	16
Freedom of Information Act 2000		21, 26
Food and Drugs (Scotland) Act 1956		17
Food Safety Act 1990		18
	SI 2002 No. 254 Health and Social Work Professions Order 2002	3
Health Act 1999		25
	SI 2005 No. 2011 Dentists Act 1984 (Amendment) Order 2005	25
	SI 2008 No. 1774 Health Care and Associated Professions (Miscellaneous Amendments) Order 2008	25

Laws	Statutory Instruments	Chapter
Health Act 2006		5, 26
	SI 2006 No. 3148 Controlled Drugs (Supervision of Management and Use) Regulations 2006	17
Health Act 2009		26
Health and Safety at Work, etc. Act 1974		21, 26
Health and Social Care Act 2001		26
Health and Social Care (Community Health and Standards) Act 2003 (England and Wales)		26
	SI 2009 No. 309 Local Authority Social Services and NHS Complaints (England) Regulations 2009	26
Health and Social Care Act 2008		25, 26
	SI 2012 No. 1640 The CQC (Healthwatch England Committee) Regulations 2012	26
Health and Social Care Act 2012		25, 26
	SI 2012 No. 1319 Health and Social Care Act (Commencement No. 1 and Transitory Provision) Order 2012	26
	SI 2012 No. 1631 NHS (Clinical Commissioning Groups) Regulations 2012 (and NHS Act 2006)	26
Human Rights Act 1998		1, 26
Limited Liability Partnership Act 2000		21
Limited Partnerships Act 1907		21
Local Government and Public Involvement in Health Act 2007		26
Local Government etc. (Scotland) Act 1994		18
Lunacy Regulation (Ireland) Act 1871		5
Medical Act 1983		8, 25
	SI 2002 No. 3135 Medical Act 1983 (Amendment) Order 2002	25

Laws	Statutory Instruments	Chapter
	SI 2004 No. 2608 General Medical Council (Fitness to Practise) Rules 2004	25
	SI 2004 No. 2611 General Medical Council (Constitution of Panels and Investigation Committee) Rules Order of Council 2004	25
	SI 2005 No. No. 402 General Medical Council (Constitution of Panels and Investigation Committee) (Amendment) Rules Order of Council 2005	25
	SI 2006 No. 1914 Medical Act (Amendment) and Miscellaneous Amendments Order 2006	25
	SI 2008 No 2554 General Medical Council (Constitution) Order 2008	25
	SI 2008 No. 3131 Medical Profession (Miscellaneous Amendments) Order 2008	25
	SI 2009 No. 2739 The General Medical Council (Licence to Practise) Regulations Order of Council 2009	8, 25
	SI 2009 No. 2751 General Medical Council (Constitution of Panels and Investigation Committee) (Amendment) Rules Order of Council 2009	25
	SI 2010 No. 2 General Medical Council (Form and Content of Registers) Regulations 2010	25
	SI 2010 No. 234 General and Specialist Medical Practice (Education, Training and Qualifications) Order 2010	25
	SI 2010 No. 344 Postgraduate Medical Education and Training (Amendment) Order of Council 2010	25
	SI 2010 No. 474 General Medical Council (Constitution of Panels and Investigation Committee) (Amendment) Rules Order of Council 2010	25
	SI 2010 No. 476 General Medical Council (Registration Appeals Panels Procedure) Rules Order of Council 2010	25
	SI 2012 No. 473 Postgraduate Medical Education and Training (Amendment) Order of Council 2012	25

Laws	Statutory Instruments	Chapter
Medicines Act 1968		2, 5
	SI 1971 No. 1445 Medicines (Retail Pharmacists – Exemptions from Licensing Requirements) Order 1971 (repealed)	3
	SI 1977 No. 670 Medicines (Bal Jivan Chamcho Prohibition) (No. 2) Order 1977	13
	SI 1978 No. 1008 Medicines (Administration of Radioactive Substances) Regulations 1978	8
	SI 1979 No. 382 Medicines (Chloroform Prohibition) Order 1979	13
	SI 1980 No. 1923 Medicines (Sale or Supply) (Miscellaneous Provisions) Regulations 1980 (repealed)	7
	SI 1980 No. 1924 Medicines (Pharmacy and General Sale) (Exemptions) Order 1980 (repealed)	9
	SI 1984 No. 769 Medicines (Products other than Veterinary Drugs) (General Sale List) Order 1984 (repealed)	7
	SI 1993 No. 832 Medicines (Applications for Manufacturer's and Wholesale Dealer's Licences) Amendment Regulations 1993 (repealed)	3
	SI 1997 No. 1830 Prescription Only (Human Medicines) Order 1997 as amended up to 2006 and repealed in part by the HMRs 2012 (Art.s 5 and 10 and Schs. 1 and 2 remain)	6, 8
	SI 2001 No. 1841 Medicines (Aristolochia and Mu Tong, Etc.) (Prohibition) Order 2001	12
	SI 2002 No. 933 Medicines (Products other than Veterinary Drugs) (General Sale List) Amendment Order 2002 (repealed)	7
	SI 2002 No. 3170 Medicines for Human Use (Kava Kava) (Prohibition) Order 2002	13
	SI 2004 No. 2779 Medicines (Vaccination against Foot and Mouth Disease) Order 2004	9
	SI 2005 No. 765 Medicines for Human Use (Prescribing) Order 2005 (repealed)	3

Laws	Statutory Instruments	Chapter
	SI 2005 No. 2750 Medicines (Traditional Herbal Medicinal Products for Human Use) Regulations 2005 (part consolidated in HMRs, remaining provisions amended SI 2004 No. 1031)	12
	SI 2005 No. 2791 Herbal Medicines Advisory Committee Order 2005 (repealed)	12
	SI 2008 No. 548 Medicines for Human Use (Prohibition) (Senecio and Miscellaneous Amendments) Order 2008	12
	SI 2008 No. 2789 Medicines (Pharmacies) (Responsible Pharmacist) Regulations 2008	5
	SI 2011 No. 2647 Medicines Act (Pharmacy) Order 2011	5
Mental Health Act 1959		5, 17
Mental Health (Scotland) Act 1960		17
Mental Health Act 2007		26
Merchant Shipping Act 1979		21
	SI 1995 No. 1802 Merchant Shipping and Fishing Vessels ((Medical Stores) Regulations 1995	21
Misuse of Drugs Act 1971		8, 17
	SI 1973 No. 798 Misuse of Drugs (Safe Custody) Regulations 1973	17
	SI 1974 No. 85 Misuse of Drugs Tribunal (England and Wales) Rules 1974	17
	SI 1997 No. 1001 Misuse of Drugs (Supply to Addicts) Regulations 1997	17
	SI 2001 No 3998 The Misuse of Drugs Regulations 2001(as amended)	8, 9
	SR 2002 No. 1 The Misuse of Drugs Regulations (Northern Ireland) 2002 (as amended)	8, 9
	SI 2003 No. 1653 Misuse of Drugs (Amendment) (No. 2) Regulations 2003	17
	SI 2005. No. 271 Misuse of Drugs (Amendment) Regulations 2005	17

Laws	Statutory Instruments	Chapter
	SI 2005 No. 2864 Misuse of Drugs and Misuse of Drugs (Supply to Addicts) (Amendment) Regulations 2005	17
	SI 2006 No. 1450 Misuse of Drugs (Amendment No. 2) Regulations 2006	17
	SI 2007 No. 2154 Misuse of Drugs and Misuse of Drugs (Safe Custody) (Amendment) Regulations 2007	17
	SI 2010 No. 2497 Misuse of Drugs (Licence Fees) Regulations 2010 (as amended)	17
	SI 2012 No. 973 Misuse of Drugs (Amendment No. 2) (England, Wales and Scotland) Regulations 2012	17
NHS Act 1946		26
NHS (Scotland) Act 1947		26
NHS Reorganisation Act 1973		26
NHS Act 1977		26
	SI 2004 No. 629 NHS (General Medical Services Contracts)(Prescription of Drugs) Regulations 2004	26
	SI 2005 No. 641 NHS (Pharmaceutical Services) Regulations 2005	26
	NHS (Scotland) Act 1978	26
	SI 2004 No. 38 NHS (Tribunal) (Scotland) Regulations 2004	26
	SI 2004 No. 115 NHS (General Medical Services Contracts)(Scotland) Regulations 2004	8
	SI 2009 No. 183 NHS (Pharmaceutical Services) (Scotland) Regulations 2009	26
	SI 2009 No. 209 NHS (Pharmaceutical Services) (Scotland) Amendment Regulations 2009	26
	SI 2011 No. 32 NHS (Pharmaceutical Services) (Scotland) Amendment Regulations 2011	26

Laws	Statutory Instruments	Chapter
	NHS and Community Care Act 1990	26
	SI 1990 No. 2160 NHS Trusts (Membership and Procedures) Regulations 1990	26
NHS Reform and Health Care Professions Act 2002		26
NHS Reform (Scotland) Act 2004		26
NHS Act 2006		24, 26
	SI 2007 No. 1320 Health Service Medicines (Information Relating to Sales of Branded Medicines, etc.) Regulations 2007	26
	SI 2008 No. 1938 Health Service Branded Medicines (Control of Prices and Supply of Information) Regulations 2008	26
	SI 2008 No. 3258 Health Service Branded Medicines (Control of Prices and Supply of Information) (No. 2) Regulations 2008	26
	SI 2010 No. 914 NHS (Pharmaceutical Services and Local Pharmaceutical Services) (Amendment) Regulations 2010	26
	SI 2011 No. 2237 NHS Commissioning Board Authority (Establishment and Constitution) Order 2011	26
	SI 2011 No. 2250 NHS Commissioning Board Authority Regulations 2011	26
	SI 2012 No. 1273 Health Education England (Establishment and Constitution) Order 2012	26
	SI 2012 No. 1399 NHS (Pharmaceutical Services) Amendment Regulations 2012	24
	SI 2012 No. 1909 NHS (Pharmaceutical Services) Regulations 2012	26
NHS (Wales) Act 2006		26
	SI 2009 No. 778 (W66) Local Health Boards (Establishment and Dissolution) (Wales) Order 2009	26

Laws	Statutory Instruments	Chapter
	SI 2009 No. 779 (W67) Local Health Boards (Constitution, Membership and Procedures) (Wales) Regulations 2009	26
	SI 2009 No. 1511 (W147) Local Health Boards (Directed Functions) (Wales) Regulations 2009	26
National Health Service Reform and Health Care Professions Act 2002		24, 25
Northern Ireland	SI 1972 No. 1265 Health and Personal Services (Northern Ireland) Order 1972	8
Northern Ireland	SR 2004 No. 140 Health and Personal Social Services (General Medical Services Contracts) (Northern Ireland) Regulations 2004	8
Nurses, Midwives and Health Visitors Act 1997		17
Pollution Prevention and Control Act 1999		21
	SI 2010 No. 675 Environmental Permitting (England and Wales) Regulations 2010	21
Poisons Act 1972		18
	SI 1982 No. 217 Poisons List Order 1982	18
	SI 1982 No. 218 Poisons Rules 1982	18
	SI 1992 No. 2293 Poisons (Amendment) Rules 1992	18
	SI 2009 No. 1077 Poisons Rules (Amendment) Order 2009	18
Prevention of Damage by Rabbits Act 1939		21
Protection of Animals Act 1911		21
Protection of Animals (Amendment) Act 1927		21
Protection of Freedoms Act 2012		21
Public Health Act 1936		17

Laws	Statutory Instruments	Chapter
Opticians Act 1989		9
Osteopaths Act 1993		3
	SI 2010 No. 231 Pharmacy Order 2010	3, 18, 22–25
	SI 2010 No. 299 Pharmacy Order (Commencement No. 1) Order of Council 2010	22, 24
	SI 2010 No. 300 General Pharmaceutical Council (Constitution) Order 2010	22
	SI 2010 No. 1367 General Pharmaceutical Council (Continuing Professional Development and Consequential Amendments) Order of Council 2010	22
	SI 2010 No. 1614 General Pharmaceutical Council (Appeals Committee Rules) Order of Council 2010	22, 24
	SI 2010 No. 1615 General Pharmaceutical Council (Fitness to Practise and Disqualification, Etc. Rules) Order of Council 2010	22, 24
	SI 2010 No. 1616 General Pharmaceutical Council (Statutory Committees and their Advisers Rules) Order of Council 2010	24
	SI 2010 No. 1618 General Pharmaceutical Council (Transfer of Property, Rights and Liabilities, Fees and Grants) Order of Council 2010	22
	SI 2010 No. 1619 The Pharmacy Order (Registration – Transitional Provisions) Order of Council 2010	22
	SI 2010 No. 1620 Pharmacy Order 2010 (Approved European Pharmacy Qualifications) Order 2010 (also under EC Act 1972)	22
	SI 2010 No. 1621 Pharmacy Order (Commencement No. 2) Order of Council 2010	22
	SI 2010 No. 1617 General Pharmaceutical Council (Registration Rules) Order of Council 2010 (also made under Medicines Act powers)	5, 22
Race Relations Act 1976		26

Laws	Statutory Instruments	Chapter
Regulatory Reform Act 2001		19
	SI 2004 No. 470 Regulatory Reform (Sunday Trading) Order 2004	19
Rehabilitation of Offenders Act 1974		24
	SI 1975 No. 1023 Rehabilitation of Offenders Act 1974 (Exceptions) Order 1975	24
Safeguarding Vulnerable Groups Act 2006		24
Social Work (Scotland) Act 1968		17
Trades Descriptions Act 1985		21
Tribunals Courts and Enforcement Act 2007		26
	SI 2010 No. 22 The Transfer of Tribunal Functions Order 2010	26
Veterinary Surgeons Act 1966		25
	SI 2010 No. 2854 Veterinary Surgeons and Veterinary Practitioners (Registration) Order of Council 2010	25
Weights and Measures Act 1985		21
Wildlife and Countryside Act 1981		21

Cases

Cases before the European Court of Justice

Case 322/01 *Deutscher Apothekerverband EV v 0800 DOCMORRIS NV and Jacques Waterval* (2003) ECJ 11/12/2003 (chapter 1)
Officier van Justitie v de Pejper [1976] ECR 613 (chapter 3)
R v Medicines Control Agency Ex p. Rhone Poulenc Rorer Ltd (C94/98) All ER (EC) 46 (chapter 3)
Upjohn 1989 C – 122/5 (chapter 2)

Cases before national courts and authorities, United Kingdom

Abullah v General Medical Council [2012] EWHC 2506 (chapter 24)
Akodu v Solicitors Regulation Authority [2009] EWHC 3588 (Admin) (chapter 24)
Balmoody v UKCC for Nurses, Midwives and Health Visitors [1998] EWHC 521 (appendix 12)
Bradshaw v General Medical Council [2010] Med L R 323 (chapter 24)
Caelham v General Medical Council [2007] EWHC 2606 (chapter 24)
Chaudhury v General Medical Council [2002] UKPC 41 (appendix 12)
Chauhan v GMC [2010] EWHC 2093 (Admin) (appendix 12)
Cheatle v General Medical Council [2009] EWHC 645 (Admin) (chapter 24)
CHRE v GDC (Marshall) [2006] EWHC 1870 (Admin) (appendix 12)
Cohen v General Medical Council [2009] EWHC 645 (Admin) (chapter 24)
Donoghue v Stevenson [1932] AC 562, 580 (chapter 23)
Dr Haikel v GMC (Privy Council Appeal No. 69 of 2011) (appendix 12)
Dwyer v Roderick, Jackson and Cross Chemists (Banbury) Ltd (unreported 10 February 1982) (box 23.4)

Eurovet VMD Annual review 2010/2011 (box 16.1)

General Medical Council v Hiew [2007] 1 W.L.R. 2007 (chapter 24)

General Medical Council v Meadow [2006] EWCA Civ 1390 (chapter 24)

Hadley v Baxendale [1854] 9 Ex 341 (chapter 1)

Harris v Registrar of Approved Driving Instructors [2010] EWCA Civ. 808 (chapter 24)

Horton v Evans and Lloyds Pharmacy Ltd [2006] EWHC 2808 QB (box 23.4)

Ibrahim [2012] EWCA Crim. 837; April 22nd 2012 (chapter 1)

Jideofo v The Law Society [2007] EW Misc 3 (31 July 2007) (chapter 24)

Joseph Lennox Holmes v RCVS [2011] UKPC 48 (chapter 25)

Lawrence v GMC [2012] EWHC 464 (Admin) (chapter 24)

Mahoney v Prestatyn Magistrates Court [2009] EWHC 3237 (Admin) (chapter 25)

Mairnovich v General Medical Council [2002] UKPC 36 (appendix 12)

Meadow v General Medical Council [2007] 2 W.L.R. 286 (chapter 24)

Norris v Weeks (1970) (*The Times Law Reports*, 6 March 1970) (box 5.1)

Nursing and Midwifery Council v Maceda [2011] EWHC 3004 (Admin) (chapter 24)

Oxford v Sanger [1965] 1 All ER 96 (box 10.1)

Pharmaceutical Society v Wright (1981) Unreported (box 9.1)

Pharmaceutical Society of Great Britain v Boots Cash Chemists (Southern) Ltd [1953] 1 All ER 482 (box 6.3)

Pharmaceutical Society of Great Britain v Dickson [1968] 2 All ER 686 (box 23.2)

Pharmaceutical Society of Great Britain v Storkwain Ltd [1986] 2 All ER 635 (box 8.4, chapter 24)

Preiss v General Dental Council [2001] 1 W.L.R. 26 (chapter 24)

Queen v Statutory Committee of the Pharmaceutical Society, ex parte Sokoh (*The Times Law Reports*, 4 December 1986) (chapter 24)

Queen v Statutory Committee of the Pharmaceutical Society, ex parte Lewis and Jefferies Ltd, Berg and Brandon (unreported) (chapter 24)

Queen on the application of Zygmunt v General Medical Council [2008] EWHC 2643 (Admin) (chapter 24)

R v Adomako [1995] A C 171 (chapter 23)

R v Department of Health, ex parte Source Informatics Ltd EWHC [1999] 4 All ER 185 (box 21.1)

R v Lee (Elizabeth) [2010] EWCA Crim. 1404; [2011] 1 W.L.R. 418 (chapter 24)

R v Patel (Hitendra) [2010] 1 W.L.R. 1011 (chapter 24)

R (on the application of Rycroft) v Royal Pharmaceutical Society of Great Britain [2011] Med L R 23 (chapter 24)

R (on the application of Sheikh) v General Dental Council [2010] Med L R 323 (chapter 24)

R v Royal Pharmaceutical Society of Great Britain, ex parte Association of Parallel Importers and Others (1989) (unreported) (box 3.1)

R (Redgrave) v Commissioner of Police for the Metropolis [2003] 1 W.L.R. 1136 (chapter 24)

R v Statutory Committee of the Pharmaceutical Society of Great Britain and Martin and Shutt Ex p. Pharmaceutical Society of Great Britain [1981] 1 W.L.R. 886 (chapter 24)

Rashid and Fatnani v General Medical Council [2007] 1 W.L.R. 1460 (appendix 12)

Roberts v Coombs [1949] KB 221 (box 8.1)

Roberts v Littlewoods Mail Order Stores Ltd [1943] All ER 1 271 (box 6.1)

Ruscillo v Council for the Regulation of Health Care Professionals [2004] EWCA Civ 1356 (chapter 24)

Summers v Congreve Horner & Co. [1992] 40 E G 144 (box 6.2)

Susie MacLeod v The Royal College of Surgeons (Privy Council Appeal No. 88 of 2005) (box 16.2)

Vali v General Optical Council [2011] EWHC 310 (Admin) (chapter 24)

Wootton v J Docter Ltd [2008] EWCA Civ. 1361 (chapter 23)

Yeong v General Medical Council [2009] EWHC 1923 (chapter 24)

Yusuf v Royal Pharmaceutical Society of Great Britain [2009] EWHC 867 (Admin) (chapter 24)

Abbreviations and acronyms

All ER	All England (Law) Reports
ALL ER (EC)	All England Reports (European Community)
AVM-GSL	Authorised Veterinary Medicine – General Sale List
BP	*British Pharmacopoeia*
BPC	British Pharmacopoeia Commission
CCG	clinical commissioning group
CE	*conformité Européene* (EC approval symbol for medical devices)
CHIP	Chemicals (Hazard Information and Packaging for Supply) (legislation)
CHRE	Council for Healthcare Regulatory Excellence (superseded by PSAHSC)
CLP	Classification, Labelling and Packaging of Substances and Mixtures (legislation)
COSHH	Control of Substances Hazardous to Health (regulations)
CPD	continuing professional development
CQC	Care Quality Commission
DEFRA	Department for Environment, Food and Rural Affairs
EC	European Commission
ECR	European Court Reports
ECJ	European Court of Justice
EEA	European Economic Area
EEC	European Economic Community
EU	European Union
EWCA Civ.	England and Wales, Court of Appeal: Civ. (civil division), Crim. (criminal division)
EWHC	England and Wales High Court: Admin (Administrative Court)
Ex	Exchequer Reports
FTP	Fitness to Practise Committee/Rules
GMC	General Medical Council

GSL	General Sale List (medicines)
GP	general practioner
GPhC	General Pharmaceutical Council
HMR	Human Medicines Regulation
IRME	ionising radiation medical exposure
LPC	local pharmaceutical committee
LPS	local pharmaceutical service
LS Law Medical	law reports published by Informa
MD	maximum dose
MDD	maximum daily dose
MHRA	Medicines and Healthcare products Regulatory Agency
MPharm	Master of Pharmacy (accredited degree)
MRL	maximum residue limit
MUR	Medication Use Review
NFA-VPS	non-food animal medicine prescribed by a veterinary, pharmacist or suitably qualified person only
NICE	National Institute for Health and Care Excellence
NHS	National Health Service
NHSCB	NHS Commissioning Board
OSPAP	Overseas Pharmacist Assessment Programme
P medicine	Pharmacy Medicine
PALS	patient advice and liaison service
PCT	primary care trust
PGD	Patient Group Direction
Pharm J	Pharmaceutical Journal
PNA	pharmaceutical needs assessment
POM	Prescription Only Medicine
POM Order	Prescription Only Medicines Order (legislation)
POM-V	Prescription Only Medicine prescribed by a veterinary prescriber only
POM-VPS	Prescription Only Medicine prescribed by a veterinary, pharmacist or suitably qualified person only
PSAHSC	Professional Standards Authority for Health and Social Care
PSNC	Pharmaceutical Services Negotiating Committee
QB	Queens Bench
RP Reg.	Responsible Pharmacist Regulation
RPS	Royal Pharmaceutical Society
RPSGB	Royal Pharmaceutical Society of Great Britain (now wound up)
RCVS	Royal College of Veterinary Surgeons
SARSS	Suspected Adverse Reaction Surveillance Scheme
SI	Statutory Instrument

SQP	suitably qualified person
UK	United Kingdom
UKPC	UK Privy Council
VAT	value added tax
VMD	Veterinary Medicines Directorate
VMR	Veterinary Medicines Regulation
W.L.R.	*Weekly Law Reports*
w/v	weight per volume
w/w	weight per weight

1

Sources of law

Thomas H John

Introduction

Since the accession of the United Kingdom (UK) (i.e. England, Scotland, Wales and Northern Ireland) to the European Treaty of Rome in 1973, almost all legislation relevant to pharmacy and medicines has derived from the European Union (EU) (formerly the European Economic Community (EEC)). Thus Europe is the highest legal authority for such law in the UK. Law emanating from the EU has then to be enacted into 'domestic' legislation to take effect in the UK. Domestic legislation in the UK operates at two levels: 'primary' legislation, that is, Acts of Parliament, and 'secondary' legislation, that is, the detailed provisions implementing the broad provisions of an Act. Public bodies are also subject to further 'Directions' made under the authority of primary and secondary legislation. This hierarchy is reflected in the processes by which law is made, how it is enforced and interpreted and how it may be challenged. This chapter provides an overview of aspects of UK law as they relate to pharmacy.

It is vital to remember that, strictly speaking, there is no such thing as 'Pharmacy Law'; rather, pharmacy as a profession and individual pharmacists are as much subject to the general law of the land as is any other individual or institution. Nevertheless, many legislative provisions are directed specifically to pharmacy and pharmacists and this is of course the central subject matter of this book.

This chapter explains how these laws are created; how they are implemented so as to apply them to our daily lives; how that implementation may be interpreted, policed and, if necessary, enforced; and, where applicable, whether any remedies may be available to individuals affected and society at large with regard to the interpretation of those laws, their policing and their enforcement.

One of the lynchpins to a democratic society such as the UK is the concept of the *separation of powers*. This concept was crystallised during and in the aftermath of the French Revolution in the late 18th century by philosophers such as Robespierre and Baron de Montesquieu. The concept holds that absolute power to regulate society should never be vested in the hands of one person or body of persons. Arguably, England was centuries ahead of these philosophers when, in 1215, King John signed the *Magna Carta* – the first time that the absolute monarch of this country ceded some of his powers to individuals besides himself.

Today, the structure of our democracy is designed to ensure that separate bodies make our laws (parliament), interpret our laws (the judiciary) and enforce our laws (the executive). These together ensure that the so-called 'rules of natural justice' are obeyed. The most important of these rules for our purposes is seen in the maxim 'no man may be a judge in his own cause'. This means that a person or body who creates a law (parliament) cannot then interpret it him or itself (this is the function of the judiciary) and cannot then go on to enforce it him or itself (that is the function of the executive, e.g. the civil service, the police and even the General Pharmaceutical Council (GPhC)). The benefits and safeguards of this arrangement for individual citizens are obvious.

European law

Following the Second World War, there was felt to be a need for trading agreements between the countries of Europe. In 1957, six states signed the Treaty of Rome, which established the EEC – now the EU. The UK acceded to the Treaty in 1973, along with Denmark and Ireland; Greece acceded in 1981 and Portugal and Spain followed in 1986. Sweden, Finland and Austria signed up to the Treaty in 1996, and Latvia, Lithuania, Estonia, Cyprus, the Czech Republic, Slovakia, Poland, Hungary, Malta and Slovenia joined in May 2004, followed by Romania and Bulgaria in 2007, bringing the total number of Member States currently to 27 (Croatia is expected to accede to the Treaty in 2013).

The Single European Act 1987 was designed to expedite a single internal market and to remove all the remaining barriers that exist to the free movement of people, goods, services and capital. It is the object of the Community to ensure that there is no impediment to these 'four freedoms' and, if there is, to remove it. Harmonisation is one method by which such obstacles can be overcome and this is shown in many of the Directives that have affected the production and distribution of pharmaceuticals.

The legislation implementing the Treaty is formulated by the Council of Ministers in four basic forms.

Regulations. These have a direct effect and are binding on all Member States and on individuals in every respect.

Directives. These are binding as to their objectives but leave to Member States the method of implementation. Such implementation may be legislative or administrative. Most directives include 'derogations': a form of exception that Member States may claim if they feel that their particular circumstances require it.

Decisions. These are binding on those to whom they are addressed and are often of an administrative nature.

Recommendations. These are self-evident and are persuasive.

The European institutions

There are five main institutions of the EU.

The *Council of Ministers* is composed of politicians of each Member State and in practice, the minister attending changes according to the item under discussion. The Council makes the ultimate decisions on European law. The Council is supported by working parties that include civil servants from each Member State and which study proposals put forward by the Council or the Commission. The working party reports are sent to the Committee of Permanent Representatives, which makes the decision whether or not to put the proposal forward to a Council meeting.

The *Commission* is made up of commissioners (civil servants), each with responsibilities for a particular area of interest, for example agriculture, internal affairs or environment. It has been called the Civil Service of the Community and proposes, executes and polices the policies of the Community as promulgated by the Council. Discussions between a commissioner's department and interested parties can lead to the formation of draft proposals. These are discussed by the Commission as a whole, which then decides on the form of any final proposal to be laid before the Council.

The *Assembly* (parliament) is a directly elected chamber of members from the 27 Member States with representation related directly to population size. It has three main functions: control over the Community's budget, power of censure over the Commission and scrutiny of the legislative process. The last function has been of importance in the promulgation of directives affecting pharmacy upon which the Assembly must be consulted. The detailed work is done by standing committees who have a *rapporteur*, responsible for preparing the draft response of the Committee and presenting it to the plenary session of the Assembly.

The *Economic and Social Committee* comprises representatives of economic and social groups in the Member States. It is divided into three groups: employers, workers (trade unions) and a variety of interest groups, which includes the professions. The Economic and Social Committee has to be consulted before any final decision can be taken on proposed legislation. The work is mainly done in various specialist expertise sections (e.g. agriculture, transport). Within each section, there are study groups that deal with specific proposals. The section produces an 'opinion', which is presented to a plenary session of the Committee before being forwarded to the Council.

The *European Court of Justice* (ECJ) is covered below, under Courts.

European law usually results from a request for action from an EU Member State. The Commission then drafts proposed legislation that passes through a lengthy debate, amendment and consultation process until the Council agrees the final form of the legislation.

British law

The scope of this book does not extend to Northern Ireland. Therefore, the law covered relates to England Scotland and Wales only, although the law in Northern Ireland often replicates British law. Law covering medicines and pharmacy practice generally applies across all of Britain but there is scope for differences. Law covering the administration of the National Health Service (NHS) differs significantly in the three component countries of Britain and may diverge further over time. There are two primary divisions in British law: statute law and common law (table 1.1). Common law itself is subdivided into criminal and civil law, but statutory law may encompass both and may or may not be accompanied by criminal, administrative or professional sanctions.

The arrangements for the NHS and for professional discipline fall into these two categories. Legislation in Britain is made in the name of the Crown – the Queen. Properties owned by and activities carried out by the state on her behalf have in the past been subject to *Crown immunity*. Crown immunity means complete immunity from prosecution and the NHS, as a manifestation of the Crown, was immune from prosecution for offences committed within the NHS by its employees, including hospital pharmacists. This is no longer true as Crown immunity was formally removed from NHS hospital services in April 1991 and all the major pharmaceutical statutory legislation now applies, including the Medicines Act and the Misuse of Drugs Acts together with the subordinate legislation made under them. The prison health services and military health services are also expected to comply with UK legislation, other than in exceptional cases (chapter 26).

Statute law

A statute, strictly speaking, is an Act of Parliament. There are two kinds, public and private, but this book is only concerned with public acts such as the Medicines Act, the Misuse of Drugs Act and the Poisons Act (appearing principally in chapters 2 to 21). Acts are commonly referred to as *primary* legislation since they are the primary authority for legislation in the UK.

Table 1.1 Summary of UK law with relevance to pharmacy				
	Statutory law			Civil law
	Criminal legislation	Administrative legislation	Professional legislation	Common law rights and duties, augmented by human rights
Enforcement agencies	Police officers, GPhC inspectors	Representatives of administrative body	Professional regulator: GPhC	Direct action by claimant
Action for breach	Prosecution in the criminal courts	Appearance before relevant tribunal	Appearance before Fitness to Practice Committee	Being sued in the civil courts
Sanctions available to society at large	Fines, community orders, imprisonment	As set out in the law including loss of remuneration, withdrawal of contractual rights or position	Placing of conditions on registration, removal from professional register	Having to pay compensation; entry in the Register of County Court Judgments
Redress available to the unsuccessful party	Appeal to a higher court	Judicial review	Appeal to a higher tribunal	Appeal to a higher tribunal

Statute law is also used to describe legislation that is subsidiary to an Act, normally in the form of Regulations or Orders in Council. These are collectively known as Statutory Instruments (SIs) or as *secondary* legislation. Once promulgated, secondary legislation has as much force in law as does primary legislation. Proposals to introduce new legislation come forward in the form of bills. Most are government bills but sometimes they are put forward by individual members of parliament (private member's bills). Before a bill is proposed, the government will normally signal its intentions in a 'white paper'. Sometimes this is preceded by a discussion document, called a 'green paper'. The programme of primary legislation is usually outlined in the Queen's speech when parliament enters a new session every autumn.

Each bill is normally introduced into the House of Commons at a formal first reading and then passes through a series of 'readings'. After the second reading, the content and object of the bill is open to debate from members. If this stage is successfully passed, the bill goes to a committee stage, which examines the detail clause by clause. These stages are then repeated in the House of Lords. Once a bill successfully passes both Houses it is submitted to the monarch for Royal Assent. This stage is invariably a formality; under the UK constitutional law, a monarch who refuses assent to a bill that has successfully passed through both Houses of Parliament (and by doing so is thereby deemed to have the assent of the UK population at large) would inevitably precipitate a constitutional crisis of a magnitude not seen in modern times. This is because of the supremacy of the UK Parliament as a law-making body.

Statutes are most often 'enabling' instruments; that is, they give powers to the executive arm of the state, usually individual Secretaries of State, to do things. Major changes to an Act can normally only be made by another Act. An SI implements the detail of broad powers given by an Act. An SI does not go through parliamentary debate but is 'tabled' in the parliament in the name of the minister and will be passed if no objections are raised.

Since the early 1980s there has been a huge annual increase in the number of SIs coming into force. For example, in 1980 a total of 178 SIs came into force. By 1990, this number had risen to 1630; there were 1744 in the year 2000 and during 2011 (the last full year for which figures are available) the number had rocketed to 2808.

Administrative law

Administrative law (appearing principally in chapter 26) is that body of law that regulates the activity of public bodies. Such bodies include NHS authorities such as primary care trusts (PCTs) in England, their predecessors and successors; local authorities; and education authorities. Every NHS body and PCT (or clinical commissioning group (CCG) from April 2013) is set up by individual Regulation under an enabling Act of Parliament and any accompanying SIs, which confer statutory powers such as the power to manage budgets, hire and fire staff and enter into contracts. These powers may not lawfully be exceeded by the public body in question. If they were to be exceeded, any party wronged may apply to the Administrative Court for *judicial review* of the action of the body in question on the ground that the decision was reached *ultra vires*, that is, in excess of its powers. Strategic health authorities, ambulance and mental health care trusts are also individually created by statute. At the time of writing, NHS Direct was a legally constituted special health authority to give it power to enter into formal contracts with PCTs (England). Administrative law comprises statutes (Acts, Regulations, Orders) supplemented by a substantial body of Directions made by senior civil servants acting under the authority of the relevant minister. Policy statements and guidelines, all of which describe the standards to which the public sector is expected to work, supplement the legal framework further. Initially, the public authority itself usually enforces administrative law; a good example would be the enforcement of the NHS dispensing contract by the PCTs in England. Enforcement is often also pursued through tribunals, appeal authorities and the courts. Sanctions are administrative such as a fine (withholding of reimbursement for dispensing NHS scripts), which reverts to the public body, or loss of contract.

As stated above, action by public bodies is susceptible to *judicial review*, a process whereby the Administrative Court (a branch of the High Court) determines whether the public body acted fairly, reasonably and within its statutory powers, rather than reviewing the factual basis on which the actual decision was reached. Three criteria are considered:

- was a decision made by a public body lawful or not that is, was it one that was within its powers?
- was it a reasonable and rational one: had the body considered all the relevant facts and ignored those that were irrelevant?
- was it based on the correct procedures laid down in a particular case, that is, did it comply with the rules of natural justice?

Decisions made in the Fitness to Practise (FTP) Committee of the GPhC and its predecessors, the Disciplinary and Statutory Committees, can be made subject to judicial review particularly if there has been a breach of proper procedures or where the penalty imposed has been irrational or unreasonable (chapter 24).

Professional law

Professional law (appearing principally in chapters 22 to 25) comprises the law underpinning the powers to discipline health professionals such as pharmacists. The authority to discipline pharmacists lies in the Pharmacy Order 2010 and its associated Rules. The notion of an expected standard of care, which is also used in civil law cases (see below), is used by professional tribunals to judge whether a professional is guilty of professional misconduct. For pharmacists, these standards may principally be found in the GPhC Standards for Conduct, Ethics and Performance (SOPs) together with standards guidelines and protocols laid down for NHS care, for example the 'standard operating procedures' for the dispensing process.

Civil law

Civil law (referred to in chapter 23) derives from the notion of duties and responsibilities owed between individual citizens (Latin *civitas*, citizen). In its turn, civil law has developed through court judgments based on common law. Common law has developed from the middle ages since the King's courts gradually took the rule of law out into the shires to make judgments over the affairs of 'common' people. Action under civil law (called a *suit*) allows an aggrieved party to sue for compensation from another citizen who is alleged to have 'wronged' him. This concept of 'a civil wrong' is known in law as *tort* (an archaic term from mediaeval French). Some types of tort are now rarely seen in courts; breach of promise, for example. Libel, slander and trespass are all civil wrongs. In healthcare practice, the most likely actions are for negligence in the form of clinical negligence. Breach of confidentiality and defamation are other examples. In a case of clinical negligence, the complainant (claimant) makes an allegation that the actions of another person (the defendant or respondent) has caused them damage or injury. To succeed, the claimant would have to prove to a defined standard (the balance of probabilities) that the health professional firstly owed him a duty of care, secondly that the duty had been breached (i.e. was lower than the standard expected) and, thirdly, that that breach had caused the injury alleged. A civil action for battery is also a possible claim in tort if a patient is treated without his or her consent.

Human rights in the UK

The Human Rights Act 1998 codified for the first time the rights enshrined in the European Convention of Human Rights. All UK courts and tribunals must now have regard to the principles of the European Convention of Human Rights when deciding cases which come before them.

The court system

The court with ultimate jurisdiction over EU law is the European Court of Justice (ECJ). This settles legal disputes involving Community legislation and its judgments are binding on each Member State. Much of its work now involves giving preliminary rulings on questions referred by the courts of the Member States.

In addition, under the auspices of the Council of Europe, there is the European Court of Human Rights, which developed separately, before the ECJ, to enforce the European Convention on Human Rights. This Convention was agreed in 1949 as a direct result of the human rights' atrocities of the Second World War. The UK was a founder member but was the last of the original signatories to enact the convention into domestic law. This was principally because the English common law conventions were held to embody adequate safeguards for human rights. Until 1998, any individual who wished to claim that their human rights had been violated had to complain for redress to the European Court of Human Rights. When the UK enacted the Convention in the Human Rights Act 1998, UK citizens then acquired the right to seek redress in the UK courts first, although the European Court of Human Rights remains an option if the complainant does not receive satisfaction in the UK.

A strict hierarchical system of UK courts means that the lowest possible tier of the court system will first make a judgment on the particular facts of a case. This judgment is binding on the parties to that case unless leave is given to appeal. On any such appeal, the higher court's decision may then set a precedent – or case law – for dealing with any similar future cases. The Appeal Court may dismiss the appeal (in which case the original judgment stands), allow the appeal (in which case the original judgment will be reversed) or grant leave to appeal to a still higher tribunal if there is one. The hierarchy of courts means that a decision on appeal that sets a precedent automatically binds all lower courts in future similar cases. More detail on the British legal system may be found in the Further reading given below.

The structure of the court system in England and Wales is shown in table 1.2.

A system of statutory tribunals also exists alongside that of the established court system. Examples include the employment tribunals, the VAT tribunals and the social care and entitlement tribunals. As with the court system, there

Table 1.2 Courts in England and Wales	
Criminal Division	**Civil Division**
Supreme Court (formerly the House of Lords)	Supreme Court
Hears appeals from the Court of Appeal and sometimes direct from the Divisional Court	Hears appeals from the Court of Appeal and sometimes direct from the High Court
Court of Appeal Criminal Division	Court of Appeal Civil Division
Hears appeals from the Crown Court on points of law or procedure only	Hears appeals from the High Court or the County Court on points of law or procedure only
Queens Bench Division (Divisional Court)	High Court Queens Bench Division
Hears appeals from the Crown Court on points of law only	Hears the more major cases of negligence (other divisions of the High Court exist, such as Family Division or Chancery, which deals with commercial matters)
Crown Court	County Court
Hears cases committed to this court and appeals from the magistrates court and generally has greater powers of sentencing than the lower court	Deals with actions involving claims for small sums of money (£5–50 000) and negligence cases where the sum at stake is less than £50 000
Magistrates Court (bench of lay magistrates assisted by a professional legal adviser)	
May sometimes sit with a district judge (formerly known as a stipendiary magistrate) and hears the less serious criminal cases	

is a hierarchy within the tribunal system. Cases go firstly to the relevant *first tier* tribunal. Any appeal from the first tier tribunal (on points of law or procedure only) will go to the *second tier* tribunal. Any further appeal goes to the Court of Appeal (Civil Division). In very rare and exceptional cases the case may be further appealed to the Supreme Court provided permission is given.

Always remember that the courts are themselves creatures of statute and only have the powers conferred on them by parliament under the doctrine of parliamentary supremacy. Courts do not *make* law, they can only *rule* on it by reason of the doctrine of separation of powers referred to above.

Scotland has a different system of courts to that in England and Wales based on its legal system's origins in Roman law (rather than the common law in England and Wales). In Scotland the lowest tiers of Court include the *Sherriff's court*, with the *Court of Session* undertaking most of the functions of the Crown and High Courts in England and Wales. However, the final domestic court of appeal for Scottish cases is still the Supreme Court, as it is for England and Wales.

How to find the law

Just as there are a vast number of statutes and secondary legislation (SIs, Orders in Council) governing our law so there is also an even larger body of case law. This is not surprising given that the original binding precedents date from the Middle Ages and will still hold as good law unless they over-ruled by any subsequent precedents.

In order to discover exactly what the law is on any given subject matter, recourse must be had, firstly, to any statutory provision and the relevant secondary legislation covering the subject and, secondly to the case law, which will give an indication on how the courts interpret those statutory provisions. Each separate source of law has a unique and distinctive method of citation, whether searching in a law library, a volume of case reports or browsing online.

Statute law

An Act of Parliament always has a *long title* which appears at its head. Sometimes there is also a more succinct *short title*. The short title may also give a brief description of the purpose behind that Act and what it is designed to achieve. The *year* it was enacted is given in a specific way related to the name of the monarch at the time it was enacted and a *chapter number* chronologically designating the point during that year when it received Royal Assent. Thus, the full citation of the Medicines Act 1968 is The Medicines Act 1968 (16 Elizabeth II: Ch. 67). It was, therefore, passed in the 16th year of Queen Elizabeth II's reign (1968) and was the 67th Act of Parliament to be passed during that year. The Act of Parliament which replaced the House of Lords by bringing the Supreme Court into being is the Constitutional Reform Act 2005 (53 Eliz. II Ch. 4) and so on. Acts are further subdivided into *Parts* setting out the broad subject areas the Act is legislating upon and, within those parts, *Sections* dealing with individual aspects of the relevant broad subject area.

An SI has a somewhat simpler method of citation involving just the year of its promulgation and a chronological number within that year. The subject matter of the SI is also generally easy to discern from a straightforward reading of its title. For example, the SI that sets out the precise structure of the GPhC is 'The General Pharmaceutical Council (Constitution) Order 2010 (SI 2010 No. 300)' meaning it was the 300th Order in Council or SI to be promulgated in the year 2010.

Provided that the name of the Act or SI one is looking for is known (or even any one or more of the other citations) it is easy to find a copy by simply going to www.legislation.gov.uk and entering the known characters. This website has copies of all UK public Acts since 1842 and most are downloadable either as '.pdf' files or as 'word' documents at no charge.

Case law

The method of citing precedents is evolving all the time and has changed significantly in recent years. Originally, approved accounts of cases (law reports) were produced by specialist journalists known as *law reporters*, who were invariably legal scholars or prominent practitioners. They were often then compiled into volumes of case reports at the end of each year. Over the years, those volumes would grow to form a *series*. Some series became obsolete or were eventually replaced by new series, often bearing the name of the new approved reporter or publisher. For example the case of *Hadley v Baxendale* (which sets out the law on the limits to the amount of damages a Claimant can sue for in a claim for breach of contract) is cited as *Hadley v Baxendale [1854] 9 Ex 341*, which means that it was reported in the year 1854 in the 9th volume of the *Exchequer Reports* (ERs) beginning at page 341. Although now nearly 160 years old, it is still good law. Common series of law reports still in publication include the *Weekly Law Reports* (often abbreviated to W.L.R) and the All England Reports (All ER), which both deal with general common law cases, and the *Industrial Relations Law Reports*, a specialist series dealing with employment law. There is as yet no series dealing specifically with pharmacy law.

Recently, a new and simpler system of citing cases now passing through the higher courts has been established. They are known collectively as *Neutral Citation Numbers* and are designed to make for easy online searches for reports of cases. A recent example is the criminal case of *Ibrahim* neutrally cited as *Ibrahim [2012] EWCA Crim. 837; April 22nd 2012*. This means the case originated from a Crown Court situated in England or Wales, it was then appealed to the England or Wales Court of Appeal (EWCA) criminal division (Crim.), and judgment was given on 22nd April and begins at page 837 of the year's record of judgments.

The student may by now very well be thinking that all the above is fine provided one knows the statute, case or citation one is looking for, but what if one only knows the subject matter? In this case, searching by the above methods is likely to be a long, not to mention, tedious process. Fortunately there is a series of encyclopaedias and case digests available that are indexed by subject matter. A widely available (in most public libraries) encyclopaedia is *Halsbury's Laws of England* and its accompanying *Halsbury's Statutes*, which, although running to around 50 separate volumes, are set out in alphabetical order of subject matter. One such volume includes a section devoted to 'pharmacy and medicine'.

A timely word of warning is appropriate here however; in addition to the vast body of law referred to above, there is also a huge body of procedural rules, guidelines and practice directions that accompany them. These rules, guidelines and practice directions govern the practical conduct of cases that come before courts and tribunals. Therefore, just as there is no substitute for taking professional advice from a competent pharmacist in matters relating to medicines, there is no substitute for taking professional legal advice if legal issues arise involving students and individual pharmacists in practice. There is a (rather 'tongue-in-cheek' but accurate nevertheless) maxim known to most practising lawyers which states simply 'he who represents himself has a fool for a client!'

Finding European law

Examples of European legislation affecting pharmacy, pharmacists and medicines are given below; further details may also be found in the reading list. Full details of the relevant British legislation appear in subsequent chapters of this book.

Most of the current UK law that applies to pharmacy practice derives from European legislation in the form of Directives, although Regulations have been made concerning, for example, the marketing authorisation of medicinal products (chapter 3). The first set of digits refers to the year of enactment; the second set refers to the number of this legal instrument within that year. All then retain either the EC (European Commission) or the EEC suffix.

European case law also has a relatively straightforward method of citation. Applications to the court are given a unique chronological reference numbers followed by 2 digits denoting the year. The name of the case is also commonly included but need not be, provided there is a citation number. Thus, the 'Doc Morris' case, which dealt with limits to the free movement of pharmaceutical goods within the EU, is cited as *Case C-322/01- Deutscher Apothekerverband EV v 0800 DOCMORRIS NV & Jacques Waterval (2003) ECJ 11/12/2003*. This means that the case was the 322nd case to be referred to the ECJ for a preliminary opinion in the year 2001 and was finally decided by the full Court and reported in the official journal of the European Communities on 11th December 2003. European legislation and case law can be consulted on the *euralex* website and copies downloaded free of charge.

Examples of European law

Free movement of pharmacists

The Pharmacy Directives concerned with the free movement of pharmacists, namely Directive 85/432/EEC, which dealt with the education and training of the pharmacist, and Directive 85/433/EEC, dealing with a pharmacist's right to establishment within the Member States, were revoked in 2005 and a consolidation directive embracing all the health professions was introduced, namely Council Directive 2005/36/EC. Each Member State is obliged to recognise, without impediment, the list of degrees (or equivalent) laid down in the Directives. Registration as a pharmacist in the UK is recognised. The competent authorities within the Member States deal with the procedure and those authorities in the UK are the GPhC and its equivalent in Northern Ireland. The new Directive 2005/36/EC also recognises a new category of registrant, namely a visiting practitioner who wants to provide services in the UK on a temporary or occasional basis.

In order for a pharmacist to move freely throughout the Community s/he must produce evidence from his/her own competent authority to the corresponding one in the host Member State that s/he:

1 is a national of a Member State of the Community or treated as such;

2a possesses a university degree (or equivalent) which was obtained following a course of study of not less than five years, at least four years of which comprised theoretical and practical training in a university, together with at least six months in-service training in a community or hospital pharmacy; or

2b has for at least three consecutive years during the previous five years been effectively and lawfully engaged in regulated pharmaceutical activity, e.g. a community pharmacy, hospital pharmacy, etc.; this is known as the acquired rights provision for those who cannot comply with point 2a above;

3 is in good physical and mental health; and

4 is of good character.

The pharmacy degrees in the UK together with the pre-registration year and the 'A'-level at university entrance are considered to be equivalent to the total five-year requirement. Directive 2005/36/EC has been implemented in Great Britain by means of Regulations and Rules made under the Pharmacy Order 2010 (chapter 22). Pharmacists seeking free movement should contact the GPhC for advice.

Production and distribution of medicinal products for human use

Council Regulation 2309/93/EEC lays down Community procedures for the authorisation and supervision of medicinal products for human and veterinary use and established the European Agency for the Evaluation of Medicinal Products. Directive 2001/83/EC, which in 2001 consolidated all the earlier Council Directives, states that the primary purpose of controls on the production and distribution of medicinal products is to safeguard public health. This consolidation has also required consequential amendments to the Medicines Act and SIs in the UK, achieved by The Medicines (Codification Amendments Etc) Regulations 2002 No. 236. The Directive defines a medicinal product and establishes that before a medicine can be put on the market it must possess a licence or marketing authorisation that has been granted on the basis of safety, quality and efficacy. In addition, the Directive covers the labelling of medicines. Commission Directive 2003/94/EC lays down the principles and guidelines of *Good Manufacturing Practice* that are applicable to all activities which require a licence under Council Directive 2001/83/EC. Good manufacturing practice means the part of quality assurance which ensures that products are consistently produced and controlled in accordance with the quality of standards appropriate to their intended use, the principles and guidelines of which are specified in Commission Directive 2003/94/EC. The Council Directive 65/65/EEC and its amending Directives were revoked by and consolidated in Council Directive 2001/83/EC. Council Regulation 2309/93/EEC, Council Directive 2001/83/EC and Commission Directive 2003/94 have been implemented in the UK under the provisions of the Medicines Act (chapters 2 and 3).

In 2004, the EU completed its review of legislation regulating medicinal products and in April 2004 published Council Directive 2004/27/EC, which amended Council Directive 2001/83/EC and Council Directive 2003/63/EC.

Council Regulation 2309/93/EC provides for marketing authorisations via the centralised procedures, the establishment of the European Agency for the Evaluation of Medicinal Products together with the setting up of a Committee for Veterinary Medicinal Products. The name of the European Agency for the Evaluation of Medicinal Products was changed to the European Medicines Agency by Council Regulation 2004/726/EC.

Analytical, toxicological and clinical standards for medicines for human use

Council Directive 2001/83/EC set up standards and protocols for the analysis, and toxicological and pharmacological tests that have to be applied to medicinal products. Clinical trials are now controlled under Council Directive 2001/20/EC.

High-technology medicinal products for human and animal use

Directive 93/41/EEC set up procedures to deal with applications for marketing authorisations involving high-technology medicinal products, in particular those derived from biotechnology.

Homoeopathic medicinal products

Council Directive 2001/83/EC is concerned with the authorisation for marketing and the labelling of homoeopathic medicinal products for human use. It also provides for a special simplified registration procedure for those traditional homoeopathic medicinal products that are placed on the market without therapeutic indications in a pharmaceutical form and dosage which do not present a risk to the public. Directive 92/74/EEC relates to homoeopathic medicinal products for veterinary use. Chapter 3 discusses the UK legislation implementing both these Directives.

Herbal Medicinal Products

In March 2004, the EU issued the Directive on Traditional Herbal Medicinal Products (Council Directive 2004/24/EC) to regulate herbal products. Member States were required to have a simplified registration scheme in force by October 2005. Directive 2004/24/EC is based on long-standing use of the product and no clinical trial evidence will be required. All herbal products already on the market can remain so for seven years (chapter 12).

Advertising, labelling and leaflets

Council Directive 2001/83/EC deals with the labelling of medicinal products and the availability of package leaflets aimed at the public. It requires that 'information supplied to users should provide a high degree of consumer protection in order that medicinal products may be used correctly on the basis of full and comprehensible information'. This was implemented in the UK on 1 January 1994 (chapter 14).

Council Directive 2001/83/EC deals with the advertising of medicinal products for human use both to the general public and to health professionals. It also deals with the question of hospitality related to sales promotion, advertising, samples, medical representatives, and so on (chapter 4).

Wholesale distribution

Council Directive 2001/83/EC covers the control of wholesale distribution of medicinal products for human use in the EC. It requires that such distribution should be subject to the possession of an authorisation to engage in the activity as a wholesaler in medicinal products and lays down the conditions for such an authorisation. Such activity is subject to licensing in the UK (chapter 3).

Colouring of medicinal products

Directive 78/25/EEC controls the colouring agents that can and cannot be added to medicinal products.

Production of medicinal products for animal use

Directive 2001/82/ECC as amended by 2004/28/EC provides that no veterinary medicinal product may be placed on the market of a Member State unless a marketing authorisation has been granted by the competent authorities of that Member State in accordance with these directives or in accordance with Regulation EC/726/2004 (UK requirements appear in chapter 16).

Directive 91/412/EEC introduced a legal requirement for a manufacturer of medicinal products for animal use to comply with the principles and guidelines of good manufacturing practice.

Regulation 90/2377/EEC lays down procedures to establish maximum residue limits (MRLs) for animal medicines in foodstuffs of animal origin.

Controlled Drugs

Council Directive 92/109/EEC applies to the manufacture and trade in scheduled substances within the EU and is implemented in the UK by the Controlled Drugs (Substances Useful for Manufacture) (Intra-Community Trade) Regulations 1993 as amended. It requires the person who manufactures or trades in these substances to be licensed and restricts the persons to whom supplies may be made. The 1993 UK Regulations treat the provisions of Council Directive 92/109/EEC as if they were requirements of Regulations by reason of the Misuse of Drug Act 1971 (Modification) Order 1990 (SI 1990 No. 2589).

Council Regulation 90/3677/EEC controls the import, export, recording and labelling of scheduled substances and the power to enter business premises to obtain evidence of irregularities. Records must be kept for two years. It also requires Member States to adopt measures to enable them to obtain information on any orders for, or activities in, scheduled substances. There is a list of scheduled substances (UK requirements appear in chapter 17).

Data protection

Council Directive 95/46/EEC extends data protection to all data maintained manually and affects the way in which patient medication records are stored. This Directive was implemented in the UK by way of the Data Protection

Act 1998, which came into force on 1 March 2000. All data, both electronic and manual, are now controlled under the 1998 Act (chapter 21).

Human rights law

The Human Rights Act 1998 applies to public authorities such as the NHS or local authorities, but it also extends to 'private bodies which exercise public functions', so private contractors dispensing NHS prescriptions would be included. Since the Act came into force, all UK laws must be interpreted to respect and protect the human rights of all UK citizens. Human rights may go beyond the scope of our common law, for example they recognise a right to privacy that does not exist in the common law.

Human rights law departs from legal convention in the UK in three main ways.

- Precedent will not necessarily bind judgments in human rights cases. The courts are expected to reflect concepts of human rights at the time of consideration rather than at the time of the complaint and thus will reflect present day attitudes and conditions.
- Statutes will be interpreted as to intention rather than 'as written'. This is a major departure from UK conventions on interpretation of statutes.
- The UK courts can issue a declaration of incompatibility so as to challenge the UK Parliament to amend the relevant statute to comply with European law.

Key human rights in relation to healthcare practice

Article numbers refer to those in the original European Convention and the text and schedules to the Human Rights Act 1998.

Article 2: The 'right to life'

The right to life is really a right not to be deprived of life except in very special circumstances. The judicial sanction of capital punishment is not a special circumstance. It should be noted that this 'right' does not equate to a right to unlimited healthcare in an effort to preserve life nor a right to death. Such rights may be cited in cases of assisted suicide or euthanasia and there are debates regarding issues such as assisted conception, contraception and abortion. Debate can also arise over resource allocation and equity in availability of treatment to all patients.

Article 3: The 'right to prohibition of torture or inhuman or degrading treatment or punishment'

At first sight, Article 3 may appear not to cover issues that have obvious relevance for healthcare but some commentators have asserted that aggressive treatment in terminal care or in some treatments of the mentally handicapped are close to being inhuman.

Article 5: the 'right to liberty'

The right to liberty is particularly relevant to the treatment of those with mental disorder, and the use of 'sectioning' and compulsory treatment is very relevant to the patient's ability to consent to treatment.

Article 6: the 'right to a fair trial'

The right to a fair trial is mostly relevant to disciplinary processes and such principles as the right to know what one is charged with, adequate time to prepare a response or defence, the right to an advocate of one's own choosing, and so on. In addition, any hearing has to be within a reasonable time and without delay, and there is a right not to incriminate oneself. The Fitness to Practise (FTP) processes within the GPhC should meet these criteria (chapter 24).

Article 8: the 'right for respect for private and family life'

Human rights issues may arise in the treatment of transsexuals and the right to practise particular forms of sexuality. This right has also been cited in relation to use of medical records in court. Article 8 is very relevant to issues of privacy in medical care, restrictions on disclosure of confidential information, and so on.

Article 9: the 'right to freedom of thought, conscience and religion'

Issues may arise where treatment is contrary to religious or cultural beliefs and practices. There also may be an issue for a 24-hour health service and religious restrictions on working at certain times or days.

Morals, ethics and law

Finally, a thought should be given to the twin concepts of 'morals' and 'ethics' as distinct from 'the law'. Detailed consideration is beyond the scope of this book and the reader is referred to the excellent volume by Professor Herbert Hart, *The Concept of Law*, which considers why and where the line is drawn between laws on the one hand and morals on the other. It is important to bear in mind that most people's ideas of morals or moral behaviour are not necessarily coterminous with the law. For example, many pharmacists were disgruntled over the recent decision by the Crown Prosecution Service to prosecute a practising pharmacist (Elizabeth Lee) for breach of section 68 of the Medicines Act 1968 after she inadvertently dispensed a product that was not what was ordered by the prescribing doctor. Many of those pharmacists no doubt believed it amoral (or even immoral) to have prosecuted in those circumstances (where the law does not require any degree of fault on the part of the dispensing pharmacist before criminal proceedings may be brought). Yet other pharmacists may consider it an immoral act to assist someone to commit suicide. Assisting a suicide is currently also unlawful but, if the law is ever relaxed to make it lawful to assist a suicide in certain defined circumstances, it does not mean that those pharmacists should have to or indeed will change their view on the morality of assisting another person to die.

The concept of ethics and ethical codes as distinct from moral codes or legal codes is beyond the scope of this book.

Summary

- Introduction to the place and legal status of the UK in the EU:
  - the concept of the separation of powers within the state
  - the concept of natural justice.
- European law: the five European institutions are the Council of Ministers, the Commission, the Assembly, the Economic and Social Committee and the ECJ. The law is produced as directives, regulations, decisions and recommendations.
- British law and the scope of UK legislation:
  - statute law, the parliamentary process and parliamentary supremacy
  - administrative law, susceptibility of public bodies
  - professional law, codes of ethics and guidelines
  - civil law, civil wrongs or torts (including negligence), battery.
- The court system:
  - the ECJ
  - the court system in England & Wales and Scotland
  - hierarchy of courts
  - case law and binding precedents
  - statutory tribunals.
- How to find the law:
  - statute law
  - case law
  - European law.
- Examples of European law.
- The distinction between laws, morals and ethics.

Further reading

Beale HL (ed.) (2004) *Chitty on Contracts*, 29th edn. London: Sweet & Maxwell.

Dugdate AM *et al.* (eds) (2002) *Clerk & Lindsell on Torts*, 18th edn. London: Sweet & Maxwell.

Hart HLA (2012). *The Concept of Law*, 3rd edn. [Clarendon Law Series.] Oxford: Oxford University Press.

Smith JC (2002) *Smith & Hogan Criminal Law*, 10th edn. London: Butterworths.

Wade ECS, Bradley EW (1996) *Constitutional and Administrative Law*, 11th edn. London: Longmans.

Wingfield J, Badcott D (2007) *Pharmacy Ethics and Decision Making*. London: Pharmaceutical Press.

Zander M (2004). *The Law Making Process*, 6th edn. [Law in context series.] Cambridge, UK: Cambridge University Press.

Websites

EU legislation: http://eur-lex.europa.eu

Legislation (can be searched on year and SI number or title): http://www.legislation.gov.uk

2

Human medicines: scope of regulation

Karen Pitchford

Consolidation of Medicines Legislation (2012)

Until August 2012, UK medicines legislation comprised the Medicines Act 1968 (the 1968 Act), around 60 principal SIs and around 130 amending SIs, which reflected developments in pharmaceuticals, wholesale trade, regulatory practice and European harmonisation. The view of the Medicines and Healthcare products Regulatory Agency (MHRA) was that the law had become fragmented and 'potentially impenetrable for users'[1] and delivered a legislative framework that was 'fragmented, complex, poorly structured and in places obsolete'.[2] Hence, a consolidation of medicines legislation was undertaken, leading to the production and enactment of the Human Medicines Regulations 2012.[3] These Human Medicines Regulations (HMRs) repealed, revoked or re-enacted most existing UK legislation regulating the authorisation, sale and supply of medicinal products for human use and consolidated their effect in one place and in rationalised form.

The Human Medicines Regulations 2012 leave parts of the 1968 Act in place, principally Part IV of the Act, which deals with the registration and conduct of pharmacies (chapter 5). Also retained are certain powers to make secondary legislation in areas that fall outside the scope of Directive 2001/83/EC (the Directive).[4] The Human Medicines Regulations 2012 provide that medicines may be supplied to the public only from pharmacies, except those medicines which can with reasonable safety be sold without the supervision of a pharmacist. The Regulations also cover matters relating to the labelling of medicines, the containers in which they are supplied and the manner in which their sale is promoted, whether by advertisement or oral representation.

[1] MHRA (2011) Impact Assessment No. 4018
[2] MHRA (2012) Explanatory Memorandum to the Human Medicines Regulations 2012
[3] Human Medicines Regulations SI 2012 No. 1916
[4] Directive 2001/83/EC of the European Parliament and of the Council on the Community Code Relating to Medicinal Products for Human Use

Certain pieces of medicines legislation have not been consolidated, including that concerned with clinical trials, the administration of radioactive medicinal products and fees charged by the MHRA for the administration of procedures under the provisions. Various orders made under section 62 of the Act to prohibit the sale, supply and importation of products containing particular substances will also remain in force along with section 62, because prohibitions of this sort are outside the scope of the Directive.

Section 104 of the 1968 Act provides for an Order to be made for the Human Medicines Regulations 2012 or the Clinical Trials Regulations to be applied to any article or substance which is not a medicinal product but is made wholly or partly for a medicinal purpose. In the past, Orders have been made in respect of surgical ligatures and sutures, dental filling substances, contact lenses and associated substances, and intrauterine contraceptive devices. However, since 1994, these substances have been considered to be medical devices rather than medicines and are now controlled under Medical Devices Regulations (see under Medical devices below).

Section 105 of the Act provides for an Order to be made for the HMRs or the Clinical Trials Regulations to be applied in respect of any substance which (a) is used as an ingredient in the manufacture of a medicinal product or (b) is capable of causing danger to the health of the community if used without proper safeguards. The order may specify which parts of the Act are to apply. Some substances used as ingredients in the manufacture of medicinal products, and certain other substances, have been controlled by orders of this kind (see appendix 1).

The Human Medicines Regulations 2012 repeal section 10(7) of the Medicines Act 1968 altogether. This section formerly exempted pharmacists from the need for a wholesale dealer's licence if wholesale dealing formed only an inconsiderable part of their business, but was not compatible with the Directive (chapter 10).

Since the Medicines Act 1968 remains partially in force, it should be read in conjunction with the Human Medicines Regulations 2012. References to Parts, Regulations and Schedules in this chapter relate to the Human Medicines Regulations 2012 and those to sections to the Medicines Act 1968, unless otherwise stated.

Neither the 1968 Act nor the Human Medicines Regulations 2012 apply to medical devices (see later in this chapter) or veterinary medicines (chapter 16).

The Human Medicines Regulations 2012

These Regulations comprise 17 Parts and 35 Schedules. This book focuses on those Parts of greatest relevance to pharmacists and those involved in pharmacy. For full details, readers should consult the actual Regulations, the accompanying Explanatory Memorandum and the MHRA website. The contents of the Regulations are set below, with where they are predominantly discussed within this book.

Part 1 General provisions: chapter 2
Part 2 Administration: chapter 2
Part 3 Manufacturing and wholesaling: chapters 3 and 10
Part 4 Requirement for authorisation: chapter 3
Part 5 Marketing authorisations: chapter 3
Part 6 Certification of homoeopathic medicinal products: chapter 11
Part 7 Traditional herbal registrations: chapter 12
Part 8 Article 126a Authorisations: chapter 3
Part 9 Borderline products: chapter 3
Part 10 Exceptions to requirement for marketing authorisation, etc.: chapter 3
Part 11 Pharmacovigilance: chapters 2 and 3
Part 12 Dealings with medicinal products: chapters 6, 7, 8 and 9
Part 13 Packaging and leaflets: chapter 14
Part 14 Advertising: chapter 4
Part 15 *British Pharmacopoeia*: chapter 15
Part 16 Enforcement: chapter 2
Part 17 Miscellaneous: chapter 2

In addition, chapter 5 covers the provisions of the Medicines Act 1968 on pharmacies, chapter 13 provisions in the Act for protection of the purchaser and chapter 16 covers the legislation on veterinary medicines.

Part 1 General provisions

Definition of medicinal product

The Regulations do not use the term 'medicine' but 'medicinal product', which is defined (HMRs Part 1, Reg.2) as:

a   any substance or combination of substances presented as having properties of preventing or treating disease in human beings; or
b   any substance or combination of substances that may be used by or administered to human beings with a view to:
   i   restoring, correcting or modifying a physiological function by exerting a pharmacological, immunological or metabolic action, or
   ii making a medical diagnosis.

Whole human blood or any human blood components are specifically excluded from the above definition.

The above definition is transposed from Directive 2001/83/EC, as amended. The European Court of Justice (ECJ) has confirmed that falling under either (a) or (b) above is sufficient to classify a product as a medicinal product,[5] ruling that 'Directive 65/65 (now Directive 2001/83) provides two definitions of the term *medicinal product*: one relating to presentation, the other to function. A product is medicinal if it falls within either of those definitions.' Directive 2004/27/EC adds a new provision to Article 2 of Directive 2001/83/EC as amended, which states, 'In cases of doubt, where, taking into account all its characteristics, a product may fall within the definition of a product covered by other Community legislation the provisions of this Directive shall apply.'

Taken together, these provisions are intended to ensure that where doubt exists over whether a product (those on the borderline between, for example, medicines and medical devices, medicines and cosmetics, medicines and food supplements, etc.) should be regulated under medicines or other sectoral legislation, the stricter medicines regulatory regime should apply. This is a broader definition than that in the HMRs and can be defined as being a medicinal product (a) by presentation and (b) by function, as outlined by the ECJ, above.

Special provisions restricting scope

Where medicines are assembled in the course of the professional practice of a doctor, dentist, nurse, midwife or herbalist for the treatment of their patients, no manufacturing licences are required (HMRs Part 1, Reg.3). Similarly where medicines are prepared under the supervision of a pharmacist and in accordance with exemptions in the retained section 10 of the 1968 Act (chapter 3), no licences are required (HMRs Part 1, Reg.4).

Classification of medicines

Regulation 5 of the HMRs provides definitions of the three classifications governing the sale or supply of medicines; these are covered in chapter 6 (Pharmacy Medicines), chapter 7 (General Sale Medicines) and chapter 8 (Prescription Only Medicines).

Licensing authority and ministers

The licensing authority is responsible for the grant, renewal, variation, suspension and revocation of licences, authorisations, certificates and registrations under the Human Medicines Regulations 2012 (Reg.6). The *licensing authority* means either or both the Secretary of State for Health (who must enforce or secure the enforcement of the Regulations and relevant EU provisions in England, Wales and Scotland) and the Minister for Health, Social

[5]Upjohn 1989 C-122/5

Services and Public Safety (who is responsible for enforcement in Northern Ireland; note that Northern Ireland will not be considered further in this chapter). Note that the Regulations apply to the whole of the UK. Generally, any function that is conferred on the licensing authority by the Regulations is to be exercised by the ministers acting jointly, although there are provisions for certain functions to be exercised by either of them acting alone or both of them acting jointly. While the ministers comprise the licensing authority, these licensing functions are carried out by either the MHRA (which is an executive agency of the Department of Health) or the European Medicines Agency (chapter 3). The MHRA is also the licensing authority for all other licences required under the Regulations (e.g. manufacturers, wholesale dealers) and is also the enforcement authority for these matters in the UK.

Advertisements relating to medicinal products

Regulation 7 of the HMRs defines an advertisement as including anything to promote the prescription, supply or use of a medicinal product. Advertising and sales promotion is discussed in chapter 4.

General interpretation

Regulation 8 of the HMRs includes definitions that apply across the whole Regulations except where there are additional lists that refer to a particular Part only (e.g. there is a further list of definitions that apply only to Part 12, concerned with 'dealings' with medicinal products; Reg.213). Most have been defined in the relevant chapter but the following used in this chapter should be noted:

Administer means administer to a human being orally, by injection or by introduction into the body in any other way or by external application (whether or not by direct application to the body), either in its existing state or after it has been dissolved or dispersed in, or diluted or mixed with a substance used as a vehicle

Hospital includes a clinic, nursing home or similar institution.

Part 2 Administration

Two advisory bodies are established under the Regulations, namely the Commission on Human Medicines (HMRs Reg.9) and the British Pharmacopoeia Commission (BPC) (HMRs Reg.11). Each advisory body must have at least eight members and may co-opt one or more additional members for the purposes of a meeting. An advisory body, or the advisory bodies acting jointly, may with the approval of the licensing authority appoint one or more subcommittees, known as expert advisory groups (see below). Each advisory body must give a report to the ministers each year (HMRs Reg.12), at a time specified by the ministers, about the performance of its functions and of those of any expert advisory group appointed by it. The Secretary of State must lay a copy of each report before parliament.

Commission on Human Medicines

The Commission on Human Medicines was established in 2005, under section 2 of the Medicines Act. The 2012 Regulations continue to provide for this body (Reg.9), the members and chair of which are appointed by the ministers, who must consult the Scottish ministers before making such appointments.

The Commission on Human Medicines must give advice to either or both of the ministers in relation to certain matters if the minister (or ministers) requests it or the Commission considers it appropriate to give it. Those matters are any relating to the execution of any duty imposed by, or to the exercise of any power conferred by, the Human Medicines Regulations 2012 or the Clinical Trials Regulations, or otherwise relating to medicinal products.

The Commission on Human Medicines must:

a give advice with respect to the safety, quality and efficacy of medicinal products and promote the collection and investigation of information relating to adverse reactions, for the purposes of enabling such advice to be given; and

b advise the licensing authority if the licensing authority:
   i is required under Schedule 11 or the Clinical Trials Regulations, to consult the Commission about any matter arising under those provisions, or
   ii consults the Commission about any matter arising under those provisions.

British Pharmacopoeia Commission

The Medicines Act established the legal status of the BPC and of the *British Pharmacopoeia* (BP) as the UK standard for medicinal products. The 2012 Regulations continue to provide for this body, the members and chair of which are appointed by the ministers, who must consult the Scottish ministers before making such appointments. The BPC must prepare, or cause to be prepared editions of the BP and any other compendia (HMRs Reg.317) and lists of British Approved Names (HMRs Reg.319) (chapter 15).

Expert advisory groups

The licensing authority may direct that either of the above advisory bodies appoint one or more subcommittees (HMRs Part 2, Reg.14), known as expert advisory groups, to assist them in their work. An advisory body may delegate any of its functions other than those of providing advice to the licensing authority in any case where the licensing authority is required to consult the advisory body under Schedule 11 to the Regulations or the Clinical Trials Regulations. An advisory body may, however, arrange for an expert advisory group to provide advice to the advisory body in relation to the performance of those functions. Regulation 14 also stipulates who may be a member of an expert advisory group and further provisions about advisory bodies and expert advisory groups are found in Schedule 2 to the Regulations.

At the time of going to press, the following expert advisory groups have been established:

- Anti-infectives/HIV/Hepatology
- Biologicals/Vaccines
- Cardiovascular/Diabetes/Renal/Respiratory/Allergy
- Chemistry, Pharmacy and Standards
- Clinical Trials
- Dermatology/Rheumatology/Gastroenterology/Immunology
- Medicines for Women's Health
- Neurology/Pain Management/Psychiatry
- Oncology and Haematology
- Paediatric Medicines
- Patient and Public Engagement
- Pharmacovigilance.

Part 11 Pharmacovigilance

Part 11 of the HMRs places general obligations on the licensing authority, with respect to pharmacovigilance, including an obligation to operate and audit a pharmacovigilance system. Further obligations are applied to the holders of marketing authorisations (chapter 3) but for a detailed account of the pharmacovigilance regime, readers are directed to the HMRs themselves and to the relevant section of the MHRA website (see end of chapter).

Regulation 178 states that the licensing authority must:

a take all appropriate measures to encourage the reporting to it of suspected adverse reactions;
b facilitate reporting through the provision of alternative reporting formats in addition to web-based formats;

c take all appropriate measures to obtain accurate and verifiable data for the scientific evaluation of suspected adverse reaction reports;

d ensure that the public is given important information on pharmacovigilance concerns relating to the use of a medicinal product in a timely manner, through publication on the UK web portal, and through other means of publicly available information as necessary; and

e ensure that all appropriate measures are taken to identify any biological medicinal product (including name and batch number) prescribed, dispensed or sold in the UK which is the subject of a suspected adverse reaction report through the methods for collecting data and, where necessary, the follow up of suspected adverse reaction reports.

Part 16: Enforcement

Part 16 of the HMRs covers enforcement. The primary duty of enforcing the Regulations in England, Wales and Scotland rests with the Secretary of State (HMRs Reg.323). There are provisions for ministers to delegate many of their functions to other authorities, but licensing requirements and those provisions which affect hospitals (except so much of the hospital as is a registered pharmacy) or the premises of a doctor's or dentist's practice are solely the responsibility of the ministers. In England, Wales and Scotland, arrangements can be made or directions given whereby local drugs authorities and/or the GPhC can have certain duties or exercise certain powers concurrently with the ministers. In Scotland, these enforcement authorities cannot themselves institute proceedings. Under Reg.323 (2), the Secretary of State may delegate (and has delegated) the duty of enforcement in connections with pharmacies and the retail distribution of medicines to the GPhC (chapters 22, 23 and 24). Other enforcement duties may be given to the GPhC and to local authorities (drugs authorities) as the appropriate ministers may decide. In addition, Part IV of the Medicines Act 1968 (Pharmacies) is retained and under that legislation, the GPhC is responsible for the maintenance of the Register of Pharmacy Premises (chapter 5) and for disciplinary control over bodies corporate and representatives of pharmacists carrying on retail pharmacy businesses (chapter 24).

The GPhC, concurrently with the minister, is also required to enforce the provisions relating to sale and supply of medicines not subject to general sale (HMRs Reg.220) and sale or supply of a Prescription Only Medicine (POM; Reg.214). The provisions relating to sale or supply of medicinal products subject to general sale (Reg.221) and sale of medicinal products from automatic machines (Reg.222) are enforced, concurrently with the minister, by the GPhC in relation to premises that are registered pharmacies and, in each area for which there is a drugs authority (see below), by that drugs authority in relation to premises that are not registered pharmacies.

Here, *premises* includes any place and a ship, aircraft, hovercraft or vehicle (Reg.323(11)).

The Secretary of State may make arrangements for either or both of the GPhC or, in respect of each area for which there is a drugs authority, the drugs authority for the area, concurrently with the Secretary of State, to enforce the following provisions:

1 compliance with standards specified in certain publications (Reg.251);
2 offences relating to dealings with medicinal products: compliance with standards specified in certain publications (Reg.255(1)(e));
3 packaging and leaflets (HMRs Part 13); and
4 requirements relating to advertising (HMRs Part 14)

Arrangements made with the GPhC in relation to HMRs Part 14, chapter 2 are to be limited to the enforcement of those provisions in respect of:

1 advertisements displayed or representations made on or in any premises where medicinal products are sold by retail or supplied in circumstances corresponding to retail sale;
2 advertisements displayed on any website associated with such premises; and
3 advertisements displayed on, or in close proximity to, a vending machine in which medicinal products are offered or exposed for sale.

Drugs authority (HMRs Reg.323 (10)) means:

a in England:
  i in relation to a non-metropolitan county, metropolitan district or London borough, the council of that county, district or borough, and
  ii in relation to the City of London (including the Inner Temple and the Middle Temple), the Common Council of the City of London;
b in Wales, the council of a county or county borough; and
c in Scotland, a council constituted in relation to a local government area under section 2 of the Local Government etc. (Scotland) Act 1994.

Under the Act, the GPhC is also required to enforce the provisions relating to:

1 prohibition of sale or supply, or importation, of medicinal products of specified description (s.62) (chapters 13 and 24)
2 sale and supply and offer of sale or supply of adulterated medicinal products (s.63)
3 sale of medicinal products not of the nature or quality demanded (s.64)
4 annual return of premises to the Registrar (s.77)
5 restrictions on use of titles, descriptions and emblems (s.78)

6 regulations imposing further restrictions on titles (s.79 (2))

7 regulations relating to requirements for containers (s.87(2))

8 regulations relating to distinctive colours, shapes and marking of medicinal products (s.88 (3)).

Inspection, sampling and seizure

A right of entry, and a right to inspect, take samples and seize goods and documents are given (HMRs Reg.325 and Reg.327) to an inspector in order to ascertain whether there has been a contravention of the Regulations. *Inspector* means a person authorised in writing by an enforcement authority for the purposes of Part 16 (enforcement) of the Human Medicines Regulations 2012 (HMRs Reg.8).

An inspector, having produced his/her identification if requested to do so, is empowered:

1 at any reasonable time, to enter premises (which includes any place and a ship, aircraft, hovercraft or vehicle) in order to determine whether there has been a contravention of any part of the Regulations which the enforcement authority is required or empowered to enforce.

2 to inspect any of the following to determine whether there has been a contravention of any provision of the Regulations which the enforcement authority must or may enforce:

a a substance or article appearing to the inspector to be a medicinal product;

b an article appearing to the inspector to be a container or package used or intended to be used to contain a medicinal product, or a label or leaflet used or intended to be used in connection with a medicinal product;

c plant or equipment, including computer equipment, appearing to the inspector to be used or intended to be used in connection with the manufacture, assembly, importation, sale, supply or advertising of, or wholesale dealing in, medicinal products;

d any process of manufacture or assembly of medicinal products;

e the way in which medicinal products, or the materials used in the manufacture of medicinal products, are tested at any stage in the process of manufacture or assembly;

f information and documents (including any that are stored electronically) relating to the manufacture, assembly, importation, sale, supply or advertising of, or wholesale dealing in, medicinal products; or

g information and documents (including any that are stored electronically) relating to the safety of medicinal products, including information and documents relating to compliance with specified parts of the Regulations;

3   to take or purchase a sample of a substance or article which appears to the inspector to be a medicinal product which is, or is intended to be, sold or supplied or a substance or article used, or intended to be used, in the manufacture of a medicinal product;

4   to require a person carrying on a business which consists of or includes the manufacture, assembly, importation, sale, supply or advertising of, or wholesale dealing in, medicinal products, or a person employed in connection with such a business, to produce information or documents relating to the business which are in the person's possession or under the person's control;

5   to take copies of information or documents mentioned, above;

6   to seize and retain a substance or article appearing to the inspector to be a medicinal product if the inspector reasonably believes that an offence under the Regulations is being or has been committed in relation to, or by means of, that substance or article;

7   to seize and retain any document (including any that are stored electronically) or anything inspected, or discovered in the course of an inspection, if the inspector reasonably believes that it may be required as evidence in proceedings; and

8   to require a person who has the authority to do so to open a container, package or vending machine or to allow the inspector to open a container, package or vending machine, for the purpose of enabling the inspector to seize a substance, article, document or other thing, as outlined above.

Where an inspector seizes a substance, article, document or other thing, s/he must, where practicable, inform the person, if any, from whom it was seized, and the occupier of the premises from which it was seized. If the seizure is from a vending machine, s/he must inform the person whose name and address are stated on the machine to be those of the machine's owner or, if no name and address are stated, the occupier of the premises on which the machine stands or to which it is affixed.

Twenty-four hours' notice must be given to the occupier if it is intended to enter any premises used only as a private dwelling. In cases where admission is refused, or such refusal is anticipated and notice of the intention to apply for a warrant has been given to the occupier, or where a request for admission, or the giving of notice, would defeat the object of the entry or where the case is one of urgency or the premises are unoccupied or the occupier is temporarily absent, a justice of the peace may issue a warrant authorising an inspector to enter premises, by force if necessary (Reg.326). Regulation 326 goes into further detail regarding who may issue a warrant and its period of validity.

An inspector entering any premises by virtue of a right of entry (Reg.325) or of a warrant under Regulation 326 may be accompanied by such persons, and take such equipment, as the inspector thinks appropriate. Where an inspector enters premises in pursuance of a warrant under Regulation 326, the inspector must, if the property is unoccupied or the occupier is temporarily absent, leave the premises as effectively secured against trespass as they were before the inspector entered.

It is an offence either to intentionally obstruct an inspector or to fail to comply with a requirement relating to inspection, sampling or seizure properly made by him or her. It is also an offence, without reasonable cause, to fail to give an inspector any other assistance or information which s/he may reasonably require in order to perform a function under the Regulations or to provide false information in relation to any such requirement (Reg.334). The Regulation goes on to say that 'Nothing in this regulation is to be read as requiring a person to answer a question or to give information if doing so might incriminate that person or the spouse or civil partner of that person' (HMRs Reg.334(8)). However, the Pharmacy Order 2010 Article 49 makes it clear that failure on the part of pharmacists or pharmacy technicians to supply information or produce any document required for a fitness to practise investigation may lead to a court order to comply (chapter 24).

An inspector who has exercised a right of entry and discloses to any other person, except in the performance of his/her duty, information about any manufacturing process or trade secret obtained by him/her in the premises commits an offence. It is similarly an offence for any person to disclose any information obtained by him/her in pursuance of the Regulations (Reg.332). An exception to this is if the inspector is or is acting on behalf of a public authority for the purposes of the Freedom of Information Act 2000.

Sampling

A detailed procedure is set out in Schedule 31 of the HMRs for dealing with samples taken by a *sampling officer* (i.e. a person authorised by an enforcement authority). A sample must be divided into three parts, two being retained by the sampling officer and the third given to the seller in the manner prescribed in the Schedule, according to the circumstances. One of the parts retained by the sampling officer may be submitted for analysis to a medicines control laboratory or to a laboratory available for the purpose in accordance with any arrangements made by the enforcing authority in question.

The laboratory to which a sample is submitted must analyse or examine the sample as soon as practicable and must issue and send to the sampling officer a certificate specifying the result of the analysis or examination. Such a certificate is to be sufficient evidence of the facts stated in the document in proceedings for an offence under the Regulations, unless another party to proceedings requires that the person who issued the certificate be called as a witness. In proceedings in Scotland, if the person who issued the certificate is called as a witness, that person's evidence is to be sufficient evidence of the facts stated in the certificate.

The second part of the sample retained by the sampling officer must be produced as evidence and, if required by either party, must be submitted for analysis to the government chemist or be sent for other examination to a laboratory specified by the court.

A sampling officer must pay the value of a sample if it is demanded by the person from whom it is taken; there is provision for arbitration about the value in case of a dispute. The taking of a sample by a sampling officer has effect as though it were a sale of a medicinal product and the provisions of section 64 of the Act relating to the protection of purchasers apply (chapter 13). Any person, other than an inspector or person authorised by an enforcement authority, who has purchased a medicinal product may submit a sample of it for analysis to the public analyst for the area where it was purchased, subject to the analyst's right to demand payment of the prescribed fee in advance. The public analyst must analyse the sample as soon as is practicable and issue a certificate in the form prescribed (HMRs Reg.330).

Part 17 Legal proceedings

Where a contravention is by reason of the act or omission of another person, that other person may be charged and convicted whether or not proceedings are taken against the person committing the contravention. A person charged with an offence who proves to the satisfaction of the court (a) that s/he exercised all due diligence to prevent the contravention and (b) that the contravention was due to the act or omission another person shall, subject to certain procedural requirements, be acquitted of the offence (HMRs Reg.335).

When an offence is committed by a body corporate, any director, secretary or other similar officer of the body corporate may be proceeded against, as well as the body corporate, if it is proved that the offence was committed with his/her consent or connivance, or was attributable to his/her neglect (Reg.338). Section 124 of the Medicines Act specifically provides that the superintendent pharmacist of a retail pharmacy business (whether or not a member of the board), and any pharmacist manager or assistant acting under his/her direction, shall be regarded as officers for this purpose. Medicinal products proved to have been found on a vehicle from which those goods are sold are presumed to have been offered for sale unless the contrary is proved (HMRs Reg.340). This presumption applies when the offences concern the offering for sale of a medicinal product contrary to the restriction on retail sales (under HMRs Regs.220 and 221). There is also a presumption in respect of the possession of medicinal products (or leaflets referring to them) on premises at which the person charged carries on a business including the supply of those goods. When the offence concerns packaging and package leaflets (Regs.268 and 269) or requirements relating to child safety (Reg.276), a person is presumed, unless the contrary is proved, to have had medicinal products in his/her possession for the purpose of sale or supply.

Warranty can be pleaded (HMRs Reg.336) as a defence to a charge of contravening Regulations 251 (compliance with standards specified in certain publications), 268 and 269 (offences relating to packaging and package leaflets), 273 (child-resistant containers for regulated medicinal products) and 275 (colouring of aspirin and paracetamol products for children).

Subject to certain formalities, a defendant can rely on warranty if s/he proves that:

a s/he purchased the substance or article in the UK as one which could lawfully be sold, supplied or offered for sale or supply or which could be lawfully sold, supplied or offered for sale or supply under the name or description or for the purpose under or for which it was sold;

b the relevant substance or article was sold with a written warranty certifying a matter specified in paragraph (a), and that if the warranty were true the alleged offence would not have been committed;

c at the time of the commission of the alleged offence the defendant had no reason to believe that the matter certified in the warranty was otherwise; and

d at the time of the commission of the alleged offence the relevant substance or article was in the same state as when the defendant purchased it.

A defendant who is an employee of the person who purchased the substance or article under warranty can rely on the same defence as his/her employer, and a name or description entered in an invoice is deemed to be written warranty that the article described can be sold under that description. It is an offence for a person to intentionally or recklessly give a purchaser a false warranty or to intentionally to apply (a) a warranty or (b) a certificate of analysis (see above) given in relation to one substance or article to a different substance or article (Reg.337). The validity of licences and licensing decisions is considered under licensing (chapter 3), and certificates issued by the Registrar relating to the premises are dealt with under pharmacies (chapter 4).

Medical devices

The Medical Devices Regulations 2002[6] made under consumer protection legislation implement the EC Medical Devices Directives into UK law. They cover such items as intrauterine devices and diaphragms, dental fillings,

[6] SI 2002 No. 618

contact lens care products, non-medicated dressings, sutures and ligatures. There are currently four sets of Medical Device Regulations implementing all of the Medical Devices Directives and amendments to date.

The Medical Devices Regulations 2002 define a *medical device* as any instrument, apparatus, appliance, software, material or other article, whether used alone or in combination, together with any accessories, including the software intended by its manufacturer to be used specifically for diagnosis or therapeutic purposes or both and necessary for its proper application, which:

a is intended by the manufacturer to be used for human beings for the purpose of:
  i diagnosis, prevention, monitoring, treatment or alleviation of disease,
  ii diagnosis, monitoring, treatment, alleviation of or compensation for an injury or handicap,
  iii investigation, replacement or modification of the anatomy or of a physiological process, or
  iv control of conception; and
b does not achieve its principal intended action in or on the human body by pharmacological, immunological or metabolic means, even if it is assisted in its function by such means, and includes devices intended to administer a medicinal product or which incorporate as an integral part a substance which, if used separately, would be a medicinal product and which is liable to act upon the body with action ancillary to that of the device.

The 2002 Regulations have been amended by Regulations in 2003[7] which cover, amongst other things, the re-classification of breast implants, in 2007[8] (which covers the re-classification of total hip, knee and shoulder joints) and in 2008[9] and in 2012[10] to meet EU obligations.

Conformity: CE marking

The Regulations place obligations on manufacturers to ensure that their devices are safe and fit for their intended purpose before they are CE marked and placed on the market in any EC Member State. The MHRA administers and enforces the legislation. *CE marking* is a mandatory conformity mark for products placed on the market in the European Economic Area (EEA). The letters *CE* are the abbreviation of the French phrase *conformité Européene*, which literally means European conformity. The CE marking on a product indicates that the manufacturer is satisfied that the product conforms to

[7]The Medical Devices (Amendment) Regulations SI 2003 No. 697
[8]The Medical Devices (Amendment) Regulations SI 2007 No. 400
[9]The Medical Devices (Amendment) Regulations SI 2008 No. 2936
[10]The Medical Devices (Amendment) Regulations SI 2012 No. 1426

all relevant essential requirements in the Directives and that it is fit for its intended purpose (Directive 93/68/EEC). In general, a medical device cannot be marketed in Europe without carrying a CE marking. A CE marking is applied by the manufacturer and means that the device meets the relevant regulatory requirements and, when used as intended, works properly and is acceptably safe.

For all but the very lowest risk devices, this must be verified by an independent certification body, called a Notified Body, before the CE marking can be affixed. The MHRA is responsible for appointing UK Notified Bodies and regularly audits them to ensure that they perform to the required standards. Custom-made devices, devices undergoing a clinical investigation and *in vitro* diagnostic medical devices for performance evaluation are exempted from the requirement for CE marking. Unless there are grounds for suspecting that a device may pose a risk to public health, Member States must not 'create any obstacles to the placing on the market or the putting into service of any medical devices as defined under the Directive bearing a legitimate CE marking' (Directive 98/79/EC). This means that a CE-marked device may have access to the whole of the Community market and manufacturers are not required to comply with any national schemes when exporting their devices to other countries in the EU.

Summary

- European Directives and Regulations together with the Medicines Act 1968 and the Human Medicines Regulations 2012 regulate the manufacture, distribution and importation of medicines for human use.
- The advisory structure for the ministers is principally the Commission on Human Medicines, which may delegate some of its functions to an expert advisory group.
- The definition of a medicinal product is set out in the Human Medicines Regulations 2012.
- The enforcement of parts of the Regulations falls upon the MHRA and the GPhC; some elements are enforced by 'drugs authorities'.
- The powers of the inspectors are laid down and stringent conditions relate to the taking of samples within a sampling procedure.
- Those liable to commit offences under the Regulations are listed together with any defences that can be raised.
- Medical devices are controlled under consumer protection legislation but are still administered by the MHRA; a CE mark means that a device is safe and fit for its intended purpose.

Further reading

Human Medicines Regulations (2012) SI 2012 No. 1916, *Explanatory memorandum*: http://www.legislation.gov.uk/uksi/2012/1916/pdfs/uksiem_20121916_en.pdf (accessed 21 November 2012).

Royal Pharmaceutical Society (2012). Support Bulletin No. 15 August 2012 Human Medicines Regulations 2012 *Pharm J*, 289: 200 (free to members or available on subscription).

Royal Pharmaceutical Society (published annually). *Medicines, Ethics and Practice: The Professional Guide for Pharmacists*. London: Royal Pharmaceutical Society (includes practice guidance on many of the topics in this chapter; free to members).

Websites

Legislation (can be searched on year and SI number or title): http://www.legislation.gov.uk

Medicines and Healthcare products Regulatory Agency: http://www.mhra.gov.uk

Royal Pharmaceutical Society (member access only; lists legal classifications of medicines and further practice guidance): http://www.rpharms.com

3

Human medicines: the licensing system

Cathal Gallagher

Licensing requirements are set out in EU Council Directives and Regulations. These directives were entered into UK law by the Medicines Act 1968, which itself enabled approximately 200 SIs to be created over the course of the next 44 years. These Regulations provided for marketing authorisations, manufacturer's licences, wholesale dealer's licences and clinical trial certificates. In August 2012, the Human Medicines Regulations 2012 (HMRs) came into force.[1] The aim was to bring the existing legislation into one set of Regulations and to simplify the way provisions are drafted. Although much of the 1968 Act and associated secondary legislation were repealed by the Human Medicines Regulations 2012, some sections/Regulations/Orders remain in force. In this chapter, the provisions of the Directives and the Act and its SIs are collated and summarised under appropriate headings. The SIs mentioned are those in force at the end of September 2012. Without the appropriate marketing authorisation, licence or certificate, it is not lawful for any person, in the course of a business carried on by him/her, to manufacture, sell, supply, export or import into the UK any of these products unless some exemption is provided in the Act or the HMRs.

Marketing authorisations for human medicines

The EEC issued proposals for a two-tiered system for obtaining marketing authorisations, which was implemented in 1994. The system comprises a centralised system and a national (Member State) system. The centralised licensing system is administered by the European Medicines Agency and is used for new active substances and certain high-technology and biotechnology products. The centralised procedure is set out in Regulation 2004/726/EC, which has direct effect on Member States without the need for any separate implementation by a Member State.

[1] Human Medicines Regulations SI 2012 No. 1916

The Member State system, which includes the mutual recognition and decentralised systems, is administered by MHRA in the UK. Council Directive 2001/83/EEC, together with the other European Pharmaceutical Directives, implemented by UK Regulations,[2] establish the procedures for the Member State system. The Regulations implement the Pharmaceutical Directives concerned by cross-reference to the Directives themselves, rather than setting out the details in full.

The decentralised procedure is applicable where a marketing authorisation does not yet exist in any of the Member States. Under the rules of this procedure, identical applications are submitted in all Member States where a marketing authorisation is sought. A 'reference' Member State, selected by the applicant, prepares draft assessment documents within 120 days and sends them to the 'concerned' Member States. Concerned Member States either approve the assessment or the application continues into arbitration procedures.

Under the mutual recognition procedure, the assessment and marketing authorisation of one reference Member State is 'mutually recognised' by other concerned Member States (i.e. other Member States recognise an existing marketing authorisation from another State). At the end of the mutual recognition procedure, a national marketing authorisation is issued in the 'concerned' Member State (e.g. by the MHRA). This mechanism is common for generic drugs.

A person may not sell or supply, or offer to sell or supply, a medicinal product otherwise than in accordance with the terms of a marketing authorisation, a certificate of registration, a traditional herbal registration or an authorisation issued for justified public health reasons under Article 126a of Directive 2001/83/EC (HMRs Reg.46(2)).

Medicinal products may include immunological products, medicinal products based on human blood or blood constituents and medicinal products based on radioisotopes (radiopharmaceuticals). However, the Human Medicines Regulations 2012 do not apply to whole human blood or any human blood component other than plasma prepared by a method involving an industrial process (HMRs Reg.2). Homoeopathic medicinal products are dealt with separately (HMRs Part 6).

Proprietary medicinal product means any ready prepared medicinal product placed on the market in the UK under a special name and in a special pack (Council Directive 2001/83/EC, Art.1 and Art.2).

Radiopharmaceutical means a medicinal product which, when ready for use, contains one or more radionuclides included for a medicinal purpose (HMRs Reg.8).

[2] The Medicines for Human Use (Marketing Authorisations etc.) Regulations SI 1994 No. 3144 as amended by SI 2002 No. 236 (both now repealed) and SI 2005 No. 2754

Blood component means red cells, white cells, platelets or plasma (HMRs Reg.8).

The holder of a marketing authorisation for a medicinal product (HMRs Reg.58(4)) may:

a sell, supply or export the product;
b procure its sale, supply or exportation;
c procure its manufacture or assembly, in accordance with the marketing authorisation.

In dealing with an application for a marketing authorisation, the licensing authority must give particular consideration to the safety, quality and efficacy of the products.

If any of the medicinal products to which the application relates is liable to be imported from a country other than one in the EEA, the material or information accompanying the application (HMRs Reg.50(3)) may include an undertaking from the manufacturer of the product to comply with the matters set out in Schedule 9 of the Regulations (HMRs Reg.50(4)). An application for a marketing authorisation for a medicinal product for human use in either of the procedures must be accompanied by the particulars set out in Council Directive 2001/83/EEC. Article 11 sets out the details of the Summary of Product Characteristics. This term means the information required to accompany any application for a marketing authorisation under Council Directive 2001/83/EEC (Art.11).

Apart from the Summary of Product Characteristics, the particulars required to be given in a full application include the kind of activity to be undertaken (e.g. selling, procuring manufacture, etc.); the pharmaceutical form of the product; its composition, physical characteristics and medicinal use; method of manufacture and assembly; quality control procedures; containers and labelling; reports of experimental and biological studies and of clinical trials and studies; any adverse reactions; and where the product is made abroad plus documentary evidence of authorisation relating to manufacture, assembly, and so on. Special additional conditions apply for applications concerning immunological products, radiopharmaceuticals and medicinal products derived from human blood or human plasma.

Abridged applications are permitted where the relevant data have been submitted in an earlier application, or data about the kind of product in question are well documented. (Renewal applications for licences and certificates are dealt with in HMRs Reg.66.) Standard conditions and obligations for marketing authorisations are prescribed in the relevant EC directives. These provisions are incorporated in the marketing authorisation unless the applicant desires that any of them shall be excluded or modified in respect of his/her product and his/her request is granted.

Revocation, variation or suspension

There is provision in the Regulations for the marketing authorisation to be revoked, varied or suspended (HMRs Reg.68). The licensing authority may impose an urgent safety restriction on the holder of a marketing authorisation (HMRs Reg.68(10)). Where this occurs, the authority must notify the suspension to the European Medicines Agency, the European Commission and all other Member States by the end of the next working day following the day on which the suspension comes into force (HMRs Reg.68(10)(b)). Providing specific conditions are met, the licensing authority may suspend the use, sale, supply or offer for sale or supply within the UK of a product to which a UK marketing authorisation relates (HMRs Reg.69).

Post-authorisation requirements

After granting of a UK marketing authorisation, the licensing authority may impose an obligation on the holder of the authorisation to conduct a post-authorisation safety study (if there are concerns about the risks of a medicinal product) or a post-authorisation efficacy study (if the understanding of the disease or the clinical methodology indicate that previous efficacy evaluations might have to be revised significantly) (HMRs Reg.61).

Where the licensing authority imposes such an obligation, it must give written notice to the holder of:

1 the imposition of the obligation;
2 the justification for the imposition;
3 the objectives and timeframe for submission and conduct of the study; and
4 the opportunity to present written observations and the time limit specified for doing so.

Generic products

A product is defined as a generic medicinal product (HMRs Reg.48(2)) when it has:

1 the same qualitative and quantitative composition in active substances; and
2 the same pharmaceutical form as the reference medicinal product; and
3 the bioequivalence with the reference product has been demonstrated by appropriate bioavailability studies.

There has to be a balance struck between allowing a person applying for a marketing authorisation for a follow-on product (e.g. a generic product) to be able to use the safety and efficacy data which has been used by the original innovator against the need for such an applicant being forced to repeat that data for the product when that information is already with the licensing authority. This balance is achieved by allowing a follow-on competitor to rely on the data for the original product only after the passage of a 'data exclusivity period'. The procedure under which a generic product can rely on the innovator's data after the end of data exclusivity period is known as an 'abridged procedure'. An applicant for a UK marketing authorisation for a relevant medicinal product that is a generic medicinal product may provide abridged information in relation to the application in accordance with Articles 10(1), (5) and (6) of Directive 2001/83/EC (HMRs Reg.51(1)).

The existing 'data exclusivity periods' under Council Directive 2001/83/EC vary from 6 to 10 years across the EU and continued to apply until November 2005, after which the amending Directive 2004/27/EC took effect. This harmonises the exclusivity period across the EU and is known as the $8 + 2 + 1$ rule. The data can be used after 8 years but the product cannot be marketed for a further 2 years. An extra year's protection can be added if the original product had therapeutic indications which were of 'significant clinical benefit' over other remedies, under the terms of Article10 (1) of 2001/83/EC (HMRs Reg.51(2)).

Borderline products

Where the licensing authority are of the opinion that a product is a relevant medicinal product,[3] they may by notice in writing serve on any person who has placed the product on the market informing him/her that the product is a relevant medicinal product and needs to be licensed together with the reasons why they are so minded. Statutory provisions provide for initial representations to be made to the licensing authority and, if necessary, for further representations to be made to an independent review body. Once a final determination has been made, the licensing authority may serve notice requiring the person not to put the product on the market or to stop marketing it from a date specified. Detailed procedures are set out in the legislation (HMRs Reg.159).

Immunity from liability for unauthorised medicinal products

In response to the suspected or confirmed spread of pathogenic agents, toxins, chemical agents or nuclear radiation which may cause harm to humans, the licensing authority may recommend or require the use of:

1 a medicinal product without an authorisation; or
2 a medicinal product with an authorisation, but for a therapeutic indication that is not permitted under the authorisation.

[3]Defined in HMRs Part 5, Reg.48 (not a registerable homoeopathic or traditional herbal medicinal product)

The holder of the marketing authorisation, a manufacturer of the product, an officer, servant or employee of the holder or manufacturer, or a healthcare professional shall not be liable to any civil liability for any loss or damage resulting from the use of the product in accordance with the recommendation or requirement (HMRs Reg.345). A 'healthcare professional' means a doctor, a dentist, a pharmacist, a registered pharmacy technician (HMRs Reg.8),[4] a registered nurse, a registered midwife, a registered optometrist, a registered osteopath,[5] a registered chiropractor,[6] a person registered with the Health and Care Professions Council,[7] (chapter 25) or a person registered as a member of a profession complementary to dentistry.[8]

Parallel importing

The importation from a Member State of the EEC of a medicinal product which is a version of one already the subject of a UK marketing authorisation is known as parallel importing. Parallel imports are imported into one Member State from another and placed on the market in the destination Member State, outside the formal channels of either the manufacturer or its licensed distributor. Parallel trade is legal under EU Law.

Legal basis for parallel imports

The legal basis for the trade in medicines can be traced back to the Treaty of Rome 1957, Article 30, which prohibits 'quantitative restrictions on imports and all measures having equivalent effect ... between member states [of the EEC]'. Furthermore, Article 31 declares that 'member states shall refrain from introducing between themselves any new quantitative restrictions or measures having equivalent effect' and Article 32 requires that, in their trade with one another, 'member states shall refrain from making more restrictive the quotas and measures having equivalent effect existing at the date of the entry into force of th[e] Treaty'. In effect, the Treaty allows neither direct restrictions, such as a complete ban, nor indirect restrictions, such as laws favouring the sale of home-produced products over those imported from other EU Member States. However, Article 36 states that the provisions of Articles 30 to 34 shall not preclude prohibitions or restrictions on imports or exports justified on 'grounds of the protection of health and life of humans, animals or plants'. This is accompanied by the qualification that '[s]uch prohibitions or restrictions shall not ... constitute a means of arbitrary discrimination or a disguised restriction on trade between member states'.

[4]Under Art. 19 (2) of the Pharmacy Order SI 2010 No. 231
[5]As defined in s.41 of the Osteopaths Act 1993
[6]As defined in s.43 of the Chiropractors Act 1994
[7]Health and Social Work Professions Order SI 2002 No. 254 (as amended)
[8]Under s.36B of the Dentists Act 1984, as amended

When the matter was referred to the ECJ,[9] it reasoned that the competent administration of the importing Member State would be clearly entitled to require the manufacturer, when they apply for a marketing authorisation, to state whether they produce several variants of the medicinal preparation under the same name for different Member States and, if such is the case, to produce similar documentation for the other variants too, identifying the differences between all these variants. It would only be if the documents produced in this way showed that there were differences which could alter the therapeutic effect that there would be any justification for treating the variants as different medicinal products.

Marketing authorisations for parallel imports

In 1982, the European Commission produced a text outlining the basic principles for an abbreviated form of marketing authorisation for parallel-traded medicines.[10] On 22 December 1986, these recommendations were passed into EU law by Community Directive 87/21/EEC, which amended Article 4 of Directive 65/65/EEC. A modified form of licence application may be considered for such a product, subject to the following conditions:

1 the product to be imported must be a proprietary medicinal product (as defined in Art.1 of Council Directive 2001/83/EC) which is not a vaccine, toxin, serum or based on human blood; a blood constituent; a radioactive isotope; or homoeopathic product as specified in the Directive;
2 it must be covered by a currently valid market authorisation granted by the regulatory body of a Member State;
3 it must have no different therapeutic effect from the product covered by the UK licence; and
4 it must be made by, or under licence to, the UK manufacturer, or by a member of the same group of companies.

If any of the above conditions is not met, the applicant will be invited to apply for a marketing authorisation in the normal way. The holder of a product licence (parallel import) does not require a separate marketing authorisation (HMRs Reg.172).

A product licence (parallel import) is granted for 5 years but normally continues in force only so long as *both* the UK marketing authorisation and the EU marketing authorisation to which it relates remain in force. If either marketing authorisation is revoked, the product licence (parallel import) will automatically fall. If a marketing authorisation is withdrawn, it may be possible to continue to market the product in the UK, but only if the product licence (parallel import) satisfies the strict criteria that the ECJ

[9] Officier van Justitie v de Peijper [1976] ECR 613
[10] Commission Communication on Parallel Imports of Proprietary Medicinal Products for which Marketing Authorisations Have Already Been Granted. C115/5. *Official Journal*, 6 May 1982

have set for the survival of the product licence (parallel import) in these circumstances. These criteria follow from a referral to the ECJ in 1998.[11] These requirements apply to the parallel importing of medicines for human use. Comparable requirements for veterinary medicines are controlled by the Veterinary Medicines Directorate (VMD), which is an Executive Agency of the Department for Environment, Food and Rural Affairs (DEFRA). Manufacturing authorisations for parallel imports apply to 'veterinary medicinal products' as defined in Directive 1002/82/EC (chapter 16).

A case in 1989 (box 3.1) has made it clear that the regulator (now the GPhC) may make additional rules concerning the use of licensed medicines on professional grounds for the protection of the public.

Box 3.1 *Importation of medicines from the EU*

R v Royal Pharmaceutical Society of Great Britain, ex parte Association of Pharmaceutical Importers and Others (1989)

In 1989 the then Royal Pharmaceutical Society of Great Britain (RPSGB) had adopted a provision in its Code of Ethics which, amongst other things, prohibited a pharmacist from substituting, except in an emergency, any other medicine for the medicine specifically ordered on a prescription, even if s/he believed that the quality and therapeutic effect were identical. In 1986, the RPSGB had published a statement to the effect that this rule applied to imported medicines as well as to medicines licensed in the UK. The Association of Parallel Importers, which represented companies which were involved in importing medicines from the European Community, maintained that the RPSGB rule infringed the provisions of the Treaty of Rome on the basis that its effect was to impose a quantitative restriction on their importing medicines – *parallel imports* – from the Community.

The ECJ held that in the absence of any Community legislation regulating the doctor–pharmacist relationship, and in particular the doctor's freedom to prescribe any medicine s/he chose, it was for each EU Member State to decide, within the limits of the Treaty, the degree to which they wish to protect the health of their people and how that was to be achieved. It was said that there was no evidence that the RPSGB rule went beyond what was necessary to achieve the objective, which was to leave the entire responsibility for the treatment of the patient in the hands of the doctor treating him/her. It followed, therefore, that the rule could also be justified under the Treaty on the grounds of the protection of public health.

---

[11]*R v Medicines Control Agency Ex p. Rhone Poulenc Rorer Ltd* (C94/98) [2000] All ER (EC) 46

Registration certificates for homoeopathic medicines for human use

Homoeopathic medicinal product means a medicinal product prepared from homoeopathic stocks in accordance with a homoeopathic manufacturing procedure described by the *European Pharmacopoeia* or, in the absence of such a description in the *European Pharmacopoeia*, in any pharmacopoeia used officially in an EEA country (HMRs Reg.8).

Certificate of Registration means a certificate granted (HMRs Reg.8). In the case of a registrable homoeopathic medicinal product, which meets the requirements laid out in HMRs Reg.102, a marketing authorisation is not required provided that a certificate of registration has been granted. Applications for a certificate of registration under the simplified procedure for a registrable homoeopathic medicinal product must be made in the manner prescribed in the Regulations (HMRs Reg.103). The application must be in writing, in English and include the particulars required by Council Directives 2001/83/EC and 2004/27/EC. Every holder of a certificate of registration must comply with all the obligations set in Council Directive 2001/83/EC, including record keeping, to facilitate withdrawal and recall (HMRs Reg.108).

A *national homoeopathic product* means a homoeopathic medicinal product which does not satisfy the conditions of HMRs Reg.102 and is indicated for the relief or treatment of minor symptoms or minor conditions in humans. Symptoms or conditions are minor 'if they ordinarily and with reasonable safety be relieved or treated without the supervision or intervention of a doctor'. The application for the grant of a UK marketing authorisation for a national homoeopathic product is required to be made in accordance with Schedule 10 of the Human Medicines Regulations 2012, including safety and efficacy data. The holder of the marketing authorisation must keep the data up to date and supply any information which entails amendment to the information.

Registration of traditional herbal medicinal products

Herbal medicinal product means a medicinal product whose only active ingredients are herbal substances or herbal preparations (or both).

Herbal preparation means a preparation obtained by subjecting herbal substances to processes such as extraction, distillation, expression, fractionation, purification, concentration or fermentation, and this includes a comminuted or powdered herbal substance, a tincture, an extract, an essential oil, an expressed juice or a processed exudate.

Herbal substance means a plant or part of a plant, alga, fungus or lichen, or an unprocessed exudate of a plant, defined by the plant part used and the botanical name of the plant, either fresh or dried, but otherwise unprocessed (HMRs Reg.8).

Traditional herbal medicinal product means a herbal medicinal product to which HMRs Reg.125 applies.

Traditional herbal registration means a registration granted by the licensing authority for a traditional herbal medicinal product under the Human Medicines Regulations 2012.

Applications for a traditional herbal registration under the simplified procedure for a traditional herbal medicinal product must be made in the manner prescribed in the Regulations (HMRs Reg.127). The application must be in writing, in English (HMRs Reg.127) and include the particulars required by Council Directives 2001/83/EC and 2004/27/EC so far as is applicable to traditional herbal medicinal products (HMRs Reg.128).

Article 126a authorisations

Where no UK marketing authorisation, certificate of registration or traditional herbal registration is in force for a product, nor is any application pending, the licensing authority may grant an Article 126a authorisation where it considers that the placing of the product on the market in the UK is justified for public health reasons (HMRs Reg.156). The product must be imported from another EU Member State in which the product is licensed in accordance with the 2001 Directive. An Article 126a authorisation remains in force for the period specified in it unless revoked before the end of that period. That period may be specified by reference to the occurrence or non-occurrence of a particular event or events, such as an epidemic infection.

Falsified Medicines Directive

On 1 July 2011, the EU adopted a new Directive on falsified medicines for human use (Directive 2011/62/EU). This Directive aims to prevent falsified medicines entering the legal supply chain and reaching patients. It introduced harmonised safety and strengthened control measures across Europe by applying new measures, including:

- obligatory features on the outer packaging of medicines to demonstrate that they are authentic;
- strengthened requirements for the inspection of the manufacturers of pharmaceutical ingredients;
- the obligation for manufacturers and distributors to report any suspicion of falsified medicines; and
- an obligatory logo that must be placed on the websites of legally operating online pharmacies, with a link to official national registers.

The Directive came into force on 21 July 2011. Member states will have to start applying these measures from January 2013 when further amendments to the Regulations can be anticipated.

Issue of licences

Manufacturer's and wholesale dealer's licences are issued by the licensing authorities: the MHRA or the European Medicines Agency (see also Council Regulation 26/2004/EC), who may grant, refuse, review, suspend, revoke or vary them (HMRs Regs.23 and 26). A licence remains in force until it is revoked by the licensing authority or surrendered by the holder (HMRs Reg.25). When an application for a licence is refused, the licensing authority must state the reasons for refusal in a notice served on the applicant (HMRs Reg.23(6)). If the holder of a licence, subsequent to its issue, contravenes any provision of that authorisation, a notice suspending or revoking it may be served on the holder (HMRs Reg.26). Similarly, a licence may be suspended where it appears to the licensing authority that it is necessary in the interests of safety (HMRs Reg.28).

Manufacturer's licences

A manufacturer's licence is required by a person who, in the course of a business carried on by him/her, manufactures, assembles or imports from a state other than an EEA country a medicinal product (HMRs Reg.17). The medicinal product, if manufactured or assembled, must be the subject of a marketing authorisation. No licence is required for the importation of a medicinal product by a person who imports a medicinal product for administration to himself or herself or to any other person who is a member of that person's household (HMRs Reg.17(6)).

Manufacture includes any process carried out in the course of making the product but does not include dissolving or dispensing the product in, or diluting or mixing it with, some other substances used as a vehicle for administration (HMRs Reg.8).

Assemble means the enclosing of the products (with or without other medicinal products of the same description) in a container which is labelled before the product is sold or supplied or, where the product (with or without medicinal products of the same description) is already enclosed in a container in which it is to be sold or supplied, labelling the container before the product is sold or supplied in it (HMRs Reg.8). Assembly has a corresponding meaning.

A licence is not required for the manufacture of chemicals and other substances used in the manufacture of ingredients of medicinal products.

Nor is a licence required for the manufacture of ingredients supplied in bulk to other manufacturers (HMRs Reg.2(3)).

Good Manufacturing Practice means the part of quality assurance which ensures that products are consistently produced and controlled in accordance with the quality of standards appropriate to their intended use, the principles and guidelines of which are specified in Directive 2003/94/EC (The Good Manufacturing Practice Directive). The licence holder must comply with the principles and guidelines for good manufacturing practice set out in the Good Manufacturing Practice Directive, and use active substances as starting materials only if those substances have been manufactured or assembled in accordance with those principles and guidelines (insofar as those principles and guidelines relate to starting materials) (HMRs Reg.37).

Applications must be made in the manner prescribed in the Regulations (HMRs Reg.21 and Sch. 3) indicating whether the licence is to relate to manufacturing or assembly or to both. The applicant must describe the products to be manufactured or assembled and give details of any manufacturing operations to be carried out. The qualifications of the production manager and of the person in charge of quality control must be given, and the name and function of the person to whom they are responsible. Where relevant, the qualifications of the person in charge of animals, and of the person responsible for the culture of any living tissue, must also be given. At least one 'qualified person' is required to be nominated whose responsibilities are set out in the Regulations (HMRs Sch. 3, Reg.21(2)).

A *qualified person* means a person who satisfies the provisions in Articles 49 and 50 of the 2001 Directive with respect to qualification and experience (HMRs Reg.8). The standard provisions for a manufacturer's licence are incorporated in every licence unless the applicant has successfully applied for any to be excluded or modified (HMRs Reg.24).

Wholesale dealer's licences

Wholesale dealing refers to selling, supplying, procuring, holding or exporting a medicinal product to a person for the purpose of selling or supplying the product, or administering it or causing it to be administered to one or more human beings or animals, in the course of a business carried on by that person (HMRs Reg.18(8) and the Veterinary Medicines Regulations (VMRs); chapter 16).[12] In simple terms, it refers to the sale or supply of a medicinal product to a person who is not the end user of that product (i.e. for redistribution).

---

[12] The Veterinary Medicines Regulations SI 2011 No. 2159

Council Directive 2001/83/EC requires a wholesale dealer's licence to be held by any person who, in the course of a business carried on by him/her (HMRs Reg.18 and VMRs):

1 sells, or offers for sale, any medicinal products by way of wholesale dealing; or

2 distributes, otherwise than by way of sale, any medicinal product, ready-made veterinary drug or industrially produced medicinal product other than a veterinary drug which has been imported but was not consigned from a Member State of the EU.

No person may distribute by way of wholesale any medicinal product which is subject to Directive 2001/83/EC (proprietary and generic medicinal products) except in accordance with a wholesale dealer's licence and from premises specified in that licence (HMRs Reg.18(3)). A wholesale dealer's licence does not authorise the distribution of a medicinal product by way of wholesale dealing, or possession for the purpose of such distribution, unless a marketing authorisation, Article 126a authorisation, certificate of registration or traditional herbal registration is in force in respect of the product (HMRs Reg.18(9)). A wholesale dealer's licence is also required for exportation of any medicinal product which is subject to the 2001 Directive (proprietary and generic medicinal products) if it is to be exported to a Member State of the EEA (HMRs Reg.18(7)(b)).

No wholesale dealer's licence is required by a person who provides facilities solely for the transport of the medicinal product, or who, in the course of his/her business as an import agent, imports a medicinal product solely to the order of another person who intends to distribute it (HMRs Reg.19(4)). Sales made by the manufacturer of a product are excluded from the definition of wholesale dealing so that s/he does not require a licence in order to sell his/her own products (HMRs Reg.19(1)(a)). Neither is a licence required by the holder of a marketing authorisation or by a person who has assembled the product to the order of the marketing authorisation holder and where the product has not left the premises of the manufacturer or assembler until the sale of the product (HMRs Reg.19(1)(b)). The requirement for a wholesale dealer's licence does not apply to the distribution of a medicinal product by way of wholesale dealing, or to the possession of a medicinal product for the purpose of such distribution, if the distribution or possession is solely for the purpose of exporting the product to states other than EEA countries (HMRs Reg.19(5)). The term *business* includes a professional practice and any activity carried on by a body of persons, whether corporate or unincorporated (HMRs Reg.8). Consequently, all sales that are made to practitioners (whether medical or dental) for use in their practices constitute sales by way of wholesale dealing.

Applications must be made in the manner prescribed in the Regulations (HMRs Reg.21 and Sch. 3) and state the classes of medicinal product which are the subject of the application and the uses for which they are intended, together with the particulars mentioned above. The applicant must also give the name and address and qualifications of the responsible person, details of an emergency plan for the recall of products and details for keeping records by way of invoices, on computer or in any other form relating to all products received or despatched.[13]

There is no statutory requirement for the responsible person to be a pharmacist, although this is desirable. However, s/he should have access to pharmaceutical knowledge and advice when it is required and have personal knowledge of:

1 the relevant provisions of the Human Medicines Regulations 2012;
2 Articles 76–85 of Directive 2001/83/EC as amended on the Community Code relating to medicinal products for human use, as amended;
3 European Commission guidelines on good distribution practice of medicinal products for human use (94/C63/03);
4 the conditions attached to the wholesale dealers licence for which s/he is nominated;
5 the products traded under the licence and the conditions necessary for their safe storage and distribution;
6 the categories of persons to whom products may be distributed; and
7 the quality system and standard operating procedures employed by the licence holder.[14]

The standard provisions for wholesale dealer's licences are incorporated in every licence unless the applicant has successfully applied for any to be excluded or modified (HMRs Reg.24).

Considerations common to manufacturer's and wholesale dealer's licences

In dealing with applications for manufacturer's or wholesale dealer's licences, the licensing authority must, in particular, take into consideration (HMRs Reg.22):

1 the operations proposed to be carried out in pursuance of the licence;
2 the premises in which those operations are to be carried out;
3 the equipment which is or will be available on those premises for carrying out those operations;

[13]The Medicines (Applications for Manufacturer's and Wholesale Dealer's Licences) Amendment Regulations SI 1993 No. 832 (now repealed)
[14]List adapted from *Notes for Applicants and Holders of a Wholesale Dealer's Licence*, MHRA Guidance Note No. 6, August 2006 available from MHRA website

4   the qualifications of the persons under whose supervision those opera-
    tions will be carried out; and
5   the arrangements made or to be made for ensuring the safe-keeping of,
    and the maintenance of, adequate records in respect of medicinal prod-
    ucts manufactured or assembled in pursuance of the licence.

Fees for licences

The fees for the various licences prescribed by the Human Medicines Regulations 2012 are made under the authority of the Medicines Act 1971 in
respect of each licence period. These are amended from time to time to reflect
increased charges and consistency with the relevant EU Directives.

Pharmacovigilance

Part 11 of the Human Medicines Regulations 2012 covers the obligations of
the licensing authority (MHRA) and marketing authorisation holders with
regard to pharmacovigilance; this implements Directive 2010/83/EU. A full
account of these requirements is outside the scope of this book but holders
of manufacturing authorisations must operate a pharmacovigilance system
to capture and evaluate all information and take all appropriate measures
to minimise and prevent risk presented by use of the medicinal product after
the authorisation is granted.

Exemptions

Exemptions for clinical trials

A *clinical trial* is an investigation or series of investigations consisting
of the administration of one or more medicinal products, where there is
evidence that they may be beneficial to a patient or patients, by one or more
doctors or dentists for the purpose of ascertaining what effects, beneficial
or harmful, the products have (HMRs Reg.8). For the manufacture or
assembly of a medicinal product to be used only for the purpose of a clinical
trial, a manufacturer's licence or a marketing authorisation is not required.
Rather, a manufacturing authorisation must be granted by the licensing
authority for the purposes of clinical trials.[15] Details of the requirements
for such an application are outlined in Part 6 and Schedule 6 of the 2004
Regulations. Notification of the supplier's intention must be sent to the
licensing authority. The notice must be accompanied by particulars of the
trial and summaries of pharmaceutical data and of reports made and tests

[15] The Medicines for Human Use (Clinical Trials) Regulations SI 2004 No. 1031, as amended
by SI 2005 No. 2754 and SI 2005 No. 2759 (now repealed) and SI 2006 No. 1928

performed as specified in Schedule 1 to the Order. There is provision for termination of the exemption in certain circumstances, usually on the grounds of safety and for appeals to a person appointed (SI 2005 No. 2754). EC Council Directive 2005/28/EEC (which is implemented by SI 2006 No. 1928) laid down the principles and detailed guidelines for good clinical practice as regards investigational medicinal products for human use.

A certificate is not required if the product to be the subject of the clinical trial is covered by a marketing authorisation and the conditions set out in SI 2004 No. 1031 are met.

Exemptions for animal test certificates

An animal test certificate authorises the conduct of a clinical trial of a veterinary medicinal product in the UK. Usually, a clinical trial involving the use of a veterinary medicinal product must be the subject of a valid animal test certificate, issued by the VMD, before it can be conducted (for information on veterinary medicines, see chapter 16). The animal test certificate holder must conduct the trial in accordance with the terms of the certificate and, under paragraph 9 of Schedule 4, may import anything specified in the animal test certificate in accordance with the conditions in that certificate.[16]

Exemptions for doctors and dentists

No licence is required where a medicinal product is manufactured or assembled by a doctor or dentist and is supplied to a patient in the course of their treatment. The medicinal product must not be manufactured or assembled on a large scale or by an industrial process (HMRs Reg.3).

Exemptions for pharmacists

The exemptions from licensing for pharmacists are contained in section 10 of the 1968 Act, to which a number of subsections were added by legislation.[17] Regulations relating to manufacturer's licences (HMRs Reg.17(1)) and marketing authorisations (HMRs Reg.46) do not apply where any provision of section 10 of the Medicines Act 1968 so provides. However, it is important to note that the HMRs repeal section 10(7) of the Medicines Act (HMRs Reg.349), which, since 1971, has exempted retail pharmacies from the need to hold a wholesale dealer's licence for 'small-scale' wholesaling. This provision was found to be incompatible with the subsequent EU

---

[16]The Veterinary Medicines Regulations SI 2011 No. 2159, Reg.25(7)

[17]The Medicines (Retail Pharmacists – Exemptions from Licensing Requirements) Order SI 1971 No. 1445 and The Medicines for Human Use (Prescribing) Order SI 2005 No. 765 (both now repealed)

Directives. Nevertheless, the MHRA has stated in May 2012 that the supply of medicines by community and hospital pharmacies to other healthcare providers in the UK who need to hold medicines for onward supply to their patients represents an important and appropriate part of professional pharmacy practice and falls within the definition of provision of healthcare services. Such transactions are not deemed by the MHRA to be 'commercial dealing'[18] (chapter 10).

In addition, the MHRA guidance continues:

> Pharmacists needing to obtain small quantities of a medicine from another pharmacist to meet a patient's individual needs may do so without the need for the supplying pharmacy to hold a Wholesale Dealer's Licence only if the transaction meets all of the following criteria:
>
> - it takes place on an occasional basis;
> - the quantity of medicines supplied is small and intended to meet the needs of an individual patient;
> - the supply is made on a not for profit basis.
>
> This restriction does not apply to the exchange of stock between pharmacies that are part of the same legal entity.

Subject to the work being done by or under the supervision of a pharmacist, no licence of any kind is required for any of the following activities being carried out in a registered pharmacy, a hospital, a health centre or a care home service.

Care home service means that given in the Regulation of Care (Scotland) Act 2001.

1 Preparing or dispensing a medicinal product in accordance with a prescription given by a practitioner, or preparing a stock of medicinal products for this purpose (s.10(1)(a)).[19] The stock of medicinal products may be procured from a manufacturer holding the appropriate special licence (see 'Special' dispensing, manufacturing and assembly exemptions below). This exemption also applies to hospitals and health centres (s.10(1) and s.10(4)).

2 Preparing or dispensing a medicinal product in accordance with a specification furnished by the person to whom the product is to be sold for administration to that person or to a person under his/her care, or an animal or herd under his/her control, or preparing a stock of medicinal products for these purposes (s.10(3)). This exemption does not cover any vaccine, plasma or serum for animal use.

---

[18] Supply of medicines by pharmacy to healthcare professionals, MHRA 4 May 2012
[19] All references in this paragraph refer to the Medicines Act 1968 (C. 67)

3 Preparing or dispensing a medicinal product for administration to a person when the pharmacist is requested to do so by or on behalf of that person in accordance with the pharmacist's own judgement as to the treatment required, and that person is present in the pharmacy at the time of the request (counter prescribing) (s.10(4)); a stock of medicinal products prepared in a registered pharmacy in accordance with 1 and 2 above and under this paragraph may be sold or supplied from any other registered pharmacy forming part of the same retail pharmacy business.

4 Preparing a medicinal product or a stock of medicinal products, not to the order of another person but with a view to retail sale or supply, provided that the sale or supply is made from the registered pharmacy where it was prepared and the product is not the subject of an advertisement (s.10(5)). In this connection, advertisement does not include words appearing on the product or its container or package or the display of the product itself, but it does include a show-card (s.10(8)).

5 Assembling a medicinal product (s.10(1)). When medicinal products are assembled in a registered pharmacy for retail sale or supply, they may not be the subject of any advertisement and may only be sold or supplied at the registered pharmacy where they are assembled or at some other registered pharmacy forming part of the same retail pharmacy business.

A retail pharmacist who is responsible for the composition of a medicinal product which s/he intends to sell or supply in the course of his/her business must hold a marketing authorisation if his/her activities fall outside the exemptions set out above. S/he must also have a manufacturer's licence or arrange for the product to be made by a manufacturer who has an appropriate licence.

Exemptions for nurses and midwives

No licence is required where a medicinal product is assembled by a registered nurse or a registered midwife if the nurse or midwife is acting in the course of his or her profession and the medicinal product is supplied to a patient in the course of the treatment of that patient, or to a patient of another doctor or dentist who is a member of the same medical or dental practice. The medicinal product must not be assembled on a large scale or by an industrial process (HMRs Reg.3).

'Specials'

A doctor, dentist, supplementary or independent prescriber does not require a licence of any kind in respect of medicinal products specially prepared by him/her for administration to a particular patient. The exemption extends to the preparation of a medicinal product at the request of another practitioner for administration to one of his/her patients. No licence of any kind is required in relation to a 'special medicinal product' of this kind if:

1 the medicinal product is supplied in response to an unsolicited order;
2 the medicinal product is manufactured and assembled in accordance with the specification of a doctor, dentist, nurse independent prescriber, pharmacist independent prescriber or supplementary prescriber;
3 the medicinal product is for use by a patient for whose treatment that person is directly responsible in order to fulfil the special needs of that patient; and
4 the conditions outlined in HMRs Reg.167 are met.

These conditions include, but are not limited to:

1 the medicinal product is supplied to a doctor, dentist, nurse independent prescriber, pharmacist independent prescriber or supplementary prescriber, or for use under the supervision of a pharmacist in a registered pharmacy, a hospital or a health centre;
2 no advertisement relating to the medicinal product is published by any person (but see chapter 14);
3 the manufacture and assembly of the medicinal product are carried out under such supervision as are adequate to ensure that the medicinal product meets the specification of the person who requires it; and
4 written records of the manufacture or assembly of the medicinal product in accordance with condition 3 are maintained and are available to the licensing authority or to the enforcement authority on request.

Mixing of medicines

The Regulations affecting the manufacturing of medicinal products do not apply to the mixing of medicines by a nurse independent prescriber, a pharmacist independent prescriber or a supplementary prescriber if the mixing of medicines forms part of the clinical management plan for an individual patient. Neither do they apply to a person acting in accordance with the written directions of a doctor, dentist, nurse independent prescriber, pharmacist independent prescriber or a supplementary prescriber if the mixing of medicines forms part of the clinical management plan for an individual patient (HMRs Reg.20).

Mixing of medicines means the combining of two or more medicinal products together for the purposes of administering them to meet the needs of an individual patient.

Hospitals

On 1 April 1991, by virtue of the National Health Service and Community Care Act 1990, all NHS hospitals lost their Crown immunity and became liable to licensing regulations. The type of activities relating to manufacture, assembly and wholesaling varies considerably from one hospital to another, and whether any particular licence is required depends on the individual activity. Certain exemptions exist where an activity takes place under the supervision of a pharmacist in a hospital (Medicines Act 1968, s.10, as amended). Hospital pharmacists requiring further details should contact the MHRA.

Summary

- All dealings in medicinal products are subject to licensing unless specifically exempted.
- Marketing authorisations or licences are needed to place a medicine on the market, to manufacture, wholesale or distribute medicinal products.
- Marketing authorisations relate to medicinal products.
- Registration certificates relate to homoeopathic remedies.
- Traditional herbal registration relates to traditional herbal medicinal products.
- Article 126a authorisations relate to unlicensed medicinal products imported from another EU Member State on public health grounds.
- A manufacturer's licence is required to manufacture, assemble or import from a state other than an EEA country a medicinal product.
- A wholesale dealer's licence is required to sell or supply a medicinal product to a person who is not the end user of that product.
- The national (decentralised) marketing authorisations are administered by the MHRA and the centralised system by the European Medicines Agency.
- A simplified system of licensing applies to parallel imports.
- Stringent requirements, set out in a Guide to Good Manufacturing Practice, apply to manufacturing licences and introduce the concept of a qualified person. Similar conditions apply to wholesale dealer's licences, which have a responsible person.
- Clinical trials are subject to certification by the licensing authority unless specifically exempted.
- Certain exemptions from licensing exist for doctors, nurses, pharmacists, other health professionals and hospitals.
- No licences are required for certain activities carried out in a pharmacy under the supervision of a pharmacist.
- Certain products are exempt from licensing, for example confectionery, food and cosmetics.
- Provisions are made for special dispensing or manufacturing services.

Further reading

Human Medicines Regulations (2012) SI 2012 No. 1916, *Explanatory memorandum*: http://www.legislation.gov.uk/uksi/2012/1916/pdfs/uksiem_20121916_en.pdf (accessed 21 November 2012).

Pharmaceutical Press (2007). *Rules and Guidance for Pharmaceutical Manufacturers and Distributors*. [The Orange Guide.] London: Pharmaceutical Press.

Royal Pharmaceutical Society (2012). Support Bulletin No. 15 August 2012 Human Medicines Regulations 2012 *Pharm J*, 289: 200 (free to members or available on subscription).

Royal Pharmaceutical Society (published annually). *Medicines, Ethics and Practice: The Professional Guide for Pharmacists*. London: Royal Pharmaceutical Society (includes practice guidance on many of the topics in this chapter; free to members).

Royal Society of Chemistry (2009). *Code of Practice for Qualified Persons*. London: Royal Society of Chemistry.

The following guides are available from the Medicines and Healthcare products Regulatory Agency (http://www.mhra.gov.uk): *Good Manufacturing Practice (manufacturers)*, *Good Pharmacovigilance Practice*, *Good Distribution Practice (wholesalers)*, *Good Clinical Practice (clinical trials)*, *Good Inspection Practice*.

Websites

EU legislation: http://eur-lex.europa.eu

Legislation (can be searched on year and SI number or title): http://www.legislation.gov.uk

Medicines and Healthcare products Regulatory Agency: http://www.mhra.gov.uk

Royal Pharmaceutical Society (member access only; lists legal classifications of medicines and further practice guidance): http://www.rpharms.com

4

Human medicines: advertising

Susan Melvin

Advertising under Part 14 of the Human Medicines Regulations 2012

Control of medicines advertising in the UK is based on a system of self-regulation underpinned by statutory powers under EU and UK law. The Human Medicines Regulations 2012[1] Part 14 implements Council Directive 2001/83/EC and ensures that a relevant medicinal product is only promoted in accordance with its marketing authorisation.

Definitions

An *advertisement* is defined as (HMRs Reg.7) anything designed to promote the prescription, supply, sale or use of that product. This includes:

a   door-to-door canvassing, visits by medical sales representatives to persons qualified to prescribe or supply medicinal products;
b   the supply of samples, the provision of inducements to prescribe or supply medicinal products by the gift;
c   offer or promise of any benefit or bonus, whether in money or in kind, except where the intrinsic value of such inducements is minimal;
d   the sponsorship of promotional meetings attended by persons qualified to prescribe or supply medicinal products; and
e   the sponsorship of scientific congresses attended by persons qualified to prescribe or supply medicinal products, including the payment of their travelling and accommodation expenses in that connection.

It does not include

a   a medicinal product's package or package leaflet;
b   reference material and announcements of a factual and informative nature, including:

[1] Human Medicines Regulations SI 2012 No. 1916

    i material relating to changes to a medicinal product's package or package leaflet,

    ii adverse reaction warnings,

    iii trade catalogues, and

    iv price lists,

       provided that no product claim is made; and

c correspondence, which may be accompanied by material of a non-promotional nature, answering a specific question about a medicinal product.

In this Regulation, 'person qualified to prescribe or supply medicinal products' has the meaning given in Reg.277(1) (interpretation: Part 14 advertising).

The term advertisement does not, however, include medicines packaging and leaflets nor catalogues and price lists provided they do not contain product claims. *Publication* in relation to an advertisement is defined in HMRs Reg.277 as the dissemination or issue of that advertisement orally, in writing or by means of an electronic communication network or in any other way and includes causing or procuring that publication by or on behalf of another person.

Requirements related to advertising

An advertisement may not be published for a medicinal product unless one of the following is in force for the product: a marketing authorisation, a certificate of registration, a traditional herbal registration or an Article 126a authorisation (chapter 3). Ministers may obtain copies of any advertisement relating to medicinal products by serving a notice on the person who issued it or caused it to be issued (HMRs Reg.304). The appropriate ministers may apply to the court for an injunction against the person concerned, or likely to be concerned, with the publication of an advertisement which is incompatible with the prohibitions imposed by HMR Reg.311.

General principles

The general requirements are as follows.

1 No person may publish an advertisement for a medicinal product unless that product has a marketing authorisation, certificate of registration, a traditional herbal registration or an Article 126a (HMRs Reg.279) and any such advertisements must be consistent with the Summary of Product Characteristics (HMRs Reg.280). This general regulation does not apply to registered homoeopathic medicinal products (HMRs Reg.301).

2 No person may publish an advertisement relating to a medicinal product unless that advertisement encourages the rational use of that product by presenting it objectively and without exaggerating its properties (HMRs Reg.280).
3 No person may publish a misleading advertisement relating to a medicinal product (HMRs Reg.280).

Duties of holders of marketing authorisations (HMRs Reg.281)

Any person who holds a marketing authorisation, a certificate of registration for a medicinal product, a traditional herbal registration or an Article 126a authorisation for a medicinal product must:

1 establish a scientific service to compile and collate all information, whether received from medical sales representatives employed by him/her or from any other source relating to that product;
2 ensure that, in relation to any such product which sales representatives promote, those medical sales representatives are given adequate training and have sufficient scientific knowledge to enable them to provide information that is as precise and as complete as possible about that product;
3 retain a sample of any advertisement for which s/he is responsible relating to that product, together with a statement indicating the persons to whom the advertisement is addressed, the method of dissemination and the date of its first publication; and
4 provide, if required and within the period specified in a notice served by the Health Ministers on him/her, any information and assistance requested by them in order to carry out their functions under Part 14 of the HMRs.

Advertisements directed to the public (HMRs Regs.282–292)

The Regulations dealing with advertisements that are directed to the public impose a range of prohibitions, restrictions and requirements, the most significant of which are set out below.

No advertisement may be published which is likely to lead to the use of a medicinal product:

1 for the purpose of inducing an abortion in women (Reg.283);
2 that is likely to lead to the use of a POM (Reg.284);
3 that contains a Controlled Drug or is in the Psychotropic Substances Convention (Reg.285);

4 that states or implies that a medical consultation or surgical intervention is unnecessary, that offers to provide a diagnosis or suggest a treatment by post or might lead to an erroneous self-diagnosis (Reg.286);

5 that suggests a guaranteed effect or no adverse reactions, uses terms or pictures that are misleading or likely to cause harm (Reg.287);

6 that wrongly implies that the product is a food or cosmetic or that its safety or efficacy is due to the fact that it is natural (Reg.288);

7 that the product is recommended by scientists, health professionals or persons who are neither of the foregoing but who, because of their celebrity, could encourage the consumption of medicinal products (Reg.289); or

8 that is directed principally at children (Reg.290).

Form and content of advertisements

No person shall publish an advertisement relating to a medicinal product unless that advertisement (HMRs Reg.291) is presented so that it is clear that the message is an advertisement and so that the product is clearly identified as a medicinal product; and includes

a the name of the medicinal product,

b if it contains only one active ingredient, the common name of the medicinal product,

c the information necessary for correct use of the product, and

d an express and clear invitation to read carefully the instructions on the package or on the package leaflet.

These provisions do not apply if the advertisement is intended as a reminder or relates to a registered homoeopathic medicinal product.

Vaccination campaigns

The Regulations as set out above do not apply to any advertisement which is part of a vaccination campaign relating to a medicinal product that is a vaccine or serum and has been approved by the Health Ministers (HMRs Reg.292).

Prohibition of supply to the public for promotional purposes

No person who is the holder of a marketing authorisation, traditional herbal registration or an Article 126a authorisation, or who carries on a medicines business, may sell or supply a medicinal product for a promotional purpose to a person who is not qualified to prescribe medicinal products (HMRs Reg.293).

Advertising to persons qualified to prescribe or supply

Persons qualified to prescribe or supply includes persons, and employees of such persons, who in the course of their profession or in the course of a business may lawfully prescribe, sell by retail or supply in circumstances corresponding to retail sale medicinal products (HMRs Reg.277).

No person may issue an advertisement relating to a medicinal product and aimed at persons qualified to prescribe or supply unless the advertisement contains the particulars set out in Schedule 30 to the HMRs (HMRs Reg.294), as summarised below:

1 the number of the marketing authorisation, certificate of registration, traditional herbal registration or Article 126a authorisation for the medicinal product;
2 the name and address of the holder of the authorisation, or the business name and address of the part of the business responsible for its sale or supply;
3 the classification of the product, i.e. POM, Pharmacy Only, or General Sale List (GSL);
4 the name of the medicinal product;
5 a list of active ingredients using their common names and placed immediately adjacent to the most prominent display of the name;
6 one or more of the indications as within the terms of the licence;
7 a succinct statement of the entries in the Summary of Product Characteristics relating to
   a adverse reactions, precautions and relevant contra-indications,
   b dosage and method of use relevant to the indications shown, and
   c the holder of a marketing authorisation, traditional herbal registration or an Article 126a authorisation;
8 the cost, excluding value added tax (VAT), of either a specified package of the product or a specified quantity or recommended daily dose, calculated by reference to any specified package of the product, except that the cost may be omitted in the case of an advertisement inserted in a publication which is printed in the UK but with a circulation outside the UK of more than 15 per cent of its total circulation; and
9 the particulars in paragraph 7 above shall be printed in a clear and legible manner and be placed in such a position in the advertisement that their relationship to the claims and indications for the product can readily be appreciated by the reader.

Abbreviated advertisements

Abbreviated advertisement means an advertisement, other than a loose insert, which does not exceed in size an area of 420 cm² in a publication sent or delivered wholly or mainly to persons qualified to prescribe or supply relevant medicinal products (HMRs Reg.295). No person may issue such an advertisement unless it:

a contains essential information as listed in Schedule 30 of the HMRs paragraphs 2–6 as set out above for advertising to persons qualified to prescribe or supply; and

b the statement 'Information about this product, including adverse reactions, precautions, relevant contra-indications, and method of use can be found at'; and

c a web site address which corresponds to that statement; and

d the name and address of the holder of the marketing authorisation, etc. relating to the product.

Written material accompanying promotions

No person may send or deliver to prescribers or suppliers of medicinal products as part of a promotion any written material (HMRs Reg.297) unless it:

1 contains essential information compatible with Schedule 30 of the HMRs; and

2 states the date on which it was drawn up or last revised.

Any such written material shall be accurate, up-to-date, verifiable and complete and not state any quotation, table or other illustrative matter taken from a medical journal or other scientific work unless it is accurately reproduced and the precise source is indicated.

Free samples for persons qualified to prescribe or supply medicinal products

A person may supply a sample only if the following conditions (A–F) are met (HMRs Reg.298).

A The recipient
  a is qualified to prescribe medicinal products, and
  b receives the sample for the purpose of acquiring experience in dealing with the product in question.

B The sample is supplied to the recipient
  a on an exceptional basis, and
  b in response to a request from, and signed and dated by, the recipient.

C Taking the year in which the sample is supplied as a whole, only a limited number of samples of the product in question are supplied to the recipient in that year.

D The sample
  a is no larger than the smallest presentation of the product that is available for sale in the UK,
  b is marked 'free medical sample – not for resale' or bears a similar description, and
  c is accompanied by a copy of the Summary of Product Characteristics.
E The sample does not contain
  a a substance which is listed in any of Schedules I, II or IV to the Narcotic Drugs Convention (where the product is not a preparation listed in Schedule III to that Convention), or
  b a substance which is listed in any of Schedules I to IV to the Psychotropic Substances Convention (where the product is not a preparation which may be exempted from measures of control in accordance with paragraphs 2 and 3 of Article 3 of that Convention).
F The supplier maintains an adequate system of control and accountability in relation to the supply of free samples.

Note that supplying samples of medicinal products to the public is unlawful.

Medical sales representatives

All sales representatives promoting medicinal products to prescribers or suppliers of medicines must give to or have available for all persons they visit a copy of the Summary of Product Characteristics. Such representatives must report all information which they receive from prescribers, including any adverse drug reactions, to the scientific service established under the Regulations (HMRs Reg.299).

Inducements and hospitality

Hospitality includes sponsorship of a person's attendance at a meeting or event and the payment of travelling or accommodation expenses (HMRs Reg.300). When products are being promoted to health professionals, no person may supply, offer or promise any gift, pecuniary advantage or benefit in kind unless it is inexpensive and relevant to the practice of medicine or pharmacy.

Hospitality may be offered at events for purely professional or scientific purposes to persons qualified to prescribe or supply relevant medicinal products provided that:

- such hospitality is strictly limited to the main scientific objective of the event; and
- it is offered only to health professionals.

It is an offence for a health professional to solicit or accept any gift, pecuniary advantage, benefit in kind, hospitality or sponsorship prohibited by the Regulations.

Advertisements for registered homoeopathic products

An advertisement relating to homoeopathic medicinal products may not mention any specific therapeutic indications (HMRs Reg.301) and may only contain the details specified in Schedule 28 to the Regulations. Nothing in Reg.291(2) (form and contents of advertisement), Reg.294 (general requirements) or Reg.295 (abbreviated advertisements) requires an advertisement relating to a homoeopathic medicinal product to which a certificate of registration relates to contain any detail not specified in Schedule 28.

Advertisements for traditional herbal medicinal products

No person may issue an advertisement for such products that are marketed in the UK under a traditional herbal registration unless it contains the statement 'Traditional herbal medicinal product for use in', followed by a statement of one or more therapeutic indications for the product consistent with the terms of the traditional herbal registration for that product, followed by 'exclusively based on long standing use' (HMRs Reg.302).

Holders of 'specials manufacturer's licences'

Specials manufacturers may not publish any advertisement, catalogue or circular relating to a special medicinal product or make any representations in respect of that product (HMRs Reg.24 and Sch.4). However, catalogues and circulars may be sent to healthcare professionals on receipt of a bona fide unsolicited order and a price list can be issued to healthcare professions without such a request.[2] A *price list* should only consist of a basic line listing providing the following information with no product claims:

- Reference number
- Drug name (British Approved Name or equivalent)
- Dosage form
- Strength
- Pack size
- Price.

[2]Information for wholesale dealers and manufacturers: advertising of unlicensed medicines, *Medicines Regulatory News* August 2010, available on the MHRA website

Monitoring of advertising

Legal provisions covering the monitoring of advertising appear in the last section of Part 14 of the Human Medicines Regulations 2012. However, the existing voluntary control under existing Codes of Advertising Practice administered by the Association of the British Pharmaceutical Industry (for POMs) and by the Proprietary Association of Great Britain (for over-the-counter medicines) continues. Complaints, in the first instance, will be referred to the appropriate self-regulatory body, but the minister has the power of civil injunction. A person holding a marketing authorisation will be required to issue corrective statements if their advertising is found to be in breach of the Regulations.

There is a schedule which gives the Health Ministers powers for determining whether or not certain advertisements, proposed or published, breach the advertising regulations. There is an opportunity for representations to be made to the Independent Regulator for Communications Industries (OFCOM) before the Health Ministers determine the case and breaches of notices issued by the Health Ministers create an offence.

Summary

- The Regulations prohibit the advertising to the public of Controlled Drugs and POMs.
- Requirements as to the information on medicinal products which has to be given to persons qualified to prescribe or supply medicines include essential information compatible with the Summary of Product Characteristics. This may be given by way of written information accompanying promotions or by promotion by medical representatives.
- A limited number only of free samples may be supplied to a person qualified to prescribe relevant medicinal products. The samples may only be supplied in response to a written request and suppliers must maintain an adequate system of control.
- No person who is the holder of a marketing authorisation or who carries on a business which consists of the manufacturing, selling or supplying medicinal products shall, for promotional purposes, sell or supply medicinal products to any member of the public.
- Hospitality given to persons qualified to prescribe or supply medicines must be reasonable in level and subordinate to the main objective of meetings held solely for scientific or professional purposes. No person may supply or promise any gift, pecuniary advantage or benefit in kind unless it is inexpensive and relevant to the practice of medicine or pharmacy.

- Conditions are set out for the advertising of homoeopathic medicinal products and for traditional herbal medicinal products.
- Monitoring of advertising is to be undertaken by self-regulatory bodies but there are also legal provisions involving the Health Ministers.

Further reading

Human Medicines Regulations (2012) SI 2012 No. 1916, *Explanatory memorandum*: http://www.legislation.gov.uk/uksi/2012/1916/pdfs/uksiem_20121916_en.pdf (accessed 21 November 2012).
Medicines and Healthcare products Regulatory Agency (2005). *Advertising and Promotion of Medicines in the UK*. [The Blue Guide]. London: The Stationery Office.
Prescription Medicines Code of Practice Authority (2012). *Association of the British Pharmaceutical Industry's (ABPI) Code of Practice*: http://www.pmcpa.org.uk/Pages/default.aspx (accessed 21 November 2012).
Proprietary Association of Great Britain (no date). *Best Practice Guidelines*, London: Proprietary Association of Great Britain.
Royal Pharmaceutical Society (published annually). *Medicines, Ethics and Practice: The Professional Guide for Pharmacists*. London: Royal Pharmaceutical Society (includes practice guidance on many of the topics in this chapter; free to members).

Websites

Association of British Pharmaceutical Industry: http://www.abpi.org.uk
Legislation (can be searched on year and SI number or title): http://www.legislation.gov.uk
Medicines and Healthcare products Regulatory Agency: http://www.mhra.gov.uk
Prescriptions Medicines Code of Practice Authority: http://www.pmcpa.org.uk
Proprietary Association of Great Britain: http://www.pagb.co.uk
Royal Pharmaceutical Society (member access only; lists legal classifications of medicines and further practice guidance): http://www.rpharms.com

5

Pharmacy businesses

Susan Melvin

Lawfully conducting a retail pharmacy business

Part IV of the Medicines Act 1968, which covers retail pharmacy businesses, has not been repealed by the Human Medicines Regulations 2012[1] but has been extensively amended by other legislation. The Health Act 2006 (s.27–s.30) amended sections 70–72 of the Medicines Act and replaced *personal control* with a requirement that each registered pharmacy is to have a *Responsible Pharmacist* in charge of the business where this relates to the sale or supply of medicines and other conditions for registration. A new section (s.72A) placed a statutory duty on the Responsible Pharmacist to ensure the safe and effective running of a pharmacy. This is discussed in more detail under Responsible Pharmacist below.

A *retail pharmacy business* means[2] a business (not being a professional practice carried on by a practitioner) which consists of or includes the retail sale of medicinal products other than medicinal products on a GSL (whether medicinal products on such a list are sold in the course of that business or not) (s.132 (1)).[3] Such a business may, subject to certain conditions, lawfully be conducted by a person (s.69) who is:

1 a pharmacist, or a partnership where each partner is a pharmacist, or, in Scotland, a partnership where one or more partners is a pharmacist; or
2 a body corporate where the business so far as concerns the keeping, preparing and dispensing of medicinal products other than medicinal products on a GSL is under the management of a superintendent who is a pharmacist and who does not act in a similar capacity for any other body corporate (s.71); or
3 a representative of a deceased, bankrupt or mentally ill pharmacist, whose name, together with the names and address of the representative, has been notified to the Registrar of the GPhC (s.72(2)).

[1] Human Medicines Regulations SI 2012 No. 1916
[2] A slightly different definition appears in the HMRs Reg.8
[3] Sections refer to the Medicines Act 1968

With regard to item 3, the following apply.

1   In relation to a pharmacist who has died, 'representative' means his/her executor or administrator and, for a period of 3 months from the date of his/her death if s/he has died leaving no executor who is entitled and willing to carry on the business, includes any person beneficially interested in his/her estate. The representative of a deceased pharmacist may carry on the business for a period of up to 5 years from the date of his/her death. Should s/he cease to be a representative before the expiry of 5 years, on completing the distribution of the deceased pharmacist's estate, his/her authority lawfully to carry on the pharmacy business would also come to an end.

2   Where a pharmacist is adjudged bankrupt or, in Scotland, sequestration of his/her estate is awarded, the trustee in bankruptcy or in the sequestration is the pharmacist's representative. S/he may carry on the pharmacist's business for a period of 3 years from the date on which s/he is adjudged bankrupt or the date of the award of sequestration, as the case may be.

3   Where a pharmacist enters into a composition or scheme or deed of arrangement with his/her creditors, or in Scotland makes a trust deed for behoof of his/her creditors, or a composition contract, then the trustee appointed under any such arrangement is the pharmacist's representative. S/he may carry on the business for a period of 3 years from the date on which s/he became entitled to do so.

4   Where a receiver is appointed for a pharmacist under Part VIII of the Mental Health Act 1959 or, in Scotland, a *curator bonis* or judicial factor is appointed for him/her on the grounds that s/he suffers from some mental disorder, or in Northern Ireland a committee, receiver or guardian is appointed in his/her case under the Lunacy Regulation (Ireland) Act 1871, then that person is the pharmacist's representative. S/he may carry on the business for 3 years from the date of his/her appointment.

A person lawfully conducting a retail pharmacy business as the representative of a pharmacist may take or use in connection with that business any title, emblem or description which the pharmacist him/herself could have used (s.78(8)) (see below). The Health Ministers may, by Order, add to, revoke or vary any of these conditions relating to the carrying on of retail pharmacy business, or provide for alternative or modified conditions. Such an Order must receive the approval of each House of Parliament (s.73).

Responsible Pharmacist

Under section 72A of the Medicines Act 1968, the Responsible Pharmacist must secure the safe and effective running of the pharmacy business at the premises in question so far as it concerns the sale or supply of medicinal products. A person may not be the Responsible Pharmacist for more than one set of premises at the same time[4] and the name of the Responsible Pharmacist for the time being with his/her registration name and number must be conspicuously displayed in the pharmacy. In addition, s/he must:

- establish, maintain and review pharmacy procedures that set out how activities are to be carried out in the pharmacy; and
- maintain a record at the pharmacy of the Responsible Pharmacist who is in charge of the pharmacy on any date and at any time; and
- comply with any other regulations made for Responsible Pharmacists.

Where the business is carried on by a pharmacist or partners, the Responsible Pharmacist must be the person carrying on the business; in a partnership, one of the partners or another pharmacist must be the Responsible Pharmacist. Where the business is carried on by a body corporate, the Responsible Pharmacist must be the superintendent or a manager subject to the directions of the superintendent and who is a pharmacist. Where the business is carried on by a representative, a pharmacist must be appointed as the Responsible Pharmacist.

Section 72A also provides that the person carrying on the business must ensure that the record of the Responsible Pharmacist is properly maintained and preserved for at least as long as is specified in Regulations (5 years, see below). This section also provides powers to specify the qualifications and experience which a pharmacist must have if s/he is to be a Responsible Pharmacist but this has not yet been implemented.

The Responsible Pharmacist Regulations

In the Responsible Pharmacist Regulations Regulations,[5] *pharmacy business* means the business in respect of which the Responsible Pharmacist has a duty under section 72A of the Medicines Act and *premises* means the premises from which the pharmacy business is carried on. *Pharmacy staff* means any pharmacist or any other person who is working at the premises in question in a role connected to the pharmacy business (Responsible Pharmacist Regulation (RP Reg.) 2). *Business hours* means the period during which the pharmacy business is operational on any day and *day* means the 24 hour period beginning and ending at midnight (RP Reg.3).

[4] A long-standing provision that the Responsible Pharmacist (formerly the pharmacist in personal control) in a pharmacy, registered for less than 3 months, could not be from an EEA country was repealed by The Medicines Act (Pharmacy) Order SI 2011 No. 2647
[5] The Medicines (Pharmacies) (Responsible Pharmacist) Regulations SI 2008 No. 2789

Absence of the Responsible Pharmacist

1   The maximum period for which the Responsible Pharmacist may be absent from the premises is 2 hours during the pharmacy business hours. If there is more than one Responsible Pharmacist during the pharmacy hours, the maximum period applies to the total period of absence for all of them.
2   The Responsible Pharmacist must not be absent unless the arrangements set out in paragraphs 3 and 4 below are in place.
3   Where it is reasonably practical for the Responsible Pharmacist to be contactable during the period of absence, arrangements must ensure that s/he can be contactable by other pharmacy staff and return with reasonable promptness if in his/her opinion it is necessary to secure the safe and effective running of the business.
4   Where it is not possible to put these arrangements into place, arrangements must be made to ensure another pharmacist is both available and contactable to advise other pharmacy staff.
5   The sale of GSL medicines may continue from the premises in the absence of the Responsible Pharmacist.

Pharmacy procedures

1   The matters which must be covered by pharmacy procedures are:
    a   the arrangements to secure that medicinal products are ordered, stored, prepared, sold or supplied by retail, and disposed in a safe and effective manner;
    b   the circumstances in which a pharmacy member of staff who is not a pharmacist may give advice on medicinal products;
    c   the identification of members of staff who are in the view of the Responsible Pharmacist competent to perform such tasks relating to the business;
    d   the keeping of records about the arrangements (mentioned in a above under recording of pharmacy procedures);
    e   the arrangements which are to apply during the absence of the Responsible Pharmacist;
    f   the steps to be taken when there is a change of Responsible Pharmacist;
    g   the procedures to be taken when there is a complaint made against the pharmacy business;
    h   the procedures which should apply when a incident occurs which may indicate that the pharmacy business is not running in a safe and effective manner; and
    i   the manner in which changes to the pharmacy procedures are notified to the pharmacy staff.

2 Pharmacy procedures must be:
  a recorded in writing, in electronic form or both;
  b available for inspection by the person carrying out the business, the superintendent (if any), the Responsible Pharmacist and pharmacy staff; and
  c reviewed regularly.

In this Regulation, *pharmacy procedures* means those procedures referred to in section 71A(3) of the Medicines Act.

Pharmacy records

The particulars to be kept are:

1 the name of the Responsible Pharmacist;
2 the registration number of the Responsible Pharmacist in the Register of Pharmacists;
3 the date and time at which the Responsible Pharmacist became the Responsible Pharmacist;
4 the date and time at which the Responsible Pharmacist ceased to be the Responsible Pharmacist;
5 in relation to any absence of the Responsible Pharmacist from the premises on a day on which they were a Responsible Pharmacist:
  a the date of the absence,
  b the time at which the absence commenced, and
  c the time at which s/he returned to the premises.

The pharmacy record must:

1 be kept in writing, in electronic form, or both;
2 be available for inspection by the person carrying out the business, the superintendent (if any), the Responsible Pharmacist and pharmacy staff;
3 be preserved by the owner of the business for a period of not less that 5 years commencing on,
  a in the case of record in electronic form the date on which it was created, or
  b in the case of written record the last day to which the record relates.

In this Regulation, *pharmacy record* means the record referred to in section 71A(4) of the Medicines Act.

Registration of pharmacy premises

Provision for the registration of pharmacies was originally under sections 74–77 of the Medicines Act but these sections have been significantly amended by Article 68 and Schedule 4 of the Pharmacy Order 2010.[6]

[6]The Pharmacy Order 2010 SI 2010 No. 231

The registrar of premises is now the Registrar of the GPhC (Art. 18) or, where appropriate, the Pharmaceutical Society of Northern Ireland. It is the Registrar's duty to keep the Register of Pharmacy Premises and, subject to the provisions described below, to enter in the Register, on payment of the prescribed fee, any premises in respect of which application is made (s.75(1)). A document purporting to be a certificate signed by the Registrar and stating that, on a specified date, specified premises were, or were not, entered in the Register shall be admissible in any proceedings as evidence (and, in Scotland, shall be sufficient evidence) that those premises were, or were not, entered in the Register on that date (s.74L).

Registered pharmacy means premises entered for the time being in Part 3 of the GPhC Register (Art. 3 and Art. 19).[7] Where a business which concerns the retail sale or supply of medicinal products is carried on in one or more separate or distinct parts of a building, each part is taken to be separate premises (s.69(2)). A departmental store or supermarket, for example, might have a department or area which is a registered pharmacy and a separate department or area (which is not a pharmacy) where GSL medicines are sold.

Conditions for registration of pharmacy premises must be fulfilled in a prescribed manner (s.74B) and as in Part 5 of the Registration Rules[8] (chapter 22). An application must be in writing and be given or sent to the Registrar with the prescribed fee. It must be made and signed by or on behalf of the person carrying on, or who intends to carry on, a retail pharmacy business at the premises to which the application relates. A separate application must be made in respect of each premises. Each application has particular requirements with which the applicant must comply.

a The applicant must specify:
   1 the applicant's full name, address and contact details (including a telephone number and electronic mail address, where possible);
   2 the full postal address of the premises to which the application relates;
   3 whether the applicant is aware that the premises to which the application relates have previously been entered in Part 3 of the Register;
   4 the name under which the retail pharmacy business that is, or is to be, carried on at the premises trades or is to trade;
   5 whether the applicant is, or will be, a person lawfully conducting a retail pharmacy business at the premises within the meaning of Part 4 of the (Medicines) Act;
   6 the date, or intended date, of the commencement of the retail pharmacy business carried on, or to be carried on, at the premises;
   7 where the retail pharmacy business is, or is to be, carried on at the premises by a representative, the name of the Responsible Pharmacist;

[7] A similar definition appears in HMRs Reg.3
[8] The GPhC (Registration Rules) Order of Council SI 2010 No. 1617

8 where the applicant is a partner in a partnership, the names of all the partners in the partnership;

9 where the applicant is a body corporate,
- the names of all of the directors of the body corporate, and
- the name of the superintendent pharmacist.

b The applicant must pay the prescribed fee in respect of the application.

c The applicant must provide:

1 a description of the premises to which the application relates;

2 details of the type of activities undertaken, or intended to be undertaken, at the premises;

3 a plan, drawn to scale, of the internal layout of the premises showing the areas in which medicinal products are intended to be sold or supplied, assembled, prepared, dispensed or stored;

4 a declaration,
- confirming that the standards set in rules under Article 7(1) of the Order in connection with the carrying on of a retail pharmacy business at a registered pharmacy are met in connection with the retail pharmacy business carried on, or intended to be carried on, at the premises, and
- providing details of any relevant offence or relevant investigation within the meaning of Article 7(6)(a) and (b) of the Order.

d The applicant must provide any other necessary supporting documents, information or evidence as mentioned in the application form.

e The application procedure also informs the applicant that, if the declaration included in the application is not completed to the satisfaction of the Registrar, the Registrar may refuse to enter the premises in Part 3 of the Register because the conditions specified in section 74B of the Act are not met.

f The applicant must sign and date the application.

The Registrar must refuse any application for the entry of premises in Part 3 of the Register if

a it is not accompanied by the necessary supporting documents, information or evidence as mentioned in the application form or subsequently required by the Registrar; or

b the applicant has not paid, or has not made arrangements with the Registrar to pay by direct debit, the prescribed fee in respect of the application.

Change of ownership

Where a change occurs in the ownership of a registered pharmacy, the registration becomes void at the end of the period of 28 days from the date on which the change occurs. If it occurs on the death of the person carrying on the business (i.e. the death of a pharmacist owner or, in the case of a partnership, one of the partners), the period is 3 months from the date of the death (s.74H).

When the registration of pharmacy premises becomes void following a change of ownership, an application for restoration to the Register may be made by the new owner. The Registrar must restore the premises to the Register if s/he is reasonably satisfied that the new owner is a person lawfully conducting a retail pharmacy business or will be so at the time s/he commences business at the premises. A fee equal to a retention fee must be paid by the new owner, but only if the retention fee for the year has not already been paid (s.74 H(5)). No description of the premises or sketch plan need be submitted.

Premises retention fees

A retention fee is payable annually in respect of any premises entered in the Register for each year subsequent to the year in which they were registered (Art. 24). In this context, year means a rolling period of 12 months beginning on the date of registration of the premises. At least 3 months before the date of registration expiry, the Registrar will send to each person carrying on a retail pharmacy business, entered in Part 3 of the register, an application form, which must be returned by that person within 2 months of the renewal date.

The GPhC may direct the Registrar to remove any premises from the Register if the person carrying on the retail pharmacy business fails to pay a retention fee within 2 months from the date on which a demand for it has been made to him/her in the prescribed manner. If, before the end of the year, or whatever period is permitted by the GPhC in any particular case, the retention fee is paid, together with any prescribed sum by way of penalty, the Registrar must restore the premises to the Register. If the GPhC so directs, the restoration shall be deemed to have had effect as from the date on which the premises were removed from the Register. (For Northern Ireland, any reference to the GPhC in this section should be construed as a reference to the Minister of Health and Social Services for Northern Ireland.)

The GPhC is responsible for making any rules relating to the registration of pharmacies (Art. 19 (3)) and for setting the standards that are to be met in connection with the carrying on of a retail pharmacy business at a registered pharmacy (Art. 7) (chapter 22).

Titles, descriptions and emblems

No person may, in connection with any business, use any title, description or emblem likely to suggest that s/he possesses any qualification with respect to the sale, manufacture or assembly of medicinal products which s/he does not in fact possess, or that any person employed in the business possesses any such qualification which that person does not in fact possess (s.78 (6)).

Furthermore, the use of certain titles and descriptions is specifically restricted as follows.

1   The description *pharmacy* may only be used in respect of a registered pharmacy or the pharmaceutical department of a hospital or a health centre. It may not be used in connection with any business, other than a pharmacy, which consists of or includes the retail sale of any goods, or the supply of any goods in circumstances corresponding to retail sale (s.78(4)). Its use in connection with a business carried on at any premises shall be taken as likely to suggest that the person carrying on the business (where that person is not a body corporate) is a pharmacist, and that any other person under whose personal control the business is carried on at those premises (so far as concerns the retail sale of medicinal products or the supply of such products in circumstances corresponding to retail sale) is also a pharmacist.

2   The titles *Pharmaceutical Chemist, Pharmaceutist, Pharmacist* may only be taken or used by pharmacists (s.78(5)), that is those on the Register held by the GPhC. These titles may not be used at any premises connected with a business which includes the retail sale or supply of any goods unless those premises are a registered pharmacy or a hospital or health centre (s.78(5)). The titles Member or Fellow of the Pharmaceutical Society, MRPharmS, or FRPharmS may only be used by members of the Royal Pharmaceutical Society (RPS).

3   The titles *Chemist and Druggist, Druggist, Dispensing Chemist* or *Dispensing Druggist* may only be taken or used by a person lawfully conducting a retail pharmacy business (s.78(2)). The taking or using of the title *Chemist* is also restricted to a person lawfully conducting a retail pharmacy business but only in connection with the sale of any goods by retail or the supply of any goods in circumstances corresponding to retail sale (s.78(2)) (see box 5.1).

> **Box 5.1** *Taking the title 'chemist'*
>
> Norris v Weeks (1970)
>
> The Pharmacy Act 1954 (s.19) read: 'it shall not be lawful for any person, unless he is a registered pharmaceutical chemist … (b) to take or use, in connection with the sale of goods by retail, the title of chemist'.
>
> A notice, about 1 ft high by 2.5 ft wide (30 cm by 75 cm) was displayed at Mr Weeks' drug store over goods intended for retail sale. It bore the wording on three lines, *Wyn's/Chemist/Sundries*. The word 'chemist' was in larger script than the other words and in a different colour. The magistrate dismissed a summons under section 19(1) (b) on the ground that, having regard to the articles displayed, the word *chemist* was merely descriptive of the type of goods sold.
>
> The High Court dismissed an appeal against this decision. It was held that an offence is committed only if a person asserts that they are a chemist or takes to themself the title 'chemist'. It could not be said that an offence is committed whenever the word 'chemist' appears.
>
> *Pharm J*, 14 March 1970 p. 268; *The Times*, 6 March 1970.

Where the person lawfully conducting the retail pharmacy business is a body corporate, these titles may only be used if the pharmacist who is superintendent is also a member of the board of the body corporate (s.78 (3)). None of these titles may be used at any premises connected with a business which includes the retail sale or supply of any goods unless those premises are a registered pharmacy (s.78(3)). The Health Ministers may by Order, and after consultation with the GPhC, impose further restrictions or requirements with respect to the use of titles, descriptions and emblems. The Health Ministers may also provide that existing restrictions shall cease to have effect or be subject to specified exceptions. Regulations for these purposes must be approved by resolution of each House of Parliament (s.79).

Standards in pharmacies

Power to regulate standards in pharmacies originally lay in sections 66–68 of the Medicines Act 1968, but these sections were repealed by the HMRs (Sch. 35). Power to set standards for pharmacies now lies with the GPhC and these are discussed more fully in chapter 22.

Summary

- Retail businesses which sell medicines not on a GSL must be registered as pharmacies. They may be owned by a pharmacist, a partnership, a body corporate or a representative of a deceased pharmacist. The concept of the Responsible Pharmacist was introduced as a new section in the Medicines Act 1968 (s.72A) with detailed Regulations.
- Detailed requirements relating to the premises, together with a fee, must be forwarded to the GPhC in order for registration to take place.
- Certain titles may only be used by pharmacists, for example pharmacist, pharmaceutical chemist.
- A body corporate may use the title dispensing chemist, chemist and druggist or chemist only if the superintendent is a member of the board, otherwise the body corporate may only use the title pharmacy in connection with its pharmacy premises.
- The GPhC, by way of rules, may impose a large range of conditions relating to premises from which medicines are sold.

Website

General Pharmaceutical Council (details of pharmacy standards):
http://www.pharmacyregulation.org

6

Human medicines: Pharmacy Medicines

Karen Pitchford

Part 12 of the Human Medicines Regulations 2012[1] is concerned with the regulation of the sale and supply of medicines. The basic principle, set out in Reg.220, is that medicinal products may be sold or supplied by retail only from registered pharmacies, unless they are products classified as GSL (chapter 7) or subject to some other exemption under the Regulations.

Regulation 220 provides that medicinal products which are not subject to general sale (i.e. which are not GSL medicines), shall not be sold or supplied, or offered for sale or supply in circumstances corresponding to retail sale by any person in the course of a business carried on by him/her unless:

1 that person is, in respect of that business, a person lawfully conducting a retail pharmacy business;
2 the product is sold, supplied or offered or offered for sale or supply on premises which are a registered pharmacy; and
3 that person, or, if the transaction is carried out on his/her behalf by another person, then that other person is, or acts under the supervision of, a pharmacist.

The above does not apply to the supply of a medicinal product in the event or anticipation of pandemic disease (see pandemic exemption, chapter 8).

NB. A retail pharmacy business must be under the control of a Responsible Pharmacist so far as it concerns the sale of medicinal products including products classified as GSL (ss.27–29 Health Act 2006, chapter 5). The meaning of *supervision* has been considered by the High Court and the Statutory Committee (see box 6.1) and is the subject of guidance from the GPhC (see box 6.2) but is currently under review at the time of going to press.

---

[1] Human Medicines Regulations SI 2012 No. 1916

Box 6.1 *The meaning of 'supervision' 1*

Roberts v Littlewoods Mail Order Stores Ltd (1943)

The Pharmacy and Poisons Act 1933 (s.18) provided: '... it shall not be lawful for a person to sell any poison in Part I of the Poisons List unless ... the sale is effected by, or under the supervision of, a registered pharmacist'. Similar wording (related to medicinal products not on a General Sale List) was included in section 52 of the Medicines Act and is now included in the Human Medicines Regulations 2012.

A sale of a Part I poison was made at a Littlewood's company pharmacy to one of the Society's inspectors while the sole pharmacist was in a stockroom upstairs and unaware that the sale was being made by an unqualified assistant. The magistrates found that the sale, though not effected by the pharmacist, was effected sufficiently under his supervision. His actual presence was not reasonably required.

The decision was reversed in the High Court, where it was held that the sale had not been supervised. Lord Caldecote said:

> ...the man who was upstairs might have been a person who was exercising personal control of a business, but I do not think that, while he was upstairs and therefore absent, he could be a person who was supervising a particular sale. It has been suggested that a man can supervise a sale without being bodily present. I do not accept that contention ... each individual sale must be, not necessarily effected by the qualified person, but something which is shown by the evidence to be under his supervision in the sense that he must be aware of what is going on at the counter, and in a position to supervise or superintend the activities of the young woman by whom each individual sale is effected.

[1943] 1 All ER 271; *Pharm J*, 30 January 1943 p. 38.

Box 6.2 *The meaning of 'supervision' 2*

Summers v Congreve Horner & Co

In their *Guidance for Responsible Pharmacists* (2010), The General Pharmaceutical Council cites the case of *Summers v Congreve Horner & Co* in considering the meaning of supervision, as applied to the assembly of medicines. The case sets out that 'supervision' can exist, *even in the absence of physical presence*.

An assistant surveyor of less than 5 years' professional experience had received that degree of supervision required by good practice in the profession of surveying for the purposes of a particular professional indemnity policy, notwithstanding that the supervisor had not actually attended at the property being surveyed. D, a firm of surveyors, sent T, a graduate with 3.5 years' practical experience, to carry out a structural survey of the house in question. T was provided with a checklist by H, a partner, and his subsequent draft report was then submitted to, discussed with and eventually approved by H, who did not, however, visit the property. When P, the purchasers, subsequently brought proceedings claiming that the report was negligent, D sought to rely upon their professional indemnity policy. The policy was expressed not to cover any claim arising from the survey, inspection or valuation of real property unless the work had been carried out (a) by a fellow or associate of one of a number of professional bodies or (b) by anyone who had not less than 5 years' experience of such work or such other person nominated by the assured to carry out such work subject always to the supervision of such work by a person qualified in accordance with (a) above. The official referee held that, save in exceptional circumstances, some attendance at the property was required in order for there to be such supervision as to bring the claim within the insurance policy; and that, there having been no attendance by H, D could not claim under the policy.

Held, allowing D's appeal by a majority, that supervision is a matter of degree, and that there had in fact been that degree of supervision required by good practice in the profession of surveying for a person of T's training and experience.

[1992] 40 E.G. 144.

The current professional convention of facilitating supervision by making sales by trained assistants and placing Pharmacy (P) Medicines behind a counter is also under review by the GPhC (chapter 22). There is case law on the meaning of the point of sale when it is effected by self-service (see box 6.3).

Selling by retail or retail sale includes all those sales which do not fall within the definition of selling by way of wholesale dealing, and supplying in circumstances corresponding to retail sale has a comparable meaning (HMRs Reg.8). Retail sale or supply, therefore, comprises all those sales or supplies of medicinal products made in the course of a business to a person who buys (or receives) them for the purpose other than that of (a) selling or supplying them or (b) administering them or causing them to be administered to one or more human beings in the course of a business carried on by him/her.

Box 6.3 *The meaning of point of sale*

Pharmaceutical Society of Great Britain v Boots Cash Chemists (Southern) Ltd (1953)

This was a case arising under the Pharmacy and Poisons Act 1933 (s.18) (see also box 6.1). It was an appeal by the Pharmaceutical Society against a judgment of the Lord Chief Justice in the High Court.

A Boots pharmacy was arranged on a 'self-service' system. A customer could select goods, including Part I poisons (roughly equivalent today to Pharmacy Medicines), from the shelves, place them in a wire basket and take them to the cash desk. Before the cashier accepted payment, a pharmacist at the cash desk could, if s/he thought fit, prevent a sale. It was suggested by the Society that a purchase was completed when a customer took an article and put it in the basket so that the pharmacist could not later intervene. That suggestion had not been accepted in the High Court by the Lord Chief Justice, who had said that self-service was no different from the normal transactions in a shop. He had continued:

> ...the mere fact that a customer picks up a bottle of medicine from the shelves in this case does not amount to an acceptance of an offer to sell. It is an offer by the customer to buy ... By using the words the sale is effected by, or under the supervision of, a registered pharmacist, it seems to me the sale might be effected by somebody not a pharmacist. If it be under the supervision of a pharmacist, the pharmacist can say: 'You cannot have that. That contains poison'. In this case I decide ... that there is no sale until the buyer's offer to buy is accepted by the acceptance of the money, and that takes place under the supervision of a pharmacist...

The Court of Appeal upheld this decision and dismissed the appeal by the Society. This means that a sale is not complete until the price is agreed with the purchaser by the person selling, and that this point of sale remains the same whether or not goods have been handed over a counter or picked up by self-service.

[1953] 1 All ER 482; *Pharm J*, 14 February 1953 p. 115.

Pharmacy Medicine defined

Certain medicinal products may only be sold or supplied from pharmacies in accordance with a prescription given by an appropriate practitioner. These products, called *Prescription Only Medicines* (POMs), are specified in a 'Prescription Only' order.[2] Any medicinal product which is not a POM or a medicinal product classified as GSL is a *Pharmacy Medicine* (P Medicine) (HMRs Reg.5). There is no definitive list of Pharmacy Medicines, as the total in the class cannot be determined. It comprises all those medicines which are covered by a marketing authorisation which specifies that the product is to be available only from a pharmacy, or which are covered by an EU marketing authorisation in which the product is not classified either as a GSL or POM, and it includes all medicines made in a pharmacy for retail sale under the exemptions from licensing granted to pharmacists under section 10 of the Medicines Act 1968 (see exemptions for pharmacists, chapter 3). Schedule 1 of the HMRs also specify certain classes of medicinal product which are to be available only from a pharmacy, that is, are not to be on general sale (chapter 7). Some GSL medicines, when presented in packs exceeding specified quantities, may only be sold or supplied from pharmacies (see retail pack sizes of certain products, chapter 7). Some POMs when presented in packs not exceeding specified quantities may only be sold or supplied from pharmacies (see Exemptions from prescription only control, chapter 8).

Exemptions in cases involving another's default

The restrictions imposed with regards to the sale of Pharmacy Medicines shall not apply to the sale or supply, or offer for sale or supply, of a medicinal product by a person if s/he, having exercised all due diligence, believes on reasonable grounds that the product is subject to general sale, that belief is due to the act or default of another person and the conditions applying to retail sale or supply of GSL medicinal products are met (HMRs Reg.244).

The conditions under which GSL medicines may be sold are described in chapter 7.

Exemption for collection and delivery arrangements

A *collection and delivery arrangement* means an arrangement whereby a person may take or send a prescription given by a doctor, dentist, nurse independent prescriber, pharmacist independent prescriber or optometrist independent prescriber to premises other than a registered pharmacy and which are capable of being closed by the occupier to exclude the public and

[2]The Prescription Only (Human Medicines) Order SI 1997 No. 1830, as amended up to 2006 and repealed in part by HMRs paragraph 71 of Sch. 34

collect or have collected on his or her behalf from such premises a medicinal product prepared or dispensed in accordance with such a prescription at a registered pharmacy by or under the supervision of a pharmacist. When an arrangement of this kind is used by a person lawfully conducting a retail pharmacy business, the supply of dispensed medicines at the non-pharmacy premises without the supervision of a pharmacist is rendered lawful by an exemption provided (HMRs Reg.248).

Summary

- Pharmacy Medicines comprise all medicinal products which are not classified as being subject to GSL or POM status or are exempt in some way from the latter.
- The legislation requires that retail sales or supplies of Pharmacy Medicines have to be made by a person conducting a retail pharmacy business, at a registered pharmacy and by, or under the supervision of, a pharmacist.
- The conditions under which Pharmacy Medicines must be sold do not apply where there is a collection and delivery arrangement in place, or where a pandemic situation exists.

Further reading

Human Medicines Regulations (2012) SI 2012 No. 1916, *Explanatory memorandum*: http://www.legislation.gov.uk/uksi/2012/1916/pdfs/uksiem_20121916_en.pdf (accessed 21 November 2012).
Royal Pharmaceutical Society (published annually). *Medicines, Ethics and Practice: The Professional Guide for Pharmacists*. London: Royal Pharmaceutical Society (includes practice guidance on many of the topics in this chapter; free to members).
Royal Pharmaceutical Society (2012). Support Bulletin No. 15 August 2012 Human Medicines Regulations 2012 *Pharm J*, 289: 200 (free to members or available on subscription).

Websites

Legislation (can be searched on year and SI number or title): http://www.legislation.gov.uk
Medicines and Healthcare products Regulatory Agency: http://www.mhra.gov.uk
Royal Pharmaceutical Society (member access only; lists legal classifications of medicines and further practice guidance): http://www.rpharms.com

7

Human medicines: General Sale Medicines

Karen Pitchford

General Sale Medicines (commonly called GSL medicines) are those which can, in the opinion of the ministers, 'with reasonable safety be sold or supplied otherwise than by or under the supervision of, a pharmacist'.[1] The effect of the Human Medicines Regulations 2012 is the same;[2] GSL medicines continue to be those that may be sold or supplied at places other than pharmacy premises and without the supervision of a pharmacist.

In the Regulations (Reg. 5), a medicinal product subject to general sale is defined as a product that is not a POM or a Pharmacy Medicine but is a product that:

a is covered by an authorisation of which it is a term that the product is to be available on general sale; or

b is covered by an EU marketing authorisation, and is not classified in the authorisation as a POM and the licensing authority has determined should be available on general sale.

Conditions applying to retail sale or supply of General Sale List medicinal products

Regulation 221 of the HMRs sets out that a person may sell or supply, or offer for sale or supply, a medicinal product that is subject to general sale at a place elsewhere than at a registered pharmacy only if the following conditions are met:

1 the place at which the medicinal product is sold, supplied, or offered for sale or supply, consists of premises of which that person is the occupier and which s/he is able to close so as to exclude the public;

---

[1] The Medicines (Products Other Than Veterinary Drugs) (General Sale List) Order SI 1984 No. 769 (now repealed)

[2] Human Medicines Regulations SI 2012 No. 1916

2 the medicinal product was made up for sale in its immediate and outer packaging elsewhere than at the place at which it is sold, supplied or offered for sale or supply and the immediate and outer packaging has not been opened since the product was made up for sale in it; and

3 if the medicinal product is of a kind specified in Schedule 15 to the HMRs (see below) and is presented for sale in accordance with the requirements specified in that Schedule for a product of that kind.

Schedule 15 relates to the retail pack sizes of certain products (see below). The above does not apply to the supply of a medicinal product in the event or anticipation of pandemic disease (see p. 00).

General Sale List Medicine defined

The classes of medicinal product on general sale for administration to human beings are set out the Medicines (Products Other Than Veterinary Drugs) (General Sale List) Order 1984 (the GSL Order), as amended. In 2002, the GSL Order was amended[3] so that, where a product has a marketing authorisation, its classification for the purposes of the GSL Order is determined by that authorisation. The GSL Order then ceased to be updated on a regular basis and it was repealed by the HMRs.

Automatic machines

Medicinal products which are subject to the GSL may be sold or offered for sale from automatic machines (HMRs Reg.222). Such machines must be located in premises which the occupier is able to close so as to exclude the public.

Retail pack sizes of certain products

Limits are imposed on the pack sizes of certain GSL products when they are sold or supplied by retail from businesses other than pharmacies. If sold outside the limits laid down, the medicinal products concerned are classed as *Pharmacy Medicines* or POMs. The limits for general sale are as follows.

Aloxiprin, aspirin and paracetamol

A medicinal product that contains aloxiprin, aspirin or paracetamol (or, where appropriate, any combination of those substances) and that is in the

[3] The Medicines (Products Other Than Veterinary Drugs) (General Sale List) Amendment Order SI 2002 No. 933 (now repealed)

Table 7.1 Retail pack sizes of aloxiprin, aspirin and paracetamol (Sch. 15 to Human Medicines Regulations 2012)

Form of product	Maximum amount
Effervescent tablets: (a) that do not contain aspirin, or (b) that do not contain more than 325 milligrams of aspirin per tablet	30 tablets
Effervescent tablets: (a) that contain more than 325 milligrams of aspirin per tablet, but (b) do not contain more than 500 milligrams of aspirin per tablet	20 tablets
Non-effervescent tablets: (a) that are enteric-coated, (b) that contain aspirin only, and (c) that do not contain more than 75 milligrams of aspirin per tablet	28 tablets
Other non-effervescent tablets or capsules	16 tablets or capsules
Powder or granules	10 sachets
Liquid preparations of paracetamol intended for persons aged 12 years and over	160 mL
Liquid preparations of paracetamol intended for persons younger than 12 years	Individual unit doses of not more than 5 mL each, to a maximum of 20 unit doses

form specified in table 7.1 must be presented for sale in a separate and individual package containing not more than the amount of the product specified in the corresponding entry.

Effervescent, in relation to a tablet or capsule, means containing not less than 75 per cent, by weight of the tablet or capsule, of ingredients included wholly or mainly for the purpose of releasing carbon dioxide when the tablet or capsule is dissolved or dispersed in water (HMRs Reg.8).

Ibuprofen

A medicinal product that contains ibuprofen and that is in the form specified in table 7.2 must be presented for sale in a separate and individual package containing not more than the amount of the product specified in the corresponding entry.

Table 7.2 Retail pack sizes of ibuprofen (Sch. 15 to Human Medicines Regulations 2012)

Form of product	Maximum amount
Tablets or capsules	16 tablets or capsules
Powder or granules	12 sachets
Liquid preparations of ibuprofen	Individual unit doses of not more than 5 mL each, to a maximum of 20 unit doses

Other Regulations[4] also listed medicinal products where limits were imposed on the pack sizes of GSL products when they were to be sold or supplied by retail from businesses other than pharmacies. These Regulations were revoked by the Human Medicines Regulations 2012. The removal of these pack size restrictions was intentional since pack size limitations, other than for paracetamol, aspirin, aloxiprin, ibuprofen and pseudoephedrine, are covered by the relevant marketing authorisations. The MHRA website includes lists of substances, according to the legal classifications of the analogous products (lists A, B and C). The lists provide, for each substance, details of the conditions for GSL, Pharmacy Medicine or POM supply of a product containing that substance and, where appropriate, additional product information recommendations and requirements. The three lists have no legal basis but are intended to provide guidance to marketing authorisation holders considering future reclassifications for their products. The lists are updated following new reclassifications.

Products not to be on general sale

The Human Medicines Regulations 2012 (Sch. 1) specify certain classes of medicinal product which are to be available only from a pharmacy: that is, which are not to be on general sale. They are:

a   a product comprising eye ointment;
b   a product that contains vitamin A, vitamin A acetate or vitamin A palmitate, in each case with a maximum daily dose equivalent to more than 7500 international units of vitamin A or 2250 micrograms of retinol; and
c   a product that contains vitamin D with a maximum daily dose of more than 400 units of antirachitic activity.

[4]The Medicines (Sale or Supply) (Miscellaneous Provisions) Regulations SI 1980 No. 1923 (now repealed)

The following medicinal products shall be available only from a pharmacy unless they are the subject of a marketing authorisation or traditional herbal registration that classifies them as medicinal products subject to general sale:

a a product that is for use as an anthelmintic;

b a product that is for parenteral administration;

c a product that is for use as an enema;

d a product that is for use wholly or mainly for irrigation of wounds, or the bladder, vagina or rectum;

e a product that is for administration wholly or mainly to children being a preparation of aloxiprin or aspirin.

f if it is a medicinal product of a kind specified in Schedule 15 (see above) but is not presented for sale in accordance with the requirements specified in that Schedule for a product of that kind to be subject to general sale.

Summary

- Medicines which in the opinion of the minister can with reasonable safety be sold other than by or under the supervision of a pharmacist are classified as GSL medicines. They may only be sold from closable premises and in their original packs.
- Certain medicines may be sold other than by or under the supervision of a pharmacist subject to certain pack sizes. These include aspirin, aloxiprin, ibuprofen and paracetamol.
- Certain medicines cannot be on general sale. These include eye ointments, most anthelmintics, parenterals, those medicines promoted as enemas or for use as irrigations, and aspirin for children.

Further reading

Human Medicines Regulations (2012) SI 2012 No. 1916, *Explanatory memorandum*: http://www.legislation.gov.uk/uksi/2012/1916/pdfs/uksiem_20121916_en.pdf (accessed 21 November 2012).

Royal Pharmaceutical Society (published annually). *Medicines, Ethics and Practice: The Professional Guide for Pharmacists*. London: Royal Pharmaceutical Society (includes practice guidance on many of the topics in this chapter; free to members).

Royal Pharmaceutical Society (2012). Support Bulletin No. 15 August 2012 Human Medicines Regulations 2012 *Pharm J*, 289: 200 (free to members or available on subscription).

Websites

Legislation (can be searched on year and SI number or title): http://www.legislation.gov.uk

Medicines and Healthcare products Regulatory Agency: http://www.mhra.gov.uk

Royal Pharmaceutical Society (member access only; lists legal classifications of medicines and further practice guidance): http://www.rpharms.com

8

Human medicines: Prescription Only Medicines

Karen Pitchford

Prescription Only Medicine defined

A *Prescription Only Medicine* (POM) means a medicinal product (HMRs Reg.5)[1] that is:

a covered by a UK marketing authorisation or an Article 126a authorisation of which it is a term that the product is to be available only on prescription;

b covered by an EU marketing authorisation and is classified in the authorisation as a POM;

c a POM by virtue of Part 1 of Schedule 1 of the Prescription Only Medicines (Human Use) Order SI 1997 No. 1830 as amended; 'the POM order'; or

d the result of the assembly, or the reformulation (including the combining with other substances), of a medicinal product that is a POM by virtue of (a) or (b), above.

Schedule 1 to the Regulations describes the classes of medicinal product which are always to be available only on prescription. They are products that are:

a for parenteral administration;

b a Controlled Drug, unless it is covered by a marketing authorisation in which the product is classified as a Pharmacy Medicine or as a medicinal product subject to general sale;

c cyanogenic substances, other than preparations for external use;

[1]Unless otherwise stated all Regs. in this chapter refer to the Human Medicines Regulations SI 2012 No. 1916

d medicinal substances that on administration emit radiation, or contain or generate any substance which emits radiation, in order that radiation may be used;

e covered by a marketing authorisation in which the product is classified as a Pharmacy Medicine or as a medicinal product subject to general sale, and consists of or contains aloxiprin, aspirin or paracetamol in the form of non-effervescent tablets or capsules (see below for exemptions);

f covered by a marketing authorisation in which the product is classified as a Pharmacy Medicine or as a medicinal product subject to general sale, and consists of or contains (in any pharmaceutical form) pseudoephedrine salts or ephedrine base or salts (see below for exemptions); or

g not covered by a marketing authorisation, and is a POM by virtue of Articles 5 and 10 of, and Schedules 1 and 2 to, the POM Order.[2]

Exemptions from Prescription Only control

Medicinal products exempt due to conditions specified in Schedule 1 of the POM Order

A medicinal product that is not the subject of a marketing authorisation is a POM for the purposes of the Human Medicines Regulations 2012 if it, or a substance in it, is listed in column 1 of Schedule 1 of the POM Order, unless there is:

a an entry in Columns 2, 3, 4 or 5 of that Schedule which contains a condition and that condition is satisfied; or

b more than one such condition which applies where that substance is used in that product and each of those conditions are satisfied.

The conditions mentioned above differ for different products but may pertain to the maximum strength, a route of administration, use for a specified purpose or in a specified class of persons, a particular pharmaceutical form or a maximum quantity that may be sold or supplied.

All these exempted medicinal products will be Pharmacy Medicines (chapter 6).

Preparations of aloxiprin, aspirin or paracetamol in the form of non-effervescent tablets or capsules exempt due to maximum strength or quantity sold or supplied

Products consisting of or containing aloxiprin, aspirin or paracetamol are exempt from POM control if the quantity of the product sold or supplied to a person at any one time does not exceed 100 tablets or capsules (HMRs Reg.236).

[2]Prescription Only Medicines (Human Use) Order SI 1997 No. 1830 (as amended)

In addition, these preparations may be exempt from POM control, if the strength of the preparation does not exceed stated maxima.[2] These are as follows:

Aspirin. If the pack size for non-effervescent tablets or capsules does not exceed 32 and the maximum strength 500 mg then the product is a Pharmacy Medicine. The total quantity sold to a person at any one time must not exceed 100.

Aspirin. If the pack size for non-effervescent tablets or capsules does not exceed 100 and the maximum strength 75 mg then the product is a Pharmacy Medicine.

Paracetamol. If the pack size for non-effervescent tablets or capsules does not exceed 32 and the maximum strength 250 mg (wholly or mainly for children under 12) or maximum strength 500 mg (for adults or children over 12), then the product is a Pharmacy Medicine. The total quantity sold to a person at any one time must not exceed 100.

Aspirin and paracetamol in preparations other than non-effervescent tablets and capsules are also Pharmacy Medicines.

Maximum strength is defined in the POM Order as either:

a the maximum quantity of a substance by weight or volume contained in a dosage unit of a medicinal product; or

b the maximum percentage of a substance contained in a medicinal product calculated in terms of weight in weight (w/w), weight in volume (w/v), volume in weight (v/w) or volume in volume (v/v) and if the maximum percentage calculated in those ways differ, the higher or highest percentage.

Maximum dose (MD) in relation to a product for internal use means the maximum quantity of the substance contained in the amount of the product that it is recommended should be taken or administered at any one time (HMRs Reg.213).

Maximum daily dose (MDD) in relation to a product for internal use means the maximum quantity of the substance contained in the amount of the product that it is recommended should be taken or administered in any period of 24 hours.

Preparations of pseudoephedrine salts or ephedrine base or salts exempt due to conditions

Products consisting of or containing pseudoephedrine salts or ephedrine base or salts that are POMs by virtue of point (f), above, are exempt from POM control, if the following conditions are met (HMRs Reg.237):

1 a product that contains pseudoephedrine salts is not sold or supplied at the same time as another medicinal product that consists of or contains ephedrine base or salts;

2 the medicinal products sold or supplied to a person at any one time do not in total contain more than:

a in the case of pseudoephedrine salts, 720 mg pseudoephedrine salts; or

b in the case of ephedrine base or salts, 180 mg ephedrine base or salts.

High dilution products

There is an exemption from POM control for high dilution products diluted to at least one part per million (6×).[2] This includes certain high diluted products which are not for parenteral administration and include aconite, arsenic trioxide, belladonna herb, ignatia bean and nux vomica seed.

Sale or supply of Prescription Only Medicines

A POM may only be sold or supplied by retail in accordance with a prescription given by an appropriate practitioner (HMRs Reg.214) (see box 8.1).

Box 8.1 *The meaning of 'acting in accordance with the directions of a practitioner'*

Roberts v Coombs (1949)

The Penicillin Act 1947 reads:

> ...no person shall sell or otherwise supply any substance to which this Act applies or any preparation of which any such substance is an ingredient or part unless (a) he is a duly qualified medical practitioner, a registered dental practitioner or a registered veterinary surgeon, or a person acting in accordance with the directions of any such practitioner or surgeon, and the substance or preparation is sold or supplied for the purposes of treatment by or in accordance with the directions of that practitioner or surgeon; or (b) he is a registered pharmacist or an authorised seller of poisons, and the substance or preparation is sold or supplied under the authority of a prescription signed and dated by any such practitioner or surgeon as aforesaid.

A shopkeeper (Coombs), who was not an authorised seller, sold penicillin ointment to customers who presented prescriptions signed and dated by a medical practitioner. The shopkeeper was charged with selling ointment containing penicillin contrary to section 1(1) of the Act, he not being one of the qualified persons mentioned in that subsection. The magistrates dismissed the summonses on the grounds that, although the shopkeeper was not a practitioner, he was a person acting in accordance with the directions of a duly qualified medical practitioner.

On appeal to the High Court it was held that a person acting in accordance with any such practitioner or surgeon was a person in the employment of a doctor or in some way actually under the direct orders of the doctor. A prescription signed and dated by a medical practitioner could be made up only by a registered pharmacist or an authorised seller of poisons.

Comment. The Penicillin Act 1947 was later replaced by the Therapeutic Substances Act 1956. The wording was subsequently retained in section 58(2)(b) of the Medicines Act 1968, which also repealed the 1956 Act. Section 58(2)(b) of the Medicines Act has subsequently been repealed by the Human Medicines Regulations 2012 and reference made within those Regulations to 'acting in accordance with the directions of such an appropriate practitioner'.

[1949] KB 221; *Pharm J*, 14 May 1949 p. 356.

In the HMRs doctors, dentists, supplementary prescribers, nurse independent prescribers and pharmacist independent prescribers are designated as appropriate practitioners in relation to any POM.

Note that in the HMRs, *doctor* means a registered medical practitioner and *dentist* means a person registered in the Dentists' Register under section 14 of the Dentists Act 1984 (as amended). Note that doctors wishing to practise medicine in the UK not only have to be registered with the General Medical Council (GMC), but are also required to hold a licence to practise issued by the GMC.[3]

Community practitioner nurse prescribers are appropriate practitioners in relation to POMs specified in Schedule 13 to the HMRs (see below). Optometrist independent prescribers are appropriate practitioners in relation to any POM other than Controlled Drugs or medicinal products that are for parenteral administration.

[3]The General Medical Council (Licence to Practise) Regulations Order of Council SI 2009 No. 2739

An *EEA health professional* means a doctor or dentist who is lawfully engaged in medical/dental practice in a relevant European country[4] and who is not otherwise a doctor or a dentist for the purpose of the Regulations (HMRs Reg.213). An EEA health professional is an appropriate practitioner in relation to any POM other than a Controlled Drug specified in Schedule 1, 2 or 3 of the Misuse of Drugs Regulations 2001[5] or in Schedule 1, 2 or 3 of the Misuse of Drugs Regulations (Northern Ireland) 2002.[6]

A *community practitioner nurse prescriber* means a registered nurse or a registered midwife against whose name is recorded in the professional register an annotation signifying that the person is qualified to order drugs, medicines and appliances from the *Nurse Prescribers' Formulary for Community Practitioners* in the current edition of the *British National Formulary* (HMRs Reg.8).

A *nurse independent prescriber* means a registered nurse or registered midwife noted in the professional register as qualified to order drugs, medicines and appliances as a nurse independent prescriber or a nurse independent/supplementary prescriber (HMRs Reg.8).

A *pharmacist independent prescriber* means a pharmacist who is noted in the relevant register as qualified to order drugs, medicines and appliances as a pharmacist independent prescriber (HMRs Reg.8).

An *optometrist independent prescriber* means a registered optometrist against whose name is recorded in the relevant register an annotation signifying that the person is qualified to order drugs, medicines and appliances as an optometrist independent prescriber (HMRs Reg.8).

A *supplementary prescriber* means a pharmacist, a registered nurse or midwife, a chiropodist, podiatrist, physiotherapist, radiographer or a registered optometrist who is noted in the relevant register as qualified to order drugs, medicines and appliances as a supplementary prescriber (or, in the case of a registered nurse or registered midwife, as a nurse independent/supplementary prescriber) (HMRs Reg.8).

The specified conditions for supplementary prescribers do not apply in relation to the prescribing and administration of medicines in accordance with the directions of another person who is an appropriate practitioner

---

[4] An EEA country other than the UK or Switzerland (although since 2008 the UK has recognised as legally valid for supply prescriptions written by a doctor or dentist registered in Switzerland). Relevant European states are Austria, Belgium, Bulgaria, Cyprus, Czech Republic, Denmark, Estonia, Finland, France, Germany, Greece, Hungary, Iceland, Ireland, Italy, Latvia, Liechtenstein, Lithuania, Luxembourg, Malta, Netherlands, Norway, Poland, Portugal, Romania, Slovakia, Slovenia, Spain and Sweden.
[5] The Misuse of Drugs Regulations SI 2001 No. 3998 (as amended)
[6] The Misuse of Drugs Regulations (Northern Ireland) SR 2002 No. 1 (as amended)

(other than a supplementary prescriber or an EEA health professional) in relation to the POM in question (Reg.216).

There are proposals to introduce independent prescribing by physiotherapists and podiatrists (box 8.2).

Box 8.2 *Proposals to introduce independent prescribing by physiotherapists and podiatrists*

A public consultation on proposals to introduce independent prescribing by physiotherapists and podiatrists was concluded in December 2011. At the time of going to press, it was expected that amendments to legislation to allow for independent prescribing by these professional groups would be laid before Parliament in the autumn of 2012 and that the first cohort of podiatrists/physiotherapists would be recruited to approved independent prescribing education programmes in autumn 2013.

Administration of Prescription Only Medicines

Regulation 214 sets out that no person shall parenterally administer a POM, otherwise than to him/herself, unless the person is an appropriate practitioner (other than an EEA health professional) or is acting in accordance with the directions of such an appropriate practitioner. However, this Regulation does not apply to the administration of:

1 certain medicines by way of parenteral injection for the purpose of saving life in an emergency (as listed in box 8.3);
2 smallpox vaccine, administered for the purpose of providing protection against smallpox virus:
   a in the event of a suspected or confirmed case of smallpox in the UK where the vaccine has been supplied by, on behalf of, or under arrangements made by the Secretary of State, the Scottish Ministers, the Welsh Ministers, the Department of Health, Social Services and Public Safety, or an NHS body,
   b to members of Her Majesty's Forces or other persons employed or engaged by them where the vaccine has been supplied by, on behalf of, or under arrangements made by, Her Majesty's Forces;
3 a radioactive medicinal product, administration of which results in a medical exposure or any other POM if it is being administered in connection with a medical exposure (see also below).

Box 8.3 *Medicinal products for parenteral administration in an emergency (HMRs Sch. 19) 2012)*

Adrenaline (epinephrine) 1:1000 up to 1 mg for intramuscular use in anaphylaxis
Atropine sulphate injection
Atropine sulphate and obidoxime chloride injection
Atropine sulphate and pralidoxime chloride injection
Atropine sulphate, pralidoxime mesilate and avizafone injection
Chlorphenamine injection
Dicobalt edetate injection
Glucagon injection
Glucose injection
Hydrocortisone injection
Naloxone hydrochloride
Pralidoxime chloride injection
Pralidoxime mesilate injection
Promethazine hydrochloride injection
Snake venom antiserum
Sodium nitrite injection
Sodium thiosulphate injection
Sterile pralidoxime

A *radioactive medicinal product* means a medicinal product which consists of, contains or generates a radioactive substance so that, when the product is administered, the radiation it emits may be used.

Medical exposure[7] means any which involves an individual being exposed to ionising radiation:

a   as part of their own medical diagnosis or treatment;
b   as part of occupational health surveillance;
c   as part of health screening programmes;
d   to patients or other persons voluntarily participating in medical or biomedical, diagnostic or therapeutic, research programmes; and
e   to individuals as part of medicolegal procedures.

Other conditions apply to the administration of a radioactive medicinal product, namely that the medicine is not a Controlled Drug and that medical exposure has been authorised by an ionising radiation medical exposure (IRME) practitioner (a registered medical practitioner, dental practitioner or

[7]The Ionising Radiation (Medical Exposure) Regulations SI 2000 No. 1059

other health professional who is entitled in accordance with the employer's procedures to take responsibility for an individual medical exposure), or, where it is not practical for an IRME practitioner to authorise the exposure, by an operator acting in accordance with written guidelines issued by an IRME practitioner. The IRME practitioner must be the holder of an appropriate certificate[8] granted by the Health Minister.

Prescriptions

A POM may only be sold or supplied by retail in accordance with a prescription given by an appropriate practitioner (HMRs Reg.214). To meet that requirement, certain conditions must be satisfied, which are slightly different for EEA health professionals (HMRs Reg.218) and other appropriate practitioners (HMRs Reg.217).

The conditions are that the prescription:

1 is signed in ink by the appropriate practitioner or the EEA health professional giving it;

2 is written in ink or otherwise so as to be indelible or (in the case of a health prescription which is not for a Controlled Drug) is written in ink or otherwise so as to be indelible or by means of carbon paper or similar material [NB EEA health professionals cannot issue health prescriptions];

3 contains the following particulars,

    a the address of the appropriate practitioner or the EEA health professional giving it,

    b the appropriate date (see below),

    c an indication of the kind of appropriate practitioner giving it or whether the EEA health professional is a doctor or dentist,

    d the name of the person for whose treatment it is given,

    e except in the case of an EEA prescription, the address of the person for whose treatment it is given, and

    f except in the case of an EEA prescription, if that person is under 12, that person's age;

4 is not dispensed after the end of the period of 6 months beginning with the appropriate date; or, in the case of a repeatable prescription, is not dispensed for the first time after the end of that period, and is dispensed in accordance with the directions contained in the prescription;

5 in the case of a repeatable prescription that does not specify the number of times it may be dispensed,

    a it is not dispensed on more than two occasions, or

---

[8]In accordance with the Medicines (Administration of Radioactive Substances) Regulations SI 1978 No. 1006

b in the case of a prescription for an oral contraceptive, it is not dispensed on more than six occasions or after the end of the period of 6 months beginning with the appropriate date; and

6 for an appropriate prescriber, who is an EEA health professional, the prescription is an EEA prescription.

If the prescription is not a health prescription for a Controlled Drug, it may be issued as an electronic prescription (HMRs Reg.219). In this case, as an alternative to fulfilling the conditions 1 and 2 specified above (for both non-EEA and EEA practitioners) the conditions are that the prescription is:

a created in an electronic form;
b signed with an advanced electronic signature; and
c sent to the person by whom it is dispensed as an electronic communication (whether or not through one or more intermediaries).

Advanced electronic signature means an electronic signature that is:

a uniquely linked to the person giving the prescription (the signatory);
b capable of identifying the signatory;
c created using means that the signatory can maintain under his/her sole control; and
d linked to the data to which it relates in such a manner that any subsequent change of the data is detectable.

Electronic communication (HMRs Reg.8) means a communication transmitted (whether from one person to another, from one device to another or from a person to a device or vice versa):

a by means of an electronic communications network within the meaning of section 32(1) of the Communications Act 2003; or
b by other means but while in an electronic form.

Repeatable prescription (HMRs Reg.213) means a prescription which contains a direction that it may be dispensed more than once.

Health prescription (HMRs Reg.213) means a prescription issued by a doctor, dentist, supplementary prescriber, nurse independent prescriber, optometrist independent prescriber, pharmacist independent prescriber or community practitioner nurse prescriber under:

a in England, the National Health Service Act 2006
b in Wales, the National Health Service (Wales) Act 2006
c in Scotland, the National Health Service (Scotland) Act 1978
d in Northern Ireland, the Health and Personal Social Services (Northern Ireland) Order 1972 No.1265.

The *appropriate date* (HMRs Reg.217) is the date on which the prescription was signed by the appropriate practitioner giving it, or, in the case of a health prescription only, the date indicated by the appropriate practitioner as being the date before which it should not be dispensed. Where a health prescription bears both dates, the later of those dates is the appropriate one. EEA health professionals cannot issue health prescriptions. so for an EEA prescription, the 'appropriate date' will always be the date on which it is signed by the EEA health professional.

Prescribing and administration by supplementary prescribers

A supplementary prescriber may give a prescription for a POM, parenterally administer a POM or give directions for the parenteral administration of a POM providing s/he is acting in accordance with the terms of a clinical management plan that relates to the patient to whom the product is prescribed/administered, has effect when the prescription is given or when the product is administered or the direction to administer is given (HMRs Reg.215) and includes the particulars specified in Schedule 14 to the HMRs. In addition, the supplementary prescriber must have access to the health records of the patient to whom the plan relates and are used by any doctor or dentist who is a party to the plan. The above does not apply if the supplementary prescriber is a community practitioner nurse prescriber and the POM prescribed or administered, or in respect of which s/he gives directions for administration, is specified in Schedule 13 to the Regulations.

A *clinical management plan* means a written plan (which may be amended from time to time) relating to the treatment of an individual patient agreed by the patient to whom the plan relates, the doctor or dentist who is a party to the plan and any supplementary prescriber who is to prescribe, give directions for administration or administer under the plan.

Due diligence clause

Where a prescription given by an appropriate practitioner does not fulfil a required condition, the sale or supply is not rendered unlawful if the person making the sale or supply, having exercised all due diligence, believes on reasonable grounds that that condition has been met (HMRs Reg.246). This due diligence clause also applies to the sale or supply made by a pharmacist in accordance with a prescription given by (HMRs Reg.228):

a another pharmacist, a registered nurse or a registered midwife, a person whose name is entered in the part of the Health and Care Professions Council Register relating to chiropodists and podiatrists, physiotherapists, radiographers (diagnostic or therapeutic) or a registered optometrist *who is not an appropriate practitioner* in relation to that POM but the pharmacist, having exercised all due diligence, believes on reasonable grounds that the person is such a practitioner; and

b a supplementary prescriber and the pharmacist, having exercised all due diligence, believes on reasonable grounds that the supplementary prescriber has complied with the requirements for prescribing by supplementary prescribers.

Forgeries

Similarly, the sale or supply by a pharmacist is not rendered unlawful if made against a forged prescription provided the pharmacist has exercised all due diligence and believes on reasonable grounds that the prescription is genuine (HMRs Reg.245) (but see box 8.4).

Box 8.4 *Sale of Prescription Only Medicines: offence of strict liability*

Pharmaceutical Society of Great Britain v Storkwain Ltd (1986)

Section 58 of the Medicines Act 1968 provides for orders to be made specifying those medicinal products which may only be sold by retail in accordance with the prescription of an appropriate practitioner.

Storkwain Ltd supplied quantities of Physeptone ampoules, Ritalin tablets and Valium tablets, all of which are POMs, on the authority of two 'prescriptions' which were, in fact, forgeries. In 1984, the Royal Pharmaceutical Society of Great Britain prosecuted the company for unlawfully selling those medicines contrary to section 58(2)(a) of the Act. It was submitted for Storkwain Ltd that they were unaware that the 'prescriptions' were not genuine. In the absence of any guilty knowledge (*mens rea*) of the forgeries on the part of the company, the magistrates dismissed the charges. The Society successfully appealed to the Court of Appeal, who held that an offence under section 58(2)(a) was one of strict liability and directed the magistrates to convict.

On further appeal by Storkwain Ltd, the House of Lords confirmed the decision of the Court of Appeal. It was held that guilty knowledge (*mens rea*) was a required ingredient of offences under certain sections of the Act, but section 58 was not one of those sections. That view was supported by the construction of section 58(4) and (5) and by section 121. The wording of the Prescriptions Only Order also conformed with that construction of the statute. An offence under section 58(2)(a) is, therefore, one of strict liability.

Comment. Section 58(4) and 58(5b) of the Medicines Act remain in force. Regulation 214 of the Human Medicines Regulations 2012 states that 'a person may not sell or supply a POM except in accordance with a prescription given by an appropriate practitioner'.

[1986] 2 All ER 635; *Pharm J*, 28 June 1986 p. 829.

Pharmacy records

A person lawfully conducting a retail pharmacy business must, in respect of every sale or supply of a POM, make or cause to be made an entry in a written or computerised record kept for that purpose (HMRs Reg.253), unless:

1 it is a sale or supply in pursuance of a health prescription or a prescription for oral contraceptives;

2 a separate record of the sale or supply is made in accordance Controlled Drugs legislation[9] (chapter 17);

3 the sale is by way of wholesale dealing and the order or invoice relating to the sale or a copy of the order or invoice is retained by the person lawfully conducting the retail pharmacy business who makes the sale;

4 in Scotland, the sale or supply is to a doctor of medicines and appliances for immediate treatment or personal administration which, under the NHS, the doctor is entitled or required to supply;[10] or

5 in Northern Ireland, the sale or supply is to a doctor of drugs, medicines and appliances for immediate treatment or personal administration which, under the NHS, the doctor is entitled or required to supply.[11]

An entry must be a written or computerised record kept for the purpose in respect of each sale or supply. The entry must be made on the day the sale or supply takes place or, if that is not reasonably practicable, on the following day.

Chapter 10 discusses records for wholesale transactions in POMs.

Particulars of prescriptions to be recorded

The particulars to be recorded in the case of a sale or supply of a POM in pursuance of a prescription given by a doctor or dentist, a supplementary prescriber, a community practitioner nurse prescriber, a nurse independent prescriber, an optometrist independent prescriber or a pharmacist independent prescriber are:

1 the date on which the POM was sold or supplied;

2 the name, quantity and, except where it is apparent from the name, the pharmaceutical form and strength of the POM sold or supplied;

[9]The Misuse of Drugs Regulations SI 2001 No. 3998 and the Misuse of Drugs Regulations (NI) SI 2002 No. 1

[10]The NHS (General Medical Services Contracts) (Scotland) Regulations SSI 2004 No. 115 (provision of drugs, medicines and appliances for immediate treatment or personal administration)

[11]The Health and Personal Social Services (General Medical Services Contracts) (Northern Ireland) Regulations SR (NI) 2004 No. 140

3 the date on the prescription and the name and address of the person giving the prescription; and

4 the name and address of the person for whom the POM was prescribed.

For second and subsequent supplies made on a repeat prescription it is sufficient to record the date of supply and a reference to the entry in the register relating to the first supply.

Additional particulars must be recorded in the case of emergency supplies to patients (see below).

Preservation of pharmacy records

The POM record must be preserved by the person lawfully conducting the retail pharmacy business for a period of 2 years from the date of the last entry in the record. Unless it is a health prescription or a prescription for a Schedule 1, 2 or 3 Controlled Drug, a prescription must be retained for 2 years from the date on which the POM was sold or supplied, or, for a repeat prescription, the date on which the medicine was supplied for the last time. Where a sale of a POM is by way of wholesale dealing, the order or invoice relating to the sale (or a copy of it) must be retained by the person lawfully conducting the retail pharmacy business who makes the sale for 2 years from the date on which the POM was sold or supplied.

Labelling of dispensed medicines

See chapter 15.

Exemptions from the need for a prescription

Exemptions for hospitals, clinics and similar settings

The requirement that a person may not sell or supply a POM except in accordance with a prescription given by an appropriate practitioner does not apply (HMRs Reg.227) when the sale or supply is made in the course of the business of a hospital, for the purpose of being administered (in the hospital or elsewhere) to a particular person in accordance with directions that:

a are in writing;

b relate to the particular person to whom the POM is to be administered; and

c are given by a person who is an appropriate practitioner in relation to that POM.

Such directions may be given by a supplementary prescriber *only* where s/he complies with any condition as to the cases or circumstances in which s/he may give a prescription for that medicine, as if the directions were a prescription. The exemption applies regardless of whether the directions satisfy the requirements for a prescription.

Exemptions for persons conducting retail pharmacy businesses

In Part 12, Ch. 3 of the HMRs, there are specific exemptions for persons lawfully conducting retail pharmacy businesses from the conditions or restrictions on the retail sale and supply of POMs. Exemptions from control for other persons are to be found in Ch. 9.

In an emergency, a person lawfully conducting a retail pharmacy business can sell or supply a POM if and so long as certain conditions are satisfied. There are two kinds of emergency supply (those made at the request of a prescriber, and those made at the request of a patient) and different conditions apply to them.

Exemption for emergency supply at the request of a prescriber

HMRs Reg.224 describe the conditions for an emergency sale at the request of a *relevant prescriber* which means any of the following:

a a doctor
b a dentist
c a supplementary prescriber
d a nurse independent prescriber
e a pharmacist independent prescriber
f a community practitioner nurse prescriber
g an optometrist independent prescriber
h an EEA health professional.

The conditions that apply for emergency supply made at the request of a relevant prescriber are that:

1 the pharmacist by or under whose supervision the POM is to be sold or supplied is satisfied that the sale or supply has been requested by a relevant prescriber (see above) who by reason of an emergency is unable to provide a prescription immediately;

2 the relevant prescriber has undertaken to provide the person lawfully conducting the retail pharmacy business with a prescription within the period of 72 hours beginning with the sale or supply;

3 the POM is sold or supplied in accordance with the directions of the relevant prescriber;

4 the POM is not a Controlled Drug specified in Schedule 1, 2 or 3 of the relevant Regulations other than a POM that consists of or contains phenobarbital or phenobarbital sodium, and is sold or supplied for use in the treatment of epilepsy (note that, in the case of an EEA prescriber, no Schedule 1, 2 or 3 Controlled Drugs may be ordered, so such prescribers may not order phenobarbital or its salts);

5 an entry is made in the Prescription Only Register (see above) on the day of the sale or supply, or, if that is not reasonably practicable, on the day following that day, stating,

   a the date on which the POM was sold or supplied,

   b the name, quantity and, except where it is apparent from the name, the pharmaceutical form and strength of the POM sold or supplied,

   c the name and address of the person giving the prescription,

   d the name and address of the person for whom the POM was prescribed,

   e the date on the prescription (this may be entered on the day that the prescription is received),

   f the date on which the prescription relating to that sale or supply is received (this may be entered on the day that the prescription is received).

Exemption for emergency supply at the request of a patient

The conditions that apply for an emergency supply made at the request of a patient set out in HMRs Reg.225 an are:

1 that the pharmacist by or under whose supervision the POM is to be sold or supplied has interviewed the person requesting it and is satisfied,

   a that there is an immediate need for the POM to be sold or supplied and that it is impracticable in the circumstances to obtain a prescription without undue delay,

   b that treatment with the POM has on a previous occasion been prescribed by a relevant prescriber for the person requesting it, and

   c as to the dose which in the circumstances it would be appropriate for that person to take;

2 that the quantity of the product sold or supplied, for a POM shown in column A of table 8.1, does not exceed that shown in column B of the table for that POM;

3 that the POM,

   a does not consist of or contain a substance specified in box 8.5,

   b is not a Controlled Drug specified in Schedule 1, 2 or 3 of the relevant Regulations other than a POM that consists of or contains phenobarbital or phenobarbital sodium, and is sold or supplied for use in the treatment of epilepsy [NB in the case of the patient of an EEA prescriber, no Schedule 1, 2 or 3 Controlled Drugs may be ordered, so the patients of such prescribers may not order phenobarbital or its salts];

4 that an entry is made in the Prescription Only Register (see above) on the day of the sale or supply, or, if that is not reasonably practicable, on the day following that day, stating

a the date on which the POM was sold or supplied,

b the name, quantity and, except where it is apparent from the name, the pharmaceutical form and strength of the POM sold or supplied,

c the name and address of the person requiring the POM, and

d the nature of the emergency;

5 that the inner or outer packaging of the POM is labelled to show

a the date on which the POM is sold or supplied,

b the name, quantity and (unless apparent from the name) the pharmaceutical strength of the POM,

c the name of the person requesting the POM,

d the name and address of the registered pharmacy from which the POM is sold or supplied, and

e the words 'Emergency Supply'.

Table 8.1 Maximum quantities that may be sold or supplied for emergency supply at the request of a patient

Column A: description	Column B: maximum quantity
A POM that: (a) is a preparation of insulin, an aerosol (a product that is dispersed from its container by a propellant gas or liquid) for the relief of asthma, an ointment or cream, and (b) has been made up for sale in a package elsewhere than at the place of sale or supply	The smallest pack that the pharmacist has available for sale or supply
An oral contraceptive.	A quantity sufficient for a full treatment cycle
An antibiotic for oral administration in liquid form	The smallest quantity that will provide a full course of treatment
A controlled drug within the meaning of Schedule 4 or 5 of the Misuse of Drugs Regulations 2001 or Schedule 4 or 5 of the Misuse of Drugs Regulations (Northern Ireland) 2002 or phenobarbital for the treatment of epilepsy	A quantity for 5 days of treatment
Any other POM	A quantity for 30 days of treatment

Box 8.5 Substances that may not be sold or supplied by a pharmacist without a prescription in response to a request for an emergency supply from a patient

Ammonium bromide
Calcium bromide
Calcium bromidolactobionate
Embutramide
Fencamfamin hydrochloride
Fluanisone
Hexobarbitone
Hexobarbitone sodium
Hydrobromic acid
Meclofenoxate hydrochloride
Methohexital sodium
Pemoline
Piracetam
Potassium bromide
Prolintane hydrochloride
Sodium bromide
Strychnine hydrochloride
Tacrine hydrochloride
Thiopental sodium

Emergency supply by a pharmacist: pandemic diseases

The restrictions on the sale or supply of a POM do not apply in certain circumstances related to pandemic diseases (HMRs Reg.226). The conditions are that the sale or supply of the POM is made by a person lawfully conducting a retail pharmacy business and:

1 the supply is made while a disease is, or in anticipation of a disease being imminently, pandemic and a serious risk, or potentially a serious risk, to human health;
2 the pharmacist by or under whose supervision the POM is to be sold or supplied is satisfied
   a that treatment with the POM has on a previous occasion been pre-scribed by a relevant prescriber for the person to be treated with it, and
   b as to the dose which in the circumstances it would be appropriate for that person to take.

Exemption for supply in the event or anticipation of pandemic disease

The restrictions on the sale or supply of a POM (or a Pharmacy Medicine or GSL medicine, chapters 6 and 7) do not apply in certain circumstances related to pandemic diseases (HMRs Reg.247). The conditions are that the supply:

1 is made while a disease is, or in anticipation of a disease being imminently, pandemic and a serious risk, or potentially a serious risk, to human health;
2 is in accordance with a protocol that
   a is approved by the ministers (chapter 2), an NHS body or the Health Protection Agency,
   b specifies the symptoms of and treatment for the disease, and
   c contains requirements as to the recording of the name of the person who supplies the product to the person to be treated ('the patient') or to a person acting on the patient's behalf, and evidence that the product was supplied to the patient or to a person acting on the patient's behalf.

Exemptions for persons conducting a retail pharmacy business making supplies under a Patient Group Direction

Patient Group Direction (PGD; HMRs Reg.213) means a written direction that relates to the sale or supply and to the administration of a description or class of medicinal product and that:

a is signed by a doctor or dentist, and by a pharmacist, and by any other person who may be required to sign it in the circumstances specified for its use; and
b relates to sale or supply and to administration to persons generally (subject to any exclusions that may be specified in the PGD).

The restrictions on retail sale, supply or administration of POMs do not apply to the sale or supply or administration of any such medicine by a person lawfully conducting a retail pharmacy business where the person sells, supplies or (as the case may be) administers the POM in accordance with a PGD pursuant to an arrangement for the supply or administration of POMs with (HMRs Reg. 233):

a the Common Services Agency, a health authority or special health authority, an NHS trust, an NHS foundation trust or a PCT;
b a police force in England, Wales or Scotland or the police service in Northern Ireland or a prison service;
c Her Majesty's forces; or

d an authority or person carrying on the business of an independent hospital, an independent clinic, an independent medical agency or, in Northern Ireland, a nursing home.

The PGD must:

1 relate to the sale or supply or (as the case may be) administration of a description or class of medicinal product by the person lawfully conducting a retail pharmacy business who sells or supplies or (as the case may be) administers the POM;

2 have effect at the time at which the POM is sold or supplied or (as the case may be) administered;

3 contain the particulars specified in Part 1 of Schedule 16 of the HMRs; if the PGD is for administration only, any restrictions on quantity may be omitted;

4 be signed on behalf of the relevant body named above (the HMRs specify the classes of person who may act as signatory), and with whom an arrangement is made;

5 where the POM is administered by the person lawfully conducting a retail pharmacy business, that person belongs to one of the classes specified in the HMRs (see appendix 3) and is designated in writing for the purpose of the administration of medicinal products under the PGD on behalf of the body with which an arrangement has been made; and

6 at the time at which the POM is supplied or administered, a marketing authorisation, Article 126a authorisation, certificate of registration or traditional herbal registration is in force in relation to it.

NB. As far as pharmacies are concerned, there is no provision to use PGDs to permit the supply or administration of Pharmacy Medicines and GSL medicines; however, such supplies are permitted in order to assist a doctor or dentist with the provision of NHS services (HMRs Reg.230).

Exemptions from Prescription Only for certain persons, including persons who supply under Patient Group Directions

These exemptions are covered in chapter 9.

Mixing of medicines

Regulation 17 of the HMRs provides that no person may manufacture, assemble or import from a state, other than an EEA state, any medicinal product or possess a medicinal product for the purpose of any of these activities except in accordance with a manufacturer's licence. However, under HMRs Reg.20 these restrictions do not apply to the mixing of medicines by:

1 a nurse independent prescriber or a pharmacist independent prescriber;
2 a supplementary prescriber, if the mixing of medicines forms part of the clinical management plan for an individual patient;
3 a person acting in accordance with the written directions of a doctor, dentist, nurse independent prescriber or pharmacist independent prescriber; or
4 a person acting in accordance with the written directions of a supplementary prescriber, if the mixing of medicines forms part of the clinical management plan for an individual patient.

Here, 'mixing of medicines' means the combining of two or more medicinal products together for the purposes of administering them to meet the needs of an individual patient.

Summary

- Certain medicines are POMs by description or class, including Controlled Drugs (unless exempted by virtue of a marketing authorisation), parenteral products and cyanogenic substances.
- In the HMRs doctors, dentists, supplementary prescribers, nurse independent prescribers and pharmacist independent prescribers are designated as appropriate practitioners in relation to any POM. Community practitioner nurse prescribers, optometrist independent prescribers and EEA health professionals are appropriate practitioners in relation to a more restricted range of POMs.
- Certain POMs may be administered parenterally for the purpose of saving life in an emergency, for example adrenaline (epinephrine) injection.
- Detailed prescription requirements are laid down and these differ slightly for prescriptions written by non-EEA and EEA practitioners.
- Detailed record keeping requirements are imposed for POMs, although there are some exemptions (e.g. for those on a health prescription or oral contraceptives).
- The HMRs allow for an emergency supply of a POM to be made at the request of a doctor, dentist, supplementary prescriber, nurse independent prescriber, pharmacist independent prescriber, community practitioner nurse prescriber, optometrist independent prescriber or an EEA health professional. The HMRs describe the conditions for such a supply to be made, for example including the exclusion of many Controlled Drugs from these arrangements.
- The HMRs allow for an emergency supply of a POM to be made at the request of a patient. The HMRs describe the conditions for such a supply to be made, for example including the exclusion of many Controlled Drugs from these arrangements and the removal of certain conditions in

the case of a declared pandemic. Detailed quantity, labelling and record conditions apply.

- The restrictions on the sale or supply of a POM (or Pharmacy Medicine or GSL, chapters 6 and 7) do not apply in certain circumstances related to pandemic diseases.
- Under certain conditions, POMs may be supplied under PGDs.
- The Regulations allow for the mixing of medicines in certain circumstances.

Further reading

Royal Pharmaceutical Society (published annually). *Medicines, Ethics and Practice: The Professional Guide for Pharmacists*. London: Royal Pharmaceutical Society (includes practice guidance on many of the topics in this chapter; free to members).

Websites

Human Medicines Regulations 2012 SI 2012 No. 1916:
    http://www.legislation.gov.uk/uksi/2012/1916/contents/made
Legislation (can be searched on year and SI number or title): http://www.legislation.gov.uk
Medicines and Healthcare products Regulatory Agency: http://www.mhra.gov.uk
Royal Pharmaceutical Society (member access only; lists legal classifications of medicines and further practice guidance): http://www.rpharms.com

9

Human medicines: exemptions from controls

Susan Melvin

Introduction

In the Human Medicines Regulations 2012, there are specified exemptions for certain classes of person from the conditions or restrictions on retail sale and/or supply[1] which apply to medicines on the GSL (HMRs Reg.221), Pharmacy Medicines (HMRs Reg.220) and POMs (HMRs Reg.214). Exemption from the restriction on the administration of POMs for parenteral use is also conferred on certain persons (HMRs Reg.214). There are also some continuing exemptions that are defined in earlier legislation.[2] The classes of person and the body exempted, the medicinal products to which the exemptions apply and the conditions (if any) which attach to the retail sale, supply or administration by these exempted persons are described in this chapter.

The sale of a POM or a Pharmacy Medicine to any of these persons in accordance with the exemptions granted to them is a sale by way of wholesale dealing (HMRs Reg.18). Persons who may engage in wholesale dealing, the extent to which it may be carried on at retail pharmacy businesses and the records to be kept in respect of wholesale transactions are described in chapter 10.

Exemption for supplies by doctors or dentists to their patients (HMRs Reg.223)

The restrictions on retail sale or supply do not apply to the sale, offer for sale or supply of any medicinal products:

1   by a doctor or dentist to a patient of his/hers, or to a person under whose care such a patient is; and

[1] Human Medicines Regulations SI 2012 No. 1916
[2] The Medicines (Pharmacy and General Sale – Exemption) Order SI 1980 No. 1924 (now repealed)

2 when the product is for the purpose of being administered to a person in accordance with directions relating to that person and those directions are given by a doctor, a dentist, a supplementary prescriber, a pharmacist independent prescriber, an optometrist independent prescriber or a community practitioner nurse prescriber.

The meaning of 'by a doctor or dentist to a patient of his' under the Medicines Act 1968 was tested in law in 1981(box 9.1)

Box 9.1 *The meaning of 'to a patient of his'*

Pharmaceutical Society v Wright (1981)

The Medicines Act requires that no person shall sell a POM product except in accordance with a prescription given by an appropriate practitioner. However, the Act provides that this provision does not apply to the sale or supply of a medicinal product to a patient of his/hers by a doctor or dentist who is an appropriate practitioner.

Once a week, Dr Wright ran a slimming clinic and those attending were given a medicinal product which was on the POM list. Many of the persons attending the clinic were patients of other doctors in the town and only attended the clinic, which was supervised by a nurse, for slimming purposes. The issue turned upon whether or not there was a doctor–patient relationship between the attendees and Dr Wright.

Mr Justice Bingham said:

> ...if a doctor acting as such, treats or gives advice to a person and assumes responsibility for that treatment or advice, that person may very well be his patient ...in determining whether the relationship does exist it is not ...of primary importance whether the person is a patient of another doctor as well nor whether the treatment or advice is given by the doctor's staff under his supervision rather than the doctor himself. Nor ... whether the relationship is a short-lived or long-lived. Nor ... need it be of primary importance whether the doctor takes less care in giving the advice or treatment than he should ...

Comment. In dismissing the appeal brought by the Pharmaceutical Society (which only became 'Royal' in 1988), Lord Donaldson, who sat with Mr Justice Bingham, said that it was for the Society to prove there was no doctor–patient relationship not for Dr Wright to prove there was.

1981, unreported.

Patient Group Directions

Certain categories of people can supply medicines under PGDs (as opposed to under the authority of a prescription) and these are listed in appendix 3. An account of the retail sale, supply or administration of medicines under a PGD by a person lawfully conducting a retail pharmacy business is covered in chapter 8. This chapter describes the supply under other versions of PGDs which appear in HMRs Regs.229, 230, 231, 232 and 234 together with Schedule 16 to the Regulations.

Supply under a Patient Group Direction by NHS bodies (HMRs Reg.229)

1 The restrictions on retail sale or supply of POMs do not apply to the supply of any such medicine in accordance with Conditions A or B, below, by

   a the Common Services Agency;

   b a health authority or special health authority,

   c an NHS trust,

   d an NHS foundation trust,

   e a PCT, or

   f a person, who is not a doctor, a dentist or a person lawfully conducting a retail pharmacy business where the person supplies a product pursuant to an arrangement with one of the persons specified in paragraphs a–e;

2 Condition A is that the product is supplied for the purpose of being administered to a person in accordance with the written directions of a doctor, dentist, nurse independent prescriber, optometrist independent prescriber or pharmacist independent prescriber relating to that person, regardless of whether the directions comply with HMRs Reg.17 (requirements for prescriptions);

3 Condition B is that

   a the product is supplied for the purpose of being administered to a person in accordance with a PGD,

   b the PGD relates to the supply of a description or class of medicinal product by the person by whom the medicinal product is supplied and has effect at the time at which it is supplied,

   c the PGD contains the particulars specified in Part 1 of Schedule 16,

   d the PGD is signed on behalf of the person specified in column 2 of the table in Part 2 of that Schedule ('the authorising person') against the entry in column 1 of that table for the class of person by whom the product is supplied,

   e the individual who supplies the product

      i belongs to one of the classes of individual specified in Part 4 of that Schedule (see appendix 3), and

    ii is designated in writing, on behalf of the authorising person, for the purpose of the supply or administration of products under the PGD; and

  f when the product is supplied, a marketing authorisation, Article 126a authorisation, certificate of registration or traditional herbal registration is in force in relation to it.

Supply under a Patient Group Direction to assist doctors or dentists (HMRs Reg.230)

Supply under a PGD to assist doctors or dentists where

a the individual supplies or (as the case may be) administers the product to assist a doctor in the provision of NHS primary medical services or a dentist in the provision of NHS primary dental services;

b the product is supplied for the purpose of being administered to a person in accordance with a PGD; and

c the following conditions are met.

The conditions are:

A the PGD relates to the supply or (as the case may be) administration of a description or class of medicinal product in order to assist the doctor or dentist in providing the services;

B the PGD has effect at the time at which the product is supplied or administered;

C the PGD contains the particulars specified in Part 1 of Schedule 16 (but with the omission of paragraph 4 in the case of a PGD relating to administration only);

D that the PGD is signed

  a by the doctor or dentist, or

  b where it also relates to supply or administration to assist one or more other doctors or dentists, by one of those doctors or dentists;

E that the PGD is signed

  a on behalf of the health authority or PCT with which a contract or agreement for the provision of those services has been made or which provides those services in the case of

    i NHS primary medical services, or

    ii NHS primary dental services in England or Wales,

  b in the case of dental services in Scotland under the National Health Service (Scotland) Act 1978, or general dental services in Northern Ireland, on behalf of the health authority with which an arrangement for the provision of those services has been made, and

c in the case of personal dental services provided under a pilot scheme in Scotland or Northern Ireland, on behalf of the health authority which is a party to the pilot scheme;

F the individual supplying the product is designated in writing for the purpose of the supply or administration of medicinal products under the PGD

    a by the doctor or dentist, or

    b where it also relates to supply to assist one or more other doctors or dentists, by one of those doctors or dentists;

G that when the product is supplied or (as the case may be) administered, a marketing authorisation, Article 126a authorisation, certificate of registration or traditional herbal registration is in force in relation to it.

Supply under a Patient Group Direction by independent hospitals etc. (HMRs Reg.231)

Regulation 231 relates to an independent hospital, an independent clinic, an independent medical agency or a nursing home (in Northern Ireland):

A applying only to England is that the registered provider at the hospital, clinic or agency is registered in compliance with section 10 of the Health and Social Care Act 2008[3] in respect of one or more of the following regulated activities

    a treatment of disease, disorder or injury,

    b assessment or medical treatment of persons detained under the Mental Health Act 1983,

    c surgical procedures,

    d diagnostic and screening procedures,

    e maternity and midwifery services, and

    f family planning;

B is that the product is sold or supplied for the purpose of being administered to a person in accordance with a PGD;

C that the PGD

    a relates to the sale or supply or (as the case may be) administration of a description or class of medicinal product by the person by whom the medicinal product is sold or supplied or administered, and

    b has effect at the time at which it is sold or supplied;

D that the PGD contains the particulars specified in Part 1 of Schedule 16 (but with the omission of paragraph 4 in the case of a PGD relating to administration only);

[3] Registered with the Care Quality Commission (England) (chapter 26)

E that the PGD is signed
    a by or on behalf of the registered provider, and
    b if there is a relevant manager for the independent hospital, clinic or medical agency, or nursing home, by that manager;
F that the individual who sells or supplies or (as the case may be) administers the product
    a belongs to one of the classes of individual specified in Part 4 of Schedule 16, and
    b is designated in writing for the purpose of the sale or supply or (as the case may be) administration of products under the PGD
        i by or on behalf of the registered provider, or
        ii if there is a relevant manager for the independent hospital, clinic or medical agency, or nursing home, by that manager;
G when the product is supplied, a marketing authorisation, Article 126a authorisation, certificate of registration or traditional herbal registration is in force in relation to it.

Supply under a Patient Group Direction by dental practices and clinics: England and Wales (HMRs Reg.232)

This paragraph applies to a dental practice or dental clinic:

a in England, in respect of which the registered provider is registered in compliance with section 10 of the Health and Social Care Act 2008[4] in respect of one or both of the following regulated activities
    i treatment of disease, disorder or injury, or
    ii diagnostic and screening procedures;
b in Wales, in which dental services are provided by private dentists and those dentists are registered with Healthcare Inspectorate Wales in accordance with the Regulations,[5] in relation to the services provided by those dentists; and
c the following conditions are met.

The conditions are:

A that the product is sold or supplied for the purpose of being administered to a person in accordance with a PGD;
B that the PGD
    a relates to the sale or supply or (as the case may be) administration of a description or class of medicinal product by the person by whom the medicinal product is sold or supplied or administered, and
    b has effect at the time at which it is sold or supplied;

[4]Registered with the Care Quality Commission (England) (chapter 26)
[5]The Private Dentistry (Wales) Regulations SI 2008 No. 1976

C that the PGD contains the particulars specified in Part 1 of Schedule 16 (but with the omission of paragraph 4 in the case of a PGD relating to administration only);

D that the PGD is signed

  a in England

    i by or on behalf of the registered provider, and

    ii if there is a relevant manager for the practice or clinic, by that manager,

  b in Wales

    i by the private dentist who is treating the person, and

    ii if there is a manager for the practice or clinic, by that manager;

E that the individual who sells or supplies or (as the case may be) administers the product

  a belongs to one of the classes of individual specified in Part 4 of Schedule 16, and

  b is designated in writing for the purpose of the sale or supply or (as the case may be) administration of products under the PGD

    i in England (a) by or on behalf of the registered provider or (b) if there is a relevant manager for the practice or clinic, by that manager, or

    ii in Wales, by the private dentist who is treating the person;

F that when the product is supplied, a marketing authorisation, Article 126a authorisation, certificate of registration or traditional herbal registration is in force in relation to it.

In relation to Wales, in this Regulation 'manager' means:

a the person who carries on the dental practice or dental clinic; or

b if there is no such person, a person who manages the practice or clinic.

Supply under a Patient Group Direction to assist the police etc. (HMRs Reg.234)

Supply can be made under a PGD to assist the police and allied services under the conditions:

A that the individual supplies or (as the case may be) administers the product to assist the provision of healthcare by, on behalf of, or under arrangements made by, one of the following bodies ('the relevant body')

  a a police force in England and Wales or in Scotland,

  b the Police Service of Northern Ireland,

  c a prison service, or

  d Her Majesty's Forces;

B that the product is supplied for the purpose of being administered to a person in accordance with a PGD;

C that the PGD relates to the supply or (as the case may be) the administration of a description or class of medicinal product to assist the provision of healthcare by, on behalf of, or under arrangements made by, the relevant body;

D that the PGD has effect at the time at which the product is supplied or (as the case may be) administered;

E that the PGD contains the particulars specified in Part 1 of Schedule 16 (but with the omission of paragraph 4 in the case of a PGD relating to administration only);

F that the PGD is signed

   a by or on behalf of a person specified in column 2 of Part 3 of Schedule 16 against the entry in column 1 for the relevant body, and

   b where the relevant body is a police force or the Police Service of Northern Ireland, by a doctor who is not employed or engaged by, and does not provide services under arrangements made with, any police force or the Police Service of Northern Ireland;

G that the individual who supplies the product is designated in writing by or on behalf of the relevant body for the purpose of the supply or (as the case may be) the administration of medicinal products under the PGD;

H that when the product is supplied, a marketing authorisation, Article 126a authorisation, certificate of registration or traditional herbal registration is in force in relation to it.

Other exemptions for sale, supply or administration by certain persons (Sch. 17 to the HMRs)

Schedule 17 is divided into five parts, which cover many exemptions from restrictions:

Part 1: sale and supply of POMs
Part 2: supply of POMs
Part 3: administration of POMs
Part 4: for certain persons who sell, supply or offer for sale or supply certain medicinal products
Part 5: for certain persons who supply certain medicinal products.

Only some of these exemptions are discussed below.

Midwives

Sale or supply

The restrictions on the sale, offer for sale or supply of any medicinal products do not apply when the sale, offer for sale or supply is in the course of the registered midwife's professional practice or being delivered or administered under arrangements made by the Secretary of State or Minister for Health, Social Services and Public Safety (HMRs Reg.223 and Part 1 (4) Sch. 17).

1 all medicinal products that are not POMs;
2 POMs contained in Schedule 17 Part 1 for sale or supply, i.e. diclofenac, hydrocortisone acetate, miconazole, nystatin or phytomenadione.

Administration

Student or registered midwives may also administer parenterally in the course of their professional practice POMs containing any of the following substances (HMRs Part 3(2) Sch. 17):

- adrenaline
- anti-D immunoglobulin
- carboprost
- cyclizine lactate
- diamorphine
- ergometrine maleate
- gelofusine
- Hartmann's solution
- hepatitis B vaccine
- hepatitis immunoglobulin
- lidocaine hydrochloride
- morphine
- naloxone hydrochloride
- oxytocins, natural and synthetic
- pethidine hydrochloride
- phytomenadione
- prochloperazine
- sodium chloride 0.9%.

The medicine shall:

a in the case of lidocaine and lidocaine hydrochloride, be administered only while attending on a woman in childbirth, and
b where administration is
   i by a registered midwife, be administered in the course of their professional practice,
   ii by a student midwife (a) be administered under the direct supervision of a registered midwife and (b) not include diamorphine, morphine or pethidine hydrochloride.

Midwives may also supply or administer POMs, Pharmacy Medicines and GSL products under PGDs (see above).

Registered nurses

Community practitioner nurse prescribers may prescribe, but not sell or supply, a limited list of POMs (HMRs Sch. 13).

Registered nurses may also supply or administer POMs, Pharmacy Medicines and GSL products under PGDs (HMRs Sch. 16).

Optometrists

Registered optometrist means a person whose name in entered in the Register of Optometrists.[6]

The restrictions on retail supply or sale do not apply to the sale or supply of certain medicinal products (those in 3 and 4 below) by registered optometrists provided they are only in the course of their professional practice and only in an emergency (HMRs Part 1(6–9) Sch. 17). The medicinal products to which this exemption applies are:

1 all medicinal products on a GSL;
2 all Pharmacy Medicines;
3 POMs that are either:
   a eye drops containing not more than 0.5 per cent chloramphenicol, or
   b eye ointment containing not more than 1.0 per cent chloramphenicol;
4 medicines which are POMs by reason only that they contain any of the following substances:
   • cyclopentolate hydrochloride
   • fusidic acid
   • tropicamide.

Supplies of these POMs may be obtained by registered optometrists for use in their practice from a retail pharmacy business subject to the presentation of an order signed by a registered optometrist. Registered optometrists may also *purchase* for use in their practice (but not for sale or supply) medicines which are POMs by reason only that they contain any one or more of the following substances (HMRs Reg.250):

• amethocaine hydrochloride
• lidocaine hydrochloride
• oxybuprocaine hydrochloride
• proxymetacaine hydrochloride.

Registered optometrists may also supply or administer POMs, Pharmacy Medicines and GSL products under PGDs (see above).

An *optometrist independent prescriber* is a registered optometrist whose name is annotated in the relevant register as qualified to order drugs and medicines.[7]

[6]Maintained under Opticians Act 1989 (as amended)
[7]Defined in HMRs Reg.8

Additional supply optometrist means a person who is registered as an optometrist and against whose name particulars of the additional supply speciality has been entered in the register.[8] They may sell or supply the following POMs in the course of their professional practice and in an emergency:

- acetylcysteine
- atropine sulphate
- azelastine hydrochloride
- diclofenac sodium
- emedastine
- homatropine hydrobromide
- ketotifen
- levocabastine
- lodoxamide
- nedocromil sodium
- olopatadine
- pilocarpine hydrochloride
- pilocarpine nitrate
- polymyxin B/bacitracin
- polymyxin B/trimethoprim
- sodium cromoglicate.

Persons lawfully conducting a retail pharmacy may sell these items on the presentation of a signed order from an additional supply optometrist.

Registered chiropodists and podiatrists

Sale or supply (HMRs Part 4(1) Sch. 17)

The restrictions on retail sale or supply do not apply to the sale or supply of certain medicinal products by registered chiropodists and podiatrists provided:

1 the sale or supply is made in the course of their professional practice; and
2 the product has been made up for sale or supply in a container elsewhere than at the place at which it is sold or supplied.

The medicinal products to which this exemption applies are:

1 medicinal products for external human use that are on a GSL; and
2 any of the following Pharmacy Medicines for external use only:
   a ointment of heparinoid and hyaluronidase, potassium permanganate crystals or solution

[8]Defined in HMRs Reg.250(10)

b products containing, as their only active ingredients, any of the following substances, at a strength, in the case of each substance, not exceeding that specified in relation to that substance:

- 9.0 per cent borotannic complex
- 10.0 per cent buclosamide
- 3.0 per cent chlorquinaldol
- 1.0 per cent clotrimazole
- 10.0 per cent crotamiton
- 5.0 per cent diamthazole hydrochloride
- 1.0 per cent econazole nitrate
- 1.0 per cent fenticlor
- 10.0 per cent glutaraldehyde
- 1.0 per cent griseofulvin
- 0.4 per cent hydrargaphen
- 2.0 per cent mepyramine maleate
- 2.0 per cent miconazole nitrate
- 2.0 per cent phenoxypropan-2-ol
- 20.0 per cent podophyllum resin
- 10.0 per cent polynoxylin
- 70.0 per cent pyrogallol
- 70.0 per cent salicylic acid
- 1.0 per cent terbinafine
- 0.1 per cent thiomersal.

Registered chiropodists or podiatrists against whose names are recorded in the relevant register annotations signifying that they are qualified to use the following medicines may sell or supply any of them in the course of their professional practice (HMRs Part 1 (6) Sch. 17):

- amorolfine hydrochloride cream: the maximum strength of amorolfine not to exceed 0.25 per cent w/w
- amorolfine hydrochloride lacquer: the maximum strength of amorolfine not to exceed 5 per cent w/v
- topical hydrocortisone the maximum strength of hydrocortisone in the medicinal product not to exceed 1 per cent w/w
- amoxicillin
- co-codamol
- co-dydramol 10/500 tablets
- codeine phosphate
- erythromycin
- flucloxacillin
- silver sulfadiazine

- tioconazole 28%
- topical hydrocortisone not exceeding 1%w/v.

Administration (HMRs Part 3(1) Sch. 17)

Registered chiropodists or podiatrists against whose names are recorded in the relevant register annotations signifying that they are qualified to use the following medicines may administer the following substances:

- adrenaline (epinephrine)
- bupivacaine hydrochloride
- bupivacaine hydrochloride with adrenaline (epinephrine) where the maximum strength of the adrenaline does not exceed 1 mg in 200 mL bupivacaine hydrochloride
- levobupivacaine hydrochloride
- lidocaine hydrochloride
- lidocaine hydrochloride with adrenaline (epinephrine) where the maximum strength of the adrenaline does not exceed 1 mg in 200 mL lidocaine hydrochloride
- mepivacaine hydrochoride
- methylprednisolone
- prilocaine hydrochloride
- ropivicaine hydrochoride.

Registered chiropodists may also supply or administer POMs, Pharmacy Medicines and GSL products under PGDs (see above).

Ambulance paramedics

Persons who are registered paramedics and administer, only for the immediate necessary treatment of sick or injured persons (HMRs Part 3 (8) Sch. 17):

- diazepam 5 mg/mL emulsion for injection;
- succinylated modified fluid gelatin 4 per cent intravenous infusion;
- medicines containing ergometrine maleate 500 micrograms/mL with oxytocin 5 IU/mL but no other active ingredient;
- POMs containing one or more of the following substances, but no other active ingredient:
  - adrenaline acid tartrate
  - adrenaline hydrochloride
  - amiodarone
  - anhydrous glucose
  - benzylpenicillin

- compound sodium lactate intravenous infusion (Hartmann's solution)
- ergometrine maleate
- furosemide
- glucose
- heparin sodium (only for the purpose of cannula flushing)
- lidocaine hydrochloride
- metoclopramide
- morphine sulphate
- nalbuphine hydrochloride
- naloxone hydrochloride
- ondansetron
- paracetamol
- reteplase
- sodium chloride
- streptokinase
- tenecteplase.

Individuals who are state registered paramedics may also supply or administer POMs, Pharmacy Medicines and GSL products under PGDs (see above).

Manufacturers of products for treatment of the hair and scalp

The holder of a manufacturer's licence for a medicinal product which is for external use in the treatment of hair and scalp conditions may sell or supply the product free from the statutory restrictions or conditions applicable to retail sales (HMRs Part 4(5) Sch. 17) provided that:

1 the licence in question contains a provision that the licence holder shall only manufacture the medicinal product for a particular person after being requested by or on behalf of that person and in that person's presence to use his/her own judgement as to the treatment required; and
2 the sale or supply is made only upon receipt of such a request.

The medicinal products to which this exemption applies are:

1 medicinal products on a GSL which are for human external use; and
2 Pharmacy Medicines which are for external use in the treatment of hair and scalp conditions and which contain any of the following substances:
   - not more than 5 per cent of boric acid
   - isopropyl myristate or lauryl sulphate
   - not more than 0.004 per cent oestrogens
   - not more than 1 per cent resorcin
   - not more than 3 per cent salicylic acid
   - not more than 0.2 per cent sodium pyrithione or zinc pyrithione.

Public analysts, sampling officers and other such persons

The restrictions on retail sale or supply do not apply to persons who sell or supply any medicinal product (HMRs Part 1 (2) Sch. 17) to any of the following:

a a public analyst appointed under section 27 of the Food Safety Act 1990 or Article 36 of the Food (Northern Ireland) Order 1989;
b an agricultural analyst appointed under section 67 of the Agriculture Act 1970(a);
c a person duly authorised by an enforcement authority under HMRs.325–328;
d a sampling officer within the meaning of HMRs Schedule 31.

The sale or supply is subject to the presentation of an order signed by or on behalf of the analyst, authorised officer, sampling officer or enforcement officer, as the case may be. It must state the status of the person signing it and the amount of the medicine required.

National Health Service drug testing

The restrictions on retail sale or supply do not apply to persons who sell or supply any medicinal product to any person employed or engaged in connection with the scheme for testing the quality and amount of the drugs, preparations and appliances supplied under the National Health Service Act 2006, the National Health Service (Scotland) Act 1978, the National Health Service (Wales) Act 2006 and the Health and Personal Social Services (Northern Ireland) Order 1972 or any subordinate legislation made under those Acts or that Order (HMRs Part 1(3) Sch. 17).

The sale or supply must be for the purpose of the relevant scheme and is subject to the presentation of an order signed on behalf of the person so employed or engaged stating:

1 the status of the person signing it; and
2 the amount of the medicinal product required.

Owners and masters of ships

The restrictions on supply (but not sale) of any medicinal product do not apply when the supply is made by the owner or the master of a ship which does not carry a doctor on board as part of her complement (HMRs Part 5(9) Sch. 17). An owner or master may also administer POMs that are for parenteral administration. The supply or administration shall be only so far as is necessary for the treatment of persons on the ship.

Offshore installations

Persons employed as qualified first-aid personnel on offshore installations may, only so far as is necessary for the treatment of persons on the installation (HMRs Part 5 (14) Sch. 17):

1 supply any medicinal product; and
2 administer all parenteral POMs.

Statutory requirements for medical treatment of employees

The restrictions on retail supply (but not sale) of medicinal products do not apply to supplies made by persons requiring medicinal products for the purpose of enabling them, in the course of any business carried on by them, to comply with any requirements made by or in pursuance of any enactment with respect to the medical treatment of employees (HMRs Part 5(8) Sch. 17). The exemption extends to the POMs and the Pharmacy Medicines specified in the relevant enactment and to medicinal products on a GSL.

The supply shall be:

1 for the purpose of enabling them to comply with any requirements made by or in pursuance of any such enactment; and
2 subject to such conditions and in such circumstances as may be specified in the relevant enactments (SI 1980 No. 1924 and SI 1997 No. 1830).

Persons employed or engaged in the lawful drug treatment services

Persons employed or engaged in the lawful drug treatment services may supply ampoules of sterile water for injection containing not more than 2 mL of sterile water (HMRs Part 5(7) Sch. 17).

Holders of Controlled Drugs authorities

The restrictions on the supply of POMs do not apply to persons authorised by licences granted under Regulation 5 of the Misuse of Drugs Regulations[9] to supply the Controlled Drugs specified in the licence (HMRs Part 5 (6) Sch. 17).

The supply shall be subject to such conditions and in such circumstances and to such an extent as may be specified in the licence. Similarly, the restrictions on the administration of POMs do not apply to persons who are authorised as members of a group by a group authority granted under Regulations 8(3) or 9(3) of the Misuse of Drugs Regulations. The exemption

[9]The Misuse of Drugs Regulations SI 2001 No. 3988 (as amended) and The Misuse of Drugs Regulations (Northern Ireland) SR 2002 No. 1 (as amended)

is limited to the administration of Controlled Drugs that are specified in the group authority and is subject to such conditions and in such circumstances and to such an extent as may be specified in the group authority.

Royal National Lifeboat Institution

The restrictions on the retail supply of any medicinal product do not apply to supply by the Royal National Lifeboat Institution or certificated first-aiders of the Institution (HMRs Part 5(1) Sch. 17). The supply of any POM shall be only so far as it is necessary for the treatment of sick or injured persons in the exercise of the functions of the Institution.

British Red Cross Society and other such organisations

The restrictions on the retail supply of Pharmacy Medicines and all medicinal products on a GSL (but *not* POMs) do not apply to supply by the bodies specified below and their certificated first-aid and certificated nursing members (HMRs Part 5(2–5) Sch. 17). In all cases the supply shall be only so far as it is necessary for the treatment of sick or injured persons. The bodies concerned are:

- British Red Cross Society
- St John Ambulance Association and Brigade
- St Andrew's Ambulance Association
- Order of Malta Ambulance Corps.

School and pre-school dental schemes

Pharmacy Medicines that are for use in the prevention of dental caries and consist of or contain sodium fluoride may be supplied in the course of 'school dental schemes', by persons carrying on the business of a school providing full-time education and in the course of 'pre-school dental schemes', by health authorities (HMRs Part 5(11 and 12) Sch. 17).

A *school dental scheme*[10] means a scheme supervised by a doctor or dentist in which medicinal products are supplied at a school to pupils of that school for the purpose of preventing dental caries. A supply may also be made to a child under 16 years of age with the consent of the parent or guardian of that child.

A *pre-school dental scheme* means a scheme supervised by a doctor or dentist in which medicinal products are supplied to parents or guardians of children under 5 years of age for use by such children for the purpose of

[10]Defined in The Medicines (Pharmacy and General Sale – Exemption) Order SI 1980 No. 1924 (now repealed)

preventing dental caries. The supplies must be made by a registered nurse or an enrolled nurse.

NB. The following are the Pharmacy Medicines affected:[11]

1 preparations of sodium fluoride for use in the prevention of dental caries in the form of:
   a tablets or drops (maximum daily dose 2.2 mg),
   b mouth rinses containing not more than 0.2 per cent (other than those for daily use),
   c mouth rinses for daily use (containing not more than 0.05 per cent),
   d dentifrices containing not more than 0.33 per cent.

Other medicinal products containing sodium fluoride are POMs and may not be sold, supplied or administered.

Mountain rescue teams

Persons who hold a certificate from the Mountain Rescue Council of England and Wales or from the Northern Ireland Mountain Rescue Co-ordinating Committee may supply all Pharmacy Medicines and GSL products as far as is necessary for the treatment of sick or injured persons in the course of mountain rescue services. They may also supply POMs in response to an order in writing signed by a doctor (HMRs Part 5(16) Sch. 17).

Occupational health schemes

Pharmacy Medicines and POMs may be supplied by a person operating an *occupational health scheme*,[12] that is, a scheme in which persons, in the course of a business carried on by them, provide facilities for their employees for the treatment or prevention of disease.

The supply must be made in the course of the scheme. The medicinal products may be supplied to the person operating the scheme in response to an order in writing signed by a doctor or a registered nurse (HMRs Part 5(10) Sch. 17).

The individual supplying or administering the medicines in the course of the scheme, if not a doctor, must be:

1 a registered nurse; and
2 where the medicinal product in question is a POM, acting in accordance with the written instructions of a doctor as to the circumstances in which POMs of the description in question are to be used in the course of the occupational health scheme.

[11] Prescription Only Medicines (Human Use) Order 1997 No. 1830 Schedule 1
[12] Defined in The Medicines (Pharmacy and General Sale – Exemption) Order SI 1980 No. 1924 (now repealed)

Operators or commanders of aircraft

The commander of an aircraft or the *operator*,[13] that is, the person for the time being having the management of the aircraft, may supply certain medicinal products but only so far as is necessary for the immediate treatment of sick or injured persons on the aircraft (HMRs Part 5(13) Sch. 17). S/he may supply any medicinal products on a GSL, any Pharmacy Medicine and POMs which are *not* for parenteral administration and which have been sold or supplied to him/her in response to an order in writing signed by a doctor. The supply of those POMs by the commander or operator shall be in accordance with the written instructions of a doctor as to the circumstances in which POMs of the description in question are to be used on the aircraft.

In addition, the commander or operator of an aircraft may administer POMs for parenteral use which have been sold or supplied to him/her in response to an order in writing signed by a doctor. The administration shall be only so far as is necessary for the immediate treatment of sick or injured person on the aircraft and shall be in accordance with the written instructions of a doctor as to the circumstances in which POMs of the description in question are to be used on the aircraft.

Universities, higher education institutions or institutions concerned with research

The restrictions on retail sale or supply do not apply to persons selling or supplying any medicinal product to a university, an institution concerned with higher education or an institution concerned with research but only for the purposes of the education or research with which the institution is concerned (HMRs Part 1(1) Sch. 17). The sale or supply is subject to the presentation of an order signed by the principal of the institution for education or research or the appropriate head of department in charge of a specified course of research. The order must state:

1 the name of the institution for which the medicinal product is required;
2 the purpose for which it is required; and
3 the total quantity required.

Supplies by holders of marketing authorisations

The restrictions on sale or supply do not apply to holders of marketing authorisations and holders of manufacturer's licences who sell or supply medicinal products referred to in the licences to pharmacists so as to enable them to prepare an entry relating to the medicinal product in question in

[13] Defined in The Medicines (Pharmacy and General Sale – Exemption) Order SI 1980 No. 1924 (now repealed)

a tablet or capsule identification guide or similar publication. No greater quantity than is reasonably necessary for that purpose may be supplied (HMRs Part 1(10) Sch. 17).

Exemptions in other legislation

Veterinary drugs

The exemptions which apply to the retail sale or supply of certain veterinary drugs are dealt with in chapter 16.

Foot and mouth disease vaccine

Specified government officers and other persons including contractors, volunteers and employees are exempt from the general restrictions of the Medicines Act in relation to Pharmacy Only and POMs in certain conditions.[14] Those conditions are when they supply foot and mouth disease vaccine as part of the government's responses to an outbreak in the UK of foot and mouth disease and complying with specified EEC measures laid down in Council Directive 2003/85/EC.

Summary

- Doctors and dentists may sell or supply all medicines to their own patients.
- NHS bodies and certain health professionals can supply medicines under PGDs. These are listed in appendix 3.
- Independent hospitals, clinics and medical agencies together with the police service, prison service and Her Majesty's Armed Forces can supply and administer under PGDs.
- For the purposes of their professional practice, midwives have a list of medicines which can be sold or supplied by them and another list of medicines which they may administer.
- In the course of their professional practice, and only in an emergency, optometrists have a list of medicines which they may sell or supply to their patients. They may also purchase for use in their practice, but not for sale or supply, a limited list of POMs.
- In the course of their professional practice, chiropodists may sell or supply to their patients any GSL product for external use and a limited list of Pharmacy Medicines. Chiropodists holding a certificate of competence in the use of analgesics may administer, in their practice, a named list of local parenteral analgesics.

[14]The Medicines (Vaccination Against Foot-and-Mouth Disease) Order SI 2004 No. 2779

- Persons who hold a certificate of proficiency in ambulance paramedic skills may parenterally administer certain medicines for the immediate, necessary treatment of the sick or injured.
- Other categories of activities also have limited lists of medicines which they may sell or supply. These include dental and occupational health schemes, owners and masters of ships, offshore installations, the Royal National Lifeboat Institution, public analysts, aircraft commanders, universities and the British Red Cross.

Further reading

Human Medicines Regulations (2012) SI 2012 No. 1916, *Explanatory memorandum*: http://www.legislation.gov.uk/uksi/2012/1916/pdfs/uksiem_20121916_en.pdf (accessed 21 November 2012).

Royal Pharmaceutical Society (published annually). *Medicines, Ethics and Practice: The Professional Guide for Pharmacists*. London: Royal Pharmaceutical Society (includes practice guidance on many of the topics in this chapter; free to members).

Websites

Legislation (can be searched on year and SI number or title): http://www.legislation.gov.uk

Medicines and Healthcare products Regulatory Agency: http://www.mhra.gov.uk

Royal Pharmaceutical Society (member access only; lists legal classifications of medicines and further practice guidance): http://www.rpharms.com

10

Human medicines: wholesale dealing

Susan Melvin

Regulations in Part 3 of the consolidated Human Medicines Regulations 2012[1] control the sale of medicinal products by way of wholesale dealing, that is, the sale or supply, or procuring, or holding or exporting it to another EEA country for the purposes of sale or supply to a person for the purpose of (a) selling or supplying them or (b) administering them to human beings in the course of a business (HMRs Reg.18(7)(b) and Reg.18(8)).

Sales of medicinal products by way of wholesale dealing can be made as set out below by:

1 the holder of a marketing authorisation; or
2 a person carrying on a business which consists (wholly or partly) of manufacturing medicinal products or of selling them by way of wholesale dealing; the sales must be made in the course of the business. (retail pharmacy owners who are not licensed as wholesalers may not sell by way of wholesale dealing; chapters 2 and 3).

Box 10.1 *The meaning of 'sale by way of wholesale dealing'*

Oxford v Sanger (1964)

The Pharmacy and Poisons Act 1933 (s.18) provided that poisons in Part I of the Poisons List could be lawfully sold only by authorised sellers of poisons. An exemption from this requirement was given in section 20(1) of the Act in respect of sales of poisons by way of wholesale dealing. Section 29 defined *sale by way of wholesale dealing* as 'sale to a person who buys for the purposes of selling again'.

---

[1]Human Medicines Regulations SI 2012 No. 1916

Sanger Ltd (wholesalers) had on five occasions sold Part I poisons to a retail shopkeeper who had subsequently sold the poisons (tablets) to the public by retail. The shopkeeper was not an authorised seller of poisons.

The wholesaler was charged with selling Part I poisons contrary to section 18 of the Act. It was contended for the prosecution that the company could not claim the benefit of the exemption for wholesale dealing as the poison had been sold to a shopkeeper who could not lawfully sell again. The magistrate dismissed the information, and an appeal to the High Court against that decision was also dismissed.

It was held in the High Court that the word *lawfully* could not be read into the definition of *wholesale dealing*. Section 20 did not lay any duty upon a wholesaler to ascertain that the retailer to whom he sold was lawfully entitled to resell. If it was desired to control wholesalers, it could and must be done by rule.

Comment. Rule 11 of the Poisons Rules made under the Poisons Act 1972 then required wholesalers who sold Part I poisons to be satisfied that their shopkeeper customers who order such poisons are authorised sellers of poisons, or that they do not intend to sell the poisons by way of retail trade. The Medicines Act 1968 (s.61) provided for similar Regulations to be made in respect of medicinal products (SI 1980 No. 1923) and HMRs Reg.44 enacts the same provisions.

[1965] 1 All ER 96; *Pharm J*, 12 December 1964 p. 599.

Conditions on sales by way of wholesale dealing

A person making sales by way of wholesale dealing must possess a wholesale dealer's licence (chapter 3). Such sales must be from a specified place and the licence holder must among other requirements (HMRs Reg.43):

1 ensure, within the limits of the holder's responsibility, the continued supply of medicinal products to pharmacies, and others who may lawfully sell them, so that the needs of patients in the UK are met;
2 keep documents to facilitate withdrawal or recall of medicinal products and maintain an emergency plan for this purpose;
3 keep records in relation to the receipt and dispatch of medicinal products of
   a the date of receipt and of despatch,
   b the name of the products,

    c the quantity of the products received or despatched, and

    d the name and address of the person from whom, or to whom, the products are sold or supplied as appropriate;

4 distribute by wholesale dealing only to persons who may lawfully sell by retail or lawfully administer those products (HMRs Reg.44);

5 have at all times at his/her disposal the services of a person – a *responsible person* – who possesses in the opinion of the licensing authority (HMRs Reg.45)

    a knowledge of the activities to be carried out and of the procedures to be performed under the licence, and

    b experience in those activities and procedures which is adequate for those purposes.

The functions of the *responsible person* shall be to ensure that the conditions under which the licence has been granted have been, and are being, complied with and that the quality of the products is maintained in accordance with the requirements of the appropriate marketing authorisation.

Prescription Only and Pharmacy Medicines by wholesale dealing

POMs and Pharmacy Medicines may be sold by way of wholesale dealing (HMRs Reg.249 and Sch. 22) to:

1 doctors or dentists;

2 any person lawfully conducting a retail pharmacy business;

3 authorities or persons carrying on the business of an independent hospital, independent clinic, independent medical agency or a hospital or health centre which is not an independent hospital or clinic or in Northern Ireland a nursing home;

4 holders of wholesale dealer's licences, or persons to whom the requirements to hold a wholesale dealer's licence do not apply by virtue of an exemption conferred by or under the Act;

5 Ministers of the Crown and government departments and officers thereof; Scottish, Welsh or Northern Irish Ministers;

6 an NHS trust or foundation trust health authority, special health authority or PCT;

7 the Common Services Agency;

8 any person who requires Pharmacy Medicines for the purpose of administering them to human beings in the course of a business where the medicines are for the purpose of being so administered pursuant to an arrangement made with an NHS trust or foundation trust, the Common Services Agency, a health authority, special health authority or PCT;

9 a person other than an exempted person who carries on a business consisting (wholly or partly) of the supply or administration of medicinal products for the purpose of assisting the provision of healthcare by or on behalf of the police force in the UK, a prison service or Her Majesty's Forces;

10 any person who is the subject of an exemption in HMRs Schedule 17 but only in respect of the medicinal products covered by the exemption (chapter 9 and HMRs Reg.250);

11 registered optometrists in that there are certain POMs which optometrists are entitled to supply to their patients or use in their practice (chapter 9); and

12 any person selling or supplying by retail, or administering, unit preparations of POMs (other than Controlled Drugs) diluted to one part in a million (6×) having been requested by or on behalf of the particular person and in that person's presence to use their own judgement as to the treatment required (see also chapter 11).

Wholesale dealing from a pharmacy

In August 2012, when the MHRA consolidated the Human Medicines Regulations 2012, the section 10(7) exemption in the Medicines Act 1968 was repealed in order to comply with EU legislation. This exemption previously allowed retail pharmacy businesses to wholesale medicines without a wholesale dealer's licence if this was an 'inconsiderable' part of their business. However, the practicalities of this removal of exemption are unclear, and at the time of going to press the MHRA had issued the following guidance (see websites at end of chapter).

> The MHRA is concerned to ensure that the repeal of the section 10(7) exemption does not adversely impact on arrangements for supply of medicines in the UK. In determining how to address this issue, the MHRA has taken careful account of the particular arrangements for delivery of healthcare in the UK which involve a wide range of individuals and in a diverse range of locations.
>
> In particular:
>
> - Many healthcare professionals and others authorised or entitled to supply medicines to the public in the UK and others authorised to receive medicines, need to hold stocks of medicines for a range of purposes including local healthcare provision and look to a local community or hospital pharmacy to supply them as part of their professional practice.
> - In contrast, some pharmacies engage in commercial trade in medicines, not solely as part of their professional practice within the UK healthcare system.

- Pharmacists may also occasionally need to obtain small quantities of a particular medicine or medicines from another pharmacist in order to meet the needs of individual patients.

MHRA enforcement

The MHRA continued to state:

> The MHRA takes the view that the supply of medicines by community and hospital pharmacies to other healthcare providers in the UK who need to hold medicines for treatment of or onward supply to their patients represents an important and appropriate part of the professional practice of both community and hospital pharmacy and falls within the definition of provision of healthcare services. In such circumstances, the MHRA will not deem such transactions as commercial dealing and pharmacies will not be required to hold a Wholesale Dealer's Licence.

> Conversely, pharmacists who wish to engage in commercial trading in medicines are entitled to do so only if they hold a Wholesale Dealer's Licence and comply with all the relevant requirements. As the authority responsible for enforcement the MHRA will take appropriate action to enforce the requirement of the legislation and will require any commercial trade in medicines to be undertaken only by holders of a Wholesale Dealer's Licence.

> Pharmacists needing to obtain small quantities of a medicine from another pharmacist to meet a patient's individual needs may do so without the need for the supplying pharmacy to hold a Wholesale Dealer's Licence only if the transaction meets all of the following criteria:

> - It takes place on an occasional basis and
> - The quantity of medicines supplied is small and intended to meet the needs of an individual patient and
> - The supply is made on a not for profit basis.

> This restriction does not apply to exchange of stock between pharmacies that are part of the same legal entity.

If the pharmacist does not possess a wholesale dealer's licence, then the only records required to be kept are a copy of the order or invoice relating to the supply or an entry made in the Prescription Only Register by the owner of the retail pharmacy business. Orders or invoices (and all orders required as a condition in connection with any exempted sale of a POM; chapter 9) must be kept for 2 years from the date of the sale or supply.

If the pharmacist does possess a wholesale dealer's licence, then all the provisions of such a possession apply (see above).

Wholesale dealing of veterinary products

See chapter 16.

Summary

- Normally, a person who sells medicines by way of wholesale dealing requires a wholesale dealer's licence, which requires special premises, records to be kept and the appointment of a responsible person whose function is to ensure that the conditions of the licence are being complied with and that the quality of the products is maintained in accordance with the requirements of the appropriate marketing authorisation.
- A pharmacist may supply medicines by way of wholesale dealing (e.g. to a doctor) provided the sales takes place on an occasional basis and the quantity of medicines supplied is small and intended to meet the needs of an individual patient and the supply is made on a not for profit basis.

Further reading

Human Medicines Regulations (2012) SI 2012 No. 1916, *Explanatory memorandum*: http://www.legislation.gov.uk/uksi/2012/1916/pdfs/uksiem_20121916_en.pdf (accessed 21 November 2012).

Royal Pharmaceutical Society (published annually). *Medicines, Ethics and Practice: The Professional Guide for Pharmacists*. London: Royal Pharmaceutical Society (includes practice guidance on many of the topics in this chapter; free to members).

Royal Pharmaceutical Society (2012). Support Bulletin No. 15 August 2012 Human Medicines Regulations 2012 *Pharm J*, 289: 200 (free to members or available on subscription).

Websites

Legislation (can be searched on year and SI number or title): http://www.legislation.gov.uk

Medicines and Healthcare products Regulatory Agency: http://www.mhra.gov.uk

Royal Pharmaceutical Society (member access only; lists legal classifications of medicines and further practice guidance): http://www.rpharms.com

11

Human medicines: sale and supply of homoeopathic medicines

Susan Melvin

Most homoeopathic medicines for human use are subject to licensing procedures but, provided certain conditions are met, a simplified system of certification is permitted under the Human Medicines Regulations 2012.[1]

In 2012, the MHRA was in consultation to amend the Product Licence of Right scheme and information requirements for marketing authorisations for homoeopathic medicinal products under national rules implementing Article 16(2) of Directive 2001/83. At the time of going to press no changes have been made.

Definition of medicinal products at high dilutions (homoeopathic medicines)

Medicinal products at high dilutions are prepared from 'unit preparations' (HMRs Reg.213).

Unit preparation means 'a preparation, including a mother tincture, prepared by a process of solution, extraction or trituration with a view to being diluted tenfold or one hundredfold, either once or repeatedly, in an inert diluent, and then used either in this diluted form or, where applicable, by impregnating tablets, granules, powders or other inert substances'.

Homoeopathic medicines for human use: licensing

See chapter 3.

[1]Human Medicines Regulations SI 2012 No. 1916 Part 6 Regs.102–124

Exemptions for medicinal products at high dilution (homoeopathic medicines)

Regulation 242 of the Human Medicines Regulations 2012 contains an exemption from the restrictions which apply to the sale or supply of Pharmacy Medicines (HMRs Reg.221; see chapter 7) or GSL medicines (HMRs Reg.222; see chapter 6) subject to a number of conditions:

1 the product is neither for parenteral administration nor a Controlled Drug;

2 the person selling or supplying the product has been requested to do so by or on behalf of a particular person and in that person's presence and the seller has used their own judgement as to the treatment required; and

3 the medicinal product consists solely of one or more unit preparations of

   a any substance where the unit preparation has been diluted to at least one part in a million (6×);

   b any substance that is listed in HMRs Part 1 of Schedule 21 where the unit preparation has been diluted to at least one part in a thousand (3×); or

   c any substance that

     i is the active substance of a medicine that is subject to general sale,

     ii is listed in HMRs Part 3 of Schedule 21, or

     iii in the case of a medicinal product for external use only, is listed in HMRs Part 4 of Schedule 21, where the unit preparation has been diluted to at least one part in ten (1×).

In addition, the restrictions on sale or supply of Pharmacy Medicine do not apply where:

1 the medicinal product is neither for parenteral administration nor a Controlled Drug;

2 the conditions regarding GSL (HMRs Reg.221) are met; and

3 the medicinal product is one that consists solely of one or more unit preparations of

   a any substance where the unit preparation has been diluted to at least one part in a million (6×),

   b any substance that is listed in HMRs Part 2 of Schedule 21 where the unit preparation has been diluted to at least one part in a million (6×), or

   c any substance that

     i is the active substance of a medicine that is subject to general sale,

     ii is listed in HMRs Part 3 of Schedule 21, or

     iii in the case of a medicinal product for external use only, is listed in HMRs Part 4 of Schedule 21, where the unit preparation has been diluted to at least one part in ten (1×).

Exemption for certain (registered) homoeopathic medicinal products (HMRs Reg.243)

Neither the restrictions on sale or supply of GSL or Pharmacy medicines apply where

a a certificate of registration is in force in relation to the product;
b the product is not an excluded product (see below); and
c the person selling or supplying the product has been requested to do so by or on behalf of a particular person and in that person's presence and the seller has used their own judgement as to the treatment required.

In addition, the restrictions on sale or supply of Pharmacy Medicines do not apply where

a a certificate of registration is in force in relation to the product;
b the conditions for GSL are met; and
c the product is not an *excluded product*, which means a product that is promoted, recommended or marketed for use as an anthelmintic; for parenteral administration; for use as eye drops; for use as an eye ointment; for use as an enema; for use wholly or mainly for irrigation of wounds or of the bladder, vagina or rectum; or for administration wholly or mainly to children being a preparation of aloxiprin or aspirin.

Medicinal products at high dilutions

Table 11.1 lists these products. Taken from HMRs Reg.242 Schedule 21.

Table 11.1 Medicinal products at high dilutions			
Part 1: unit preparations diluted to at least one part in a thousand (3×)	**Part 2: unit preparations diluted to at least one part in a million (6×)**	**Part 3: unit preparations diluted to at least one part in ten (1×)**	**Part 4: unit preparations diluted to at least one part in ten (1×) for external use**
Agaricus muscarius	Adonis vernalis	Abies excelsa	Adonis vernalis
Ailanthus glandulosa	Agaricus bulbosus	Abies nigra	Agricus bulbosus
Apocynum cannabinum	Agaricus muscarius	Abies nobilis	Agricus muscarius
Aurum Iodatum	Agnus castus	Acalpha indica	Agnus castus
Belladonna	Ailanthus glandulosa	Agate	Allanthus glandulosa
Bismuth subgallate	Alum	Alisma plantago aq.	Alum
Bryonia alba dioica	Amethyst	Alstonia scholaris	Amethyst
Calcium fluoride	Ammonium iodide	Aluminium	Ammonium iodide
Cantharis	Amygdalae amarae	Amber (Succinum)	Amygdalae amarae
	Apatite	Ambra grisea	Apatite

(continued overleaf)

Table 11.1 *(continued)*

Part 1: unit preparations diluted to at least one part in a thousand (3×)	Part 2: unit preparations diluted to at least one part in a million (6×)	Part 3: unit preparations diluted to at least one part in ten (1×)	Part 4: unit preparations diluted to at least one part in ten (1×) for external use
Cerium oxalicum	Apocynum androsaemifolium	Ammonium phosphate	Apocynum androsaemifolium
Chelidonium majus	Apocynum cannabinum	Angostura vera	Apocynum cannabinum
Chenopodium oil	Argentite	Anthoxanthum	Argentite
Cina	Argentum chloride	Apis mellifera	Argentum chloride
Colocynthis	Argentum iodide	Aqua marina	Argentum iodide
Convallaria majalis	Arnica	Aqua mellis	Artemisia cina
Gelsemium sempervirens	Artemisia cina	Aralia racemosa	Aspidium filix-mas
Hyoscyamus niger	Aspidium filix-mas	Aranea diadema	Aspidium anthelmintica
Lycopodium	Aspidium anthelmintica	Arum maculatum	Aurum sulphide
Manganese acetate	Aurum sulphide	Arum triphyllum	Balsamum copaivae
Ranunculus bulbosus	Balsamum copivae	Asarum	Balsamum peruvianum
Terebinthinae oleum	Balsamum peruvianum	Asperula odorata	Barium citrate
	Barium citrate	Astacus fluviatillis	Barium sulphate
	Barium sulphate	Auric Chloride	Bismuth metal
	Bismuth metal	Badiaga	Bismuth subgallate
	Bismuth subgallate	Beech (*Fagus sylvestris*)	Bismuth subnitrate
	Bismuth subnitrate	Bellis perennis	Boletus laricis
	Boletus laricis	Berberis aquifolium	Bovista
	Bovista	Borago officinalis	Cade oil
	Cade oil	Butyric acid	Calcium fluoride
	Calcium fluoride	Calcium metal	Carduus marianus
	Cantharis	Calcium chloride	Cedar wood oil
	Carduus marianus	Calcium oxide	Cerium oxalicum
	Cedar wood oil	Calcium sulphate	Chalcocite
	Cerium oxalicum	Castoreum	Chalcopyrite
	Chalcocite	Ceanothus americanus	Chelidonium majus
	Chalcopyrite	Cedron	Chenopodium oil
	Chelidonium majus	Cerato (*Ceratostigma willmottiana*)	Colocynthis
	Chenopodium oil	Cherry Plum (*Prunus cerasifera*)	Convallaria majalis
	Colocynthis	Chestnut, red and sweet	Copper silicate, Nat
	Convallaria majalis	Cholesterinum	Crotalus horridus
	Copper silicate, Nat.	Chrysolite	Cucurbita
	Crotalus horridus	Cistus canadensis	Cucumis melo
	Cucurbita	Clematis erecta	Datura stramonium
	Cucumis melo	Conchae vera	Derris
	Datura stramonium	Conchiolinum	Diamond

(continued overleaf)

Table 11.1 (continued)

Part 1: unit preparations diluted to at least one part in a thousand (3×)	Part 2: unit preparations diluted to at least one part in a million (6×)	Part 3: unit preparations diluted to at least one part in ten (1×)	Part 4: unit preparations diluted to at least one part in ten (1×) for external use
	Derris	Corallium rubrum	Ephedra vulgaris
	Diamond	Crab apple	Ferric acetate
	Ephedra vulgaris	Crocus sativus	Ferrous iodide
	Ferric acetate	Erbium	Ferrous oxalate
	Ferrous iodide	Erigeron canadense	Ferrous sulphide
	Ferrous oxalate	Fuligo	Formic acid
	Ferrous sulphide	Genista tinctoria	Gall
	Formic acid	Geum urbanum	Gelsemium
	Gall	Glycogen	sempervirens
	Gelsemium	Gnaphalium	Gneiss
	sempervirens	leontopodium	Hamamelis virginiana
	Gneiss	Gold	Hepar sulfuris
	Granatum	Gorse (Ulex europaeus)	Hyoscyamus niger
	(Pomegranate) bark	Graphites	Iris florentine
	Harmamelis virginiana	Gratiola officinalis	Jaborandi
	Hepar sulfuris	Gymnocladus	Juniperus sabina
	Hyoscyamus niger	(American coffee tree)	Kaolinite
	Iris florentine	Haematoxylon	Lachmanthus tinctoria
	Jaborandi	campechianum	Lapis albus
	Juniperus sabina	Hecla lava (ash from	Lycopodium
	Kalinite	Mount Hecla)	Magnesium
	Lachmanthus tinctoria	Hedeoma pulegioides	Magnesium acetate
	Lapis albus	Hedra helix	Magnesium chloride
	Lycopodium	Heliotrope	Magnetite
	Magnesium	Heracleum spondylium	Manganese acetate
	Magnesium acetate	Herniaria	Nicotiana tabacum
	Magnesium chloride	Hornbeam (Carpinus	Nicotiana tabacum oil
	Magnetite	betulus)	Oleander
	Manganese acetate	Iberis amara	Opuntia vulgaris
	Nicotiana tabacum	Impatiens	Oxalic acid
	Nicotiana tabacum oil	Iris germanica	Petroleum
	Oleander	Iris pseudacorus	Phellandrium
	Opuntia vulgaris	Jacaranda procera	aquaticum
	Oxalic acid	Jatropha curcas	Pix liquida
	Petroleum	Juncus communis	Platinum
	Phellandrum	Justica adhatoda	Platinum chloride
	aquaticum	Lamium album	Potassium hydroxide
	Pix liquida	Laurus nobilis oil	Potassium silicate
		Laurocerasus	Pyrethrum

(continued overleaf)

Table 11.1 *(continued)*

Part 1: unit preparations diluted to at least one part in a thousand (3×)	Part 2: unit preparations diluted to at least one part in a million (6×)	Part 3: unit preparations diluted to at least one part in ten (1×)	Part 4: unit preparations diluted to at least one part in ten (1×) for external use
	Platinum	Ledum palustre	Pyrolusite
	Platinum chloride	Lilium tigrinum	Ranunculus acris
	Potassium hydroxide	Lonicera caprifolium	Ranunculus bulbosus
	Potassium silicate	Lysimachia vulgaris	Ranunculus flammula
	Pyrethrum	Magnesium phosphate	Ranunculus repens
	Pyrolusite	Magnesite	Ranunculus scelerantus
	Ranunculus acris	Magnolia	Rhodium oxynitrate
	Ranunculus bulbosus	Marum verum	Rhododendron
	Ranunculus flammula	Melilotus officinalis	chrysanthemum
	Ranunculus repens	Menispermum	Rhus toxicidendron
	Ranunculus sceleratus	canadense	Salicylic acid
	Rhodium oxynitrate	Pephitis putorius	Scrophularia aquatica
	Rhododendron	Mercurialis perennis	Sodium aluminium
	chrysanthemum	Mimulus (*Mimullis*	chloride
	Rhus toxicodendron	*guttatus*)	Sodium auro-chloride
	Salicylic acid	Moschus	Sodium hypochlorite
	Scrophularia aquatica	Myrica gale	Sodium nitrate
	Sodium aluminium	Myrtus communis	Squill
	chloride	Ocimum basilicum	Stannum metal
	Sodium auro-chloride	Olive	Sulphur iodide
	Sodium hypochlorite	Oxalis acetosella	Tannic acid
	Sodium nitrate	Pangamic acid	Terebinthinae oleum
	Squill	Paullinia cupana	Topaz
	Stannum metal	Penthorum sedoides	Uric acid
	Staphisagria	Pollen (mixed)	Zinc hypophosphite
	Sulphur iodide	Polygonatum	Zinc isovalerate
	Tamus communis	multiflorum	
	Tannic acid	Polygonum aviculare	
	Terebinthinae oleum	Polypodium vulgare	
	Theridion	Primula vulgaris	
	Thuja occidentalis	Prunella vulgaris	
	Topaz	Ptellea trifoliata	
	Uric acid	Ratanhia	
	Zinc hypophosphite	Robinia pseudoacacia	
	Zinc isovalerate	Rubia tinctorum	
		Rumex acetosella	
		Sal marina	
		Sarcolactic acid	
		Sarracenia purpurea	
		Scleranthus	
		(*Scleranthus annuus*)	

(continued overleaf)

Table 11.1 (continued)			
Part 1: unit preparations diluted to at least one part in a thousand (3×)	**Part 2: unit preparations diluted to at least one part in a million (6×)**	**Part 3: unit preparations diluted to at least one part in ten (1×)**	**Part 4: unit preparations diluted to at least one part in ten (1×) for external use**
		Silica	
		Silphium laciniathum	
		Sodium benzoate	
		Spongia marina	
		Star of Bethlehem (*Ornithogalum umbellatum*)	
		Ulmus campestris	
		Vine	
		Walnut (*Juglerus regia*)	
		Water violet (*Hottonia palustris*)	
		Wild oat	
		Wild rose	

Summary

- Most homoeopathic medicines are on the GSL and may be sold from any retail shop which is closable to the public.
- Certain listed homoeopathic medicines may be sold if the seller is requested by a customer to use the seller's own judgement as to the treatment required. There are certain excluded categories.

Further reading

Human Medicines Regulations (2012) SI 2012 No. 1916, *Explanatory memorandum*: http://www.legislation.gov.uk/uksi/2012/1916/pdfs/uksiem_20121916_en.pdf (accessed 21 November 2012).

Royal Pharmaceutical Society (published annually). *Medicines, Ethics and Practice: The Professional Guide for Pharmacists*. London: Royal Pharmaceutical Society (includes practice guidance on many of the topics in this chapter; free to members).

Royal Pharmaceutical Society (2012). Support Bulletin No. 15 August 2012 Human Medicines Regulations 2012 *Pharm J*, 289: 200 (free to members or available on subscription).

Websites

Legislation (can be searched on year and SI number or title): http://www.legislation.gov.uk

Medicines and Healthcare products Regulatory Agency: http://www.mhra.gov.uk

Royal Pharmaceutical Society (member access only; lists legal classifications of medicines and further practice guidance): http://www.rpharms.com

12

Human medicines: herbal medicines

Susan Melvin

In March 2004, the European Commission issued a Directive on Traditional Herbal Medicinal Products (2004/24/EC), which amended Council Directive 2001/83/EC as far as herbal products were concerned. The Human Medicines Regulations 2012[1] enacts these requirements for traditional herbal medicines in HMRs Part 7 and Schedule 29.

If a herbal product is not registered as a medicinal product, it could be sold in the UK as a food or cosmetic, in which case it does not have to comply with medicines legislation. If it is a medicinal product it can either be registered as a traditional herbal medicine or be licensed with a marketing authorisation or product licence in the usual way (chapter 3). Traditional herbal medicines do not make claims about efficacy whereas a product with a product licence will have to do so.

A Herbal Medicines Advisory Committee has been established[2] in accordance with the 2001 Directive to give advice:

1 with respect to safety, quality and efficacy in relation to human use of herbal medicinal products, other than any product
   a   in respect of which a marketing authorisation, product licence or certificate of registration has been granted, or
   b   which is the subject of an application for such an authorisation, licence or certificate;
2 with respect to safety, quality and efficacy in relation to human use of any herbal medicinal product
   a   in respect of which a marketing authorisation, product licence of certificate of registration has been granted,

---

[1] Human Medicines Regulations SI 2012 No. 1916
[2] The Herbal Medicines Advisory Committee Order SI 2005 No. 2791 (now repealed)

b which is the subject of an application for such an authorisation, licence or certificate where the Health Minister or the licensing authority request such advice or provide the committee with information relating to that product, or

c in relation to the sale, supply, manufacture or assembly of medicinal products under section 12 of the Act, which provides exemptions from the requirements to have a product, manufacturing or wholesale dealer's licences for herbal remedies which are sold under consultation, and for remedies which are not industrially produced and are sold without any written recommendations for their use.

Definitions

The Human Medicines Regulations 2012 (Reg.8) has the following definitions.

Herbal medicinal product means a medicinal product whose only active ingredients are herbal substances or herbal preparations (or both).

Herbal preparation means a preparation obtained by subjecting herbal substances to processes such as extraction, distillation, expression, fractionation, purification, concentration or fermentation, and includes a comminuted or powdered herbal substance, a tincture, an extract, an essential oil, an expressed juice or a processed exudate.

Herbal substance means a plant or part of a plant, alga, fungus or lichen, or an unprocessed exudate of a plant, defined by the plant part used and the botanical name of the plant, either fresh or dried, but otherwise unprocessed.

Registration of traditional herbal medicines

Traditional herbal medicinal product means a herbal medicinal product to which HMRs Reg.125 applies. The conditions laid down are that a registration procedure is established for the product (chapter 3) which fulfils the following criteria. The product must meet the following conditions:

A if by virtue of its composition and indications the product is appropriate for use without the need for a medical practitioner to
  a diagnose the condition to be treated by the product,
  b prescribe the product, or
  c monitor the product's use;
B if the product is intended to be administered at a particular strength and in accordance with a particular posology;
C if the product is intended to be administered externally, orally or by inhalation;
D if the product

a has been in medicinal use for a continuous period of at least 30 years, and

b has been in medicinal use in the EU for a continuous period of at least 15 years,

c it is immaterial for the purposes of condition D whether or not during a period mentioned in that condition
  i the sale or supply of the product has been based on a specific authorisation, or
  ii the number or quantity of the ingredients (or any of them) has been reduced;

E if there is sufficient information about the use of the product as mentioned in condition D (referred to in this Part as its 'traditional use'), so that (in particular)
  a it has been established that the traditional use of the product is not harmful, and
  b the pharmacological effects or efficacy of the product are plausible on the basis of long-standing use and experience.

Subject to several exceptions, no traditional herbal medicinal product may be placed on the market or distributed by way of wholesale dealing unless a traditional herbal registration in respect of the product has been granted.

Traditional herbal registration means a registration granted by the licensing authority for a traditional herbal medicinal product under the Human Medicines Regulations 2012 (chapter 3).

Exemption from registration (herbal practitioners[3])

The Regulations regarding registration do not apply to a herbal medicinal product under the following conditions:[4]

1 where a herbal medicinal product is manufactured or assembled by a person ('A') (paragraph 6) if
  a the manufacture or assembly takes place on premises occupied by A and from which A can exclude the public,
  b the product is for administration to a person ('B') and A has been requested by or on behalf of B, and in B's presence, to use A's judgement as to the treatment required,
  c the product does not contain a substance specified in Part 1 of Schedule 20,

---

[3]It is expected that proposals to register herbal practitioners will be published in late 2012/early 2013
[4]HMRs Regs.3(6) and 3(9)

d the product does not contain a substance listed in Part 2 of that Schedule, unless the product is sold or supplied

   i in or from containers or packages labelled to show a dose not exceeding the maximum dose or maximum daily dose specified in column 2 of that Part, or

   ii in the case of a product for external use only, with a percentage of the substance in the product that does not exceed the percentage specified in column 3 of that Part; and

e the condition in paragraph (9) is met.

2 paragraph 9 condition is that the medicinal product is not manufactured or, as the case may be, assembled

   a on a large scale, or

   b by an industrial process.

If the product is manufactured under Reg.3(6) then there are no labelling requirements although good practice would be to label them.

Labelling for traditional herbal medicinal products

HMRs Reg.265(1) and Schedule 29 set out additional requirements for the labels of traditional herbal medicines:

1 a statement to the effect that the product is a traditional herbal medicine, for the use of specific purposes by reason of long-standing use; and

2 a statement that the user should consult a doctor or other healthcare practitioner if symptoms persist during use of the medicinal product, or if adverse effects not mentioned on the package or package leaflet occur.

Where the traditional herbal medicine is not a GSL medicine it must be labelled to show the capital letter 'P' within a rectangle within which there is no other matter of any kind.

Exemptions from full labelling in certain circumstances

HMRs Reg.265(2) goes on to specify that no information need appear on:

1 any package in the form of a transparent wrapping or cover provided the container is labelled and clearly visible; or

2 any package in the form of wrapping paper, paper bag or similar covering provided the enclosed container is labelled accordingly;

3 any container which is for export;

4 any container which is an ampoule or other container of not more than 10 mL normal capacity which is enclosed in a package which is labelled accordingly; or

5 for packages in themselves in the form of a bubble or blister, or a sheet or strip of like packages, and required to be labelled 'P', the requirement shall be met if the letter is displayed at frequent intervals on the strip or sheet.

Herbal remedy

Under section 132(1) of the Medicines Act 1968, a *herbal remedy* is a medicinal product consisting of a substance produced by subjecting a plant or plants to drying, crushing or any other process, or of a mixture whose sole ingredients are two or more substances so produced, or of a mixture whose sole ingredients are one or more substances so produced and water or some other inert substance.

Exemptions from controls on retail sale

There is an exemption for herbal remedies in Regulation 241 of the HMRs from the restrictions on retail sale and supply of medicinal products in HMR Regs.220 and 221 (chapters 6 and 7). The exemption applies to anything done at premises of which the person carrying on the business in question is the occupier and which s/he is able to close so as to exclude the public (HMRs Reg.241).

The effect of this is that any shopkeeper can sell:

a any herbal remedy on the GSL; or
b any herbal remedy which is exempted by virtue of being listed in Schedule 20 Part 1 or under the circumstances given in Part 2.

Schedule 20 conditions on retail sale or supply

Schedule 20 to the HMRs is in two parts, reflecting the different degrees of control over the retail sale or supply of the substances in each part (table 12.1). Part 1 sets out the substances that may only be sold by retail at registered pharmacies and by or under the supervision of a pharmacist; Part 2 sets out the substances that may only be sold by retail from registered pharmacies and by or under the supervision of a pharmacist except when manufactured by herbal practitioners under HMRs Reg.3(6) (see above).

Banned herbal remedies

The following banning orders were made under section 62 of the Medicines Act 1968 or the European Communities Act 1972 and have not been consolidated into the HMRs.

Aristolochia

The various forms of *Aristolochia* were made POMs on 13 January 1997[5] (chapter 8). Since then the sale, supply and importation of medicinal products consisting or containing a plant belonging to the species of the genus

[5] Prescription Only Medicines (Human Use) Order 1997

Table 12.1 Restrictions in respect of certain herbal remedies (Sch. 20 of the Human Medicines Regulations 2012[a])

PART 1

Botanical source	Common name		
Apocynum cannabinum	Canadian hemp		
Areca catechu	Areca		
Artemisia cina	Santonica		
Brayera anthelmintica	Kousso		
Catha edulis	Catha		
Chenopodium ambrosioides var anthelminticum	Chenopodium		
Crotalaria berberoana	Crotalaria fulva		
Crotalaria spectabilis	Crotalaria spect.		
Cucurbita maxima	Cucurbita		
Delphinium staphisagria	Stavesacre seeds		
Dryopteris filix-mas	Male fern		
Duboisia leichardtii, Duboisia myoporoides	Duboisia		
Ecballium elaterium	Elaterium		
Embelia ribes, Embelia robusta	Embelia		
Erysimum canescens	Erysimum		
Holarrhena antidysenterica	Holarrhena		
Juniperus sabina	Savin		
Mallotus philippinensis	Kamala		
Pausinystalia yohimbe	Yohimbe bark		
Punica granatum	Pomegranate bark		

(continued overleaf)

Table 12.1 *(continued)*

PART 1

Botanical source	Common name		
Rhus radicans	Poison ivy		
Scopolia carniolica			
Scopolia japonica	Scopolia		
Strophanthus courmonti, Strophanthus emini, Strophanthus gratus, Strophanthus hispidus, Strophanthus kombe, Strophanthus nicholsoni, Strophanthus sarmentosus	Strophanthus		
Ulmus fulva, Ulmus rubra	Slippery elm bark (whole or unpowdered)		
Viscum album	Misletoe berry		

PART 2

Column 1		Column 2	Column 3
Substance			
Botanical source	**Common name**	**Maximum dose (MD) and maximum daily dose (MDD)**	**Percentage**
Aconitum balfourni, Aconitum chasmanthum, Aconitum deinorrhizum, Aconitum lycoctonum, Aconitum napellus, Aconitum spicatum, Aconitum stoerkianum, Aconitum uncinatum var *japonicum*	Aconite		1.3%
Adonis vernalis	Adonis vernalis	100 mg (MD), 300mg (MDD)	
Aspidosperma quebrachoblanco	Quebracho	50 mg (MD), 150 mg (MDD)	
Atropa acuminata, Atropa belladonna	Belladonna herb, Belladonna root	In the form of belladonna herb: 50 mg (MD), 150 mg (MDD); in the form of belladonna root: 30 mg (MD), 90 mg (MDD)	

(continued overleaf)

Table 12.1 *(continued)*

PART 2

Column 1		Column 2	Column 3
Substance			
Botanical source	**Common name**	**Maximum dose (MD) and maximum daily dose (MDD)**	**Percentage**
Chelidonium majus	Celandine	2 g (MD), 6 g (MDD)	
Cinchona calisaya, Cinchona ledgerana, Cinchona micrantha, Cinchona officinalis, Cinchona succirubra	Cinchona bark	250 mg (MD), 750 mg (MDD)	
Colchicum autumnale	Colchicum corm	100 mg (MD), 300 mg (MDD)	
Conium maculatum	Conium fruits, conium leaf		7.0%
Convallaria majalis	Convallaria	150 mg (MD), 450 mg (MDD)	
Datura innoxia, Datura stramonium	Stramonium	50 mg (MD), 150 mg (MDD)	
Ephedra distachya, Ephedra equisetina, Ephedra gerardiana, Ephedra intermedia, Ephedra sinica	Ephedra	600 mg (MD), 1800 mg (MDD)	
Gelsemium sempervirens	Gelsemium	25 mg (MD), 75 mg (MDD)	
Hyoscyamus albus, Hyoscyamus muticus, Hyoscyamus niger	Hyoscyamus	100mg (MD), 300 mg (MDD)	
Lobelia inflata	Lobelia	200 mg (MD), 600 mg (MDD)	
Pilocarpus jaborandi, Pilocarpus microphyllus	Jaborandi		5.0%
Rhus toxicodendron	Poison oak		10.0%
Senecio jacobaea	Ragwort		10.0%

[a]This schedule has no associated Explanatory Memorandum.

Aristolochia or belonging to any of the species *Akebia quinata, Akebia trifoliata, Clematis armandi, Clematis montana, Cocculus laurifolius, Cocculus orbiculatus, Cocculus trilobus* and *Stephania tetrandra*, or consisting of or containing an extract from such a plant, are prohibited.

The ban was extended in 2001.[6] The prohibition relating to *Aristolochia* does not apply to the importation from an EEA country if the product originates in a EEA country or originates from outside the EEA but is in free circulation in EU Member States and is being, or is to be, exported to a third country or to an EEA country other than the UK[7] or possesses a traditional herbal registration.[8]

Mu Tong and Fangji

The sale, supply and importation of medicinal products is prohibited where, at the time of the sale, supply or importation, the label on the container or package, or any document accompanying the product indicates in any language that the product consists of or contains Mu Tong or Fangji or that the product consists of or contains *Akebia quinata, Akebia trifoliata, Clematis armandi, Clematis montana, Cocculus laurifolius, Cocculus orbiculatus, Cocculus trilobus* and *Stephania tetrandra*, or an extract from such a plant.

The prohibition relating to Mu Tong and Fangii does not apply to the importation from an EEA country if the product originates in a EEA country or originates from outside the EEA but is in free circulation in EU Member States and is being, or is to be, exported to a third country or to an EEA country other than the UK or possesses a traditional herbal registration (as above).

Kava-kava

The sale, supply and importation of any medicinal product for human use which consists or contains a plant or part of a plant belonging to the species *Piper methysticum* (known as kava-kava) or an extract from such a plant is prohibited.

The prohibition relating to *Piper methysticum* does not apply to the importation from an EEA country if the product originates in a EEA country or originates from outside the EEA but is in free circulation in EU Member States and is being, or is to be, exported to a third country or to an EEA country other than the UK or possesses a traditional herbal registration (as above).

[6] The Medicines (Aristolochia and Mu Tong etc.) (Prohibition) Order SI 2001 No. 1841
[7] The Medicines for Human Use (Prohibition) (Senecio and Miscellaneous Amendments) Order SI 2008 No. 548
[8] The Medicines (Traditional Herbal Medicinal Products for Human Use) Regulations SI 2005 No. 2750

Senecio

This sale, supply and importation of any medicinal product for human use which consists or contains a plant belonging to the species *Senecio* or an extract from such a plant is prohibited.

The prohibition relating to *Senecio* does not apply where the product is:

a for external use only and not a teething preparation, throat spray or pastilles, throat lozenge or tablet, nasal spray, inhalation or drops;

b sold or supplied to public analyst, a sampling officer, an enforcement officer or a food safety officer;

c imported from an EEA country if the product originates in a EEA country or originates from outside the EEA but is in free circulation in EU Member States and is being, or is to be, exported to a third country or to an EEA country other than the UK; or

d the subject of a product licence, a marketing authorisation, a certificate of registration as a homoeopathic substance or a traditional herbal registration (SI 2008 No. 548).

Summary

- There is a Herbal Medicines Advisory Committee established to deal with the safety and quality of herbal products other than products which possess a marketing authorisation, product licence or certificate of registration.
- Ordinary shopkeepers can sell herbal remedies on the GSL and herbal remedies which are merely dried, crushed or comminuted without any written recommendation, but this excludes those in Schedule 20 of the HMRs.
- Herbal practitioners can sell herbal remedies of the kind described above which shopkeepers can sell and also those remedies containing substances in and subject to the requirements of Part 2 of the Schedule 20 of the HMRs.
- Herbal remedies containing substances in Part 1 or Part 2 of the Schedule 20 to the HMRs may be sold from pharmacies.
- There is a simple registration procedure established for traditional herbal medicinal products.
- Certain herbals have been banned, e.g. *Aristolochia*, Mu Tong, Fangji, *Piper methysticum* (kava-kava) and *Senecio*.

Further reading

Barnes J *et al.* (2007). *Herbal Medicines* 3rd edn. London: Pharmaceutical Press.

Website

National Institute of Medical Herbalists: http://www.nimh.org.uk

13

Human medicines: prohibitions for protection of the purchaser

Susan Melvin

Prohibition orders

The Medicines Act 1968 provides power (s.62) for the appropriate ministers to make a prohibition, either total or limited in some way, on the sale, supply or importation of specified classes of medicinal product or of particular medicinal products if it appears to them necessary to do so in the interest of safety. Before making such an Order, the ministers are required to consult the appropriate committee (or the Commission on Human Medicines) and to consider representations made by other organisations which have been consulted. These requirements may be waived if, in the opinion of the ministers, it is essential to make the Order with immediate effect to avoid serious danger to health. An Order made without consultation is effective for 3 months only but may be renewed.

Any person who, otherwise than for performing or exercising a statutory duty or power, is in possession of such a medicinal product, knowing or having reasonable cause to suspect that it was sold, supplied or imported in contravention of the Order, is guilty of an offence (s.67) (see also chapter 2).

Section 62 Orders

Bal Jivan Chamcho

The sale, supply or importation of Bal Jivan Chamcho is prohibited. This is a baby tonic in the form of a dark brown aromatic solid substance affixed to a spoon-shaped metal appliance. The prohibition[1] does not apply to importation from a Member State of the EU or if it originated in a state

[1] The Medicines (Bal Jivan Chamcho Prohibition) (No. 2) Order SI 1977 No. 670

within the EEA. Neither does the prohibition apply to the sale or supply to a public analyst, a sampling officer or a person duly authorised by an enforcement authority under the Act.

Herbal products

Four other section 62 banning orders have been made in relation to herbal medicines, namely for *Aristolochia*, Mu Tong or Fangji,[2] Kava-kava[3] and Senecio[4] (see also chapter 12).

Chloroform

The sale or supply of medicinal products for human use which consist of or contain chloroform is prohibited[5] subject to the following exceptions. A sale or supply made:

1   by a doctor or dentist to a patient of his/hers, where the medicinal product has been specially prepared by that doctor or dentist for administration to that particular patient;
2   by a doctor or dentist who has specially prepared the medicinal product at the request of another doctor or dentist for administration to a particular patient of that other doctor or dentist;
3   from a pharmacy or hospital where the medicinal product has been specially prepared in accordance with a prescription given by a doctor or dentist for a particular patient;
4   to a hospital, a doctor or a dentist for use as an anaesthetic;
5   to a person who buys it for the purpose of reselling it to a hospital, a doctor or a dentist for use as an anaesthetic;
6   where the medicinal product contains chloroform in a proportion of not more than 0.5 per cent (w/w) or (v/v);
7   where the medicinal product is solely for use in dental surgery;
8   where the medicinal product is solely for use by being applied to the external surface of the body which for the purpose of this Order does not include any part of the mouth, teeth or mucous membranes;
9   where the medicinal product is for export; or
10 where the medicinal product is sold for use as an ingredient in the preparation of a substance or article in a pharmacy, a hospital or by a doctor or dentist.

For the purposes of sale or supply (but not of importation) of medicines for human use, the exemption limits for chloroform given in the POM and

---

[2] The Medicines (Aristolochia and Mu Tong etc.) (Prohibition) Order SI 2001 No. 1841
[3] The Medicines for Human Use (Kava-kava) (Prohibition) Order SI 2002 No. 3170
[4] The Medicines for Human Use (Prohibition) (Senecio and Miscellaneous Amendments) Order SI 2008 No. 548
[5] The Medicines (Chloroform Prohibition) Order SI 1979 No. 382

GSL Orders are over-ridden by this Order. The practical effect is that only products falling within items 6 and 8 above may be sold by retail to the general public. But for the purposes of record keeping, the exemption levels in the POM Order still apply, so that records are required to be kept only of sales or supplies of products for internal use which contain more than 5 per cent of chloroform w/w or v/v as appropriate.

Section 104 and Section 105 Orders

Section 104 and section 105 Orders are covered in chapter 2 and appendices 1 and 2.

Adulteration of medicinal products

The Medicines Act (s.63) makes it an offence:

1 to add any substance to, or abstract any substance from, a medicinal product so as to affect injuriously the composition of the product, with intent that the product shall be sold or supplied in that state; or

2 to sell or supply, or offer or expose for sale or supply, or have in possession for the purpose of sale or supply, any medicinal product whose composition has been injuriously affected by the addition or abstraction of any substance (s.63).

Protection for purchasers of medicinal products

It is also an offence to sell (or supply on a practitioner's prescription) to the prejudice of the purchaser (or patient) any medicinal product which is not of the nature or quality demanded by the purchaser (or specified in the prescription) (s.64).

There is no offence if the medicinal product contains some extraneous matter, the presence of which is proved to be an inevitable consequence of the process of manufacture, nor is it an offence where:

1 a substance has been added to, or abstracted from, the medicinal product which did not injuriously affect the composition of the product and was not carried out fraudulently; and

2 the product was sold having attached to it, or to a container or package in which it was sold, a conspicuous notice of adequate size and legibly printed specifying the substance added or abstracted.

While this section of the Medicines Act remained unused for many years after the Act was passed, it has recently been used to prosecute pharmacists and other staff where an error has been made in dispensing a prescription (chapter 24). At the time of writing, this section was being reviewed by MHRA.

Summary

- The sale or supply of some medicinal products is either prohibited (e.g. Bal Jivan Chamcho) or prohibited subject to exceptions (e.g. chloroform).
- It is an offence to adulterate, by way of addition or abstraction, a medicinal product or to sell, supply or possess an adulterated product.
- It is an offence to sell or supply to the prejudice of the purchaser (or patient) any medicinal product which is not of the nature or quality demanded by the purchaser (or specified on a prescription).

Further reading

Human Medicines Regulations (2012) SI 2012 No. 1916, *Explanatory memorandum*: http://www.legislation.gov.uk/uksi/2012/1916/pdfs/uksiem_20121916_en.pdf (accessed 21 November 2012).

Royal Pharmaceutical Society (published annually). *Medicines, Ethics and Practice: The Professional Guide for Pharmacists*. London: Royal Pharmaceutical Society (includes practice guidance on many of the topics in this chapter; free to members).

Royal Pharmaceutical Society (2012). Support Bulletin No. 15 August 2012 Human Medicines Regulations 2012 *Pharm J*, 289: 200 (free to members or available on subscription).

Websites

EU legislation: http://eur-lex.europa.eu

Legislation (can be searched on year and SI number or title): http://www.legislation.gov.uk

Medicines and Healthcare products Regulatory Agency: http://www.mhra.gov.uk

Royal Pharmaceutical Society (member access only; lists legal classifications of medicines and further practice guidance): http://www.rpharms.com

14

Human medicines: labelling, packaging, leaflets and identification

Susan Melvin

Regulations and penalties

Provisions covering packaging and leaflets for medicinal products are largely found in Part 13 of the Human Medicines Regulations[1] (Regs.257–276) and Schedules 24 to 29, although there are still some residual sections of the Medicines Act 1968 that are relevant to this chapter.

Regulations apply to:

1 packaging requirements (HMRs Reg.257 and Sch. 24)
2 the labelling of packages (Sch. 24)
3 the display of distinctive marks on containers and packages (HMRs Reg.262)
4 leaflets (Sch. 27)
5 colour or shape (Medicines Act (s.88(1)); and
6 distinctive marks to be displayed on such products (Medicines Act s.88(1)).

For the same purposes and also for preserving the quality of the products, Regulations may prohibit the sale of medicinal products in containers which do not comply with specified requirements, in particular as to the strength, shape or pattern of the containers or of the materials of which they are made (Medicines Act s.87).

It is an offence (HMRs Reg.269) for any person in the course of a business carried on by him/her to supply, offer to supply or have in their possession to supply a product knowing or having reasonable cause to believe

[1] Human Medicines Regulations SI 2012 No. 1916 (HMRs)

1 that a package or package leaflet supplied does not comply with the marketing authorisation; or

2 that the product is not accompanied by a package leaflet when one is required.

Any person contravening the labelling regulations (see below) is liable on summary conviction to a fine of up to £5000 and, on conviction or indictment, to a fine or to imprisonment for a term not exceeding 2 years or to both (HMRs Reg.271).

Definitions

The terms defined here are those used in the HMRs in connection with labelling which are not explained elsewhere in the text (HMRs Reg.8 and Reg.213).

Common name in relation to a medicinal product, active substance or excipient means:

a its International Nonproprietary Name recommended by the World Health Organization; or

b if such a name does not exist, its usual common name (HMRs Reg.8).

The *quantity* can be expressed in terms of the dilution of the unit preparation for a *homoeopathic product* (i.e. a product prepared in accordance with the methods of homoeopathic medicine or similar system which is sold or supplied as a homoeopathic product and is so described by the person who sells or supplies it) (HMRs Reg.264 and Sch. 28).

Immediate packaging in relation to a medicinal product means the container or other form of packaging immediately in contact with the medicinal product (HMRs Reg.8).

A *container*, in relation to a medicinal product, means the bottle, jar, box, packet or other receptacle which contains or is to contain it, not being a capsule, cachet or other article in which the product is or is to be administered; and where any such receptacle is or is to be contained in another such receptacle, it includes the inner receptacle but not the outer (s.132 Medicines Act).

It should be noted that a capsule, cachet or other article in which a medicinal product is to be administered is not normally a container, but if the capsule etc. is not to be administered, then it is a container.

A *package*, in relation to any medicinal products, means any box, packet or other article in which one or more containers of the products are to be enclosed, and where any such box, package or other article is, or is to be itself, enclosed in one or more other boxes, packets or other articles, it includes each of the boxes, packets or other articles in question (HMRs Reg.8).

In effect, the inner receptacle which actually contains the medicinal products is a container; every outer receptacle is a package.

Labelling, in relation to a container or package of medicinal products, means affixing to or otherwise displaying on it a notice describing or otherwise relating to the contents (HMRs Reg.8).

External use means its use by application to the skin, teeth, mucosa of the mouth, throat, nose, ear, eye, vagina or anal canal in circumstances where local action only is necessary and systemic absorption is unlikely to occur, but it does not include its use by means of a throat spray, nasal spray, nasal inhalation or teething preparation or by means of throat pastilles, throat lozenges or nasal drops. (HMRs Reg.213).

Specified publication means the *European Pharmacopoeia*, BP (or other official compendia which may in the future be produced under the Medicines Act) and the list of British Approved Names (HMR Reg.321).

Labelling and packaging

The regulations apply at all stages of distribution, except where otherwise stated. Medicinal products which are Controlled Drugs must also be labelled in accordance with the Misuse of Drugs Regulations 1985 (see chapter 17).

General labelling provisions for medicinal products

All labelling of containers and packages must be:

1 legible, comprehensible and indelible (HMRs Reg.257(6)); and
2 either in the English language only or in English and in one or more other languages provided that the same particulars appear in all the languages used (HMRs Reg.266).

Where the holder of a marketing authorisation for a relevant medicinal product proposes to alter the labelling relating to it in any respect, s/he must notify the licensing authority and, unless the licensing authority has notified him/her that it does not approve the alterations, s/he may, after a period of 90 days from the date of notification by him/her, supply the product with the altered labelling (HMRs Reg.267).

Standard labelling particulars for medicinal products

The standard requirements for the labelling of containers and packages of relevant medicinal products are set out in Council Directive 2001/83/EC and HMRs Reg.257 and Schedule 24. There are modifications for small containers and blister packs (see below).

The standard requirements are as follows (Part 1):

1 the name of the medicinal product;
2 the strength and pharmaceutical form of the product;
3 where appropriate, whether the product is intended for babies, children or adults;

4 where the product contains up to three active substances, the common name of each active substance;

5 a statement of the active substances in the product, expressed qualitatively and quantitatively per dosage unit or according to the form of administration for a given volume or weight, using their common names;

6 the pharmaceutical form and the contents by weight, by volume or by number of doses of the product;

7 a list of

  a all excipients when the product is injectable or is a topical or eye preparation, or

  b in any other case, those excipients known to have a recognised action or effect and included in the guidance published pursuant to Article 65 of the 2001 Directive;

8 the method of administration of the product and if necessary the route of administration;

9 where appropriate, space for the prescribed dose to be indicated;

10 a warning that the product must be stored out of the reach and sight of children;

11 any special warning applicable to the product;

12 the product's expiry date (month and year), in clear terms;

13 any special storage precautions relating to the product;

14 any special precautions relating to the disposal of an unused product or part of a product, or waste derived from the product, and reference to any appropriate collection system in place;

15 the name and address of the holder of the marketing authorisation, Article 126a authorisation or traditional herbal registration relating to the product and, where applicable, the name of the holder's representative;

16 the number of the marketing authorisation, Article 126a authorisation or traditional herbal registration for placing the medicinal product on the market;

17 the manufacturer's batch number; and

18 in the case of a product that is not a POM, instructions for use.

The outer packaging may be labelled to show symbols, diagrams or pictures designed to clarify certain information mentioned in 1 to 18 above and other information compatible with the Summary of Product Characteristics which is useful to the patient (HMRs Reg.261).

The name of the medicinal product must also be expressed in Braille format on the outer packaging of the product. A holder of a marketing authorisation, Article 126a authorisation or traditional herbal registration must ensure the package leaflet is available on request in formats suitable for blind and partially-sighted persons (HMRs Reg.259).

In addition, EU Member States may require certain additional labelling, for example the price of the product, the reimbursement conditions and the classification, such as POM.

Summary of Product Characteristics means the information required to accompany any application for a marketing authorisation under Council Directive 2001/83.EC (HMRs Reg.8).

Blister packs for medicinal products

Where the container of a relevant medicinal product is a blister pack and is enclosed within a package which complies with the standard labelling (see above), the container must be labelled with (HMRs Reg.257 and Sch. 24 Part 2):

1 the name of the medicinal product;
2 the strength and pharmaceutical form of the product;
3 where appropriate, whether the product is intended for babies, children or adults;
4 where the product contains up to three active substances, the common name of each active substance;
5 the name of the holder of the marketing authorisation, Article 126a authorisation or traditional herbal registration relating to the product;
6 the product's expiry date (month and year); and
7 the manufacturer's batch number.

Small containers for medicinal products

Where the container of a medicinal product is *not* a blister pack but is too small to include all the standard particulars for medicinal products it must be labelled with (HMRs Reg.257 and Sch. 24 Part 3):

1 the name of the medicinal product;
2 the strength and pharmaceutical form of the product;
3 where appropriate, whether the product is intended for babies, children or adults;
4 where the product contains up to three active substances, the common name of each active substance;
5 the method of administration of the product and if necessary the route of administration;
6 the product's expiry date (month and year); and
7 the manufacturer's batch number.

Standard labelling requirements for containers and packages for radiopharmaceuticals (HMRs Reg.262)

Containers and packages for radiopharmaceuticals must be labelled with the standard particulars for relevant medicinal products together with the following additional particulars:

1 the carton and container must be labelled in accordance with regulations for the safe transport of radioactive materials laid down by the International Atomic Energy Agency and the labelling on the shielding and the vial must comply with the rest of the provisions of this legislation;
2 the label on the shielding must
   a include the information specified in Part 1 of Schedule 24,
   b explain in full the codings used on the vial,
   c indicate, where necessary, for a given time and date, the amount of radioactivity per dose or per vial, and
   d indicate the number of capsules or, for liquids, the number of millilitres per container;
3 the label on the vial must include
   a the name or code of the medicinal product, including the name or chemical symbol of the radionuclide,
   b the batch identification and expiry date of the product,
   c the international symbol for radioactivity,
   d the name and address of the manufacturer, and
   e the amount of radioactivity; as mentioned in paragraph 2(c).

Medicines on prescription

The packaging of medicines dispensed on prescription must be labelled to show the following particulars (HMRs Reg.258 and Sch. 25 Part 1):

1 where the product is to be administered to a particular individual, the name of that individual;
2 the name and address of the person who sells or supplies the product;
3 the date on which the product is sold or supplied;
4 unless paragraph 5, applies, such of the following particulars as the appropriate practitioner who prescribed the product may specify
   a the name of the product or its common name,
   b directions for use of the product, and
   c precautions relating to the use of the product;
5 this paragraph applies if the pharmacist, in the exercise of professional skill and judgement, is of the opinion that the inclusion of one or more of the particulars mentioned in paragraph 4 is inappropriate;

6 where paragraph 5 applies, the pharmacist may include such particulars, of the same kind as those mentioned in paragraph 4, as the pharmacist thinks appropriate.

Paragraphs 5 and 6 above are sometimes described as 'Medicines Optimisation'.

A container need not be labelled if it is enclosed in a package which is labelled with the required particulars.

Medicines Optimisation

Schedule 25 of the HMRs extends previous provisions to allow pharmacists to use their discretion when labelling dispensed medicines. A pharmacist may, if s/he is of the opinion that the inclusion of any of the particulars above is inappropriate, include other particulars of the same kind as the pharmacist thinks appropriate (HMRs Sch. 25 Part 1(5) and (6)).

Packaging for transport, delivery and storage

The packaging requirements required for transport, delivery and storage must appear on the outer package, that is to say, the package enclosing the package immediately enclosing the container (HMRs Reg.258 and Sch. 25 Part 2). The required particulars are:

1 any special handling and storage particulars;
2 the expiry date of the product; and
3 the manufacturer's batch number.

Packaging of Pharmacy and Prescription Only Medicinal products

All Pharmacy and POM medicinal products when sold or supplied by retail, held for such sale or distributed by wholesale must bear the following the capital letter 'P' or 'POM' within a rectangle containing no other matter on the packaging (HMRs Reg.258 and Sch. 25 Part 3).

Packaging requirements for medicines containing paracetamol (HMRs Sch. 25 Part 4)

The following must appear on the package if the product contains paracetamol:

1 except where the name of the product includes the word '*paracetamol*' and appears on the container or package, the words '*Contains paracetamol*';

2 the words 'Do not take more medicine than the label tells you to. If you do not get better, talk to your doctor' (these words must appear adjacent to either the directions for use or the recommended dosage);

3 unless it is wholly or mainly intended for children who are 12 years old or younger (i.e. it is a product for children 12 and over), the words 'Do not take anything else containing paracetamol while taking this medicine', and

  a if a package leaflet accompanying the product includes the words in quotation marks in paragraph 16 of Schedule 27 (package leaflets), the words 'Talk to a doctor at once if you take too much of this medicine, even if you feel well', or

  b if no package leaflet accompanies the product or the package leaflet does not include those words, the words 'Talk to a doctor at once if you take too much of this medicine, even if you feel well. This is because too much paracetamol can cause delayed, serious liver damage';

4 and is wholly or mainly intended for children who are 12 years old or younger, the words 'Do not give anything else containing paracetamol while giving this medicine', and

  a if a package leaflet accompanying the product includes the words in quotation marks in paragraph 17 of Schedule 27 (package leaflets), the words 'Talk to a doctor at once if your child takes too much of this medicine, even if they seem well'; or

  b if no package leaflet accompanies the product or the package leaflet does not include those words, the words 'Talk to a doctor at once if your child takes too much of this medicine, even if they seem well. This is because too much paracetamol can cause delayed, serious liver damage'.

Those phrases must be in a prominent position.

Medicines manufactured by pharmacies under section 10 of the Medicines Act 1968

Pharmacies are permitted to manufacture medicines without the need for marketing authorisations or licences subject to conditions under section 10 of the Medicines Act 1968 (chapter 3). In these circumstances the medicines must bear packaging details as set out below (HMRs Sch. 26 Part 2):

1 where the product is to be administered to a particular individual, the name of that individual;

2 the name and address of the person who sells or supplies the product;

3 the date on which the product is sold or supplied;

4 where the product is prescribed by an appropriate practitioner, such of the following particulars as the appropriate practitioner who prescribed the product may specify, unless paragraph 5 applies
   a the name of the product or its common name,
   b directions for use of the product, and
   c precautions relating to the use of the product;
5 this paragraph applies if a pharmacist, in the exercise of professional skill and judgement, is of the opinion that the inclusion of one or more of the particulars specified in paragraph 4 by the appropriate practitioner who prescribed the product is inappropriate;
6 where paragraph 5 applies, the pharmacist may include such particulars, of the same kind as those mentioned in paragraph 4, as the pharmacist thinks appropriate; and
7 where the product is not prescribed by an appropriate practitioner, directions for use of the product, but these may be omitted in circumstances where section 10(3) of the Medicines Act1968 applies.

Labelling of medicinal products for clinical trials

Where a medicinal product is for administration in a clinical trial (chapter 3), the labelling on the container and package must sufficiently identify the clinical trial, the product (if more than one product is supplied in the course of the trial) and such designation as will identify the person to whom the product is to be administered. It must also show the name and address of the premises where the clinical trial is to be carried out (or the name and address of the product licence holder) and particulars required to be stated on the labels by the product licence or clinical trial certificate.

Standard labelling requirements for containers and packages of homoeopathic medicinal products

All containers and packages for homoeopathic products must be labelled clearly and make reference to their homoeopathic nature by clear use of the words *homoeopathic medicinal product*. In addition, they must carry the following particulars and no others (HMRs Reg.264 and Sch. 28):

1 the scientific name of the stock or stocks followed by the degree of dilution, making use of the symbols of the pharmacopoeia used in relation to the homoeopathic manufacturing procedure described therein for that stock or stocks;
2 the name and address of the holder of the certificate of registration and, where different, the name and address of the manufacturer;
3 the method of administration and, if necessary, route;
4 the expiry date of the product in clear terms, stating the month and year;

5 the pharmaceutical form;
6 the contents of the sales representation;
7 any special storage precautions;
8 any special warning necessary for the product concerned;
9 the manufacturer's batch number;
10 the registration number allocated by the licensing authority;
11 the words *Homoeopathic medicinal product without approved therapeutic indications*; and
12 a warning advising the user to consult a doctor if the symptoms persist during the use of the product.

Package leaflets

General requirements

All leaflets included in the package or container of any medicinal product must comply with HMRs Reg.260 and Schedule 27.

All particulars must be drawn up in accordance:

1 with the Summary of Product Characteristics, and
2 contain all the information specified and in the Order specified in Schedule 27.

The particulars must be legible, clear and easy to use, and the applicant for, or holder of, a marketing authorisation Article 126a authorisation or traditional herbal registration relating to the product must ensure that target patient groups are consulted in order to achieve this.

The particulars which must be included are as follows:

1 the name of the medicinal product;
2 the strength and pharmaceutical form of the product;
3 where appropriate, whether the product is intended for babies, children or adults;
4 where the product contains up to three active substances, the common name of each active substance;
5 the pharmaco-therapeutic group or type of activity of the product, in terms easily comprehensible for the patient;
6 the product's therapeutic indications;
7 a list of,
   a contra-indications,
   b appropriate precautions for use,
   c interactions with other medicinal products which may affect the action of the product,

   d interactions with other substances, including alcohol, tobacco and foodstuffs, which may affect the action of the product, and

   e special warnings, if any, relating to the product;

8 the list mentioned in paragraph 7 must

   a take into account the special requirements of particular categories of users (including, in particular, children, pregnant or breastfeeding women, the elderly and persons with specific pathological conditions),

   b mention, if appropriate, possible effects on the ability to drive vehicles or to operate machinery, and

   c list any excipients,

      i if knowledge of the excipients is important for the safe and effective use of the product, and

      ii the excipients are included in the guidance published pursuant to Article 65 of the 2001 Directive;

9 instructions for proper use of the product including, in particular,

   a the dosage,

   b the method and, if necessary, route of administration,

   c the frequency of administration (including, if necessary, specifying times at which the product may or must be administered),

   d the duration of treatment if this is to be limited,

   e symptoms of an overdose and the action, if any, to be taken in case of an overdose,

   f what to do if one or more doses have not been taken,

   g an indication, if necessary, of the risk of withdrawal effects, and

   h a specific recommendation to consult a doctor or pharmacist, as appropriate, for further explanation of the use of the product;

10 a description of the adverse reactions which may occur in normal use of the medicinal product and, if necessary, the action to be taken in such a case;

11 a reference to the expiry date printed on the packaging of the product with

   a a warning against using the product after that date,

   b if appropriate, details of special storage precautions to be taken,

   c if necessary, a warning concerning visible signs of deterioration,

   d the full qualitative composition (in active substances and excipients), and the quantitative composition in active substances, using common names, of each presentation of the medicinal product,

   e for each presentation of the product, the pharmaceutical form and content in weight, volume or units of dosage,

f the name and address of the holder of the marketing authorisation, Article 126a authorisation or traditional herbal registration relating to the product and, if applicable, the name of the holder's appointed representative, and

g the name and address of the manufacturer of the product;

12 where the product is authorised under different names in different EU Member States in accordance with Articles 28 to 39 of the 2001 Directive, a list of the names authorised in each Member State;

13 For medicinal products included in the list referred to in Article 23 of Regulation (EC) No. 726/2004, the statement: '*This medicinal product is subject to additional safety monitoring*';

14 the statement: '*Also you can help to make sure that medicines remain as safe as possible by reporting any unwanted side effects via the internet at www.mhra.gov.uk/yellowcard. Alternatively you can call Freephone 0808 100 3352 (available from 10 a.m. to 2 p.m. Mondays to Fridays) or fill in a paper form available from your local pharmacy*'; and

15 the date on which the package leaflet was last revised.

The licensing authority may decide that certain therapeutic indications need not be included in a leaflet where the dissemination of such information might have serious disadvantages for the patient.

The outer packaging and the package leaflet of a medicinal product may include (HMRs Reg.261):

1a symbols, diagrams or pictures designed to clarify information mentioned in Part 1 of Schedule 24 or in Schedule 27, and

b other information, compatible with the Summary of the Product Characteristics, which is useful to the patient; and

2 symbols, diagrams, pictures or additional information included in accordance with this regulation must not include any element of a promotional nature.

Leaflets for medicines containing paracetamol (HMRs Sch. 27 Part 2)

If a medicinal product contains paracetamol, unless the product is wholly or mainly intended for children 12 years old or younger, the words '*Talk to a doctor at once if you take too much of this medicine even if you feel well. This is because too much paracetamol can cause delayed, serious liver damage*' must be used.

If a medicinal product contains paracetamol and is wholly or mainly intended for children 12 years old or younger, the words '*Talk to a doctor at once if your child takes too much of this medicine even if they seem well. This is because too much paracetamol can cause delayed, serious liver damage*' must be used.

Leaflets for radiopharmaceuticals and radiopharmaceutical-associated products

A leaflet enclosed with a radiopharmaceutical or radiopharmaceutical-associated product must include, in addition to the general requirements (see above) the following (HMRs Reg.263):

1 details of any precautions to be taken by the user and the patient during the preparation and administration of the product; and
2 details of any special precautions to be taken in respect of the disposal of the container and its unused contents.

Leaflets for homoeopathic medicinal products

Any leaflet enclosed in or supplied with the packaging of a homoeopathic product which is placed on the market in accordance with a certificate of registration must bear the words '*homoeopathic medicinal product*'. In addition the leaflet must carry the following particulars and no others (HMRs Sch. 13 Reg.264 and Sch. 28):

1 the scientific name of the stock or stocks followed by the degree of dilution, making use of the symbols of the pharmacopoeia used in relation to the homoeopathic manufacturing procedure described therein for that stock or stocks;
2 the name and address of the holder of the certificate of registration and, where different, the name and address of the manufacturer;
3 the method of administration and, if necessary, route;
4 the expiry date of the product in clear terms, stating the month and year;
5 the pharmaceutical form;
6 the contents of the sales representation;
7 any special storage precautions;
8 any special warning necessary for the product concerned;
9 the manufacturer's batch number;
10 the registration number allocated by the licensing authority preceded by the capital letters 'HR';
11 the words '*Homoeopathic medicinal product without approved therapeutic indications*'; and
12 a warning advising the user to consult a doctor if the symptoms persist during the use of the product.

Requirements relating to child safety (HMRs Regs.272–276)

Regulated medicinal products means (HMRs Reg.272) medicinal products containing, aspirin, paracetamol or more than 24 mg of elemental iron, which are in the form of tablets, capsules, pills, lozenges, pastilles, suppositories or oral liquids, except for:

1 effervescent tablets containing not more than 25 per cent of aspirin or paracetamol by weight;
2 medicinal products in sachets or other sealed containers which hold only one unit of dose;
3 medicinal products that are not intended for retail sale by a retail pharmacy or supplied in pursuance of a prescription; and
4 for export.

It is an offence to sell or supply regulated medicinal products otherwise than in containers that are opaque or dark-tinted, and child-resistant (HMRs Reg.273). Non-reclosable containers are child resistant if they have been evaluated in accordance with, and comply with:

1 British Standard EN 14375:2003 published by the British Standard Institution on 18 April 2005; or
2 any equivalent or higher technical specification for non-reclosable child-resistant packaging recognised for use in the EEA.

Reclosable containers are child resistant if they have been evaluated in accordance with and comply with:

1 British Standard EN ISO 8317:2004 published by the British Standard Institution on 11 May 2005; or
2 any equivalent or higher technical specification for reclosable child-resistant packaging recognised for use in the EEA.

The Regulations do not apply to products where (HMRs Reg.274) the sale or supply is carried out:

a by or under the supervision of a pharmacist;
b on premises which are a registered pharmacy; and
c either
  i in accordance with a prescription given by an appropriate practitioner where it is not reasonably practicable to provide the regulated medicinal products in containers that are both opaque or dark-tinted and child resistant, or
  ii at the request of a person who is aged 16 or over and specifically requests that the regulated medicinal products not be contained in a child-resistant container.

They also do not apply to the sale or supply of regulated medicinal products:

a by a doctor or dentist to a patient, or the patient's carer, for the patient's use;

b by a doctor or dentist to a person who is an appropriate practitioner, at the request of that person, for administration to a patient of that person; or

c in the course of the business of a hospital or health centre, where the sale or supply is for the purposes of administration, whether in the hospital or health centre or elsewhere, in accordance with the directions of an appropriate practitioner.

The sale or supply of a medicinal product containing aspirin or paracetamol of any colour other than white is prohibited if it is a product for children aged 12 or under, and, in the case of paracetamol, it is in a solid form (including tablets, capsules, pills, lozenges, pastilles or suppositories) (HMRs Reg.275).

Use of fluted bottles

The HMRs have repealed the requirement for certain liquid medicinal products for external use to be sold or supplied in fluted bottles.

Summary

- There are detailed labelling requirements for relevant medicinal products for human use, which includes all medicines which have been granted, or had renewed, marketing authorisations (product licences) since January 1994. These do not include those medicines dispensed against a prescription or official formula, or for research or trials.
- There are additional warning labels for paracetamol.
- There are modified labelling provisions for medicinal products which are in small containers, blister packs, homoeopathic products and for radio-pharmaceuticals.
- Abbreviated labelling provisions exist for medicines dispensed against a prescription given by a practitioner.
- There are separate labelling requirements for ingredients, contract manufacture and assembly, chemist's nostrums, import and export, surgical materials and clinical trials.
- Every container or package of medicinal products must contain a patient leaflet. Detailed requirements exist for the contents of these leaflets.
- Special leaflets provisions exist for homoeopathic medicinal products.
- Special requirements apply to the sale of medicinal products in unit-dose form which contain aspirin or paracetamol. These products must be packed in child-resistant containers, i.e. opaque reclosable resistant containers or bubble/blister packs.

Further reading

Human Medicines Regulations (2012) SI 2012 No. 1916, *Explanatory memorandum*: http://www.legislation.gov.uk/uksi/2012/1916/pdfs/uksiem_20121916_en.pdf (accessed 21 November 2012).

Royal Pharmaceutical Society (published annually). *Medicines, Ethics and Practice: The Professional Guide for Pharmacists*. London: Royal Pharmaceutical Society (includes practice guidance on many of the topics in this chapter; free to members).

Websites

Legislation (can be searched on year and SI number or title): http://www.legislation.gov.uk

Medicines and Healthcare products Regulatory Agency: http://www.mhra.gov.uk

Royal Pharmaceutical Society (member access only; lists legal classifications of medicines and further practice guidance): http://www.rpharms.com

15

Human medicines: pharmacopoeias and compendia

Susan Melvin

Part 15 of the HMRs[1] covers pharmacopoeias and compendia which contain the standards for 'official' (British or European) medicinal products and pharmaceutical substances.

British Pharmacopoeia and compendia

Until 1970, the BP was compiled by the GMC under the Medical Act 1956 when the copyright was assigned to Her Majesty (Medicines Act, s.98). A committee now established under Regulation 11 of the HMRs, known as the BPC, prepares new editions[2] of the BP and any amendments to such editions.

The BPC must prepare editions of the BP containing such relevant information relating to substances, combinations of substances and articles as detailed below (HMRs Reg.317(1 and 2)):

1 substances, combinations of substances and articles (whether medicinal products or not) which are or may be used in the practice of medicine or surgery (other than veterinary medicine or veterinary surgery), dentistry and midwifery; and

2 substances, combinations of substances and articles used in the manufacture of substances and articles listed under 1 above.

The BPC may also publish a compendium other than the BP if it thinks this appropriate (HMRs Reg.317(3)). Information relating to substances and articles used in veterinary medicine and surgery (whether veterinary drugs or not) is published in a separate compendium, the *British Pharmacopoeia (Veterinary)*.

[1] Human Medicines Regulations SI 2012 No. 1916
[2] The next BP at the time of writing comes into force from the 1 January 2013

Lists of names

The BPC is authorised to prepare lists of suitable names for substances and articles for placing at the head of monographs in the BP or in the compendia (HMRs Reg.318). The publication of any such lists supersedes any previously published list.

Publication

If the Commission on Human Medicines so recommends, the BP, the compendia and the lists of names must be published and made available for sale to the public by the appropriate ministers. Every copy must specify the date from which it is to take effect, and notice must be given in the *London*, *Edinburgh* and *Belfast Gazettes* not less than 21 days before that date (HMRs Reg.320(1 and 2)). Apart from the BP and the compendia, other publications containing relevant information may be prepared at the discretion of the Commission on Human Medicines (HMRs Reg.319).

European Pharmacopoeia

The *European Pharmacopoeia* is published under the direction of the Council of Europe (Partial Agreement) in accordance with the Convention on the Elaboration of a European Pharmacopoeia held in 1964. In 1973, the standards in the *European Pharmacopoeia*, together with any amendments or alterations published in the *Gazette*, took precedence over the standards in other publications. The Health Ministers may publish amendments to the BP when necessary to give effect to the Convention but, should a difference exist at any time between the two pharmacopoeias, the standard of the *European Pharmacopoeia* would prevail (HMRs Reg.320(3)).

Compliance with official standards

It is unlawful for any person, in the course of a business carried on by him/her:

a to sell a medicinal product which has been demanded by the purchaser by, or by express reference to, a particular name; or

b to sell or supply a medicinal product in pursuance of a prescription given by a practitioner in which the product required is described by, or by express reference to, a particular name; or

c to sell or supply a medicinal product which, in the course of the business, has been offered or exposed for sale by, or by express reference to, a particular name, if that name is at the head of the *relevant monograph* in a specified publication, or is an approved synonym for such a name, and the product does not comply with the standard specified in that monograph (HMRs Regs.251 and 255).

It is also an offence if the name in question is the name of an active ingredient of the product and, in so far as the product consists of that ingredient, it does not comply with the standard specified (HMRs Reg.251(4)). A name is taken to be an approved synonym for a name at the head of a monograph in the *European Pharmacopoeia* if, by a notice published in the *Gazette* and not subsequently withdrawn, it is declared to be approved by the Commission on Human Medicines as a synonym for that name (HMRs Reg.251).

The publications to which these requirements extend are the *European Pharmacopoeia*, the BP and any compendium published under Part 15 of the HMRs. For the purpose of complying with official standards, the *relevant monograph* is ascertained as follows (HMRs Reg.252).

1 If a particular edition of a particular publication is specified together with the name of the medicinal product, then the relevant monograph is (a) the monograph (if any) headed by that name in that edition of the publication or (b) if there is no such monograph in that edition, the *appropriate current monograph* (if any) headed by that name.

2 If a particular publication, but not a particular edition, is specified, together with the name of the medicinal product, then the relevant monograph is (a) the monograph (if any) headed by that name in the current edition of the specified publication or (b) if there is no such monograph in the current edition of the publication, the *appropriate current monograph* headed by that name, or (c) if there is no *appropriate current monograph*, then the monograph headed by that name in the latest edition of the specified publication which contained a monograph so headed.

3 If no publication is specified together with the name of the medicinal product, the relevant monograph is *the appropriate current monograph*, if any.

Appropriate current monograph, in relation to a particular name, means the monograph (if any) headed by that name, or by a name for which it is an approved synonym, in the current edition of the BP, or a compendium published under Part 15 of the HMRs.

Current means current at the time when the medicinal product in question is demanded, described in a prescription, or offered or exposed for sale; and the current edition of a publication is the one in force at that time, together with any amendments, alterations or deletions. Any monograph shall be construed in accordance with any general monograph, notice, appendix, note or other explanatory material applicable to the monograph which is contained in the relevant edition of the publication (HMRs Reg.252(5–7)).

Specified publications

The HMRs use the term *specified publication* to mean (HMRs Reg.321):

a *European Pharmacopoeia*
b *British Pharmacopoeia*
c the Cumulative List of Recommended International Nonproprietary Names
d any other compendium or list prepared under HMRs Regs.317 or 318.

When reference is made in a marketing authorisation, manufacturer's or wholesale dealer's licence, an Article 126a authorisation, a certificate of registration or a traditional herbal registration (chapters 3, 11 and 12) to a specified publication, but no particular edition is mentioned, then it is to be construed as the current edition.

The *British National Formulary* and other formularies under the *British National Formulary* are published jointly by the British Medical Association and the Pharmaceutical Press and are not 'official' publications under the HMRs.

Summary

- The BP comprises information consisting of descriptions and standards for substances and articles which may be used in medicine other than veterinary medicine together with substances and articles used in the manufacture of medicinal products.
- The *European Pharmacopoeia*, where appropriate, takes precedence over the standards in other publications.
- It is an offence to sell, supply or dispense a medicinal product of a particular name if that name is at the head of a monograph in a pharmacopoeia, and the product does not comply with the standard specified in that monograph.

Further reading

Human Medicines Regulations (2012) SI 2012 No. 1916, *Explanatory memorandum*: http://www.legislation.gov.uk/uksi/2012/1916/pdfs/uksiem_20121916_en.pdf (accessed 21 November 2012).

Royal Pharmaceutical Society (published annually). *Medicines, Ethics and Practice: The Professional Guide for Pharmacists*. London: Royal Pharmaceutical Society (includes practice guidance on many of the topics in this chapter; free to members).

Royal Pharmaceutical Society (2012). Support Bulletin No. 15 August 2012 Human Medicines Regulations 2012 *Pharm J*, 289: 200 (free to members or available on subscription).

Websites

Legislation (can be searched on year and SI number or title): http://www.legislation.gov.uk

Medicines and Healthcare products Regulatory Agency: http://www.mhra.gov.uk

Royal Pharmaceutical Society (member access only; lists legal classifications of medicines and further practice guidance): http://www.rpharms.com

16

Veterinary medicines

Gordon Hockey

The VMRs[1] set out the legal framework in the UK for the authorisation, marketing and supply of veterinary medicines. The VMD, an executive agency of the DEFRA, licenses veterinary medicines and the manufacturers. The VMRs are issued under the European Communities Act 1972 and until recently have been annual. Unless otherwise stated, references to sections relate to the current VMRs, which came into force on 1 October 2011.

A Veterinary Products Committee provides scientific advice on any aspect of veterinary medicines requested by the VMD, on behalf of the Secretary of State. The Committee's main role is to provide advice on applications for marketing authorisations and animal test certificates (for clinical trials of veterinary medicines), and to monitor veterinary pharmacovigilance activities through the Suspected Adverse Reaction Surveillance Scheme (SARSS). The Veterinary Residues Committee provides advice on the residue surveillance programmes.

The VMD provides Veterinary Medicine Guidance notes on aspects of the VMRs as well as links to the relevant UK and EU legislation on its website (see the end of this chapter).

Scope of the Veterinary Medicines Regulations

A *veterinary medicinal product* (veterinary medicine) means (VMRs Reg.2[2]):

1 any substance or combination of substances presented as having properties for treating or preventing disease in animals; or
2 any substances or combination of substances which may be used in, or administered to, animals with a view to restoring, correcting or modifying physiological functions by exerting a pharmacological, immunological or metabolic action or by making a medical diagnosis.

[1] The Veterinary Medicines Regulations SI 2011 No. 2159
[2] VMRs Reg.2, originally from consolidated Directive 2001/82/EC, as amended by Directive 2004/28/EC

In addition:

1 'animal' means all animals, other than man, and includes birds, reptiles, fish, molluscs, crustacea and bees'; and
2 'horse' means all species of Equidae and a horse is a food-producing animal unless it has been declared not intended for slaughter for human consumption in accordance with various 'passport' regulations.

Products may be medicinal by presentation or function and are subject to the VMRs even if also subject to other legislation.
The VMRs do not apply to (VMRs Reg.3):

1 an inactivated immunological veterinary medicine that is manufactured, on the instructions of a veterinary surgeon, from pathogens or antigens obtained from an animal and used for the treatment of that animal;
2 veterinary medicines based on radioactive isotopes; and
3 a product intended for administration in the course of a procedure licensed under the Animal (Scientific Procedures) Act 1968, but if animals are to the put into the human food chain the only products that may be administered are those within their marketing authorisation and those administered in accordance with an animal test certificate.

Offences

Offences under the VMRs include the following:

1 to place a veterinary medicine upon the market unless that product has a marketing authorisation granted by the Secretary of State (VMRs Reg.4);
2 to administer a veterinary medicine to an animal unless;
   a the product has a marketing authorisation authorising its administration in the UK and the administration is in accordance with the marketing authorisation, or
   b it is administered in accordance with Schedule 4 (cascade) or Schedule 6 (exemptions for small pet animals) (VMRs Reg.8);
3 to supply a veterinary medicine that has passed its expiry date (VMRs Reg.7(2));
4 to open a package (including the outer package) before it has been supplied to the final user, other than permitted by Schedule 3 (VMRs Reg.7(3));
5 to supply a medicinal product authorised for human use for administration to an animal other than in accordance with a prescription given by a veterinary surgeon for administration under the cascade (VMRs Reg.7(4));
6 to possess a veterinary medicine not supplied in accordance with Schedule 3 (VMRs Reg.7(5)); and
7 to advertise a veterinary medicine contrary to the VMRs.

Improvement notices (VMRs Reg.38) and seizure notices (VMRs Reg.41) must be made public (VMRs Reg.42) and prosecutions are reported in the VMD's Marketing Authorisations Veterinary Information Service, which is available on the VMD's website (see the end of this chapter). The most significant prosecution in recent years was reported in the VMD's Annual Review 2010/2011 (see box 16.1)

Box 16.1 *The Eurovet case and illegal import*

Eurovet convictions for the illegal importation and supply of veterinary medicines were reported in *VMD Annual Review 2010/2011*.

In July 2011, 13 people were convicted in Europe's largest illegal veterinary medicines business to date, which smuggled more than £6 million of veterinary medicines into the UK. The two ring-leaders were sentenced to 28 months' and 20 months' imprisonment. Other sentences varied from 13 months' imprisonment to suspended sentences and unpaid work. Investigations by the DEFRA Investigation Services began in 2006 and identified approximately 4000 customers of the company Eurovet; more than 20 tonnes of medicines were seized from the company's premises in Picardy. The VMD have stated that:

> The company in this case had no connection or involvement whatsoever with the bona-fide veterinary medicines company Eurovet Animal Health BV or its UK branch Eurovet Animal Health Limited based in Cambridge.

Marketing authorisations (VMRs Part 2 and Sch. 1)

There are four types of marketing authorisation system: centralised, decentralised, multi-recognition and national. Applications for a European marketing authorisation through the centralised system are made to the European Medicines Agency and the procedure is compulsory for veterinary medicine for use as growth or yield enhancers. Applications for veterinary medicines are evaluated through the Committee for Veterinary Medicines[3] and the decision to grant a marketing authorisation is made by the European Commission.

The decentralised scheme is available where the applicant wishes to license a product for more than one EU Member State, and the multi-recognition procedure applies where the medicine is authorised in one EU Member State

[3] Established by EU Regulation 726/2004

already. The national scheme applies where registration is only required in one state. Application for a marketing authorisation for a medicinal product for animal use in any of the procedures must be accompanied by the appropriate particulars.[4]

Marketing authorisations for food-producing species

If the veterinary medicine is intended for food-producing species and contains one or more pharmacologically active substances not yet included for the species in question in Commission EU Regulation 37/2010, a document certifying that a valid application for the establishment of MRLs must have been submitted to the VMD in accordance with EC Regulation 470/2009 of the European Parliament and of the Council (VMRs Sch. 1, para. 2(3)(p)). Special provisions apply to the administration of veterinary medicines to horses where there is no authorised veterinary medicine and the provisions of cascade do not apply, provided that the administration is recorded in the horse's passport (VMRs Sch. 4, para. 3).

Homoeopathic veterinary medicines (VMRs Sch. 1, Part 9 and Sch. 3, para. 10(4))

The VMRs set out a simplified marketing authorisation procedure for veterinary homoeopathic products and provide that a homoeopathic remedy may be prepared extemporaneously and supplied directly to the end user by a pharmacist in a registered pharmacy in accordance with a homoeopathic manufacturing procedure described in the official *European Pharmacopoeia*.

Exemptions for small pet animals (VMRs Sch. 6)

These exemptions apply solely to aquarium animals, cage birds, ferrets, homing pigeons, rabbits, small rodents and terrarium animals. A veterinary product intended solely for one of these categories of pets may be placed on the market, imported or administered without a marketing authorisation provided it complies with certain conditions, including the following:

1 the Secretary of State may approve the active substance in a veterinary medicine manufactured in accordance with the Schedule, unless the active substance requires veterinary control;
2 the product must not be an antibiotic;
3 the product must not contain any narcotic or psychotropic drug;
4 the product is not for treatments or pathological processes that require precise prior diagnosis or the use of which may cause effects that impede or interfere with subsequent or therapeutic measures;

[4]See, in particular, VMRs Schedule 1, Part 1, Reg.2(2), which refers to requirements set out in Council Directive 2001/82/EEC

5 the product must comply with detailed labelling requirements set down in the Schedule; and

6 the method of administration must be oral or topical or (in the case of a product for fish) by addition to the water.

The manufacturer, importer or retailer must notify DEFRA within 15 days and keep a record after learning of any serious adverse reaction to such a product and failure to comply is an offence.

Pharmacovigilance (VMRs Sch. 1, Part 8)

A marketing authorisation holder must have an appropriately qualified person for pharmacovigilance who resides in a EU Member State and whose responsibilities include establishing a system that ensures information about adverse events, for example adverse reactions, is collected and collated by the manufacturer. These are reported to the Secretary of State at least every 3 years or more frequently as appropriate, for example for newer veterinary medicines or serious adverse events.

In addition, there is the SARSS, managed by the VMD, which collates and evaluates reports of suspected adverse events submitted on the (yellow) SARSS forms. Veterinary surgeons and veterinary nurses, pharmacists and suitably qualified persons/prescribers (SQPs) and animal owners may all submit SARSS forms.

Classification of veterinary medicines (VMRs Sch. 3, para. 1)

In the VMRs, there are four classes of veterinary medicine together with authorised suppliers namely:

POM-V: Prescription Only Medicines prescribed by a veterinary surgeon (or veterinary practitioner);

POM-VPS: Prescription Only Medicines prescribed by a veterinary surgeon, pharmacist or SQP;

NFA-VPS: non-food animal medicine (e.g. for pets) prescribed by a veterinary surgeon, pharmacist or SQP;

AVM-GSL: Authorised Veterinary Medicines on the General Sale List.

The Secretary of State must specify the classification of the veterinary medicine when granting a marketing authorisation but may vary it by compulsory variation or at the request of the holder of the authorisation. The classification rules are briefly:

1 products must be classified as POM-V:
   a if containing narcotic or psychotropic substances, or
   b for administration following a diagnosis or clinical assessment by a veterinary surgeon;

2 products must be classified as POM-V or POM-VPS:

   a for food-producing animals, subject to certain exceptions, for example where there is no risk to human or animal health as regards residues or the development of resistance to antimicrobial or anthelmintic substances even when the products are used incorrectly,

   b to avoid unnecessary risk for the target species, the person administering the product, or the environment,

   c if the product may impede or interfere with subsequent diagnosis or therapeutic measures, or

   d if the product contains a new active substance that has not been included in an authorised veterinary medicine for 5 years.

A list of authorised veterinary medicines is available on the VMD website. The details of the classification and supply of veterinary medicines, wholesale dealers and sheep dip are set out in Schedule 3.

Wholesale supply of veterinary medicines (VMRs Sch. 3, para. 2)

Wholesale supply is regulated as:

1 only a holder of a marketing authorisation, the holder of a manufacturing authorisation or the holder of a wholesale dealer's authorisation may supply veterinary medicine by wholesale or be in possession of it for that purpose;

2 they may only supply to a person who may supply veterinary medicines either by wholesale or retail;

3 if supply is made to SQPs, the supply must be made to them on that person's approved premises;

4 a wholesale dealer may break open any package (other than the immediate package of a veterinary product);

5 it is irrelevant whether or not the supply is for profit; and

6 a retailer may supply another retailer with such products for the purpose of alleviating a temporary shortage that could be detrimental to animal welfare.

Retail supply of veterinary medicines

Retail supply means any supply other than to or from the holder of a wholesale authorisation and whether or not for payment.

1 POM-V products may only be supplied by a veterinary surgeon or a pharmacist and must be supplied in accordance with a prescription from a veterinary surgeon.

2 POM-VPS products may only be supplied by a veterinary surgeon, pharmacist or a SQP and must be in accordance with a prescription from one of those persons.

3 NFA-VPS products may be supplied without a prescription but may only be supplied by a veterinary surgeon, a pharmacist or a SQP.

4 AVM-GSL products have no such supply restrictions (VMRs Sch. 3, para. 3).

Any person who prescribes a POM-V or POM-VPS product (or prescribes and supplies it) or supplies an NFA-VPS product must (VMRs Sch. 3, para. 7):

- before doing so, be satisfied that the person who will use the product is competent to do so safely, and intends to use it for a purpose for which it is authorised;
- when doing so, advise on its safe administration and any warnings or contra-indications on the label or package leaflet; and
- not prescribe (or in the case of a NFA-VPS product, supply) more than the minimum amount required for the treatment. (It is a defence to show the manufacturer does not supply a smaller container under its marketing authorisation and that the person prescribing or supplying is not authorised to break open the package before supply).

Veterinary medicines that are also Controlled Drugs are subject to the Misuse of Drugs Act 1971 and associated Regulations, although generally not the enhanced restrictions introduced following the independent private inquiry into Dr Shipman by Dame Janet Smith.[5]

Prescription and supply requirements

Prescription Only Medicine prescribed by a veterinary prescriber

A veterinary surgeon who prescribes a veterinary medicine classified as POM-V must first carry out a clinical assessment of the animal and the animal must be under his/her care; failure to do so is an offence. This does not apply in relation to the administration of such a product to a wild animal where the administration is authorised by the Secretary of State (VMRs Sch. 3, para. 3).

The Royal College of Veterinary Surgeons (RCVS) provides an interpretation of 'under his/her care' that is endorsed by the VMD as meaning:[6]

a the veterinary surgeon must have been given the responsibility for the health of the animal or herd by the owner or the owner's agent;

b that responsibility must be real and not nominal;

---

[5] *The Shipman Fourth Report: The Regulation of Controlled Drugs in the Community*, published in July 2004

[6] Note 2, Veterinary medicines, supporting guidance to the Code of Conduct for veterinary surgeons, available on the RCVS website at the end of this chapter

c the animal or herd must have been seen immediately before prescription or recently enough or often enough for the veterinary surgeon to have personal knowledge of the condition of the animal or current health status of the herd or flock to make a diagnosis and prescribe;
d the veterinary surgeon must maintain clinical records of that herd/flock/individual.

The RCVS interpretation was subject to judicial scrutiny in an appeal from the RCVS Disciplinary Committee to the Privy Council (box 16.2).

Box 16.2 The meaning of 'under the care of a veterinary surgeon'

Susie Macleod v The Royal College of Veterinary Surgeons (Appeal No. 88 of 2005)

The appeal concerned Mrs Macleod's vaccination clinic that was staffed by veterinary nurses and had no resident veterinary surgeon. The RCVS Disciplinary Committee found on the facts that veterinary medicines were prescribed and supplied to animals that were not under the care of a veterinary surgeon, as interpreted by the RCVS Guide (now Code) to Professional Conduct, and directed that her name be suspended from the register of veterinary surgeons. At the appeal, their Lordships said that the RCVS interpretation was clear and provided an accurate and helpful interpretation; and that 'the detailed findings made by (the RCVS Disciplinary Committee) and the expression of opinion contained in its judgment that (Mrs Macleod's) actions were capable of jeopardising animal welfare give sustainable grounds for reaching its ultimate decision . . . '. However, Mrs Macleod's appeal was successful for other reasons and the Privy Council reduced the direction that her name be suspended from the register to a reprimand.

Prescription Only Medicine prescribed by a veterinary prescriber, pharmacist or suitably qualified person

A veterinary medicine classified as POM-V or POM- VPS must be prescribed, but a prescription may be oral or written. Unless supplied by the person who prescribes the medicine, the prescription must be written (VMRs Sch. 3, para. 5(1)).

A written prescription must be in ink or other indelible format and must include (VMRs Sch. 3, para. 6):

a the name, address, and telephone number of the person prescribing the product;
b the qualifications enabling the person to prescribe the product;

c the name and address of the owner or keeper;
d the identity (including the species) of the animal or group of animals to be treated;
e the premises at which the animals are kept if this is different from the address of the owner or keeper;
f the date of the prescription;
g the signature or other authentication of the person prescribing the product;
h the name and amount of the product prescribed;
i the dosage and administration instructions;
j any necessary warnings;
k the withdrawal period if relevant; and
l if it is prescribed under the cascade, a statement to that effect.

A prescription for a Controlled Drug (POM-V) is valid for 28 days and for any other drug is valid for 6 months or such shorter period as may be specified in the prescription. If the prescription is a repeatable, it must specify the number of times the product may be supplied (VMRs Sch. 3, para. 6(3 and 4)).

The person supplying the product may only supply the product specified on the prescription, must take all reasonable steps to be satisfied that the prescription has been written and signed by a person entitled to prescribe the product and must take all reasonable steps to ensure the it is supplied to the person named in the prescription. It is an offence to alter a written prescription unless authorised to do so by the person who signed it (VMRs Sch. 3, para. 5(2)).

If a veterinary medicine is prescribed (and supplied) in accordance with the marketing authorisation, no additional labelling is required by the VMRs, and it is an offence if any of the relevant information is not clearly visible at the time of supply. There is no offence if a veterinary surgeon amends the product label or a pharmacist amends the label in accordance with a prescription from a veterinary surgeon, for example by adding a dispensing label, provided that the unamended manufacturer's information remains clearly visible (VMRs Sch. 3, para. 12(2 and 3)).

If the veterinary medicine is supplied in a container other than that specified in the marketing authorisation, the container must be suitably labelled by the veterinary surgeon or pharmacist and additional information supplied (which may include a copy of the Summary of Product Characteristics or the package leaflet) to enable the product to be used safely (VMRs Sch. 3, para. 12 (3)).

The cascade (VMRs Sch. 4)

If there is no veterinary medicine in the UK for a condition, the veterinary surgeon responsible for the animal may, in particular to avoid unacceptable suffering, treat the animal concerned under the following cascade in the following order (VMRs Sch. 4, para. 1):

1 a veterinary product authorised in the UK for use with another animal species or for another condition in the same species; or
2 if and only if there is no such product that is suitable, either
   a a medicinal product authorised in the UK for human use, or
   b a veterinary product not authorised in the UK but authorised in another Member State of the EC for use with any animal species (if for food-producing animal must be for a food-producing species); or
3 if there is no such product that is suitable, a veterinary product prepared extemporaneously by a pharmacist, a veterinary surgeon or a person holding manufacturing authorisation authorising the manufacture of that type of product.

A veterinary medicine that is administered outside its marketing authorisation or has no marketing authorisation must be prescribed by a veterinary surgeon under the cascade (VMRs Part 1, Reg. 8(b)). This includes medical products authorised for human use.

Unless the prescribing veterinary surgeon supplies or administers the veterinary medicine to the animal, the person supplying it, for example a pharmacist or another veterinary surgeon, must label the product with the following information (VMRs Sch. 3, para. 13):

1 the name and address of the pharmacy or veterinary surgery or approved premises supplying the product;
2 the name of the veterinary surgeon who prescribed it;
3 the name and address of the animal owner;
4 the identification (including the species) of the animal or group of animals;
5 the date of supply;
6 the expiry date of the product, if applicable;
7 the name or description of the product, which should include at least the name and quantity of the active ingredients;
8 the dosage and administration instructions;
9 any special storage precautions;
10 any necessary warnings for the user, target species, administration or disposal of the product;
11 the identity (including the species) of the animal or group of animals;
12 the withdrawal period, if relevant; and
13 the words '*Keep out of reach of children*' and '*For animal treatment only*'.

A veterinary surgeon prescribing or administering a veterinary medicine to a food-producing animal must specify an appropriate withdrawal period (VMRs Sch. 3, para. 2(1)).

Supply by veterinary surgeons and pharmacists (VMRs Sch. 3, paras. 8, 9 and 10)

A veterinary surgeon must supply veterinary products from a veterinary practice premises registered with the RCVS under the VMRs. A pharmacist may supply a veterinary product which is classified POM-V, POM-VPS or NFA-VPS from premises registered as a pharmacy or a veterinary practice and may supply those classified as POM-VPS or NFA-VPS from premises approved as SQP retailers premises.

A veterinary surgeon or pharmacist supplying veterinary products (other than AVM-GSL) must be present when the product is handed over unless s/he authorises each transaction individually before the product is supplied and s/he is satisfied that the person handing it over is competent to do so.

A pharmacist may:

a supply veterinary products prepared in a pharmacy in accordance with the prescriptions of a pharmacopoeia and supplied to the end user;

b supply certain homoeopathic remedies prepared extemporaneously in a pharmacy provided they are supplied to the end-user; and

c can break open any package containing a veterinary medicine other than the immediate package.

On 25 May 2012, the VMD launched a voluntary Accredited Internet Retailer Scheme to facilitate self-regulation of UK-based Internet retailers selling veterinary medicines. The aim of the scheme is to ensure that animal owners buying veterinary medicines over the Internet have appropriate advice from a veterinary surgeon, pharmacist or SQP and they buy medicines authorised for use in the UK. Details of the scheme are available on the VMD website (see the end of this chapter).

Supply by suitably qualified persons (VMRs Sch. 3, para. 14)

A *suitably qualified person* is a person who is trained and registered to be able to sell a limited range of veterinary medicines and often works from a pet shop, saddler or agricultural merchant's premises. SQPs prescribe and supply veterinary medicines classified as POM-VPS and NFA-VPS.

The Secretary of State may recognise bodies that are suitable to maintain a register, for example the Animal Medicines Training Regulatory Authority.

The Secretary of State must be satisfied that the body:

1 has in place a system for ensuring that the person applying for registration has had adequate training to act as an SQP;

2 has adequate standards in deciding whether to register an SQP;

3 maintains a programme of continuing professional development (CPD) for persons registered with it; and

4 operates an adequate appeal system if it intends to refuse to register anyone with appropriate qualifications or to remove anyone from the register.

The supply of veterinary medicines by an SQP must take place from premises approved by the Secretary of State as being suitable for the storage and supply of such products. An SQP may also make supplies from a registered pharmacy or a registered veterinary practice premises. An SQP may break open any package (other than an immediate package) containing a veterinary product.

An SQP who supplies POM-VPS or NFA-VPS products must:

a hand over or dispatch the product personally;
b ensure that when the product is handed over or dispatched s/he is in a position to intervene; or
c check that the product allocated for supply is in conformity with a prescription and satisfy himself/herself that the person handing over the product is competent so to do.

The list of registered SQPs and the premises approved for sales by the Secretary of State is available on the VMD website (see end of this chapter).

The Secretary of State has the power to remove the approval of SQP premises if they are no longer suitable for the storage and supply of veterinary medicines. An SQP who considers that his/her registered premises no longer complies with its approval conditions must notify the Secretary of State and failure to do so is an offence.

The Secretary of State has issued a *Code of Practice for SQPs* (VMRs Sch. 3, para. 14(7)) and the Animal Medicines Training Regulatory Authority, as a recognised body, must take appropriate action in accordance with its disciplinary code if an SQP registered with it does not comply with the Code. The Code of Practice sets out the standards which SQPs are expected to meet and supplements the legal requirements with other provisions relating to personnel, sale and storage arrangements and standards of premises. The Code is available on the VMD website (see end of this chapter).

Records of receipt and supply for Prescription Only Medicines

Any person who sells or receives veterinary medicines classified as POM-V and POM-VPS must keep all documents and/or the relevant information relating to the transaction that show (VMRs Part 3, Reg.23(1)):

1 the date;
2 the name of the product;

3 the batch number (except that, in the case of a product for a non-food-producing animal, this need only be recorded on the date s/he receives the batch or the date s/he starts to use it);

4 the quantity;

5 the name and address of supplier or recipient; and

6 if there is a written prescription, the name and address of the person who wrote the prescription and a copy of the prescription.

If the documents do not include this information the person must make a record of the missing information as soon as reasonably practicable following the transaction. The records must be kept for at least 5 years and be made available on request to any person having a duty of enforcement (VMRs Reg.23(3 and 4)).

There are strict record-keeping provisions relating to those who keep food-producing animals and veterinary surgeons who prescribe for them (VMRs Part 3).

Records and storage by wholesalers

A registered wholesaler must keep detailed records of all incoming and outgoing sales including disposal for at least 3 years. These must include the (VMRs Reg.22):

1 date and nature of the transaction;

2 name of the product;

3 manufacturer's batch number;

4 expiry date;

5 quantity; and

6 name and address of supplier or recipient.

The wholesale premises must be weatherproof, secure and lockable, clean and free from contaminants. The holder of the authorisation must have the services of technically competent staff and an effective recall system. The authorisation, which may cover more than one site, must list the type of products dealt with, where they are stored, the name and address of the person holding the authorisation, the address of the premises and the name of the qualified person under the relevant provisions (VMRs Sch. 3, Part 2).

Annual audit (VMRs Sch. 3, para. 15)

At least once a year, every person entitled to supply veterinary products on prescription must carry out a detailed audit and incoming and outgoing products must be reconciled with products currently held stock, any discrepancies being recorded. This is particularly so for Controlled Drugs. Guidance issued by the VMD provides that a system linking incoming and outgoing transactions with stock held, with an annual or more frequent stock-take, for example for tax purposes, should meet the annual audit requirement.[7]

Advertising of veterinary products (VMRs Reg.10)

It is an offence to advertise a veterinary medicine if the advertisement is misleading or carries a claim not in the Summary of Product Characteristics. It is also an offence to advertise a human medicine for administration to animals, including sending a price list of human medicines or the medicines to a veterinary surgeon or veterinary practice. There is a defence for publishers (VMRs Reg.12). However, a wholesaler may send a list of human medicines with prices to a veterinary surgeon provided that the list has been requested by the veterinary surgeon and the list states clearly that the products do not have a marketing authorisation as a veterinary product and may only be prescribed and administered under the cascade.

Advertising of Prescription Only Medicines (VMRs Reg.11)

Regulation 11 of the Veterinary Medicines Regulations covers both products classified as POM-V and those classified as POM-VPS. It is an offence to advertise veterinary medicines that are available on a veterinary prescription only or contain psychotropic drugs or narcotics.

In the case of POM-V medicines, the prohibition does not apply to price lists or to advertisements aimed at veterinary surgeons, veterinary nurses, pharmacists or professional keepers of animals.

In the case of POM-VPS medicines, the prohibition does not apply to price lists or to advertisements aimed at veterinary surgeons, pharmacists, registered SQPs, other veterinary healthcare professionals, professional keepers of animals or owners or keepers of horses.

Importation of veterinary medicines (VMRs Reg.9)

Authorised veterinary medicines may be imported into the UK only by:

1 the holder of the marketing authorisation for the veterinary medicine;
2 the holder of a relevant manufacturing authorisation;
3 an authorised wholesale dealer provided that the authorisation covers the product and the holder of the marketing authorisation has been notified in writing in advance of the importation;
4 a veterinary surgeon or pharmacist; and
5 a SQP appropriately registered, but only for veterinary medicines that s/he may supply.

[7]See also the VMD, Veterinary Medicines Guidance Note No. 3

There are no restrictions on the importation of AVM-GSL products.

Unauthorised veterinary medicines may be imported into the UK only if permitted by Regulation 25 of the Veterinary Medicines Regulations. This includes provision for a veterinary surgeon to import such products in accordance with an appropriate certificate granted by the Secretary of State, for the purpose of administration under the cascade to animals that are the responsibility of the veterinary surgeon. The product may be imported by the veterinary surgeon personally or by using a wholesale dealer or pharmacist.

Labelling requirements for veterinary medicines (VMRs Sch. 1, Part 7)

All labels and leaflets must be in English but may contain other languages provided they give identical information in all languages. The regulations require the following information to appear in legible characters on the immediate packaging:

1 the name, strength and pharmaceutical form of the veterinary medicine;
2 name and strength of each active substance, and of any excipient, if this is required under the Summary of Product Characteristics;
3 route of administration (if not immediately apparent);
4 batch number;
5 expiry date;
6 the words '*for animal treatment only*' and if appropriate '*to be supplied only on a veterinary prescription*';
7 the contents by weight, volume or number of dose units;
8 the marketing authorisation number;
9 the name and address of the market authorisation holder or if there is a distributor authorised in the marketing authorisation, the distributor;
10 suitably labelled space to record discard date (if relevant);
11 target species;
12 the distribution category;
13 the words '*keep out of reach of children*';
14 storage instructions;
15 the in-use shelf-life (if appropriate);
16 for food-producing species, the withdrawal period for each species or animal product concerned;
17 any warning specified in the marketing authorisation;
18 disposal advice;
19 full indications;
20 dosage instructions;
21 contra-indications;
22 further information required by the marketing authorisation; and
23 if the product is one where the dose needs to be specified for the animal being treated, a space for this.

If all these are on the immediate package, there is no necessity for any out-packaging or a package leaflet (VMRs Sch. 1, Part 7, para. 48(2)).

In the case of reduced labelling, the full information must be on an outer packaging and if this is not practicable then in a leaflet accompanying the product (VMRs Sch. 1, Part 7, para. 49(4)). The leaflet must contain all the information 1–23 as above except the expiry date and the batch number (VMRs Sch. 1, Part 7, para. 50(1)).

Labelling of ampoules (VMRs Sch. 1, Part 7, para. 51)

For containers such as ampoules or other unit dose forms, where the container cannot bear legibly the required information, the following information must be shown on the immediate package:

1 the name of the veterinary medicine;
2 the name and strength of the active ingredient;
3 the batch number;
4 route of administration, if not immediately apparent;
5 the expiry date; and
6 the words *'for animal treatment only'* or, if appropriate, *'to be supplied only on a veterinary prescription'*.

Small containers other than ampoules (VMRs Sch. 1, Part 7, para. 52)

For small immediate packaging containing a single dose, other than ampoules, on which it is impossible to give the required information the immediate package must be labelled with the batch number and the expiry date.

Sale of sheep dips (VMRs Sch. 3, Part 2)

The Regulations apply to any veterinary medicine that is a sheep dip of any type and it is an offence to use sheep dip unless it is done by, or under the supervision and in the presence of, a person qualified to use sheep dip, which is a person who holds either:

- A Certificate of Competence in the Safe Use of Sheep Dips showing that Parts 1 and 2 of the assessment referred to in the certificate have been satisfactorily completed, or
- National Proficiency Tests Council Level 2 Award in the Safe Use of Sheep Dip (Qualification and Credit Framework).

For England, Wales and Northern Ireland, the certificate must be issued by the National Proficiency Tests Council, the National Proficiency Tests Council part of the City and Guilds Group or City and Guilds National Proficiency Tests Council. In Scotland, the certificate must be issued by one of those organisations or the Scottish Skills Testing Service.

The sale of sheep dip must be to a person (or to a person acting on behalf of a person) who is qualified to use it. The supplier must keep a record of that person's certificate number as soon as is reasonably practicable and retain it for 3 years from the date of the sale.

If the active ingredient is an organophosphorus compound, the supplier must give to the buyer:

- a double-sided laminated notice meeting the specification set out in the regulations as to advice on sheep dipping (unless the notice has been provided to the buyer within the previous 12 months and the supplier knows or has reasonable cause to believe the buyer still has it available for use); and
- two pairs of gloves, either as described in the notice or providing demonstrably superior protection to the user against exposure to the dip than would be provided by the gloves described.

The notice must be at least A4 size with laminated cover and must tell the reader:

1 to read and act in accordance with instructions, including instructions on measuring and diluting concentrate;
2 that sheep dip is absorbed through the skin and always to wear the recommended protective clothing including gloves and have a spare set of clothing;
3 always to wash protective clothing before taking it off;
4 to direct any questions to the supplier or manufacturer; and
5 in a diagram, the recommended protective clothing.

Medicated feeding stuffs and specified feed additives (VMRs Sch. 5)

A veterinary surgeon, pharmacist or, in the case of a product classified as POM-VPS, a SQP may supply a veterinary medicine for incorporation into feeding stuffs. The supply must be to an approved premixture manufacturer or to an approved feeding stuffs manufacturer if the approval permits the rate of incorporation specified on the label of the veterinary medicine (if the manufacturer is the end user the supply must be in accordance with a prescription).

Schedule 5 includes detailed rules on medicated feeding stuffs and Schedule 5 covers specified feed additives, including those on incorporation, top dressing and prescriptions.

Fair trading

A set of regulations concerning supply and prescribing of veterinary medicines has been issued by the Department of Trade and Industry under competition law,[8] which for 3 years between 31 October 2005 and 30 Octobeer 2008 prohibited the veterinary surgeon from charging a client a fee for a prescription (Reg.3(2)).

These Regulations continue to provide that a

1 veterinary surgeon may not discriminate between a client to whom s/he provides a prescription and a client to whom s/he does not as far as the price s/he charges for any relevant veterinary medicine (broadly veterinary medicines classified as POM-V) and fees for supplying services other than the giving of a prescription (Reg.6); and

2 a manufacturer or wholesaler may not discriminate unreasonably between veterinary surgeons and pharmacists ((Reg.4) in:
   a the price that they charge for the supply of relevant veterinary medicine,
   b any discount or rebate in connection with such a supply, or
   c any other terms or conditions upon which they supply.

In addition, a manufacturer must at intervals of not more than 3 months notify in writing the relevant veterinary surgeon and pharmacist of the net price at which s/he supplies veterinary medicines. Net price means the list price less any discount and should state whether it includes VAT (Reg.4).

Summary

- Veterinary surgeons and practitioners may sell or supply any medicinal product for administration by them, or under their direction, and for POM-V medicines they must first carry out a clinical examination and the animal or herd must be under their care.
- There are four classes of veterinary medicines with several classes of sellers:
   a POM-V products may only be supplied by a veterinary surgeon or a pharmacist and must be supplied in accordance with a prescription from a veterinary surgeon,
   b POM-VPS products may only be supplied by a veterinary surgeon, pharmacist or a SQP and must be in accordance with a prescription from one of those persons,
   c NFA-VPS products are for non-food-producing animals and may be supplied without a prescription but may only be supplied by a veterinary surgeon, a pharmacist or a SQP, and
   d AVM-GSL products are authorised on the GSL and there are no supply restrictions.

[8]The Supply of Relevant Veterinary Medicinal Products Order 2005 (SI 2005 No. 2751)

- There are detailed rules governing the classes of veterinary medicines concerned with the questions of prescribing, supplying and advertising.
- There are rules concerning fair trading to allow pharmacists and veterinary surgeons to compete for business.
- Details are laid down for the registration, and training of SQPs and the premises from which they may supply veterinary medicines.
- There is a code of practice for SQPs.
- There are controls over the supply of sheep dips.

Further reading

Kayne S (2011). *An Introduction to Veterinary Medicines*. Glasgow: Saltire Books.

Veterinary Medicines Directorate (2011). *Veterinary Medicines Guidance Notes*. London: Veterinary Medicines Directorate: http://www.vmd.defra.gov.uk/public/vmr.aspx (accessed 21 November 2012).

Veterinary Medicines Directorate (2012). *Veterinary Medicines Advice for Pharmacists*. London: Veterinary Medicines Directorate: http://www.vmd.defra.gov.uk/pdf/leaflet_pharmacists.pdf (accessed 21 November 2012).

Veterinary Medicines Regulations (2011) SI 2011 No. 2159: http://www.legislation.gov.uk/uksi/2011/2159/pdfs/uksi_20112159_en.pdf (accessed 21 November 2012).

Websites

Animal Medicines Training and Regulatory Authority: http://www.amtra.org.uk

Department for Environment, Food and Rural Affairs: http://www.defra.gov.uk

Legislation (can be searched on year and SI number or title): http://www.legislation.gov.uk

Royal College of Veterinary Surgeons: http://www.rcvs.org.uk

Veterinary Medicines Directorate: http://www.vmd.defra.gov.uk

17

Controlled Drugs

Cathal Gallagher

The Misuse of Drugs Act 1971 consolidates and extends previous legislation and controls the export, import, production, supply and possession of dangerous or otherwise harmful drugs, termed *Controlled Drugs*. The 1971 Act is also designed to deal with the control and treatment of addicts and to promote education and research relating to drug dependence. It extends to Northern Ireland (s.38).

In relation to drugs, the Act is largely restrictive in its terms although it does provide for licences to be issued for importation and exportation (s.3). Apart from that, the general effect is to render unlawful all activities in the drugs which are controlled under the Act, except as provided in the Regulations made under the Act. The extent to which these Regulations relax the restrictions is dealt with later in this chapter.

Advisory Council on Misuse of Drugs

The Advisory Council on Misuse of Drugs was formally established (under s.1) from 1 February 1972, replacing the former Advisory Committee on Drug Dependence which had no statutory authority. It advises the ministers, that is the Secretary of State for the Home Affairs Department, and the ministers responsible for health and education in England, Wales, Scotland and Northern Ireland.

The Advisory Council consists of not fewer than 20 members appointed by the Secretary of State (usually for a term of 3 years) after consultation with such organisations as s/he considers appropriate, including at least one person appearing to the Secretary of State to have wide and recent experience in each of the following:

1 the practice of medicine (other than veterinary medicine);
2 the practice of dentistry;
3 the practice of veterinary medicine;

4 the practice of pharmacy;
5 the pharmaceutical industry;
6 chemistry, other than pharmaceutical chemistry.

The Advisory Council also contains individuals that appear to the Secretary of State to have wide and recent experience of social problems connected with the misuse of drugs (Sch. 1 to the Act). The Secretary of State appoints one of the members of the Advisory Council to be chairman, and the Council may appoint committees and include on them persons who are not members of the Council. There are currently 24 council members.

The Advisory Council is required to keep under review the situation in the UK with respect to drugs which are being, or appear to them likely to be, misused (s.1). If it considers that misuse could cause harmful effects which might constitute a social problem, it has a duty to advise the ministers on the action to be taken. In particular it must advise on measures:

1 to restrict the availability of such drugs or to supervise the arrangements for their supply;
2 to enable persons affected by the misuse of such drugs to obtain proper advice, and to secure the provision of proper facilities and services for the treatment, rehabilitation and aftercare of such persons;
3 to promote co-operation between the various professional and community services which, in the opinion of the Council, have a part to play in dealing with social problems connected with the misuse of such drugs;
4 to educate the public (and in particular the young) in the dangers of abusing such drugs, and to give publicity to those dangers; and
5 to promote research into, or otherwise to obtain information about, any matter which in the opinion of the Council is of relevance for the purpose of preventing the misuse of such drugs or dealing with any social problem connected with their misuse. The Secretary of State has authority to conduct or assist in conducting such research (s.32).

The Advisory Council also has a duty to advise on any matter relating to drug dependence or misuse of drugs which any of the ministers may refer to it. In particular, the Advisory Council is required to advise the Secretary of State on communications relating to the control of any dangerous or otherwise harmful drug received from any authority established under a treaty, convention or other agreement to which HM Government is a party. Before any Regulations are made under the Act, the Advisory Council must be consulted (s.31(3)).

Class A, B and C drugs

The drugs subject to control are listed in Schedule 2 to the Act and the term Controlled Drug means any substance or product so listed. The Schedule is divided into three parts or classes largely on the basis of decreasing order of harmfulness: Part I (class A), Part II (class B) and Part III (class C). This division into three classes is solely for the purpose of determining penalties for offences under the Act (s.25) (see appendix 4).

Changes may be made to the list of Controlled Drugs subject to consultation with the Advisory Council. Amendment is made by an Order in Council which must be approved by an affirmative resolution of each House of Parliament (s.2).

It should be noted that the classification of Controlled Drugs for purposes of the regimes of control which must be applied to drugs when used for lawful purposes appears in the Schedules to the Misuse of Drugs Regulations 2001.[1] This classification is of importance to practitioners and pharmacists in their daily work and is set out in appendix 5.

Restrictions and exemptions

The importation or exportation of Controlled Drugs is prohibited, except in accordance with a licence issued by the Secretary of State or when permitted by Regulations (s.3). Certain activities are specifically declared to be unlawful:

1 producing a Controlled Drug (s.4);
2 supplying or offering to supply a Controlled Drug to another person (s.4);
3 possessing a Controlled Drug (s.5); and
4 cultivating any plant of the genus *Cannabis* (s.6).

Producing a Controlled Drug means producing it by manufacture, cultivation or any other method, and supplying includes distribution (s.37). For the purposes of the Act, the things which a person has in his/her possession are taken to include anything subject to his/her control which is in the custody of another (s.37). Cannabis (except in the expression cannabis resin) means any plant of the genus *Cannabis* or any part of any such plant (by whatever name designated) except that it does not include cannabis resin or any of the following products after separation from the rest of the plant (Criminal Law Act 1977, s.52), namely:

1 mature stalk of any such plant;
2 fibre produced from mature stalk of any such plant; and
3 seed of any such plant.

Exemptions from these controls may be authorised by the Secretary of State, who may:

1 by Regulations exempt any specified Controlled Drug from any of the restrictions on import, export, production, supply or possession (s.7);

[1] The Misuse of Drugs Regulations SI 2001 No. 3998

2 by Regulations make it lawful for persons to produce, supply or possess Controlled Drugs to the extent which s/he thinks fit (s.7); and

3 permit by licence or other authority any of the activities in 2 and prescribe any conditions to be complied with (s.7).

The Secretary of State must exercise his/her powers to make Regulations so as to secure appropriate exemptions for the possession, supply, manufacture or compounding of Controlled Drugs by practitioners, pharmacists and persons lawfully conducting retail pharmacy businesses, and for prescribing and administration by practitioners (s.7). The term practitioner (except in the specific expression 'veterinary practitioner') means a doctor, dentist, veterinary practitioner or veterinary surgeon (s.37).

If the Secretary of State considers that it is in the public interest for a drug to be used only for the purposes of research or other special purposes, s/he may make an order to that effect. It is then unlawful for a practitioner, pharmacist or a person lawfully conducting a retail pharmacy business to do anything in relation to that drug except under licence. In this connection, doing things includes having things in one's possession. When making an order of this kind, the Secretary of State must act on the recommendation of the Advisory Council or after consulting that Council (s.7). Licence fees are prescribed in regularly updated SIs.[2]

The 2001 Regulations list 'exempted' products, which means a preparation or other product consists of one or more parts any of which contains a Controlled Drug where:

1 the preparation or other product is not designed for administration of the Controlled Drug to a human being or animal;

2 the Controlled Drug in any component part is packaged in such a form or in combination with other active or inert substances in such a manner that it cannot be recovered by readily applicable means or in a yield which constitutes a risk to health; or

3 no one component part of the product or combination contains more than 1 mg of the Controlled Drug or 1 microgram in the case of lysergide or any other N-alkyl derivative of lysergamide.

Other exemptions will apply, for example to *in vitro* diagnostic devices or kits used by laboratories for the detection of drugs of misuse or for clinical diagnosis or other products containing very small quantities of Controlled Drugs (e.g. radioactive research compounds). The provisions of the Act will apply to the possession of a stock of Controlled Drugs for the purpose of producing kits and other exempted products. The safe custody Regulations will also apply to any stock of Schedule 1 and 2 Controlled Drugs and stocks of buprenorphine, diethylpropion, flunitrazepam and temazepam held for the propose of manufacture of the exempted products.

[2] The Misuse of Drugs (Licence Fees) Regulations SI 2010 No. 2497 (as amended)

Supply of articles for administering or preparing Controlled Drugs

The following persons:

- a practitioner;
- a pharmacist;
- a person employed or engaged in the lawful provision of drug treatment services;[3]
- a supplementary prescriber acting under and in accordance with the terms of a clinical management plan;[4] and
- a nurse independent prescriber[5]

may supply or offer to supply the following articles:

- a swab;
- utensils for the preparation of a Controlled Drug;
- citric acid;
- a filter;
- ampoules of water for injection.

only when supplied or offered for supply in accordance with the Medicines Act and its Regulations.

Provisions for preventing misuse

The Secretary of State may make such Regulations as appear to him/her necessary or expedient for preventing the misuse of Controlled Drugs (s.10). In particular s/he may make provisions that:

1 require precautions to be taken for the safe custody of Controlled Drugs;
2 impose requirements as to the documentation of transactions involving Controlled Drugs, and require copies of documents relating to such transactions to be furnished to the prescribed authority;
3 require the keeping of records and the furnishing of information with respect to Controlled Drugs and in such circumstances and in such manner as may be prescribed;
4 provide for the inspection of any precautions taken or records kept in pursuance of Regulations under this section;
5 relate to the packaging and labelling of Controlled Drugs;
6 regulate the transport of Controlled Drugs and the methods used for destroying or otherwise disposing of such drugs when no longer required;

[3] The Misuse of Drugs (Amendment) (No. 2) Regulations SI 2003 No. 1653
[4] The Misuse of Drugs (Amendment) Regulations SI 2005 No. 271
[5] The Misuse of Drugs (Amendment No. 2) (England, Wales and Scotland) Regulations 2012 No. 973

7 regulate the issue of prescriptions containing Controlled Drugs and the supply of Controlled Drugs on prescriptions, and require persons issuing or dispensing prescriptions containing such drugs to furnish to the prescribed authority such information relating to those prescriptions as may be prescribed;

8 require any doctor who attends a person who s/he considers, or has reasonable grounds to suspect, is addicted (within the meaning of the Regulations) to Controlled Drugs of any description to furnish to the prescribed authority such particulars with respect to that person as may be prescribed; and

9 prohibit any doctor from administering, supplying and authorising the administration and supply to persons so addicted, and from prescribing for such persons, such Controlled Drugs as may be prescribed, except and in accordance with the terms of a licence issued by the Secretary of State in pursuance of the Regulations.

In addition to making Regulations about safe custody, the Secretary of State may also, by notice in writing, require the occupier of any premises where Controlled Drugs are kept to take further precautions as specified in the notice (s.11).

Information concerning misuse

Doctors, pharmacists and persons lawfully conducting retail pharmacy businesses in any area may be called upon to give particulars of the quantities of any dangerous or otherwise harmful drugs (not necessarily controlled under the Act) which have been prescribed, administered or supplied over a particular period of time. The Secretary of State may call for this information if it appears to him/her that a social problem exists in that area caused by a drug or drugs.

A notice in writing may be served on the persons concerned specifying the period and requiring particulars of the drug to be furnished in such a manner and within such time as set out in the notice. Pharmacists may be required to give the names and addresses of the prescribing doctors but may not be required to identify the patients concerned. It is an offence to fail, without reasonable excuse, to give the information required or to give false information (s.17).

Prohibitions on possession, prescribing and supply

Directions following convictions

Where a pharmacist or practitioner has been guilty of any offence under the Act or of any offence under the Customs and Excise Act 1952 or the

Customs and Excise Management Act 1979 relating to the unlawful importation or exportation of Controlled Drugs, the Secretary of State may make
a direction in respect of him/her. If s/he is a practitioner, the direction will
prohibit him/her from having in his/her possession, prescribing, administering, manufacturing, compounding and supplying, and from authorising the
administration and supply of the Controlled Drugs specified in the direction.
If s/he is a pharmacist, the direction will prohibit him/her from having in
his/her possession, manufacturing, compounding and supplying and from
supervising and controlling the manufacture, compounding and supply of
the Controlled Drugs specified in the direction (s.12).

A copy of any such direction given by the Secretary of State must be
served on the person to whom it applies and notice of it must be published in
the *London*, *Edinburgh* and *Belfast Gazettes*. A direction takes effect when
a copy has been served on the person concerned and it is then an offence for
him/her to contravene it. The Secretary of State may cancel or suspend any
direction which s/he has given. S/he may also bring a suspended direction
into force again by cancelling its suspension (ss.12, 13 and 16).

Conviction for an offence under the Act committed by a pharmacist or
other person who is a director, officer or employee of a body corporate
carrying on a retail pharmacy business renders that body liable to disqualification under Part 4 of the Pharmacy Order 2010 and consequent removal of
its premises from the Register of Pharmacies (chapter 24).

Prohibitions affecting doctors

If a doctor contravenes the Regulations relating to notification of addicts
or the prescribing of Controlled Drugs for addicts, s/he does not commit
any offence under the Act. The Secretary of State may, however, make a
direction prohibiting him/her from prescribing, administering or supplying,
or authorising the administration or supply of, the Controlled Drugs specified
in the direction. The doctor commits an offence if s/he contravenes that
direction (s.13).

Irresponsible prescribing

If the Secretary of State is of the opinion that a practitioner has been
prescribing, administering or supplying, or authorising the administration or
supply of, any Controlled Drugs in an irresponsible manner, s/he may give a
direction in respect of the practitioner concerned prohibiting him/her from
prescribing, administering and supplying or authorising the administration
and supply of the Controlled Drugs specified in the direction (s.13).

Tribunals, advisory bodies and professional panels

Before s/he gives a direction prohibiting a doctor or other practitioner from
prescribing, administering or supplying Controlled Drugs, the Secretary of

State must, except when the direction is based on a conviction, follow the procedure set out in the Act (ss.14, 15 and 16). S/he must refer the case to a tribunal consisting of four members of the practitioner's profession and with a lawyer as chairman (Sch. 3). Legislation under section 59 prescribes the procedure to be followed before tribunals.[6] If, as a result of the tribunal's finding, that the practitioner has been found to be responsible for the contravention or conduct alleged, the Secretary of State then proposes to make a direction; the practitioner must be informed and given the opportunity to make representations in writing within 28 days. If the practitioner so does, then the case must be referred to an advisory body of three appointed persons, one being a member of the practitioner's profession. After receiving the advice of that body, the Secretary of State may (a) advise that no further proceedings be taken; (b) refer the case back to the same, or another, tribunal; or (c) give a direction under section 13 as described above (s.14). Although the legal underpinning for such tribunals is still in place, the last case was disposed in 1994.

In a case of irresponsible prescribing, if the Secretary of State considers circumstances require that a direction be given with the minimum of delay, s/he may refer the matter to a professional panel consisting of three members of the practitioner's profession appointed by the Secretary of State. The panel must afford the practitioner an opportunity to appear before it and, after considering the circumstances of the case, must report to the Secretary of State whether or not it believes there are reasonable grounds for thinking that there has been conduct as alleged. If the panel considers there are such grounds, the Secretary of State may give a direction at once which is effective for a period of 6 weeks. S/he must also refer the case at once to a tribunal, in accordance with the procedures outlined above. The period of operation of the temporary direction may be extended from time to time by a further 28 days if the tribunal consents. After the tribunal, or the advisory body as appropriate, has considered the case, the Secretary of State may, if s/he thinks fit, make a permanent direction, if that is the advice given to him/her. If no such direction is given, the temporary prohibition will cease (s.15).

Offences, penalties and enforcement

Schedule 4 to the Act is a tabulated summary of offences under the Act and the penalties applicable to them. The level of penalty for offences which concern a Controlled Drug varies according to the class (A, B or C) into which the drug falls, the generally more harmful drugs attracting greater penalties.

[6]The Misuse of Drugs Tribunal (England and Wales) Rules SI 1974 No. 85

The occupier or manager of any premises commits an offence (s.8) if s/he knowingly permits or suffers any of the following to take place on the premises:

1 producing or supplying, or attempting to produce or supply, or offering to supply any Controlled Drug in contravention of the Act;
2 preparing opium for smoking; and
3 smoking cannabis, cannabis resin or prepared opium.

It is an offence (s.9) for any person to:

1 smoke or otherwise use prepared opium; or
2 frequent a place used for the purpose of opium smoking; or
3 have in his/her possession
   a any pipes or other utensils made or adapted for use in connection with the smoking of opium, being pipes or utensils which have been used by him/her or with his/her knowledge and permission in that connection or which s/he intends to use or permit others to use in that connection, or
   b any utensils which have been used by him/her or with his/her knowledge and permission in connection with the preparation of opium for smoking.

Other offences are described in some detail in Schedule 4. Those relating to contravention of Regulations or of conditions of any licence, or of directions relating to safe custody of Controlled Drugs, are of special concern to practising pharmacists (ss.11 and 18). A person commits an offence if in the UK s/he assists in or induces the commission in any place outside the UK of an offence punishable under the provisions of a corresponding law in force in that place (s.20).

Corresponding law means a law stated, in a certificate purporting to be issued by or on behalf of the government of a country outside the UK, to be a law providing for the control and regulation in that country of the production, supply, use, export and import of (ss.20 and 36):

1 drugs and other substances in accordance with the provisions of the Single Convention on Narcotic Drugs signed at New York on 30 March 1961; or
2 dangerous or otherwise harmful drugs in pursuance of any treaty, convention or other agreement or arrangement to which the government of that country and of the UK are parties.

The unlawful import and export of Controlled Drugs is an offence under the Customs and Excise Management Act 1979, which provides penalties for improper importation or exportation or for fraudulent evasion of any prohibition or restriction affecting Controlled Drugs. Attempting to commit an offence under any provision of the Act or inciting or attempting to incite another to commit such an offence are also offences. They attract the same penalty as the substantive offences (ss.19 and 25).

Where any offence under the Act committed by a body corporate is proved to have been committed with the consent or connivance of, or to be attributable to any neglect on the part of, any director, manager, secretary or other similar officer of the body corporate, or any person purporting to act in any such capacity, s/he, as well as the body corporate, is guilty of the offence and is liable to be proceeded against accordingly (s.21).

Proof that the accused neither knew of nor suspected, nor had reason to suspect, the existence of some fact which it is necessary for the prosecution to prove is a defence in connection with the offences of production, supply or possession of Controlled Drugs, cultivation of cannabis or possession of opium pipes and utensils. When it is necessary, in connection with any offence, to prove that a substance or product is a Controlled Drug, the accused may prove that s/he believed it to be a different Controlled Drug. This, in itself, will not constitute a defence unless there could have been no offence had the drug been of that description (s.28).

It is also a defence for a person accused of unlawful possession of a Controlled Drug to prove that s/he took possession of it to prevent another person committing an offence, and that s/he took steps to destroy it as soon as possible, or that s/he took possession of the drug to hand it over to some authorised person as soon as possible (s.5).

A constable, or other person authorised by the Secretary of State, has power to enter any premises used for the production and supply of Controlled Drugs and inspect books and documents and any stocks of drugs. An inspector of the GPhC is authorised by the Secretary of State to inspect books and documents. It is an offence to conceal any such books, documents or stock.

A constable may also, on the authority of a warrant, enter any premises named in the warrant, by force if necessary, and search them and any person found therein, seizing any Controlled Drug or any document relevant to the transaction if s/he has reasonable grounds to consider that an offence under the Act has been committed (s.23).

A constable may arrest a person who has committed an offence under the Act, or whom s/he suspects has committed an offence, if that person's name and address are unknown to him/her or cannot be ascertained, if s/he suspects the name and address are false or if s/he has reasonable cause to think that the person may abscond unless arrested (s.24). S/he may detain for the purposes of search any person whom s/he has reasonable grounds to suspect is in unlawful possession of a Controlled Drug. S/he may also stop and search any vehicle or vessel for the same reason and may seize anything which appears to be evidence of an offence under the Act (s.23).

It is an offence intentionally to obstruct a person exercising their powers of examination or search. Failure to produce any book or document without reasonable excuse is also an offence, and proof of the reasonableness of the excuse rests with the person offering it as a defence (s.23).

Upon a conviction, anything relating to the offence may be forfeited and destroyed or otherwise dealt with by order of the court, subject to any person claiming to be the owner showing cause why the order should not be made (s.27). The Drug Trafficking Offences Act 1986 provides for the confiscation of the proceeds of drug trafficking received by convicted persons.

Scheduled substances: precursors

Scheduled substances means those substances which are useful for the manufacture of Controlled Drugs.

Council Regulation 90/3677/EEC controls the import, export, recording and labelling of scheduled substances and the power to enter business premises to obtain evidence of irregularities. Records must be kept for 2 years. It also requires EU Member States to adopt measures to enable them to obtain information on any orders for, or activities in, scheduled substances. There is a list of scheduled substances. The EC Regulation was implemented by the Criminal Justice (International Co-operation) Act 1990 (s.12), which created the offences of manufacturing or supplying scheduled substances knowing or suspecting they are to be used in or for the unlawful production of a Controlled Drug. Regulations made under the 1990 Act (s.13) enable the other requirements of the EC Regulation to be investigated and enforced.[7]

Council Directive 92/109/EEC, which is complementary to the above EC Regulation, applies to the manufacture and trade in scheduled substances within the EU and was implemented in the UK in 1993.[8] It requires the person who manufactures or trades in these substances to be licensed and restricts the persons to whom supplies may be made. The 1993 UK Regulations as amended treat the provisions of Council Directive 92/109/EEC as if they were requirements of Regulations made under section 13 of the 1990 Act.

[7]The Controlled Drugs (Drug Precursors)(Community External Trade) Regulations SI 2008 No. 296
[8]The Controlled Drugs (Substances Useful for Manufacture) (Intra–Community Trade) Regulations SI 1993 No. 2166, as amended by SI 2004 No. 850

Powers of the Secretary of State

The power of the Secretary of State to make Regulations is exercised by statutory instruments (ss.7, 10, 22 and 31). Regulations may make provision for different cases and circumstances and for different Controlled Drugs and different classes of person. The opinion, consent or approval of a prescribed authority or of any person may also be made material to a Regulation, for example the approval of a chief officer of police is required in connection with certain safekeeping requirements for drugs (s.31). Any licence or other authority issued by the Secretary of State for the purposes of the Act may be made subject to such conditions as s/he thinks proper and may be modified or revoked at any time (s.30).

The application of any provision of the Act which creates an offence and those provisions of the Customs and Excise Management Act 1979 that apply to the importation and exportation of Controlled Drugs may, in prescribed cases, be excluded by Regulation. Similarly, any provision of the Act or any Regulation or Order made under it may, by Regulation, be made applicable to servants and agents of the Crown (s.22).

Most of the Regulations are designed to render lawful various activities in connection with Controlled Drugs which would otherwise be unlawful under the Act. For example, they are necessary to enable doctors, pharmacists and others to prescribe, administer, manufacture, compound or supply Controlled Drugs as appropriate to their particular capacities. They also govern such matters as the safekeeping of Controlled Drugs and their destruction, the notification of addicts and the supply of Controlled Drugs to addicts.

Regimes of control

The drugs controlled under the Act are classified in the Misuse of Drugs Regulations 2001[9] into five schedules in descending order of control, the most stringent controls applying to drugs in Schedule 1. All the schedules are set out fully in appendix 5 and the controls applying to each are outlined below.

Schedule 1

Schedule 1 lists Controlled Drugs which may not be used for medicinal purposes, their production and possession being limited, in the public interest, to purposes of research or other special purposes. Certain limited classes

[9]The Misuse of Drugs Regulations SI 2001 No. 3998 (as amended; references refer to these Regulations)

of person have a general authority to possess these drugs in the course of their duties, for example constables or carriers (Reg.6). Other persons may only produce, supply or possess the drugs within the authority of a licence issued by the Secretary of State. The requirements of the Misuse of Drugs Regulations relating to (a) documentation, (b) keeping of records, (c) preservation of records, (d) supply on prescription, (e) marking of containers and (f) procedure for destruction apply in full to these drugs in Schedule 1.

Schedule 2

Schedule 2 includes the opiates (such as heroin, morphine and methadone) and the major stimulants (such as the amphetamines). A licence is needed to import or export drugs in this schedule but they may be manufactured or compounded by a practitioner, a pharmacist, a person lawfully conducting a retail pharmacy business acting in their capacity as such, or a person holding an appropriate licence. A pharmacist may supply a Schedule 2 drug to a patient (or the owner of an animal) only on the authority of a prescription in the required form issued by an appropriate practitioner (Regs.15 and 16).

The drugs may only be administered to a patient by a doctor or dentist, or by any person acting in accordance with the directions of a doctor or dentist (Reg.7). Requirements as to safe custody in pharmacies and control over destruction apply to these drugs, and the provisions relating to the marking of containers and the keeping of records, must also be observed (Regs.18 and 19).

Schedule 3

Schedule 3 includes the barbiturates (except quinalbarbitone (secobarbital), which is a Schedule 2 Controlled Drug) and a number of minor stimulant drugs, such as benzphetamine, and other drugs which are not thought likely to be so harmful when misused as the drugs in Schedule 2. The controls which apply to Schedule 2 also apply to drugs in Schedule 3, except that:

1 they may also be manufactured by persons authorised in writing by the Secretary of State;
2 there is a difference in the classes of person who may possess and supply them;
3 the requirements as to destruction do not apply to retail dealers; and
4 entries in a register of Controlled Drugs need not be made in respect of these drugs but invoices or like records must be kept for a period of 2 years (see below).

Schedule 4, Part I

Part I of Schedule 4 contains the benzodiazepine tranquillisers. The restrictions applicable to Schedule 3 drugs apply to these drugs with the relaxations 1 to 5 as given for Schedule 4 Part II drugs below. There is no restriction on imports and exports.

Schedule 4, Part II

Part II of Schedule 4 contains the anabolic and androgenic steroids and derivatives, together with an andrenoceptor stimulant and polypeptide hormones. The restrictions applicable to Schedule 3 drugs apply to them with the following relaxations:

1 there is no restriction on the possession of any Schedule 4 Part II drug when contained in a medicinal product;
2 prescription and labelling requirements under the Misuse of Drugs Act do not apply, but the provisions of the Medicines Act do apply;
3 records need not be kept by retailers;
4 destruction requirements apply only to importers, exporters and manufacturers;
5 there are no safe custody requirements; and
6 there is no restriction on imports or exports provided they are imported or exported by a person for self-administration.

The requirement under 6 above that the drugs specified in Part II of Schedule 4 must be in the form of a medicinal product was removed in 2012.[10]

Schedule 5

Schedule 5 specifies those preparations of certain Controlled Drugs for which there is only negligible risk of abuse. There is no restriction on the import, export, possession or administration of these preparations, and safe custody requirements do not apply to them. A practitioner or pharmacist, acting in his/her capacity as such, or a person holding an appropriate licence, may manufacture or compound any of them.

No record in the register of Controlled Drugs need be made in respect of Schedule 3, 4 or 5 drugs obtained by a retail dealer, but the invoice, or a copy of it, must be kept for 2 years. Producers and wholesale dealers must retain invoices of quantities obtained and supplied (Reg.24(1)). No authority is required to destroy these drugs, and there are no special labelling

[10]The Misuse of Drugs (Amendment No. 2) (England, Wales & Scotland) Regulations SI 2012 No. 973

requirements, although Medicines Act labelling requirements apply. A retail dealer is defined as a person lawfully conducting a retail pharmacy business or a pharmacist engaged in supplying drugs to the public at a NHS health centre.

Poppy-straw

Poppy-straw, which includes poppy heads, is listed as a Controlled Drug in Schedule 2 to the Act, where it is defined as 'all parts, except the seeds, of the opium poppy, after mowing'. It is not included in any of the Schedules to the Regulations. Although a licence is required to import or export poppy-straw, its production, possession and supply are free from control (Reg.4). Concentrate of poppy-straw, which means the material produced when poppy-straw has entered into a process for the concentration of its alkaloids, is included in Schedule 1 to the Regulations to which apply the stringent controls described above.

Import and export

Controlled Drugs may only be imported or exported in accordance with the terms and conditions of a licence issued by the Secretary of State (s.3 of the Act) but drugs in Schedules 4 Part II and Schedule 5 are exempted from this requirement (Reg.4). Drugs in Schedule 4 Part I are subject to certain restrictions (see below). Unlawful import or export is an offence under the Customs and Excise Management Act 1979 (see below).

Possession and supply

It is unlawful for any person to be in possession of a Controlled Drug unless:

1 s/he holds an appropriate licence from or is registered by the Secretary of State (Reg.10);
2 s/he is a member of a class specified in the Regulations and is acting in his/her capacity as a member of that class (Regs.6 and 10); or
3 the Regulations provide that possession of that drug or group of drugs is not unlawful.

Possession of poppy-straw or drugs in Schedule 5 and medicinal products in Schedule 4 are not controlled (Reg.4).

The classes of person who may possess or supply Controlled Drugs are given in table 17.1, with an indication of the range of drugs they may possess and/or supply. A person authorised to supply may supply only those persons authorised to possess, and such supply is subject to any provisions of the Medicines Act 1968 which apply to the drug being supplied.

Table 17.1 Possession and supply of Controlled Drugs

	Class of person	Possession	Supply
1	A person holding an appropriate licence from the Home Office	S1 S2 S3 S4 S5	S1 S2 S3 S4 S5
2	A constable when acting in the course of his/her duty	S1 S2 S3 S4 S5	S1 S2 S3 S4 S5
3	A person engaged in the business of a carrier when acting in the course of that business	S1 S2 S3 S4 S5	S1 S2 S3 S4 S5
4	A person engaged in the business of a postal operator when acting in the course of that business (SI 2003 No. 1653)	S1 S2 S3 S4 S5	S1 S2 S3 S4 S5
5	An officer of Customs and Excise when acting in the course of his/her duty as such	S1 S2 S3 S4 S5	S1 S2 S3 S4 S5
6	A person engaged in the work of any laboratory to which the drug has been sent for forensic examination when acting in the course of his/her duty as a person so engaged	S1 S2 S3 S4 S5	S1 S2 S3 S4 S5
7	A person engaged in conveying the drug to a person authorised by the regulations to have it in his/her possession (see under Requisitions)	S1 S2 S3 S4 S5	S1 S2 S3 S4 S5
8	A person possessing a drug for administration in accordance with the directions of a practitioner (e.g. on a prescription) [The Home Office takes the view that it is unlawful for a doctor to possess a Controlled Drug on the strength of a prescription issued by him/herself and naming him/herself as patient (*Pharm J* 8 October 1977 p. 328)]	S2 S3 S4 S5	
9	A person authorised under a group authority	S2 S3 S4 S5	S2 S3 S4 S5
10	A practitioner	S2 S3 S4 S5	S2 S3 S4 S5
11	A nurse independent prescriber or pharmacist independent prescriber (SI 2012 No. 973)	S2 S3 S4 S5	S2 S3 S4 S5
12	A pharmacist	S2 S3 S4 S5	S2 S3 S4 S5
13	A person lawfully conducting a retail pharmacy business	S2 S3 S4 S5	S2 S3 S4 S5
14	The person in charge or acting person in charge of a hospital or care home which is wholly or mainly maintained by a public authority out of public funds or by a charity or by voluntary subscriptions (c.f. 25 below) may not supply if there is a pharmacist responsible for dispensing and supply of drugs	S2 S3 S4 S5	S2 S3 S4 S5

(continued overleaf)

Table 17.1 *(continued)*

	Class of person	Possession	Supply
15	The senior or acting senior registered nurse for the time being in charge of a ward, theatre or other department in a hospital or care home which is wholly or mainly maintained by a public authority out of public funds or by a charity or by voluntary subscriptions, in the case of drugs supplied to him/her by a person responsible for the dispensing of medicines at the hospital or care home (c.f. 26 below) *Senior* or *acting senior registered nurse* includes any male nurse occupying a similar position Supply subject to direction by doctor or dentist	S2 S3 S4 S5	S2 S3 S4 S5
16	A person who is in charge of a laboratory, the recognised activities of which consist in, or include, the conduct of scientific education or research and which is attached to a university, university college or a hospital as described in 13 or to any other institution approved for the purpose by the Secretary of State (c.f. 27 below)	S2 S3 S4 S5	S2 S3 S4 S5
17	A public analyst appointed under section 89 of the Food and Drugs Act 1955 or section 27 of the Food and Drugs (Scotland) Act 1956	S2 S3 S4 S5	S2 S3 S4 S5
18	A sampling officer within the meaning of the Food and Drugs Act 1955 or the Food and Drugs (Scotland) Act 1956	S2 S3 S4 S5	S2 S3 S4 S5
19	A sampling officer within the meaning of Schedule 3 to the Medicines Act 1968	S2 S3 S4 S5	S2 S3 S4 S5
20	A person employed or engaged in connection with a scheme for testing the quality or amount of the drugs, preparations and appliances supplied under the National Health Service Act 1946 or the National Health Service (Scotland) Act 1947 and the Regulations made thereunder	S2 S3 S4 S5	S2 S3 S4 S5
21	A person authorised by the General Pharmaceutical Council (under Reg.8(2)(c) of the Pharmacy Order 2010) for the purposes of sections 108 and 109 of the Medicines Act 1968	S2 S3 S4 S5	S2 S3 S4 S5
22	The owner or master of a ship (which is not carrying a doctor) for the purposes of complying with the Health and Safety at Work, etc. Act 1974 or the Merchant Shipping Acts. *Master of ship* includes every person (except a pilot) having command or charge of any ship	S2 S3 S4 S5	S2 S3 S4 S5

(continued overleaf)

Table 17.1 *(continued)*

	Class of person	Possession	Supply
23	The master of a foreign ship in port in Great Britain possessing drugs as necessary for the equipment of his/her ship and authorised by the local medical officer of health	S2 S3 S4 S5	
24	The installation manager of an offshore installation possessing drugs for the purpose of compliance with the Health and Safety at Work etc. Act 1974, or the Mineral Workings (Off-Shore Installations) Act 1971. S/he may supply to (a) any person who may lawfully supply the drug; (b) any person on the installation whether employed there or not; (c) any constable for destruction	S2 S3 S4 S5	S2 S3 S4 S5
25	The person in charge or acting person in charge of a hospital or care home (c.f. 13 above). May not supply if there is a pharmacist responsible for dispensing and supply of drugs	S3 S4 S5	S3 S4 S5
26	The senior or acting senior registered nurse for the time being in charge of a ward, theatre or other department in a hospital or care home in the case of drugs supplied to him/her by a person responsible for the dispensing and supply of medicines at the hospital or care home (c.f. 15 above). Supply subject to direction by doctor or dentist	S3 S4 S5	S3 S4 S5
27	A person in charge of a laboratory the recognised activities of which consist in, or include, the conduct of scientific education or research (c.f. 16 above)	S3 S4 S5	S3 S4 S5
28	A person whose name is entered in a register maintained by the Home Office relating to Schedule 3 drugs	S3 S4 S5	S3 S4
29	A person authorised in writing by the Secretary of State	S5	S5
30	Registered practising midwives (see supply to midwives and administration, p. 00) [Reg.11]. Any Controlled Drug s/he may lawfully administer under the Medicines Act Regulations		
31	A person licensed under the Wildlife and Countryside Act 1981	S2 S3	S2 S3

(continued overleaf)

	Class of person	Possession	Supply
	Table 17.1 *(continued)*		
32	A registered nurse (SI 2003 No. 2429)		A registered nurse may supply in accordance with a Patient Group Direction any drug specified in Schedule 4 and 5 to a person who can lawfully possess that drug except anabolic steroids or any preparation for injection
33	A registered nurse (SI 2003 No. 2429)		A registered nurse may supply in accordance with a Patient Group Direction diamorphine for the treatment of cardiac pain to a person admitted as a patient to a coronary care unit or an accident and emergency department of a hospital
34	A supplementary prescriber (SI 2005 No. 271)		A supplementary prescriber may administer a Controlled Drug when acting in accordance with the terms of a clinical management plan without the directions of a doctor or dentist

Standard operating procedures

All healthcare providers including retail pharmacies must have up-to-date standard operating procedures in place[11] that cover the following:

1 who has access to Controlled Drugs;
2 where Controlled Drugs are stored;
3 security in relation to the storage and transportation of Controlled Drugs, as required by the legislation;
4 disposal and destruction of Controlled Drugs;
5 record keeping, including
   a maintaining relevant registers of Controlled Drugs under the legislation, and
   b maintaining a record of Controlled Drugs specified in Schedule 2 to the Misuse of Drugs Regulation 2001 as amended and that have been returned from patients together with details of name and address of patient and method and date of destruction (see below);
6 who is to be alerted if complications arise which may include details of when and how the relevant accountable officer should be informed of incidents.

[11] The Controlled Drugs (Supervision of Management and Use) Regulations SI 2006 No. 3148

Other general authorities to possess and supply include:

1 any person who is lawfully in possession of a Controlled Drug may supply that drug to the person from whom s/he obtained it;

2 any person who is in possession of a Schedule 2, 3, 4 or 5 drug which has been supplied for him/her by, or on the prescription of, a practitioner may supply that drug to any doctor, dentist or pharmacist for the purpose of destruction;

3 any person who is in lawful possession of a Schedule 2, 3, 4 or 5 drug which has been supplied by, or on the prescription of, a veterinary surgeon or veterinary practitioner for the treatment of animals may supply that drug to any veterinary surgeon, veterinary practitioner or pharmacist for the purpose of destruction;

4 any of the following persons may supply or administer a specified Controlled Drug under a Patient Group Direction (PGD):

  a a person who holds a certificate of proficiency in ambulance paramedic skills issued by, or with the approval of, the Secretary of State or a person who is a state registered paramedic,

  b a registered health visitor,

  c a registered midwife,

  d a registered optometrist,

  e a state registered chiropodist,

  f a person who is registered in the Register of Orthoptists under the Health Professions Council,

  g a person who is registered in the Register of Physiotherapists under the Health Professions Council, or

  h a person who is registered in the Register of Radiographers under the Health Professions Council.

Midwives and pethidine

A registered midwife who has, in accordance with the Nurses, Midwives and Health Visitors Act 1997, notified to the local supervising authority his/her intention to practise may, as far as is necessary for the practice of his/her profession or employment as a midwife, possess and administer any Controlled Drug which the Medicines Act 1968 permits him/her to administer. Supplies may only be made to him/her, or possessed by him/her, on the authority of a midwife's supply order, that is, an order in writing specifying the name and occupation of the midwife obtaining the Controlled Drug, the purpose for which it is required and the total quantity to be obtained (Reg.11[12]). It must be signed by the appropriate medical officer, which means:

[12]References now revert to the Misuse of Drugs Regulations 2011 except where stated

1 a doctor who is for the time being authorised in writing for the purpose of Regulation 11 by the local supervising authority for the region or area in which the Controlled Drug was, or is to be, obtained; or
2 a person appointed by that authority to exercise supervision over certified midwives within their area, e.g. a non-medical supervisor of midwives.

A midwife may surrender any stocks of Controlled Drugs in his/her possession which are no longer required by him/her to a doctor falling within category 1 above (Reg.11) or to the person from whom s/he obtained them (Reg.6).

The midwife must, on each occasion on which s/he obtains a supply of a Controlled Drug, enter in a book kept by him/her solely for this purpose, (a) the date and (b) the name and address of the person from whom the drug was obtained, the amount obtained and the form in which it was obtained. When administering any Controlled Drug to a patient, s/he must enter in the same book as soon as practicable the name and address of the patient, the amount administered and the form in which it was administered (Reg.21). A midwife's supply order must be retained for 2 years by the pharmacist who supplies the Controlled Drug and s/he must make an appropriate entry in his/her register of Controlled Drugs (Regs.19 and 22).

Requisitions

Standard requisition forms are now produced by the NHS but there is no legal requirement for them to be used. If a non-standard requisition form is used, all the legal requirements must be complied with. The requisition must be signed by the recipient, state his/her name, address and profession or occupation, and must specify the total quantity of the drug and the purpose for which it is required.

A requisition in writing must be obtained by a supplier before s/he delivers any Controlled Drug except those in Schedules 4 and 5, poppy-straw or any drug in Schedule 3 contained in or comprising a preparation which (a) is required for use as a buffering agent in chemical analysis, (b) has present both a substance in the Schedule and a salt of that substance, and (c) is pre-mixed in a kit (Reg.14(7)). A supplier, in this context, means any person who is not a practitioner supplying such a Controlled Drug, otherwise than on prescription, or by way of administration, to any of the following recipients:

1 a practitioner;
2 the person in charge or acting person in charge of a hospital or care home;
3 a person who is in charge of a laboratory;
4 the owner of a ship, or the master of a ship which does not carry a doctor among the seamen employed in it;

5 the master of a foreign ship in a port in Great Britain;

6 the installation manager of an off-shore installation (Reg.14(4));

7 a supplementary prescriber;[13]

8 a nurse independent prescriber;

9 a pharmacist independent prescriber;[14]

10 a senior or acting senior registered nurse in charge of a ward, department or care home who obtains supply from the hospital; the requisition must be maintained in the dispensary and a copy left with the nurse; and

11 an operating department practitioner, who can obtain from the pharmacy in his/her hospital.

The recipient must mark the requisition with the suppliers name and address, keep a copy for 2 years and send the original documents to the NHS Business Services Authority. This also applies to the non-standard forms.

A wholesale dealer, that is, a person who carries on the business of selling drugs to persons who buy to sell again, when supplying a pharmacist does not require a requisition. The supplier must be reasonably satisfied that the signature is that of the person purporting to have signed the requisition and that s/he is engaged in the profession or occupation stated (Reg.14(2)).

Where a supplier, who is not a practitioner, supplies a Controlled Drug for which a requisition is required, s/he may not supply it to any person sent on behalf of the recipient to collect the drug unless that person (a) is authorised to have the drug in his/her possession, otherwise than as a messenger; or (b) produces to the supplier a statement in writing signed by the recipient to the effect that s/he is empowered by the recipient to receive the drug on his/her behalf, and the supplier is reasonably satisfied that the document is genuine (Reg.14(1)).

Where a recipient is a practitioner who represents that s/he urgently requires a Controlled Drug for the purpose of his/her profession, the supplier, if s/he is reasonably satisfied that the practitioner requires the drug and is by reason of some emergency unable to furnish a written requisition, may deliver the drug on an undertaking by the practitioner to furnish a written requisition within the next 24 hours. Failure to do so is an offence on the part of the practitioner (Reg.14(2)).

A requisition furnished by the master of a foreign ship must contain a statement that the quantity of drug to be supplied is the quantity necessary for the equipment of the ship (Reg.14(5)) signed by the proper officer of the port health authority or, in Scotland, the medical officer designated under section 14 of the National Health Service (Scotland) Act 1978 by the health board within whose jurisdiction the ship is.

---

[13] The Misuse of Drugs (Amendment) (No. 2) Regulations SI 2003 No. 1653
[14] The Misuse of Drugs (Amendment) Regulations SI 2005 No. 271

A requisition furnished by the matron or acting matron of a hospital or care home must also be signed by a doctor or a dentist employed or engaged in that hospital or care home (Reg.14(5)).

A senior or acting senior registered nurse for the time being in charge of any ward, theatre or other department of a hospital or care home who obtains a supply of a Controlled Drug from the person responsible for dispensing and supplying medicines at that hospital or care home must furnish a requisition in writing signed by him/her which specifies the total quantity of the drug required. S/he must retain a copy or note of the requisition. The person responsible for the dispensing and supply of medicines must mark the requisition in such a manner as to show that it has been complied with and must retain the requisition in the dispensary (Reg.14(6)).

Prescriptions for Controlled Drugs

Prescription means a prescription used by a doctor for the medical treatment of a single individual, by a dentist for the dental treatment of a single individual, a nurse independent prescriber for the medical treatment of a single individual, a pharmacist independent prescriber for the medical treatment of a single individual or by a veterinary surgeon or veterinary practitioner for the purposes of animal treatment. No prescription requirements are laid down for any Controlled Drug in Schedules 4 or 5 to the Regulations except for temazepam.

A person shall not issue a prescription other than a health prescription or a veterinary prescription for temazepam unless it is written on a prescription form provide by a PCT or equivalent body for the purpose of private prescribing and it specifies the identification number and address of the person issuing it.[15] In the case of other Controlled Drugs (i.e. those in Schedules 2 and 3), a prescription must not be issued unless it complies with the following requirements:

1 be written so as to be indelible, be dated and be signed by the person issuing it with his/her usual signature and dated by him/her (it is unlikely that a carbon copy, even one bearing an original signature would be sufficient to satisfy the indelibility requirement);[16]
2 except in the case of a health prescription, it must specify the address of the person issuing it;
3 it must have written thereon, if issued by a dentist, the words '*for dental treatment only*' and, if issued by a veterinary surgeon or a veterinary practitioner, a declaration that the Controlled Drug prescribed is for an animal under his/her care;

[15] The Misuse of Drugs (Amendment No. 2) Regulations SI 2006 No. 1450
[16] The Misuse of Drugs and the Misuse of Drugs (Supply to Addicts) (Amendment) Regulations SI 2006 No. 2864

4 it must specify the name and address of the person for whose treatment it is issued or, if it is issued by a veterinary surgeon or veterinary practitioner, the name and address of the person to whom the Controlled Drug prescribed is to be delivered;

5 it must specify the dose to be taken, and

   a in the case of a prescription containing a Controlled Drug which is a preparation, it must specify the form and, where appropriate, the strength of the preparation, and either the total quantity (in both words and figures) of the preparation or the number (in both words and figures) of dosage units, as appropriate, to be supplied,

   b in any other case, it must specify the total quantity (in both words and figures) of the Controlled Drug to be supplied; and

6 in the case of a prescription for a total quantity intended to be dispensed by instalments, it must contain a direction specifying the amount of the instalments of the total amount which must be dispensed and the intervals to be observed when dispensing (Reg.15(1)).

A prescription issued for the treatment of a patient in a hospital or care home and written on the patient's bed card or case sheet need not specify the address of the patient (Reg.15(3)). When a drug is administered from stock held in the ward, the prescription requirements do not apply.

A Controlled Drug, except those in Schedules 4 and 5, must not be supplied by any person on a prescription (Reg.15):

1 unless the prescription complies with the provisions set out above;

2 unless the prescriber's address on the prescription is within the UK;

3 unless the supplier is either acquainted with the prescriber's signature, and has no reason to suppose that it is not genuine, or has taken reasonably sufficient steps to satisfy him/herself that it is genuine;

4 before the date specified on the prescription; and

5 later than 28 days after the date specified on the prescription unless it is an instalment prescription (see below).[17]

Prescriptions (other than those for drugs in Sch. 4 or Sch. 5) which contain a direction that specified instalments of the total amount may be supplied at stated intervals must not be supplied otherwise than in accordance with the directions (Regs.16 (4) and 23 (3)):

1 the first instalment must be supplied not later than 13 weeks after the date specified in the prescription;

2 the prescription must be marked with the date at the time when each instalment is supplied;

3 the prescription must be retained for 2 years after the supply of the last instalment; and

4 repeat prescriptions as such are not provided for, in that the total quantity of drug prescribed must be stated on the prescription.

[17]The Misuse of Drugs (Amendment No. 2) Regulations SI 2006 No. 1450

A pharmacist may supply a Controlled Drug if the prescription contains minor typographical errors or spelling mistakes or if it does not comply with the provisions of Regulation 15 provided that:[18]

1 having exercised all due diligence, s/he is satisfied on reasonable grounds that the prescription is genuine;
2 having exercised all due diligence, s/he is satisfied on reasonable grounds that the supply of the drug is in accordance with the intention of the person issuing the prescription;
3 s/he amends the prescription in ink or otherwise indelibly to correct the minor errors or mistakes or so that the prescription complies with the Regulation 15 requirements;
4 s/he marks the prescription so that the amendment s/he has made is attributable to her/him; and
5 items 1–4 above apply if the total quantity or number of doses is specified in either words or figures but not if both words and figures are missing.

EEA prescribers, who are appropriate practitioners within the meaning of section 58(2)(a) of the Medicines Act 1968 may give prescriptions for Controlled Drugs in Schedules 4 or 5 only.[19]

A person supplying temazepam in accordance with an electronic prescription shall at the time of supply enter on the form by electronic means the date on which the drug was supplied.[20]

A person who is asked to supply a Controlled Drug specified in Schedule 2 must first ascertain whether the person collecting the drug is the patient, the patient's representative or a healthcare professional acting in his/her professional capacity:[21]

1 where the person is the patient or the patient's representative, s/he may (a) request evidence of identity, or (b) refuse to supply if he is not satisfied as to identity; and
2 where the person is a healthcare professional, s/he may (a) request the identity of the person, (b) obtain that person's name and address or (c) supply even if not satisfied as to identity.

A copy of every prescription other than a health or veterinary prescription must be sent to the relevant NHS service agency.

Nothing in the Regulations relating to prescriptions (Regs.15 and 16) has effect in relation to prescriptions issued for the purposes of a scheme for testing the quality and amount of the drugs, preparations and appliances supplied under the NHS or to any prescriptions issued to sampling officers under the Food and Drugs (Scotland) Act 1956 or the Medicines Act 1968 (Reg.17).

[18] The Misuse of Drugs (Amendment No. 2) Regulations SI 2006 No. 1450
[19] The Medicines for Human Use (Prescribing by EEA Practitioners) (Amendment) (No. 2) Regulations SI 2010 No. 2785
[20] The Misuse of Drugs Regulations SI 2001 Reg.16(3)
[21] The Misuse of Drugs (Amendment No. 2) Regulations SI 2006 Reg.6

A person is not in lawful possession of a drug if s/he obtained it on a prescription which s/he obtained from the prescriber (a) by making a false statement or declaration or (b) by not disclosing to the doctor that s/he was being supplied with a Controlled Drug by or on the prescription of another doctor (Reg.10(2)).

Marking of containers

The container in which a Controlled Drug, other than a preparation, is supplied must be plainly marked with the amount of drug contained in it. If the drug is a preparation made up into tablets, capsules or other dosage units, the container must be marked with the amount of Controlled Drug(s) in each dosage unit and the number of dosage units in it. For any other kind of preparation, the container must be marked with the total amount of the preparation in it and the percentage of Controlled Drug(s) in the preparation (Reg.18(1)). These requirements do not apply to (a) poppy-straw, (b) Controlled Drugs in Schedules 4 and 5, (c) Controlled Drugs supplied on the prescription of a practitioner or for administration in a clinical trial or a medicinal test on animals, or (d) any Schedule 3 drug in a preparation used as a buffering agent in chemical analysis or which has present in it both a substance in that Schedule and a salt of that substance or is pre-mixed in a kit (Reg.18(2), as amended).

Registers and records

There is no statutory format for the register provided the following information is recorded. However the National Pharmacy Association does produce a register which complies with the requirements.

Register means either a bound book, which does not include any form of loose-leaf register or card index (Reg.2), or a computerised system which is in accordance with best practice guidelines endorsed by the Secretary of State for Health.[22]

Minimum information to be recorded regarding Controlled Drugs obtained

An entry in a register of Controlled Drugs must be made in respect of every quantity of any drug in Schedules 1 and 2 which is obtained or supplied (whether by way of administration or otherwise), the name and address of the supplier and the date received. This requirement applies to any person authorised to supply those drugs except a senior or acting senior registered nurse for the time being in charge of a ward, theatre or other department in a hospital or care home, or a person licensed to supply by the Secretary of State if the licence does not require a register to be kept (Reg.19).

[22] The Misuse of Drugs and the Misuse of Drugs (Supply to Addicts) (Amendment) Regulations SI 2005 No. 2864

Minimum information to be recorded regarding Controlled Drugs supplied

The following information must be recorded:

1 date supplied;
2 name and address of person supplied;
3 quantity of drug supplied;
4 person collecting Schedule 2 drug, for example patient/representative or name and address of healthcare professional collecting (see below); and
5 proof of identity of person collecting Controlled Drugs requested or obtained (Yes/No).

In the case of a drug on the schedules supplied on a prescription, an entry should be made as to whether the person who has collected the drug was the patient, the patient's representative or a healthcare professional acting on behalf of the patient (Reg.6 of 2006 Regulations) and:

a if the person who collected the drugs was a healthcare professional acting of behalf of the patient, that person's name and address; or
b if the person who collected the drugs was the patient or the patient's representative, whether evidence of identity was requested of that person and whether evidence of identity was provided by that person.

Nothing prevents the use of the register to record additional information to that required or allowed under these provisions. Entries in the register must be made in chronological sequence. A separate register or separate part of the register must be used in respect of each class of drugs. A separate page should be used in respect of each strength and form of that drug and the head of each such page should specify the class of the drug, its strength and form.[23] Dexamphetamine, for example, may be entered under amphetamine, but a separate part of the register is required for methylamphetamine. Separate sections can be used, if desired, in respect of different drugs or different strengths of a drug falling within the same class (Reg.19).

The class of drugs recorded must be specified at the head of each page of the register and entries must be made on the day of the transaction or the following day. No cancellation, obliteration or alteration of any entry may be made, and corrections must be by way of marginal notes or footnotes, which must be dated. Every entry and every correction of such an entry must be in ink or be otherwise indelible or shall be in a computerised form in which every entry is attributable and capable of being audited and which is in accordance with best practice guidelines endorsed by the Secretary of State.[24]

[23] The Misuse of Drugs and Misuse of Drugs (Safe Custody) (Amendment) Regulations SI 2007 No. 2154
[24] Misuse of Drugs and the Misuse of Drugs (Supply to Addicts) (Amendment) Regulations 2005 (SI 2005 No.2864), reg.10

A register must not be used for any other purpose and must be kept at the premises to which it relates, and where the register is in a computerised form, it must be accessible from those premises. A separate register must be kept in respect of each set of premises of the business. There may only be one such register for each premises unless the Secretary of State has approved the keeping of separate registers in different departments (Reg.20).

Where a supply is made to a member of the crew of a ship or a person on an off-shore installation, an entry, specifying the drug, in the official log book or installation log book is a sufficient record. These books are required to be kept under the Merchant Shipping Acts. In the case of a ship which is not required to carry an official log book, a report signed by the master of the ship is sufficient if it is delivered as soon as may be to the superintendent of a mercantile marine office.

Return of Controlled Drugs from patients

A pharmacist or practitioner need not legally record any prescribed drug returned to him/her for destruction, but good pharmaceutical practice would suggest that an entry is made in the drugs register giving the date of receipt; quantity, strength and name of the Controlled Drug; name and address of person who returned the stock; and the date of destruction (see below). Standard operating procedures should be available for these returns from patients and relate to the above information and details of storage and destruction.

Running balances

At present there is no legal requirement to keep running balances. However, it is strongly recommended that they be kept in accordance with a standard operating procedure pending future legislation.

Furnishing of information

Particulars of stocks, receipts and supplies of Controlled Drugs must be furnished on request to any person authorised in writing by the Secretary of State. The register, the stocks of drugs and other relevant books and documents must also be produced if requested (Reg.25). If records are held in a computerised form, a copy of the computerised form must be supplied if requested.[25] Inspectors of the GPhC are authorised for this purpose in relation to registered pharmacies. Those required to furnish information are:

1 practitioners;
2 wholesale dealers;
3 retail dealers;

[25] The Misuse of Drugs and the Misuse of Drugs (Supply to Addicts) (Amendment) Regulations SI 2005 No. 2864

4 persons in charge of hospitals, care homes or laboratories;

5 persons authorised under the Act or Regulations to produce, import or export any Controlled Drug;

6 persons authorised under Regulation 9(4)(a) to supply drugs in Schedules 3 and 4 (Reg.26(2));

7 supplementary prescribers;[26] and

8 nurse independent prescribers.[27]

Professional personal records relating to the physical or mental health of an individual are exempt.

Preservation of records

All registers and midwives' record books must be preserved for 2 years from the date on which the last entry is made therein. Every requisition, order or prescription (other than a health prescription) on which a Controlled Drug is supplied must be preserved for 2 years from the date on which the last delivery is made (Reg.23).

For Controlled Drugs in Schedules 3 and 5 to the Regulations, it is sufficient if every invoice is preserved for 2 years from the date on which it is issued. Producers and wholesalers must keep invoices in respect of Schedule 3 and 5 drugs obtained or supplied by them, and retail dealers must keep invoices in respect of the drugs they obtain. Copies of invoices (e.g. on microfilm) may be retained in place of the original document (Reg.24).

Destruction of Controlled Drugs

Persons who are required to keep records in respect of Controlled Drugs in Schedules 1, 2, 3 or 4 may only destroy them in the presence of a person authorised by the Secretary of State either personally or as a member of a class. Among the classes of authorised person for this purpose are police officers, inspectors of the Home Office and of the GPhC and, for stock kept in a hospital, the regional pharmaceutical officer or the senior administrative officer employed on duties connected with the administration of the hospital concerned (see Role of Accountable Officers, below). An Accountable Officer cannot be an authorised person.

Particulars of the date of destruction and the quantity destroyed must be entered in the register of Controlled Drugs and signed by the authorised person in whose presence the drug was destroyed. The authorised person may take a sample of the drug which is to be destroyed, and destruction must be carried out according to his/her directions.

[26]The Misuse of Drugs (Amendment) Regulations SI 2005 No. 271
[27]The Misuse of Drugs (Amendment No. 2) (England, Wales and Scotland) Regulations SI 2012 No. 973

A pharmacist or practitioner may destroy prescribed drugs returned by a patient or the patient's representative without legally being required to make any record and without the presence of an authorised person (but see registers and records above).

The master of a ship or installation manager of an off-shore installation may not destroy any surplus drugs but may dispose of them to a constable or to a person who is lawfully entitled to supply them (i.e. to any pharmacist or licensed dealer who could have supplied them to him/her) (Reg.26).

Accountable Officers

Regulations made under the Health Act 2006[28] introduced the concept of an accountable officer as the final amendment to the legislation following the *Shipman Report* (chapter 25).[29]

Accountable officer means a fit, proper and suitable experienced person appointed or nominated by a designated body to ensure the safe, appropriate and effective management and use of Controlled Drugs within organisations subject to their oversight.

A designated body (i.e. a trust or heath board) must nominate or appoint an accountable officer who is responsible to its registered manager and is not involved in the management or use of Controlled Drugs themselves. The accountable officer must have regard to:

1 best practice, and establish and operate, or ensure that his designated body establishes and operates, the safe management and use of Controlled Drugs by his designated body;
2 ensuring that a body or person acting on behalf or providing services under arrangements made with his designated body establishes and operates appropriate arrangements for securing the safe management and use of Controlled Drugs;
3 ensuring that his designated body or those providing services have up-to-date standard operating procedures in place in relation to the management and use of Controlled Drugs; such standard operating procedures must comply with the statutory requirements (see above);
4 ensuring adequate destruction and disposal of Controlled Drugs and appoint authorised persons for this;
5 ensuring monitoring and auditing of Controlled Drugs;
6 ensuring adequate training of persons handling Controlled Drugs;
7 ensuring the monitoring and audit and use of Controlled Drugs by individuals and ensure their performance;

[28] The Controlled Drugs (Supervision of Management and Use) Regulations SI 2006 No. 3148
[29] The Department of Health issued a consultation in October 2012 on changes to these Regulations to anticipate the changes in NHS structure in England from April 2013

8 maintaining a record of concerns regarding individuals; and
9 sharing information with trusts, GPhC, police, etc.

Accountable officers have the right of access, carry out periodic inspections of premises, investigate concerns and take action if there are well-founded concerns. Accountable officers must make annual reports to their designated body, always act to protect the safety of patients and the general public and are immune from civil action when sharing information if disclosure is made in good faith.

Substance misusers

There are separate Regulations relating to addicts and the supply of certain Controlled Drugs to them although amendments also appear in a number SIs cited above.[30] A person is regarded as being addicted to a drug 'if, and only if, s/he has, as a result of repeated administration, become so dependent on a drug that s/he has an overpowering desire for the administration of it to be continued'. The expression drug in this context means those specified in the Regulations namely:

1 cocaine, dextromoramide, diamorphine, dipipanone, hydrocodone, hydromorphone, levorphanol, methadone, morphine, opium, oxycodone, pethidine, phenazocine and piritramide;
2 any stereoisomeric form of a substance specified in item 1 above, except dextrorphan;
3 any ester or ether of a substance specified in items 1 or 2 above not being a substance for the time being specified in Part II of Schedule 2 to the Misuse of Drugs Act 1971;
4 any salt of a substance specified in any of items 1 to 3 above; and
5 any preparation or other product containing a substance or product specified in any of items 1 to 4 above.

Except for the treatment of organic injury or disease or unless s/he is licensed so to do by the Secretary of State, no doctor, nurse independent prescriber or pharmacist independent prescriber may administer or authorise the supply of cocaine, diamorphine or dipipanone, or the salts of any of these, to an addicted person.[31]

There is provision for addicts to receive daily supplies of cocaine, heroin, dextromoramide, dipipanone, methadone and pethidine on special prescription forms (FP(10)HP) issued by drug addiction clinics. There is also provision for supplies of all Schedule 2 Controlled Drugs for the treatment

[30] The Misuse of Drugs (Supply to Addicts) Regulations SI 1997 No. 1001 (as amended)
[31] Added by The Misuse of Drugs (Amendment No. 2) (England, Wales and Scotland) Regulations SI 2012 No. 973

of addiction to be issued by general medical practitioners on special prescription forms (FP (10) MDA or in Scotland GP 10). These are administrative arrangements made under the NHS and do not form part of the Misuse of Drugs Regulations.

Safe custody of Controlled Drugs

The Regulations relating to safe custody apply to all Controlled Drugs with the following exceptions:[32]

1   any drug in Schedules 4 and 5;
2   any liquid preparations, apart from injections, which contain any of the following
    a   amphetamine
    b   benzphetamine
    c   chlorphentermine
    d   fenethylline
    e   mephentermine
    f   methaqualone
    g   methylamphetamine
    h   methylphenidate;
3   any of the following
    a   cathine
    b   ethchlorvynol
    c   ethinamate
    d   mazindol
    e   meprobamate
    f   methylphenobarbitone (methylphenobarbital)
    g   methyprylone
    h   pentazocine
    i   phentermine
    j   any 5,5-disubstituted barbituric acid
    k   any stereoisomeric form of a substance specified in a to j above
    l   any salt of a substance specified in a–k above; and any preparation or other product containing a substance or product specified in a–k above.

The premises to which the safe custody requirements apply are:

1   any premises occupied by a retail dealer for the purposes of his/her business;
2   any care home within the meaning of Part VI of the Public Health Act 1936 or the Care Homes Registration (Scotland) Act 1938;

[32] The Misuse of Drugs (Safe Custody) Regulations SI 1973 No. 798 (as amended)

3 any residential or other establishment provided under or by virtue of section 59 of the Social Work (Scotland) Act 1968;

4 any mental care home within the meaning of Part III of the Mental Health Act 1959; and

5 any private hospital within the meaning of the Mental Health (Scotland) Act 1960

The occupier and every person concerned in the management of any of these premises must ensure that all Controlled Drugs (except those mentioned above) are, so far as circumstances permit, kept in a locked safe, cabinet or room which is so constructed and maintained as to prevent unauthorised access to the drugs. This requirement does not apply in respect of any Controlled Drug which is for the time being constantly under the direct personal supervision of:

a a pharmacist in the premises of a retail dealer (e.g. when dispensing prescriptions); or

b the person in charge of the premises or any member of his/her staff designated by him/her for the purpose in the case of other premises to which the Regulations apply.

The relevant requirements which apply to safes, cabinets and rooms where Controlled Drugs are kept are in Schedule 2 to the Regulations.

The owner of a pharmacy may, as an alternative, elect to apply to the police for a certificate that his/her safes, cabinets or rooms provide an adequate degree of security. Applications must be made in writing. After inspection by the police, and if the degree of security is found to be adequate, a certificate, renewable annually, may be issued. The certificate will specify conditions to be observed and may be cancelled if there is a breach of any condition, if the occupier has refused entry to a police officer or if there has been any change of circumstances lowering the degree of security.

Quite apart from these special requirements, which affect only certain classes of premises, a person having possession of any Controlled Drug to which the safe custody Regulations apply must ensure that, as far as circumstances permit, it is kept in a locked receptacle which can be opened only by him/her or by a person authorised by him/her. This requirement does not apply to a carrier in the course of his/her business or to a person engaged in the business of the Post Office when acting in the course of that business, or to a person to whom the drug has been supplied on the prescription of a practitioner for his/her own treatment or that of another person or an animal.

Summary

Table 17.2 summarises Controlled Drugs legislation.

Table 17.2 Summary of the Misuse of Drugs Regulations

	Schedule 1	Schedule 2	Schedule 3	Schedule 4, Part I	Schedule 4, Part II	Schedule 5
Administration	By licence only	To a patient by a doctor, dentist, supplementary prescriber, nurse independent prescriber or pharmacist independent prescriber, or by any person acting in accordance with the directions of a doctor, dentist, supplementary prescriber, nurse independent prescriber or pharmacist independent prescriber	To a patient by a doctor, dentist, supplementary prescriber, nurse independent prescriber or pharmacist independent prescriber, or by any person acting in accordance with the directions of a doctor, dentist, supplementary prescriber, nurse independent prescriber or pharmacist independent prescriber	To a patient by a doctor, dentist, supplementary prescriber, nurse independent prescriber or pharmacist independent prescriber, or by any person acting in accordance with the directions of a doctor, dentist, supplementary prescriber, nurse independent prescriber or pharmacist independent prescriber	To a patient by a doctor, dentist, supplementary prescriber, nurse independent prescriber or pharmacist independent prescriber, or by any person acting in accordance with the directions of a doctor, dentist, supplementary prescriber, nurse independent prescriber or pharmacist independent prescriber	No restriction
Import and export	By licence only	By licence only	By licence only	No restriction when contained in a medicinal product	No restriction	No restriction
Possession	By licence only	See under Possession and supply (p. 000)	See under Possession and supply (p. 000)	No restriction	No restriction	No restriction
Supply	By licence only	See under Possession and supply (p. 000)	See under Possession and supply (p. 000)	See under Possession and supply (p. 000)	See under Possession and supply (p. 000)	See under Possession and supply (p. 000)
Emergency supply	No	No	No, except phenobarbital for epilepsy	Yes	Yes	Yes

Table 17.2 (*continued*)

	Schedule 1	Schedule 2	Schedule 3	Schedule 4, Part I	Schedule 4, Part II	Schedule 5
Production	By licence only	Licence holders, pharmacists, practitioners and owners of pharmacies	Licence holders, authorised persons, pharmacists, practitioners and owners of pharmacies	Licence holders, authorised persons, pharmacists, practitioners and owners of pharmacies	Licence holders, authorised persons, pharmacists, practitioners and owners of pharmacies	Licence holders, pharmacists, practitioners and owners of pharmacies
Prescription requirements	By licensed persons only	Yes	Yes, except temazepam	Do not apply	Do not apply	Do not apply
Register	Yes	Yes	No register, but records to be kept by licensed and authorised persons; invoices to be kept by retail dealers, wholesalers, hospitals, care homes and laboratories	No register, but licensed producers and authorised suppliers must keep records of imports and exports	No register, but licensed producers and authorised suppliers must keep records of imports and exports	No register, but licensed producers, wholesalers, and retail dealers must keep invoices

Table 17.2 (continued)

	Schedule 1	Schedule 2	Schedule 3	Schedule 4, Part I	Schedule 4, Part II	Schedule 5
Labelling requirements	Yes	Yes	Yes	No	No	No
Destruction requirements	Yes	Yes, but do not apply to drugs returned by patients	Apply only to imports, exports, and licensed manufacturers	Apply only to imports, exports and licensed manufacturers	Apply only to imports, exports and licensed manufacturers	Do not apply
Safe custody requirements	Yes, except quinalbarbital [secobarbital]	Yes (except certain liquids, quinalbarbital [secobarbital] and temazepam) (see p. 000)	No (except temazepam buprenorphine and diethylpropion) (see p. 000)	No	No	No
Requisition requirements	Yes	Yes	No	No	No	No

Further reading

National Prescribing Centre (2009 updated October 2010) *A Guide to Good Practice in the Management of Controlled Drugs in Primary Care, England*, 3rd edn. Liverpool: National Prescribing Centre.

Royal Pharmaceutical Society (published annually). *Medicines Ethics and Practice: The Professional Guide for Pharmacists*. London: Royal Pharmaceutical Society (includes practice guidance on many of the topics in this chapter; free to members).

Websites

Legislation (can be searched on year and SI number or title): http://www.legislation.gov.uk

Royal Pharmaceutical Society: http://www.rpharms.com (member access only; lists legal classifications of medicines and further practice guidance are included).

National Prescribing Centre (guides and reports on Controlled Drugs in prisons, ambulance and paramedic services and private prescribing as well as a handbook for accountable officers): http://www.npc.co.uk

18

Poisons

Karen Pitchford

Review of Poisons legislation

In April 2011, the government introduced a 'Red Tape Challenge, aimed at reducing the overall burden of regulation, across a range of areas. Poisons legislation was considered as part of the Retail spotlight theme and, following the review, a commitment was made to improve aspects of the legislation. As this book went to press, the Home Office were in the process of reconstituting the Poisons Board (see below), which had not previously met since 1993. Hence, changes to Poisons legislation may be expected but the potential form and content of these changes are not clear at the time of going to press.

Legal framework

The Poisons Act 1972 and the Poison Rules (SI 1982 No. 218, as amended) made under it are concerned with the sale of poisons. The Poisons Act does not extend to Northern Ireland.

A poison means a non-medicinal poison (Rule 2) and is defined in the Act (s.11) as a substance which is included in Part I or Part II of the Poisons List Order,[1] made under the Act, and which is neither a medicinal product as defined under Regulation 2 of the Human Medicines Regulations 2012[2] nor a substance which is treated as a medicinal product by virtue of an Order made under section 104 or section 105 of the Medicines Act (chapter 2) nor a veterinary medicinal product as defined by Regulation 2 of the Veterinary Medicines Regulations 2006[3] (chapter 16).

Other definitions within the Poisons Act include *the board* (s.11); this means, in relation to a body corporate, persons controlling the body by whatever name it is called (e.g. the management committee of a co-operative

---

[1] The Poisons List Order SI 1982 No. 217
[2] Human Medicines Regulations SI 2012 No. 1916
[3] Veterinary Medicines Regulations SI 2011 No. 2159

society). The Act also follows the definitions of the Medicines Act for 'persons lawfully conducting a retail pharmacy business' and a 'registered pharmacy' (chapter 5). A more restricted meaning is given to 'sale by way of wholesale dealing'; in relation to poisons, this means sale to a person who buys for the purpose of selling again (chapter 10).

Meaning of poison

Three cases concerned the interpretation of certain sections of the Pharmacy Act 1868 (now repealed). It was held by the High Court that a compound containing a poison, as well as the actual poison, was subject to the Act. The principal point at issue was the meaning of the word *poison* as used in that Act and similarly used in the current Poisons Act 1972. Further detail of these earlier cases can be found *in Pharmacy Law and Ethics*, 8th edition.

The Poisons Board

The Act (s.1) provides for the continuation of an advisory committee first established under the Pharmacy and Poisons Act 1933 called the Poisons Board. It consists of at least 16 members and the Secretary of State has powers to appoint up to three additional members if s/he thinks fit. The board must include five persons appointed by 'the Council of the Pharmaceutical Society of Great Britain' (words taken from statute), of whom one shall be a person engaged in the manufacture for sale by way of wholesale dealing of pharmaceutical preparations. Since the Royal Pharmaceutical Society of Great Britain (RPSGB) has been dissolved, the five pharmaceutical nominations for the newly constituted Board (see note above) have been received from the RPS and the GPhC. Members of the Poisons Board hold office for 3 years and the Secretary of State appoints one of the members as the chairman. The quorum is 11 and the Board has power to appoint replacements for casual vacancies. The Board makes its own regulations as to procedure, subject to the approval of the Secretary of State (s.1).

The Poisons List

The Poisons List Order, as amended (see appendix 6) contains the Poisons List, which is a list of substances treated as poisons for the purposes of the Act (s.2).

This list is divided into two parts. Essentially, the classification of poisons as Part I or Part II relates to who may lawfully sell certain poisons and to premises from which they may be sold:

Part I consists of poisons where sale is restricted to persons lawfully conducting a retail pharmacy business (subsequently referred to as Part I poisons).

Part II consists of poisons which may only be sold either by a person lawfully conducting a retail pharmacy business or by a person whose name is entered in a local authority's list as a *listed seller* (subsequently referred to as Part II poisons).

NB. Some substances in the Poisons List also have medicinal uses or are included in medicinal products (e.g. sodium fluoride, nicotine). When sold as medicinal products, they are controlled under the Medicines Act 1968 and the Human Medicines Regulations 2012 but when sold for non-medicinal purposes they are subject to the Poisons Act 1972 and to the Poisons Rules. Note, also, that unless otherwise stated, an unqualified reference to a poison includes a substance containing that poison.

Local authorities' lists

Every local authority is obliged to keep a list of the names and business addresses of persons, *listed sellers*, who are entitled to sell Part II poisons and must enter on the list all those persons who make an application. A local authority has the power (a) to refuse to enter, or to remove from the list, a name if, in its opinion, the person is not fit to be on the list, and (b) to remove a name for non-payment of any fee determined by the authority. A person aggrieved by such a decision can appeal to the Crown Court or, in Scotland, to the Sheriff (s.5). A local authority's list, which is open to inspection without fee, must include particulars of the premises and of the names of the persons listed.

The Act provides for the payment of reasonable fees as determined by the authority for a person making application for his/her name to be included on the list, for the making of any alteration in the list in relation to the premises in respect of which his/her name is entered and also for further annual payments of fees for having his/her name retained on the list (s.6(2), as amended).

If a person whose name is on a local authority's list is convicted of any offence which in the opinion of the court renders him/her unfit to have his/her name so listed, the court may, as part of the sentence, order his/her name to be removed and him/her to be disqualified from being on the list for a specified period. Any person whose name is on a local authority list may not use in connection with his/her business any title, emblem or description reasonably calculated to suggest that s/he is entitled to sell any poisons which s/he is not entitled to sell (s.6).

Local authority means (a) in relation to England, the council of a county, metropolitan district, or London borough or the Common Council of the City of London, (b) in relation to Wales, the council of a county or county borough and (c) in relation to Scotland, a council constituted under section 2 of the Local Government etc. (Scotland) Act 1994 (s.11 (2), as amended).

Inspection and enforcement

The Pharmacy Order 2010[4] amends the Poisons Act and makes it the duty of the GPhC to secure compliance with the provisions of the Poisons Act 1972 and the Poisons Rules by registered pharmacists and persons carrying on a retail pharmacy business. This is achieved by the GPhC inspectorate (chapter 22).

An inspector appointed by the GPhC to ensure compliance by pharmacists and persons carrying on retail businesses has (a) power at all reasonable times to enter any registered pharmacy and (b) power to enter any premises in which s/he has reasonable cause to suspect that a breach of the law has been committed in respect of any Part I poison. Whether in a retail pharmacy business or any other premises, an inspector has power to make such examination and inquiry and to do such other things (including the taking, on payment, of samples) as may be necessary to ascertain that the Act and the rules are being complied with.

It is the duty of every local authority, by means of inspection and otherwise, to take all reasonable steps to secure compliance with the provisions of the Poisons Act and its rules, as far as they concern Part II poisons, (a) by persons not being persons lawfully conducting a retail pharmacy business, and (b) by any persons lawfully conducting a retail pharmacy business in so far as that business is carried on at premises which are not a registered pharmacy. Each local authority must appoint inspectors for these purposes.

An inspector appointed by the GPhC may, with the consent of the GPhC, also be appointed by a local authority to be an inspector for the purposes of this section of the Act (s.9, as amended).

For the purposes of enforcement, an inspector appointed by a local authority has power at all reasonable times to enter any premises on the local authority's list and any premises where s/he has reasonable cause to suspect that a breach of the law has been committed in respect of any Part II poison (s.9). An inspector appointed by a local authority in England or Wales has power, with the consent of the authority, to institute proceedings before a court of summary jurisdiction, in the name of the authority, and to conduct any proceedings so instituted by him/her (s.9, as amended).

It is an offence for any person wilfully to delay or obstruct an inspector, to refuse to allow a sample to be taken, or to fail without reasonable excuse to give any information which the Poisons Act requires him/her to give to an inspector (s.9). It is specifically provided that nothing in the Poisons Act authorises an inspector to enter or inspect the premises of a doctor, a dentist, a veterinary surgeon or a veterinary practitioner unless those premises are a shop (s.9).

[4]The Pharmacy Order SI 2010 No. 231

A document purporting to be a certificate sent by a public analyst appointed under section 27 of the Food Safety Act 1990 or a person appointed by the Secretary of State (in Scotland, the Lord Advocate) to make analyses for the purposes of the Poisons Act is admissible in any proceedings under the Act as evidence of the matters stated therein, and either party may require the person who has signed the certificate to be called as a witness (s.8, as amended).

Penalties and legal proceedings

Any person who contravenes or fails to comply with the Poisons Act, or any of the provisions made under the Poisons Rules, is liable on summary conviction to a fine not exceeding £2500, and for continuing offences to a further fine not exceeding £200 for every day subsequent to the day on which s/he is convicted of the offence (s.8, as amended and the Criminal Justice Acts 1982 and 1991). For the misuse of titles (s.6) and obstruction of an inspector (s.9) the maximum fine is £500.

In the case of proceedings against a person under the Poisons Act or Poisons Rules for or in connection with the sale, exposure for sale or supply of a poison effected by an employee, it is not a defence that the employee acted without the authority of the employer and any material fact known to the employee is deemed to have been known to the employer (s.8).

Information in respect of any offence under the Poisons Act or Poisons Rules must be laid within 12 months of the commission of the offence. There is an additional provision that the Secretary of State may institute proceedings within a period of 3 months after the date on which evidence sufficient in his/her opinion to justify a prosecution for an offence comes to his/her knowledge (s.8).

The Poison Rules

The Poisons Act (s.7) provides that the Secretary of State may, after consultation with or on the recommendation of the Poisons Board, make rules (see appendix 7) in respect of any of the following:

1 the sale, whether wholesale or retail, or the supply of poisons by or to any persons or classes of person and in particular but without prejudice to the generality of the foregoing provisions
   a for regulating or restricting the sale or supply of poisons by persons whose names are entered in a local authority's list and for prohibiting the sale of any specified poison or class of poisons by any class of such persons, and
   b for dispensing with or relaxing with respect to any poisons any of the preceding provisions of this Act relating to the sale of poisons;

2 the storage and labelling of poisons (but see chapter 20);

3 the containers in which poisons may be sold or supplied;

4 the addition to poisons of specified ingredients for the purpose of rendering them readily distinguishable as poisons;

5 the compounding of poisons, and the supply of poisons on and in accordance with a prescription duly given by a doctor, a dentist, a veterinary surgeon or a veterinary practitioner;

6 the period for which any books required to be kept for the purpose of this Act are to be preserved;

7 the period for which any certificate for the purchase of a poison given under section 3 of the Act (see appendix 8) is to remain in force; and

8 for prescribing anything which is by the Act to be prescribed by rules.

The Secretary of State may issue to the Poisons Board a direction that, before recommending rules under 1a, 2, 3 and 4 above, the Board must first consult a body representative of persons engaged in the manufacture of poisons or preparations containing poisons.

The power to make rules or Orders under the Act is exercised by SIs. The current rules are set out in the Poison Rules 1982, as amended (see appendix 7). Apart from their general classification into Part I or Part II poisons, poisons may be, in addition, divided into classes by their inclusion in certain Schedules to the Poison Rules.

There are eight Schedules to the rules and they are described, briefly, below. More detailed reference is made later in this volume (see also appendix 7).

Schedule 1. This is a list of poisons which are subject to special restrictions relating to storage, conditions of sale, and keeping of sales records.

Schedule 4. This includes a list of articles exempted from control as poisons (Rule 8). Essentially, if an article is subject to the provisions of Schedule 4, it is not subject to control under the Poisons Act.

Schedule 5. Some Part II poisons may be sold by listed sellers only in certain forms. The details are given in this Schedule (see appendix 7).

Schedule 8. This shows the form of application for inclusion in a local authority's list of sellers of Part II poisons.

Schedule 9. This shows the form of the list kept by a local authority of listed sellers of Part II poisons.

Schedule 10. This shows the form of the certificate for the purchase of a Schedule 1 poison.

Schedule 11. This shows the form of the entry to be made in the poisons book on sale of a Schedule 1 poison.

Schedule 12. This includes details on further restrictions on the sale and supply of certain poisons, including the forms of authority required for certain of these poisons.

NB. Schedules 2, 3, 6 and 7 were deleted in 1985.[5] Packaging and labelling of poisons is now controlled under the Chemicals (Hazard Information and Packaging for Supply) (CHIP) Regulations 2009[6] and the Classification, Labelling and Packaging of Substances and Mixtures (CLP Regulations; chapter 20).[7]

Sale and supply of poisons

General requirements

Except in certain circumstances (see Sales exempted by the Poisons Act, below), it is unlawful for a person to sell any substance which is a Part I poison unless (s.3):

1 s/he is a person lawfully conducting a retail pharmacy business;
2 the sale is effected on the premises which are a registered pharmacy; and
3 the sale is effected by or under the supervision of a pharmacist.

It is unlawful for a person to sell any substance which is a Part II poison unless (s.3):

1 s/he is a person lawfully conducting a retail pharmacy business and the sale is effected on premises which are a registered pharmacy; or
2 his/her name is entered in a local authority list in respect of the premises on which the poison is sold.

As sales of poisons must be effected on registered or listed premises, it is not lawful for sales to take place from door to door, although a sale through the post from registered or listed premises would appear to be lawful.

The conditions required for persons lawfully to conduct 'a retail pharmacy business' are described in chapter 5. Such persons may sell at a registered pharmacy any poison whether it is in Part I or Part II of the Poisons List. The sale of a Part I poison from retail premises must be made by or under the supervision of a registered pharmacist (s.3). Each sale, if not made by the pharmacist personally, must be effected under his/her supervision in the sense that s/he should be in a position to intervene to prevent the sale.

Listed sellers may not sell any Part II poison which has, since being obtained by them, been subject to any form of manipulation, treatment or processing as a result of which the poison has been exposed, nor may they sell any poison included in Schedule 1, unless the sale is effected by him/herself or by a responsible deputy (Rule 10).

[5] by the Poisons Rules (Amendment) Order SI 1985 No. 1077
[6] The Chemicals (Hazard Information and Packaging for Supply) Regulations SI 2009 No. 716
[7] The Classification, Labelling and Packaging EC Regulation 1272/2008

A *responsible deputy* means a person nominated as a deputy on the listed seller's form of application or any person substituted, by notice in writing to the local authority, for the person originally nominated. Not more than two deputies can be nominated at the same time in respect of one set of premises (Rule 10).

A listed seller may not sell (Rule 10):

1 any poison included in the first column of Part A of Schedule 5 (see appendix 7) unless the article or substance is in the form specified in the second column of that Part; or
2 any poison included in Part B of Schedule 5 (see appendix 7) unless the purchaser is engaged in the trade or business of agriculture, horticulture or forestry and requires the poison for the purposes of that trade or business.

Containers

Rule 20 of the rules which set out provision for containers has been repealed.[8] Provision for containers which have to bear tactile danger warnings are contained in the CLP Regulations or the earlier CHIP Regulations (chapter 20).

Storage of poisons

A poison included in Schedule 1 (see appendix 7) must be stored in any retail shop or premises used in connection with a retail shop:

1 in a cupboard or drawer reserved solely for the storage of poisons;
2 in a part of the premises which is partitioned off or otherwise separated from the remainder of the premises and to which customers are not permitted to have access; or
3 on a shelf reserved solely for the storage of poisons and no food is kept directly under the shelf.

Schedule 1 poisons used in agriculture, horticulture or forestry must not be stored on any shelf, or in any part of the premises where food is kept, or in any cupboard or drawer unless the cupboard or drawer is reserved solely for the storage of poisons to be used in agriculture, horticulture or forestry (Rule 21).

[8] The Poisons (Amendment) Rules SI 1992 No. 2293

Labelling of hydrogen cyanide

It is an offence to sell or supply any compressed hydrogen cyanide unless the container is labelled with the words '*Warning: this container holds poisonous gas and should only be opened and used by persons having expert knowledge of the precautions to be taken in its use*' (Rule 18). This does not apply to sale or supply of compressed hydrogen cyanide to be exported to purchasers outside the UK.

Labelling and packaging of poisons which are 'chemicals'

Substances in the Poisons List are also subject to the CLP Regulations (chapter 20). The provisions of the Poisons Act and rules relating to labelling, containers and storage do not apply to these substances except:

1 the special warning label for compressed hydrogen cyanide (see above); and
2 the storage requirements for poisons on retail premises (see above).

Schedule 1 Poisons

Sales of poisons included in Schedule 1 to the Poisons Rules are subject to requirements additional to those applying to Part I and Part II poisons.

Knowledge of the purchaser

The purchaser of a Schedule 1 poison must be either (s.3):

1 certified in writing in the prescribed manner, by a person authorised in the Poisons Rules to give such a certificate, to be a person to whom the poison may properly be sold; or
2 known by the seller, or by a pharmacist employed by him/her at the premises where the sale is effected, to be a person to whom the poison may properly be sold.

Any householder is a person authorised to give a certificate as in 1 above (Rule 25). If the householder giving the certificate is not known to the seller to be a responsible person of good character, then the certificate is required to be endorsed by a police officer in charge of a police station.

NB. The police officer certifies that the householder, not the purchaser, is a responsible person of good character. The form of the certificate is laid down in Schedule 10 (see appendix 8) and the certificate has to be retained by the seller (Rule 25).

For certain sales or supplies of Schedule 1 poisons, the requirement of knowledge of the purchaser by the seller is deemed to be satisfied if the purchaser is known by the person in charge of the premises in which the poison is sold, or of the department of the business in which the sale is effected, to be a person to whom the poison may properly be sold or supplied. This relaxation applies to:

1 sales of Part II, Schedule 1 poisons made by listed sellers (Rule 5);
2 supplies of commercial samples of Schedule 1 poisons (Rule 6); and
3 sales of Schedule 1 poisons exempted under section 4 of the Act (Rule 6) (see below).

Records

The seller must not deliver a Schedule 1 poison until s/he has made, or caused to be made, the required entry in the poisons book and the purchaser has signed it (s.3). The entries must be made in the manner and form prescribed in Schedule 11 (Rule 26; see appendix 7). The particulars to be recorded are the:

1 date of the sale;
2 name and quantity of the poison supplied;
3 purchaser's name and address and their business trade or occupation;
4 purpose for which the poison is stated to be required;
5 date of certificate (if any); and
6 name and address of persons giving certificate (if any).

The poisons book must be retained for 2 years from the date on which the last entry was made (Rule 27). A signed order may be accepted in lieu of the purchaser's signature in certain circumstances (see below).

Signed orders

A person who requires a Schedule 1 poison for the purpose of their trade, business or profession may give the seller a signed order in lieu of his/her signature in the poisons book (Rule 6). The seller must obtain, before completion of the sale, the order in writing signed by the purchaser stating:

1 their name and address;
2 their trade, business or profession;
3 the purpose for which the poison is required; and
4 the total quantity of the poison to be purchased.

The seller must be reasonably satisfied that the signature is that of the person purporting to have signed the order and that the person carries on the trade, business or profession stated in the order being one in which the poison is used. The seller must make the entry in the poison book before delivery. S/he must include the words *signed order* in place of the signature and add a reference number by which the order can be identified.

When a person represents that s/he urgently requires a poison for his/her trade, business or profession, the seller may, if s/he is reasonably satisfied that there is an emergency and the purchaser is unable to supply a signed order, or to attend to sign the entry in the book, before delivery, supply the poison on an undertaking by the purchaser that the purchaser will supply a signed order within 72 hours. Failure to comply with an undertaking or the making of false statements in order to obtain Schedule 1 poisons without a signed order are contraventions of the Poison Rules (Rule 6).

Exemptions from Schedule 1 requirements

The requirements described above as to the knowledge of the purchaser by the seller and entry in the poisons book with signature of the purchaser or supplier of a signed order do not apply to:

1 the sale of poisons to be exported to purchasers outside the UK;
2 the sale of any article by its manufacturer, or by a person carrying on a business in the course of which poisons are regularly sold by way of wholesale dealing if
   a the article is sold or supplied to a person carrying on a business in the course of which poisons are regularly sold or regularly used in the manufacture of other articles, and
   b the seller or supplier is reasonably satisfied that the purchaser requires the article for the purpose of that business (Rule 6);
3 the sale of nicotine, its salts or its quaternary compounds (a Part II, Sch. 1 poison) in the form of agricultural or horticultural insecticides consisting of nicotine dusts containing not more than 4 per cent w/w of nicotine (Rule 5);
4 the sale of articles containing barium carbonate, zinc phosphide or alpha-chloralose where the article is prepared for the destruction of rats or mice (Rule 7).

Schedule 1 poisons subject to additional restrictions (Rule 12)

Certain Schedule 1 poisons are subject to additional restrictions on sale or supply (Sch. 12); they include strychnine (its salts or quaternary compounds), fluoroacetic acid (any salt thereof or fluoroacetamide), thallium, zinc phos-phide, sodium arsenites or potassium arsenites. They may be sold or supplied only:

1 for export to purchasers outside the UK; or
2 to persons or institutions concerned with scientific education or research or chemical analysis for the purpose of that education research or analy-sis; or
3 by way of wholesale dealing.

In addition, sales are permitted in the circumstances described below under the name of each particular poison.

Since September 2006, *strychnine* no longer has approval from the Chemicals Regulation Directorate for purchase or use for mole control. There is, however, provision for the supply for the purpose of killing foxes in an infected area under the Rabies (Control) Order 1974.[9] Details regarding the requirements for such sales are given in appendix 7 (Sch. 12, Part 1, para. 5).

Fluoroacetic acid, its salts or fluoroacetamide may be sold for use as a rodenticide in certain circumstances which are detailed in appendix 7 (Sch. 12, Part 1, para. 6).

Salts of thallium, potassium and sodium arsenites, the cyanides of cal-cium, potassium and sodium, and *zinc phosphide* are also included in Schedule 12 but like strychnine are no longer approved by the Chemicals Regulation Directorate.

Calcium, potassium and sodium cyanides and *sodium and potassium arsenites* may only be sold in any of the circumstances described in section 4 of the Act (Rule 14; see Sales exempted by the Poisons Act, below).

Sales exempted by the Poisons Act, including wholesale dealing

Section 4 of the Poisons Act exempts certain categories of sales of poisons from the provisions of the Act, except as provided by the Poisons Rules. The principal effect is that sales of poisons falling within these categories are not required to be made from pharmacies or the premises of listed sellers and, for Part I poisons, the supervision of a pharmacist is not required. Except as indicated, the provisions as to Schedule 1 poisons do apply to these exempted sales (Rule 6).

The exempted categories are as follows.

1 Sales of poisons by way of wholesale dealing, that is, sales made to a person who buys for the purpose of selling again. (NB. 'Wholesale deal-ing' has a wider meaning in the Human Medicines Regulations 2012.) A wholesaler who sells a Part I poison to a shopkeeper must have reasonable

[9] The Rabies (Control) Order SI 1974 No. 2212

grounds for believing that the purchaser is a person lawfully conducting a retail pharmacy business. If not, then the wholesaler must obtain a statement signed by the purchaser, or a person authorised by the purchaser, to the effect that the purchaser does not intend to sell the poison on any premises used for or in connection with his/her retail business (rule 11).

2 Sales of poisons to be exported to purchasers outside the UK.

3 Sale of an article to a doctor, dentist, veterinary surgeon or veterinary practitioner for the purposes of his/her profession.

4 Sale of an article for use in connection with any hospital, infirmary, dispensary or similar institution approved by an Order of the Secretary of State.

5 Sale of an article by a person carrying on a business, in the course of which poisons are regularly sold either by way of wholesale dealing or for use by purchasers in their trade or business to

   a a person who requires the article for the purpose of his/her trade or business,

   b a person who requires the article for the purpose of enabling him/her to comply with any requirements made by or in pursuance of any enactment with respect to the medical treatment of persons employed by him in any trade or business carried on by him/her,

   c a government department or an officer of the Crown requiring the article for the purposes of the public service, or any local authority requiring the article in connection with the exercise by the authority of any statutory powers, or

   d a person or institution concerned with scientific education or research, if the article is required for the purposes of that education or research.

Automatic machines

It is unlawful for a poison to be exposed for sale in, or to be offered for sale by means of, an automatic machine (s.3).

Summary

- The Poisons Board advises the Secretary of State as to which substances should be in the Poisons List.
- The Poisons List is divided into two parts. Poisons in Part I may be sold only from retail pharmacies by or under the supervision of a pharmacist whereas Part II poisons can be sold from retail pharmacies and other shopkeepers who are listed with the local authority (listed sellers).
- There are eight active Schedules. Schedule 1 contains poisons to which special restrictions apply relating to sale, storage and the keeping of records. The seller must have special knowledge of the purchaser and

record the transaction and obtain the purchaser's signature in a poisons book. Special provisions are made for signed orders in lieu of the purchaser's signature and for storage of poisons (away from the public).

- Special conditions apply to the sale of strychnine. It may only be sold by way of wholesale, or to persons or institutions concerned with education or research, for export or to a person who has obtained a written authority from the appropriate agricultural authority in England, Scotland or Wales. It is no longer approved for killing moles. The form of the written authority is set out in Schedule 12.
- Sodium and potassium arsenites, thallium, zinc phosphide, and the cyanides are no longer approved by the Chemicals Regulation Directorate.

Websites

Chemicals Regulation Directorate: http://www.pesticides.gov.uk/home.asp
Department for Environment, Food and Rural Affairs: http://www.defra.gov.uk
Home Office: http://www.homeoffice.gov.uk/

19

Alcohol and denatured alcohol

Susan Melvin

The law relating to alcohol and denatured alcohol is contained mainly in the Customs and Excise Management Act 1979, the Alcoholic Liquor Duties Act 1979 and the Denatured Alcohol Regulations SI 2005 No. 1524.

Intoxicating liquor means alcohol, wine, beer, cider and any other fermented, distilled or spirituous liquor, but (apart from cider) does not include any liquor for the sale of which, by wholesale, no excise licence is required.

The term *alcohol* means 'alcohol of any description and includes all liquor mixed with alcohol and all mixtures, compounds or preparations made with alcohol but does not include denatured alcohol'.

Retail sales of intoxicating liquor

Intoxicating liquor may be sold[1] only by a person holding a personal licence (NCPLH[2]) granted in England and Wales by the licensing authority or in Scotland by the Licensing Board acting is the licensing authority. The authority has an absolute discretion in the granting of such licences.

The premises from which the alcohol is sold must hold a premises licence and have a Designated Premises Supervisor (DPS). Restrictions on hours of opening are dependent on the premises licence granted by the authority.

NB. A licence is not required for the sale by retail of alcohol made up in a medicine by a pharmacist or a sale to a trader for the purpose of that trade.

Alcohol duty

Alcohol and all goods containing alcohol imported into the UK are liable to a customs duty, and all alcohol made in the UK by a licensed distiller

---

[1] See Licensing Act 2003 (E & W); Licensing (Scotland) Act 2005
[2] National Certificate for Personal Licence Holders

are liable to an excise duty (Customs and Excise Management Act 1979). Exemption from Customs and Excise duty exists for alcohol used in making denatured alcohol (see below).

A *reduced rate of duty* is payable if any person can prove to the Commissioner of Customs and Excise that s/he has used alcohol, upon which the full duty has been paid, solely for the purpose of manufacturing or preparing any article recognised by the Commissioner as being used for medical or scientific purposes. This concession is granted subject to any conditions which the Commissioner may impose by means of regulations. The guidelines have been made and are contained in the Alcohol Regulations[3] (see below).

A person wishing to claim repayment of a portion of the duty must comply with the following (as set out in Part VIII of the Alcohol Regulations): s/he must not *receive* at his/her premises any alcohol except (a) alcohol accompanied by a permit or certificate; or (b) alcohol which, if not required to be accompanied by a permit or certificate on removal, are accompanied by an invoice or similar document containing particulars of the alcohol and the duty paid, and the name and address of the supplier (Reg.63).

A claimant must *store* separately (a) alcohol recovered from alcohol in respect of which s/he has or intends to make a claim; (b) any other recovered alcohol; (c) any other alcohol (Reg.65). S/he is not allowed to mix alcohol recovered from alcohol, in respect of which s/he has or intends to make a claim, with any other alcohol except for use in the manufacture or preparation of a medicine which is recognised as such by the Commissioners, or for scientific purposes (Reg.65). On each container in which s/he stores alcohol or recovered alcohol, the claimant must permanently and legibly mark the capacity of the container. Each container has to be stored to give convenient access to a Customs and Excise officer (Reg.64).

The claimant is required to keep a *stock book* in an approved form (Reg.66) and is required to make immediate entries in respect of:

1 alcohol received at the premises, brought back into stock for use or recovered on the premises;
2 alcohol or recovered alcohol intended to be delivered from, or to be used on, the premises; and
3 any article made with alcohol (Reg.67).

The pharmacist both in retail and hospital is mainly concerned with alcohol other than recovered alcohol. Separate accounts must be kept for alcohol and recovered alcohol in a stock book. Specimen stock-book rulings are illustrated in figures 19.1 and 19.2.

---

[3]The Alcohol Regulations SI 1952 No. 2229 (as amended; not available online)

Date	Permit No.	Name and address of supplier	Quantity received	Strength o.p.

Figure 19.1   Alcohol received.

Repayment of duty not claimed plus sales			Repayment of duty claimed			Recognised article made	
Date	Quantity	Strength	Date	Quantity	Strength	Name	Quantity

Figure 19.2   Alcohol used or sold.

If a person uses alcohol in the *manufacture or preparation of any recognised medicine* (e.g. homoeopathic medicine), entries must be made in a stock book recording (Reg.66):

1 all alcohol received at his/her premises;
2 all alcohol and mixtures brought back into stock for use in the manufacture or preparation of a recognised medicinal article, being alcohol or mixtures previously entered in the stock book as having been used and in respect of which s/he has in accordance with the Alcoholic Liquor Duties Act 1979 refunded any duty repaid;
3 all alcohol delivered from his/her premises;
4 all alcohol used on his/her premises, the purposes for which they are used and the quantities used for each purpose;
5 the name and quantity of each recognised medical article made;

6 the name and quantity of any other article made; and

7 any other use of the alcohol.

Separate particulars are required for alcohol used for scientific purposes (Reg.66).

It is an offence for a claimant to cancel, obliterate or, except with the permission of a Customs and Excise officer, alter any entry in the book (Reg.68). The book must be left on the premises while in use and for 12 months following the final entry, together with all books, invoices and other trade documents containing any information on which entries in the book are based. The claimant must at all reasonable times allow an officer to inspect the book, invoices and documents, and take extracts therefrom or make entries in the book (Reg.69). Unless the Commissioners permit otherwise, the claimant, if not a rectifier, must take stock and balance the account of alcohol in his/her stock book at the end of each month (Reg.70) or when required to do so by an officer.

A claimant must not deliver from his/her premises or use for any purpose other than manufacture or preparation of a recognised medicinal article or for a scientific purpose any alcohol in respect of which s/he has made or intends to make a claim (Reg.71). Claims for recovery of duty must be made on the approval form obtainable from a Customs and Excise officer. The claim must be signed by the claimant or a person duly authorised by the claimant, and must be made within 3 months of the date on which the alcohol was used. Claims cannot be made more frequently than twice a month in respect of alcohol used on any one set of premises (Reg.73).

When in doubt concerning any provisions of the alcohol Regulations, pharmacists are advised to consult the local officer of Customs and Excise.

Denatured alcohol

Denatured alcohol is alcohol which is mixed with other substances in accordance with Regulations made by the Commissioners under the Alcoholic Liquor Duties Act 1979.

There are three types of denatured alcohol but the pharmacist is generally concerned only with two: completely denatured alcohol (formerly mineralised methylated spirits) and industrial denatured alcohol (formerly industrial methylated spirits).

The Alcohol Regulations[4] set particulars for the supply, receipt, sale, storage, and so on of all types of denatured alcohol, although the provisions for licensing and inspection are to be found in the Act itself. In addition, the Commissioners issue notices for guidance and these can be obtained from local Customs and Excise offices. No person may methylate, or wholesale,

[4]The Denatured Alcohol Regulations SI 2005 No. 1524

denatured alcohol of *any type* unless they hold a licence as a methylator from the Commissioners authorising them to do so.

The local Customs and Excise officer may enter and inspect in the daytime the premises of any person authorised by the Regulations to receive alcohol, and may inspect and examine any of the alcohol stored there. The local officer is empowered to take samples of alcohol and any goods containing denatured alcohol, provided a reasonable price is paid for the sample.

It is unlawful:

1   to prepare, attempt to prepare or sell any alcohol for use as a beverage or mixed with a beverage;
2   to use alcohol in the preparation of any article capable of being used as a beverage or as a medicine for internal use;
3   to sell or possess any such article; and
4   to purify or attempt to purify any alcohol, or recover or attempt to recover the alcohol therein, by means of distillation, condensation or in any other manner unless permitted to do so by the Commissioners.

Nothing in the statute prevents the use of alcohol in the making for external use only of any article sold or supplied in accordance with Regulations.

If required to do so by the Commissioners, the retailer must keep an account, in a prescribed form, of his/her stock of alcohol (Reg.27). The retailer is required to keep alcohol under proper control or under the control of a responsible person appointed by the retailer and held under lock or otherwise stored to the satisfaction of the local officer.

On the closure or transfer of a business, or on the death of the retailer, the stock of alcohol must be disposed of in an approved manner and within a reasonable time to the satisfaction of the Commissioners (Reg.26).

Industrial denatured alcohol (formerly industrial methylated spirits)

The Regulations require that industrial denatured alcohol must consist of 95 parts by volume of alcohol together with 5 parts by volume of wood naphtha (Reg.15). The formulation of denatured alcohol that is supplied must be approved by the UK or an EU Member State.

A person lawfully conducting a retail pharmacy business cannot receive industrial denatured alcohol for sale by him/her or for export unless s/he has made application to the proper officer in the required form, which is available from the local office of Customs and Excise, and has supplied such information as may be required. The proper officer may make the certificate of authority subject to conditions (Reg.25) and restrict it to the receipt of denatured alcohol for certain purposes only. Pharmacists *must* comply with the conditions of the certificate. The certificate of authority may be revoked or varied for any reasonable cause at any time (Reg.24). The authorised uses for which industrial denatured alcohol may be sold are set out in HM Customs and Excise Notice No. 473 dated July 2005.

The proper officer may authorise a pharmacist to receive industrial denatured alcohol and:

1 use it to make any article approved by the proper officer;
2 dispense it, or articles made from it, on a prescription; and
3 sell or supply it, other than on a prescription, for medical or scientific purposes.

Sales of industrial denatured alcohol may be made:

1 to any person authorised to receive it in any quantity not exceeding 20 litres provided that a written statement is received from the user that s/he is authorised to receive it;
2 in any quantity not exceeding 3 litres to a doctor, dentist, nurse, chiropodist, veterinary surgeon or any other person entitled by law to provide medical or veterinary services in the UK, provided that a written order signed by such a person is received;
3 of not more than 20 litres to persons outside the UK; and
4 for medical or veterinary purposes on a prescription or order of a medical practitioner, dentist or veterinary surgeon or practitioner.

Similarly, a pharmacist may supply or sell articles:

1 which have been manufactured by that pharmacist using industrial denatured alcohol in accordance with the conditions imposed in the certificate of authority; or
2 which are so manufactured in accordance with the certificate of authority and are sold or supplied on a prescription.

Industrial denatured alcohol must be purchased from an authorised methylator in quantities of not less than 20 litres. Alternatively, not more than 20 litres at a time can be obtained from an authorised user (e.g. a wholesale chemist).

An authorised user, such as a pharmacist, must keep records of his dealings with industrial denatured alcohol in accordance with any conditions imposed by the Regulations or a proper officer, who must be allowed to inspect such records at any reasonable time. An annual return of all industrial denatured alcohol received and used or supplied must be made to the proper officer on request. Records must be kept for 2 years.

All stocks must be kept under lock and key under the control of the pharmacist. The local Customs and Excise may require a pharmacist to comply with special storage requirements.

All bottles and other containers in which industrial denatured alcohol or articles containing it are supplied must be labelled in accordance with the CLP Regulations (chapter 20). If supplied or dispensed for medical use the

Received or set aside as a separate stock for sale			Sold		
Date	Whence received	Quantity	Date	Whether sold on requisition for use of a doctor etc., on written order	Quantity

Figure 19.3 Specimen form of account for guidance of pharmacists when selling industrial denatured spirits other than on prescription.

label must also include '*For external use, not to be taken*' or words to the same effect.

A specimen form of account is shown in figure 19.3.

Completely denatured alcohol (formerly mineralised methylated spirits)

The Regulations require that completely denatured alcohol must consist of 90 parts by volume of alcohol together with 9.5 parts by volume of wood naphtha and 0.5 part of crude pyridine. To every 1000 litres of the mixture must be added 3.75 litres of petroleum oil and not less than 1.5 g by weight of powdered aniline dye (methyl violet).

Completely denatured alcohol can be purchased from a methylator or, in small quantities, from a wholesaler. No restrictions are placed on the retailing of completely denatured alcohol in England and Wales. The weekend restrictions on sale were removed in 2004.[5] The local officer of Customs and Excise visits the premises to satisfy him/herself as to the suitability of the premises for the storage of completely denatured alcohol.

Scotland: sale of completely denatured alcohol and surgical alcohol

For many years, there were additional restrictions on the retail sale of methylated alcohol and surgical alcohol in Scotland. These included the

[5] The Regulatory Reform (Sunday Trading) Order 2004 SI 2004 No. 470

need for sellers to register and keep records and contained additional labelling requirements. These restrictions were removed in 1998.[6] The 2005 Regulations now apply to Scotland and are similar to those in England and Wales. However it remains an offence to sell completely denatured alcohol in Scotland to a person who is under 14 years of age.

Summary

- The law relating to denatured alcohol and the rules regarding the duty on products are outlined.
- The term denatured alcohol includes alcohol of any description including liquors mixed with spirits and all mixes with spirits but not industrial spirits.
- Intoxicating liquor comprises any fermented, distilled or spirituous liquor but (apart from cider) does not include any liquor that does not require a licence for wholesale.
- There are three types of denatured alcohol but the pharmacist is generally concerned with two: completely denatured alcohol and industrial denatured alcohol; there are specific Regulations for these alcohols governing the supply, receipt, sale, storage, and so on, of all types of denatured alcohol.

Website

HM Revenue and Customs: http://www.hmrc.gov.uk

[6]The Deregulation (Methylated Alcohol Sale by Retail) (Scotland) Regulations SI 1998 No. 1602 (s.87)

20

Chemicals

Susan Melvin

The CLP Regulations[1] for chemicals is in a state of transition and is due to be complete by the 1 June 2015. The requirements of the CLP Regulations are included in the latest of a series of regulations on hazard information and packaging for supply, known collectively as the CHIP Regulations[2] and made under the European Communities Act 1972. Chemicals classified under the CHIP Regulations as being harmful to health are also subject to the Control of Substances Hazardous to Health Regulations[3] (the COSHH Regulations).

Definitions

Dangerous substances means a substance listed in Table 3.2 of Part 3 of Annex VI of the CLP Regulations.

Preparations means mixtures or solutions of two or more substances and *dangerous preparation* means a preparation which is in one or more categories of danger in Column 1 of Schedule 1 to the CHIP Regulations.

Supply, in relation to a substance or preparation, means making that substance or preparation available to another person and includes importation of the substance or preparation into Great Britain.

Application of the Regulations and exceptions

The CHIP Regulations apply to the classification, packaging and labelling of any substance or preparation which is dangerous subject to the following exceptions of relevance to pharmacy:

a a medicinal product;
b a veterinary product;
c an investigational medicinal product;

[1] Classification, Labelling and Packaging EC Regulation 1272/2008
[2] The Chemicals (Hazard Information and Packaging for Supply) Regulations SI 2009 No. 716
[3] The Control of Substances Hazardous to Health Regulations SI 2002 No. 2677 (as amended)

d a substance specified in an Order made under sections 104 or 105 of the Medicines Act 1968;

e a Controlled Drug;

f a cosmetic product;

g in the form of waste to which Regulations apply;

h a food or animal feeding stuff;

i a radioactive substance;

j a substance intended for export to a country which is not a Member State of the EU;

k a medical device which is invasive or used in direct contact with the human body; or

l munitions, including fireworks (only Regs. 6–11 do not apply).

Most of the substances controlled as dangerous substances in the approved supply list are chemicals and only a few are likely to be encountered in pharmacy. A selection of the substances taken from the approved supply list is given in appendix 8. It comprises:

1 those dangerous substances which are also controlled by the Poisons Act 1972 (chapter 18); and

2 other dangerous substances which may be held in stock in a pharmacy.

A pharmacy dealing with a request for any chemical not shown in appendix 8 should refer to the approved supply list and Regulations or seek advice from the Health and Safety Executive or pharmacy body. It should be borne in mind that substances sold as medicinal products or pesticides are not subject to the labelling requirements of the CHIP Regulations 2009, as amended.

Inspection and enforcement

The provisions are enforced as if they were health and safety regulations made under the Health and Safety at Work Etc. Act 1974. Where a dangerous substance is supplied in or from a registered pharmacy, the enforcing authority is the GPhC. The enforcing authority in relation to supplies made in any shop, market stall or other retail outlet is the local weights and measures authority and in all other cases the Health and Safety Executive.

Classification

Substances or preparations which are dangerous to supply have to be classified by the manufacturer. The manufacturer must decide what kind of danger the chemical presents and allocate to it a phrase describing the general nature of the risk attached to it (a *risk phrase*).

Each substance or preparation is classified in the approved list as to its category of danger (Sch. 1):

1 *physicochemical properties*: explosive, extremely flammable, highly flammable or flammable, and oxidising;
2 *health effects*: very toxic, toxic, harmful, irritant, corrosive, sensitising, carcinogenic, mutagenic and toxic for reproduction; and
3 dangerous to the environment.

All substances and preparations which are classified as carcinogenic, mutagenic or toxic for reproduction, together with certain solvents (e.g. chloroform and carbon tetrachloride), have to be labelled 'Restricted for professional users' and, therefore, cannot be sold to the general public.

Pharmacists will normally not have to classify dangerous substances or preparations as this will have been done by the supplier. However, if a pharmacist still produces preparations to his/her own formulation then s/he will have to classify the dangers.

Each classification of danger will carry with it indications of danger, particular risks and safety precautions which will be required when such substances or preparations are labelled and sold.

Indications of danger

There are 10 categories of indications of danger. Each category has its own symbol which must be in black on an orange/yellow background. The symbols are shown in appendix 8 and are:

1 explosive: an exploding bomb;
2 extremely flammable, highly flammable: a flame;
3 very toxic, toxic: a skull and cross-bones;
4 corrosive: a hand and a piece of metal being dissolved by liquid dropping from two test tubes;
5 oxidising: a flame over a circle;
6 irritant, harmful: a St Andrew's cross; and
7 dangerous to the environment: a tree and a fish.

Indications of particular risks

Each dangerous substance or preparation is classified in the CLP Regulations as to the indications of particular risks with which the receptacle must be labelled. These include, for example: *'reacts violently with water'*, *'irritating to the eyes'*, *'harmful if swallowed'*, *'explosive when mixed with a combustible material'*, *'sensitising'*, *'carcinogenic'* (see appendix 8).

Indications of safety precautions required

Each dangerous substance or preparation is classified in the CLP Regulations as to the indication of safety precautions with which the receptacle must be labelled. These include, for example, *'keep out of the reach of children'*, *'wear suitable protective clothing'*, *'never add water to this product'* (see appendix 8).

Packaging

It is unlawful to supply any person with a substance or preparation dangerous to supply unless it is in a receptacle which is designed, constructed, maintained and closed so as to prevent its escape when subjected to the stresses and strains of normal handling. This does not prevent the fitting of a suitable safety device (Reg.11). When the receptacle is fitted with a replaceable closure, the latter must be so designed so that the receptacle can be repeatedly reclosed without the contents escaping. The packaging must be made of materials which are neither adversely affected by the substance nor liable in conjunction with that substance to produce another substance which is a risk to the health and safety of the public (Reg.11).

Receptacle means a container together with any material, wrapping and component, including any closure or fastener associated with the container which enables the container to perform its containment function.

Package means the package in which a substance or preparation is supplied and which is liable to be individually handled during the course of the supply and includes the receptacle containing the substance or preparation and any other packaging associated with it and any pallet or other device which enables more than one receptacle containing a substance or preparation to be handled as a unit, but does not include:

1 a freight container (other than a tank container), a skip, a vehicle or other article of transport equipment; or
2 in the case of supply by way of retail, any wrapping such as a paper or plastic bag into which the package is placed when presented to the purchaser.

Child-resistant closures

Child-resistant closures must be used on certain products when sold to the general public. These substances or preparations include those that are classified as *'toxic'*, *'very toxic'* or *'corrosive'*, and methanol above 3 per cent.

Tactile danger warnings

In order to aid the blind and partially sighted, a tactile danger warning such as a raised triangle, must be used on packaging when products classified as '*harmful*', '*highly flammable*', '*extremely flammable*', '*toxic*', '*very toxic*' and '*corrosive*' are sold to the general public.[4]

Labelling for supply

Labelling for supply must be in English, unless supply is to another EU Member State, when it has to be in the language of that state. It must be clearly and indelibly marked on a part of the package reserved for that purpose and securely fixed with its entire surface in contact with the package. Where it is impracticable to attach a label in this way, because the package is an awkward shape or is too small, then it may be attached in some other appropriate manner.

The colour and nature of the markings on the label must be such that the symbols required (see below) stand out from the background so as to be readily noticeable and the wording be of such a size and spacing as to be easily read. The package must be labelled so that the particulars can be read horizontally when the package is set down normally.

The dimensions of the label must be in accordance with table 20.1.

Any symbol required to be shown must be printed in black on an orange/yellow background and its size, including the orange/yellow background, must be at least equal to one-tenth of the area of a label and in any case shall not be less than 100 mm^2. Where because of the size of the label it is not reasonably practicable to provide safety phrases on the label, that

Table 20.1 Label dimensions for supply	
Capacity of package	Dimensions of label
3 litres or less	If possible at least 52 mm × 74 mm
Exceeding 3 litres but not exceeding 50 litres	At least 74 mm × 105 mm
Exceeding 50 litres but not exceeding 500 litres	At least 105 mm × 148 mm
Exceeding 500 litres	At least 148 mm × 210 mm

[4] As required in The Chemicals (Hazard Information and Packaging for Supply) (Amendment) Regulations SI 2000 No. 2381

information may be given on a separate label or on a sheet accompanying the package.

No *dangerous substance* (e.g. a chemical) may be supplied unless it is in a package which clearly shows the following particulars:

1 the name and full address and telephone number of a person in a Member State who is responsible for supplying the substance, whether s/he is the importer, manufacturer or distributor;
2 the name of the substance in accordance with the CLP Regulations;
3 the following particulars:
   a the indication(s) of danger and the corresponding symbol(s) (if any),
   b the risk phrases (set out in full),
   c the safety phrases (set out in full),
   d the EC number and, in the case of a substance dangerous for supply which is listed in Part 3 of Table 3.2 of Annex VI of the CLP Regulations, the words *EC label*.

NB. The risk and safety phrases need not be shown on packages of 125 mL or less except if the substance is classified as '*flammable*', '*highly flammable*', '*oxidising*' or '*irritant*'.

No *dangerous preparation* (e.g. a mixture of substances) may be supplied unless it is in a package which clearly shows the following particulars (Reg.7):

1 the name and full address and telephone number of a person in a Member State who is responsible for supplying the preparation whether s/he is he importer, manufacturer, or distributor;
2 the name of the preparation as it appears in Table 3.2 of Part 3 Annex VI of the CLP Regulation;
3 the following particulars:
   a the indication(s) of danger and the corresponding symbol(s) (if any),
   b the risk phrases (set out in full),
   c the safety phrases (set out in full), and
   d in the case of a preparation intended for sale to the public, the nominal quantity.

Figure 20.1 shows an example of a label.

Data sheets

Safety data sheets have to be provided when substances and preparations which are subject to the REACH (Registration, Evaluation, Authorisation and Restriction of Chemicals) Regulations[5] are supplied for the first time in

[5]The REACH (Registration, Evaluation, Authorisation and Restriction of Chemicals) Enforcement Regulations SI 2008 No. 2852

Completely Denatured Alcohol	
	Highly flammable Toxic by inhalation and if swallowed Keep locked up and out of reach of children Keep container tightly closed Keep away from sources of ignition-no smoking
	Avoid contact with skin In case of accident or if you feel unwell, seek medical advice immediately and show label where possible
EEC 250 659 6	
Tel: 0101 1111	**A.N.Other MRPharmS** **1 High Street** **Blanktown** 500 ml

Figure 20.1   example of a label.

connection with work, for example a supply to a doctor for use in his/her practice, to a health centre or to factories. This is to ensure that the recipient can take any necessary precautions relating to the protection of health and safety at work and relating to the protection of the environment.

The supplier must ensure that the data sheet is kept up to date and revise it in line with any new health or safety information. A revised data sheet must be supplied to a customer who has received a supply within the last 12 months. Data sheets do not have to be given when supplies are made to the general public for private use.

Control of substances hazardous to health

The COSHH Regulations impose duties on employers to protect employees and other persons who may be exposed to substances hazardous to health and impose certain duties on employees concerning their own protection in the workplace. The Regulations implement a number of European Directives and are consistent particularly with Council Directive 80/1107/EEC, which provides for protection of workers from risks related to exposure from chemical, physical and biological agents.

The Regulations apply to any place of work including hospital or community pharmacies, pharmaceutical laboratories or administrative offices. They cover virtually any substance (except those subject to specific legislation such as asbestos, ionising radiation) but are particularly relevant to pesticides, chemicals, harmful microorganisms and medicines. Persons consuming medicines are not covered by the Regulations.

The COSHH Regulations require that an assessment of risk is made of substances used and procedures operated in the workplace.

Risk means the likelihood that the potential for harm to the health of a person will be attained under the conditions of use and exposure and also the extent of that harm. A high-level hazard could arise from mishandling a low-risk substance, for example licking the fingers while handling metallic mercury. The level of hazard is usually greater following ingestion and becomes progressively less through inhalation to skin contamination from leakage and spillage.

Every employer must ensure that the exposure of their employees to substances hazardous to health is either prevented or, where this is not reasonably practicable, is adequately controlled. *Substances hazardous to health* are those as defined in the CHIP Regulations.

Every employer must not carry out work which is liable to expose his/her employees to any hazardous substance unless s/he has made a suitable and sufficient assessment of the risks created by that work and the steps needed to avoid risk as set out in the Regulations. Where employees are exposed to risk, the employer must ensure that they are under suitable health surveillance.

Manufacturers of substances which may be hazardous to health must provide full details (e.g. labels, leaflets, data sheets, instruction manuals) of the precautions to be taken when handling the substance.

Employers must take measures to train and inform staff of the dangers, to prevent or minimise exposure where possible and, if necessary, to monitor exposure and implement a health surveillance programme for all those exposed. Risk can be reduced by avoiding the substance altogether, using a safer substance or the same substance in a safer form, by enclosing the process and extracting the by-products, by improving ventilation or hygiene facilities, by instituting safer handling procedures or by introducing personal protective equipment such as gloves, masks and respirators. In cases of difficulty, advice should be sought from the local area office of the Health and Safety Executive or from the local authority environmental health officer.

Summary

- The CLP Regulations for chemicals are in a state of transition and are due to be complete by the 1st June 2015.
- Requirements for labelling are listed in Table 3.2 of Part 3 of Annex VI of the CLP Regulations.
- The CHIP Regulations, as amended, require that all substances and preparations defined as dangerous to supply must be classified, usually by the supplier, as to the kind of danger the chemical presents and be allocated a phrase describing the general nature of the risk.

- All substances and preparations defined as dangerous to supply must be supplied in packages which comply with the standards set out in the Regulations, including child-resistant closures and tactile warnings.
- All packages must be labelled with the appropriate symbols of danger, the relevant risk phrases and safety precautions.
- The COSHH Regulations impose duties on employers to protect employees and other persons who may be exposed to substances hazardous to health and impose certain duties on employees concerning their own protection in the workplace.
- Employers must take measures to train and inform staff of the dangers, to prevent or minimise exposure where possible and, if necessary, to monitor exposure and implement a health surveillance programme for all those exposed.

Further reading

Health and Safety Executive (2002). *CHIP for Everyone*. London: HSE Books.

Health and Safety Executive (2002). *The Idiot's Guide to CHIP*. London: HSE Books.

Health and Safety Executive (2005). *Control of Substances Hazardous to Health Approved Code of Practice*. London: HSE Books.

Health and Safety Executive (2009). *Approved Classification and Labelling Guide: Chemicals (Hazard Information and Packaging for Supply) Regulations 2009 (CHIP 4) (L131)*, 6th edn. London: HSE Books.

Health and Safety Executive (2010). *Read the Label: How to Find Out if Chemicals are Dangerous*. [Leaflet INDG352(rev1).] London: HSE Books (single copy free or priced packs of 15): http://www.hse.gov.uk/pubns/indg352.pdf (accessed 21 November 2012).

Websites

COSHH Essentials: http://www.coshh-essentials.org.uk/

Health and Safety Executive: http://www.hse.gov.uk/chip; http://www.hse.gov.uk/coshh

21

Miscellaneous legislation affecting pharmacy

Joy Wingfield

The principal statutes concerning medicines, Controlled Drugs, poisons, alcohol and chemicals have been explained in chapters 2 to 20. There remain several enactments, and other measures, which are relevant to pharmacy. Some are of general application; others may apply only to one of the branches of pharmacy practice. This chapter comprises notes on some relevant statutes and regulations. The law outlined is that applying in England and Wales, but similar provisions apply in Scotland. The notes are grouped under appropriate subject headings, as follows:

- data protection and freedom of information
- pharmacy ownership
- workplace law
- consumer protection law
- health and safety law
- environmental law
- merchant shipping: medical scales
- jury service.

Data protection and freedom of information

Data Protection Act 1998

The Data Protection Act 1998 regulates the 'processing' of 'personal data'.

Personal data means any information whereby a living individual can be identified.

Processing means virtually any activity such as obtaining, recording or holding the data; carrying out operations or sets of operations on the data; organisation, adaptation or alteration of the data; retrieval; consultation or use of the data; and alignment, combination, blocking, erasure or destruction of the data.

Unlike the earlier Act of 1984, which applied only to 'computerised' data, the 1998 Act additionally covers paper records and filing systems and, indeed, any storage system structured so that data relating to a living individual can be retrieved.

The person to whom the data relates is called the *data subject*. The person who determines how and for what purposes the personal data is processed is called the *data controller*; anyone else who actually processes the data is called a *data processor* (s.1). The 1998 Act also imposes additional controls on *sensitive personal data*, which includes any information, including opinion, relating to the physical or mental health or condition of the data subject (s.2).

The Act is administered by the Information Commissioner (formerly Data Protection Registrar, then Commissioner) who maintains a Register of *Registrable Particulars* notified by data controllers, who pay an annual fee (s.18). Data controllers must comply with the eight *data protection principles* set out in the Act (Sch. 1). These principles have the force of law. Briefly, the principles require that personal data shall be:

1   obtained and processed fairly and lawfully and shall not be processed at all unless certain conditions are met (see below);
2   obtained and processed for, or in ways compatible with, one or more lawful purpose;
3   adequate, relevant and not excessive in relation to that purpose or purposes;
4   accurate and kept up to date;
5   kept for no longer than necessary;
6   processed in accordance with the rights of data subjects under the Act (see below);
7   protected against unauthorised or unlawful processing and against accidental loss, destruction or damage; and
8   not transferred (with certain exceptions) outside the EEA unless the recipient country operates the same controls on data protection as applies within the EEA.

The Information Commissioner may refuse to register notification if s/he considers that these principles will be contravened (s.22). Processing personal data without notification is a criminal offence (s.21).

The Act imposes conditions which must be met even before processing of personal data can be contemplated (see principle 1 above). Generally, no personal data may be processed at all unless either the data subject has given consent or one of a series of other conditions has been met. These include 'the need to pursue the legitimate interests of the controller' *provided* these are not prejudicial to the interests of the data subject (Sch. 2). This condition should be applicable to all uses of personal data in pharmacy practice. In addition, where the data are also *sensitive* personal data, either *explicit consent* must be obtained from the data subject or such consent may not be needed if the processing is 'necessary for medical purposes' and is undertaken by:

1 a health professional, or
2 a person who in the circumstances owes a duty of confidentiality which is equivalent to that which would arise if that person were a health professional.

Medical purposes includes the purposes of preventative medicine, medical diagnosis, medical research, the provision of care and treatment and the management of healthcare services (Sch. 3).

Therefore, virtually all personal data used in pharmacy practice are 'sensitive' but 'explicit consent' (which implies a written explanation, a consent form and a decision freely made in appreciation of all its consequences) is not deemed necessary for patient medication records at least, provided all personnel who may process such data are bound by the health professional's duty of confidentiality. The definition of *health professional* in the Act includes pharmacists (s.69).

The Act sets out explicit rights of data subjects and others (s.7; see principle 6 above). Data controllers must, on receipt of a written request accompanied by a fee:

1 inform the data subject if personal data are being processed;
2 give data subjects a description of the data which are being processed, for what purposes and to whom the data will be disclosed; and
3 provide data subjects with that information in an intelligible form within 40 days of the request.

Data subjects also have a right to prevent processing of their data for marketing purposes (s.11) and to be notified if 'automated' decisions are taken in relation to, for example, work performance, creditworthiness, reliability or conduct (s.12). Rights are also conferred to allow data subjects to claim compensation from the data controller for failure to comply with any of the requirements of the Act or to fail to rectify, block, erase or destroy any inaccurate data (s.14).

There are exemptions allowing the data controller to exclude information relating to an individual other than the data subject, to allow some latitude where provision of copy records is very difficult or impossible to achieve, to protect trade secrets (s.8) and to withhold data if they are likely to cause substantial damage or distress to the data subject or any other person (s.10). Regulations made under section 7 also allow data controllers to decline to disclose data if this would be likely to cause serious harm to the physical or mental health or condition of the data subject or any other person. Information should not normally be disclosed without data subject consent unless it has been established that the data subject is incapable of managing his/her own affairs and the person requesting disclosure has been appointed by a court to manage those affairs.[1]

Parents, guardians or carers may seek disclosure of information about data subjects other than themselves for whom they undertake parental or carer responsibility. If the data subject is a child or anyone else who is likely to understand fully his or her rights to confidentiality, then consent should be established if at all possible. The maximum fee for arranging access to automated health records is £10, although £50 is the maximum if paper records are included.[2]

A further condition for the processing (which includes disclosure) of sensitive personal data is in accordance with circumstances specified by the Secretary of State (para. 10, Sch. 3 of the Act). This could, therefore, include disclosure where it is necessary for the prevention or detection of crime or for protecting the public against dishonesty, malpractice, incompetence or mismanagement where seeking the consent of the data subject would prejudice those purposes.[3]

Additional controls[4] over the processing of personal data electronically introduced two new rules for email marketing: all marketing messages must disclose the sender's identity and provide a valid address for opt-out requests and unsolicited messages, and, in most circumstances, require prior consent from the recipient.

In 2007, a detailed Code of Practice on information security management was introduced for NHS providers of healthcare, as part of their *information governance* arrangements. This Code applies to both managed NHS services and contractors who provide services for the NHS and covers all forms of patient health records, administrative information, radiographs ('X-rays'), photographs, digital media such as DVDs and removable memory sticks, networked computer records and email, text and other message types.

Access to health records

Most of the provisions of the Access to Health Records Act 1990 are now within the Data Protection Act 1998, but the 1990 Act continues to provide that a personal representative of a deceased person or anyone who has a claim arising out of a patient's death can also claim access to 'sensitive personal data' maintained in health records.

Generally speaking, the requirements of data protection legislation do not apply to any information which relates to a data subject who has died

[1] The Data Protection (Subject Access Modification) (Health) Order SI 2000 No. 413
[2] The Data Protection (Subject Access) (Fees and Miscellaneous Provisions) Regulations SI 2000 No. 191
[3] The Data Protection (Processing of Sensitive Personal Data) Order SI 2000 No. 417
[4] The Privacy and Electronic Communications (EC Directive) Regulations SI 2003 No. 2426

(but see above) nor to data which have been 'anonymised' (i.e. have been detached from any details or any links whatsoever which could identify a living individual). A legal case has been brought to clarify the limits on the use of anonymised data when derived from patient medication records held by community pharmacists (see box 21.1).

Box 21.1 *Sale of prescription data*

R v Department of Health, ex parte Source Informatics Ltd (2000)

Source Informatics Ltd proposed a scheme whereby after they, Source Informatics, had obtained the prescribers' consent, pharmacists, for a fee, would supply anonymised information contained on NHS prescriptions for the purposes of market research. The Department of Health in a policy document entitled *The Protection and Use of Patient Information* had made clear that under common law and the Data Protection Act principles the general rule was that information given in confidence may not be disclosed without the consent of the provider of the information (i.e. doctor or pharmacist). It also stated that anonymisation, with or without aggregation, did not remove the duty of confidence towards patients who are the subject of the data, namely details on their prescriptions written by the doctor and dispensed by the pharmacist. The High Court ([1999] 4 All ER 185) agreed with the Department of Health. The Court of Appeal on judicial review reversed the decision and Mr Justice Simon Brown said:

> the patient has no proprietorial claim to the prescription form or to the information it contains ... [he has] no right to control its use provided only and always that his privacy is not put at risk ...

He concluded by saying:

> Participation in Source's scheme by doctors and the pharmacists would not in my judgment expose them to any serious risk of successful breach of confidence proceedings by a patient.

Comment. This case was not appealed and it would seem that the Data Protection Act does not normally cover data which have been anonymised, that is, detached from any details which could identify a living individual.

The Times, 18 January 2000.

Freedom of Information Act 2000

The Freedom of Information Act 2000 seeks to promote the openness and accountability of public authorities. Whereas the Data Protection Act is concerned to protect the privacy of individuals and their personal data, the Freedom of Information Act gives people the right to seek information from public authorities about how they carry out their duties, why they make the decisions they do and how they spend public money. Public authorities would include NHS trusts and PCTs. Such trusts must adopt and maintain a publication scheme, setting out details of information it will routinely make available, how the information can be obtained and whether there is any charge for it. Each trust must comply, normally within 28 days, with requests for the information that it holds unless an exemption from disclosure applies. Exemptions include personal data covered by the Data Protection Act (see above), information provided to the public authority in confidence and some limited protection from disclosure which may jeopardise commercial interests. From 1 January 2009, pharmacies providing NHS services were required to adopt a model publication scheme approved by the Information Commissioner.

Pharmacy ownership

A full explanation has been given in chapter 5 of the controls applied by the Medicines Act 1968 to the conduct of 'retail pharmacy businesses'. As such, a business can be owned by an individual pharmacist, a partnership of pharmacists or a body corporate (i.e. a company); it is desirable that the legal status of partnerships and companies should be understood. Only a brief explanation can be given here and any pharmacist contemplating ownership should seek advice from a suitably specialised lawyer or from the business law pages on the website of the Department for Business, Innovation and Skills (formerly the Department for Business, Enterprise and Regulatory Reform, formerly the Department of Trade and Industry).

Partnerships

A partnership is defined in the Partnership Act 1890 as the relationship which exists between persons carrying on a business in common with a view of profit. In contrast to a company (see below), a partnership, or *firm*, is simply a number of individuals each of whom has a responsibility for the affairs and the liabilities of the firm as a whole.

In England and Wales, a partnership (firm) does not have a legal status of its own as does a company. This means that the private assets of each partner can be called upon to satisfy any of the firm's debts. All the partners are liable for any debts incurred by one partner acting on behalf of the firm.

In Scotland, a partnership has a status similar to that of a body corporate (i.e. it *is a legal person distinct from the partners of whom it is composed*). It is for this reason that in a partnership owning a retail pharmacy in England and Wales, all the partners must be pharmacists, whereas in a Scottish partnership only one partner need be a pharmacist (chapter 5).

A partnership can arise in either of two ways: by express agreement or by implied agreement between two or more persons. A partnership can be implied if two or more persons work together in such a way as to fall within the definition as set out in the Act. Generally, if they share in the management of the business and share the profits, then the law will recognise them as partners.

When a partnership is formed to run a retail pharmacy, it is invariably a partnership of express agreement, and the conditions of the partnership are set out in a partnership contract or articles. The articles can be altered at any time with the consent of all the partners, whether this is express or implied. The only exception is where the articles restrict the right to vary (e.g. that no change may be made for 2 years).

A partnership can be formed where one of the partners may limit their responsibility for the firm's debts, leaving the other partners to share the unlimited liability. This partner is often referred to as a *sleeping partner*, as s/he takes no part in the management of the firm. Partnerships of this type are not common and are governed by the Limited Partnerships Act 1907. If a person wishes to limit their liability in this way today, they are more likely to invest in a limited company. Once again, it is stressed that before contemplating forming a partnership, pharmacists should take legal advice and have any partnership contract drawn up by a solicitor.

The Limited Liability Partnership Act 2000 allowed the creation of limited liability partnerships within England, Scotland and Wales to retain the organisational flexibility and tax treatment of a partnership but also derive benefit from the separate legal personality of a company with limited liability. Limited liability partnerships must register and submit annual accounts to Companies House.

Companies

A company (or corporation aggregate or *body corporate*) is a body of persons combined or incorporated for some common purpose. The most common example is a registered trading company, that is, a company which has been incorporated under the relevant Companies Act. The notes given here can only outline the general principles of company law, with some special reference to certain aspects which particularly affect pharmacy businesses. Incorporation as a company enables a group of people to act and to trade in the same way as an individual owner. It also enables them to trade with limited liability to the individual shareholder. Once incorporated, a company is *a legal person* and quite distinct from its members. It can own property, employ persons and be a creditor or debtor just like a human being. This is a fundamental principle of company law.

The promoters of a company must file (electronic submission became permitted in 2006) the following documents with the Register of Companies:

1 memorandum of association;
2 articles of association;
3 list of directors and name of secretary;
4 statement of the nominal share capital;
5 notice of the address of the registered office; and
6 declarations by a solicitor or a person named in the articles as a director or secretary that all the requirements of the Companies Acts in respect of registration have been complied with.

If all the documents are in order, the Registrar will issue a certificate of incorporation, which is conclusive evidence that the company has been registered and that the requirements of the Act have been complied with.

There are at least three types of company: a public company, a private limited company and a private unlimited company. Most pharmacists will be concerned with the private company, whether limited or not.

A *private company* needs only one director but if there is a sole director, s/he cannot also be the company secretary. Shares and debentures in a private company cannot be offered to the public.

An *unlimited company* is one where there is no limit on the members' liability to contribute to the assets in order to satisfy the company's debts.

Memorandum of association

The memorandum of association regulates the external affairs of the company and must include five clauses, namely those relating to the name, registered office, objects, liability and capital of the company. It must be signed by each subscriber.

The name of a private limited company must end with the word *limited*. For a public limited company, the last words must be *public limited company* or *plc*.

There is a general freedom of choice of the company name, but a company cannot be registered under the Act by a name which includes, otherwise than at the end of its name, the word *limited, unlimited* or *public limited company* or the Welsh equivalents (e.g. *cfyngedig*). Where *cfyngedig* is used, the fact that the company is a limited company must be stated in English and in legible characters on all official company stationery and publications, and in a notice conspicuously displayed in every place where the company's business is carried on.

No name may be used which the Registrar considers offensive or which, if used, would constitute a criminal offence. In the latter category would fall a retail company which is not conducting a retail pharmacy business and which wished to use the title *chemist*.

Certain words and expressions may only be used in company or business names with the approval of the Secretary of State or other relevant body specified in Regulations. For the word *chemist* the GPhC is the relevant body, but, when *chemist* or *chemistry* is used in an industrial sense, it is the Royal Society of Chemistry. Similarly, for the word *apothecary* the relevant body in England and Wales is the Worshipful Society of Apothecaries and in Scotland, the GPhC.

Articles of association

The articles regulate the internal affairs of the company (i.e. the rights of shareholders and the manner in which the business of the company is conducted). A model set of articles is set out in Regulations made under the Act. It may be used by a company as it is or adapted as required. If no articles are submitted with the application for registration, the statutory ones will apply. The articles of a company are freely alterable by special resolution, subject to certain safeguards.

The legal effect of the memorandum and articles is that they bind the company and its members as if they had been signed and sealed by each individual member and contained covenants on the part of each member to observe all the provisions of the memorandum and articles.

Directors

The first directors of a company are usually appointed in accordance with the articles; if not they are appointed by the original subscribers to the company. Subsequent appointments are usually governed by a procedure laid down in the articles. It must be stressed that a pharmacist becoming a director should be fully aware of the contents of the memorandum and articles of association of the company s/he joins. Directors must exercise their powers as directors for the benefit of the company. A director has a duty to the company to exercise such skill and care as s/he possesses. If appointed in a specific capacity calling for a particular skill (e.g. a pharmacist who is a director of a body corporate), s/he must exercise that skill in a reasonable manner for the benefit of the company. Directors are not bound to give continuing and unremitting attention to the company's affairs and are justified in trusting the officers of the company to perform their duties honestly.

A pharmacist who becomes superintendent chemist (pharmacist) of a company will almost invariably be appointed a director, and a knowledge of the powers and duties of directors is essential. For example, if a company fails to make its annual return then the company and/or any of its officers or directors is liable to a default fine. A pharmacist who resigns as a superintendent chemist should ensure that s/he also resigns as a director. Instances have occurred where a pharmacist, some years after having resigned as a superintendent chemist, has been prosecuted for failing to make an annual return as s/he had remained a director of the company.

Business Names Act 1985

A *business name* is a name used by a business which is other than (a) for a sole trader, his/her surname; (b) for a partnership, the surnames or corporate names of all members of the partnership, or (c) for a corporate business, the names of the company concerned. Certain additions are permitted (e.g. forenames or initials). Where a business name is used, the true name(s) and address(es) of the owner(s) must appear on all business stationery and that information must be prominently displayed at the business premises. The use of certain types of business name require the written approval of the Secretary of State and regulations may specify certain words or expressions which may only be used with the approval of a government department or some other relevant body.

Workplace law

Workplace law covers both *employment law* and a range of *anti-discrimination and public protection law* and these can affect pharmacists and sometimes their staff in the workplace. Knowledge of employment law is important to pharmacists both in their capacity as employer and as an employee. Employment rights derive from two main areas: those created by Acts of Parliament (statutory employment rights) and those created by decisions of courts over time (common law rights; chapter 1).

Statutory employment rights

Employment rights cover rights such as equal pay; sick pay; the right not to be unlawfully discriminated against on the grounds of sex or marital status, sexual orientation, race, disability, religion or belief, age, trade union membership, or part-time or fixed term status; not to suffer a detriment for making a protected disclosure in the public interest ('whistle blowing'); and not to be dismissed unfairly. Employees have also been granted rights to a written statement of the terms of employment, of the reasons for dismissal, to minimum disciplinary procedures, to be accompanied at a disciplinary hearing, to an itemised pay statement, for time off for public duties, for time off for antenatal care, for time off for care of dependants, to a minimum wage, to a minimum period of notice for termination of employment, to maternity leave and pay, to paternity leave and pay, to request flexible working and to entitlement to rest breaks and restrictions on weekly working time. This list is not exhaustive.

The rights are enforceable by employees through the Employment Tribunal. Some rights require the employee to have a qualifying period of service before the rights can be enforced in the Employment Tribunal. The compensation that can be awarded by the tribunal is sometimes subject to a statutory minimum or a statutory cap depending on the nature of the claim. However, in other claims, the tribunal considers what is just and equitable in all the circumstances having regard to the loss sustained by the employee.

In the context of employment law, *disability* means 'a physical or mental impairment which has a substantial and long-term adverse effect on a person's ability to carry out normal day-to-day activities'. *Day-to-day activities* involve mobility; manual dexterity; physical co-ordination; ability to lift, carry or move ordinary objects; speech, hearing or eyesight; memory; or ability to concentrate, learn, understand or perceive physical danger. Therefore, the definition includes those with hearing or visual impairment, those with learning disabilities or mental illness and those with long-term illnesses such as severe arthritis, human immunodeficiency virus infection, multiple sclerosis and muscular dystrophy. Certain conditions are excluded, notably addiction to alcohol, nicotine or non-therapeutic drugs.

Common law rights

In the employment context, the principal common law claim is where an employee claims that the employer has acted in breach of the contract of employment. Employment Tribunals can deal with breach of contract claims where the breach has arisen or is outstanding on the termination of the employment. There is a limit of £25 000 on the awards a tribunal can make in these circumstances. Alternatively, employees can make claims either in the County Court or High Court (chapter 1), depending on the amount of damages claimed and other certain criteria applied by the courts.

European law

Sometimes, UK national law is in conflict with EU legislation. In these instances, the case may be referred to the ECJ (chapter 1), the decisions of which will be binding on UK courts and tribunals. Decisions of the ECJ may also result in amendments to national law.

Further information on this complex and fast changing area of law can be obtained at the websites at the end of this chapter.

Vicarious liability

The term *vicarious liability* in this context signifies the liability which an employer may incur to a customer for damage caused by an employee in the course of his/her employment. This, in legal terms, is the relationship between *master* and *servant* and means that the 'master' cannot only order or require *what* must be done but also *how* it shall be done.

All employee pharmacists should have a contract of employment, but in many areas pharmacists themselves will decide *how* a task should be performed and this will often be a matter for the pharmacist's own professional judgement. Therefore, if an employee pharmacist makes a mistake or is so careless as to cause *damage* (e.g. injury, fear, anxiety, etc.) to a patient or customer, the employer would probably be liable. However, if the act or omission fell into the realm of professional judgement, the pharmacist may also incur additional personal liability and might be accountable to the GPhC and/or to his/her employer to justify his/her actions. This is why pharmacists are advised to carry their own professional indemnity insurance or ensure that they practise only in an establishment which is covered by such insurance.

Access to goods, facilities and services

The Equality Act 2010 has replaced previous anti-discrimination laws with a single Act which bans unfair treatment and helps to achieve equal opportunities in the workplace and in wider society. The Act covers nine 'protected characteristics' which may not be used as a reason to treat people unfairly. They are:

- age
- disability
- gender reassignment
- marriage and civil partnership
- pregnancy and maternity
- race
- religion or belief
- sex
- sexual orientation.

The Equality Act sets out the different ways in which it is unlawful to treat someone, such as direct and indirect discrimination, harassment, victimisation and failing to make a reasonable adjustment for a disabled person. The Act prohibits unfair treatment in the workplace when providing goods, facilities and services; when exercising public functions; in the disposal and management of premises; in education; and by associations (such as private clubs). The Act has been brought into force gradually; for example, from October 2010 breastfeeding mothers gained protection from harassment if they wish to feed in public places, pay secrecy clauses were made unenforceable and the definition of gender reassignment was changed by removing the requirement for medical supervision. In April 2011, the public sector (which includes the NHS, NHS contractors and regulators such as the GPhC) gained a duty positively to promote equality in their recruitment and promotion policies and in all other public activities. From October 2012, it will be unlawful to discriminate on the basis of age unless the practice is covered by an exception from the ban, or good reason can be shown for the differential treatment ('objective justification'). The health and social care services do not have any such general exceptions.

Vetting of healthcare workers

Legislation designed to protect children and vulnerable adults from abuse has meant that persons working in either health or social care are now subject to several vetting processes before employment. These include criminal record checks with the Criminal Records Bureau to preclude or possibly constrain the employment of those with relevant convictions. In 2008, a substantial programme of 'vetting' health and social care workers and approving their involvement in 'regulated' and 'controlled' activities was introduced but this has since been reviewed and scaled down when the Conservative–Liberal Democrat Coalition Government came to power in 2010. From December 2012, subject to Parliamentary approval of the necessary legislation,[5] a new non-departmental public body (merged from the Criminal Records Bureau and the Independents Safeguarding Authority) called the Disclosure and Barring Service will take over both criminal record checks, overseeing the scope of redefined 'regulated activities' involving close working with vulnerable groups, including children which a barred person must not do.

Consumer protection law

Detailed information on consumer protection law may be found on the Department for Business, Innovation and Skills website (given at the end of this chapter). All retailers are subject to controls on price, description and the safety of the goods they sell. The majority of the law in this area is enforced by the local authority, usually the trading standards departments. In some cities, those duties may be shared with the local environmental health officer. The general principle of most of this law is that it makes it a criminal offence to mislead consumers as to the description, price or safety of goods and services. The majority of the criminal offences in this area are strict liability offences, coupled to a defence of due diligence. It is,

[5] Regulations to be made under the Protection of Freedoms Act 2012

therefore, vitally important that processes and procedures are in place so that a pharmacist can show that s/he took reasonable steps and precautions to check that descriptions of goods and services were accurate or that the goods s/he sold were safe. The following topics may be of interest.

Trades Descriptions Act 1968

The Trades Descriptions Act makes it an offence to falsely describe goods or services in the course of a trade or business. The law is wide enough to cover all forms of description and it should be noted that the retailer is to some extent in double jeopardy as there is an offence for supplying goods to which a false description has been applied as well as an offence of applying a false description to goods. Particular care needs to be taken where verbal descriptions are being applied to goods, as the individual becomes personally liable for those descriptions should they subsequently prove to be inaccurate. With regard to services, it is an offence to knowingly make a false statement.

Product liability

The Consumer Protection Act 1987 creates liability without fault on the part of the producer for damage caused by a defect in their product. Four classes of person may face liability for a defective product: the manufacturer, the importer, the person who holds themselves out as the manufacturer or, in the event of none of the former being identified, the person supplying the product to the victim. The first three groups have a primary liability; the supplier has a secondary liability based upon their inability to identify a primary producer. When medicines might be the subject of an action in the courts (there have been very few cases under the Act), the primary producer will normally be the product licence holder. The supplying pharmacist should, therefore, ensure that s/he has adequate systems and records to ensure that the licence holder or manufacturer can always be identified with some certainty. Liability probably does not arise from repackaging licensed medicines or from supplying them against a prescription, provided the source is known.

The supplying pharmacist will carry full liability for 'own branded' goods in which the pharmacy's name and address are affixed to containers of medicines made up elsewhere and not so identified. The supplying pharmacist also carries full liability when s/he prepares his/her own remedies for a patient under section 10 of the Medicines Act (chapter 3). In these circumstances, it is advisable to maintain full manufacturing records so that the producer of the ingredients can always be identified. Claims may be made for up to 3 years after the 'relevant date' – when the victim became aware of the facts – subject to a maximum of 10 years from the date of putting the product into circulation.

Price control

Customers' rights on pricing are protected in two areas of consumer protection law: controls on misleading price indications and requirements to display price, and in certain circumstances unit price, in close proximity to the goods. It is an offence to give a misleading price indication and it is, therefore, important for any pharmacist involved in retailing to be aware of the Code of Practice for Traders on Price Indications. This code provides guidance to retailers on what constitutes 'misleading' and how 'offer' prices can be constructed. A second obligation is simply a requirement to display a price in such a way that customers see it without having to ask in close proximity to all goods available for sale. If those goods are required to be sold by weight or measure, then there is an obligation to give a unit price (cost per kilogram or litre) as well as the actual selling price. Unit price controls do not apply to medicines. Within pharmacies, cosmetics, toiletries and food supplements are the items most likely to be affected. Unit price controls apply only in larger stores (over $280\,m^2$). Details of the controls are complicated and subject to change. Advice on price indications should, therefore, be sought from the local trading standards department.

Safety of goods

Consumer protection law also creates an obligation to provide customers with goods that are safe. Any reasonably foreseeable risks arising out of the goods should have been dealt with by the manufacturer and addressed either by changing the design of the goods to make them safer or by issuing warnings or instructions that deal with the issue. Where local authorities find unsafe goods, as well as prosecuting they can also serve enforcement notices requiring that the products are removed from the marketplace.

Weights and Measures Act 1985

The Weights and Measures Act 1985 and the Regulations made under it control the manner in which goods should be weighed, measured and retailed. They also control the way quality indications should be given on the packaging. The legislation lays down specific construction criteria for equipment and measures and sets down the accuracy tests that the equipment must pass if it is to be used for selling goods. The Regulations also set out a detailed regime for the packaging of goods, and those pharmacists involved in packing bulk goods should consult the BIS website (see end of chapter) as well as seeking guidance from the local trading standards department. The selling of goods deficient in weight or volume is a strict liability offence but defences are available.

Competition Act 1998

The Competition Act 1998 reflects a worldwide trend to open up markets, stimulate competition and establish transparent and fair marketing arrangements. It seeks to do this by outlawing agreements between businesses and decisions taken by businesses on concerted practices that affect trade in the UK or Europe. Those decisions are not allowed to have as their object or effect the prevention, distortion or restriction of competition within the UK. An example of such a practice would be people acting together directly or indirectly to fix the purchase or selling process. The rules not only affect retailers but also trade associations or any other group of persons acting together in a way as to distort competition. The fines under the Competition Act can be very high, as the maximum ceiling on the fine is 10 per cent of company turnover.

In pharmacy, the advent of the Competition Act led to the abolition of *resale price maintenance* on the price at which medicines available over the counter could be supplied.[6] At that time, this Act also affected the profession's Code of Ethics. The rules of trade associations and professional bodies are covered by the anti-competitive prohibitions in the Act unless they are specifically exempted in Schedule 4. For historical reasons, pharmacy was not included in Schedule 4 (although some other health professions were) and the Code of Ethics for pharmacy had to comply with the provisions of the Act. Prior to 2002, the Codes of Ethics contained several restraints, in the public interest, on the promotion and supply of medicines but there are none in subsequent codes (former RPSGB) or standards (GPhC). In August 2012, the Office of Fair Trading announced that it had obtained assurances from eight NHS trusts that they would cease sharing commercially sensitive information about their private patient unit prices.[7] This was held to have the 'potential to facilitate collusion' and create an illegal cartel to maintain prices.

Bribery Act 2010

Bribery is broadly defined in the Act as giving someone a financial or other advantage to encourage that person to perform their functions or activities improperly or to reward that person for having done so. An organisation (company, trust, etc.) could be liable under the Bribery Act if a very senior person (e.g. a managing director) commits a bribery offence. It could also be liable where someone who performs services for it (e.g. an employee or an agent) pays a bribe specifically to get business, keep business or gain a business

---

[6] *Pharm J*, 16 August 1997 p. 236; 25 October 1997 p. 676.
[7] OFT *Welcomes Action by NHS Trusts to Ensure Compliance with Competition Law*, Press release, Office of Fair Trading 12 August 2012

advantage for the organisation. A defence is provided if the organisation can show that it had adequate processes in place to prevent bribery.

Websites providing detailed information on trading and other retail law are given at the end of this chapter.

Health and safety law

Health and Safety at Work Act 1974

The Health and Safety at Work Act 1974 is extremely broad and basically sets out the requirements for a 'duty of care' for everyone in the workplace, including the protection of the health and safety of the public against the risks to health arising from work activities. It, therefore, applies to employers, employees, owners/occupiers of premises, suppliers and the self-employed. The Act provides a framework for other health and safety legislation. Detailed requirements are set out in specific Regulations. These Regulations are themselves supported by an Approved Code of Practice that expands the requirements contained within individual Regulations by providing detailed interpretation and guidance. Approved Codes of Practice are the main working documents for those with health and safety responsibilities.

Employers have a duty of care under the Health and Safety at Work Etc. Act 1974, together with its associated Regulations, to ensure, so far as is reasonably practicable, the health, safety and welfare of employees while they are at work. The main areas covered are:

- safe plant and machinery (work equipment) and safe operating procedures;
- safe use, handling and storage and transport of articles and substances;
- provision of information, instruction, training and supervision;
- provision and maintenance of a safe place of work with safe means of access and egress; and
- for an employer with more than four employees, provision of a written policy for health and safety and details of the arrangements for carrying out the requirements of the policy.

Employers, including the self-employed (e.g. a locum pharmacist), and owners/occupiers have a similar duty to safeguard the health and safety of others who are not employees but who may be affected by his/her business activities. 'Others' include customers, visitors and the general public. Employees themselves also have a duty under the Act to take reasonable care for their own health and safety and for that of anyone else who may be affected by what they (employees) do or fail to do. There is also a duty to co-operate with their employer on health and safety issues.

Enforcement of health and safety requirements is undertaken by inspectors from the Health and Safety Executive for 'industrial premises' or by officers from the local authorities for 'retail premises'. Both regulatory groups have the powers to inspect, investigate cases of non-compliance, warn and issue 'improvement notices' or 'prohibition notices' as well as prosecute offenders.

It is beyond the scope of this book to provide much detail about health and safety legislation. However, it is important to raise the awareness of *risk assessment* as the basic 'tool' for identifying and managing risk. Areas where risks might arise in pharmacy practice include:

- work equipment (Provision and Use of Work Equipment Regulations);
- substances (COSHH Regulations, ch. 20); and
- manual handling (Manual Handling Operations Regulations).

To manage health and safety risks, it is necessary to identify the risks. The risk-assessment process achieves this by examining the workplace itself and work activities (tasks). Hazards (things with the potential to cause harm) are noted and the associated consequences (severity) of each hazard ranked should the harm be inflicted. For each hazardous situation, the types of person at risk are also identified. An assessment is also made of the likelihood of the harm actually occurring, again ranked according to likelihood. An assessment of the risk is then made for each situation based on the equation:

Risk = Consequence × Likelihood for each category of persons at risk

The basic principles of risk assessment are detailed in a Health and Safety Executive Approved Code of Practice *Management of Health and Safety at Work Regulations 1999*, to which reference should be made. Persons compiling risk assessments must be trained and have sufficient knowledge and experience of the process such that they are able to demonstrate their competence to the persons at risk depending upon the assessment and any regulatory inspector. Consideration should always be given to engaging suitable experts to do this work for anything other than situations where there are low consequences from workplace hazards. A key outcome of risk assessment is to require the identification and implementation of control measures to reduce risks to as low a level as is reasonably practicable. Control measures may range from hardware (e.g. guards for machinery) to procedural matters (e.g. operating procedures) to personal protective equipment (e.g. gloves/goggles). Risk can be eliminated only if a hazard is eliminated. Substituting something less hazardous (e.g. less-toxic cleaning materials) can reduce risk.

Regulatory inspectors would expect to see 'suitable and sufficient' risk assessments during any visit. It is important to review risk assessments and other health and safety arrangements periodically, or in the event of an accident or even a 'near miss', to see if the assessment and control measures are still valid and whether they can be improved to reduce risks to health and safety further. All such assessments should be discussed with employees who are 'at risk'.

Websites providing detailed information on health and safety law are given at the end of this chapter.

Environmental law

DEFRA is the government department responsible for a vast range of public services and controls such as air quality, noise pollution, litter, energy and chemicals. This section provides an overview of two areas that are relevant to pharmacy practice: controls on waste and the protection of animals and birds. Controls on poisons are covered in chapter 18.

Controls on waste

The Environmental Protection Act 1990 introduced a *duty of care* which applies to all persons who import, produce, carry, keep, treat or dispose of controlled waste. This, therefore, applies to pharmacists, who necessarily handle waste or unwanted medicines in the course of their practice. The duty of care lies on all holders of waste at every stage in its history, such that a pharmacist having held controlled waste may only pass it on to an *authorised person*, such as registered carriers, permit/licence holders or someone who is exempt from either being a registered carrier or operating under a permit/licence. Further, s/he must transfer with the waste such a written description of the waste – a transfer note, setting out the type and quantity of the waste – as will enable others to dispose of the waste appropriately and avoid committing an offence under the Act.

Controlled waste includes household, industrial and commercial waste of any kind, whether conventionally thought of as polluting or not. The Controlled Waste Regulations[8] define *clinical waste* as, amongst other things, 'waste from a healthcare activity (including veterinary healthcare) that (a) contains viable micro-organisms or their toxins which are known or reliably believed to cause disease in humans or other living organisms or (b) contains or is contaminated with a medicine that contains a biologically active pharmaceutical agent . . .'.

The Regulations also define the type of waste (household, industrial or commercial) based on its source. This is significant, because while a local authority has a duty to collect household waste, the Regulations allow a charge to be made for collection and sometimes disposal of some household wastes specified in Schedule 1 of the Regulations. Clinical waste produced

[8] The Controlled Waste Regulations SI 2012 No. 811

in a domestic property, for example, may incur a collection charge, but its disposal attracts no charge. Producers of commercial or industrial wastes are more likely to have to use private contractors for this purpose. Under the Environmental Protection Act 1990, permits or licences are required for the storage, transfer, treatment and disposal of waste. A permit or licence is not generally required to store waste on the premises at which it was produced.

Further Regulations set out arrangements that may be made[9] and which, if they comply with the conditions specified, will be exempt from section 33(1)(a) of the Environmental Protection Act 1990 (the restriction on knowingly permitting the deposit of controlled waste on any land without an environmental permit). One such exemption is for the 'temporary storage at a collection point'. This exemption allows a community pharmacy to temporarily store waste in a secure container where returned medicines have been received from domestic premises. This exemption does not require registration, but waste disposal companies collecting waste from pharmacies will need to be satisfied that the pharmacy is complying with the conditions specified.

Under this exemption, wastes of different types should not be mixed. Where practicable for example, blisters of unused or unwanted medicines should be removed from the cardboard cartons so that they can be sent for incineration, whereas the cardboard cartons (and any patient information leaflets) can be sent for recycling. Discharge of pharmaceutical waste to sewer must have the prior agreement of the water authorities. Non-pharmaceutically active products (such as saline bags) may be discharged but, at the other extreme, cytotoxic or ecotoxic products would not be permitted. The agreement of the water authorities may depend on the amounts and types of discharge upstream and downstream of the pharmacy.

Hazardous Waste Regulations[10] essentially replaced the 1996 Special Waste Regulations. Hazardous waste is classified as hazardous waste by the Hazardous Waste Regulations 2005 and the List of Wastes Regulations 2005 if it has hazardous properties. In pharmacy, the main hazardous properties seen in medicinal waste are cytotoxic or cytostatic products. The Regulations require the producer of the hazardous waste to keep hazardous waste separate from non-hazardous waste, and to segregate hazardous from non-hazardous waste if mixed wastes are received. This poses a challenge to a pharmacy that accepts unwanted medicines from patients, as the pharmacy would need to be able to identify whether any waste received is hazardous in order to carry out this segregation.

In England and Wales, producers of hazardous waste must notify the Environment Agency that it is a producer, but if a pharmacy produces less than 500 kg per year (taking into account not only medicines, but all

---

[9] Schedule 15 of the Environmental Permitting (England and Wales) Regulations SI 2010 No. 675
[10] The Hazardous Waste (England and Wales) Regulations SI 2005 No. 894 (as amended)

other hazardous waste such as fluorescent tubes, computer monitors, etc.), then it is exempt from notification. Movement of hazardous waste is tightly controlled, and must be accompanied by a detailed consignment note which describes the waste sufficiently to allow safe ultimate disposal.

Controlled Drugs

The special restrictions on the destruction of Controlled Drugs under the Misuse of Drugs Act 1971 were considered in chapter 17. Controlled Drugs, whether stock or returned by patients, are subject to the same considerations described above for other returned medicines and advice, so disposal via the sewage system would not generally be permitted. Further, the Misuse of Drugs Act requires that Controlled Drugs be denatured in such a way as to render the drug irretrievable, such as use of specially designed Controlled Drug denaturing kits. The denaturing of Controlled Drugs would be classified as 'treatment' of waste, which would require a permit, but the 2010 Regulations (see above) set out an exemption for sorting and denaturing Controlled Drugs for disposal. This exemption must be registered with the Environment Agency.

Sharps

Sharps can be returned to a pharmacy, but the health and safety of staff and persons using the pharmacy is paramount, and procedures must protect from risk of injury. The European Directive 2010/32/EU sets out requirements to prevent sharps injuries in the healthcare sector. This directive must be implemented through domestic legislation by May 2013. This focuses on risk assessment, and then elimination, prevention and protection. Under this directive, the practice of recapping of needles will be prohibited (this is aimed at healthcare workers, and is designed to minimise the number of needlestick injuries).

Controls to protect animals and birds

Animals in research

The Animal (Scientific Procedures) Act 1986 makes provision for the protection of animals used for experimental or scientific procedures.

A *protected animal* for the purposes of the Act means *any living vertebrate other than a human*.

A *regulated procedure* is any experimental or other scientific procedure applied to a protected animal which may have the effect of causing that animal pain, suffering, distress or lasting harm.

The Act provides for a system of (a) personal licences, (b) project licences and (c) scientific establishment licences. Before issuing any licence, the Secretary of State must consult one of the inspectors appointed under the

Act (s.9). The breeding and sale of animals for experimental purposes is also controlled.

The Act specifies the type of programmes for which project licences may be issued, including, amongst other things, the prevention, diagnosis or treatment of disease; certain educational purposes; and forensic enquiries. Projects may only be carried out by licensed persons on licensed scientific establishments. The Act deals specifically with humane methods of killing experimental animals. The Animals Procedures Committee has the duty of advising the Secretary of State on matters concerned with the Act. S/he may consult the Committee on the question of licences and on the preparation of codes of practice. Regulations[11] implementing European Directive 2010/63/EC came into force in December 2012.

Wild animals and farm livestock

Where under the Animal (Cruel Poisons) Act 1962, the Secretary of State has specified that a poison cannot be used for destroying animals without causing undue suffering and that other suitable methods of destroying them exist, s/he may, by regulations, prohibit or restrict the use of that poison for destroying animals or animals of a particular description.

Regulations have been made which prohibit the use of yellow phosphorus and red squill for the destruction of animals.[12] The Regulations also prohibit the use of strychnine for killing any animals including moles. The supply of these substances for prohibited purposes could constitute aiding and abetting an offence under the Act.

NB. Where the minister believes or suspects that rabies exists in any area, s/he may by an Order made under the Rabies Act 1974 declare that area to be an *infected area* for purposes connected with the control and eradication of that disease. S/he may also take steps to secure destruction of foxes in an *infected area* and an officer of DEFRA and any person authorised in writing by the minister may enter any land for the purpose of carrying out such destruction. Where the minister exercises this power, methods of destruction may be used (e.g. the use of strychnine) which would apart from these provisions be unlawful.[13] The Protection of Animals Act 1911 provides that it is unlawful wilfully to administer, or cause or procure to be administered, to any animal a poisonous or injurious drug or substance. Similarly, it is unlawful to sell or offer or expose for sale any grain or seed which has been rendered poisonous except for *bona fide* use in agriculture. It is also an offence to place upon any land or in any building any poison or any fluid or edible matter (not being seed or grain) which has been rendered poisonous. It is a defence to prove that the poison was placed for the purpose of destroying

[11] The Animals (Scientific Procedures) Act 1986 Amendment Regulations SI 2012 No. 3039
[12] The Animals (Cruel Poisons) Regulations SI 1963 No. 1278
[13] Rabies (Control) Order SI 1974 No. 2212

insects and other invertebrates where it is found necessary in the interest of public health or agriculture, or to preserve other animals, and that adequate precautions have been taken to prevent injury to dogs, cats, other domestic animals and wild birds.[14]

A defence also exists where a person uses poisonous gas in a rabbit hole or places in a rabbit hole a substance which by evaporation or any contact with moisture generates poisonous gas (e.g. Cymag).[15] These defences are not valid where the poison concerned is prohibited by the Animal (Cruel Poisons) Act 1962 (see above). It is also a defence under the Wildlife and Countryside Act 1981 to prove that what was done was performed in accordance with a licence granted under that Act.

In relation to wildlife, the Wildlife and Countryside Act 1981 prohibits certain methods of killing or taking of wild birds and wild animals, including the laying of 'any poisonous, poisoned or stupefying substance'. The prohibition does not apply to anything done under or in accordance with the terms of a licence granted by the appropriate authority. The appropriate authority varies according to the purpose of the licence (e.g. if the licence is issued for the purpose of preventing the spread of disease, then the appropriate authority is the Agriculture Minister). Such a licence may be issued by the Agriculture Minister for the killing or taking of certain wild birds (e.g. feral pigeons, house sparrows, etc.) using the chemical alpha-chloralose. Alpha-chloralose can be sold to local authorities and to *bona fide* pest control companies who have had issued to them by the Agriculture Minister a licence which allows them to compound and use their own bait. Farmers have been known to make approaches to pharmacists for supplies of alpha-chloralose; although the pharmacist may lawfully supply this chemical under poison legislation, a supply made for the purpose of stupefying birds could be an offence under the Wildlife and Countryside Act 1981. Pharmacists receiving requests for alpha-chloralose or stupefying bait should, before supplying, contact the RPS for further details.

Merchant shipping: medical scales

Regulations implement Council Directive 92/29/EEC and make for the minimum safety and health requirements for improved medical treatment so far as the Directive relates to the carriage of medicines and other medical stores at sea.[16] They cover the carrying of appropriate medical stores on board ships, including fishing vessels.

[14]Protection of Animals (Amendment) Act 1927
[15]Prevention of Damage by Rabbits Act 1939
[16]The Merchant Shipping and Fishing Vessels (Medical Stores) Regulations SI 1995 No. 1802 (as amended)

A *ship* in this context means a UK ship other than pleasure vessels used for non-commercial purposes and not manned by professional crews and ships employed in inland navigation.

The master of any ship which does not carry a doctor is required to make arrangements for securing medical attention on board ship to be given by himself or by some other person appointed by him/her for the purpose. There are minimum requirements for the medicines and medical stores to be carried before a ship may put to sea and the *scale of medicines* to be carried depends upon whether or not there is a duly qualified medical practitioner in the ship's complement.

The various scales are provided for in the 1995 Regulations and in Merchant Shipping Notices M.1607 and M.1608. The Regulations also specify requirements for the packaging, labelling and storage of medicines and other medical items (e.g. disinfectants). The containers must be labelled amongst other things, with:

1 the name of the medicine, in English, as indicated in the respective scale;
2 the expiry date, where appropriate;
3 any storage requirements;
4 name and address of supplier, product licence number and batch number; and
5 any further information required by the notices.

The containers of capsules and tablets must be capable of reclosure so as to prevent the ingress of moisture.

A ship in the UK may be detained if a person empowered under the Act to inspect the medical stores is not satisfied that the required stores are being carried.

Orders made under the Misuse of Drugs Act 1971 and the Medicines Act 1968 permit the owner or master of a ship which does not carry a doctor as part of its complement to obtain certain Controlled Drugs and any other POMs which are necessary for the treatment of persons on the ship. The medical scales issued under the Merchant Shipping Act are minimum requirements only.

Jury service

All persons normally resident in the UK and aged between 18 and 70 years who are registered as parliamentary or local government electors are, with very few exceptions, liable for jury service. Schedule 33 (under s.321 of the Criminal Justice Act 2003) sets out the exemptions, which are broadly persons who are mentally disordered; persons who are or have been subject to certain detention, custody, prison or court martial sentences; and, as a discretionary exemption, persons who are needed for military service at the material time. Pharmacists have no occupational exemption. Details of what jury service entails and the payment and expenses arrangements can be found on the Court Service website at the end of this chapter.

In Scotland, pharmacists may be eligible for exemption from jury service. Exemption is not automatic and the pharmacist who wishes to be excused must give written notice to the clerk of the court from whom the citation is received, indicating his/her right and desire to be so excused. Details can be found on the Scottish Courts website at the end of the chapter.

Summary

- This chapter outlines enactments and other measures which can be relevant to pharmacy. Some are of general application and others may apply only to one of the branches of pharmacy practice.
- Data protection and freedom of information legislation covers virtually all personal data used in pharmacy practice. Under the legislation, health professionals, including pharmacists, have a duty of confidentiality.
- The law covering being an owner, an employer or an employee is outlined as is the law relating to running a retail business and health and safety issues.
- There are controls on disposal of waste, on supply of pesticides and to protect animals and birds.
- The carriage of appropriate medical stores on board ships to fulfil minimum safety and health requirements for medical treatment where a ship does not carry a doctor is covered by scales that specify the medicines to be included.

Further reading

Austen N, Hawkins A (2007). Get your Company Act together. *Pharmacy Today*, April, pp. 26–27.

Davies J (2005). In good company. *Chemist and Druggist*, 26 November, p. 38.

Day C (2007). To err can be expensive. *Pharmacy Magazine*, July, p. 49.

Exten-Wright J, Stansfield T (2008) Employing overseas workers. *Chemist and Druggist*, 8 November, pp. 35–37.

Fradgley S, Smith J (2012) Purple waste: how a hospital trust deals with hazardous waste medicines *Pharm J*, 288: 417–418.

Ministry of Justice (2011). *Guidance on the Bribery Act 2010*. London: Ministry of Justice: http://www.justice.gov.uk/downloads/legislation/bribery-act-2010-guidance.pdf (accessed 21 November 2012).

Mooney H (2011). Beware of those bearing gifts (about the Bribery Act 2011). *Health Service Journal*, 1 December, p. 21.

Muir J (2002). Sometimes things go wrong: the concept of unfair dismissal. *Pharm J*, 268: 445–447.

Pate R, Anderson M (2011). Good relationships must come first (about the Bribery Act). *Pharm J*, 287: 572.

Richman C, Castensson S (2008). Impact of waste pharmaceuticals: an environmental hazard or 'greenwash'? *Pharm J*, 280: 335–337.

Rosenbloom K *et al.* (2005) The Disability Discrimination Act. *Pharm J*, 275: 747–750.

Santillo M (2012). What you need to know about the new EU legislation on needlestick injuries. *Pharm J*, 288: 760–761.

Wakeman R (2007). Clean up your act. *Pharmacy Today*, June, pp. 6–7.

Weinbren, E (2012). Pharmacy wins three-year battle against disproportionate staff vetting plans. *Chemist and Druggist*, 8 May (online).

Wilkinson E (2012). How to be disability friendly. *Chemist and Druggist*, 7th July, p. 23.

Websites

Advisory, Conciliation and Arbitration Service: http://www.acas.gov.uk

Chemist and Druggist: http://www.chemistanddruggist.co.uk

Consumer Regulations: http://www.crw.gov.uk

Department for Business, Innovation and Skills: http://www.bis.gov.uk/

Department for Environment, Food and Rural Affairs: http://www.defra.gov.uk

Environment Agency (waste disposal):
    http://www.environment-agency.gov.uk/business/topics/waste/default.aspx

Equality Act, Home Office: http://homeoffice.gov.uk/equalities/equality-act/

Government websites: http://www.direct.gov.uk/en/index.htm

Health and Safety Executive: http://www.hse.gov.uk

Home Office (proposals to update animal experimentation legislation):
    http://scienceandresearch.homeoffice.gov.uk/animal-research/legislation/

Home Office (vetting, disclosure and barring):
    http://www.homeoffice.gov.uk/crime/vetting-barring-scheme/

Jury service: http://www.courtservice.gov.uk

Jury service in Scotland: http://www.scotcourts.gov.uk

Local authority circulars: http://www.hse.gov.uk/lau/lacs/index.htm

Ministry of Justice: http://www.justice.gov.uk

National Pharmacy Association (leaflets and guidance on disposal of hazardous waste):
    http://www.npa.org.uk

Office of Fair Trading: http://www.oft.gov.uk

Office of the Information Commissioner: http://www.informationcommissioner.gov.uk

Pharmaceutical Journal: http://www.pjonline.com

Trading Standards Departments: http://www.tradingstandards.gov.uk

22

Pharmacy regulation

Dai John

The GPhC became the independent regulator for pharmacists, pharmacy technicians and pharmacy premises in Great Britain on 27 September 2010. Prior to this date, the RPSGB had dual regulatory and professional leadership roles. Pharmacy was the last of the healthcare professions to have an independent regulator in Great Britain. The GPhC has appointed a director in each of Scotland and Wales, recognising the divergence in Great Britain health policy and delivery.

The General Pharmaceutical Council

The role of the GPhC (also referred to as the Council) is to protect, promote and maintain the health, safety and wellbeing of members of the public by upholding standards and public trust in pharmacy. Article 4 (3) of the Pharmacy Order 2010[1] identifies the principal functions of the GPhC:

a   to establish and maintain a register of pharmacists, pharmacy technicians and premises at which a retail pharmacy business is, or is to be, carried on;
b   to set and promote standards for the safe and effective practice of pharmacy at registered pharmacies;
c   to set requirements by reference to which registrants must demonstrate that their fitness to practise is not impaired;
d   to promote the safe and effective practice of pharmacy by registrants (including, for example, by reference to any code of conduct for, and ethics relating to, pharmacy);
e   to set standards and requirements in respect of the education, training, acquisition of experience and CPD that it is necessary for pharmacists and pharmacy technicians to achieve in order to be entered in the Register or to receive an annotation in the Register and to maintain competence; and
f   to ensure the continued fitness to practise of registrants.

[1] The Pharmacy Order SI 2010 No. 231; all references in this chapter are to the Pharmacy Order unless otherwise stated

The GPhC is a 'body corporate' (defined in chapter 21) which became a legal entity on 10 February 2010, with the chair and the other 13 members of the Council appointed by the Appointments Commission as designate appointments in 2009. This was formalised by the Pharmacy Order 2010 and the General Pharmaceutical Council (Constitution) Order 2010[2] and other 'commencement' orders.[3] The Pharmacy Order 2010 was enacted under powers conferred by sections 60, 62(4) and 62(4A) of, and Schedule 3 to, the Health Act 1999, as read with paragraph 1A of Schedule 2 to the European Communities Act 1972. The Council has a Great Britain rather than a UK jurisdiction; that is, it has regulatory powers in England, Scotland and Wales. The Pharmaceutical Society of Northern Ireland is the pharmacy regulator for Northern Ireland, although the two organisations work collaboratively via a Memorandum of Understanding (see websites at the end of this chapter). The GPhC has adopted the principle that in the conduct of public business in Wales, it will treat the English and Welsh languages on a basis of equality to fulfil its obligations under the Welsh Language Act 1993 (see website at the end of this chapter).

The main powers and responsibilities of the GPhC derive from the Pharmacy Order 2010 and the Rules made under the Order. The GPhC has powers and responsibilities for the registration of pharmacy premises and for enforcing certain provisions under the Medicines Act 1968 and the Poisons Act 1972. To carry out its functions effectively the GPhC works in close collaboration with a number of other individuals and organisations. These include other regulators, other organisations such as those representing patients and the public, professional bodies such as the RPS, educators and employers. The GPhC works with a number of government agencies to avoid duplication of effort and to improve patient safety; these include the police, Care Commission in Scotland, Care Quality Commission (CQC), Health Inspectorate Wales, the Counter Fraud and Security Management Services of the NHS (this is now known as NHS Protect and is part of the NHS Business Services Agency), the Crown Prosecution Service, Her Majesty's Inspectorate of Prisons, National Patient Safety Agency (and its successor) and the National Treatment Agency for Substance Misuse, together with the MHRA and the Veterinary Medicines Directorate (VMD) (see website resources).

The Professional Standards Authority for Health and Social Care[4]

The Professional Standards Authority for Health and Social Care (PSAHSC) oversees the work of the GPhC and eight other healthcare regulators and

[2]SI 2010 No. 300
[3]SI 2010 Nos. 299, 1618, 1619 and 1621
[4]Formerly called the Council for Healthcare Regulatory Excellence

promotes the health and wellbeing of patients and the public in the regulation of health professionals. The PSAHSC is also empowered to receive details of all the decisions of the GPhC's fitness to practise cases and, subject to certain conditions, to refer cases to the High Court or to the Court of Session in Scotland. (The PSAHSC is more fully discussed in chapters 24 and 25.)

The Pharmacy Order 2010

This Pharmacy Order 2010 makes provision for establishing the GPhC and sets out the arrangements for regulating pharmacists and pharmacy technicians in Great Britain. It also amends and supplements various provisions in Part 4 of the Medicines Act 1968 (C. 67), and in section 9 of the Poisons Act 1972 in respect of the regulation and inspection of registered pharmacies in Great Britain. The Order also implements in part the European Council Directive 2005/36/EC, as amended by Council Directive 2006/100/EC, on pharmacy professional qualification recognition.

The Order comprises eight parts with an associated six schedules:

Part 1 Preliminary matters
Part 2 The Council and its Committees
Part 3 Registered Pharmacies: Standards in retail pharmacies
Part 4 Registration
Part 5 Education, training and acquisition of experience and continuing professional development
Part 6 Fitness to practise
Part 7 Proceedings
Part 8 Miscellaneous:

    Schedule 1 Constitution of the General Pharmaceutical Council
    Schedule 2 Visiting Practitioners from relevant European States
    Schedule 3 The Directive: Designation of competent authority etc.
    Schedule 4 Amendments, repeals and revocations
    Schedule 5 Transitional Provisions
    Schedule 6 Savings (primary and secondary legislation).

The term registrant is used in the Order and refers to a pharmacist and/or pharmacy technician, as appropriate. Article 3(2) defines what is meant by the practise of the profession, that is, 'a person practises as a pharmacist or a pharmacy technician if, while acting in the capacity of or purporting to be a pharmacist or a pharmacy technician, that person undertakes any work or gives any advice in relation to the preparation, assembly, dispensing, sale, supply or use of medicines, the science of medicines, the practice of pharmacy or the provision of healthcare'. A registrant must have appropriate indemnity cover in respect of liabilities which may be incurred as a result of practising as a pharmacist or pharmacy technician (Art.32(1)). It is an offence for anyone, including a pharmacy student or pre-registration trainee to use the title 'pharmacist' or 'pharmacy technician' unless they are registered.

A person commits an offence (Art.38(2)) who:

a uses the title 'pharmacist' or '*fferyllydd*' (its equivalent in the Welsh language) without being entered as a pharmacist in Part 1 or 4 of the Register;

b uses the title 'pharmacy technician' or '*technegydd fferylliaeth*' (its equivalent in the Welsh language) without being entered as a pharmacy technician in Part 2 or 5 of the Register; or

c uses a title in respect of a particular annotation, which is a prescribed specialist title, where that person does not have an entry in any part of the Register with that particular annotation.

Constitution Order

The Constitution Order[5] made under Article 4(2) of the Pharmacy Order requires that the Council consists of seven registrant members who are registered as pharmacists or pharmacy technicians and seven lay[6] members. There are limitations on the period for which members may serve on the Council (Art.3). The GPhC is to make provision with regard to the education and training of the Council members in standing orders (Art.4). Certain categories of people, for example people who have been convicted of certain types of offences, are disqualified from being members of the Council (Art.5) and once members have been appointed, there are certain circumstances in which they may be removed (Art.6) or suspended from office (Art.7). Provisions relating to the chair (including powers to appoint a deputy chair) of the Council can be found in Articles 8, 9 and 10. There are also provisions relating to the proceedings of the Council including its quorum, which is eight members (Arts.11 and 12). Members of Council are appointed by the appointments commission to ensure a balance of qualities, skills and experience, and to reflect the diversity of the public and of the pharmacy profession.

Functions of the General Pharmaceutical Council

The GPhC's functions may best be grouped as the setting and enforcement of standards for pharmacy premises, education and training for entry on to the GPhC registers of registrants, registration, and maintenance of their fitness

---

[5] SI 2000 No. 300

[6] Lay members are defined in Schedule 1 to the principal Order as 'members who are not and never have been entered in the register of any regulatory body and do not hold qualifications which would entitle them to apply for registration under this Order'

to practise. The requirements for pharmacy registration are largely set out in chapter 5, but standards and enforcement are covered below. Details of these functions are set out in the Order and its schedules and in Registration Rules made under the Pharmacy Order 2010,[7] supplemented by standards and guidance formulated by the GPhC under the authority of the Order and Registration Rules. The requirements are very detailed and the standards are under regular review so reference should be made to the GPhC website for the current requirements at any time. The following is an overview of the legal underpinning for the first three of the GPhC's functions; chapter 23 looks at the range of measures which affect the professional conduct of pharmacy professionals and a full account of the fitness to practise arrangements and their application is given in chapter 24.

Standards for pharmacy premises and their enforcement

The GPhC must set standards for 'the carrying on a retail pharmacy business at a registered pharmacy' (Art.7). Up to mid-2012, the Council had issued only interim standards which are summarised in box 22.1

Box 22.1 *Summary of interim standards for owners and superintendent pharmacists of retail pharmacy businesses*

For those responsible for providing pharmacy services within an organisation they must ensure that all the standards set out in document are met, whether or not those matters are delegated to others. The relevant text is given below.

1. Management and leadership responsibilities

> Owners and superintendent pharmacists have overall responsibility for setting out the standards and policies for the provision of pharmacy services by their organisations. Where a body corporate owns a pharmacy business, a superintendent pharmacist must be appointed to manage the pharmaceutical aspects of the business.

> Superintendent pharmacists have legal obligations under the Medicines Act 1968. The role of superintendent pharmacist is a key position carrying full-time responsibility and accountability within a company.

---

[7]The GPhC (Registration Rules) Order of Council SI 2010 No. 1617 'Registration Rules'

Specific responsibilities are identified for those who are a member of a board of a body corporate (Arts.1.1 to 1.3), owners or super-intendent pharmacists (Arts.1.4 and 1.15) and for superintendent pharmacists (Arts.1.16 to 1.18).

2. Policies, procedures and records

For the safe and effective running of a pharmacy it is essential that appropriate policies, procedures and records are established, maintained and reviewed. You must ensure that all legal and professional requirements are met in relation to the pharmacy services.

There are requirements relating to record-keeping mechanisms (Arts.2.1 to 2.3), to standard operating procedures (Arts.2.4 and 2.5), incident-reporting mechanisms (Arts.2.6 and 2.7) and handling complaints and managing concerns (Arts.2.8 to 2.10).

3. Pharmacy staff

Employees must be supported when carrying out their professional and legal duties. They must be provided with training and development opportunities to strengthen and improve their knowledge, skills and competencies. You must make sure that staff are employed, managed and trained appropriately.

Further information is provided on employing, managing or leading others (Arts.3.1 to 3.7) and for training staff (Arts.3.8 to 3.10).

4. Pharmacy premises

The pharmacy premises from which services are provided must be safe and fit for purpose. You must ensure that the premises you own, or are the superintendent for, are appropriate for the professional services being provided.

There are specific sections relating to the conditions of the premises (Arts.4.1 and 4.2); to the availability of facilities and equipment at the premises (Arts.4.3 and 4.4); the conditions in which medicinal products are to be stored (Art.4.5); arrangements for the obtaining, handling, use, supply and security of medicinal products or medical devices (Arts.4.6 to 4.13); and, as applicable, in relation to operating an internet pharmacy service (Arts.4.14 and 4.15).

NB. In September 2012, the Council announced that it had agreed new standards for registered pharmacies which set out the required outcomes that pharmacy owners and superintendent pharmacists must meet when operating a registered pharmacy. These standards are to be implemented from September 2013 and appear in appendix 9 and on the GPhC website.

However, after a consultation process during 2012, the GPhC published its new standards, which will be effective from September 2013. These appear in appendix 9.

The GPhC must establish an inspectorate (Art.8) and must make provision in Rules about the intervals at which inspectors may conduct routine inspections of registered pharmacies and the circumstances in which inspectors may conduct special inspections of, and visits to, registered pharmacies (Art.9). The powers of a Council inspector are set out in Article 11 and to intentionally obstruct them in exercising their powers is an offence (Art.12). The inspector may serve an improvement notice on the person conducting a retail pharmacy business (Art.13) subject to certain conditions; further Articles detail offences committed by partnerships, appeals against improvement notices and the powers of the courts on appeal. At the time of writing the Council were consulting on how they would implement their powers on inspections and enforcement of standards.

In addition to the general standards, the GPhC has issued *guidance* to owners and superintendent pharmacists on their responsibilities in ensuring compliance with the Responsible Pharmacist Regulations (chapter 5).

The Schedule to the Registration Rules makes detailed provision in respect of applications relating to Part 3 of the Register (registered pharmacies). These applications relate to entries of premises and their renewal and restoration. Applications must be made on the relevant application form and have to be accompanied by a fee determined by GPhC. Applications for the voluntary removal of an entry will usually be refused where there is an ongoing investigation or there are outstanding proceedings relating to the retail pharmacy business carried on at the registered pharmacy. The Registration Rules also set out the procedure to be followed if an entry relating to a pharmacy premises has been fraudulently procured or incorrectly made.

Education and training

Parts 4 and 5 of the Order set out the obligations of the GPhC to appoint a Registrar (Art.18), to establish, maintain and ensure access to the Register and to maintain the Register in the appropriate form and content (Art.19). The Register is in five parts:

Part 1 relating to pharmacists other than visiting practitioners
Part 2 relating to pharmacy technicians other than visiting practitioners
Part 3 relating to premises
Part 4 relating to pharmacists who are visiting practitioners
Part 5 relating to pharmacy technicians who are visiting practitioners.

Parts 4 and 5 also provide for entitlement to entry in Part 1 or Part 2 of the Register, in particular the requirements and standards for education and training of all registrants, both before and after registration. The GPhC does not register pharmacy support staff such as dispensing assistants and medicine counter assistants, but it does accredit courses for them. Part 5 requires the GPhC to set the requirements for appropriate qualifications, to hold assessments and to appoint examiners (Art.44). In connection with all aspects of education and training, the GPhC may appoint visitors to inspect any site at which relevant education or training is provided and to examine the associated assessments or tests of competence (Art.45). Education and training providers must provide the Council with relevant information when required (Art.46) and the GPhC may refuse or withdraw approval of a course, qualifications and institutions as a result of any visitor's report (Art.47).

Parts 3, 4 and 5 of the Order should be read in conjunction with the Registration Rules, which provide the detail in relation to registration issues. Part 2 of the Registration Rules requires the Register to be kept in writing and securely, although certain information is also available online in a searchable format. Part 2 also contains provisions relating to the recording of fitness to practise matters in the Register, for example if conditions have been imposed by the FTP Committee (chapter 24). Registrants are required to notify the Registrar in writing of any changes to their name or contact details. Part 3 of the Registration Rules makes detailed provision in respect of the form and manner of various applications in relation to entries in the Register and include annotations in respect of specialisations (so far the only annotations are as a pharmacist independent prescriber or a pharmacist supplementary prescriber). Applications must be made on the relevant application form (available on the GPhC website) and must to be accompanied by the fee prescribed in Rules made under Article 36 of the Pharmacy Order 2010, which are reviewed annually by Council.[8] Pharmacists who have completed

---

[8] For example, the fees for 2013 appear in the GPhC (Registration and Renewal) Rules Order 2012 made under Article 36 and 66(1)(c) of the Pharmacy Order

the relevant approved education and training as a supplementary prescriber and/or independent prescriber apply to the GPhC with evidence so that the appropriate annotation to their entry is made in the Register (chapter 8 and the GPhC website). Applications, including those regarding annotations, must generally be refused if they are not made within the prescribed time limit and if the prescribed fee is not paid (Part 3). Provision is made for the voluntary removal of entries (including annotations) in the Register for pharmacists and pharmacy technicians. Applications for the voluntary removal of an entry from the Register will generally be refused where there is an ongoing investigation or there are outstanding proceedings relating to a registrant's fitness to practise.

Part 4 of the Registration Rules contains a procedure to be followed by the Registrar for dealing with Register entries relating to registrants that may have been fraudulently procured or incorrectly made, or where the fitness to practise of a registrant was impaired at the time of the registrant's entry in the Register but was not declared.

Registration as a pharmacist

Registration in the UK can be achieved through one of two routes:

a   UK accredited 4-year Master of Pharmacy (MPharm) degree, successful completion of 52 weeks of pre-registration training in England, Scotland or Wales and having passed the GPhC's registration assessment; or

b   a UK-accredited 4-year MPharm degree, successful completion of 52 weeks of pre-registration training in Northern Ireland[9] and having passed the Pharmaceutical Society of Northern Ireland's registration examination.

Accreditation of UK pharmacist training

If a UK MPharm degree or an Overseas Pharmacist Assessment Programme (OSPAP) (see below) is not accredited (or is not provisionally accredited) by the GPhC, then this means that the graduates will not be eligible to be registered as a pharmacist. The GPhC accreditation process involves peer review, site visits, provider self-assessment and public reports. Course providers are required to periodically submit for re-accreditation. Article 42 of the Order requires the GPhC to produce standards for the initial education and training of pharmacists for MPharm and OSPAPs; these are summarised in box 22.2.

---

[9] Formerly referred to as 'reciprocity' arrangements

Box 22.2 Summary of standards for initial education and training of pharmacists

These standards provide universities with the standards for the initial education and training of pharmacists. There are requirements for submitting a degree for accreditation, which are published in the GPhC's *Accreditation and Recognition Manual*, published separately. The time between starting an MPharm degree and registration normally must be no more than 8 years.

Standard 1 Patient and public safety. There must be clear procedures to address concerns about patient safety arising from initial pharmacy education and training. Concerns must be addressed immediately.

Standard 2 Monitoring, review and evaluation of initial education and training. The quality of pharmacy education and training must be monitored, reviewed and evaluated in a systematic and developmental way.

Standard 3 Equality, diversity and fairness. Initial pharmacy education and training must be based on principles of equality, diversity and fairness. It must meet the requirements of all relevant legislation.

Standard 4 Selection of students and trainees. Selection processes must be open and fair and comply with relevant legislation. Processes must ensure that students and trainees are fit to practise as students or trainees at the point of selection. Selection includes recruitment and admissions.

Standard 5 Curriculum delivery and the student experience. The curriculum for MPharm degrees and the pre-registration scheme must deliver the outcomes in Standard 10. Most importantly, curricula must ensure that students and trainees practise safely and effectively. To ensure this, pass criteria must describe safe and effective practice.

Standard 6 Support and development for students and trainees. Students and trainees must be supported to develop as learners and professionals during their initial education and training.

Standard 7 Support and development for academic staff and pre-registration tutors. Anyone delivering initial education and training should be supported to develop in their professional role.

Standard 8 Management of initial education and training. Initial pharmacist education and training must be planned and maintained through transparent processes which must show who is responsible for what at each stage.

Standard 9 Resources and capacity. Resources and capacity are sufficient to deliver outcomes.

Standard 10 Outcomes. The outcomes for the initial education and training of pharmacists are listed in this standard.

In addition to the standards themselves, the document also lists criteria that need to be met for each standard, the evidence required in support of meeting the standards and guidance on meeting the standard. There are also prerequisites for meeting particular standards.

The standards document also contains a number of appendices and some further information:

Appendix 1 Indicative syllabus

Appendix 2 European requirements for the initial education training of pharmacists

Appendix 3 National and European requirements for master's level qualifications

Appendix 4 Sites for pharmacist pre-registration training.

Students are required to comply with the Council code of conduct for students. The code is based on the GPhC's document Standards of Conduct, Ethics and Performance. Indeed the wording of the seven principles is identical but the sub-elements sometimes differ so as to be of relevance to, and in the appropriate context for, pharmacy students. For example, Article 3.1 reads 'recognise diversity and respect the cultural differences, values and beliefs of others, including students and staff', whereas the standards for conduct, ethics and performance for registrants state at Article 3.1, 'Recognise diversity and respect people's cultural differences and their right to hold their personal values and beliefs' (chapter 23).

In addition, the GPhC has issued guidance to schools of pharmacy on developing and applying consistently fitness to practise procedures for students. Pharmacy students, as student health professionals, have certain privileges and responsibilities, for example through dealing with patients, some of whom would be classed as vulnerable. Schools of pharmacy are responsible for ensuring that students have opportunities to learn and practise to the high standards expected of them, and that they are required to be fit to practise (in terms of health and good character). It may well be, in the public interest, that an individual's conduct, for example, is not compatible with registration with the GPhC. The GPhC guidance on fitness to practise procedures states that the schools should make students aware of the requirements for registration as a pharmacist, including those relating to health and good character. In part, this is to contextualise the requirement for student fitness to practise procedures (see website references at the end of the chapter).

A number of UK universities have GPhC-accredited MPharm degrees, and a number of schools of pharmacy offer an accredited MPharm degree that is taught, in part, overseas at a partner university, currently with partner universities in Malaysia. Students enrolled on the latter, commonly referred to as 2+2 programmes, study the first 2 years of the MPharm at the partner university and join the university's UK MPharm course for years three and four. Students who graduate from a GPhC-accredited 2+2 MPharm course are eligible to enter pre-registration training in the UK and, as such, may follow the UK route to registration allowing them to practise as a pharmacist in the UK (subject to finding employment and UK Border Agency requirements). Institutions offering both types of programmes are listed on the GPhC website.

Pharmacists qualified in Northern Ireland

Reciprocity continues to exist between the Pharmaceutical Society of Northern Ireland and the GPhC (Art.20(4)). Details of additional documentation and supporting evidence that must be submitted to the GPhC can be found on the GPhC website.

Pharmacists qualified from European Economic Area countries

Regulations provide for the registration of those who are a national of an EEA country and have qualified as a pharmacist in an EEA country other than the UK.[10] Details of additional documentation and supporting evidence that must be submitted to the GPhC can be found on the GPhC website.

Pharmacists qualified from outside the European Economic Area

For those who qualified as a pharmacist outside of the EEA or for those who have an EEA pharmacist qualification (other than a UK-recognised pharmacist qualification) but are not a national of an EEA country, they must have successfully completed (a) an OSPAP, (b) 52 weeks of pre-registration training approved by the GPhC, and (c) the GPhC registration assessment. Further information, including details of those universities offering the OSPAP programme is available from the GPhC website.

Pre-registration pharmacist training

In addition to approval of qualifications, the GPhC is required to set out the conditions for a period of training, together with successful completion of a registration assessment, to be undertaken prior to registration. An integrated 'sandwich' course combining 4 years of academic study with the equivalent of

[10]The Pharmacy Order 2010 (Approved European Pharmacy Qualifications) Order SI 2010 No. 1620

12 months of training in practice is an alternative approach. In future years, this integrated programme may become the norm.[11] Pre-registration training must be managed by an approved pre-registration tutor at an accredited training site. All trainees are required to achieve competence in a defined set of performance standards during their training, namely personal effectiveness, interpersonal skills and knowledge and understanding relating to medicines and health. The pre-registration year (or two 6-month periods for sandwich programmes) assesses competence in practice and establishes the individual's ability to apply knowledge; to develop and demonstrate new knowledge and skills; and to demonstrate appropriate attitudes and behaviours in practice. Individuals have a maximum of three attempts to pass the Registration Assessment. Further details of the conditions for pre-registration training and the registration assessment may be found on the GPhC website.

Registration as a pharmacy technician

Pharmacy technician training involves completing both a knowledge and competency-based qualification. This can be achieved either by undertaking GPhC-accredited courses or qualifications recognised by the GPhC. A summary of the current standards for the initial education and training of pharmacy technicians is set out in box 22.3.

Box 22.3 *Standards for initial training of pharmacy technicians*

The 14 standards set out the criteria against which the GPhC reviews (and approves or otherwise) pharmacy technician qualifications and training programmes.

1 There must be clear procedures to address immediately any concerns about patient safety arising from pharmacy technician education and training involving patients and the public.
2 All selection procedures must be open, fair and designed to identify those applicants who will practise safely and effectively and uphold the standards of the profession.
3 All aspects of pharmacy technician education and training must be based on principles of equality, diversity and fairness and meet the requirements of all relevant legislation.
4 The quality of pharmacy technician education and training must be monitored, reviewed and evaluated in a systematic way.

---

[11] Under the Modernising Pharmacy Careers Programme, currently hosted by Medical Education England but due to be come under Health Education England during 2013

5 Trainees must be supported to acquire the necessary skills and experience through induction, effective supervision, an appropriate and realistic workload, personal support and time to learn.

6 Those involved in providing the teaching and learning must be supported to acquire the necessary skills and experience through induction, effective mentoring, continuing professional development and personal support.

7 Education and training must be planned and maintained through transparent processes which show who is responsible at each stage.

8 The education and training facilities, infrastructure, leadership and other staffing must be sufficient to deliver outcomes.

9 The programme must develop the required skills, knowledge and understanding.

10 The programme must be delivered at Qualifications and Credit Framework level 3, Scottish Credit and Qualifications Framework level 6 or equivalent.

11 The curriculum must remain relevant to current practice and national standards.

12 The assessment strategy must assure appropriate standards of assessment.

13 The assessment strategy must ensure that trainees can demonstrate the required outcomes and practise safely and effectively according to the standards of proficiency and other relevant standards and guidance when they register.

14 There must be effective monitoring and evaluation mechanisms in place to ensure appropriate standards in the assessment.

Student pharmacy technicians must abide by the GPhC Code of Conduct for pre-registration trainee pharmacy technicians. Once they are registered, they must abide by the standards for conduct, ethics and performance (see below). Applications for registration with the GPhC as a pharmacy technician can be made if the person has GPhC-approved qualifications and meets the work experience requirements, or if they are an EEA national with an EEA pharmacy technician qualification (see website references at end of the chapter).

Other conditions for registration as a pharmacy professional

As well as completing the appropriate qualification, training and assessment requirements and paying the appropriate fee, the applicant must provide evidence of his/her identity, that his/her fitness to practise is not impaired by reason of physical or mental health and in certain cases evidence as to his/her good character and good repute (Arts.20–23 of the Order). A registrant must have in force an adequate and appropriate arrangement that provides cover in relation to that registrant in respect of liabilities which may be incurred by that registrant when practising (Art.32). Other articles in Part 4 make provision for visiting registrants (Art.33), and temporary registrations in the case of emergencies (Art.34).

Registration appeals

Certain registration decisions are appealable and these are set out in Article 39. The GPhC must operate an Appeals Committee to deal with these appeals (Art.40) and further appeal is permitted to the courts (Art.41). Further details of these processes are set out in GPhC Rules[12] and on the GPhC website. The Appeals Committee must, as soon as is reasonably practicable, send the person bringing the appeal the Committee's decision and the reasons for it and of any right of appeal. Rule 10 provides that the burden of proof is on the appellant and that the civil standard of proof applies (chapter 1). At the time of going to press, there has been one case heard by the Appeals Committee (box 22.4).

Box 22.4 *Registration Appeal case: pharmacy technician*

Tuesday, 18th October 2011

The appellant appealed against a decision of the Registrar on 11 July 2011 not to enter her as a pharmacy technician in Part 2 of the Register maintained by the Council. By virtue of Article 39(1)(b) of the Order, a decision by the Registrar not to enter a person in Part 2 of the Register is an appealable decision. This was a meeting of the Appeals Committee and not a hearing and so it did not hear oral evidence.

On 5 December 2005, the appellant had pleaded guilty at Croydon Magistrates' Court to four offences of making a false representation with a view to obtaining a benefit under the social security legislation for herself. The offences were committed in the period 2001 to 2004. She was sentenced to a community punishment order for 100 hours in respect of each offence and was also sentenced to a fine. The appellant applied to the RPSGB for voluntary registration as a pharmacy technician in 2008. In her application dated 24 May 2008 she declared

---

[12] The GPhC (Appeals Committee Rules) Order of Council SI 2010 No. 1614 'Appeals Rules'

that she had been convicted of a criminal offence which related to the overpayment of benefit. On receipt of this information, the then RPSGB Registrar investigated the circumstances of the conviction and following that investigation decided on 2 October 2008 to refuse the appellant's application to be entered in the Register.

In February 2011, the appellant then made an application to be entered in the Council's Register. In that application at paragraph 3.1 she was asked 'Have you ever applied previously for registration with the Royal Pharmaceutical Society of Great Britain (RPSGB) or the General Pharmaceutical Council (GPhC), either as a pharmacy technician . . . ?' The appellant ticked the 'No' box.

She was also asked: 'Have you previously been convicted or cautioned for a criminal offence in the British Islands or elsewhere . . . ?' The appellant ticked the 'No' box.

Further on in the application the appellant made a number of declarations as follows

'7.2 The information that I have provided in this application for registration is complete, true and accurate . . . '

'I understand that [7.6] If I am found to have given false or misleading information in connection with my application for registration in the Register, this may be treated as misconduct, which may result in my removal from the Register.'

The Registrar wrote to the appellant on 11 July 2011 to notify her of his decision to refuse her application for registration as a pharmacy technician. In giving his reasons, he referred to the appellant's failure to declare her conviction and a previous application for registration with the Society; her declarations on the application form and to her understanding of the consequences of giving false or misleading information at 7.6 of the application form.

He also referred to the conviction in the following terms

In your application of 24 May 2008 you disclosed your conviction at Croydon Magistrates' [sic] in December 2005 for making dishonest representations to obtain benefit. Following careful consideration by the Registrar of the former pharmacy regulator [the Society], your application for registration was refused. You were notified of the Registrar's decision by letter dated 2 October 2008. Reasons for the decision to refuse included not only the serious nature of the offences and that they were committed whilst you were practising as a pharmacy technician but also:

i your failure to provide evidence of your insight into the offences,

ii your lack of understanding of the offences' relevance to the practice of pharmacy, and

iii your decision not to provide supporting testimonials despite being given the opportunity to do so.

In concluding his reasons for refusing to register the Registrar wrote

The GPhC's standards of conduct, ethics and performance require registrants to act with honesty and integrity to maintain public trust and confidence in the profession. In all the circumstances, I consider that you have demonstrated a failure to meet this standard and that granting your application would undermine public confidence in the regulation of the pharmacy profession and may bring the profession into disrepute.

Rule 10 of the Appeal Rules establishes that the Appellant bears the burden of establishing that the appealable decision should be overturned and Rule 10(2) sets out that

If the appeal is against a decision to refuse to enter the appellant … in the Register, the Committee may only decide to enter, or direct the Registrar to enter, the appellant … in the Register if the appellant has proved that the appellant is … entitled to be so entered.

Article 20(1)(a)(ii) of the Pharmacy Order states that a person is entitled to be entered in Part 2 of the register as a pharmacy technician if, amongst other matters, the Registrar is satisfied that the person's fitness to practise is not impaired. Article 51 (1) of the same order states that 'A person's fitness to practise is to be regarded as "impaired" for the purposes of this Order only by reason of' and then sets out 14 criteria, including misconduct and a conviction in the British Islands for a criminal offence.

The representations of the appellant included statements relating to remorse and regret of her actions and 'mistakes'. She stated that she believed that her conviction had no bearing on her ability to carry out a role as a pharmacy technician to the highest possible standard.

Written submissions on behalf of the Council argued that the appellant 'deliberately told untruths to her regulatory body by positively asserting that she had no previous convictions and that she does not in her notice of appeal address the issue why she did not mention her previous application for registration'.

> Having carefully considered all the evidence submitted together with the submissions made by both the appellant and the respondent the decision of the committee is to dismiss the appeal. The committee noted that the Council had argued that both misconduct and a conviction, in fact four convictions, were present here triggering consideration of impairment of fitness to practise. The committee recognised that the convictions were in respect of behaviour several years ago and also noted that the offences did not, on the information supplied to it, require proof of dishonesty to establish a conviction. The committee therefore regarded the convictions as not establishing dishonest behaviour by the appellant in 2001, 2002 and 2004. The committee did however regard the appellant's behaviour in knowingly submitting an application for registration in 2011 that was wrong in a number of respects as dishonest, which the appellant accepts. The committee also noted that the appellant's behaviour both in relation to the matters for which she was convicted and in relation to her application in 2011 all involved her over a period of ten years in making false representations in order to secure an advantage to herself; benefits to which she was not entitled in the case of the convictions and to improve her chances of being registered in the case of the application this year.

The committee concluded that it was 'not satisfied that the appellant has proved that her fitness to practice is not impaired' and informed the appellant of her right of appeal, under Article 41(1) of the Pharmacy Order, against its decision.

See chapter 24 for information relating to impaired fitness to practise.

Continuing professional development

Part 5 of the Order contains powers to regulate training both before and after registration (Arts.42 and 43) through CPD and, in due course, through revalidation. At the time of writing, the processes for revalidation were under consideration but standards for CPD have been published and apply to all registrants (box 22.5).

> *Box 22.5* *Standards for continuing professional development*
>
> The CPD requirements apply to all pharmacy professionals and the CPD record is expected to cover the full scope of practice and roles. The CPD standards are as follows.
>
> **1.1** Keep a record of your CPD that is legible, either electronically online at the website www.uptodate.org.uk, on another computer, or as hard copy on paper and in a format published or approved by us and carrying the CPD approved logo.
>
> **1.2** Make a minimum of nine CPD entries per year which reflect the context and scope of your practice as a pharmacist or pharmacy technician.
>
> **1.3** Keep a record of your CPD that complies with the good practice criteria for CPD recording published in Plan and Record by us (www.uptodate.co.uk).
>
> **1.4** Record how your CPD has contributed to the quality or development of your practice using our CPD framework.
>
> **1.5** Submit your CPD record to us on request.

Rules made under Article 43 of the Pharmacy Order[13] mean that an appearance before the FTP Committee is possible (subject to the following of procedures as laid out in rules) for failing to submit appropriate CPD records in response to a request by the Council.

English language competency

At present, the GPhC cannot require evidence of English language competency from EEA nationals wishing to register with the GPhC as a pharmacy professional. Once registered, however, registrants are required to practise pharmacy in Great Britain in accordance with the GPhC's Standards of Conduct, Ethics and Performance (see below), specifically Principle 7, which states 'Make sure that you and everyone you are responsible for have the language skills to communicate and work effectively with colleagues'. Practising pharmacy in breach of these standards could result in fitness to practise proceedings (chapter 24). However, entry requirements to UK MPharm and OSPAP programmes require evidence of English language proficiency.

---

[13] The GPhC (CPD and Consequential Amendments) Order of Council SI 2010 No. 1367

Remaining parts of the Pharmacy Order 2010

Parts 6 and 7 of the Pharmacy Order are concerned with standards of conduct ethics and performance (Art.48; see chapter 23) and powers and processes to deal with allegations of impaired fitness to practise (chapter 24). Part 8 of the Order provides powers for the GPhC to charge reasonable fees in connection with its functions (Art.65) and to make Rules in connection with its functions (Art.66). Article 67 designates the GPhC as the competent authority in respect of Directive 2005/36/EC.

Other standards and guidance

Much of the GPhC standards and guidance relates to the behaviour and conduct of registrants – pharmacists and pharmacy technicians – and these are covered in greater detail in chapter 23. Some set out obligations on registrants and require the owner and pharmacist superintendent to support registrants in achieving them (the legal requirements for Responsible Pharmacists are covered in chapter 5). A glossary of terms used in the standards and guidance is available on the GPhC website. For convenience, a list of standards and guidance available at the time of writing is given below.

Standards

Conduct, ethics and performance (chapter 23)
Standards for registered pharmacies (see box 22.1 and appendix 9)
CPD (see box 22.5)
Initial education and training for pharmacists (see box 22.2)
Initial education and training for pharmacy technicians (see box 22.3)
Proficiency; still under development.

Guidance

Consent (chapter 23)
Maintaining clear sexual boundaries (chapter 23)
Owners and superintendents who employ Responsible Pharmacists (see above)
Patient confidentiality (chapter 23)
The provision of pharmacy services affected by religious or moral beliefs (chapter 23)
Raising concerns (chapter 23)
Responding to complaints and concerns (chapter 23)
Responsible Pharmacists (chapter 23).

Summary

- The primary role of the GPhC is to protect, promote and maintain the health, safety and wellbeing of members of the public by upholding standards and public trust in pharmacy. It achieves this in a number of ways such as
    - approving qualifications for registrants,
    - accrediting education and training providers,
    - maintaining a register of pharmacists, pharmacy technicians and pharmacy premises,
    - establishing and promoting standards for registered pharmacies,
    - monitoring pharmacy professionals' fitness to practise and dealing in a proportionate and fair way with complaints and concerns, and
    - setting standards and providing guidance.

- The GPhC derives its powers from the Pharmacy Order 2010 and Rules made under the Order.

Websites

Association of Pharmacy Technicians UK: http://www.aptuk.org
General Pharmaceutical Council (details of pharmacy standards): http://www.pharmacyregulation.org

The GPhC is a public body and all its activities are mostly available to the public and professionals alike (some exceptions are hearings on fitness to practise that are held in private). The material appearing on its website is expanding rapidly at the time of going to press and it may not be helpful to give precise locations as these may change. However, the following guide may help readers to locate many of the documents referred to in the chapter text:

- Memorandum of Understanding with Pharmaceutical Society of Northern Ireland: see under, about us
- Organisations which Council works with: see under, about us
- Welsh language scheme: see under, pharmacy regulation
- UK and overseas registration: see under, registration
- All standards: see under, standards
- Student registrant code of conduct: see under, education
- Accredited institutions and courses: see under, education
- Pre-registration training: see under, education

Guild of Healthcare Pharmacists: http://www.ghp.org.uk
Legislation (can be searched on year and SI number or title): http://www.legislation.gov.uk
National Pharmacy Association (for pharmacy owners and their employees): http://www.npa.org.uk
Pharmacists Defence Association (for individual pharmacists): http://www.the-pda.org
Professional Standards Authority for Health and Social Care (formerly Council for Healthcare Regulatory Excellence http://www.chre.org.uk: (to change December 2012).
Royal Pharmaceutical Society: http://www.rpharms.com

23

Professional conduct

Dai John and David H Reissner

This book only makes reference to ethics in relation to the GPhC's standards and guidance on conduct, ethics and performance and its application to professional conduct or misconduct. A wider exposition of pharmacy ethics, its underpinning moral philosophy and how it interfaces with healthcare law is beyond the scope of this book. However, interested readers are referred to the Further reading at the end of the chapter. The concept of good professional conduct and misconduct is now embodied in the wider disciplinary term 'impaired fitness to practise', which is the basis for all disciplinary referrals within the pharmacy profession (chapter 24) and indeed all other health professions.

The term 'profession' was formerly applied only to the church, the law and medicine – the three 'learned' professions. The meaning of the term is now broader, as is apparent from the definition in the Oxford English Dictionary: 'a vocation in which a professed knowledge of some department of learning is used in its application to the affairs of others, or in the practice of an art founded upon it'. In modern usage, it seems that almost all occupations that require some measure of intellectual training can be described as professions. However, an organised profession requires more than the mere existence of an intellectual discipline. The essence of professionalism is the relationship of trust which exists between the practitioner and the person who receives his/her advice or services. The recipient, relying entirely on the knowledge of the practitioner, must be able to have complete trust in his/her services and the impartiality of his/her advice. It follows that there must be an established minimum standard of knowledge for practitioners, and that there must be agreement amongst them about standards of behaviour in their professional work. This means that there must be a body which determines the standard of education and establishes the code of conduct. In the past, this body has been representative of practitioners and subject to their control but since the various scandals of the late 1990s, healthcare professional regulators put the public interest first and include practitioners amongst many other interested parties to arrive at the standards required (chapter 25).

The profession of pharmacy

If the characteristics described are accepted as the elements of a profession, then pharmacy meets the essential requirements, which are four in number (box 23.1).

Box 23.1 Elements of a profession

An intellectual discipline and a standard of knowledge. Pharmacy is of ancient origin. In Great Britain, it was never clearly separated from medicine until the formation of the Pharmaceutical Society of Great Britain in 1841. Membership of the Society was, from the first, by examination, but it was not until the Pharmacy Act 1868 that all newcomers to the profession who wished to practise were required to pass a qualifying examination, whether or not they intended to become members of the Society. Today, a university degree in pharmacy together with 12 months of practical training is required before registration as a pharmacist (see chapter 22).

A representative body of practitioners. The GPhC is the regulatory body for pharmacists and pharmacy technicians. The standards of conduct, ethics and performance for pharmacists and pharmacy technicians reflect not just of the views of pharmacists and pharmacy technicians, but also of those who support, regulate and use pharmacy services.

Standards of conduct. There are accepted standards of conduct, ethics and performance known throughout the profession. They are enforceable by virtue of the Pharmacy Order 2010 via the GPhC's fitness to practise procedures. The GPhC's FTP Committee takes into account the standards of conduct, ethics and performance when considering professional conduct but is not bound by it (chapter 24).

Service and advice. Pharmacists have traditionally been mainly concerned with the supply to the public of medicines, either in response to a prescription or other authority or sold over the counter. In these supplies, the pharmacist should give whatever advice is necessary in the interest of the patient or customer. Increasingly, pharmacists are also concerned with the provision of services specifically to improve health and the management and use of medicines, usually accompanied by advice or recommendations, intervention and support for patients and fellow health professionals. Some pharmacists have prescribing rights.

The existence of a body of independent private practitioners has been held to be essential if an occupation is truly to be regarded as a profession. The argument is that only the relationship between an independent practitioner and his/her client is a fully professional one, and an employed practitioner must inevitably be subject to external pressures, either consciously or un-consciously, according to the conditions of his/her employment. No pharmacist, whether employed in public service or in the service of a body corporate engaged in retail pharmacy, would accept that his/her standards or his/her judgment are in any way affected by the fact that s/he is an employee. Indeed, some might argue that a pharmacist in public service is free from some of the commercial pressures which may influence the judgment of the independent practitioner. Even so, there is some force in the argument that the existence of a number of independent practitioners is indispensable for the full development of the profession.

Trade and profession

There is a deep-rooted feeling that trading and professional activities are incompatible. Yet what is the difference between making a living from selling one's professional services and making a living from the buying and selling of goods? The professional person might have some difficulty in explaining his/her objections to commerce without casting doubts on the integrity of the tradesperson. Although there is an element of snobbery in it, there is undoubtedly a difference between the trading outlook and the professional outlook. The tradesperson, however honest, is principally concerned with the profitability of his/her business. His/her main object is to achieve as large a financial return as possible. S/he holds his/her customers to be the best judges of what they want and s/he seeks to satisfy their demands. The old common law maxim applicable to *trade* (contracts of sale) was 'let the buyer beware'.

Professional people working in their special field of knowledge where their advice is crucial must often be the judges of what is best for their clients or customers, although patients are increasingly encouraged to take part in and exercise choice over healthcare decisions. Indeed this principle is now accepted in the 2010–2012 NHS reforms, which promote the policy of 'no decision about me without me'.[1] If professionals do this according to the standards of their profession, then the advice they give must, at times, be to the practitioners' own financial disadvantage. It is recognition of this essential trust by the public which confers any special status the professional person may have.

Some pharmacists, such as many of those who work in hospitals or in teaching, do not engage in trade, although within the context of the NHS

---

[1] Available on the Department of Health website: www.dh.gov.uk

(chapter 26) they are increasingly involved in marketing their services and operating within budgets and business constraints similar to those applied in retailing. However, the majority of pharmacists in retail pharmacy businesses practise pharmacy in a trading environment. In addition to the supply of medicines and the provision of other professional services, they sell many other goods. Theirs is a trading profession, a description applied by Lord Wilberforce in the Dickson case of the 1960s (box 23.2).

Box 23.2 The Dickson case

Pharmaceutical Society of Great Britain v Dickson (1968)

The background to the case was as follows. Arising out of a recommendation of the Report on the General Practice of Pharmacy (*Pharm J*, 20 April 1963), a motion was put to the Annual General Meeting of the Pharmaceutical Society in 1965 in the following terms:

New pharmacies should be situated only in premises which are physically distinct, and should be devoted solely to:

i   Professional services, as defined
ii Non-professional services, as defined, and
iii such other services as may be approved by the Council, and
iv the range of services as may be approved by the Council;
    and the range of services in existing pharmacies, or in
    pharmacy departments of larger establishments should not
    be extended beyond the present limits except as approved by
    the Council.

At a special general meeting held at the Royal Albert Hall to consider the recommendation on 25 July 1965, RCM Dickson (a director of Boots Pure Drug Co. Ltd) sought an injunction to restrain the holding of the meeting. He also claimed that the motion was outside the scope of the Society's powers and was a restraint of trade. Application for an injunction was refused by the High Court and a motion supporting the recommendation was passed by 5020 votes to 1336. However, the order of the High Court declared:

That it is not within the powers, purposes or objects of the
Pharmaceutical Society of Great Britain ... to enforce or carry
out or attempt to enforce or carry out the provisions of the
motion ... on the ground that the said provisions are in restraint
of trade.

The Court of Appeal dismissed an appeal by the Society against the order. On further appeal to the House of Lords, the order given by the High Court was affirmed. It was held that:

The proposed restriction, although intended to be binding in honour only, might be a basis for disciplinary action. The courts had the power and the duty to determine its validity.

It was not within the powers or purposes of the Society to control selling activities which did not interfere with the proper performance of professional pharmaceutical duties.

The only relevant object in the Society's Charter was 'to maintain the honour and safeguard and protect the interests of the members in the exercise of the profession of pharmacy' and the proposed rules of conduct had too slender a connection or link to that object.

The proposed restrictions were beyond the powers of the Society as they were in restraint of trade and had not been shown to be reasonable.

This decision did not affect the Society's powers to regulate professional conduct in pharmacy; a function now of the GPhC.

NB The Pharmaceutical Society became 'Royal' in 1988

[1968] 2 All ER 686 *Pharm. J*, 1 June 1968 p. 651. This was an appeal by the Society to the House of Lords against an Order of the Court of Appeal ([1967] All ER 558; *Pharm J*, 4 February 1967 p. 113), which upheld a judgment of the High Court (Chancery Division) ([1966] 3 All ER 404; *Pharm J*, 2 July 1966 p. 22).

The conflict between professional and commercial methods in pharmacy has its origin in the economic need for most pharmacists to engage in ordinary trade as well as pharmacy, together with the fact that any corporate body which complies with certain requirements has the legal right to establish a retail pharmacy business (chapter 5). The Pharmaceutical Society of Great Britain,[2] as the regulating body at the time of the Dickson case, had throughout its history resisted any pressures of the commercial world that appeared to be adverse to the profession. However, the advent of competition law (chapter 21) limited the extent to which any regulator can impose ethical constraints on commercial activities, for example on the promotion and supply of medicines.

[2] The Society was not granted its 'Royal' prefix until 1988

Professional ethics and law

Ethics is the science of morals, or moral philosophy. The principles, written or unwritten, that are accepted in any profession as the basis for proper behaviour are the ethics of the profession. Rules of law and rules of ethics are commonly held to differ because law is enforced by the state while ethical rules are only morally binding. However, law and ethics are not opposites. The law itself has a basis in ethics; in general, it reflects the moral standards of the community. Criminal law comprises those rules of conduct which the community (through parliament) has decided must be observed on pain of a penalty, such as a fine or imprisonment. Criminal law, therefore, includes the[3] Medicines, Poisons and Misuse of Drugs Acts, where transgression may result in prosecution. Other parliamentary legislation creates administrative law, which gives power to public bodies to regulate certain activities carried out on behalf of the public. The NHS Terms of Service is an example. A breach may result in an administrative sanction following investigation under the NHS complaints procedures (chapter 26).

Moral obligations are also recognised by the state through common law, which essentially enshrines certain duties which individuals owe to one another. Breach of these duties may result in action through the civil law courts to seek compensation for a 'civil wrong'. The most familiar of these is probably an action alleging negligence on the part of a health practitioner. Negligence is just one of a range of torts, or civil wrongs, and is discussed in more detail later in this chapter. Other torts which might arise in pharmacy practice are breach of confidentiality and defamation. Pharmacists, as they become integrated into the healthcare team, will increasingly come into possession of sensitive information and will be expected to observe strict confidentiality over the use and disclosure of such information and refrain from using it in ways which may lower the standing of the subject in the eyes of the community (i.e. defamation).

However, the state does not attempt to enforce every rule of social behaviour, nor does it interfere in those matters which are by common consent left to the consciences of individuals (e.g. religious observance) or in those standards which are agreed amongst a profession provided they can be seen to be necessary for the further protection of the public.

Former codes of ethics

Ever since the foundation of the Pharmaceutical Society of Great Britain in 1841, there has been concern about the need to maintain and improve standards of conduct in pharmacy. The advantage of having a written code

---

[3] Many offences formerly in the Medicines Act 1968 are now to be found in the Human Medicines Regulations 2012

was recognised, but nothing positive emerged until the changes made by the Pharmacy and Poisons Act 1933 gave the Society wider authority, including the power to take disciplinary action and to remove names from the Register of Pharmaceutical Chemists (an equivalent term to pharmacists). A proposal for a code of ethics made by the Teesside branch of the Society in 1937 was widely discussed, but it was found difficult to strike the right balance between a general description of good behaviour and the expression of specified principles in clear-cut terms. The document which was finally accepted by the profession was the first attempt at a written code. An amended version of this *Statement upon Matters of Professional Conduct* was later published in the *Pharmaceutical Journal* (17 June 1944). Other amendments led to the publication of revised versions in 1953, 1964, 1970, 1984, 1992 and 2007. Since October 2010, the setting of standards and guidance for pharmacists and pharmacy technicians became the responsibility of the GPhC and this chapter looks first at the professional control exercised by the regulator.

Standards of Conduct, Ethics and Performance

As explained in chapter 22, the GPhC has the duty to set standards as the basis by which a registrant's fitness to practise may be assessed.[4] The GPhC must also make Rules setting out the criteria to which the FTP Committee (chapter 24) is to have regard when considering whether a registrant is fit to practise.[5] The legislation makes it clear that failure to comply with such standards is not, of itself, evidence of misconduct (one of the grounds for alleging impaired fitness to practise) but is to be taken into account in any fitness to practise proceedings against a registrant. A summary of the GPhC's Standards is set out in box 23.3.

Box 23.3 Summary of standards of conduct, ethics and performance

This document sets out the standards of conduct, ethics and performance that pharmacy professionals must follow. The Council uses the term 'pharmacy professionals' for pharmacists and pharmacy technicians registered with them.

It is important that pharmacy professionals meet the standards and are able to practise safely and effectively. Their conduct will be judged against the standards and failure to comply could put registration at risk. When the Council receives complaints or concerns against a pharmacy professional it is these standards

---

[4] Article 48 of the Pharmacy Order SI 2010 No. 231
[5] The GPhC (Fitness to Practise and Disqualification, Etc. Rules) Order SI 2010 No. 1615 (FTP Rules)

that are considered when deciding whether or not any action against that individual is necessary. The Council stresses that these standards apply in whichever sector of the profession a pharmacist or technician practices and so they also apply in education, research and other settings, even if the professional is not involved interacting directly with patients or the public.

There are seven standards and pharmacy professionals must comply with each. Within each standard there are a number of components (number in parentheses).

1   Make patients your first concern (10)
2   Use your professional judgement in the interests of patients and the public (5)
3   Show respect for others (9)
4   Encourage patients and the public to participate in decisions about their care (7)
5   Develop your professional knowledge and competence (5)
6   Be honest and trustworthy (9)
7   Take responsibility for your working practices (12).

Included within this standards documents the Council states:

We do not dictate how you should meet our standards. Each standard can normally be met in more than one way and the way in which you meet our standards may change over time. The standards are of equal importance.

You are professionally accountable for your practice. This means that you are responsible for what you do or do not do, no matter what advice or direction your manager or another professional gives you. You must use your professional judgement when deciding on a course of action and you should use our standards as a basis when making those decisions.

You may be faced with conflicting professional or legal responsibilities. In these circumstances you must consider all possible courses of action and the risks and benefits associated with each one to decide what is in the best interests of patients and the public.

Each standard is underpinned by statements which expand on how observance of the standard should be manifested in day to day practice. However, the application of ethical standards can be challenging, particularly when two competing ethical principles may be present in a given situation. A significant understanding is needed of the moral theory underpinning professional behaviour coupled with possession of skills in resolving professional dilemmas and taking decisions and an appreciation of competing accountabilities both in law and through professional regulation; for more information see the Further reading list at the end of this chapter.

Guidance

The GPhC has seen fit to publish additional guidance in certain areas of practice where the application of the Standards may not be sufficient to support practice. The guidance that has been published at the time of going to press is given below; however, the Council is committed to a regular review of all its standards and guidance so readers should check on the GPhC website for the latest versions.

Responsible Pharmacists

The legislation on Responsible Pharmacists is covered in chapter 5. In addition the GPhC has published guidance on Standard 7.7 of the Standards of Conduct, Ethics and Performance, which states, 'You must make sure that you keep to your legal and professional responsibilities and that your workload or working conditions do not present a risk to patient care or public safety'.

This guidance is intended to complement guidance for owners and superintendent pharmacists who employ Responsible Pharmacists (chapter 22).

Consent (available in the Welsh language)

The guidance document enlarges on Standard 3.6 of the Standards of Conduct, Ethics and Performance, which states 'You must get consent for the professional services you provide and the patient information you use'.

The guidance describes what is meant by consent, the two types of consent (explicit and implied), ways in which consent can be obtained, and capacity or otherwise to give consent (including assessment of capacity).

Maintaining clear sexual boundaries (available in the Welsh language)

The guidance document enlarges on Standard 3.9 of the Standards of Conduct, Ethics and Performance, which states 'You must maintain proper professional boundaries in your relationships with patients and others you come into contact with during the course of your professional practice and take special care when dealing with vulnerable people'.

The guidance outlines the importance of maintaining clear sexual boundaries. It describes the power imbalance which normally exist between a patient and a pharmacy professional, identifies that cultural and other reasons can lead to differences in what individuals see as appropriate or inappropriate and also provides guidance on the use of a chaperone, which is defined within the guidance (at 5.1):

A chaperone is a person (usually the same sex as the patient) who is present as a safeguard for the patient and the healthcare professional. They are also a witness to the patient's continuing consent for the procedure. Their role may vary depending on the needs of the patient, the pharmacy professional and the examination or procedure being carried out.

Patient confidentiality (available in the Welsh language)

The guidance document enlarges on Standards 3.5, 3.7 and 3.8 of the Standards of Conduct, Ethics and Performance, which state:

3.5 Respect and protect people's dignity and privacy. Take all reasonable steps to prevent accidental disclosure or unauthorised access to confidential information. Never disclose confidential information without consent unless required to do so by the law or in exceptional circumstances.

3.7 Use information you obtain in the course of your professional practice only for the purposes you were given it, or where the law says you can.

3.8 Make sure you provide the appropriate levels of privacy for patient consultations.

The guidance contains information on the duty of confidentiality, protecting confidential information and disclosing information (with consent and under circumstances where there has not been consent).

The provision of pharmacy services affected by religious and moral beliefs

The guidance document includes guidance for pharmacy professionals and for those who employ them. It includes guidance for those who hold such beliefs on what they should do before (or if) they accept employment as well as what to do in the when circumstances arise.

Raising concerns (available in the Welsh language)

The guidance document enlarges on Standards 1.2, 2.4 and 7.11 of the Standards of Conduct, Ethics and Performance, which state:

1.2 You must take action to protect the well-being of patients and the public.

2.4 You must be prepared to challenge the judgement of your colleagues and other professionals if you have reason to believe that their decisions could affect the safety or care of others.

7.11 You must make the relevant authority aware of any policies, systems, working conditions, or the actions, professional performance, or health of others if they may affect patient care or public safety. If something goes wrong or if someone reports a concern to you, make sure that you deal with it appropriately.

The guidance outlines the importance of raising concerns, how to raise a concern and the legal aspects, including an outline of the Public Interest Disclosure Act 1998, which protects employees who raise genuine concerns in the workplace. Furthermore, it provides additional guidance for employers.

Responding to complaints and concerns

The guidance document covers dealing with complaints and concerns raised by patients, the public and other healthcare professionals. Dispensing errors are frequently the basis for complaints to the GPhC and so it has published guidance on how to minimise the risk of a dispensing error occurring, what to do if a dispensing error occurs and what to afterwards (error review or root cause analysis).

Negligence

Taken together, the standards and associated guidance from the GPhC set the 'standard of care' and hence the 'duty of care' expected of practising pharmacists and pharmacy technicians. These terms are also used widely in the civil law, which is concerned with duties owed between one citizen and another, particularly in matters of *negligence*. The extent to which a healthcare professional did, or did not, discharge his/her duty of care towards a patient, or other recipient of his/her services is the key consideration in negligence cases and the award of compensation if a failure of duty of care is found. Readers should also note that the two processes, a fitness to practise inquiry by the GPhC and an action in negligence in the civil courts, are not exclusive. The same failure of duty of care may lead to both. If a failure in care leads to a death then allegations may also be heard in the criminal courts as charges of 'gross negligence manslaughter' and/or 'corporate manslaughter'. These are discussed at the end of this chapter and a discussion of types of law can also be found in chapter 1. Furthermore, errors that result in a death may lead to a prosecution under section 64 of the Medicines Act 1968 (see chapters 13 and 24) and any errors could lead to a performance tribunal under the NHS law governing the community pharmacy contract (chapter 26).

Professional or clinical negligence

A pharmacist, or any member of the pharmacy staff, may be faced with an action for negligence in the civil courts. The essence of the tort of negligence is that there is on the part of the defendant a legal duty of care which s/he has failed to meet, as a result of which the plaintiff has suffered damage. The duty to take care was described in the case of *Donoghue v Stevenson*[6] thus:

> You must take reasonable care to avoid acts or omissions which you can reasonably foresee would be likely to injure your neighbour. Who, then, in law is my neighbour? The answer seems to be ... persons who are so closely and directly affected by my act that I ought reasonably to have them in contemplation as being so affected when I am directing my mind to the acts or omissions which are called in question.

The law imposes a duty to take care in a variety of circumstances. As sellers of goods, community pharmacists have a duty to take reasonable care to warn customers of any potential dangers arising from them. Quite apart from this general duty on all sellers of goods, there is a special relationship between pharmacists and their customers in respect of transactions involving pharmaceutical knowledge. Reliance is placed upon the special skill and knowledge of the pharmacist when selling, dispensing or prescribing medicinal products. The law would expect him/her to exercise that degree of competence which the average member of the profession is required to possess. This is known as the 'duty of care'. A pharmacist occupying a special position in any branch of pharmacy would be expected to have a degree of ability commensurate with that position. Pharmacists consistently, and with good reason, press for recognition as experts upon drugs and medicines, and for the right to take a greater part in the health services. Every right has its correlative duty, and pharmacists, as they achieve greater recognition, must expect the law to require from them a higher degree of skill. It is probable that they will, as a consequence, be more liable to actions for professional negligence.

Four High Court decisions illustrate this point well (box 23.4). The apportioning of liability is now an accepted principle in dispensing negligence cases, as demonstrated in the more recent cases in box 23.4, the 'Epilim case' and the 'dexamethasone case'.

---

[6][1932] Appeal Court 562, 580

Box 23.4 Four High Court decisions illustrating issues of liability to actions for professional negligence

The 'Migril case'

A woman who suffered gangrene in both feet, requiring extensive surgery, as a result of receiving an overdose of Migril (ergotamine tartrate, cyclizine hydrochloride and caffeine citrate) prescribed for migraine was awarded over £130 000 damages.

The owner of the pharmacy, who admitted negligence, was held liable for 45 per cent of the damages awarded. The judge, Mr Justice Stuart-Smith, in making the award said that the pharmacist owed a duty to the patient to ensure that drugs were correctly prescribed and that the pharmacist should have spotted the doctor's error and queried the prescription with the prescriber. He said:

> Pharmacists ... have to exercise an independent judgment to ensure that the drug is apt for the patient as well as that it conforms to the physician's requirements. It is an active duty and ... it is what the chemist writes on the label that is the critical thing so far as the patient is concerned. The patient will often forget, or not pay attention to what the doctor may say at the time of prescribing, but he or she relies on the written instructions on the bottle given by the chemist.

It is clear from the judgment that a pharmacist must not be deterred in querying prescriptions with the prescriber by any adverse response on the part of the prescriber, who may resent his/her decisions being questioned. The legal and professional responsibility of the pharmacist to verify and question prescriptions has been highlighted and established by this case.

Dwyer v Roderick, Jackson and Cross Chemists (Banbury) Limited (unreported, 10 February 1982); *Pharm J*, 20 February 1982 p. 205

The 'Daonil case'

In another case in 1988, a patient visited his doctor for his regular prescription for inhalers and tablets. At the same time, he was prescribed Amoxil (amoxicillin) for a chest infection. When he took the handwritten prescription to the pharmacy, the pharmacist misread Amoxil as Daonil (glibenclamide) and the patient suffered irreversible brain damage.

Mr Justice Auld in awarding a total of £100 000 damages (apportioned according to perceived responsibility for negligence as to 75 per cent against the pharmacist and 25 per cent against the doctor) said that even assuming that the prescription was unclear, the pharmacist should have been alerted to the fact that Daonil was being recommended in the wrong dosage and quantity. He should also have noticed that the man who collected the drugs did not claim exemption from paying a NHS prescription charge for the Daonil, although diabetics were entitled to exemption from prescription charges. It was not enough for pharmacists to blindly dispense drugs without giving thought to what they were doing. Giving the decision in the High Court, Mr Justice Auld held that a doctor had a duty to his/her patient to write a prescription sufficiently legibly so as to reduce the likelihood of it being misread by a busy or careless pharmacist. But the pharmacist, in turn, was under a duty to give some thought to the prescriptions s/he was dispensing. If there was an ambiguity in the prescription, s/he should not dispense a drug without first satisfying him/herself that it was the correct one.

Lord Justice Auld said:

> The GP should have taken account of the possibility that a poorly written prescription might be misinterpreted by the pharmacist: Every now and then the competent or tired and/or flustered and/or distracted pharmacist might very well mechanically dispense a prescription which in more alert and quieter moments he would question...

> It is accepted that a prescription which is so written as to invite or reasonably permit mis-reading by a pharmacist under ordinary working conditions (which it is accepted may be less than ideal) falls below the necessary standard...

> ... it is well-established that the pharmacist, if in any doubt at all, should contact the doctor before [dispensing]...

> ... Looking at the case as a whole ... the chain of causation from Dr Miller's bad handwriting was not broken and the consequence of his writing a word which could reasonably be read as 'Daonil', even with the other factors [which should have caused the pharmacist to realise the prescription was not for Daonil] is not enough to make it beyond reasonable forseeability that Daonil would be prescribed.

Pharm J, 26 March 1988 p. 404

The 'Epilim case'

In a settlement in the High Court in Manchester on 28 February 2000, the claim arose from a negligently written prescription, in November 1999, for Epilim (sodium valproate) 500 mg tablets where the strength, and hence the dosage and administration instructions, were incorrect. The pharmacy's professional indemnity insurer agreed to pay 25 per cent of the settlement (£225 000) plus costs) for the pharmacist's failure to detect and correct the error. The prescribing doctor was held liable for the remaining 75 per cent of the compensation paid to the patient.

Shipman V Mayfair Chemists (Hyde) Limited; *Chemist and Druggist*, 4 March 2000 p. 5

The 'dexamethasone case'

In 2006, despite patient medication records showing a series of previous supplies of dexamethasone 0.5 mg, a pharmacist dispensed a prescription that had incorrectly been written for dexamethasone 4 mg. This error was compounded when the patient returned home to to the USA and her physician continued to prescribe 4 mg tablets for her, based on the label on her supply made in the UK. She suffered severely from Cushing's syndrome which led to the loss of her business and personal difficulties. The trial judge said:

> ... the dramatic increase in strength should have alerted Mr
> Gabla to the need to go behind the guidance in the BNF [*British
> National Formulary*] and to question the correctness of the
> prescription with Dr Evans or Mrs Horton ... the prescription
> did not have to be dispensed urgently ... The accepted wisdom is
> that whenever pharmacists dispense a prescription, they should
> consider whether the medication being prescribed is suitable for
> the patient ... If the prescription ... had been for a patient who
> had not had previous prescriptions dispensed by the branch, it
> may have been sufficient for Mr Gabla to check in the BNF ... a
> significant increase raised at the very least the possibility that the
> prescription might be inaccurate. The question was no longer
> whether the strength of the dexamethasone being prescribed came
> within its usual therapeutic range.

In this case, nearly £1.5 million compensation was awarded and was apportioned between the UK doctor and the employer of the pharmacist. (See also box 23.5 for expansion on the term 'professional assessment' in the comments made by the judge in this case.)

Horton v Evans and Lloyds Pharmacy Limited [2006] EWHC 2808 (QB); [2007] LS Law Medical 212; (2007) 94 B.M.L.R. 60; [2007] P.N.L.R. 17

Pharm J, 18 November 2006 p. 595; 17 March 2007 p. 302

The 'dexamethasone case' in box 23.4 also provides an indication of meaning for the term *professional assessment* in relation to the dispensing of a prescription (box 23.5).

Box 23.5 *Meaning of professional assessment*

In the 'dexamethasone case' described in box 23.4, comment was made by the judge on what is meant by the term 'professional assessment' (in the service specifications accompanying the former RPSGB's Code of Ethics) in relation to the dispensing of prescriptions. He said:

> The accepted wisdom is that whenever pharmacists dispense a prescription they should consider whether the medication prescribed is suitable for the patient. That is what the Royal Pharmaceutical Society of Great Britain's Code of Medicines, Ethics and Practice[1] requires pharmacists to do – namely 'Every prescription must be professionally assessed by a pharmacist to determine the suitability for the patient'. That is recognised by Lloyds because its branch procedures manual is to the same effect. These requirements mirror pharmacists' obligations under common law. As Stuart-Smith J said in *Dwyer v Roderick* (10 February1982)[2] 'pharmacists ... have to exercise an independent judgement to ensure that the drug is apt for the patient as well as that it conforms to the physicians requirements.

The defence raised the issue that the pharmacist had noted the strength on the prescription was large, had checked in the BNF, found that a 4 mg dosage was within the usual therapeutic range and had, therefore, dispensed the prescription without referring to the doctor. The judge dealt with this defence thus:

It was true that the prescription was for a strength of dexamethasone which could be properly prescribed, but the dramatic increase in strength should have alerted the pharmacist to the need to go behind the guidance in the BNF and to question the correctness of the prescription with Dr Evans or Mrs Horton ... It was no longer whether the strength came within its usual therapeutic range and could for that reason be said to be suitable for Mrs Horton.

If the patient already has a patient medication record on the computer, previous prescription medication details on the PMR should be studied in order to check that there has been no change to the strength or dose of the patient's medication. Any changes should be queried with the patient or the prescriber.

In these circumstances I have no doubt that what the pharmacist should have done was to follow the instruction in the branch procedure manual and question the correctness of the prescription with Dr Evans or Mrs Horton. Had he done that, Dr Evans' mistake would have been discovered. In failing to do that the pharmacist fell below the standards which could reasonably have been expected of a reasonably careful and competent pharmacist.

[1] Reproduced in the RPSGB *Medicines, Ethics and Practice* guide until July 2010.
[2] The 'Migril case', described in box 23.4.

A patient may hold a pharmacy owner vicariously liable for the acts or omissions of a pharmacist, but individual pharmacists owe patients an independent duty of care. As such, if a pharmacy owner is sued by a patient, the pharmacy owner is entitled to claim an indemnity from a pharmacist (whether an employee or a self-employed locum) responsible for an error, or a contribution to any damages payable to the patient.[7]

Criminal negligence

Although negligence is most likely to be considered in the civil courts in an action for compensation for harm caused by a pharmacist's duty of care, if the failure is associated with the death of a patient, a pharmacist may

[7]See, for example, *Wootton v J Docter Ltd* [2008] EWCA Civ. 1361; [2009] *LS Law Medical* 63; this was a case in which no actual indemnity or contribution was ordered because the court held that, although a dispensing error had been made, it had not caused the patient any injury or loss

be charged with the serious criminal offence of manslaughter if the error is considered to be gross negligence. The 'leading case' in relation to health professionals is that involving a hospital doctor, an anaesthetist, in 1995.[8] The case was considered by the House of Lords, which held:

> The question is whether it (the defendant's conduct) should be characterised as gross negligence and therefore a crime; and whether, having regard to the risk of death involved, the defendant's conduct was so bad in all the circumstances as to amount to a criminal act or omission.

Put colloquially, the question was whether the defendant was 'criminally negligent'. Until 2000, there had been no modern case in which a pharmacist had been prosecuted following a dispensing error linked to the death of a patient. However, this position changed following charges of manslaughter brought in that year (the Peppermint Water case) against a pharmacist and a pre-registration graduate who failed to prevent a fatal dispensing error when preparing a mixture for an infant. The mixture was erroneously compounded using concentrated instead of double-strength chloroform water. When the case came to court, the Crown Prosecution Service agreed to drop the charges of manslaughter and to substitute prosecutions under section 64 of the Medicines Act (chapter 13) for supplying a medicine not of the nature and quality demanded.[9] Since that time, it has become increasingly common for pharmacists and their staff to be involved in Coroner's inquests following deaths associated with medication and to be at risk of charges of criminal negligence if their failings may have led directly to the death.

Following a patient's death in 2005, a pharmacist Phillip Dean was accused of criminal negligence manslaughter associated with the supply of an unintended dose of 100 mg Oramorph (morphine sulphate) rather than 10 mg. The prosecution asserted that because Mr Dean did not check that what he was dispensing was intended by the doctor he was grossly negligent. Mr Dean said that he knew such a high dose of morphine could cause serious harm but that he had dispensed that strength since; two general practitioners (GPs), a nurse and even medical experts all concluded that what appeared to have been written on the prescription was indeed '100mg'. Mr Dean was acquitted.[10]

Corporate manslaughter

The Corporate Manslaughter and Corporate Homicide Act 2007 came into force in 2008 and may mean that manslaughter charges will be laid against

[8] *R v Adomako* [1995] 1 A.C. 171
[9] *Pharm J*, 4 March 2000 p. 356; 11 March 2000 pp. 389–392; 18 March 2000 p. 427
[10] *Chemist and Druggist*, 3rd January 2008, available online

managers, directors and superintendents of companies or NHS bodies, such as hospital trusts and primary care organisations, if death occurs through major failures in management arrangements, such as staffing, training or resources.

Summary

- Pharmacy is regarded as a profession because its members are bound by regulated standards of education and standards of conduct, ethics and performance.
- There are seven key standards with supporting guidance in many areas.
- Pharmacists' activities are subject to criminal law, administrative law, civil law and fitness to practise arrangements based on the GPhC's Standards and supporting guidance.
- Several legal cases now demonstrate the duty of care owed by pharmacists to their clients.

˙Further reading

Reissner D (2008). Fatal distraction. *Chemist and Druggist*, 29 March, p. 15 (http://www.chemistanddruggist.co.uk).

Rodgers R, John D (2006). Paternalism to professional judgement: the history of the Code of Ethics. *Pharm J*, 276: 721.

Wingfield J (2007). Consent: the heart of patient respect. *Pharm J*, 279: 411–414.

Wingfield J (2007). New emphasis in the Code of Ethics. *Pharm J*, 279: 237–240.

Wingfield J (2007). When confidences should be kept and what constitutes an exception. *Pharm J*, 279: 533–536.

Wingfield J, Badcott D (2007). *Pharmacy Ethics and Decision Making*. London: Pharmaceutical Press.

Websites

Chemist and Druggist (a weekly publication mostly concerned with community pharmacy): http://www.chemistanddruggist.co.uk

General Pharmaceutical Council (details of pharmacy standards): http://www.pharmacyregulation.org

The GPhC is a public body and all its activities are mostly available to the public and professionals alike (some exceptions are hearings on fitness to practise that are held in private). The material appearing on its website is expanding rapidly at the time of going to press and it may not be helpful to give precise locations as these may change. However, standards and guidance may be found under 'standards'.

Royal Pharmaceutical Society: http://www.rpharms.org

The RPS is a membership organisation for pharmacists and the *Pharmaceutical Journal* is provided free to its members. The RPS also issues annually the Medicines, Ethics and Practice Guide which is intended to assist members in interpretation of the law and standards of practice in real life situations.

24

Fitness to practise

David H Reissner

The role of the General Pharmaceutical Council

The role of the GPhC (chapter 22) is to protect the health, safety and wellbeing of patients and people who use pharmacy services. Its principal functions (Art.4)[1] include:

a establishing and maintaining a register of pharmacists, pharmacy technicians and premises at which a retail pharmacy business is, or is to be carried on;

b setting and promoting standards (chapters 22 and 23) for the safe and effective practice of pharmacy;

c setting requirements by reference to which registrants must demonstrate that their fitness to practise is not impaired;

d promoting the safe and effective practice of pharmacy by registrants (including, for example, by reference to any code of conduct for, and ethics relating to, pharmacy); and

e ensuring the continued fitness to practise of registrants.

Fitness to practise

Although not a legal definition, the GPhC defines 'fitness to practise'[2]:

> as a person's suitability to be on [its] register without restrictions. In practical terms, this means maintaining appropriate standards of proficiency, being of good character and in good enough health to practise safely and effectively, and adhering to principles of good practice as set out in [its] standards and guidance, and other relevant best practice advice.

---

[1] Article 4 of the Pharmacy Order 2010 (all Articles are from the Pharmacy Order 2010 unless otherwise stated)

[2] The GPhC *Annual Fitness to Practise Report 2011–2012*

Specific occasions when fitness to practise falls to be considered

The Council will consider the fitness to practise of a registrant specifically:

a   when a registrant first applies for registration (Art.23(1)(5);

b   if it is shown to the satisfaction of the Registrar that a registrant's fitness to practise is impaired as a result of prescribed circumstances (see below) or because of a problem with the registrant's physical or mental health (Art.30) at the time of entry or renewal of an entry in the Register;

c   where an allegation is made to the Council that a registrant's fitness to practise is impaired (Art.52); or

d   the GPhC has information that calls into question a registrant's fitness to practise, even though no allegation has been made to that effect (Art.52).

Under the FTP Rules,[3] a registrant must notify the GPhC's Registrar in writing within 7 days if (Rule 4), amongst other things, s/he

a   is convicted of any criminal offence;

b   accepts a caution;

c   becomes subject to an investigation into their fitness to practise by another regulatory body;

d   becomes the subject of any fraud investigation in relation to the Health Service; or

e   is the subject of a ruling that renders him or her unable to practise within the NHS on fitness to practise grounds.

Failure to give disclosure may itself be considered misconduct, and the courts have upheld the serious view taken by regulators of such failure because it strikes at the heart of the registration process and the reliability of the Register; the failure to disclose is highly relevant to whether an applicant is fit to practise.[4]

Grounds for finding impairment

A person's fitness to practise may only be regarded as 'impaired' by reason of (Art.51):

a   misconduct;

b   deficient professional performance (which includes competence);

c   adverse physical or mental health which impairs their ability to practise safely and effectively or which otherwise impairs their ability to carry out the duties of a pharmacist or a pharmacy technician in a safe and effective manner;

[3] The General Pharmaceutical Council (Fitness to Practise and Disqualification etc. Rules) Order of Council SI 2010 No. 1615
[4] *Harris v Registrar of Approved Driving Instructors* [2010] EWCA Civ. 808

d failure to comply with a reasonable requirement imposed by an individual assessor or an assessment team in connection with carrying out a professional performance assessment:

e a conviction or police caution for a criminal offence,[5] or being bound over to keep the peace; or

f a determination of impairment of unfitness to practise by another regulatory body or inclusion in a barred list.[6]

Misconduct

Misconduct may relate to professional practice, including dispensing errors (see below), but the meaning of 'misconduct' is much wider. Specifically in relation to pharmacy practice, in a case in which a pharmacist failed to query an ambiguous prescription for a mixture that contained a fatal overdose of pethidine, the High Court held that misconduct is simply to be defined as 'incorrect or erroneous conduct of any kind provided that it is of a serious nature judged according to the rules written or unwritten governing the profession'.[7]

Since this decision, the term 'misconduct' has found its way into pharmacy legislation, and the courts have considered the meaning of misconduct on numerous occasions. If misconduct is alleged to have occurred at a pharmacy, the fact of being superintendent pharmacist[8] of a body corporate that owns a pharmacy, or ownership of a pharmacy,[9] is not sufficient on its own to justify referring an allegation of misconduct against either.

Misconduct in pharmacy legislation

There are express statutory references to misconduct in the legislation governing the practice of pharmacy. Specifically, if a registrant fails to comply with standards of conduct, ethics or performance set by the GPhC (see chapter 22), any such failure is not, of itself, to be taken to constitute misconduct. However, it is to be taken into account in any fitness to practise proceedings (Art.48 (3).

Responsible Pharmacists at registered premises have a legal duty to secure the safe and effective running of the pharmacy business, so far as [this]

---

[5] The conviction may occur anywhere in the world but, in the case of a conviction outside the British Islands must be for something that would be a criminal offence in the British Islands
[6] Under the Safeguarding Vulnerable Groups Act 2006
[7] Mr Justice Webster in *The Queen v Statutory Committee of the Pharmaceutical Society, ex parte Sokoh*, *The Times*, 4 December 1986
[8] *The Queen v The Statutory Committee of the Pharmaceutical Society of Great Britain, Ex parte Lewis and Jeffreys Limited, Berg and Brandon* (unreported, Mr Justice Woolf, 20 December 1982)
[9] *Akodu v Solicitors Regulation Authority* [2009] EWHC 3588 (Admin)

concerns the sale or supply of all medicines at those premises; and to keep certain records. The Responsible Pharmacist must also maintain and keep under review procedures designed to secure the safe and effective running of the business at the relevant premises.[10] Failure to comply with any such requirements will not automatically be regarded as misconduct, but it may constitute misconduct for the purpose of any fitness to practise proceedings.[11]

Before the introduction of the legal requirement for Responsible Pharmacists,[12] it was common practice to bring disciplinary proceedings against companies that owned a pharmacy where something untoward had occurred and against the superintendent pharmacist of that company. Fitness to practise proceedings are now brought less often against companies or superintendents. Since then, the principal focus has been on Responsible Pharmacists.

Dispensing errors as misconduct or as deficient professional performance

The question of whether a single dispensing error can be misconduct has been considered by the High Court, which ruled that a single error is capable of constituting misconduct if it is sufficiently serious, although whether it crosses the threshold of seriousness depends on the facts of individual cases.[13] The modern approach may be summarised in the words of Lord Cooke[14] in a dental appeal:

> It is settled that serious professional misconduct does not require moral turpitude. Gross professional negligence can fall within it. Something more is required than a degree of negligence enough to give rise to civil liability but not calling for the opprobrium that inevitably attaches to the disciplinary offence.

The GPhC does not express a view whether single dispensing errors are misconduct, but is not likely to refer single errors to its FTP Committee, because the GPhC thinks that single dispensing errors do not raise fitness to practise concerns unless there are significant other factors.[15] Such other factors may include the seriousness of harm to a patient.

The case of Aukse Austinskaite[16] may be thought to represent the modern approach to dealing with dispensing errors. Ms Austinskaite was a pharmacist who admitted a series of dispensing errors. The Council contended that her fitness to practise was impaired on the alternative grounds

[10] Section 72A Medicines Act 1968
[11] Section 72B Medicines Act 1968
[12] Introduced by amending the Medicines Act 1968 with effect from 1 October 2009
[13] See end of chapter for finding cases cited in this chapter
[14] *Preiss v General Dental Council* [[2001] 1 W.L.R 26
[15] General Pharmaceutical Council's *Annual Report 2011–2012*
[16] 16 April 2012 (*Pharm J*, 15 September 2012 p. 307)

of deficient professional performance or misconduct. The FTP Committee followed a ruling of the High Court[17] that where charges of misconduct and deficient professional performance are founded on the same facts, then the Committee can only find impairment on one of those grounds, not on both.

The Committee noted that deficient professional performance has been defined in these terms[18] in a GMC case involving a medical practitioner:

> It connotes a standard of professional performance which is unacceptably low and which (save in exceptional circumstances) has been demonstrated by reference to a fair sample of the [pharmacist's] work

The Committee went on to rule that 'not every instance of deficient professional performance . . . will necessarily give rise to impairment'. The Committee had regard to the fitness to practise criteria (see below) and concluded that, on the facts of the case, the registrant presented an actual risk to patients and the frequency and gravity of the dispensing errors were such that she might well bring the profession of pharmacy into disrepute. The case was thus dealt with as deficient professional performance, rather than as misconduct.

Convictions and other misconduct

The 'double jeopardy' rule does not apply to fitness to practise proceedings.[19] The FTP Committee may find facts proved on the balance of probabilities even though a registrant may have been acquitted of an offence in a criminal court where the burden of proof – beyond reasonable doubt – was higher. Convictions and misconduct need not be related to the practice of pharmacy, so there are no limitations on the scope of allegations, including convictions of students,[20] that may lead to consideration of whether fitness to practise is impaired. Examples of modern cases that have led to fitness to practise proceedings include:

- failure to disclose to the GPhC convictions for theft,[21] for motoring offences,[22] or for drug misuse;[23]

[17] *Vali v General Optical Council* [2011] EWHC 310 (Admin)

[18] *Caelham v General Medical Council* [2007] EWHC 2606, [2008] *LS Law Medical* 96

[19] *R (Redgrave) v Commissioner of Police for the Metropolis* [2003] 1 W.L.R 1136

[20] Pharmacy students had been involved in a fracas at the London School of Pharmacy. They were found guilty of unlawful wounding and each given a conditional discharge (which is not classed as a conviction). The High Court held that it was open to the Pharmaceutical Society to bring a case alleging misconduct in disciplinary proceedings, relying on the same facts as were before the criminal court; *R v Statutory Committee of the Pharmaceutical Society of Great Britain and Martin and Shutt Ex p. Pharmaceutical Society of Great Britain* [1981] 1 W.L.R. 886

[21] Maria Del Rosario Ferrero Alvarez-Rementaria (*Pharm J*, 3 March 2012 p. 284)

[22] Jasmeet Kaur Brar (*Pharm J*, 3 March 2012 p. 283)

[23] Patrick O'Sullivan (*Pharm J*, 24 March 2012 p. 395)

- sexual activity with a 14-year old girl;[24]
- sexually touching a patient during acupuncture treatment;[25]
- touching a patient in a consulting room[26] (not with a sexual motive, but because the pharmacist lacked appropriate expertise); and
- convictions for drink driving or for doing an act to pervert the course of justice.[27]

First registration and good character

Before being registered with the GPhC, an applicant must satisfy registration requirements to establish that they are fit to practise the profession (Art.23(1)(d)). The same obligation is placed both on applicants who have never been on the Register of the RPSGB or the GPhC and on those formerly on the Register of the RPSGB but who were not on the register at the date its regulatory functions were taken over by the GPhC;[28] for example, in the case of the latter because they had been removed at the direction of the Statutory Committee or the Disciplinary Committee following a finding of misconduct that rendered them unfit to be on the Register.

Guidance[29] given to the GPhC (and other regulators) by the Professional Standards Authority For Health and Social Care (PSAHSC) (when it was known as the Council for Healthcare Regulatory Excellence (CHRE)[30]) is that there are four key elements which form the basis this assessment. These are whether an applicant has acted, or there is reason to believe they are liable in future to act:

a in such a way that puts at risk the health, safety or wellbeing of a patient or other member of the public;

b in such a way that his/her registration would undermine public confidence in the profession;

c in such a way that indicates an unwillingness to act in accordance with the standards of the profession; or

d in a dishonest manner.

The same principles for assessing fitness to practise in the case of someone already registered apply to the case of an applicant for registration.[31]

---

[24]Hailmarim Lakew (*Pharm J*, 7 January 2012 p. 14

[25]Jasbinder Singh Bansal (*Pharm J*, 7 January 2012 p. 14)

[26]Asif Ghafoor (*Pharm J*, 28 January 2012 p. 122)

[27]Vijay Ratilal Mistry (*Pharm J*, 5 May 2012 p. 570)

[28]This was on 27 September 2010

[29]*A Common Approach to Good Character Across the Health Professions Regulators*, December 2008, available on CHRE website

[30]Renamed on 1 December 2012 as the Professional Standards Authority for Health and Social Care Professions

[31]*Jideofo v The Law Society* [2007] EW Misc 3 (31 July 2007)

However, in contrast to the position of an existing registrant, the burden is on the applicant to satisfy the Registrar that s/he is fit to practise.

If the Registrar of the GPhC refuses registration on fitness to practise grounds, the reasons for refusal must be given (Art.24(3)(b)). The applicant has a right of appeal (Art.40) to the Registration Appeals Committee provided the appeal is brought within 28 days of the date on which the written statement of the reasons for the decision was sent. The procedure governing appeals is set out in separate Rules.[32]

Interim orders

Where the Registrar[33] or the Investigating Committee considers that the FTP Committee should consider making an interim order (Art.53(3)(c)) suspending the registrant from practice pending a full fitness to practice hearing, the allegation must be referred to the FTP Committee. The FTP Committee must hold a hearing and give the registrant reasonable notice. The notice period is nevertheless usually very short. The registrant is entitled to attend and be represented at the hearing.

The FTP Committee will approach applications for interim orders on the basis of the evidence available so far and the nature of the allegations, and it will make a decision on the basis that the allegation is true, without deciding the facts of the case. It is not the responsibility of the Committee to make findings of fact or to resolve factual disputes, even if the registrant contends that the evidence is weak.[34] Out of fairness to registrants who have not been found guilty of any offence or misconduct, hearings are held in private.

The Committee may make an immediate order suspending the registrant from practice for up to 18 months or may impose conditions of practice pending a full fitness to practise hearing if it is satisfied that it is necessary for the protection of members of the public or is otherwise in the public interest or is in the interests of the registrant (Art.56). No member of the FTP Committee that has made an interim order may sit as a member of the Committee at a final hearing of the allegation.[35]

[32] The General Pharmaceutical Council (Appeals Committee Rules) Order of Council SI 2010 No. 1614 (Appeals Rules)
[33] Rule 6(4) of FTP Rules
[34] *Abdullah v General Medical Council* [2012] EWHC 2506; the High Court (Mr Justice Lindblom) held that Parliament had entrusted to the GMC's Interim Orders Panel the power to make decisions on a doctor's freedom to practise while his fitness to do so was investigated, using its own experience and expertise and its own knowledge of the public's expectations of the medical profession. The allegations against the doctor were very serious. There was a need to maintain public confidence in the medical profession or the medical regulator, and action would sometimes have to be taken to protect public confidence even where there was no immediate risk to patients
[35] Paragraph 5 of Schedule 1 of the Pharmacy Order 2010

If an interim order is made, the GPhC will be expected to prepare its case for a final hearing during the lifetime of the order. If the Council has not been able to bring the case to a final hearing within that time and if it is unable to do so within the 18-month maximum period of suspension the FTP Committee can impose, the Council may apply to the High Court for an interim order to be extended. The High Court has power to extend an extension by up to a further 12 months (Art.56(5)). The High Court has generally been willing to grant extensions while the regulator completes the preparation of its case for a final hearing, although not always for the period sought by the regulator. In one of the leading cases,[36] in which an extension was granted, the High Court held that the court could take into account the gravity of the allegations, the nature of the evidence, the seriousness of the risk of harm to patients, the reasons why the case had not been concluded and the prejudice to the practitioner if an interim order were continued. However, there are examples of refusal, such as in a case in which, by the time a previous 3-month extension granted by the court had expired, the regulator had still not even decided whether to formulate charges against the registrant. The judge took into account that the order had been considered necessary to protect the public from harm but much of the delay was unexplained, and he held that this could not be decisive for all time.[37]

Examples of cases in which registrants have been suspended under interim orders (mostly heard in private and not reported) include:

- a pharmacist about to stand trial for a putting counterfeit Viagra on the market, presumably because of concern about public confidence in the profession when the trial was reported in the press if it became known that the defendant was a practising pharmacist;[38]
- a pharmacist who had made a single but fatal dispensing error, after the case had been reported in a local newspaper;[39]
- a pharmacist accused of taking financial advantage of a vulnerable adult; and
- allegations that a doctor had made false accusations, fabricated and altered original documents and lied to a disciplinary investigator were sufficient to justify an interim suspension of his registration on grounds that such allegations would likely undermine public confidence in the profession.[40]

An interim order was refused in a case where the registrant had been arrested and bailed following an allegation of domestic violence but not yet

---

[36] *General Medical Council v Hiew* [2007] 1 W.L.R. 2007

[37] *Nursing and Midwifery Council v Maceda* [2011] EWHC 3004 (Admin)

[38] In the event, the pharmacist's conviction in the Crown Court was quashed by the Court of Appeal: *R v Patel (Hitendra)* [2010] 1 W.L.R 1011

[39] *Cambridge News*, 21 June 2008 (http://www.cambridge-news.co.uk/Cambridge/Pharmacy-to-blame-for-death-coroner.htm)

[40] *Bradshaw v General Medical Council* [2010] Med. L.R. 323

charged at the time of the application for an interim order. The Committee was at pains to emphasise that it was not engaged in a fact-finding exercise, and that the allegations were vehemently denied by the registrant. The Committee ruled that in considering an allegation of domestic violence in the context of whether an order is necessary for the protection of members of the public, the existence of a threat to the safety of members of the family cannot be regarded as the existence of a threat to the public at large; suspension from practice as a pharmacist would not protect family members.

As to whether suspension would be necessary in the public interest, the High Court has held in the case of a dental practitioner convicted of conspiracy to defraud[41] that 'it is ... likely to be a relatively rare case where a suspension order will be made on an interim basis on the ground that it is in the public interest' because of the impact on a registrant's ability to earn a living. The Court held that, in the absence of necessity for suspension at an interim stage, 'the question of public perception and public confidence could be reflected by an appropriate decision by the Panel, if so minded, at the final hearing when all the facts had been fully explored, all the mitigation fully advanced and the position finally assessed at [the final hearing]'. Indeed, in a case of non-clinical allegations, it has been held that only something that would impinge more directly on members of the public, such as murder, rape or abuse of children, would justify interim suspension for the purpose of public protection.[42]

Registrants have a right of appeal (Art.58) to the High Court against interim orders. Any such appeal must be brought within 28 days of the date on which written notice of the reasons for the decision was sent to the registrant, or such longer period as the court may allow. In the event of an appeal, the interim order will not take effect until the expiry of the date for appealing or, in the even of an appeal, its final disposal (Art.59). However, the FTP Committee may order a suspension until its interim order comes into effect if it is satisfied that it is necessary to do so for the protection of members of the public or is otherwise in the public interest or in the interests of the registrant.

The FTP Committee must review interim orders within 6 months and must keep orders under review. Registrants may request an earlier review once 3 months have passed (Art.56). On a review, the Committee may continue, vary or revoke the interim order.

Initial action in respect of allegations

If the GPhC has information or receives information or an allegation that a registrant's fitness to practise is or might be impaired, the Registrar must

[41] R (on the application of Sheikh) v General Dental Council [2010] Med. L.R. 323
[42] Bradshaw as in citation 40

normally refer the information or allegation to the Council's Investigating Committee (Art.52) unless the allegation falls within the Council's threshold criteria (Art.52 and Rule 6 of FTP Rules) for not making a referral (box 24.1) or unless more than 5 years have elapsed since the most recent events referred to in the allegation. If more than 5 years have elapsed, the Registrar may only refer the case if s/he considers that it is necessary for the protection of the public, or otherwise in the public interest for the allegation to be referred.

Box 24.1 GPhC threshold criteria in fitness to practise allegations

The threshold criteria are that cases are not to be referred to the Investigating Committee unless one of the following statements is true:

Principle 1, make patients your first concern:
- there is evidence that the registrant's conduct or performance caused moderate or severe harm or death, which could and should have been avoided;
- there is evidence that the registrant deliberately attempted to cause harm to patients and the public or others;
- there is evidence that the registrant was reckless with the safety and wellbeing of others.

Principle 2, use your professional judgment in the interests of patients and the public:
- there is evidence that the registrant put their own interests, or those of a third party, before those of their patients;
- there is evidence that the registrant culpably failed to act when necessary in order to protect the safety of patients.

Principle 3, show respect for others;
- there is evidence that the registrant failed to respect the human rights of patients, or demonstrated in their behaviour attitudes which are incompatible with registration as a pharmacy professional;
- there is evidence that the registrant failed to maintain appropriate professional boundaries in their relationship with patients and/or others.

Principle 4, encourage patients and the public to participate in decisions about their care:
- there is evidence that the registrant damaged or put at significant risk the best interests of patients by failing to communicate appropriately with patients or others.

Principle 5, develop your professional knowledge and competence:

- there is evidence that the registrant practised outside of their current competence;
- there is evidence that the registrant failed to maintain their knowledge and skills in a field relevant to their practice;
- there is evidence of a course of conduct, which is likely to undermine public confidence in the profession generally or put patient safety at risk, if not challenged by the regulatory body.

Principle 6, be honest and trustworthy:
- there is evidence that the registrant behaved dishonestly;
- there is evidence of behaviour on the part of the registrant which is likely to undermine public confidence in the profession generally, if not challenged by the regulatory body.

Principle 7, take responsibility for your working practices:
- there is evidence that the registrant has practised in a way that was systemically unsafe or has allowed or encouraged others to do so, where he or she has responsibilities for ensuring a safe system of working;
- there is evidence of adverse physical or mental health which impairs the registrant's ability to practise safely or effectively.

If the Registrar is in doubt as to whether the above criteria have been met, he shall refer the case to the Investigating Committee.

When making a referral to the Investigating Committee, the Registrar is under an obligation to make any referral to the Investigating Committee within a reasonable time, but failure to do so would not invalidate the referral or provide grounds to set it aside unless a fair disciplinary process is no longer possible.[43]

The Investigating Committee

The Investigating Committee consists of a lay member who is the chair, two lay members who are deputy chairs, two other lay members; and five registrant members.[44] They have a 4-year term of office. The quorum

[43] *R (on the application of Rycroft) v Royal Pharmaceutical Society of Great Britain* [2011] Med. L.R. 23

[44] A 'lay member' is defined in Rule 1 of the General Pharmaceutical Council (Statutory Committees and their Advisers Rules) Order of Council SI 2010 No. 1616 (Statutory Committee Rules) as a member who is not, and has never been, entered in the Register of any regulatory body and does not hold qualifications which would entitle them to apply for entry in the Council's Register.

comprises three members and must include a chair or deputy chair, a registrant and a lay member. The Committee must sit with a legal adviser.[45]

The Investigating Committee meets in private. Its primary function is to decide whether an allegation ought to be considered by the FTP Committee (Art.53). The Committee may not hear oral evidence. Instead, registrants will be given at least 21 days in which to make written representations. In relation to a heath allegation, the Committee may require the registrant to agree to be examined by a nominated medical practitioner.

In deciding whether to refer an allegation to the FTP Committee, the Investigating Committee will follow published referral criteria (see appendix 10). The criteria require the Investigating Committee to form a view whether there is a real prospect proving the facts alleged and whether, if proved, those facts would amount to impairment of fitness to practise.

The Investigating Committee's powers include giving a warning and giving advice (including advice to a person against whom an allegation has not been made, such as a pharmacist's employer). Where the Committee determines that the allegation ought to be considered by the FTP Committee or a registrant has requested a referral, the Committee must refer the case to the FTP Committee. In the event of such a referral, the Registrar must inform the person who made the allegation.

Prosecutions

Many breaches of the Human Medicines Regulations 2012 are criminal offences (Reg.255). The GPhC has power to enforce many of the relevant provisions of the Regulations (Reg.323). If the Investigating Committee considers that the Council should consider exercising any of its powers to bring criminal proceedings, it must notify the Registrar accordingly (Art.53(4)). The Council has published a prosecution policy (see appendix 11). Its view is that taking a proportionate and cost-effective approach means using alternatives to prosecution, including seeking voluntary compliance and non-criminal regulatory interventions, for example fitness to practise proceedings, where appropriate.

When offences are committed, these usually involve strict liability,[46] meaning that offences may be committed unintentionally. The Council's powers to prosecute are not exclusive. Prosecutions have also been brought by the Crown Prosecution Service. In the case of dispensing errors, prosecutions have typically alleged that a pharmacist has supplied a product to the

---

[45]Rule 21 of the Statutory Committee Rules

[46]See, for example, *Pharmaceutical Society of Great Britain v Storkwain Limited* (although after the House of Lords upheld a conviction for unwittingly dispensing a forged prescription, a due diligence was introduced, which is now in Regulation 245 of the Human Medicines Regulations 2012

prejudice of the patient that is not of the nature or quality demanded[47] (and chapter 13). It is not only pharmacists who may be prosecuted. Where a dispenser had selected an incorrect drug and passed it to a pharmacist, who then authorised an incorrect prescription, both the dispenser and the pharmacist have been convicted of an offence.[48] The High Court held that the dispenser could not avoid conviction by arguing that the pharmacist was more in control of the supply, had higher qualifications and a more important position, nor did the pharmacist's failure to carry out the necessary checks break the chain of supply.

In another case, that of Elizabeth Lee,[49] who made a non-fatal dispensing error for which she initially received a suspended prison sentence[50] in respect of labelling offences, such had been the concern in pharmacy circles about the fairness of this sentence that the Crown Prosecution Service was forced to review its policy on prosecution and publish guidance to prosecutors.[51] In future, while dispensing errors continue to be criminal offences, the Crown Prosecution Service will apply a detailed analysis before deciding whether to prosecute, taking into account such factors as whether a simple error was made, whether there was recklessness and whether remedial action was taken. If a pharmacist or pharmacy technician is convicted of an offence, then that offence will never be spent for the purpose of the Rehabilitation of Offenders Act 1974.[52] The issue of whether pharmacists and pharmacy employees should be at risk of conviction for dispensing errors has been the subject of considerable debate and is currently under review by the MHRA.

Disqualification

In the case of an allegation against a body corporate, if the Investigating Committee considers there is a real prospect that the FTP Committee will make a direction for disqualification,[53] the Investigating Committee may refer the matter to the FTP Committee for disqualification proceedings (see Sanctions, below). Such proceedings are rare and are only likely to be brought in the case of a business conducted in wholesale disregard of the

[47] Section 64 of the Medicines Act 1968
[48] *Mahoney v Prestatyn Magistrates' Court* [2009] EWHC 3237 (Admin)
[49] *R v Lee (Elizabeth)* [2010] EWCA Crim. 1404; [2011] 1 W.L.R. 418. Mrs Lee was charged under s.64 (chapter 13) and under s.85 of the Medicines Act 1968 (chapter 14) but only the second charge was heard. Mrs Lee resigned from the register of the former RPSGB and was not the subject of further enquiry
[50] The sentence was overturned on appeal and replaced by a fine of £300, *R v Lee (Elizabeth)* [2010] EWCA Crim. 1404; [2011] 1 W.L.R. 418
[51] Available on the Crown Prosecution Service website (see end of chapter)
[52] Rehabilitation of Offenders Act 1974 (Exceptions) Order SI 1975 No. 1023
[53] Rule 9(7)(b) of the FTP Rules

rules governing the profession or in flagrant disregard of the need to protect patients and the public.

Disposal of allegations without hearings

Following a decision of the Investigating Committee to refer an allegation to the FTP Committee, the person responsible for presenting the Council's case may conclude that the case should not proceed to a hearing, for example because there is insufficient evidence to justify a finding that a registrant's fitness to practise is impaired, or because the decision to refer was legally flawed because the Investigating Committee failed to take into account a relevant consideration, such as delay. In that event, the Investigating Committee must be informed and the Committee may rescind the referral,[54] after giving any complainant an opportunity to comment. The Investigating Committee is not bound to rescind the referral and on occasions has declined to do so.

The Fitness to Practise, Committee

The FTP Committee is to consist of

- a lay member who is the chair;
- eight lay members who are deputy chairs;
- 11 other lay members; and
- 20 registrant members.

The quorum for the FTP Committee comprises the chair or a deputy chair and at least two other members. The number of registrant members who are members of that formation of the Committee must not exceed the number of lay members by more than one. A member who has sat on the Committee when granting an interim order may not sit in subsequent proceedings in the case.[55] Usually, hearings (other than case management meetings) are conducted by a committee comprising a legally qualified Chair, a registrant member and a lay member.

The Committee may seek advice from a clinical adviser on a health-related issue or any other specialist adviser on issues within their speciality.[56] The Committee may be expected to rely on the specialist knowledge of registrant members, but with the following in mind:[57]

the rules of natural justice preclude expert members from giving evidence to themselves which the parties have no opportunity to challenge

[54]Rule 38 of the FTP Rules
[55]Rule 19 of the Statutory Committee Rules
[56]Rule 23 of the FTP Rules
[57]*Lawrence v GMC* [2012] EWHC 464 (Admin)

and ... where a specialist tribunal drawing on its own knowledge and experience independently identified an important fact or matter which may influence its decision but which has not been the subject of evidence adduced by the parties, it should state this openly and give the parties an opportunity to seek to adduce evidence and/or make submissions on it.

Indeed, a decision of the former Statutory Committee was quashed because when its members deliberated in private they consulted *Martindale* without reference to the parties concerned on a point that was not covered by the professional knowledge of the pharmacists on the Committee.[58]

Procedure prior to hearings

As soon as reasonably practicable after an allegation has been referred by the Investigating Committee or the Registrar, the Council must serve on the registrant finalised particulars of the allegation, sufficiently particularised to enable them to understand the allegation, together with any witness statements, expert reports or other documents relied on by the Council, and any evidence or documents in the Council's possession that may assist the registrant in the preparation of his or her defence. As soon as reasonably practicable after service by the Council, the registrant must serve on the Council any witness statements, expert reports and other documents the registrant relies on.[59]

There are rules for case management and, if a direction is required any party may request a management meeting, for example as to compliance with the rules, the disclosure of evidence, issues as to witnesses or to seek a ruling of law. At such meetings, the chair of the FTP Committee, sitting alone, may give directions in order to secure the just, expeditious and effective running of the proceedings before the Committee. Such hearings may take place by telephone conference, rather than personal attendance.[60]

Fitness to practise hearings

At fitness to practise hearings,[61] both the GPhC and the registrant may be represented by a solicitor or barrister or, in the case of the Council, by an employee.[62] A registrant may also be represented by a person from a defence organisation or trade union. At the start of any hearing to determine whether a registrant's fitness to practise is impaired (defined as a 'principal hearing'),

---

[58] *Fletcher and Lucas v Pharmaceutical Society of Great Britain, Pharm J*, July 1978 p. 93
[59] Rule 14 of the FTP Rules
[60] Rule 20 of the FTP Rules
[61] Rule 35 of the FTP Rules
[62] Rule 43 of the FTP Rules

the FTP Committee must determine any preliminary legal arguments. The chair will then establish whether the registrant makes any admissions and, if so, will announce that the facts admitted have been found proved. Where facts are in dispute, the case for the Council is then presented to the Committee and evidence will be given in support. The registrant will then present his or her case and may call evidence. The burden of proving disputed facts is on the Council. The standard of proof is the civil one (see also chapter 1): facts must be proved on the balance of probabilities[63] even where a criminal offence is alleged. After hearing any submissions as to the findings it should make, the Committee will deliberate privately before announcing its findings of fact in public.

The Committee must receive further evidence and hear any further submissions from the parties as to whether, on the basis of the facts found proved, the registrant's fitness to practise is impaired (see the section on Impairment above as to the exclusive reasons that must be proved in order for fitness to practise to come under consideration). The Committee will then deliberate in private.

Fitness to practise criteria

When deciding whether the requirements as to fitness to practise are met in relation to the registrant, the FTP Committee must have regard[64] to whether or not the conduct or behaviour that has been found proved:

a presents an actual or potential risk to patients or to the public;
b has brought, or might bring, the profession of pharmacy into disrepute;
c has breached one of the fundamental principles of the profession of pharmacy; or
d shows that the integrity of the registrant can no longer be relied upon.

In cases where it is alleged that a registrant's fitness to practise may be impaired by health factors, the Committee must have regard to whether or not there is evidence of actual or potential self-harm; or harm to patients or to the public.

The determination of fitness to practise has been considered by the courts in a number of key cases.[65] The courts have held that the task of the Committee is to take account of any conviction or misconduct of the practitioner

---

[63] Rule 42 of the FTP Rules
[64] Rule 5 of the FTP Rules
[65] *Meadow v General Medical Council* [2007] 2 W.L.R 286; *Cohen v General Medical Council* [2008] EWHC 581 (Admin); *Cheatle v General Medical Council* [2009] EWHC 645 (Admin); *Yeong v General Medical Council* [2009] EWHC 1923; The Queen on the Application of *Zygmunt v General Medical Council* [2008] EWHC 2643 (Admin); [2009] *LS Law Medical* 219

and to consider it in the light of all the other relevant factors known to them in answering whether by reason of the registrant's misconduct, conviction, deficient professional performance, and so on his or her fitness to practice is impaired. This is a process of looking forward, as well as back, and taking into account the practitioner's efforts to address his or her problems and reduce the risk of recurrence. Even if an isolated dispensing error is found to be misconduct, the Committee may conclude that the chance of it being repeated in the future is so remote that a registrant's fitness to practise is not impaired.[66] In the case a series of errors, such as that of Aukse Austinskaite (see above), the Committee noted that its 'task [was] to determine not whether at some time in the past the registrant's fitness to practise was impaired, but whether it was currently impaired'. The Committee took the view that the concept of 'remediability' is applicable to cases where impairment might arise from deficient professional performance caused by a consistent tendency to make dispensing errors. On the facts of that case, the Committee found that the registrant's fitness to practise was impaired.

The FTP Committee may find that the registrant's fitness to practise is not impaired but may nevertheless issue a warning or advice to them or any other involved person. If the FTP Committee decides that the registrant's fitness to practise is impaired, it must announce its finding in public and give reasons for that decision. The Committee may then receive further evidence and hear any further submissions as to the appropriate sanction, if any, to be imposed.

Sanctions

Submissions as to sanction[67] may include any mitigating circumstances and any relevant matters in the registrant's history, such as previous adverse findings. The Committee may receive submissions not only from the parties at this stage but also from any other person, perhaps a patient, who has a direct interest in the proceedings. The Committee may:[68]

a give a warning to the registrant;

b give advice to any other person or body involved on any issue related to the allegation;

c give a direction that the registrant's name be removed from the Register (except when impairment is only by reason of health);

d give a direction that the registrant's entry in the Register be suspended for a specific period up to a maximum of 12 months; or

---

[66] *Cohen v General Medical Council* [2008] EWHC 581 (Admin); [2008] *LS Law Medical* 246

[67] The registrant or person representing the registrant may present arguments as to what sanction (or outcome) may be appropriate to the case

[68] (Article 54 of the Pharmacy Order 2010

e direct that the registrant's entry in the Register be conditional upon complying with such requirements as the Committee thinks fit, such conditions may run for up to 3 years; examples of conditions include undertaking training, practising under supervision or not holding the position of superintendent pharmacist.

The Committee will take into account published guidance on indicative sanctions (appendix 12). This guidance emphasises that the purpose of sanctions is not to punish the registrant but to protect the public and maintain confidence in the profession of pharmacy and proper standards of behaviour. Aggravating features include dishonesty,[69] sexual misconduct in relation to professional duties and lack of insight. Mitigating features include repayment of any misappropriated funds, ill health at the time of misconduct or deficient professional performance, open and frank admissions at an early stage, demonstrating insight and the absence of actual or potential harm to patients or the public.

In reaching its decision, the Committee will attach greater weight to the interests of the public than the interests of the registrant. The Committee will aim to apply sanctions proportionately. In other words, it will impose a sanction that is no more severe than necessary to achieve its purpose. The Committee will therefore usually consider its powers in ascending order of seriousness to determine whether, starting with a warning, this would be sufficient to address the impairment it has found.

Similar procedures will be followed where an allegation is made in respect of a body corporate that carries on a retail pharmacy business. If the body corporate or one of its officers or employees has been convicted of an offence or has been guilty of misconduct which would render the person concerned unfit to be a pharmacist, the FTP Committee may direct that the body corporate be disqualified from running a retail pharmacy business at all its premises or at specific premises.

After deliberating in private, the Committee will announce its decision in public. The outcome of cases will often be case specific, depending on the Committee's view of the gravity of cases, and the insight of the registrant, taking the Indicative Sanctions guidance into account. It does not necessarily follow, therefore, that a registrant who has been convicted of an offence of dishonesty will be removed from the Register. Some registrants found to

---

[69]In *Yusuf v Royal Pharmaceutical Society of Great Britain* [2009] EWHC 867 (Admin), Mr Justice Munby dismissed an appeal against removal from the Register, saying 'there may be cases of misconduct – even dishonesty – in a non-professional context where a disciplinary tribunal could, in appropriate circumstances, conclude that some penalty short of the ultimate penalty suffices. A trivial act of shoplifting in a 'moment of madness' by a professional person of otherwise blameless character is very different indeed from the wholesale misconduct and dishonesty in a professional context of which the appellant was her found guilty'.

have acted dishonestly will be removed; others have received suspensions of varying lengths.

Examples of suspension in modern times include:

- 3 months for failure to inform the Registrar of convictions for driving offences[70]
- 6 months for failing to inform the Registrar after accepting a police caution for theft[71]
- 2 months for practising while not registered[72]
- 12 months for a series of dispensing errors by a pharmacy technician[73]
- 9 months for sexually touching a woman during acupuncture treatment[74]
- 1 month for a conviction for driving while disqualified[75]
- 5 months for sending offensive and distasteful emails; and offensive PMR entries[76]
- 2 months for subjecting a colleague to a campaign of harassment[77]
- 12 months for sexual assault on two females.[78]

As an illustration of the Committee's approach to sanctions in a case involving dispensing errors, the case of Aukse Austinskaite (referred to above), may be useful. The Committee noted that the dispensing errors were 'comparatively large in number...and included serious errors in the form of exposure of the patients to risk...' However, the Committee considered removal, which not only carries a lasting stigma but would also prevent the registrant from practising for at least 5 years, would be too severe and a disproportionate sanction. The Committee considered that the registrant should be given an opportunity to come back to pharmacy and 'learn to do the job properly'. The Committee directed a suspension for a period of 12 months, saying that in view of her good testimonials she did not deserve to have her name removed, and that the public interest did not demand the removal of her name.

The case of Glackin sheds light on the approach to drug misuse.[79] The registrant's fitness to practise was found to be impaired because of cocaine use. The Chair of the Committee said, 'Regular, even if infrequent misuse of drugs, presents a risk to health and might therefore prejudice patients.

[70] Jasmeet Kaur Brar (*Pharm J*, 3 March 2012 p. 283)

[71] Maria Del Rosario Ferrero Alvarez-Rementaria, (*Pharm J*, 3 March 2012 p. 284)

[72] Sukhjinder Singh Aujla (*Pharm J*, 3 March 2012 p. 284)

[73] Moira JayneTuckwood (*Pharm J*, 3 March 2012 p. 283)

[74] Jasbinder Singh Bansal (*Pharm J*, 7 January 2012 p. 14)

[75] Faraz Khan (*Pharm J*, 7 January 2012 p. 15)

[76] Matthew Jonathan Smith (*Pharm J*, 23 June 2012 p. 762)

[77] Narinderpal Bal (*Pharm J*, 23 June 2012 p. 763)

[78] Roshan Lal (*Pharm J*, 23 June 2012 p. 763)

[79] Brendan Ambrose Glackin (*Pharm J*, 30 June 2012 p. 795)

It is bound to undermine public confidence in the profession, it breaches a fundamental tenet of the profession and it is contrary to the Code of Ethics'. Ordering a 12-month suspension, the Committee said that, when a review took place, the registrant would need to provide evidence that he had kept his knowledge up to date and complied with CPD requirements; proof of attendance at a return to practise course; reports concerning any work he had carried out; and a report from his GP concerning his health, insofar as it might affect his fitness to practise, with particular reference to drug abuse.

A suspension or a direction to remove a registrant's name from the Register will not normally take effect until the 28-day period for appealing has expired. The Committee may order the suspension or removal to have immediate effect if it is satisfied that this is necessary for the protection of members of the public or is otherwise in the public interest or in the interests of the registrant (Art.60).

Effect of suspension

If the FTP Committee imposes a suspension, it will conduct a review hearing before the expiry of the extension. At the review hearing, the Committee may decide to remove the registrant's name from the Register or extend the suspension by up to 12 months; if the registrant has already been suspended for at least 2 years, the Committee may suspend the registrant indefinitely. At the end of any period of suspension, the Committee may impose conditions of practice. In the Austinskaite case, referred to above, the Committee said that if, when her suspension was reviewed, there was no evidence that the registrant had any intention of learning to practise to an accepted level of competence, it may be that the Committee would decide to remove her name at the review hearing. If she were able to provide the Committee with evidence of competence, it would probably permit her to return to practice.

It has been argued that since a suspended pharmacist must be treated as not being entered in the Register (Art.19 (8) the effect of suspension is to prevent a pharmacist who owns an NHS pharmacy in his or her own name from providing services and thus put him/her at risk of removal from the pharmaceutical list (in other words, losing their NHS 'contract').[80] However, it is thought that the better view is that a suspended pharmacist may continue to own an NHS pharmacy but may not personally provide NHS services during the period of suspension. This view would be consistent with section 132(8) of the National Health Service Act 2006.

---

[80]Regulation 74(1)(b) of the National Health Service (Pharmaceutical Services) Regulations SI 2012 No. 1399

Costs

Before a principal hearing or a restoration hearing (see below) takes place, a party may serve the other party and the secretary to the committee a schedule of costs and expenses related to or connected with the hearing. This must be done no less than 24 hours before the date of the hearing. After announcing the Committee's decision, the chair may invite representations as to whether costs or expenses should be assessed against either party.

In practice, the Committee does not routinely award costs and there is no principle that costs are paid by the 'loser' to the 'winner'. Costs will usually be awarded only because of the way one of the parties has conducted itself. For example, costs have been awarded against the RPS (when it was the regulator) because a case ought not to have been brought against two out of three registrants who were partners in a pharmacy business but who were not alleged to have been involved in the misconduct by a third partner.[81] In another case,[82] a registrant had made false expense claims to an employer. He made admissions of dishonesty when interviewed by the police. When fitness to practise proceeding were brought, he contested the allegations and a hearing was listed for 2 days. On the first day of the hearing, the registrant accepted that the account he had given to the police was correct and the hearing was completed that day. The expense of arranging the second day was, therefore, wasted. The Committee held that it was unreasonable to have contested the allegations up to the morning of the first day of the hearing, and ordered the registrant to pay the wasted costs.

Where the Committee orders a party to pay costs or expenses, the chair may summarily assess the costs or expenses or require the parties to agree a figure or have them assessed by a person appointed by the secretary.

Appeals

There is a right of appeal (Art.58) to the High Court against decisions to direct removal from the Register, suspension and the imposition of conditions of practice. A notice of appeal must be lodged at the High Court within 28 days, beginning with the date on which written notice of the reasons for the decision was sent to the appellant. There is no power to extend this period.

Appeals to the High Court take the form of a re-hearing,[83] although it is not usual for the court to hear witness evidence. Fresh evidence is not normally admitted, and the court will usually deal with appeals by reference to a transcript of the fitness to practise proceedings. Unless the FTP Committee is found to have made an error of law or its decision was not

[81]Tanna (*Pharm J*,, 1 March 2008 p. 235)
[82]Shiraz Mughal, 12 September 2011
[83]Paragraph 22.3(2) of the Practice Direction of Part 52 of the Civil Procedure Rules

supported by the evidence, the High Court will accord the FTP Committee an appropriate measure of respect in relation to its rulings, while being ready in appropriate cases to substitute its own decision for that of the Committee.[84]

Professional Standards Authority for Health and Social Care

The fitness to practise role of the GPhC is overseen by the PSAHSC (formerly the CHRE). If the PSAHSC considers that a fitness to practise decision is unduly lenient, and that it would be desirable for the protection of members of the public for the PSAHSC to do so, the PSAHSC may refer the case to the High Court.[85] The test for referral is not whether a decision was lenient, but was unduly lenient, because the findings of professional misconduct were inadequate or because the penalty did not adequately reflect the findings of professional misconduct that had been made, or both. When deciding if a decision was unduly lenient, the High Court will consider whether the sanction was one which a disciplinary tribunal, having regard to the relevant facts and to the object of the disciplinary proceedings, could reasonably have imposed.[86]

Restoration to the Register and registration following removal

In the case of a person whose name has been removed from the Register at the direction of the FTP Committee, no application for restoration may be made before the expiration of 5 years from the date of removal or within 12 months from the date of an earlier application.[87] The Registrar will refer any application for restoration to the FTP Committee. The burden of proof in a restoration application is on the applicant. who must prove that s/he is entitled to be registered.

A person whose name was removed from the Register before the GPhC became the regulator will not have been on the Council's Register. As such, an application for restoration cannot be made, and such a person would have to apply for registration to the Registrar. There is no time restriction of the kind that applies to applications for restoration. Initially, the Registrar usually determines such applications without a hearing. If an application is refused, there is a right of appeal to the Registration Appeals Committee (see also chapter 22). The procedures that have to be followed in order to

[84] *General Medical Council v Meadow* [2006] EWCA Civ. 1390
[85] Section 29 of the National Health Service Reform and Health Care Professions Act 2002
[86] *Ruscillo v Council for the Regulation of Health Care Professionals* [2004] EWCA Civ. 1356; [2005] 1 W.L.R. 717
[87] Article 57(2) of the Pharmacy Order 2010

appeal are set out in Regulations.[88] Appeals take the form of a re-hearing, which may be on paper. The appellant may request a hearing and may give oral evidence. The burden and standard of proof in the case of an appeal to the Registration Appeals Committee is on the appellant, who must establish that the Registrar's refusal should be overturned.[89]

Summary

- The GPhC will consider fitness to practise on an application for first registration and when it receives information or an allegation that fitness to practise may be impaired.
- Allegations of impairment are usually based on a conviction, misconduct, deficient professional performance or health.
- Dispensing errors may be misconduct or deficient professional performance, but single errors are not usually referred for fitness to practise proceedings unless very serious.
- Allegations are usually passed by the GPhC's Registrar to the Investigating Committee, which will decide whether to refer the case to the FTP Committee.
- The FTP Committee may impose an interim suspension while awaiting a full hearing if it considers this necessary for the protection of the public or is otherwise in the public interest.
- At a full (or 'principal') hearing, the FTP Committee will decide the facts and whether a registrant's fitness to practise is impaired.
- If a registrant's fitness to practise is found to be impaired, the FTP Committee can give advice, a warning, impose conditions of practice, suspend for up to 12 months or direct the registrant's removal from the GPhC's Register.
- In deciding on the appropriate and proportionate sanction, the FTP Committee will have regard to published guidance ('Indicative Sanctions').
- The FTP Committee has power to order the GPhC or a registrant to pay costs.
- A registrant has a right of appeal to a court against a decision to suspend or to remove from the Register.
- Following removal from the Register, an application for restoration cannot be made before 5 years have elapsed.

Further reading

Glynn J, Gomez D (2012). *Regulation of Healthcare Professionals*. London: Sweet & Maxwell.

[88] The General Pharmaceutical Council (Appeals Committee Rules) Order of Council SI 2010 No. 1614 (Appeals Rules)
[89] Rule 10 of the Appeals Rules

Websites

Chemist and Druggist (a weekly publication for community pharmacy but also publishes short
reports of some fitness to practise cases): http://www.chemistanddruggist.co.uk
Crown Prosecution Service: http://www.cps.gov.uk
Crown Prosecution Service (guidance on prosecution policy):
http://www.cps.gov.uk/legal/l_to_o/medicines_act_1968/
General Pharmaceutical Council: http://www.pharmacyregulation.org
General Pharmaceutical Council (details of pharmacy standards):
http://www.pharmacyregulation.org

The GPhC carries an online register which contains details of any publicly available fitness to
practise hearings and their outcomes. To find a case, go to the home page and enter the name
(or the registration number if known and still valid) into the register search function. A link
to the fitness to practise case will appear against the registrant's name if available. The GPhC
also publishes every 2 months *Regula+e*; this carries updates on the Council's activities as
well as lessons to be learned from selected fitness to practise cases.

Legislation: http://www.legislation.gov.uk
Royal Pharmaceutical Society: http://www.rpharms.org

- fitness to practise procedures: http://www.pharmacyregulation.org/raising-
  concerns/hearings/committees/fitness-practise-committee
- fitness to practise cases: http://www.pharmacyregulation.org/search/search_decisions

The RPS is a membership organisation for pharmacists and the *Pharmaceutical Journal* is provided free to its members. Fitness to practise cases are often the subject of short reports in
the *Pharmaceutical Journal*. The RPS also issues annually the *Medicines, Ethics and Practice Guide*, which is intended to assist members in interpretation of the law and standards of
practice in real life situations.

25

Regulation of other health professions

Gordon Hockey

Medical scandals and convergence of regulation

During the 1990s and into the first years of the 21st century, a series of scandals, mostly involving doctors, led to a radical overhaul of the regulation of all health professions, including pharmacy. Space does not permit a full account here but the following overview is well supported by website resources (see end of chapter) covering the detailed inquiries that followed the scandals. One of the first inquiries, in 2001, was the Kennedy Inquiry,[1] which investigated a flawed system at an NHS hospital, which 'led to around one-third of all the children who underwent open-heart surgery receiving less than adequate care. More children died than might have been expected in a typical (comparative) unit'. The inquiry criticised in particular the presence of a 'club culture' and the absence of any agreed means of assessing the quality of care, of standards for evaluating performance or of clarity as to who in the NHS was responsible for monitoring the quality of care. This last finding led to the development of clinical governance within the NHS (now termed quality and performance; chapter 26) and then in private healthcare. A second inquiry, at Alder Hey Hospital in Liverpool,[2] set out to inquire into the removal, retention and disposal of human tissue and organs following coroners' and hospital postmortem examinations and the extent to which the Human Tissue Act 1961 had been complied with. In this Inquiry, it was found that the doctors and staff at Alder Hey had failed to provide suitable advice, counselling and support necessary to affected families and showed a lamentable grasp of the modern concepts of consent and involvement of patients, parents and relatives in medical care.

[1]Kennedy 2001, *The Report of the Public Inquiry into Children's Heart Surgery at the Bristol Royal Infirmary 1984–1995: Learning from Bristol*
[2]Redfern et al. 2001, *The Royal Liverpool, Children's Inquiry*

To some extent, the above two inquiries pale into insignificance beside a third, the Shipman Inquiry,[3] at least in relation to the number of deaths caused. Dr Harold Shipman, by all accounts a benign caring GP with a single-handed practice in Hyde, a small town in a pleasant part of northwest England, was eventually proven to have murdered at least 200 of his patients and more were suspected. When he was eventually imprisoned for life after nearly 30 years of practice, he hanged himself, thus taking any further information about numbers or his motives to his grave. Two of the key outcomes of the Shipman Inquiry were a series of recommendations to modify the legislation regarding Controlled Drugs to limit the likelihood of such unnoticed diversion occurring again and changes to the regulation of doctors (and subsequently all the main healthcare professions). A further series of inquiries were published into the conduct of Clifford Ayling,[4] Richard Neale[5] and, jointly, William Kerr and Michael Haslam.[6] These revealed both appalling flaws in the professional behaviour of a few doctors and the failure of those in positions of authority or the regulator (the GMC) to detect signs of this behaviour and to take timely and effective action to protect patients from it.

The convergence of healthcare regulation has been assisted by the establishment of the PSAHSC,[7] a super-regulator (formerly the CHRE) which, since 2002, has provided increasing oversight of the individual healthcare regulators, and 'section 60' orders,[8] which, since 1999, have provided a relatively swift mechanism to change the primary legislation governing the individual healthcare regulators.

Professional Standards Authority for Health and Social Care

Largely as a result of political concern about the unsatisfactory nature of self-regulation of doctors, the government established the PSAHSC, which is now charged with promoting the interests of users of healthcare in the

[3] Smith J 2002–2005, *The Shipman Inquiry* (six individual reports)
[4] Department of Health 2004, *Committee of Inquiry: Independent Investigation into how the NHS Handled Allegations about the Conduct of Clifford Ayling*
[5] Department of Health 2004, *Committee of Inquiry to Investigate how the NHS Handled Allegations about the Performance and Conduct of Richard Neale*
[6] Department of Health 2005, *The Kerr/Haslam Inquiry, Full Report*
[7] The Professional Standards Authority for Health and Social Care. This was established as the Council for the Regulation of Health Care Professionals under the National Health Service Reform and Health Care Professions Act 2002 and renamed the Council for Healthcare Regulatory Excellence by the Health and Social Care Act 2008, before being renamed again as the Professional Standards Authority for Health and Social Care by section 222 of the Health and Social Care Act 2012
[8] Health Act 1999

UK and users of social care and social work services in the England, as well as other members of the public in relation to the performance by the regulatory bodies of health professionals.[9] PSAHSC oversees the medical, dental, nursing, optical, chiropractic, osteopathic and health profession councils plus the GPhC and the Pharmaceutical Society of Northern Ireland (the main healthcare professions). Its role is to review and scrutinise the regulatory systems of the main health and social care professions, to drive up standards and to foster harmonisation of regulatory practice and outcomes. PSAHSC may, investigate, report on the performance and audit the fitness to practise cases of each regulatory body, and may recommend changes to the way in which the body performs its functions. It may refer to the High Court those bodies whose disciplinary committees appear to be too lenient in dealing with the public's complaints against health professionals.[10] It may also advise and audit any health or social care regulator or any body which has functions (whether or not relating to health or social care) corresponding to those of a regulatory body.[11]

PSAHSC/CHRE will also advise the Secretary of State and Health Ministers in Scotland, Wales and Northern Ireland on regulatory policy and from time to time carries out special reviews. These have included reviews of significant failings at the Nursing and Midwifery Council (2008), the General Teaching Council (England) (2009) and the General Social Care Council (2010), which are available on the website of CHRE (which will change into PSAHSC at 1 December 2012; see the end of the chapter). It is notable that two of the three regulators have closed following the reviews. On 1 April 2012, the General Teaching Council for England Teaching Agency closed and the Teaching Agency, an executive agency of the Department for Education, became responsible for the regulation of the teaching profession. On 1 August 2012, the General Social Care Council closed and the Health Professions Council, renamed as the Health and Care Professions Council,[12] became responsible for regulation of social workers in England.

Section 60 Orders

Section 60 of the Health Act 1999[13] provides powers to change the regulation of the main healthcare professions by Order in Council. This has accelerated

[9] Section 25 of the National Health Service Reform and Health Care Professions Act 2002, as amended by section 223 of the Health and Social Care Act 2012

[10] Section 26 of the National Health Service Reform and Health Care Professions Act 2002

[11] Section 25B of the National Health Service Reform and Health Care Professions Act 2002, as amended by the Health and Social Care Act 2012

[12] Health and Social Care Act 2012

[13] as amended by the Health and Social Care Act 2008 and the Health and Social Care Act 2012

the pace of legislative change because it avoids the need for new primary legislation. Such Orders in Council may:

a modify the regulation of any profession, so far as appears to be necessary or expedient for the purpose of securing or improving the regulation of the profession or the services which the profession provides or to which it contributes; and

b regulate any other profession which appears to be concerned (wholly or partly) with the physical or mental health of individuals and to require regulation in pursuance of this section.

Many changes have since been made to the statutory regulations of the main healthcare regulators, including, for example, the establishment of the GPhC by the Pharmacy Order 2010.[14]

Law Commission proposals on regulation

In 2012, the Law Commission undertook a review on the regulation of health (in the UK) and social care professionals (in England) and consulted on proposals to introduce a single Act of Parliament to provide the legal framework to replace all the individual governing statutes and orders.[15] The intention was to simplify and modernise the current complex arrangements for professional regulation and impose consistency across the regulators by giving government the power to make regulations for any of the regulators or merge or abolish existing regulators or establish a new regulator. The report was still awaited at the time of going to press.

The General Medical Council

The GMC, which is the sole registering authority in the UK for the medical profession, was established by the Medical Act 1858, as amended.[16] Its main objective is to protect, promote and maintain the health and safety

[14]Pharmacy Order SI 2010 No. 231

[15]Law Commission, Scottish Law Commission and the Northern Ireland Law Commission 2012, *Regulation of Health Care Professionals: Regulation of Social Care Professionals in England*

[16]The Medical Act 1983, as amended by the Medical Act 1983 (Amendment) Order SI 2002 No. 3135, the Medical Act (Amendment) and Miscellaneous Amendments Order SI 2006 No. 1914, The Health Care and Associated Professions (Miscellaneous Amendments) Order SI 2008 No. 1774, the Medical Profession (Miscellaneous Amendments) Order SI 2008 No. 3131, the General and Specialist Medical Practice (Education, Training and Qualifications) Order SI 2010 No. 234, and the Health and Social Care Act 2008

of the public (s.1A). The GMC Council comprises 12 members, 6 lay and 6 medical, all appointed by an independent appoinments process.[17]

The GMC has power to regulate medical education (Part I and II) and to provide advice for members of the medical profession on standards of professional conduct or on medical ethics (s.35) and powers to make regulations with respect to the form and keeping of the Register, whether a licence to practise is held (Part IIIA) and details of entry on a Specialist Register (s.34). Practitioners must pay registration fees and annual retention fees, which are set out in regulations made by the GMC under section 32 of the Medical Act 1983.

The Register, registration and licence to practise

The GMC has a Register of Medical Practitioners with provision for full or provisional registration as appropriate and in accordance the following four lists (s.2 and s.30).

The *Principal Register* includes those with:

- qualifying examinations and primary UK qualifications (s.3);
- full registration under the EEA system (s.14A);
- provisional registration, including those from the EEA (s.15 and s.15A);
- from the EEA with qualifications accepted by another Member State of the EEA (s.19A), and,
- those directed to be registered fully or partially as EEA nationals with overseas primary qualifications (s.19 and 21), with full or provisional registration with an overseas qualification (s.21B and 2s.1C).

The *Temporary Register* is related to emergencies declared by the Secretary of State (s.18A):

- temporary visiting eminent specialists (s.27A) and special purposes (s.27B); and
- visiting medical practitioners from another Member State of the EEA or Switzerland (Sch. 2A).

The GMC also holds a General Practitioner Register and a Specialist Register.[18]

---

[17]Articles 2, 3 and 8 of the General Medical Constitution (Constitution) Order SI 2008 No. 2554, as amended by the General Medical Council (Constitution) (Amendment) Order SI 2012 No. 1654

[18]The various medical specialties are set out in the Postgraduate Medical Education and Training (Amendment) Order of Council SI 2010 No. 473, as amended by the Postgraduate Medical Education and Training (Amendment) Order of Council SI 2012 No. 344

The Registrar must include the doctor's name and address and date of registration but the register that is published (electronically or otherwise) must include only information about registered qualifications, any licence to practise, inclusion in any specialist list and other such particulars as the GMC may direct. The GMC may make regulations setting out the detailed form and content of the registers (s.31(1 and 2).[19] There are appeals procedures against registration and training decisions (primarily Sch. 3A and additional rules[20]).

The GMC has power to make regulations with respect to the grant, refusal to grant and the withdrawal of a licence to practice, which is part of the provisions for the revalidation of medical practitioners.[21] There is an appeals procedure to the Registration Appeals Panel (Sch. 3B).

Revalidation

Licensed doctors will have to revalidate, usually every 5 years, by having regular appraisals that are based on the GMC core guidance for doctors, Good Medical Practice. Revalidation will be introduced across the UK in early December 2012, and the majority of licensed doctors should be revalidated for the first time by the end of March 2016. All doctors, whether GPs, hospital doctors or employed in the private sector, are required to revalidate. Employers or those bodies that contract with doctors must appoint a responsible officer who will implement the GMC's requirements for appraisal and recommendations on revalidation.

Professional discipline

A medical practitioner's fitness to practise shall be regarded as 'impaired' for the purposes of this Act by reason only of (s.35C):

a misconduct;

b deficient professional performance;

c a conviction or caution in the British Islands for a criminal offence, or a conviction elsewhere for an offence which, if committed in England and Wales, would constitute a criminal offence;

d adverse physical or mental health; or

e a determination by a body in the UK responsible under any enactment for the regulation of a health or social care profession to the effect that his fitness to practise as a member of that profession is impaired, or a determination by a regulatory body elsewhere to the same effect.

[19] The General Medical Council (Form and Content of the Registers) Regulations SI 2010 No. 2
[20] The General Medical Council (Registration Appeals Panels Procedure) Rules Order of Council SI 2010 No. 476
[21] The General Medical Council (Licence to Practise) Regulations Order of Council SI 2009 No. 2739

The provisions apply even if the matter occurred outside the UK or at a time the person was not registered or the information was obtained as part of revalidation procedures.

The GMC fitness to practise procedures, including those for interim orders, are set out in the Act (primarily Part V and Sch. 4) and supporting regulations.[22] Interim orders are imposed where necessary for the protection of the public, or in the interests of the doctor, and the doctor's registration may be suspended, or made subject to conditions.

Insurance

The GMC guidance on practice, *Good Medical Practice* (see GMC website address at end of chapter), provides that doctors 'must take out adequate insurance or professional indemnity cover for any part of your practice not covered by an employer's indemnity scheme, in your patients' interests as well as your own' (para. 34).

Titles and descriptions

Only fully registered persons may hold certain appointments as physicians, surgeons or other medical officers (e.g. in the naval, military or air services or in the prison service) (s.47) or recover in any court of law any charge made for medical or surgical advice or attendance (s.46). A certificate required by law to be from a physician, surgeon, licentiate in medicine and surgery, or other medical practitioner is not valid unless the person signing it is fully registered (s.48).

Any person commits an offence if s/he wilfully and falsely pretends to be or takes or uses the name or title of physician, doctor of medicine, licentiate in medicine and surgery, bachelor of medicine, surgeon, GP or apothecary, or any name, title, addition or description implying that s/he is registered under any provision of the 1983 Act, or that s/he is recognised by law as such (s.49 and s.49A). Nothing in the Act prejudices or in any way affects the lawful occupation, trade or business of chemists and druggists, or of dentists, so far as they extend to selling, compounding and dispensing of medicines (s.54).

---

[22] Primarily the GMC (Fitness to Practise) Rules 2004 (No. 2608)as amended by the General Medical Council (Constitution of Panels and Investigation Committee) Rules Order of Council SI 2004 No. 2611, The General Medical Council (Constitution of Panels and Investigation Committee) (Amendment) Rules Order of Council SI 2005 No. 402, The General Medical Council (Constitution of Panels and Investigation Committee) (Amendment) Rules Order of Council SI 2009 No. 2751, the General Medical Council (Constitution of Panels and Investigation Committee) (Amendment) Rules Order of Council 2010 SI 2010 No. 474, The General Medical Council (Registration Appeals Panels Procedure) Rules Order of Council SI 2010 No. 476

Disclosure of information

Regulations give the GMC power to require disclosure of information that would assist in the carrying out their functions in respect to fitness to practise (s.35A).

In addition, the GMC is obliged to notify specified persons when formal proceedings are initiated against a doctor in respect of his/her fitness to practise where they consider it in the public interest (s.35B).

The General Dental Council

The practice of dentistry is controlled by the Dentists Act 1984 through the General Dental Council, whose constitution, as amended,[23] comprises 12 registered dentists or dental care professionals and 12 lay members, all appointed by the Privy Council. The functions in respect of education, registration and discipline are similar to those of the GMC.

The practice of dentistry is deemed to include the performance of any such operation and the giving of such treatment, advice or attendance as is usually performed or given by dentists, and any person who performs any operations or gives any treatment, advice or attendance on or to any person as preparatory to or for the purpose of or in connection with the fitting, insertion or fixing of dentures, artificial teeth or other dental appliances is deemed to have practised dentistry within the meaning of the Act (s.37).

The General Dental Council also registers dental care professionals: dental therapists and dental hygienists,[24] dental nurses, dental technicians, clinical dental technicians and orthodontic therapists.[25]

The Dentists Register

The Dentists Register must be made available to the public as the Registrar considers appropriate (s.22 as substituted[26]) and the following are the main groups entitled to be registered (s.15–17, as amended[27]):

[23] The General Dental Council (Constitution) Order SI 2009 No. 1808
[24] General Dental Council (Professions Complementary to Dentistry) (Dental Hygienists and Dental Therapists) Regulations Order of Council SI 2006 No. 1677
[25] The General Dental Council (Professions Complementary to Dentistry) Regulations Order of Council SI 2006 No. 1440
[26] The Dentists Act 1984 (Amendment) Order SI 2005 No. 2011
[27] The Dental Qualifications (Recognition) Regulations SI 1996 No. 1496, The European Primary and Specialist Dental Qualifications Regulations SI 1998 No. 811, Council Regulation (EEC) No. 312/76, The European Qualifications (Health Care Professions) Regulations SI 2003 No. 3148, The European Qualifications (Health and Social Care Professions and Accession of New Member States) Regulations SI 2004 No. 1947, The Dentists Act 1984 (Amendment) Order SI 2005 No. 2011, The European Qualifications (Health and Social Care Professions) Regulations SI 2007 No. 3101

1 any person who is a graduate or licentiate in dentistry of a dental authority;
2 any person who is a national of a EEA country and holds an appropriate European diploma;
3 any person who holds a recognised overseas diploma; and
4 any person with a relevant enforceable community right or EEA applicants who complies with third country qualifications.

An applicant must satisfy the Registrar as to his/her identity, good character and good physical and mental health. An overseas applicant under item 3 above must also satisfy the Registrar that s/he has the necessary skill and knowledge, and knowledge of English, which, in the interests of him/herself and patients is necessary for the practice of dentistry in the UK.

The holder of a recognised overseas diploma may, without meeting any additional requirements, be temporarily registered in the Dentists Register for a specified period for the purpose of practising dentistry in a specified hospital or institution. The Register must include a note of the restriction.

Similar provisions apply for dental care professionals (s.36C[28]).

Professional discipline

A dentist's fitness to practise may be considered impaired (s.27) and a dental care professional's (s.36N[29]) by:

a misconduct;
b deficient professional performance;
c adverse physical or mental health;
d a conviction or caution in the UK for a criminal offence, or a conviction elsewhere for an offence which, if committed in England and Wales, would constitute a criminal offence;
e the person having
  i accepted a conditional offer under section 302 of the Criminal Procedure (Scotland) Act 1995 (fixed penalty: conditional offer by procurator fiscal), or
  ii agreed to pay a penalty under section 115A of the Social Security Administration Act 1992 (penalty as alternative to prosecution);
f the person, in proceedings in Scotland for an offence, having been the subject of an order under section 246(2) or section 246(3) of the Criminal Procedure (Scotland) Act 1995 discharging him absolutely; or

[28] The Dentists Act 1984, as amended by The Dentists Act 1984 (Amendment) Order SI 2005 No. 2011
[29] The Dentists Act 1984, as amended by The Dentists Act 1984 (Amendment) Order SI 2005 No. 2011

g a determination by a body in the UK responsible under any enactment for the regulation of a health or social care profession to the effect that the person's fitness to practise as a member of that profession is impaired, or a determination by a regulatory body elsewhere to the same effect.

The Dentists Act 1984 as amended[30] and the Fitness to Practise Regulations 2006[31] set out the procedures to be followed by the General Dental Council's Investigating Committee, Health Committee, Professional Conduct Committee, Professional Performance Committee and Interim Orders Committee. The Rules relate to proceedings against both dentists and members of professions complementary to dentistry and cover proceedings relating to a practitioner's fitness to practise and also those relating to whether entry to the Dentists Register or the Dental Care Professionals Register has been fraudulently procured.

Insurance

A registered dentist or a dental care professional must have adequate and appropriate insurance throughout the period of registration (s.36L[32]).

Titles and descriptions

Only registered dentists and medical practitioners may use the titles dentist, dental surgeon or dental practitioner. It is an offence for other persons to use such titles. Similarly, no person, including a medical practitioner, may use the term registered dentist unless s/he is so registered (s.39). Dentists, however, have no legal right or title to be registered under the Medical Act 1983 and may not assume any title implying a right to practise medicine or general surgery (s.7).

The practice of dentistry is restricted to registered dentists and medical practitioners (s.38). It is no longer lawful for a pharmaceutical chemist to extract a tooth in the case of emergency.

Registered dental professionals may only use in connection with his/her premises any description reasonably calculated to suggest possession of a professional status or qualification in fact possessed and any title for which s/he is registered in the Dental Care Professionals Register.

---

[30] The Dentists Act 1984, as amended by The Dentists Act 1984 (Amendment) Order SI 2005 No. 2011

[31] The General Dental Council (Fitness to Practise) Rules SI 2006 No. 1663

[32] The Dentists Act 1984, as amended by The Dentists Act 1984 (Amendment) Order SI 2005 No. 2011

Other healthcare regulators

The other healthcare regulators are as follows and regulate the corresponding professionals:

General Chiropractic Council: chiropractors
General Optical Council: optometrists, dispensing opticians
General Osteopathic Council: osteopaths
GPhC: pharmacists, pharmacy technicians
Health and Care Professions Council: arts therapists, biomedical scientists, chiropodists/podiatrists, clinical scientists, dietitians, hearing aid dispensers, occupational therapists, operating department practitioners, orthoptists, paramedics, physiotherapists, practitioner psychologists, prosthetists/orthotists, radiographers, social workers, speech and language therapists
Nursing and Midwifery Council: nurses, midwives
Pharmaceutical Society of Northern Ireland: pharmacists.

These regulators have similar provisions to those for dentists and pharmacists.

The Council of the Royal College of Veterinary Surgeons

Veterinary surgeons are subject to more traditional registration that equates with the registration of healthcare practitioners from the late 1990s and early 2000s, with a strengthened Code of Conduct for veterinary surgeons based on changes to the regulation of health and social care professionals (see below).

The Veterinary Surgeons Act 1966 is the principal statute dealing with the management of the veterinary profession in relation to registration, education and professional conduct. The Council of the RCVS, the controlling body, includes 24 persons elected by the members, four appointed by the Privy Council and two appointed by each university in the UK that grants a veterinary degree recognised by the Privy Council.

Veterinary surgery means the art and science of veterinary surgery and medicine and includes the diagnosis of diseases in, and injuries to, animals, including tests performed on animals for diagnostic purposes; the giving of advice based upon such diagnosis; the medical or surgical treatment of animals; and the performance of surgical operations on animals (s.27).

The RCVS regulates veterinary nurses through its Royal Charter[33] and contract provisions with registered veterinary nurses.

[33]Supplemental Royal Charter 1967

The Register of Veterinary Surgeons

The Registrar of the RCVS, who is appointed by the Council of the College, maintains the Register. It is published as often as the Council thinks fit, but in any year in which a full Register is not produced, alterations to it must be published instead (s.9). It comprises four lists (s.2).

1   The General List of persons entitled to be registered as graduates in veterinary surgery of universities recognised by the Privy Council (s.3) or as students of other universities who have passed the examinations held by the RCVS (s.4) or persons from the EU who hold recognised European qualifications (s.5(a and b)).
2   The Commonwealth List of persons entitled to be registered as holding some Commonwealth qualification (s.6).
3   The Foreign List of persons entitled to be registered as holding some foreign qualification (s.6).
4   The Temporary List of persons registered to practise veterinary surgery temporarily, subject to such restrictions as to place and circumstances as the Council of the Royal College may specify (e.g. persons who have passed the examinations for a degree but have not yet formally graduated, or the holders of Commonwealth or foreign qualifications not otherwise registerable). It is not lawful for a temporarily registered person to practise except in accordance with the restrictions specified in the RCVS Council's direction (s.7).

The details required for registration, and the powers to register and deregister members are set out in Regulations.[34]

Professional discipline

Veterinary surgeons and practitioners may be removed from the Register for criminal offences or 'disgraceful conduct in any professional respect'. There is a Preliminary Investigation Committee and a Disciplinary Committee and provision for suspension of registration as well as removal from the Register (s.16); appeals against a direction are made to the Privy Council (s.17). DEFRA has consulted on a Legislative Reform Order planned for the end of 2012, which will ensure that members of the Preliminary Investigation Committee and the Disciplinary Committee are not also members of RCVS Council, a move endorsed by the Privy Council in a recent appeal case.[35] The RCVS has introduced fitness to practise regulation through the Veterinary Surgeons Act 1966 and health and performance protocols linked to the *Code*

[34]The Veterinary Surgeons and Veterinary Practitioners (Registration) Regulations Order of Council 2010 SI 2010 No. 2854
[35]*Joseph Lennox Holmes v RCVS* [2011] UKPC 48

of Professional Conduct for veterinary surgeons (see the RCVS website at the end of this chapter).

Insurance

The RCVS Code of Professional Conduct states that 'veterinary surgeons must ensure that all their professional activities are covered by professional indemnity insurance or equivalent arrangements' (para. 3.4).

Restrictions on practice and use of titles

No one may practise, or hold themselves out as practising or being prepared to practise, veterinary surgery unless they are registered as a veterinary surgeon or are in the supplementary register as a veterinary practitioner (s.19). It is an offence for an unregistered person to use the titles 'veterinary surgeon' or 'veterinary practitioner' or any name, title, addition or description implying that s/he is qualified to practise veterinary surgery (s.20).

The Act provides some limited exceptions, for example for veterinary nurses (Sch. 3) and medical practitioners and dentists (s.19).

Summary

- The history of professional regulation suggests that it might have had greater emphasis on self-protection than self-regulation.
- The introduction of a super regulator has brought greater consistency and accountability to the healthcare regulators.
- A simplified mechanism to introduce new primary legislation, the Section 60 Orders, has seen a rapid change in the legal framework for regulators.
- There are moves (through the Law Commission) to introduce a single Act of Parliament to govern the regulation of healthcare professionals.
- The regulation of healthcare professionals' fitness to practise is primarily in the public interest.
- Other regulators, for example the RCVS, strive towards similar fitness to practise regulation.

Further reading

Department of Health (2004). *Committee of Inquiry to Investigate how the NHS Handled Allegations about the Performance and Conduct of Richard Neale*. London: The Stationery Office: http://www.dh.gov.uk/en/Publicationsandstatistics/Publications/PublicationsPolicyAndGuidance/DH_4088995

Department of Health (2004). *Committee of Inquiry: Independent Investigation into how the NHS Handled Allegations about the Conduct of Clifford Ayling*. London: The Stationery Office: http://www.dh.gov.uk/en/Publicationsandstatistics/Publications/PublicationsPolicyAndGuidance/DH_4088996

Department of Health (2005). *The Kerr/Haslam Inquiry, Full Report*. London: The Stationery Office: http://www.dh.gov.uk/en/Publicationsandstatistics/Publications/PublicationsPolicy AndGuidance/DH_4115349

Glynn J, Gomez D (2012). *Regulation of Healthcare Professionals*. London: Sweet & Maxwell.

Kennedy I (2001). *The Report of the Public Inquiry into Children's Heart Surgery at the Bristol Royal Infirmary 1984–1995: Learning from Bristol*. London: The Stationery Office: http://www.bristol-inquiry.org.uk/final_report/the_report.pdf, accessed 21 November 2012.

Law Commission, Scottish Law Commission and the Northern Ireland Law Commission (2012). *Regulation of Health Care Professionals: Regulation of Social Care Professionals in England*. [Joint Consultation Paper LCCP 202/SLCDP 153/NILC.] London: The Stationery Office.

Redfern M *et al.* (2001). *The Report of the Royal Liverpool Children's Inquiry*. London: The Stationery Office (http://www.rlcinquiry.org.uk/ (accessed 21 November 2012).

Ritchie J (2000). *An Inquiry into Quality and Practice within the National Health Service Arising from the Actions of Rodney Ledward*. London: The Stationery Office: http://www.dh.gov.uk/en/Publicationsandstatistics/Publications/PublicationsPolicy AndGuidance/DH_4093337 (accessed 21 November 2012).

Smith J. *The Shipman Inquiry* [six reports]. London: The Stationery Office, 2002–2005: http://www.shipman-inquiry.org.uk/home.asp (accessed 21 November 2012).

Websites

Council for Healthcare Regulatory Excellence (becoming the Professional Standards Authority for Health and Social Care on 1 December 2012): http://www.chre.org.uk/

General Dental Council: http://www.gdc-uk.org/

General Medical Council: http://www.gmc-uk.org/

General Optical Council: http://www.optical.org/

General Pharmaceutical Council: http://pharmacyregulation.org/

Health Professions Council: http://www.hpc-uk.org/

Nursing and Midwifery Council: http://www.gnmc-uk.org/nmc/main/home.html

Pharmaceutical Society of Northern Ireland http://www.psni.org.uk/

Royal College of Veterinary Surgeons: http://www.rcvs.org.uk

26

NHS law and organisation

Sarah ME Cockbill, Stephen Lutener, Edward Mallinson and Joy Wingfield

At the time of going to press the NHS in England was undergoing significant changes that were due to be completed by April 2013. Most of these changes were clarified during 2012 but the implementing legislation was expected to be laid towards the end of 2012 or in early 2013. Because the changeover may not be fully completed by April 2013, we have retained references to the 'old' system but for detailed discussion, readers should refer to the 9th edition of this book.

Legislative framework for the NHS

The National Health Service (NHS) Act 1946 made it the duty of the Minister of Health (now the Secretary of State for Health) in England, and later the Secretary of State for Wales to:

- promote the establishment in England and Wales of a comprehensive health service designed to secure improvement in the physical and mental health of the people of England and Wales and the prevention, diagnosis and treatment of illness;
- provide or secure the provision of services to do this; and
- provide these services free of charge unless otherwise expressly provided in any other Act.

In Scotland, a similar health service was established by the NHS (Scotland) Act 1947, the minister responsible being the Secretary of State for Scotland.

The service was reorganised into a single management structure in England and Wales by the NHS Reorganisation Act 1973 and in Scotland by the NHS (Scotland) Act 1978. The 1978 Act for Scotland is still the basis for the NHS in Scotland although there have been a number of later amendments (notably the NHS Reform (Scotland) Act 2004). For England and Wales, the provisions of the 1946 Act and most of the provisions of the 1973

Act, including those affecting pharmaceutical services, were consolidated into the NHS Act 1977. The 1977 Act has been effectively replaced by the consolidated NHS Act 2006 (for England) and the NHS (Wales) Act 2006. All three Acts (for England, Scotland and Wales) retain broadly the same duty upon the relevant government minister as set out in 1946 (but see the impact of the Health and Social Care Act 2012 in England below).

NHS Act 2006

In Part 1 of the NHS Act 2006, the Secretary of State must promote in England a comprehensive health service designed to secure improvement in the physical and mental health of the people of England, and in the prevention, diagnosis and treatment of physical and mental[1] illness. The Secretary of State's duties also extend to providing:

- hospital accommodation;
- other accommodation for the purpose of any service provided under the Act;
- medical, dental, ophthalmic, nursing and ambulance services;
- facilities for the care of expectant and nursing mothers and young children;
- facilities for the prevention of illness, the care of persons suffering from illness and the aftercare of persons who have suffered from illness; and
- services for the diagnosis and treatment of illness.

Under the NHS Act 2006, the Secretary of State may direct that any of his/her functions be carried out by a strategic health authority, a PCT, an NHS trust or a special health authority by way of statutory 'Directions' (see below). Broadly, the NHS is operated under NHS contracts between one health service body 'the commissioner' and another 'the provider'. These contracts are not generally enforceable at law but only through appeal to the Secretary of State. From April 2013, strategic health authorities and PCTs were due to be abolished by sections 33 and 34, respectively, of the Health and Social Care Act 2012, from which time the NHS Commissioning Board (NHSCB) was expected to take over the commissioning of the four primary care services: GPs, pharmacies, opticians and dentists.

Arrangements for the NHS contractual framework (henceforward called a contract) for community pharmacy service and local pharmaceutical service (LPS) appear in Part 7 of the NHS Act 2006 and are dealt with in more detail later in this chapter (but note that while the contractual framework for community pharmacy services is not a contract in law, the LPS is a legal contract). From April 2013, the main responsibility for commissioning of

---

[1] The phrase 'physical and mental' has been added by the Health and Social Care Act 2012

community pharmacy services rests with the NHSCB, administered through its local area teams.

Part 8, section 169 of the 2006 Act continued the arrangements for appeals, and the Secretary of State directs the NHS Litigation Authority to exercise any of his/her functions relating to the determination of appeals. Secretary of State Directions require the NHS Litigation Authority to determine appeals concerning applications for entry onto pharmaceutical lists, and in relation to appeals against determinations over the hours of opening of NHS community pharmacies.[2] The Authority also considered appeals concerning performers' lists and decisions made by PCT disciplinary committees but this has now transferred to the first-tier tribunal within the Ministry of Justice.[3] Part 9 contains the provisions for prescription charges to be paid by certain people presenting NHS prescriptions in the community. Part 10 makes a series of requirements concerning the protection of the NHS from fraud, such as compulsory disclosure of documents and information. Part 12 includes details of how the public and patients will have an input into NHS planning and operation and Part 13 contains provisions enforcing controls on the maximum price of medicines (the Pharmaceutical Price Regulation Scheme) and other medical supplies to the NHS. The Department of Health negotiates the Pharmaceutical Price Regulation Scheme on behalf of the whole of the UK. Part 14 contains sections covering interpretation and defined expressions and brought the Act into force on 1 March 2007.

Earlier legislation relevant to pharmacy

Health Act 1999

Although the provisions of the Health Act 1999 which are directly related to the management of the NHS are now incorporated into the NHS Act 2006, there remain some other sections of the 1999 Act that are relevant to pharmacy. These include the statutory duty of quality on NHS bodies and services (termed *quality and performance* or *clinical governance*) and enabling powers to regulate healthcare professions, including pharmacy. Section 60 of the Health Act 1999 in particular provided power to change the regulatory and disciplinary powers of the RPSGB. The section 60 and 62 order making powers were later used to make the Pharmacy Order 2010, which transferred the regulatory and disciplinary powers of the RPSGB to the GPhC in September 2010 (chapters 22, 23 and 24).

---

[2] The National Health Service Litigation Authority (Functions relating to Pharmaceutical Services and Local Pharmaceutical Services) (England) Directions 2012
[3] Under the Transfer of Tribunals Order SI 2010 No. 22

Health and Social Care Act 2001

Again, most of the NHS provisions in the Health and Social Care Act 2001 have been subsumed into the NHS Act 2006, but section 63 amends the Medicines Act and adds pharmacists to the groups of health practitioners who are able to authorise a prescription for a POM (see independent and supplementary prescribing in chapters 8 and 9).

National Health Service Reform and Health Care Professions Act 2002

As its name suggests, the NHS reforms in the National Health Service Reform and Health Care Professions Act 2002 are now in the National Health Service Act 2006, but the 2002 Act also provided for the establishment of the Council for the Regulation of Healthcare Professions, later the CHRE and then renamed under the Health and Social Care Act 2012 as the PSAHSC. This body oversees the regulatory and disciplinary roles of all the healthcare professions (chapters 22, 23 and 24).

Health and Social Care (Community Health and Standards) Act 2003 (England and Wales Only)

Once again, a significant number of provisions relating to the NHS in this Act now appear in the NHS Act 2006. However, the 2003 Act replaced an earlier provision in the Health and Social Care Act 2001 creating the Commission for Health Improvement (now superseded) with a wider body, the Commission for Health Care Audit and Inspection (or as it preferred to be called, the Healthcare Commission). In addition, a parallel inspection body for social care inspection, the Commission for Social Care Inspection was set up. These bodies were later combined; see Health and Social Care Act 2008 below.

Health Act 2006

The Health Act 2006 became rather famous for introducing a ban on smoking in public premises but it also contained a wide range of provisions affecting the NHS and other matters. For pharmacists, the most important provisions are in Part 3, which contained powers to change the Regulations under the Misuse of Drugs Act (chapter 17) following the Shipman scandal (chapter 25). Section 30 inserted a new section into the Medicines Act 1968 to change the requirement for a pharmacist to be in 'personal control' of a pharmacy to there being a 'Responsible Pharmacist' for each pharmacy (chapter 5). Moreover, section 26 of the Health Act 2006 inserts further sections into the Medicines Act 1968 to change the interpretation of 'supervision' in sections 10 and 52 of the 1968 Act. Consultation was expected on these changes in 2008 and 2009, but no real progress had been made by September 2012.

Health and Social Care Act 2008

The Health and Social Care Act 2008 introduced changes in two areas affecting pharmacy. First, it established the GPhC (chapters 22, 23 and 24). Second, the 2008 Act changed the name of the over-arching regulator for healthcare professions to the CHRE (the Health and Social Care Act 2012 makes further changes, see below) and combined into the CQC the roles of the Commission for Health Care Audit and Inspection (the Healthcare Commission), the Commission for Social Care Inspection (see above) and the Mental Health Act Commission.

Health Act 2009

The Health Act 2009 brought in the NHS Constitution (section 1) and quality accounts (section 8) (to report on the quality of NHS services provided by an NHS body). Although Quality Accounts have been prepared by a small number of NHS bodies, the cost and the complexity has caused a review, and at September 2012 they have not rolled out widely, and do not have to be prepared by primary care providers.

Impending legislation in England

Health and Social Care Act 2012

The most fundamental change to the NHS since its inception was introduced by the Health and Social Care Act 2012.[4] This section looks at the layout and content of the Act, where relevant to pharmacy; later policy directions implicit in the Act are considered and then the likely structure of the NHS in England – as far as was known at the time this book went to press (end September 2012). Much of the Act substitutes for, amends or replaces existing provisions in the 2006 NHS Act. Part 1 of the 2012 Act is concerned with the health service in England and sets out the duties of the Secretary of State, the role and duties of the new NHSCB, of new CCGs and new roles for local authorities such as county and metropolitan councils to undertake the provision of public health services. A small but significant change in Part 2 (s.59) is the repeal of the 1987 AIDS (Control) Act and its Regulations, which prohibited the marketing of diagnostic tests for the human immunodeficiency disease.

[4] The Health and Social Care Act (Commencement No 1 and Transitory Provision) Order SI 2012 No. 1319

In Part 3, Monitor (a body corporate originally concerned with the authorisation of foundation trusts; see below) acquires new duties to promote the provision of a healthcare service which 'is economic, efficient and effective and maintains and improves quality . . . ' and to promote competition between providers of healthcare services where this is in the interest of the patient. In Part 3 too are provisions for registration of most healthcare providers with the CQC. Part 4 proposes the eventual abolition of all NHS trusts as they are all expected to reach foundation trust status by April 2013.

Part 5 establishes a Committee of the CQC to be called Healthwatch England, whose role is to provide the Secretary of State, the NHSCB, Monitor and English local authorities with advice, information and assistance on the views of local healthwatch organisations and people who use health or social care services. In addition, local authorities must establish health and wellbeing boards, which, together with local healthwatch, will inform their 'joint strategic needs assessment'[5] and develop the local health and wellbeing strategy for the locality. Changes to the arrangements for the award of contracts for pharmaceutical services appear in Part 6, and the establishment of the National Institute for Health and Care Excellence (NICE) as a corporate body, together with a formalised role in developing quality standards for healthcare, appears in Part 8. Part 10 lists certain public bodies that are to be abolished (most notably the National Patient Safety Agency, although its functions will be transferred to the NHSCB) and Part 11 includes a duty of co-operation between Monitor and the CQC in their respective functions. Some 23 schedules then cover the detail of these provisions.

Despite the major changes in the structure of the health service, the Secretary of State continues to be required to exercise the functions conferred by the Act so as to secure that services are provided in accordance with the Act, and the Secretary of State retains ministerial responsibility to parliament for the provision of the health service in England.

Consequently, the above legislation all forms the legal basis for the NHS in England. The NHS (Wales) Act 2006 as amended applies to the NHS in Wales, and as time passes, the NHS in Wales is diverging from that applying in England. The National Health Service (Scotland) Act 1978 as amended applies to NHS Scotland.

NHS directions and policy statements

In addition to the statute law set out above, power is also given to the Secretary of State for Health (or equivalent ministers in Wales and Scotland) to make additional 'directions' written by senior civil servants acting under the authority of the relevant minister. Policy statements and guidelines, all of

---

[5] Section 116 of the Local Government and Public Involvement in Health Act 2007

which describe the standards to which the public sector is expected to work, supplement the legal framework further (see under the managed service later in this chapter and also chapter 1).

NHS policy and planning

Government ministers and health departments continually issue large quantities of strategic and planning documents, supplemented with guidance and procedures as to how policy should be implemented. Where changes to legislation are required, the government will issue a white paper (in England, chapter 1) or similar blueprints in Scotland and Wales setting out how policy goals will be secured. Major changes in previous decades were covered in earlier editions of this book; this edition only covers the changes brought in after 2010 by the Conservative–Liberal Democrat Coalition Government. However, a constant feature of reforms of the NHS in England since the 1980s has been the management of the relationship between commissioners and providers of healthcare. In essence, commissioners buy healthcare and providers provide it. The process of commissioning involves identifying health need, researching how it can be addressed, setting specifications for the services then needed, contracting with providers to provide them and reassessing performance in addressing the identified need. Pharmacists are mainly engaged in provision of pharmacy services within hospitals or community pharmacies, but many are also involved in the commissioning side, particularly in relation to the management of drug budgets and optimal use of medicines.

The proposed reforms were described in July 2010 in the White Paper called *Equity and Excellence: Liberating the NHS*.[6] This detailed how power would be devolved from Whitehall to patients and professionals: 'Professionals would be free to focus on improving health outcomes and patients would get more choice and control so that services are more responsive'. The White Paper established the principle of 'no decisions about me without me' and proposed that strategic health authorities and PCTs would be phased out from April 2013. The NHSCB would be established to commission primary care services. The White Paper recognised the important and expanding role for pharmacy – making better use of medicines, and in supporting better health. Local authorities would be given responsibility for commissioning public health services at local level.

Under the Act, every GP practice will be a member of a CCG, working with other healthcare professionals and in partnership with local communities and local authorities to commission the majority of NHS services for their patients. The NHSCB will calculate practice-level budgets, allocate

[6]Department of Health 2010, *Equity and Excellence: Liberating the NHS*

them directly to the commissioning groups and hold them to account for the use of NHS resources and for commissioning outcomes. The NHSCB was established in shadow form as a special health authority (the National Health Services Commissioning Board Authority) on 31 October 2011,[7] and it was intended to transition to the NHSCB in October 2012 before taking full statutory responsibility for commissioning on 1 April 2013, at which time PCTs were expected to cease to exist.

The government's strategy for public health was the subject of another White Paper: *Healthy Lives, Healthy People*, published on 30 November 2010.[8] This set out the long-term vision for the future of public health in England and was intended to change the way in which public health was improved. It aimed to tackle obesity, sexually transmitted diseases, problem drug use, rising levels of harm from alcohol, smoking and poor mental health. Although the White Paper proposed a shift from central control to local empowerment a new national public health service, Public Health England would support local innovation, help disease control and protection and share information on innovations from around the world. The White Paper also recognised pharmacists' role in improving public health and identified their potential to improve health and wellbeing and to reduce health inequalities.

Following the White Papers, the Health and Social Care Bill was published in early 2011 but was extensively challenged, particularly by clinicians. In April 2011, the normal legislative processes were paused, to allow a review led by a 'Future Forum', chaired by Professor Steve Field, a former Chairman at the Royal College of General Practitioners.

The Future Forum conducted a listening exercise along four themes in order to listen and advise on the modernisation plans:

- the role of choice and competition for improving quality;
- how to ensure public accountability and patient involvement in the new system;
- how new arrangements for education and training can support the modernisation process; and
- how advice from across a range of healthcare professions can improve patient care.

The Forum's report set out core recommendations including protecting the values of the NHS and the rights of patients as set out in the NHS Constitution; removal of political interference and creating greater transparency about the spending of public money; protection against conflicts of interest;

---

[7]The NHS Commissioning Board Authority (Establishment and Constitution) Order SI 2011 No. 2237 and the NHS Commissioning Board Authority Regulations SI 2011 No. 2250

[8]Department of Health 2010, *Healthy Lives, Healthy People*

increasing more effective multiprofessional involvement in the design and commissioning of services; recognising a role for clinical and professional networks and establishing multispeciality clinical senates to provide strategic advice to commissioners; the use of competition as a tool for supporting choice, promoting integration and improving quality; and better integration of commissioning across health and social care.

The NHS Constitution

First published in January 2009 and revised in March 2010, the NHS Constitution established the principles and values of the NHS in England. It sets out patient and staff rights and responsibilities and is intended to ensure that it delivers high-quality healthcare that is free for everyone. The Constitution was updated in 2012 to highlight the importance of 'whistleblowing' (raising concerns about aspects of the service which may endanger patient care or safety). There are seven key principles to the NHS Constitution:

1 the NHS provides a comprehensive service, available to all irrespective of gender, race, disability, age, sexual orientation, religion or belief;
2 access to NHS services is based on clinical need, not an individual's ability to pay;
3 the NHS aspires to the highest standards of excellence and professionalism;
4 NHS services must reflect the needs and preferences of patients, their families and their carers;
5 the NHS works across organisational boundaries and in partnership with other organisations in the interest of patients, local communities and the wider population;
6 the NHS is committed to providing best value for taxpayers' money and the most effective, fair and sustainable use of finite resources; and
7 the NHS is accountable to the public, communities and patients that it serves.

All people who work in the NHS or who deliver NHS services are expected to observe and implement the principles set out in the NHS Constitution.

NHS structure in Great Britain

Like the legislation that underpins it, the structure of the NHS undergoes constant change. Although the structures and titles vary significantly in England, Wales and Scotland, all have organisations that plan and commission local health services and deliver family health practitioner services, plus organisations that provide secondary (mostly hospital) care. Reference should be made to websites at the end of the chapter for the latest information on NHS developments in each home country.

NHS structure in England

The Department of Health

The Department of Health has five ministers (the most senior is called the Secretary of State for Health) who work with the Departmental Board consisting of the Permanent Secretary and the department's four head policy advisers together with five non-executive members to form the strategic and operational leadership of the Department. An Executive Board, consisting of the civil servants who sit on the Departmental Board, supports the Permanent Secretary.

The Board is responsible for advice to ministers, setting Department of Health standards and establishing governance frameworks. Key national clinical priorities, such as cancer and cancer networks, mental health, older peoples' services or diabetes services are led by national clinical directors (often termed 'czars' by the media). In addition, there are six 'heads of professions', including a Chief Pharmaceutical Officer. The Department of Health works with a wide range of 'arms-length bodies' (also called non-departmental public bodies or more often, quasi-autonomous non-governmental organisations – QUANGOs) to deliver its objectives: examples include the MHRA (see chapter 2), special health authorities (a type of independent NHS trust which provides services nationally on behalf of the NHS), and tribunals such as the NHS Litigation Authority. These 'arms-length bodies' are constantly evolving.

The Department of Health oversees three distinct services: the NHS, the Public Health Service and the Social Care Services. Pharmacists can expect to be involved professionally in the first two of these.

Figure 26.1 gives an overview of expected health service structures in England from April 2013.

National Health Service Commissioning Board

The NHS Commissioning Board Authority (a special health authority) was established on 31 October 2011 to make all the preparations for the establishment in law of the NHSCB (expected in October 2012) and to take on its statutory responsibilities from April 2013.[9] The Board has a duty concurrently with the Secretary of State to promote a comprehensive health service designed to secure improvement in the physical and mental health of the people of England, and in the prevention, diagnosis and treatment of physical and mental illness. The duty does not extend into public health functions (which remain with Public Health England and at local level with the local authorities).

[9] NHS Commissioning Board Authority (Establishment and Constitution) Order 2011 SI No 2237, NHS Commission Board Authority Regulations 2011 SI No. 2250

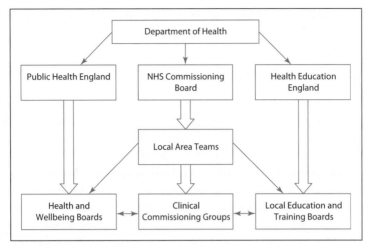

Figure 26.1 Expected NHS structure in England.

The Board is required to arrange for the provision of services in accordance with the 2012 Act and must exercise its functions relating to CCGs so as to secure the provision of those services provided by CCGs. The Board must exercise its functions so as to ensure that each provider of primary medical services (a GP) is a member of a CCG and that all areas of England are covered by CCGs whose areas do not overlap. A lengthy authorisation process for each CCG was in progress when this book went to press.

The NHS Commissioning Board Authority has a chair, appointed by the Secretary of State, and at least five other appointees of the Secretary of State. These are non-executive members. These non-executive members appoint a Chief Executive together with other executive members, such that the total number of these executive members is less than the number of non-executive members. The Chief Executive's appointment is subject to the consent of the Secretary of State, and the first Chief Executive Officer was required to be appointed by the Secretary of State. The Board Authority may publish guidance for CCGs, but it must publish guidance for CCGs on the discharge of their commissioning functions. Before it publishes guidance on commissioning, it must consult the Healthwatch England committee of the CQC.

Clinical networks and senates

At the time of writing, it was proposed that the NHSCB will host clinical networks, which will advise on distinct areas of care, such as cancer or maternity services. The NHSCB will also host new clinical senates (likely to be 12) which will provide multidisciplinary input to strategic clinical decision making to support commissioners, and embed clinical expertise at the heart of the NHSCB. The purpose of these groups is to ensure that CCGs and the NHSCB itself have access to a broad range of expert clinical input to support and inform their commissioning decisions. The relationship between the NHSCB and clinical networks and senates is likely to change as the new commissioning system matures.

Regions and local area teams

As the NHS prepared for the changes in April 2013, the former strategic health authorities were clustered into four NHSCB regions: North, South, Midlands and East and London. The former PCTs were also grouped into around 50 clusters, which, in turn, are planned to become 27 local area teams delivering the role of the NHSCB at a subnational level. The local area teams will take on direct commissioning responsibilities for GP services, dental services, pharmacy and certain aspects of optical services. Some local area teams will take the lead on commissioning of specialised services and some will carry out commissioning for military and prison health. As the local area teams develop, they will expect to provide a core for the local professional networks. These will bring together clinicians and include representatives from local representative committees, most notably local pharmaceutical committees (LPCs; see below). Local professional networks for pharmacy will provide clinical leadership in medicines optimisation to the local area teams and help to develop the role of local community pharmacy.

Clinical commissioning groups

A CCG is responsible for providing services for the purposes of the health service in its area.[10] It is essentially a group of primary medical services providers. When a group of providers of primary medical services is ready to form a CCG, it must apply to the NHSCB, providing a copy of the CCG's constitution. Its constitution must specify the name of the CCG, the members of the group and the area of the group. It must specify the arrangements made by the CCG for the discharge of its functions. The constitution must also specify the procedure to be followed by the CCG in making decisions, and the arrangements it makes to ensure that there is transparency about its decisions and the manner in which they are made. The board of the CCG must appoint an accountable officer who is responsible for ensuring that the CCG complies with its statutory obligations, complies with any provisions published by the NHSCB relevant to the CCG and exercises its functions in a way which provides good value for money.

The CCG is required to exercise its functions in a way that promotes the NHS Constitution, and it must promote awareness of the NHS Constitution among patients, staff and members of the public. It must exercise its functions with a view to securing continuous improvement in the quality

[10]NHS (Clinical Commissioning Groups) Regulations 2012 SI No. 1631

of services provided, and in particular secure continuous improvement in the effectiveness, safety and quality of patient experience that are achieved from the provision of the services. CCGs must also promote the involvement of patients and their carers in decisions relating to the prevention or diagnosis of illness in the patients, or the care or treatment of patients as well as enabling patients to make choices about their treatment. CCGs must obtain appropriate advice from persons who (taken together) have a broad range of professional expertise in the prevention, diagnosis or treatment of illness, and the protection or improvement of public health. Although there is no formal requirement to include a pharmacist on the CCG board, a pharmaceutical input is likely to be necessary to ensure a proper range of professional expertise.

In relation to any health services which are provided under arrangements made by a CCG, the CCG must make arrangements to ensure public involvement in the planning of the commissioning arrangements; in the development and consideration of proposals by the CCG for changes in the commissioning arrangements (if these are going to affect the public) and in decisions of the CCG affecting the operation of the commissioning arrangements where the implementation of the decisions would have an impact on the public. A CCG must prepare and publish an annual commissioning plan setting out how it proposes to exercise its functions, providing a copy to the NHSCB and to any relevant health and wellbeing board. In preparing a commissioning plan, the CCG must consult individuals for whom it has responsibility and any relevant health and wellbeing boards. The CCG must also publish an annual report on how it has discharged its functions in the previous financial year and send a copy to the NHSCB. The NHSCB will conduct a performance assessment of each CCG, each financial year. At the time of writing, there were 212 CCGs in the authorisation process.

Commissioning support services/units

Although CCGs cannot delegate or subcontract their responsibility for commissioning local health services for their population, the 2010 reform programme recognised that both they and the NHSCB would require support to deliver the complex process of commissioning. This is likely to be in the form of clinical support service bodies to provide the non-clinical specialist skills needed to commission effectively. During 2011, commissioning support was undertaken predominantly by NHS staff working in PCT clusters; during 2012, a variety of models have evolved: delivery in-house by CCG staff, sharing of services hosted by one CCG but available to one or more neighbouring CCGs, staff-led (mostly from the PCTs) enterprises or joint working arrangements with local authorities or the independent or voluntary sector. Each commissioning support service unit has to meet a number of quality checkpoints devised by the NHSCB, and successful ones will be 'hosted' by the NHSCB for up to 3 years from April 2013 to ensure they are sufficiently robust to become independent of the NHS. The ultimate intention is that CCGs should have a choice of high-quality and flexible support services to assist them in their commissioning duties. At the time of writing, there were likely to be around 23 commissioning support services/units in existence from April 2013.

NHS trusts

A trust is an NHS body which is permitted, by individual Orders under the NHS Acts, to assume responsibility for the ownership and management of health service bodies. A trust is run by a board, which may engage staff and set rates of pay and may borrow capital and dispose of assets. However, this freedom is constrained in that the staff remains NHS employees and the premises remain NHS property. Secondary care trusts are essentially providers of healthcare; their services were principally commissioned by PCTs or GP practices through practice-based commissioning but their services will be commissioned mainly by CCGs after April 2013.

There are several types of trust, taking legal responsibility for providing particular health services in particular localities. The most familiar perhaps are acute trusts, which essentially manage hospitals delivering secondary healthcare. Some acute trusts are regional or national centres for more specialised (tertiary) care or are attached to universities and train health professionals (teaching trusts). There are also ambulance trusts, providing emergency access to healthcare, and mental health trusts, often working closely with local authority social services to provide health and social care for people with mental health problems. A small number of care trusts have also been established to deliver social care, mental healthcare and primary healthcare in a given locality

Foundation trusts

In 2012, there were 144 NHS foundation trusts, registered by the CQC and licensed by Monitor, of which the majority are acute trusts, with 41 mental health trusts and 3 ambulance trusts. These are non-profit-making, public benefit corporations which were created to devolve decision making to local organisations and communities. NHS foundation trusts are subject to NHS standards, but because they are not directed by government, they have greater freedom to decide their own strategy, and are accountable to their local communities and their commissioners through their board of governors. The government decided that all hospital NHS trusts should become NHS foundation trusts, and the Health and Social Care Act 2012 will abolish all the NHS trusts once they have become, merged with or been acquired by an NHS foundation trust.

Health services in prisons and the armed forces

Formerly under the auspices of the Home Office and the Ministry of Defence, respectively, services for prisoner and offender health and military health (along with certain public health services commissioned by the NHSCB such as screening, vaccinations and child health for children under 5 years) will be the subject of more Department of Health guidance during 2012, probably through one or more local area teams (see above). A commitment exists to ensure that the nature and quality of healthcare services provided in these areas are of a quality at least to the level of those in the 'mainstream' NHS.

Special health authorities

Special health authorities are health authorities that provide a health service to the whole of England, not just to a local community. The NHS reforms in 2012–2013 abolished some special health authorities, created some new ones, transferred some of their roles to other bodies and created some on a temporary basis. Examples include:

- the Health Protection Agency was established in 2003 to protect the public from threats to their health from infectious diseases. Due to be abolished in April 2013, its role will be undertaken by Public Health England;
- the National Institute for Health and Clinical Excellence (NICE) will change from a special health authority to a new body corporate – the National Institute for Health and Care Excellence (which will also be known as NICE);
- the Health Education Authority was established in June 2012 (see below); and
- the NHS Commissioning Board Authority was established in October 2011; it was replaced by the NHSCB from October 2012.

NHS Direct

NHS Direct was established in 1999 as a directly funded Department of Health body; in 2007, it became an NHS trust. There is now an NHS Direct Wales and NHS24 for Scotland. NHS Direct provides 24-hour nurse-led telephone help on health advice plus an online website. It also provides mobile apps for advice on the move.

NHS 111

NHS 111 is a new three-digit telephone service that was introduced during 2012 on a pilot basis to improve access to NHS urgent care services. It is intended that this service is used by patients for medical advice where the health concern is not sufficiently serious or urgent to use the 999 service. As CCGs take over the commissioning of services, it is anticipated that they may commission NHS 111 locally.

Walk in centres

A number of pilot NHS walk-in centres were established during 1999 and 2000; again led by nurses, these aim to improve access to primary healthcare services. Legally they are equivalent to NHS hospital outpatient units so supplies of medicines and collection of prescription charges may be made on the spot to patients who use the centres. If appropriately trained, nurse prescribers in walk-in centres may also issue NHS prescriptions. Most NHS walk-in centres also supply a range of medicines under PGDs (chapters 8 and 9).

NHS Choices

NHS Choices is an online collection of information about the NHS. It contains a directory of pharmacies, GPs, NHS trusts, and so on. It allows users to quickly locate health services in their area. The website also contains healthy living advice.

Public Health England

Public Health England will be an executive agency of the Department of Health and will 'provide strategic leadership and vision for the protection and improvement of the nation's health.' It will work with the NHSCB, local authorities and local health and wellbeing boards to develop national priorities in public health. It will appoint Directors of Public Health (jointly with local authorities) who are responsible for the health of the population of the local authority.

Health and wellbeing boards

Each local authority must establish a health and wellbeing board for its area. The board will consist of the director of adult social services, director of children's services, a representative of the local healthwatch organisation, a representative of each relevant CCG, at least one councillor of the local authority and other persons that the local authority thinks appropriate. These boards are intended to encourage local authorities to integrate health and local government services. The responsibility for preparing a 'pharmaceutical needs assessment' (PNA) as a basis for awarding community pharmacy contracts (see below) will pass from the local PCT to the local authority from April 2013, and the health and wellbeing board will influence the commissioning of public health services locally.

Health Education England

Bodies and processes to manage the postgraduate training and numbers in the medical and nursing workforce have been part of NHS planning for some time through medical deaneries and university contracts for training. The 2010 reforms propose the establishment of Health Education England,[11] a new national leadership organisation responsible for ensuring that education, training, and workforce development drives the highest quality public health and patient outcomes. It is intended that Health Education England will take over this role from April 2013.

Local education and training boards

Local education and training boards are intended to take over the postgraduate training and workforce planning roles of the former strategic health authorities from April 2013, working under the direction of Health Education England. They will be the vehicle for local providers and professionals to improve the quality of local education and training outcomes to meet the needs of service providers, patients and the public.

The political intention is for the NHSCB and Public Health England to work together at national level with Health Education England to ensure there is an adequately trained workforce available to deliver health and public health services. At local level the CCG, the local authority planners (health and wellbeing boards informed by Healthwatch) and the local education and training boards are also required to co-operate to support national strategic plans.

Managed health services and the private sector

The term 'managed service' generally implies services paid for 'out of the public purse', that is through the payment of taxes to the state. In that sense, pharmacists who work within PCTs, NHS trusts (mostly hospitals but see above), most prison health services and health services for the armed forces are working in the managed sector. Increasingly, pharmacists working for GP practices are subject to NHS management. By contrast, pharmacists in community practice are employed privately but their NHS services are subject to NHS management arrangements. The private sector (such as private hospitals run by a range of insurers and provident societies or care homes providing nursing care run by commercial agencies) is financed by shareholders and by direct payments from the service users.

Boundaries between these sectors, at least in the provision of health services, have become increasingly blurred, and management and measurement

---

[11]Established in June 2012 under the the Health Education England (Establishment and Constitution) Order SI 2012 No. 1273

of the quality of these services is converging. Since April 1991 (removal of Crown immunity; chapter 1), the major statutes concerning medicines (including Controlled Drugs) and related matters now apply to NHS hospitals as well to hospitals and care homes providing nursing care which are privately owned. Prison services, whether state or privately run, are expected to comply with UK law as far as is practicable, as are military health services, even when operating overseas. In addition, it is now relatively common for an NHS trust to register the hospital dispensary or pharmacy department with the GPhC as a Registered Pharmacy (chapter 5), thus enabling it to engage in over-the-counter sales to patients, relatives and staff.

Trusts and other public bodies are legally responsible for the services they provide. Litigation against them is increasing and it is important that pharmacists employed in these sectors of pharmacy understand not only the legislation but also the criteria against which accepted standards of care may be judged. The common law principles of negligence (chapter 23) and professional responsibility apply to pharmacists in the managed sector and they should be aware of the differences between managerial responsibility (master–servant relationship) and professional obligations.

Quality and performance in the NHS

There are three main mechanisms intended to assure the quality of NHS and public healthcare: the development of outcome frameworks, the work of independent regulators and the involvement of patients and the public. All were in place at the time of writing, but their operation, role and scope will be strengthened and deepened following the implementation of further reforms from April 2013. Outcomes frameworks have developed from the concept of clinical governance, which was introduced by the Health Act 1999 and strengthened by subsequent NHS Acts. The concept of clinical governance is now embedded in a wide range of mechanisms for maintaining the competence of health professionals and ensuring the quality of health services provided both within the NHS and in the private sector.

Outcomes frameworks

Following the 2010 White Paper, an NHS Outcomes Framework for 2011–12 was published setting out five domains of health for which specific outcomes would be expected from commissioners and providers:

Domain 1: preventing people from dying prematurely
Domain 2: enhancing quality of life for people with long term conditions
Domain 3: helping people to recover from episodes of ill-health or following injury
Domain 4: ensuring people have a positive experience of care
Domain 5: treating and caring for people in a safe environment and protecting them from avoidable harm.

The Outcomes Framework will be reviewed and updated each year to drive improvements through the whole of the NHS. The Secretary of State 'mandate' to the NHSCB (published for consultation in July 2012) builds on these outcomes to set 'levels of ambition' for the NHSCB to work towards once it is fully operational. Since December 2010, annual NHS Commissioning Outcomes Frameworks have been published setting out the outcomes and corresponding indicators of good performance in commissioning that will be used to hold the NHSCB to account by the Secretary of State for Health. In January 2012, a similar Public Health Outcomes Framework was published and sets the outcomes expected of Public Health England. Although not strictly relevant to pharmacists, an Adult Social Care Outcomes Framework was launched in March 2011, representing agreed outcome measures between the Department of Health, the Association of Directors of Adult Social Services and the Local Government Association.

Quality and Outcomes Frameworks have been in place since 2004 as measures of the performance of GPs offering medical services in the community; many have suggested that the Quality and Outcomes Frameworks should be developed to reflect and promote the involvement of community pharmacists in the delivery of such outcomes. In February 2012, proposals for a Health Education England Education Outcomes Framework will include academia, employers and providers of NHS services in their joint development.

National Institute for Health and Care Excellence

The original version of NICE was set up in 1999 to reduce variation in the availability and quality of NHS treatments and care: the so-called 'postcode lottery'. Its role has changed in subsequent years and under the 2012 reforms it will have a slightly different title (but retains the same acronym). It produces evidence-based guidance on which medicines, treatments, procedures and devices represent the best quality care value for the NHS. It also produces public health guidance recommending best ways to encourage healthy living, promote wellbeing and prevent disease. It is developing a library of 150 quality standards, which will be reflected in new Commissioning Outcomes Frameworks, in Quality and Outcomes Frameworks and in the Commissioning for Quality and Innovation Payment Framework. NICE manages NHS Evidence, a web-based service that provides access to authoritative clinical and non-clinical evidence and examples of best practice in healthcare.

Regulators

The Care Quality Commission

The CQC regulates, inspects and reviews all adult social care services in the public, private and voluntary sectors in England. Under the Health and Social Care Act 2008, the CQC has powers to register providers of NHS care and has a wide range of enforcement powers to achieve compliance with registration requirements; it may require a ward or service to be closed until safety requirements are met as well as being able to suspend or de-register services where absolutely necessary. The inclusion of the functions of the Mental Health Act Commission in the remit of the CQC strengthens the oversight of patients subject to compulsory detention for mental health reasons. Under the Health and Social Care Act 2012, the CQC and Monitor (see below) will operate a joint licensing regime for providers of NHS services. Community pharmacies will not have to register with the CQC provided they are engaged only in 'dispensing and associated activities', nor will registration be required for 'diagnostic testing of the simplest kind'. However, prescribing, clinical services or services designed to promote health and wellbeing may become subject to registration requirements. Registration of GP practices opened in July 2012 and is expected to come into force from April 2013.

Monitor

Until 2012, Monitor was the body responsible for licensing NHS foundation trusts. Section 62 of the Health and Social Care Act 2012 provides that its new role will expand to become the sector regulator for healthcare, except for those healthcare providers that are exempt (NB. community pharmacies were, in August 2012, expected not to be subject to regulation by Monitor when the Department of Health consulted on the licensing provisions). The main duty of Monitor will be to protect and promote the interests of people who use healthcare services by promoting provision of healthcare services which are economic, efficient and effective, and which maintain or improve the quality of the services. It will work with CQC in a joint licensing and registration regime for health service providers.

Patient and public involvement

Under the Local Government and Public Involvement in Health Act 2007 (Part 14), previous public involvement bodies were phased out and local involvement networks (LINks), funded by local authorities to 'give citizens a stronger voice in how their health and social care services are delivered', were established under the Local Involvement Networks Regulations 2008. Subsequently, the 2012 Act established Healthwatch England as a committee of CQC and it was launched in 2012[12] to advise the Secretary of State, the NHSCB, Monitor and local authority's health and wellbeing boards. It has the power to recommend that the CQC takes action where there are concerns about health or social care. At local level, it is anticipated that

[12]The CQC (Healthwatch England Committee) Regulations 2012 SI No. 1640

local involvement networks will become Local Healthwatch during 2012. Providers of health services, including trusts and community pharmacies, are expected to allow reasonable access to members of healthwatch teams to 'enter and view and observe the carrying-on of activities' and to respond to reports issued by the Local Healthwatch.

Patient complaints

In relation to complaints (and general advice), each trust has been required since September 2003 to set up a 'patients advice and liaison service' (PALS) to provide information, advice and support to help patients, families and their carers to get the most out of the NHS. This may include giving advice and support on the making of complaints and referral to the Independent Complaints Advocacy Service; this service aims to secure consistent national standards and performance indicators for the handling of complaints. Since 1993, there has been a Health Service Commissioner (Ombudsman) to consider complaints about clinical matters and complaints involving practitioners. The Ombudsman can only consider complaints related to NHS care in England which have had a response from the practitioner. There are separate Ombudsmen for Scotland and Wales.

In December 2008, the Department of Health announced plans for a single complaints system to cover all health and adult social care services in England. This is now enshrined in statute.[13] The arrangements required of pharmacies (and other providers of health and social care) must ensure:

- complaints are dealt with efficiently;
- complaints are properly investigated;
- complainants are treated with respect and courtesy;
- complainants receive, so far as is reasonably practical
  - assistance to enable them to understand the procedure in relation to complaints, or
  - advice on where they may obtain such assistance;
- complainants receive a timely and appropriate response;
- complainants are told the outcome of the investigation of their complaint; and
- action is taken if necessary in the light of the outcome of a complaint.

The arrangements for PALS have not been changed by the 2012 Act but they should be able to commission information and advice from the Local Healthwatch from the autumn of 2012.

[13]The Local Authority Social Services and National Health Service Complaints (England) Regulations SI 2009 No. 309

Pharmaceutical Price Regulation Scheme

A voluntary regulatory scheme to allow the NHS to have access to good quality, proprietary medicines at reasonable prices while allowing a fair return for the pharmaceutical industry has been in place since 1957. The current scheme applies to the whole of the UK. It is underpinned by sections 260–266 of the NHS Act 2006 (see above) and Regulations.[14] While the bulk of the industry participates in the voluntary scheme, those that do not are subject to statutory controls.[15] The legislation allows the NHS to control the prices it will pay to any company which chooses not to sign up to the voluntary agreement or fails to reach agreement. The implementing Regulations will be renewed annually to comply with the requirements of Council Directive 89/105/EEC. In March 2011, the Department of Health undertook a consultation on a new approach to the regulation of the prices of medicines supplied to the NHS called 'value-based pricing'. In its response after the consultation, the Department of Health stated that it would look to begin negotiations on this approach 'sometime in 2012'.

The pharmacy contractual framework in England

Made initially under Part III of the NHS Act 1977, later replaced by Part 7 of the NHS Act 2006, the principal Regulations covering the provision of pharmaceutical services in England are the NHS (Pharmaceutical Services) Regulations 2012.[16] These Regulations replaced earlier Regulations in 2005,[17] which had introduced four exemptions from the restrictions on award of contracts which had been in place since 1987. The 2012 Regulations retained an exception for distance-selling pharmacies (i.e. those operating wholly by mail order or Internet) but removed three of the exemptions (for pharmacies undertaking to open for the provision of pharmaceutical services for at least 100 hours per week, for pharmacies in large out of town retail developments and for pharmacies in new one-stop primary care centres). The 2012 Regulations also replaced the 'necessary or expedient' test for new pharmacies, by requiring most new pharmacy applications to be assessed against the PNA.

The 2012 Regulations incorporate, among other things, provisions to enable any person to receive such drugs, medicines and appliances as are ordered and include the contract conditions or the Terms of Service

---

[14]Health Service Branded Medicines (Control of Prices and Supply of Information) Regulations SI 2008 No. 1938, Health Service Medicines (Information Relating to Sales of Branded Medicines, etc.) Regulations SI 2007 No. 1320

[15]Health Service Branded Medicines (Control of Prices and Supply of Information) (No. 2) Regulations SI 2008 No. 3258

[16]SI 2012 No. 1909, the '2012 Regulations'

[17]The NHS (Pharmaceutical Services) Regulations SI 2005 No. 641 'The 2005 Regulations'

for pharmacists – a term that also includes persons lawfully conducting a retail pharmacy business (chapter 5). The PCT is required to prepare a list, the pharmaceutical list, of the names and addresses of all those pharmacists who have undertaken to provide pharmaceutical services in an area, together with the services provided. In this context, 'pharmacists' includes all pharmacy contractors: including company-owned pharmacies, partnerships and sole proprietors. Because of the structural reforms expected to be completed by April 2013, it will be necessary for the 2012 Regulations to be amended to recognise the new commissioning relationships when PCTs cease to exist. For the purpose of the remainder of this chapter, the Regulations described are the NHS (Pharmaceutical Services) Regulations 2012, but it is expected that references in those Regulations to PCTs will be replaced by references to the NHSCB. The descriptions of the Regulations below make that substitution. Where Regulation numbers or paragraph numbers are referenced, these are of the 2012 Regulations, and these may differ when updated Regulations are laid. Therefore, readers should consult the legislation website for the up to date Regulations.

Any pharmacist who wishes to be included in the list must apply to the NHSCB in the prescribed form.

Pharmaceutical needs assessments

Prior to the September 2012 Regulations, an application (other than minor relocations, changes of ownership or one which fell into the four exemptions listed above) would only be granted for a pharmacy if the PCT was satisfied that it is necessary or expedient to grant the application in order to secure, in the neighbourhood in which the applicants premises are to be located, the adequate provision of pharmaceutical services specified in the application. Proposals to modify these exemptions were included in the Pharmacy in England White Paper published in 2008, and the Health Act 2009 amended the NHS Act 2006 to require PCTs to prepare PNAs. From April 2013, subject to the amendment of the 2012 Regulations, the duty to prepare and publish PNAs will transfer to the health and wellbeing boards of the local authorities. The Health Act 2009 also provides that these PNAs would, when the legislation is brought fully into force, form the basis for the determination of applications carried out by PCTs.

The 2005 Regulations were amended in 2010[18] to require PCTs to prepare PNAs and the first PNAs were required to be published by 1 February 2011. The government laid the 2012 Regulations in the summer of 2012, coming into force on 1 September 2012. Under these Regulations, the PCT would assess whether the application met a current or future need identified in

[18] National Health Service (Pharmaceutical Services and Local Pharmaceutical Services) (Amendment) Regulations SI 2010 No. 914

the PNA, would secure improvements or better access to pharmaceutical services, or would bring about unforeseen benefits not envisaged when the PNA was published. The applications would be granted only if the PCT was satisfied as to conditions relating to the PNA. These responsibilities will pass to the NHSCB from April 2013.

The 2012 Pharmaceutical Services Regulations

The 2012 Regulations retain the exemption (but re-phrased as an 'exception') for distance-selling pharmacies. The Health and Social Care Act 2012 made provision for the duties of the PCT to maintain pharmaceutical lists, and for the determination of applications to be transferred to the NHSCB. The Act also made provision to change the PNA-based test, once the responsibility for determining applications rests with the NHSCB. The effect of the change is to allow the NHSCB to grant an application that proposes to meet a current or future need only if it is satisfied that it is necessary to do so.

Part 2 sets out the requirements for the production of PNAs. The first PNAs were produced by PCTs, but from March 2013 they are expected to be the responsibility of the health and wellbeing board of the local authority.

Part 3 contains the requirement for maintenance of, and applications for inclusion in, pharmaceutical lists. 'Routine' applications (defined in Reg.12) will be assessed against the PNA with applications undertaking to meet current or future needs being assessed under Regulations 13–16. Applications that seek to secure improvements or better access are dealt with under Regulations 17 and 19 and applications that offer improvements or better access to pharmaceutical services that were not foreseen when the PNA was published are dealt with in Regulations 18 and 19.

Part 4 sets out the 'excepted' applications. These include relocation applications that do not result in significant change to pharmaceutical services provision (Reg.24), distance-selling pharmacies (Reg.25) and change of ownership applications (Reg.26).

Part 5 contains some grounds for refusing different types of application, for example where there are already pharmacy premises on the same or adjacent site, or to defer applications if the area has been designated for the purpose of developing a LPS arrangement.

Part 6 provides for refusal, deferral or to impose conditions on applications on fitness to practise grounds.

Part 7 covers determinations as to whether or not an area is a controlled locality (a rural area) in which a patient may request that their doctor provides a dispensing service. In these areas, applications from pharmacies or doctors are granted only if to do so would not prejudice the provision of pharmaceutical services, LPS or primary medical services (Reg.44).

Procedures for applications are set out in Schedules 2 and 3.

Part 8 sets out the arrangements for doctors to dispense.

Part 9 sets out some conditions that are to be imposed on chemists, such as requirements relating to co-operation with the NHSCB over local resolution of disputes (Reg.68). The principal terms of service for chemists are in Schedule 4 for retail pharmacy businesses and Schedule 5 for appliance contractors.

The terms of service in Schedule 4 include obligations to provide the 'essential services' that must be available at each pharmacy, including dispensing and repeat dispensing services, disposal of unwanted drugs, signposting to other providers where necessary, provision of public health advice and promotion of healthy lifestyles. As well as providing these essential services, a retail pharmacy business must also have an acceptable system of clinical governance and provide information about fitness matters.

Part 10 includes arrangements for dealing with breaches of terms of service by chemists, who may be issued with a breach notice (Reg.71, where a failure to comply with the terms of service cannot be remedied) or a remedial notice (Reg.70, where the chemist can remedy the breach). A withholding of payment may also be imposed (Reg.72). In serious cases, including those where there is repeated failure to comply with the terms of service, this can lead to removal from the pharmaceutical list (Reg.73).

These new powers replace the enforcement arrangements that applied under the NHS (Service Committees and Tribunal) Regulations 1992.

Part 11 set out the fitness to practise arrangements.

Part 12 contains the financial provisions relating to remuneration and reimbursement of chemists, including the requirement to publish the Drug Tariff (Reg.89). Prescription pricing is carried out by NHS Business Services Authority Prescription Services, which calculates and makes payments to pharmacy and appliance contractors. The Authority also produces prescribing and costs information for the NHS. The Pharmaceutical Directorate of NHS Business Authority produces the Drug Tariff.

Part 13 sets out the miscellaneous matters such as revocations and transitional arrangements.

Terms of Service of pharmacists

Essential services
The Terms of Service appear in Schedule 4 to 2012 Regulations; Part 2 of the Schedule sets out the essential services which must be provided by every NHS community pharmacy. This includes the dispensing of prescriptions and repeat dispensing. This may be against a paper prescription or an electronically transferred prescription bearing the prescriber's advanced electronic signature. The pharmacist must supply any drugs except those called 'scheduled drugs' (popularly known as the Black List), which comprises medicines in certain categories that cannot be prescribed for supply against NHS prescriptions. The categories were originally indigestion remedies, laxatives,

analgesics for mild to moderate pain, bitters and tonics, vitamins and the benzodiazepine tranquillisers and sedatives. The Black List is made under 2004 Regulations[19] and the list now includes many other medicines and, subject to exceptions, so-called 'lifestyle' drugs such as Viagra (sildenafil) and Propecia (finasteride). Some of the scheduled drugs can be supplied in certain circumstances; for example Viagra can be prescribed for men suffering from certain medical conditions. A full list of the drugs affected is also to be found in Part XVIIIA and B of the Drug Tariff.

All supplies of medicines (and appliance where relevant) must be made with reasonable promptness. The pharmacist is expected to give an estimate of the time when drugs or appliances will be ready if asked.

In a case of urgency, a pharmacy may (but is not compelled to) dispense a medicine (not a Controlled Drug) requested by a doctor without a signed prescription provided that the doctor undertakes to supply a signed prescription or transmit an electronic prescription within 72 hours.

Prescription charges

Pharmacy staff are required to check at the point of dispensing, where an exemption has been claimed other than on age grounds, whether patients have evidence of their entitlement to exemption from the prescription charge. Where the patient cannot produce satisfactory evidence, the 'evidence not seen' box on the reverse of the prescription form must be marked with an X, but the prescription need not be refused. Any fees collected by the pharmacist are later debited from the payments s/he subsequently receives from the pricing authorities. At the time of writing, the exemption categories were of four types (full details are to be found in Part XVI of the Drug Tariff):

- persons who are exempt on age grounds;
- holders of a range of exemption certificates;
- persons who receive, or are partners of someone receiving, state benefits; and
- persons receiving no-charge contraceptives.

Providing ordered drugs or appliances

The pharmacist must only supply the drugs or appliances as ordered on the prescription (para. 8) but, provided they are not Controlled Drugs (other than those specified in Schedule 4 or 5 of the Misuse of Drugs Regulations 2001), the pharmacist may exercise his professional skill and knowledge to remedy deficiencies in dosage or strength and where quantity is not stated to supply treatment for up to 5 days.

Changes made in July 2012 require the pharmacist to supply in manufacturer's original packs where the amount specified on the prescription

[19]The NHS (General Medical Services Contracts) (Prescription of Drugs) Regulations SI 2004 No. 629

corresponds to an original pack. Where the amount prescribed differs from an original pack, the pharmacist must dispense the amount ordered unless the product is available only in a special container (any container with an integral means of application or from which it is not practicable to dispense an exact quantity) or where the drug is sterile, effervescent or hygroscopic, a liquid preparation for addition to bath water, a coal tar preparation, or a viscous preparation. In these cases, the pharmacy may round the quantity dispensed to the nearest special container quantity (unless it is a Controlled Drug). All supplies of a manufactured medicine must be made with a patient information leaflet. The supply must be under the direct supervision of the pharmacist (this may also be affected if and when 'supervision' under the Medicines Act is reinterpreted and if the 2012 Regulations are amended). The pharmacist must supply the drug in a suitable container, if needed, free of charge.

A pharmacist may refuse to provide the supply (para. 9):

- where s/he reasonably believes that the prescription is forged;
- where to supply would be contrary to the pharmacist's clinical judgement;
- where the pharmacist or others on the premises are subject to or threatened with violence;
- where the person presenting the prescription commits or threatens to commit a criminal offence; or
- where there are irregularities or there are other circumstances in a repeat dispensing service which mean that a repeat supply is not appropriate (in this case, the pharmacist must refuse to dispense).

The pharmacist must ensure that appropriate advice on use and information is given to patients about their supplies (para. 10) to enable them to use the medicines appropriately. This may include advice on safe-keeping and safe destruction, providing guidance about only requesting repeats of items that are actually needed and details of any items or part-items that are owed. Records must be kept of supplies made and of any clinically significant advice, interventions or referrals made. If the supply of an item is refused by the pharmacist, the prescriber must be informed; where a repeat prescription is denied, the patient must be referred back to the prescriber for further advice.

Electronic prescribing or electronic transfer of prescriptions

A significant proportion of community pharmacies are able to receive 'Release 1' electronic prescriptions, which may be transmitted electronically but still require the existence of a paper form for the supply to be completed. Implementation of 'Release 2' of the electronic prescription service in which the prescription is only transmitted electronically was enabled in 17 'initial implementer PCTs' at the beginning of December 2008[20] and

[20] The Primary Medical Services (Electronic Prescription Authorisation) Directions 2008

this number had increased to about half of PCTs (83) by mid-2012. Paragraph 11 of the Terms of Service require a pharmacist to inform patients about the electronic prescription service whether or not s/he is participating in the service and, if not participating, to inform the patient of at least two other pharmacies in the area who are (if known). The terms of service also requires the pharmacist to record the name of the pharmacy nominated by the patient to receive his or her electronic prescription, where the patient wishes to use that service and the pharmacist is enabled for 'Release 2' of electronic prescription service.

Supply of 'specified' appliances

Where a 'specified appliance' is supplied, there are additional requirements. A 'specified appliance' means

a any of the following appliances listed in Part IXA of the Drug Tariff
   i a catheter appliance (including a catheter accessory and maintenance solution),
   ii a laryngectomy or tracheostomy appliance,
   iii an anal irrigation system,
   iv a vacuum pump or constrictor ring for erectile dysfunction, or
   v a drainage wound pouch;
b an incontinence appliance listed in Part IXB of the Drug Tariff; or
c a stoma appliance listed in Part IXC of the Drug Tariff.

Where a pharmacy supplies these, a home delivery service must be provided for these products. The pharmacy must offer to deliver the specified appliance to the patient's home and, if that offer is accepted, the delivery must be made with reasonable promptness and at an agreed time. The delivery must be in a package which displays no writing or other markings which could indicate its content; and the manner of delivery (e.g. the delivery van) of the package must not convey the type of appliance being delivered.

When a specified appliance is provided, the pharmacy must also provide a reasonable supply of appropriate supplementary items (such as disposable wipes and disposal bags).

The pharmacy must also ensure there are facilities for a patient receiving specified appliances to obtain expert clinical advice regarding the appliance. In appropriate circumstances the pharmacist must refer the patient who seeks advice to a prescriber or must offer the patient an 'appliance use review' (see below). If the pharmacist cannot provide specified appliances or an appliance use review, the patient can be referred or signposted to another provider who can.

Other essential services

Paragraphs 13, 14 and 15 of the Terms of Service require that a pharmacist shall accept and dispose of unwanted drugs (returned from households) in the appropriate manner. The PCT prior to 2013 was required to arrange and fund the disposal of the waste, and it is expected that this duty will transfer to the NHSCB.

The pharmacist must comply with the legislation applicable to waste (chapter 21). The pharmacist must segregate the different wastes (solids, liquids and aerosols) if required to do so by the waste contractor and must ensure that transfer notes and consignment notes are preserved in accordance with the waste legislation.

The pharmacist must ensure staff handling waste are appropriately trained and must provide equipment to deal with spills close by the storage.

The pharmacy may accept waste from households (which includes medicines from care homes) for disposal and may also dispose of out-dated or obsolete stock which was held for the purpose of dispensing as part of the NHS-funded arrangements. While waste medicines can be accepted from care homes that provide nursing care, this is not part of the NHS-funded scheme, and the pharmacy would need to ensure that legislation was being complied with by the care home, for example the home had furnished transfer or consignment notes.

Further guidance on waste can be obtained through the Pharmaceutical Services Negotiating Committee (PSNC) website (see end of chapter).

Paragraphs 16 to 18 require the pharmacist to promote public health messages to the public and to undertake prescription-linked interventions, backed up by leaflets and referral if necessary for patients who have diabetes, are at risk of coronary heart disease, who smoke or who are overweight. Records of any clinically significant advice must be made in a form that facilitates audit and follow-up care. This service involves both opportunistic interventions as well as participating in up to six public health campaigns a year.

Paragraphs 19 and 20 set out the pharmacist's duty to provide information to users of the pharmacy about other health and social care providers and organisations ('signposting') where advice is requested which the pharmacy cannot provide itself.

Paragraphs 21 and 22 set out how the pharmacist shall also provide advice and support to people caring for themselves or their families. This includes providing advice on the purchase of appropriate over the counter medicines.

Hours of opening

Pharmacies are required to be open for the provision of pharmaceutical services for 40 core hours per week unless the NHSCB allows a variation, or the contract was granted under the exemption requiring 100 core hours a week (see control of entry above) (para. 23). A pharmacy can open additional hours (called supplementary hours). Unless the pharmacy is a distance-selling (Internet or mail order) pharmacy, a notice showing the hours when the pharmacy is open for the provision of pharmaceutical services must be exhibited. At times when the business is closed, a notice must be displayed which lists the addresses of the other pharmacies and their opening hours.

Pharmacies wishing to amend their core hours must apply to the NHSCB and, if they wish to amend their additional (supplementary) hours, they must notify the NHSCB at least 90 days in advance. Arrangements for Bank Holidays and Christmas are also specified; they are complex and interested readers are referred to the PSNC website for full details.

Clinical governance and fitness to practise

Paragraph 28 of the Terms of Service requires that the pharmacist shall 'participate in an acceptable system of clinical governance', which must comprise:

A *patient and public involvement programme*. This is met by means of a practice leaflet for the public giving information about the pharmacy services available from each premises, a requirement to promote the NHS services provided, the undertaking of an approved community pharmacy patient questionnaire, having arrangements for monitoring drugs or appliances that are out of stock, adopting monitoring arrangements to ensure compliance with the Equality Act 2010, and co-operating with any statutory inspection or review.

A *clinical audit programme*. The pharmacy must implement at least one pharmacy-based and one NHSCB-chosen audit per year.

A *risk management programme*. This includes the appointment of a clinical governance lead; procedures to manage the quality of stock and equipment, appropriate standard operating procedures, child protection procedures, vulnerable adult protection procedures, a patient safety incident and near-miss recording and reporting system, arrangements for dealing with communications concerning patient safety such as MHRA drug alerts, waste disposal arrangements for confidential waste and monitoring of compliance with health and safety legislation (chapter 21).

A *clinical effectiveness programme*. The programme would include advice with repeat dispensing arrangements.

A *staffing and staff management programme*. This includes induction and training, checking of qualifications and references and addressing poor performance for all staff; identifying and supporting development needs of staff; and whistle-blowing procedures;

An *information governance programme*. This provides for compliance with approved procedures for information management and security, and submission of an annual self-assessment of compliance via approved data submission arrangements.

A *premises standards programme*. This includes a system for maintaining cleanliness at the pharmacy which is designed to ensure that the risk to people at the pharmacy of healthcare-acquired infection is minimised, and arrangements for compliance in the areas of the pharmacy in which patients receive NHS services with any approved particulars that are designed to ensure that those areas are an appropriate environment in which to receive healthcare.

The pharmacist must conform to the generally accepted professional standards within the pharmacy profession (para. 29) and must not give, promise or offer any person any gift or reward (whether by way of a share of or dividend on the profits of the business, or by way of discount, rebate or otherwise) as an inducement for any kind of prescriptions to be presented to a particular pharmacy (para. 30). The pharmacist and his/her staff must not give, promise or offer to any relevant person (e.g. a GP or a member of the GP's staff) any gift or reward (including by way of a share of, or dividend on, the profits of the pharmacist's business, or by way of discount or rebate) as an inducement to the person recommending to any person that they present a prescription to the pharmacy, nominates the pharmacy for the purposes of the Electronic Prescription Service, or request that the pharmacy provides them with any directed service.

The pharmacist (including the superintendent pharmacist and other pharmacists who are directors of a pharmacy company) must notify the NHSCB about any convictions or adverse fitness to practise incidents as they arise. It should also be noted here that the NHS Act 2006 (s.166) states that Regulations may require that a person listed in the pharmaceutical list must hold approved indemnity cover. This has not been incorporated into the 2012 Regulations but it is required in the conditions for being a practising registered pharmacist (chapter 22), and because paragraph 29 of the NHS Terms of Service requires an NHS pharmacy to provide pharmaceutical services and exercise any professional judgement in connection with such services in conformity with the standards generally accepted in the pharmaceutical profession, it follows that the NHS effectively also requires appropriate indemnity arrangements.

Inspection and access to information
Paragraph 35 specifies that the pharmacist must allow persons authorised by the NHSCB to enter and inspect his/her pharmacy at any reasonable time for the purpose of ensuring compliance with the Terms of Service and auditing and monitoring of any pharmaceutical services. This does not extend to entry of parts of the premises used solely for residential purposes, and the confidentiality of patient information should be protected.

Directed services
Regulation 11 sets out the general provisions relating to the Terms of Service, and these include any 'directed services' that the pharmacy undertakes to provide. Directed services are those provided in accordance with the Secretary of State Directions.[21] These may be for advanced services (for which a national tariff has been set) or for enhanced services (where the fee is agreed

[21]These include the Pharmaceutical Services (Advanced and Enhanced Services) (England) Directions 2012 (this and any later amendments are available on the PSNC and Department of Health websites)

between the local commissioner and the contractor). These Directions set out the conditions that apply to the advanced services that were in place at the time of writing, namely the Medicines Use Review (MUR) (or a prescription intervention that leads to an MUR), the New Medicine Service, the Appliance Use Review Service and the Stoma Appliance Customisation Service.

The Medicines Use Review service. This was the first of the advanced services which can be provided by accredited pharmacists from premises that meet accreditation requirements for confidential consultation areas. The service includes reviews undertaken periodically (usually no more frequently than annually) as well as those arising in response to significant prescription intervention during the dispensing process. The MUR is intended to help patients to use their medicines more effectively. This is achieved by improving patient knowledge, concordance and use of medicines by establishing the patient's actual use, understanding and experience of taking their medicines; identifying, discussing and assisting in resolving poor or ineffective use of their medicines; identifying side effects and drug interactions that may affect patient compliance; and improving the clinical and cost effectiveness of prescribed medicines and reducing medicine wastage. In 2011, in order to ensure maximum benefit from the service, a target was introduced, requiring a percentage of all MUR consultations to be carried out on a nationally specified target population. These were patients recently discharged from hospital, patients taking high-risk medicines and patients with respiratory disease.

The New Medicine Service. This service was introduced in 2011 to provide support for people with long-term conditions, who are newly prescribed a medicine, in order to improve medicines adherence. It was initially focused on asthma and chronic obstructive pulmonary disease, type 2 diabetes, antiplatelet/anticoagulant therapy and hypertension. The service was time limited and commissioned until March 2013, but subject to the service being shown to be of value to the NHS, it may continue. Academic institutions were commissioned to carry out an evaluation of the service. The service includes the provision of advice when providing for the first time a specified medicine for one of the specified conditions and the making of an arrangement for a further discussion about 2 weeks later, and a final discussion at about 4 weeks from the initial supply.

Appliances advanced services. The two appliance-based advanced services provide invaluable support for patients using specified appliances or who require stoma appliances to be customised to ensure a better fit. These services are provided mainly by Dispensing Appliance Contractors.

The PSNC website provides further detailed information on the advanced services.

Enhanced services (locally commissioned services)

The 2012 Directions list 20 services that may be the subject of arrangements for enhanced services. These include:

- monitoring and screening for patients taking anticoagulants
- advice and support for patients in care homes
- smoking cessation services
- services to school staff and children
- home delivery of medicines
- needle and syringe exchange schemes
- services using PGD authorisations (chapters 8 and 9)
- full medication reviews
- minor ailment services.

Several of these may become nationally required services if and when the proposals in the White Paper Pharmacy in England are implemented (see above).

Local pharmaceutical services

PCTs or in due course the NHSCB may commission any other services (LPS schemes) from pharmacies, usually services not traditionally associated with pharmacy, to address local needs. These are most commonly contracts for 'essential small pharmacies' where there is insufficient demand for a viable business without some financial support. The Essential Small Pharmacy LPS contract parallels the arrangements for pharmaceutical services and, in particular, the terms of service for pharmacy contractors. The original contracts were directed by the Secretary of State to begin on 1 April 2006 and to end on 31 March 2011. An extension of 2 years was added in 2010 and in September 2012, Directions were issued extending the contracts until March 2015.

Local pharmaceutical committees

The LPCs are recognised under section 167 of the NHS Act 2006 as representative of the persons providing pharmaceutical services in the locality of one or more PCTs. When the Health and Social Care Act 2012 comes into force, the NHSCB will recognise an LPC formed for an area which is representative of the persons providing pharmaceutical services in the area for which the LPC is formed.

Those LPCs which have adopted the model constitution promulgated by the PSNC in 2009 comprise usually 13 members (although it is for each LPC to determine the optimum number). Some LPCs have adopted a constitution that allows for both pharmacists and non-pharmacist members, elected or appointed by contractors in accordance with the 'model constitution'. From 2009, the numbers of members representing independently owned or multiple-owned pharmacies should be proportional to the number of pharmacies owned within each sector. Full details are available on the PSNC website.

Each LPC appoints its own secretary or chief officer and the appointment has to be notified to the PCT and to the PSNC. The LPC also appoints a chair, a vice-chair and a treasurer. These officers need not be members of the LPC. The term of office for members of the LPC is 4 years and the LPC has power to appoint members in the event of casual vacancies. A person ceases to be a member of the LPC if s/he ceases to be engaged in the section of the NHS which s/he represents. His/her seat must be declared vacant if s/he has been absent without reasonable cause from three consecutive meetings of the LPC, or for more than 50% of the ordinary meetings of the LPC.

The duties of an LPC include governance and finance, representation of pharmacy contractors, support for pharmacy contractors, and relationships with other bodies, in the interests of pharmacy contractors.

Governance and finance

The LPC is required to conduct its affairs in accordance with accepted principles of good governance (e.g. in accordance with the Nolan principles), ensuring that the appropriate structures and resources are in place to discharge its duties in a proper manner: it must maintain appropriate management and administrative structures to ensure that the LPC's business is carried out efficiently and effectively; it should respond to any request for an inquiry by a contractor who believes that the LPC or an officer of the committee has acted unconstitutionally; and it will request the PCT or NHSCB to allot to the LPC such sums as are required to defray the Committee's administrative expenses.

Representation of pharmacy contractors

The LPC will receive, and where appropriate should respond to, national or local consultations which are relevant to the pharmacy contractors in its area. It should appoint or nominate representatives to any committee, subcommittee, working group or other body on which representation of pharmacy contractors is required and should make representations to the commissioners and to the PSNC on matters of importance to pharmacy contractors.

Support for pharmacy contractors

The LPC should ensure transparency and equality of information and opportunity for all pharmacy contractors in matters relating to the local purchasing of pharmaceutical services, ensure appropriate arrangements are in place to advise any pharmacy contractor who needs help or assistance on NHS matters, provide appropriate levels of guidance and support to pharmacy contractors or groups of pharmacy contractors in the formulation of bids for funds held at any level, advise on submissions for LPS and local commissioning, and consider any complaint made by any pharmacy contractor against another pharmacy contractor involving any question of the efficiency of the pharmaceutical services as empowered by Regulations.

Relationships with other bodies, in the interests of pharmacy contractors

The LPC should aim to establish effective liaison with other bodies concerned with the health service in its area, collaborate as appropriate with PSNC on all matters relating to the provision of local pharmaceutical services and aim to collaborate with other pharmaceutical bodies including LPCs and other non-pharmaceutical bodies to the benefit of pharmacy contractors. The LPC must prepare an annual report and accounts and must circulate them to the electors in the area and to the PSNC.

Pharmaceutical Services Negotiating Committee

The PSNC is recognised by the Secretary of State as being representative of pharmacy contractors in England on NHS matters. It negotiates terms and conditions of service for pharmacy contractors. The PSNC has 31 members: 13 independent contractor members elected on a regional basis from England, 1 member from Wales, 2 independent members appointed by the National Pharmacy Association, 12 members appointed by the Company Chemists Association, and 3 non-Company Chemists Association multiple pharmacy members elected by owners of multiple pharmacy businesses who are not members of the Company Chemists Association. The PSNC has four subcommittees, concerned with funding and contract, service development, LPC and implementation support and resource development and finance. The PSNC has also set up the Pricing Audit Centre, which carries out both random and routine checking and special checks at the request of a contractor of the pricing of prescriptions by NHS Business Services Authority Prescription Services.

NHS structure in Wales

NHS law and organisation in Wales

In Wales, the statutory powers of the NHS are defined by the NHS (Wales) Act 2006 and the subordinate legislation, the NHS Wales Shared Services Directions 2011 (the Directions), which came into force on 1 April 2011. The 2006 Act brings together a range of regulatory requirements relating to the establishment and implementation of a Welsh NHS. It defines the duty of Welsh Ministers to promote an effective, efficient and economical provision of certain administrative, professional and technical services (the shared services) as well as giving them a general power to provide these services. It allows Welsh Ministers to give directions to NHS bodies on the way in which they are established and regulated as well as how they should exercise those functions that have been delegated to them. These directions may be communicated by way of SIs (i.e. Regulations, Orders, etc.), by Ministerial letter (previously through a series of Welsh health circulars), other form of written instruction or may be issued as guidance. Any instruction or guidance issued has the same legal standing as a direction and must, therefore, be treated as mandatory by NHS bodies, which have a legal duty to comply.

The Directions define the provision of particular services, the provision of services otherwise than in Wales, terms of NHS contracts, and provision of services otherwise than by Welsh Ministers. The aforementioned Directions also make provision for the constitution and membership of NHS bodies in Wales. They also set out more detailed procedures and administrative arrangements for these bodies, forming the basis on which they determine their standing orders and other operating arrangements. Therefore, it may be seen that organisational roles and responsibilities are clearly defined within and between NHS bodies as well as between NHS bodies and any community partners.[22]

Whilst the NHS Act 2006 applies equivalent legislation to the NHS in England to that set out in the NHS (Wales) Act 2006, it also contains some legislation that applies to both England and Wales. Key sections of this Act include section 72, which places a duty on NHS bodies to co-operate with each other in exercising their functions, and section 82, which places a duty on NHS bodies and local authorities to co-operate with one another in order to secure and advance the health and welfare of the people of England and Wales. As may be expected, all NHS bodies in Wales are required to take cognisance any wider, relevant legislative framework.[23]

---

[22]Legislation specific to Wales: National Health Service Trusts (Membership and Procedure) Regulations 1990 and subsequent amendments, NHS in Wales Accounts Directions (issued under s.178, Sch. 9, para. 3(1) of the National Health Service (Wales) Act 2006), the Local Health Boards (Constitution, Membership and Procedures) (Wales) Regulations SI 2009 No. 779 (W 67), the Local Health Boards (Establishment and Dissolution) (Wales) Order SI 2009 No. 778 (W66), the Local Health Boards (Directed Functions) (Wales) Regulations SI 2009 No. 1511 (W147)

[23]Relevant UK primary legislation: Health and Safety at Work, etc. Act 1974, Race Relations Act 1976, Access to Health Records Act 1990, Computer Misuse Act 1990, Data Protection Act 1998, Human Rights Act 1998. Freedom of Information Act 2000, Health and Social Care (Community Health and Standards) Act 2003, Children Act 2004, Equality Act 2006, National Health Service Act 2006, National Health Service (Wales) Act 2006, Companies Act 2006, Corporate Manslaughter and Corporate Homicide Act 2007. Mental Health Act 2007

The current NHS Wales came into being on 1 October 2009 and involved the creation of the seven new health boards:

Abertawe Bro Morgannwg University Health Board
Aneurin Bevan Health Board
Betsi Cadwaladr University Health Board
Cardiff & Vale University Health Board
Cwm Taf Health Board
Hywel Dda Health Board
Powys Teaching Health Board.

There are also three NHS trusts, each of which provides services on an all-Wales basis:

Public Health Wales NHS Trust
Velindre NHS Trust
Welsh Ambulance Services NHS Trust.

There are no longer any Regional Offices within the NHS Wales structure.

Responsibilities and accountability

The Welsh Government's Health and Social Services Directorate General has responsibility for the issuing of instructions and guidance to NHS bodies in relation to the conduct of certain activities. Welsh Ministers have established arrangements for providing for the delivery and strategic planning of shared services as well as a governance framework. They have also made arrangements for the reporting and monitoring of performance of the shared services by the NHS Wales Shared Services Partnership Committee (the Committee). The Health Boards and Trusts have now delegated responsibility and accountability for the continued development, operational management and performance of shared services to the Director, NHS Wales Shared Services ('the Director of Shared Services'), who has been appointed on their behalf. The Director is accountable to the Chief Executive of the NHS in Wales.

Other key Welsh Government personnel have accountability as follows (figure 26.2). The Minister for Health and Social Services is held accountable for the performance of NHS Wales by the National Assembly for Wales. The Chief Executive of NHS Wales is also the Director General of Health Social Services and Children within the Welsh Government. The post-holder is designated by the Permanent Secretary of the Welsh Government as the Accounting Officer for the NHS in Wales, and is an Additional Accounting Officer in respect of his/her role as Director General. As Chief Executive of NHS Wales, s/he is accountable to the Minister for Health and Social Services.

Chairs, vice-chairs and other independent members on NHS boards are held to account by the Minister for Health and Social Services for their personal performance in fulfilling their roles and responsibilities through annual

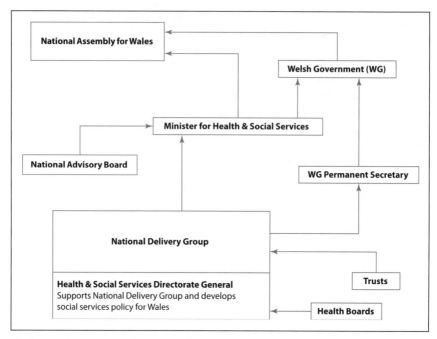

Figure 26.2 NHS structure in Wales.

accountability agreements linked to the conduct of personal performance management arrangements. Chief executives and executive directors of NHS bodies are held to account for their personal performance by their boards, and to the Chief Executive, NHS Wales.

Individuals within NHS bodies have their responsibilities and accountability defined within a clear framework of delegation, and their performance is regularly reviewed and reported upon through an NHS wide personal performance management system. Professional staff working within the NHS are also accountable to their professional bodies.

Shared service provision

The NHS Wales Shared Services Partnership is an organisation designed to deliver healthcare to the people of Wales through the provision of a comprehensive range of services and to support the statutory bodies of NHS Wales. This support is intended to be customer focused and includes the following services:

- audit and assurance
- e-business
- contractor
- employment
- facilities
- legal and risk

- prescribing
- procurement
- Welsh Risk Pool.

Welsh Health Boards and NHS Trusts have collaborated over the operational arrangements for the provision of the NHS Shared Services and have agreed the terms of a Co-operation Agreement for implementation of these services, setting out how they will work together to ensure that the arrangements are introduced and operate effectively by collective decision making. The relevant Directions[24] set out, at Schedule 4, the services that make up the Shared Services Portfolio from 1 April 2011. The Shared Services Partnership Committee will approve all changes to the Shared Services Portfolio. Table 26.1 shows the Trust or Health Board currently responsible for the implementation of each of the Shared Services.

Pharmacy organisation in Wales

The Shared Service relevant to pharmacy is the Prescribing Services Unit, which is responsible for reimbursement services to pharmacies, GPs and appliance contractors for the medicines and devices they provide on NHS prescriptions. Additionally, they are responsible for the provision of prescribing and dispensing information to NHS staff delivering medicines management services.

Table 26.1 Welsh Shared Services	
Health Boards and NHS trusts	**Shared Services**
Cwm Taf Health Board	Welsh Health Estates
Betsi Cadwaladr Health Board	Welsh Health Legal Services and the Welsh Risk Pool
Powys Teaching Health Board	Contractor Services
Velindre NHS Trust	Prescribing Services Unit
Hywel Dda Health Board	Capital and PFI audit and consultancy services
Abertawe Bro Morgannwg University Health Board	Welsh Health Supplies
All health boards and trusts	Procure to Pay Services, comprising: Accounts Payable and Procurement Services, Payroll and Recruitment Services, Internal Audit Services

NHS Wales e-Governance Manual

[24] The NHS Wales Shared Services Directions 2011 (2011 No. 13)

Community pharmacy contract

Any NHS community pharmacy contract will be awarded after application to and consideration by the Health Board in which it is proposed to establish the pharmacy. Any appeal related to decisions made by the Health Board will be considered by the Welsh Ministers under the NHS (Pharmaceutical Services) Regulations 1992 (as amended) SI No. 662.[25]

Community Pharmacy Wales

Negotiation on reimbursement and national service payments are undertaken by Community Pharmacy Wales. The status of Community Pharmacy Wales as a negotiating body for Welsh pharmacy contractors was legally established in April 2004; full details of its constitution and activities are available on the relevant website at the end of this chapter. Wales has adopted a community pharmacy contractual framework that is similar to that in England, particularly with regard to essential, advanced and enhanced service levels. However, the detailed arrangements, especially fees and some services, diverge from those in England. For example, Wales no longer charges for NHS prescriptions and has not adopted the Local Pharmaceutical Schemes (LPS), the New Medicine Service or the exemptions to control of entry that applied to England prior to the 2012 Regulations (see above). Conversely, Wales has a discharge medicine review service but England does not. These differences are current at the time of going to press but other differences in the provision of services will emerge and readers are advised to check the websites for Community Pharmacy Wales and NHS Wales for current information.

NHS structure in Scotland

NHS law and organisation in Scotland

Scotland has had its own Parliament since July 1999 and it has powers to make primary legislation on healthcare. The NHS in Scotland has always operated separately from the service in England and Wales. Although the principal Act remains the NHS (Scotland) Act 1978, this has now been modified by the NHS Reform (Scotland) Act 2004. NHS Scotland policy is developed and administered through the Scottish Government Health Department via 14 territorial 'unified' NHS boards. Primary and secondary care are separate divisions within the unified NHS boards, with representation from each local authority to improve management of health and social care. In addition, there is oversight of the board's activities by

---

[25] As this book went to press, the Welsh Government announced a consultation on new Regulations to replace the 1992 Regulations; these will retain the 'necessary and expedient' test for control of entry and add new requirements concerning fitness to be included in the pharmaceutical list. The consultation closes on 22 November 2012

NHS Healthcare Improvement Scotland. This was established by the Public Services Reform (Scotland) Act 2010 and brings together NHS Quality Improvement Scotland and the Scottish Health Council, the latter becoming a committee of NHS Healthcare Improvement Scotland.

The functions of the NHS boards include the planning and provision of healthcare services and the management of pharmacy contracts. The Scottish Health Council monitors the performance of the NHS boards and promotes public involvement in healthcare. Each board also supports community health partnerships, which are coterminous with local authority boundaries and which focus on planning and provision of local health services. Each community health partnership has on its committee a place for a registered pharmacist whose name is included in, or who is fully or substantially employed by a person or body whose name is included in, a pharmaceutical list prepared by an NHS board. Most NHS boards have the services of a pharmacist, called variously a 'consultant' or 'specialist' in pharmaceutical public health and who provides strategic pharmacy advice to the NHS board. The overall control of pharmaceutical services within each NHS board lies with the board's director of pharmacy. In addition, all NHS boards have an area pharmaceutical committee. These committees comprise pharmacists who work in both the hospital and community sectors and are representative of the professionals working, or living, in the area.

The Practitioner Services Division of NHS National Services Scotland manages payments for pharmacy contractors. Responsibility for inspection and audit of healthcare lies with the NHS Healthcare Improvement Scotland. The Scottish Health Council represents the patient's voice in healthcare and may inspect both primary and secondary care establishments. Figure 26.3 outlines NHS structure in Scotland.

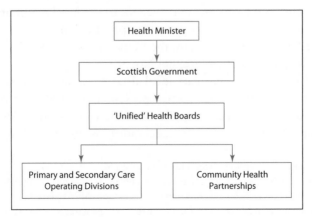

Figure 26.3 NHS structure in Scotland.

Pharmacy organisation in Scotland

Negotiation on remuneration and reimbursement on behalf of Scotland's community pharmacy contractors is carried out by *Community Pharmacy Scotland* (previously known as the Scottish Pharmaceutical General Council). This body negotiates nationally on behalf of 14 area pharmacy contractor committees, one for each NHS board. The Community Pharmacy Contract in Scotland is radically different from that in either England or Wales and its scope is to be found in the Smoking, Health and Social Care (Scotland) Act 2005 (asp.13). The Scottish contract comprises services in four areas.

Minor Ailment Service. This is a scheme whereby patients who are registered with a Scottish GP and who are exempt from prescription charges (with some exceptions) may register with a community pharmacy and receive over-the-counter medicines within a formulary, free of charge, following consultation with the pharmacist.

Public Health Service. This involves community pharmacists and staff in national programmes to promote healthy lifestyles and public health interventions such as smoking cessation, chlamydia screening and supply of emergency hormonal contraception.

Acute Medication Service. This essentially is the dispensing of acute prescriptions.

Chronic Medication Service. This covers the dispensing of repeat prescriptions and the management of patients' medication in conjunction with their GP.

The implementation of the Chronic Medication Service was slowly taking place at the time of writing (end September 2012) but was not complete.

The Terms of Service for chemists in Scotland are laid down in the NHS (Pharmaceutical Services) (Scotland) Regulations,[26] as amended.[27] Amendments include arrangements for the provision of the Chronic Medication Service element of the contract and changes to the handling of applications for Pharmacy Contracts. Arrangements for disciplinary service committees and tribunals are covered by the National Health Service (Tribunal) (Scotland) Regulations 2004 (SI 2004 No. 38).

Control of entry to pharmaceutical lists in Scotland differs from that in England and Wales. There is no provision for 100-hour pharmacies under the Regulations and all applications are considered under the terms of paragraph 5(10) of the 2009 Regulations, as amended,[28] by the NHS

[26] NHS (Pharmaceutical Services) (Scotland) Regulations SI 2009 No. 183

[27] NHS (Pharmaceutical Services) (Scotland) Amendment Regulations SI 2009 No. 209, NHS (Pharmaceutical Services) (Scotland) Amendment Regulations SI 2011 No. 32

[28] An application made in any case other than one to which paragraph (3) or (4) applies shall be granted by the board after the procedures set out in Schedule 3 have been followed, only if it is

Board Pharmacy Practices Committee. While there are three pharmacists on the committee, (two contractor representatives and one who is neither a contractor nor an employee thereof) nominated by the area pharmaceutical committee, none has a vote on the final outcome.[29] Appeals on the decisions of the Pharmacy Practices Committee are made to the National Appeal Panel, which comprises a legally qualified chair (appointed by Scottish Ministers),[30] one pharmacist[31] and one lay member[32] nominated by the health boards. Here, however the pharmacist is a voting member of the panel.

Summary

- The statutory framework for NHS services differs between England, Scotland and Wales, although the objectives are similar.
- The NHS is a mixed market of commissioning and provision of services by a range of health service bodies, overseen by civil service departments reporting to governments.
- NHS trusts, mostly hospitals, provide NHS secondary care in England and Wales; in Scotland, the provision of secondary care comes under the acute operational divisions of the NHS boards.
- PCTs in England and local health boards in Wales secure the provision of primary care, including pharmaceutical services, through 'contracts' with local owners of pharmacies; it is expected that from April 2013, the commissioning of primary care in England will transfer to the NHSCB; in Scotland and Wales, this activity has passed to NHS boards.
- It is expected that when the NHS reforms are complete in 2013, health and wellbeing boards appointed within local authorities will prepare PNAs, which will be used in the determination of pharmacy applications, and they will also be responsible for local public health commissioning.
- CCGs (groups of providers of primary medical services) will commission many services locally for the populations for whom they are responsible.

---

satisfied that the provision of pharmaceutical services at the premises named in the application is necessary or desirable in order to secure adequate provision of pharmaceutical services in the neighbourhood in which the premises are located by persons whose names are included in the pharmaceutical list

[29]NHS (Pharmaceutical Services) (Scotland) Amendment Regulations SI 2011 No. 32, Sch. 4(7)(2)

[30]NHS (Pharmaceutical Services) (Scotland) Amendment Regulations SI 2011 No. 32, Sch. 4(10)(1 and (2)

[31]NHS (Pharmaceutical Services) (Scotland) Amendment Regulations SI 2011 No. 32, Sch. 4(11)(b)

[32]NHS (Pharmaceutical Services) (Scotland) Amendment Regulations SI 2011 No. 32, Sch. 4(11)(c)

- There are controls over the granting of rights to provide NHS pharmaceutical services, mainly based on the need to secure adequate provision of those services, as identified in the PNA for the area.
- Persons providing NHS pharmacy services must comply with conditions set out in the NHS chemists' Terms of Service.
- Specifications for the amount and conditions which apply to payments under the NHS chemists' Terms of Service are set out in the Drug Tariff.
- Negotiations for payments take place nationally through the PSNC, Community Pharmacy Wales or Community Pharmacy Scotland and locally through LPCs or their Welsh or Scottish equivalents.
- The public interest in the NHS is represented by local involvement networks and the PALS in England, community health councils in Wales and local health councils in Scotland. 'Local involvement networks' will become Local Healthwatch during 2013.

Further reading

Department of Health (2008). *Pharmacy in England Building on Strengths: Delivering the Future*. London: The Stationery Office.
Department of Health (2009). *High Quality Care for All: Our Journey So Far*. London: Department of Health: http://www.dh.gov.uk/publications (accessed 21 November 2012).
Department of Health (2010). *Equity and Excellence: Liberating the NHS*. London: Department of Health: http://www.dh.gov.uk/prod_consum_dh/groups/dh_digitalassets/ @dh/@en/@ps/documents/digitalasset/dh_117794.pdf (accessed 21 November 2012).
Department of Health (2010). *Healthy Lives, Healthy People: Our Strategy for Public Health in England*. London, The Stationery Office: http://www.dh.gov.uk/en/ Publicationsandstatistics/Publications/PublicationsPolicyAndGuidance/DH_121941 (accessed 21 November 2012).
Department of Health (2011). *NHS Future Forum: Summary Report on Proposed Changes to the NHS*. London: Department of Health: http://www.dh.gov.uk/prod_consum_dh/groups/ dh_digitalassets/documents/digitalasset/dh_127540.pdf (accessed 21 November 2012).
Scottish Executive (2002). *The Right Medicine: A Strategy for Pharmaceutical Care in Scotland*. Edinburgh: Scottish Executive.
Welsh Assembly Government (2002). *Remedies for Success: A Strategy for Pharmacy in Wales*. Cardiff: Welsh Assembly Government.

Websites

Care Quality Commission: http://www.cqc.org.uk/
Community Pharmacy Scotland: http://www.communitypharmacyscotland.org.uk/
Community Pharmacy Wales: http://www.cpwales.org.uk/
Department of Health (England):
http://www.dh.gov.uk/en/Healthcare/Medicinespharmacyandindustry/index.htm
General Pharmaceutical Council: http://www.pharmacyRegulation.org/
Health Education England: http://www.hee.nhs.uk/
Health Inspectorate Wales: http://www.hiw.org.uk/
Monitor: http://www.monitor-nhsft.gov.uk
National Institute for Clinical Excellence: http://www.nice.org.uk
National Patient Safety Agency: http://www.npsa.nhs.uk
NHS 24: http://www.nhs24.com/

NHS Choices: http://www.nhs.uk/Pages/HomePage.aspx
NHS Constitution: http://www.dh.gov.uk/en/Publicationsandstatistics/Publications/
    PublicationsPolicyAndGuidance/DH_132961
NHS Direct Wales: http://www.nhsdirect.wales.nhs.uk/
NHS Direct: http://www.nhsdirect.nhs.uk/
NHS Prescription Service (England): http://www.nhsbsa.nhs.uk/prescriptionservices.aspx
NHS Primary Care Commissioning: http://www.pcc.nhs.uk
NHS Scotland: http://www.scotland.gov.uk/Topics/Health/NHS-Scotland/
NHS Wales: http://www.nhswalesgovernance.com
NHS Wales: http://www.wales.nhs.uk
Parliamentary and Health Service Ombudsman (England): http://www.ombudsman.org.uk/
Patient Advice and Liaison Services: http://www.pals.nhs.uk/
Pharmaceutical Services Negotiating Committee: http://www.psnc.org.uk
Public Services Ombudsman for Wales: http://www.ombudsman-wales.org.uk/
Scottish Public Services Ombudsman: http://www.spso.org.uk/

Appendix 1

Medicines Act 1968: section 104 and 105 Orders

Various articles and substances are treated as medicinal products (chapter 2) by virtue of Orders made under the Act, as follows:

Section 104(1) Orders

Orders made under section 104(1) of the Act can extend the application of specified provisions of the Human Medicines Regulations 2012 or Clinical Trials Regulations to articles and substances which are not medicinal products as defined in the 2012 Regulations but which are manufactured, sold, supplied, imported or exported for use wholly or partly for a medical purpose (see principally chapters 2 and 3). Two Orders under this section are still extant.

The Medicines (Radioactive Substances) Order 1978 (SI 1978 No. 1004) extends the application of the provisions relating to the holding of licences to the following articles and substances:

a interstitial and intracavitary appliances (other than nuclear powered cardiac pacemakers) which contain or are to contain a radioactive substance sealed in a container (otherwise than solely for the purpose of storage, transport or disposal) or bonded solely within material and including the immediate container or bonding that are designed to be inserted into the human body or body cavities;

b surface applicators, that is to say plates, plaques and ophthalmic applicators which contain or are to contain a radioactive substance sealed in a container (otherwise than solely for the purpose of storage, transport or disposal) or bonded solely within material and including the immediate container or bonding that are designed to be brought into contact with the human body;

c any apparatus capable of administering neutrons to human beings when the neutrons are administered in order to generate a radioactive substance in the person to whom they are administered for the purpose of diagnosis or research;

d other substances or articles (not being an instrument, apparatus or appliance) which consist of or contain or generate a radioactive substance and which:

  i consist of or contain or generate that substance in order, when administered, to utilise the radiation emitted therefrom, and

  ii are manufactured, sold or supplied for use wholly or mainly by being administered to one or more human beings solely by way of a test for ascertaining what effects it has when so administered.

The meaning of administer in relation to any apparatus in (c) above is modified to include the exposure of the body or any part of the body to the neutrons issued by the apparatus.

The second Order, the Medicines (Cyanogenetic Substances) Order 1984 (SI 1984 No. 187), extends to cyanogenetic substances the application of those provisions of the Human Medicines Regulations 2012 or Clinical Trials Regulations relating to dealings with products (including sale, supply or importation), the packaging and promotion of products and miscellaneous and supplementary provisions. Licensing requirements are not applied. Cyanogenetic substances means preparations which:

a are presented for sale or supply under the name of, or as containing, amygdalin (laetrile or vitamin B_{17}); or

b contain more than 0.1 per cent by weight of any substance having the formula either α-cyanobenzyl-6-Oβ-D-glucopyrosol-D-glucopyranoside or α-cyanobenzyl-Oβ-D-glucopyranosiduronic acid.

Section 105(1)(a) Orders

Orders made under section 105(1)(a) of the Act extend the application of specified provisions of the Human Medicines Regulations 2012 or Clinical Trials Regulations to certain substances which are not medicinal products but which are used in the manufacture of medicinal products.

Section 105(1)(b) and 105(2) Orders

Orders made under section 105(1)(b) and 105(2) of the Act extend the application of specified provisions of the Act to substances which, if used without proper safeguards, are capable of causing damage to the health of the community, or of causing danger to the health of animals generally or of one or more species of animals. One Order has been made under this section, but has subsequently been repealed by the Human Medicines Regulations 2012.

Appendix 2

Prohibition of non-medicinal antimicrobial substances

Antimicrobial substances were brought within the control of the Medicines Act 1968 (and now under the Human Medicines Regulations 2012 and the Clinical Trials Regulations) by an Order under section 105 (see appendix 1). This was to stop the unregulated import and supply of crude antibiotic material as a 'chemical' by making no medicinal claims for it.

The Medicines (Prohibition of Non-Medicinal Antimicrobial Substances) Order 1977 (SI 1977 No. 2131) prohibits, subject to certain exceptions, the sale or supply of the following antimicrobial substances; the prohibition applies whether or not the substance is contained in any other substance or article, unless it is a medicinal product or an animal feeding stuff.

Amphomycin
Bacitracin
Candicidin
Capreomycin
Chloramphenicol
Cycloserine
Erythromycin
Framycetin
Furaltadone
Furazolidone
Fusidic acid
Griseofulvin
Hachimycin
Nalidixic acid
Nitrofurantoin
Nitrofurazone
Novobiocin
Nystatin

Oleandomycin
Paromomycin
Spectinomycin
Spiramycin
Tylosin
Vancomycin
Viomycin
Virginiamycin

NB. In this Part:

a a reference to any substance, other than furaltadone, shall be construed as a reference to the substance for which such name is shown in the current edition of the list of names prepared and published under section 100 of the Act; and

b furaltadone means (6)-5-morpholino-methyl-3-(5-nitrofurylideneamino)-2-oxazolidine.

Permitted sales or supplies

Sale or supply of prohibited substances (table A2.1) is permitted in the circumstances described below:

a where a sale by way of wholesale dealing is made to
  i a veterinary surgeon or veterinary practitioner,
  ii a person lawfully conducting a retail pharmacy business,
  iii a holder of a manufacturer's licence granted under Part II of the Act, or
  iv a person carrying on the business of selling by way of wholesale dealing;
b where the sale or supply is to any of the following
  i a public analyst appointed under section 27 of the Food Safety Act 1990,
  ii an agricultural analyst appointed under section 67 of the Agriculture Act 1970,
  iii a person duly authorised by an enforcement authority under sections 111 and 112 of the Act,
  iv a sampling officer within the meaning of Schedule 3 to the Act, or
  v universities, other institutions concerned with higher education or institutions concerned with research;
c griseofulvin when sold or supplied in a product which is for use as a fungicide or for use in the manufacture of fungicides for horticultural purposes and containing other ingredients in such a quantity as to render the product unfit for any medicinal purpose and unpalatable to such a degree as to prevent consumption by human beings;

Table A2.1 Meaning of prohibited substances

Class of substance	Meaning
Amphotericins	Antimicrobial substances or mixtures of such substances produced by *Streptomyces nodosus*
Cephalosporins	Antimicrobial substances containing in their chemical structure a fused dihydrothiazine β-lactam nucleus
Gentamicins	Any antimicrobial basic substance or mixture of such substances produced by the strain *Micromonospora purpurea*, which on 1 September 1967 was numbered NRRL2953 in the culture collection of the Northern Utilisation Research and Development Branch of the United States Department of Agriculture
Kanamycins	Any antimicrobial substance or mixture of such substances produced by *Streptomyces kanamyceticus*
Lincomycins	Antimicrobial substances produced by *Streptomyces lincolnensis* var. *lincolnensis*. These substances are the basic amides of hygric acid or of a substituted hygric acid with 6-amino-6,8-dideoxy-1-thiogalacto-octopyranose or with substituted 6-amino-6,8-dideoxy-1-thiogalacto-octopyranose
Neomycins	Antimicrobial substances or mixtures of such substances produced by *Streptomyces fradiae* which are complex organic bases and which yield on hydrolysis with mineral acids the base neamine
Penicillins	Any antimicrobial acid which contains in its structure a fused thiazolidine β-lactam nucleus
Polymixins	Any antimicrobial substance produced by any strain of *Bacillus polymyxa*
Rifamycins	A group of related antimicrobial macrolactams produced by the growth of *Streptomyces mediterranei* and containing the chemical structure of 11-acetoxy-7,9,15-trihydroxy-13-methoxy-2,6,8,10,12-penta-methyl-pentadeca-2,4,14-trienoic acid amide attached by the nitrogen atom and by the oxygen atom in the 15-position, respectively, to the 7- and 2-positions of a 5,6,9-trioxygenated 2,4-dimethyl-1-oxonaphtho-(2,1β)-furan
Ristocetins	Antimicrobial substances produced by a strain of a *Nocardia* species referred to as *Nocardia lurida*
Streptomycins	Any antimicrobial complex organic base or mixture of such bases produced by *Streptomyces griseus* which (a) yields on hydrolysis with mineral acids the base streptidine (meso-1-3-diguanidocyclohexane-2,4,5,6-tetraol), and (b) yields on hydrolysis by a 4% solution of sodium hydroxide the substance maltol (3-hydroxy-2-methyl-8-pyrone)
Sulphanilamide	Sulphanilamide being *p*-aminobenzenesulphonamide, having any of the hydrogen atoms of either or both nitrogen atoms substituted by an equal number of univalent atoms or radicals
Tetracyclines	Antimicrobial bases which contain the chemical structure naphthacene-2-carboxamide, hydrogenated to any extent and having each of the positions 1, 3, 10, 11, 12 and 12a substituted by a hydroxyl or an oxo group

d streptomycins as for griseofulvin plus when used, sold or supplied for use as a preservative in a product used in the artificial breeding of animals;

e sulphanilamide when, as the derivative sulphaquinoxaline (not exceeding 0.5 per cent), it is sold or supplied in a product for the destruction of rats or mice, or for the manufacture of such a product. The product must also contain warfarin or its sodium or triethanolamine derivative;

f sulphanilamide when, as the derivative methyl-4-aminobenzenesulphonyl carbamate, it is sold or supplied for use in the manufacture of herbicides or contained in a product used as a herbicide for agricultural, horticultural or forestry purposes or for use in or near water or on uncultivated land; and

g amphotericins, gentamicins, kanamycins, lincomycins, nystatin, penicillins, spectinomycin and tylosin when used, sold or supplied for use as a preservative in a product used in the artificial breeding of animals.

Appendix 3

Patient Group Directions

Taken from the Human Medicines Regulations 2012 No. 1916 (Regs. 229, 230, 231, 232, 233 and 234 and Sch. 16)

Particulars to be included in a Patient Group Direction

The following particulars are to be included:

1 the period during which the Direction is to have effect;
2 the description or class of medicinal product to which the Direction relates;
3 the clinical situations which medicinal products of that description or class may be used to treat or manage in any form;
4 whether there are any restrictions on the quantity of medicinal product that may be sold or supplied on any one occasion and, if so, what restrictions;
5 the clinical criteria under which a person is to be eligible for treatment;
6 whether any class of person is excluded from treatment under the Direction and, if so, what class of person;
7 whether there are circumstances in which further advice should be sought from a doctor or dentist and, if so, what circumstances;
8 the pharmaceutical form or forms in which medicinal products of that description or class are to be administered;
9 the strength, or maximum strength, at which medicinal products of that description or class are to be administered;
10 the applicable dosage or maximum dosage;
11 the route of administration;
12 the frequency of administration;
13 any minimum or maximum period of administration applicable to medicinal products of that description or class;
14 whether there are any relevant warnings to note and, if so, what warnings;

15 whether there is any follow-up action to be taken in any circumstances and, if so, what action and in what circumstances;

16 arrangements for referral for medical advice; and

17 details of the records to be kept of the supply, or the administration, of products under the Direction.

Classes of individuals by whom supplies may be made

The following groups may make supplies under a PGD:

pharmacists
registered chiropodists and podiatrists
registered dental hygienists
registered dental therapists
registered dietitians
registered midwives
registered nurses
registered occupational therapists
registered optometrists
registered orthoptists
registered orthotists and prosthetists
registered paramedics
registered physiotherapists
registered radiographers
registered speech and language therapists.

Appendix 4

Schedule 2 to the Misuse of Drugs Act 1971 classifies Controlled Drugs into three lists (Class A, Class B and Class C) for the purpose of the level of penalties for offences under the Act. The penalties are given in Schedule 3 (not reproduced here). Since the Act came into force, numerous additions have been made, by Orders, to the original list of drugs in Schedule 2.

In this appendix, a date shown against any drug indicates the year it was added to the list.

For the Schedules to the Misuse of Drugs Regulations, which classify Controlled Drugs according to the relevant regimes of control, see appendix 6.

Part I Class A drugs

1 a The following substances and products, namely:

Acetorphine
Alfentanil (1984)
Allylprodine
Alphacetylmethadol
Alphameprodine
Alphamethadol
Alphaprodine
Anileridine
Benzethidine
Benzylmorphine (3-benzylmorphine)
Betacetylmethadol
Betameprodine
Betamethadol

Betaprodine

Bezitramide

4-Bromo-2,5-dimethoxy-α-methylphenethylamine (1975)

Bufotenine

Carfentanil (1986)

Clonitazene

Coca leaf

Cocaine

4-Cyano-2-dimethylamino-4,4-diphenylbutane

4-Cyano-1-methyl-4-phenylpiperidine

Desomorphine

Dextromoramide

Diamorphine

Diampromide

Diethylthiambutene

N,N-Diethyltryptamine

Difenoxin (1-(3-cyano-3,3-diphenylpropyl)-4-phenylpiperidine 4-
    carboxylic acid) (1975)

Dihydrocodeinone-O-carboxymethyloxime

Dihydroetorphine

Dihydromorphine

Dimenoxadole

Dimepheptanol

Dimethylthiambutene

2,5-Dimethoxy-α,4-dimethylphenethylamine

N,N-Dimethyltryptamine

Dioxaphetyl butyrate

Diphenoxylate

Dipipanone

Drotebanol (3,4-dimethoxy-17-methylmorphinan-6β,14-dioi) (1973)

Ecgonine, and any derivative of ecgonine which is convertible to ecgo-
    nine or to cocaine

Ethylmethylthiambutene

Eticyclidine (1984)

Etonitazene

Etorphine

Etoxeridine

Etryptamine (1998)

Fentanyl

Furethidine

Hydromorphinol

Hydromorphone

Hydroxypethidine

N-Hydroxytenamphetamine (1990)
Isomethadone
Ketobemidone
Levomethorphan
Levomoramide
Levophenacylmorphan
Levorphanol
Lofentanil (1986)
Lysergamide
Lysergide and other N-alkyl derivatives of lysergamide
Mescaline
Metazocine
Methadone
Methadyl acetate
Methylamphetamine (2006)
Methyldesorphine
Methyldihydromorphine (6-methyldihydromorphine)
4-Methylaminorex (1990)
2-Methyl-3-morpholino-1,1-diphenylpropanecarboxylic acid
1-Methyl-4-phenylpiperidine-4-carboxylic acid
Metopon
Morpheridine
Morphine
Morphine methobromide, morphine N-oxide and other pentavalent
    nitrogen morphine derivatives
Myrophine
Nicomorphine (3,6-dinicotinoylmorphine)
Noracymethadol
Norlevorphanol
Normethadone
Normorphine
Norpipanone
Opium, whether raw, prepared or medicinal
Oxycodone
Oxymorphone
Pethidine
Phenadoxone
Phenampromide
Phenazocine
Phencyclidine (1979)
Phenomorphan
Phenoperidine
4-Phenylpiperidine-4-carboxylic acid ethyl ester

Piminodine

Piritramide

Poppy-straw and concentrate of poppy-straw

Proheptazine

Properidine (1-methyl-4-phenylpiperidine-4-carboxylic acid isopropyl ester)

Psilocin

Racemethorphan

Racemoramide

Racemorphan

Remifentanil

Rolicyclidine (1984)

Sufentanil (1983)

Tapentadol (2011)

Tenocyclidine (1984)

Thebacon

Thebaine

Tilidate (1983)

Trimeperidine

b Any compound (not being a compound for the time being specified in paragraph (a) above) structurally derived from tryptamine or from a ring-hydroxytryptamine by substitution at the nitrogen atom of the side-chain with one or more alkyl substituents but no other substituent;

The following phenethylamine derivatives, namely:

Allyl(α-methyl-3,4-methylenedioxyphenethyl)amine

2-Amino-1-(2,5-dimethoxy-4-methylphenyl)ethanol

2-Amino-1-(3,4-dimethoxyphenyl)ethanol

Benzyl(α-methyl-3,4-methylenedioxyphenethyl)amine

4-Bromo-β,2,5-trimethoxyphenethylamine

N-(4-sec-Butylthio-2,5-dimethoxyphenethyl)hydroxylamine

Cyclopropylmethyl(α-methyl-3,4-methylenedioxyphenethyl)amine

2-(4,7-Dimethoxy-2,3-dihydro-1 H-indan-5-yl)ethylamine

2-(4,7-Dimethoxy-2,3-dihydro-1 H-indan-5-yl)-1-methylethylamine

2-(2,5-Dimethoxy-4-methylphenyl)cyclopropylamine

2-(1,4-Dimethoxy-2-naphthyl)ethylamine

2-(1,4-Dimethoxy-2-naphthyl)-1-methylethylamine

N-(2,5-Dimethoxy-4-propylthiophenethyl)hydroxylamine

2-(1,4-Dimethoxy-5,6,7,8-tetrahydro-2-naphthyl)ethylamine

2-(1,4-Dimethoxy-5,6,7,8-tetrahydro-2-naphthyl)-1-methylethylamine

α,α-Dimethyl-3,4-methylenedioxyphenethylamine

α,α-Dimethyl-3,4-methylenedioxyphenethyl(methyl)amine

Dimethyl(α-methyl-3,4-methylenedioxyphenethyl)amine

N-(4-Ethylthio-2,5-dimethoxyphenethyl)hydroxylamine

4-Iodo-2,5-dimethoxy-α-methylphenethyl(dimethyl)amine

2-(1,4-Methano-5,8-dimethoxy-1,2,3,4-tetrahydro-6-naphthyl)ethylamine

2-(1,4-Methano-5,8-dimethoxy-1,2,3,4-tetrahydro-6-naphthyl)-1-methylethylamaine

2-(5-Methoxy-2,2-dimethyl-2,3-dihydrobenzo[b]furan-6-yl)-1-methylethylamaine

2-Methoxyethyl(α-methyl-3,4-methylenedioxyphenethyl)amine

2-(5-Methoxy-2-methyl-2,3-dihydrobenzo[b]furan-6-yl)-1-methylethylamine

β-Methoxy-3,4-methylenedioxyphenethylamine

1-(3,4-Methylenedioxybenzyl)butyl(ethyl)amine

1-(3,4-Methylenedioxybenzyl)butyl(methyl)amine

2-(α-Methyl-3,4-methylenedioxyphenethylamino)ethanol

α-Methyl-3,4-methylenedioxyphenethyl(prop-2-ynyl)amine

N-Methyl-N-(α-methyl-3,4-methylenedioxyphenethyl)hydroxylamine

O-Methyl-N-(α-methyl-3,4-methylenedioxyphenethyl)hydroxylamine

α-Methyl-4-(methylthio)phenethylamine

β,3,4,5-Tetramethoxyphenethylamine

β2,5-Trimethoxy-4-methylphenethylamine

c Any compound (not being methoxyphenamine or a compound for the time being specified in paragraph (a) above) structurally derived from phenethylamine, an N-alkylphenethylamine, α-methylphenethylamine, an N-alkyl-α-methylphenethylamine, α-ethylphenethylamine, or an N-alkyl-α-ethylphenethylamine by substitution in the ring to any extent with alkyl, alkoxy, alkylenedioxy or halide substituents, whether or not further substituted in the ring by one or more other univalent substituents;

d Any compound (not being a compound for the time being specified in paragraph (a) above) structurally derived from fentanyl by modification in any of the following ways

   i by replacement of the phenyl portion of the phenethyl group by any heteromonocycle whether or not further substituted in the heterocycle,

   ii by substitution in the phenethyl group with alkyl, alkenyl, alkoxy, hydroxy, halogeno, haloalkyl, amino or nitro groups,

   iii by substitution in the piperidine ring with alkyl or alkenyl groups,

   iv by substitution in the aniline ring with alkyl, alkoxy, alkylenedioxy, halogeno or haloalkyl groups,

    v by substitution at the 4-position of the piperidine ring with any alkoxycarbonyl or alkoxyalkyl or acyloxy group (SI 1986 No. 2230), or

   vi by replacement of the N-propionyl group by another acyl group;

  e Any compound (not being a compound for the time being specified in paragraph (a) above) structurally derived from pethidine by modification in any of the following ways:

    i by replacement of the 1-methyl group by an acyl, alkyl whether or not unsaturated, benzyl or phenethyl group, whether or not further substituted,

   ii by substitution in the piperidine ring with alkyl or alkenyl groups or with a propano bridge, whether or not further substituted,

  iii by substitution in the 4-phenyl ring with alkyl, alkoxy, aryloxy, halogeno or haloalkyl groups,

   iv by replacement of the 4-ethoxycarbonyl by any other alkoxycarbonyl or any alkoxyalkyl or acyloxy group, or

    v by formation of an N-oxide or of a quaternary base.

2 Any stereoisomeric form of a substance for the time being specified in paragraph 1 above not being dextromethorphan or dextrorphan.

3 Any ester or ether of a substance for the time being specified in paragraph 1 or 2 above, not being a substance for the time being specified in Part II of this Schedule.

4 Any salt of a substance for the time being specified in any of paragraphs 1 to 3 above.

5 Any preparation or other product containing a substance or product for the time being specified in any of paragraphs 1 to 4 above.

6 Any preparation designed for administration by injection which includes a substance or product for the time being specified in any of paragraphs 1 to 3 of part II of this Schedule.

Part II Class B drugs

1 **a** The following substances and products:

Acetyldihydrocodeine
Amphetamine
Cannabinol (2008)
Cannabinol derivitaves (2008)
Cannabis and cannabis resin (2008)
Codeine
Dihydrocodeine
Ethylmorphine (3-ethylmorphine)
Glutethimide (1985)
Lefetamine (1986)

Mecloqualone (1984)
Methaqualone (1984)
Methcathinone (1998)
Methylphenidate
Methylphenobarbitone [methylphenobarbital] (1984)
Nicocodine
Nicodicodine (6-nicotinoyldihydrocodeine) (1973)
Norcodeine
Pentazocine (1985)
Phenmetrazine
Pholcodine
Propiram
Zipeprol (1998)

aa Any compound (not being bupropion, cathinone, diethylpropion, pyrovalerone or a compound for the time being specified in paragraph (a) above) structurally derived from 2-amino-1-phenyl-1-propanone by modification in any of the following ways,

  i by substitution in the phenyl ring to any extent with alkyl, alkoxy, alkylenedioxy, haloalkyl or halide substituents, whether or not further substituted in the phenyl ring by one or more other univalent substituents,

  ii by substitution at the 3-position with an alkyl substituent, or

  iii by substitution at the nitrogen atom with alkyl or dialkyl groups, or by inclusion of the nitrogen atom in a cyclic structure (2010);

ab Any compound structurally derived from 2-aminopropan-1-one by substitution at the 1-position with any monocyclic, or fused-polycyclic ring system (not being a phenyl ring or alkylenedioxyphenyl ring system), whether or not the compound is further modified in any of the following ways:

  i by substitution in the ring system to any extent with alkyl, alkoxy, haloalkyl or halide substituents, whether or not further substituted in the ring system by one or more other univalent substituents,

  ii by substitution at the 2-amino nitrogen atom with alkyl or dialkyl groups, or

  iii by inclusion of the 2-amino nitrogen atom in a cyclic structure (2010);

b Any 5,5-disubstituted barbituric acid;

c 2,3-Dihydro-5-methyl-3-(4-morpholinylmethyl)pyrrolo[1,2,3-*de*]-1,4-benzoxazin-6-yl]-1-naphthalenylmethanone (2009),

3-Dimethylheptyl-11-hydroxyhexahydrocannabinol (2009),

9-Hydroxy-6-methyl-3-[5-phenylpentan-2-yl]oxy-5,6,6a,7,8,9,10,
    10a-octahydrophenanthridin-1-yl] acetate (2009),
9-(Hydroxymethyl)-6,6-dimethyl-3-(2-methyloctan-2-yl)-
    6a,7,10,10a-tetrahydrobenzo[c]chromen-1-ol (2009),
Nabilone (2009),
Any compound structurally derived from 3-(1-naphthoyl)indole or
    1H-indol-3-yl-(1-naphthyl)methane by substitution at the nitro-
    gen atom of the indole ring by alkyl, alkenyl, cycloalkylmethyl,
    cycloalkylethyl or 2-(4-morpholinyl)ethyl, whether or not further
    substituted in the indole ring to any extent and whether or not sub-
    stituted in the naphthyl ring to any extent (2009),
Any compound structurally derived from 3-(1-naphthoyl)pyrrole
    by substitution at the nitrogen atom of the pyrrole ring by
    alkyl, alkenyl, cycloalkylmethyl, cycloalkylethyl or 2-(4-
    morpholinyl)ethyl, whether or not further substituted in the
    pyrrole ring to any extent and whether or not substituted in the
    naphthyl ring to any extent (2009),
Any compound structurally derived from 1-(1-naphthylmethyl)indene
    by substitution at the 3-position of the indene ring by
    alkyl, alkenyl, cycloalkylmethyl, cycloalkylethyl or 2-(4-
    morpholinyl)ethyl, whether or not further substituted in the indene
    ring to any extent and whether or not substituted in the naphthyl
    ring to any extent (2009),
Any compound structurally derived from 3-phenylacetylindole
    by substitution at the nitrogen atom of the indole ring with
    alkyl, alkenyl, cycloalkylmethyl, cycloalkylethyl or 2-(4-
    morpholinyl)ethyl, whether or not further substituted in the indole
    ring to any extent and whether or not substituted in the phenyl ring
    to any extent (2009), and
Any compound structurally derived from 2-(3-hydroxycyclohexyl)
    phenol bysubstitution at the 5-position of the phenolic ring
    by alkyl, alkenyl, cycloalkylmethyl, cycloalkylethyl or 2 (4-
    morpholinyl)ethyl, whether or not further substituted in the
    cyclohexyl ring to any extent (2009).

2   Any stereoisomeric form of a substance for the time being specified in
    paragraph 1 of this Part of this Schedule;
    a   any ester or ether of cannabinol or of a cannabinol derivative (2008).

3   Any salt of a substance for the time being specified in paragraph 1 or 2 or
    2a of this Part of this Schedule.

4   Any preparation or other product containing a substance or product for
    the time being specified in any of paragraphs 1 to 3 of this Part of this
    Schedule, not being a preparation falling within paragraph 6 of Part I of
    this Schedule.

Part III Class C drugs

1 **a** The following substances, namely:

Alprazolam

Amineptine (2011)

Aminorex (1998)

Benzphetamine

Bromazepam (1985)

Brotizolam (1998)

Camazepam (1985)

Cathine (1986)

Cathinone (1986)

Chlordiazepoxide (1985)

Clorphentermine

Clobazam (1985)

Clonazepam (1985)

Clorazepic acid (1985)

Clotiazepam (1985)

Cloxazolam (1985)

Delorazepam (1985)

Dextropropoxyphene (1983)

Diazepam (1985)

Diethylpropion (1984)

Estazolam (1985)

Ethchlorvynol

Ethinamate (1985)

Ethyl loflazepate (1985)

N-Ethylamphetamine

Fencamfamin (1986)

Fenethylline (1986)

Fenproporex (1986)

Fludiazepam (1985)

Flunitrazepam (1985)

Flurazepam (1985)

Gamma-butyrolactone (2009)

Halazepam (1985)

Haloxazolam (1985)

4-Hydroxyl-*n*-butyryl acid (2003)

Ketamine (2005)

Ketazolam

Loprazolam (1985)

Lorazepam (1985)

Lormetazepam (1985)

Mazindol (1985)
Medazepam (1985)
Mefenorex (1985)
Mephentermine
Meprobamate (1985)
Mesocarb (1998)
Methyprylone (1985)
Midazolam (1990)
Nimetazepam (1985)
Nitrazepam (1985)
Nordazepam (1985)
Oxazepam (1985)
Oxazolam (1985)
Pemoline (1989)
Phendimetrazine
Phentermine (1985)
Pinazepam (1985)
Pipradol
Prazepam (1985)
Pyrovalerone (1986)
Temazepam (1985)
Tetrazepam (1985)
Triazolam (1985)
Zolpidem.
5α-Androstane-3,17-diol (2009)
Androst-4-ene-3,17-diol (2009)
1-Androstenediol (2009)
5-Androstene-3,17-diol
1-Androstenedione (2009)
4-Androstene-3,17-dione
5-Androstenedione (2009)

b Atamestane
Bolandiol
Bolazine
Boldenone
Boldione (2009)
Bolenol
Bolmantalate
1,4-Butanediol (2009)
Calusterone
4-Chloromethandienone
Clostebol
Danazol (2009)

Desoxymethyltestosterone (2009)
Drostanolone
Enestebol
Epitiostanol
Ethylestrenol
Fluoxymesterone
Formebolone
Furazabol
Gestrinone (2009)
3-Hydroxy-5α-androstan-17-one (2009)
Mesbolone
Mestanolone
Mesterolone
Methandienone
Methandriol
Methenolone
Methyltestosterone
Metribolone
Mibolerone
Nandrolone
19-Norandrostenedione (2009)
19-Nor-4-androstene-3,17-dione
19-Nor-4-androstene-3,17-diol
19-Norandrosterone (2009)
Norboletone
Norclostebol
Norethandrolone
19-Noretiocholanolone (2009)
Oripavine (2009)
Ovandrotone
Oxabolone
Oxandrolone
Oxymesterone
Oxymetholone
Prasterone
Propetandrol
Prostanozol (2009)
Quinbolone
Roxibolone
Silandrone
Stanozolol
Stenbolone
Testosterone

Tetrahydrogestrinone (2009)

Thiomesterone

Trenbolone

c Any compound (not being trilostane or a compound for the time being specified in paragraph (b) above) structurally derived from 17-hydroxyandrostan-3-one or from 17-hydroxy-estran-3-one by modification in any of the following ways

   i by further substitution at position 17 by a methyl or ethyl group,

   ii by substitution to any extent at one or more positions 1, 2, 4, 6, 7, 9, 11 or 16, but at no other position,

   iii by unsaturation in the carbocyclic ring system to any extent, provided that there are no more than two ethylenic bonds in any one carbocyclic ring,

   iv By fusion of ring A with a heterocyclic system,

   v 1-Benzylpiperazine or any compound structurally derived from 1-benzylpiperazine or 1-phenylpiperazine by modification (i) by substitution at the second nitrogen atom of the piperazine ring with alkyl, benzyl, haloalkyl or phenyl groups or (ii) by substitution in the aromatic ring to any extent with alkyl, alkoxy, alkylenedioxy, halide or haloalkyl groups (2009);

d Any substance which is an ester or ether (or, where more than one hydroxyl function is available, both an ester and an ether) of a substance specified in paragraph (b) above or described in paragraph (c) above;

e The following:

Chorionic gonadotrophin (HCG)

Clenbuterol

Non-human chorionic gonadotrophin (HCG)

Somatrem

Somatrophin

Somatotrophin

Zeranol (2009)

Zilpaterol (2009).

2 Any stereoisomeric form of a substance for the time being specified in paragraph 1 of this Part of this Schedule, not being phenylpropanolamine.

3 Any salt of a substance for the time being specified in paragraph 1 or 2 of this Part of this Schedule.

4 Any preparation or other product containing a substance for the time being specified in any of paragraphs 1 to 3 of this Part of this Schedule, Part IV.

Part IV Meaning of certain expressions used in this Schedule

For the purposes of this Schedule, the following expressions (which are not among those defined in section 37(1) of this Act) have the meanings hereby assigned to them.

Cannabinol derivatives means the following substances, except where contained in cannabis or cannabis resin, namely tetrahydro derivatives of cannabinol and 3-alkyl homologues of cannabinol or of its tetrahydro derivatives.

Coca leaf means the leaf of any plant of the genus *Erythroxylon* from whose leaves cocaine can be extracted either directly or by chemical transformation.

Concentrate of poppy-straw means the material produced when poppy-straw has entered into a process for the concentration of its alkaloids.

Medicinal opium means raw opium which has undergone the process necessary to adapt it for medicinal use in accordance with the requirements of the BP, whether it is in the form of powder or is granulated or is in any other form, and whether it is or is not mixed with neutral substances.

Poppy-straw means all parts, except the seeds, of the opium poppy, after mowing.

Raw opium includes powdered or granulated opium but does not include medicinal opium.

Appendix 5

Misuse of Drugs Regulations 2001 (as amended): Controlled Drugs classified for regimes of control

The five Schedules of Controlled Drugs appended to the Misuse of Drugs Regulations 2001 (SI 1985 No. 3998, as amended) are reproduced in this appendix. It should be used in conjunction with chapter 17 and, in particular Table 17.2. They provide a full explanation of the regulations, and how they affect the drugs in the various Schedules.

Schedule 1

Controlled Drugs subject to the requirements of Regulations 14, 15, 16, 18, 19, 20, 23, 26 and 27.

1 **a** The following substances and products, namely:

4-Bromo-2,5-dimethoxy-α-methylphenethylamine
Bufotenine (2009)
1,4-Butanediol
Cannabinol: not being dronebenol or its stereoisomers
Cannabinol derivatives
Cannabis and cannabis resin
Cathinone
Coca leaf
Concentrate of poppy-straw
[2,3-Dihydro-5-methyl-3-(4-morpholinylmethyl)pyrrolo[1,2,3-*de*]-
1,4-benzoxazin-6-yl]-1-naphthalenylmethanone (2009)
3-Dimethylheptyl-11-hydroxyhexahydrocannabinol (2009)
N,N-Diethyltryptamine

2,5-Dimethoxy-4α-dimethylphenethylamine

N,N-Dimethyltryptamine

Eticyclidine

Etryptamine (1998)

Fungus (of any kind) which contains psilocin or an ester of psilocin (2005)

Gamma-butyrolactone (2009)

9-Hydroxy-6-methyl-3-[5-phenylpentan-2-yl] oxy-5,6,6α,7,8,9,10, 10a-octahydrophenanthridin-1-yl acetate (2009)

9-(Hydroxymethyl)-6,6-dimethyl-3-(2-methyloctan-2-yl)-6α,7,10,10α-tetrahydrobenzo[c]chromen-1-ol (2009)

N-Hydroxytenamphetamine

Lysergamide

Lysergide and other N-alkyl derivatives of lysergamide

Mescaline

Methcathinone (1998)

4-Methylaminorex

Psilocin

Raw opium

Rolicyclidine

Tenocyclidine;

b Any compound (not being a compound for the time being specified in paragraph (a) above) structurally derived from tryptamine or from a ring-hydroxy tryptamine by substitution at the nitrogen atom of the sidechain with one or more alkyl substituents but no other substituents;

c The following phethylamine derivatives, namely:

Allyl(α-methyl-3,4-methylenedioxyphenethyl)amine

2-Amino-1-(2,5-dimethoxy-4-methylphenyl)ethanol

2-Amino-1-(3,4-dimethoxyphenyl)ethanol

Benzyl(α-methyl-3,4-methylenedioxyphenethyl)amine

4-Bromo-β,2,5-trimethoxyphenethylamine

N-(4-sec-Butylthio-2,5-dimethoxyphenethyl)hydroxylamine

Cyclopropylmethyl(α-methyl-3,4-methylenedioxyphenethyl)amine

2-(4,7-Dimethoxy-2,3-dihydro-1 H -indan-5-yl)ethylamine

2-(4,7-Dimethoxy-2,3-dihydro-1 H -indan-5-yl)-1-methylethylamine

2-(2,5-Dimethoxy-4-methylphenyl)cycloprophlamine

2-(1,4-Dimethoxy-4-naphthyl)ethylamine

2-(1,4-Dimethoxy-4-naphthyl)-1-methylethylamine

N-(2,5-Dimethoxy-4-propylthiphenethyl)hydroxylamine

2-(1,4-Dimethoxy-5,6,7,8-tetrahydro-2-naphthyl)ethylamine

2-(1,4-Dimethoxy-5,6,7,8-tetrahydro-2-naphthyl)-1-methylethylamine α,α-Dimethyl-3,4-methylenedioxyphenethylamine

α,α-Dimethyl-3,4-methylenedioxyphenethyl(methyl)amine

Dimethyl(α-methyl-3,4-methylenedioxyphenethyl)amine

N-(4-Ethylthio-2,5-dimethoxyphenethyl)hydroxylamine

2-(1,4-Methano-5,8-dimethoxy-1,2,3,4-tetrahydro-6-
naphthyl)ethylamine

2-(1,4-Methano-5,8-dimethoxy-1,2,3,4-tetrahydro-6-naphthyl)-1-
mathylethylamine

2-(5-Methoxy-2,2-dimethyl-2,3-dihydrobenzo[*b*]furan-6-yl)-1-
methylethylamine

2-Methoxyethyl(α-methyl-3,4-methylenedioxyphenethyl)amine

2-(5-Methoxy-2-methy-2,3-dihydrobenzo[*b*]furan-6-yl)-1-
methylethylamine

β-Methoxy-3,4-methylenedioxyphenethylamine

1-(3,4-Methylenedioxybenzyl)butyl(ethyl)amine

1-(3,4-Methylenedioxybenzyl)butyl(methyl)amine

2-(α-Methyl-3,4-methylenedioxyphenethylamino)ethanol

N-Methyl-N-(α-methyl-3,4-methylenedioxyphenethyl)hydroxylamine

O-Methyl-N-(α-methyl-3,4-methylenedioxyphenethyl)hydroxylamine

α-Methyl-4-(methylthio)phenethylamine

β,3,4,5-Tetramethoxyphenethylamine

β2,5-Trimethoxy-4-methylphenethylamine

d Any compound (not being methoxyphenamine or a compound
for the time being specified in paragraph (a) above) structurally
derived from phenethylamine, an N-alkylphenethylamine,
α-methylphenethylamine, an N-alkyl-α-methylphenethylamine,
α-ethylphenethylamine or an N-alkyl-α-ethylphenethylamine by substitution in the ring to any extent with alkyl, alkoxy, alkylenedioxy or
halide substituents, whether or not further substituted in the ring by
one or more other univalent substituents;

e Any compound (not being a compound for the time being specified
in Sch. 2) structurally derived from fentanyl by modification in any of
the following ways, that is to say

   i by replacement of the phenyl portion of the phenethyl group by
any heteromonocycle whether or not further substituted in the
heterocycle,

   ii by substitution in the phenethyl group with alkyl, alkenyl,
alkoxy, hydroxy, halogeno, haloalkyl, amino or nitro groups,

   iii by substitution in the piperidine ring with alkyl or alkenyl groups,

   iv by substitution in the aniline ring with alkyl, alkoxy, alkylenedioxy, halogeno or haloalkyl groups,

   v by substitution at the 4-position of the piperidine ring with any
alkoxycarbonyl or alkoxyalkyl or acyloxy group, or

vi by replacement of the N-propionyl group by another acyl group;

f Any compound (not being a compound for the time being specified in Sch. 2) structurally derived from pethidine by modification in any of the following ways

  i by replacement of the 1-methyl group by an acyl, alkyl whether or not unsaturated, benzyl or phenethyl group, whether or not further substituted,

  ii by substitution in the piperidine ring with alkyl or alkenyl groups or with a propano bridge, whether or not further substituted,

  iii by substitution in the 4-phenyl ring with alkyl, alkoxy, aryloxy, halogeno or haloalkyl groups,

  iv by replacement of the 4-ethoxycarbonyl by any other alkoxycarbonyl or any alkoxyalkyl or acyloxy group, or

  v by formation of an N-oxide or of a quaternary base;

g 1-Benzylpiperazine or any compound (not being a compound for the time being specified in Part II of this Schedule) structurally derived from 1-benzylpiperazine or 1-phenylpiperazine by modification in any of the following ways

  i by substitution at the second nitrogen atom of the piperazine ring with alkyl, benzyl, haloalkyl or phenyl groups, or

  ii by substitution in the aromatic ring to any extent with alkyl, alkoxy, alkylenedioxy, halide or haloalkyl groups (2009),

h Any compound structurally derived from 3-(1-naphthoyl)indole or 1H-indol-3-yl-(1-naphthyl)methane by substitution at the nitrogen atom of the indole ring by alkyl, alkenyl, cycloalkylmethyl, cycloalkylethyl or 2-(4-morpholinyl)ethyl, whether or not further substituted in the indole ring to any extent and whether or not substituted in the naphthyl ring to any extent (2009);

i Any compound structurally derived from 3-(1-naphthoyl)pyrrole by substitution at the nitrogen atom of the pyrrole ring by alkyl, alkenyl, cycloalkylmethyl, cycloalkylethyl or 2-(4-morpholinyl)ethyl, whether or not further substituted in the pyrrole ring to any extent and whether or not substituted in the naphthyl ring to any extent (2009);

j Any compound structurally derived from 1-(1-naphthylmethyl)indene by substitution at the 3-position of the indene ring by alkyl, alkenyl, cycloalkylmethyl, cycloalkylethyl or 2-(4-morpholinyl)ethyl, whether or not further substituted in the indene ring to any extent and whether or not substituted in the naphthyl ring to any extent (2009);

k Any compound structurally derived from 3-phenylacetylindole by substitution at the nitrogen atom of the indole ring with alkyl, alkenyl, cycloalkylmethyl, cycloalkylethyl or 2-(4-morpholinyl)ethyl, whether or not further substituted in the indole ring to any extent and whether or not substituted in the phenyl ring to any extent (2009);

l   Any compound structurally derived from 2-(3-hydroxycyclohexyl)phenol by substitution at the 5-position of the phenolic ring by alkyl, alkenyl, cycloalkylmethyl, cycloalkylethyl or 2-(4-morpholinyl)ethyl, whether or not further substituted in the cyclohexyl ring to any extent (2009);

m   Any compound (not being bupropion, diethylpropion, pyrovalerone or a compound for the time being specified in paragraph (a) above) structurally derived from 2-amino-1-phenyl-1 propanone by modification in any of the following ways

   i   by substitution in the phenyl ring to any extent with alkyl, alkoxy, alkylenedioxy, haloalkyl or halide substituents, whether or not further substituted in the phenyl ring by one or more other univalent substituents,

   ii   by substitution at the 3-position with an alkyl substituent, or

   iii   by substitution at the nitrogen atom with alkyl or dialkyl groups, or by inclusion of the nitrogen atom in a cyclic structure (2010);

n   Any compound structurally derived from 2-aminopropan-1-one by substitution at the 1-position with any monocyclic, or fused-polycyclic ring system (not being a phenyl ring or alkylene-dioxyphenyl ring system), whether or not the compound is further modified in any of the following ways

   i   by substitution at the 3-position with an alkyl substituent,

   ii   by substitution at the 2-amino nitrogen atom with alkyl or dialkyl groups, or

   iii   by inclusion of the 2-amino nitrogen atom in a cyclic structure (2010).

o   Any compound (not being pipradrol) structurally derived from piperidine, pyrrolidine, azepane, morpholine or pyridine by substitution at a ring carbon atom with a diphenylmethyl group, whether or not the compound is further modified in any of the following ways, that is to say:

   i   by substitution in any of the phenyl rings to any extent with alkyl, alkoxy, haloalkyl or halide groups;

   ii   by substitution at the methyl carbon atom with an alkyl, hydroxyalkyl or hydroxy group;

   iii   by substitution at the ring nitrogen atom with an alkyl, alkenyl, haloalkyl or hydroxyalkyl group.

2   Any stereoisomeric form of a substance specified in paragraph 1.

3   Any ester or ether of a substance specified in paragraph 1 or 2.

4   Any salt of a substance specified in any of paragraphs 1 to 3.

5   Any preparation or other product containing a substance or product specified in any of paragraphs 1 to 4, not being a preparation specified in Schedule 5.

Schedule 2

Controlled Drugs subject to the requirements of Regulations 14, 15, 16, 18, 19, 20, 21, 23, 26 and 27.

1 The following substances and products, namely:

Acetorphine
Alfentanil
Allylprodine
Alphacetylmethadol
Alphameprodine
Alphamethadol
Alphaprodine
Amineptine (2010)
Anileridine
Benzethidine
Benzylmorphine (3-benzylmorphine)
Betacetylmethadol
Betameprodine
Betamethadol
Betaprodine
Bezitramide
Carfentanil
Clonitazene
Cocaine
4-Cyano-2-dimethylamino-4,4-diphenylbutane
4-Cyano-1-methyl-4-phenylpiperidine
Desomorphine
Dextromoramide
Diamorphine
Diampromide
Diethylthiambutene
Difenoxin
Dihydrocodeinone-O-carboxymethyloxine
Dihydroetorpine
Dihydromorphine
Dimenoxadole
Dimepheptanol
Dimethylthiambutene
Dioxaphetyl butyrate
Diphenoxylate
Dipipanone
Dronabinol
Drotebanol

Ecgonine, and any derivative of ecgonine which is convertible to ecgonine or to cocaine

Ethylmethylthiambutene

Etonitazene

Etorphine

Etoxeridine

Fentanyl

Furethidine

Hydrocodone

Hydromorphinol

Hydromorphone

Hydroxypethidine

Isomethadone

Ketobemidone

Levomethorphan

Levomoramide

Levophenacylmorphan

Levorphanol

Lofentanil

Medicinal opium

Metazocine

Methadone

Methadyl acetate

Methyldesorphine

Methyldihydromorphine (6-methyldihydromorphine)

2-Methyl-3-morpholino-1,1-diphenylpropanecarboxylic acid

1-Methyl-4-phenylpiperidine-4-carboxylic acid

Metopon

Morpheridine

Morphine

Morphine methobromide, morphine N-oxide and other pentavalent nitrogen morphine derivatives

Myrophine

Nabilone (2009)

Nicomorphine

Noracymethadol

Norlevorphanol

Normethadone

Normorphine

Norpipanone

Oripavine (2009)

Oxycodone

Oxymorphone

Pethidine
Phenadoxone
Phenampromide
Phenazocine
Phencyclidine
Phenomorphan
Phenoperidine
4-Phenylpiperidine-4-carboxylic acid ethyl ester
Piminodine
Piritramide
Proheptazine
Properidine
Quinalbarbitone [secobarbital]
Racemethorphan
Racemoramide
Racemorphan
Remifentanil
Sufentanil
Tapentadol (2010)
Thebacon
Thebaine
Tilidate
Trimeperidine
Zipeprol.

2 Any stereoisomeric form of a substance specified in paragraph 1 not being dextromethorphan or dextrorphan.

3 Any ester or ether of a substance specified in paragraph 1 or 2, not being a substance specified in paragraph 6.

4 Any salt of a substance specified in any of paragraphs 1 to 3.

5 Any preparation or other product containing a substance or product specified in any of paragraphs 1 to 4, not being a preparation specified in Schedule 5.

6 The following
Acetyldihydrocodeine
Amphetamine
Codeine
Dextropropoxyphene
Dihydrocodeine
Ethylmorphine (3-ethylmorphine)
Fenethylline
Glutethamide
Lefetamine
Mecloqualone
Methaqualone
Methylamphetamine

Methylphenidate
Nicocodine
Nicodicodine (6-nicotinoyldihydrocodeine)
Norcodeine
Phenmetrazine
Pholcodine
Propiram
Quinalbarbitone (secobarbital).

7 Any stereoisomeric form of a substance specified in paragraph 6.

8 Any salt of a substance specified in paragraph 6 or 7.

9 Any preparation or other product containing a substance or product specified in any of paragraphs 6 to 8, not being a preparation specified in Schedule 5.

Schedule 3

Controlled Drugs subject to the requirements of Regulations 14, 15, 16, 18, 22, 23, 24, 26 and 27.

1 a The following substances:

Benzphetamine
Cathine
Chlorphentermine
Diethylpropion
Ethchlorvynol
Ethinamate
Flunitrazepam (1998)
Mazindol
Mephentermine
Meprobamate
Methylphenobarbitone [methylphenobarbital]
Methyprylone
Pentazocine
Midazolam (2007)
Phendimetrazine
Phentermine
Pipradrol
Temazepam

b Any 5,5-disubstituted barbituric acid, not being quinalbarbitone [secobarbital].

2 Any stereoisomeric form of a substance specified in paragraph 1, not being phenylpropanolamine.

3 Any salt of a substance specified in paragraph 1 or 2.

4 Any preparation or other product containing a substance specified in any of paragraphs 1 to 3, not being a preparation specified in Schedule 5.

Schedule 4, Part I

Controlled Drugs excepted from the prohibition on importation, exportation and, when in the form of a medicinal product, possession and subject to the requirements of Regulations 22, 23, 25, 26 and 27.

1 The following substances and products:

Alprazolam
Aminorex
Bromazepam
Brotizolam
Camazepam
Chlordiazepoxide
1-(3-Chlorophenyl)piperazine (2009)
1-(3-Chlorophenyl)-4-(3-chloropropyl)piperazine (2009)
Clobazam
Clonazepam
Clorazepic acid
Clotiazepam
Cloxazolam
Delorazepam
Diazepam
Estazolam
N-Ethylamphetamine
Ethyl loflazepate
Fencamfamin
Fenproporex
Fludiazepam
Flurazepam
Halazepam
Haloxazolam
4-Hydroxy-*n*-butyric acid
Ketamine (2005)
Ketazolam
Loprazolam
Lorazepam
Lormetazepam
Medazepam
Mefenorex
Mesabolene (2003)
Mesocarb
Nimetazepam
Nitrazepam
Nordazepam

Oxabolene (2003)
Oxazepam
Oxazolam
Pemoline
Pinazepam
Prazepam
Pyrovalerone
Tetrazepam
Triazolam
Zolpidem.

2 Any stereoisomeric form of a substance specified in paragraph 1.
3 Any salt of a substance specified in paragraph 1 or 2.
4 Any preparation or other product containing a substance or product specified in any of paragraphs 1 to 3, not being a preparation specified in Schedule 5.

Schedule 4, Part II

Controlled Drugs excepted from the prohibition on possession when in the form of a medicinal product; excluded from the application of offences arising from the prohibition on importation and exportation when imported or exported in the form of a medicinal product by any person for administration to himself; and subject to the requirements of Regulations 22, 23, 26 and 27.

1 The following substances and products:
5α-Androstane-3,17-diol (2009)
Androst-4-ene-3,17-diol (2009)
1-Androstenediol (2009)
5-Androstene-3,17-diol
1-Androstenedione (2009)
4-Androstene-3,17-dione
5-Androstenedione (2009)
Atamestane
Bolandiol
Bolasterone
Bolazine
Boldenone
Boldione (2009)
Bolenol
Bolmantalate
Calusterone
4-Choromethandienone
Clostebol

Danazol (2009)
Desoxymethyltestosterone (2009)
Drostanolone
Enestebol
Epitiostanol
Ethyloestrenol
Fluoxymesterone
Formebolone
Furazabol
Gestrinone (2009)
3-Hydroxy-5α-androstan-17-one (2009)
Mebolazine
Mepitiostane
Mestanolone
Mesterolone
Methandienone
Methandriol
Methenolone
Methyltestosterone
Metribolone
Mibolerone
Nandrolone
19-Nor-5-androstene-3,17-diol
19-Norandrostenedione (2009)
19-Norandrostene-3,17-dione
19-Norandrosterone (2009)
Norboletone
Norclostebol
Norethandrolone
19-Noretiocholanolone (2009)
Ovandrotone
Oxandrolone
Oxymesterone
Oxymetholone
Prasterone
Propetandrol
Prostanozol (2009)
Quinbolone
Roxibolone
Silandrone
Stanolone
Stanozolol
Stenbolone

Testosterone
Tetrahydrogestrinone (2009)
Thiomesterone
Trenbolone.

2 Any compound (not being trilostane or a compound for the time being specified in paragraph 1 of this part of this Schedule) structurally derived from 17-hydroxyandrostan-3-one or from 17-hydroxyestran-3-one by modification in any of the following ways:

a by further substitution at position 17 by a methyl or ethyl group;

b by substitution to any extent at one or more positions 1, 2, 4, 6, 7, 9, 11 or 16, but at no other position;

c by unsaturation in the carbocyclic ring system to any extent, provided that there are no more than two ethylenic bonds in any one carbocyclic ring;

d by fusion of ring A with a heterocyclic system.

3 Any substance which is an ester or ether (or, where more than one hydroxyl function is available, both an ester and an ether) of a substance specified in paragraph 1 or described in paragraph 2 of this Part of the Schedule.

4 The following:

Chorionic gonadotrophin (HCG)
Clenbuterol
Non-human chorionic gonadotrophin (HCG)
Somatrem
Somatotrophin
Zeranol (2009)
Zilpaterol (2009).

5 Any stereoisomeric form of a substance specified or described in any of paragraphs 1 to 4 of this Part of this Schedule.

6 Any salt of a substance specified or described in any of paragraphs 1 to 5 of this Part of this Schedule.

7 Any preparation of other product containing a substance or product specified or described in any of paragraphs 1 to 6 of this Part of the Schedule, not being a preparation specified in Schedule 5.

Schedule 5

Controlled Drugs excepted from the prohibition on importation, exportation and possession and subject to the requirements of Regulations 24 and 25.

1 (1) Any preparation of one or more of the substances to which this paragraph applies, not being a preparation designed for administration by injection, when compounded with one or more other active or inert ingredients and containing a total of not more than 100 milligrams of the substance or substances (calculated as base) per dosage unit or with a total concentration of not more than 2.5 per cent (calculated as base) in undivided preparations.

(2) The substances to which this paragraph applies are acetyldihydrocodeine, codeine, dihydrocodeine, ethylmorphine, nicocodine, nicodicodine (6-nicotinoyldihydrocodeine), norcodeine, pholcodine and their respective salts.

2 Any preparation of cocaine containing not more than 0.1 per cent of cocaine calculated as cocaine base, being a preparation compounded with one or more other active or inert ingredients in such a way that the cocaine cannot be recovered by readily applicable means or in a yield which would constitute a risk to health.

3 Any preparation of medicinal opium or of morphine containing (in either case) not more than 0.2 per cent of morphine calculated as anhydrous morphine base, being a preparation compounded with one or more other active or inert ingredients in such a way that the opium or, as the case may be, the morphine cannot be recovered by readily applicable means or in a yield which would constitute a risk to health.

4 Any preparation of dextropropoxyphene, being a preparation designed for oral administration, containing not more than 135 milligrams of dextropropoxyphene (calculated as base) per dosage unit or with a total concentration of not more than 2.5 per cent (calculated as base) in undivided preparations.

5 Any preparation of difenoxin containing, per dosage unit, not more than 0.5 milligrams of difenoxin and a quantity of atropine sulphate equivalent to at least 5 per cent of the dose of difenoxin.

6 Any preparation of diphenoxylate containing, per dosage unit, not more than 2.5 milligrams of diphenoxylate calculated as base, and a quantity of atropine sulphate equivalent to at least 1 per cent of the dose of diphenoxylate.

7 Any preparation of propiram containing, per dosage unit, not more than 100 milligrams of propiram calculated as base and compounded with at least the same amount (by weight) of methylcellulose.

8 Any powder of ipecacuanha and opium comprising:

10 per cent opium, in powder,

10 per cent ipecacuanha root, in powder, well mixed with

80 per cent of any other powdered ingredient containing no Controlled Drug.

9 Any mixture containing one or more of the preparations specified in paragraphs 1 to 8, being a mixture of which none of the other ingredients is a Controlled Drug.

Appendix 6

The Poisons List Order 1982

Non-medicinal poisons are listed in the Schedule to this Order (SI 1982 No. 217, as amended) made under the Poisons Act 1972. Those substances in Part I of the list may not be sold by retail except by a person lawfully conducting a retail pharmacy business. Those in Part II of the list may only be sold by a person lawfully conducting a retail pharmacy business or by a person whose name is entered in a local authority's list (listed sellers).

The Poisons List: Part I

Aluminium phosphide

Arsenic; its compounds, other than those specified in Part II of this list

Barium, salts of, other than barium sulphate and the salts of barium specified in Part II of this list

Bromomethane

Chloropicrin

Fluoroacetic acid; its salts, fluorocetamide

Hydrogen cyanide; metal cyanides, other than ferrocyanides and ferricyanides

Lead acetates; compounds of lead with acids from fixed oils

Magnesium phosphide

Mercury, compounds of, the following: nitrates of mercury; oxides of mercury; mercuric cyanide oxides; mercuric thiocyanate; ammonium mercuric chlorides; potassium mercuric iodides; organic compounds of mercury which contain a methyl (CH_3) group directly linked to the mercury atom

Oxalic acid

Phenols (phenol; phenolic isomers of cresols, xylenols, monoethylphenols) except in substances containing less than 60 per cent w/w of phenols; compounds of phenol with a metal, except in substances containing less than the equivalent of 60 per cent w/w of phenols

Phosphorus, yellow

Strychnine; its salts, its quaternary compounds
Thallium, salts of.

The Poisons List: Part II

Aldicarb
Alpha-chloralose
Ammonia
Arsenic, compounds of; the following: calcium arsenites, copper acetoarsenite, copper arsenates, copper arsenites, lead arsenates
Barium, salts of; the following: barium carbonate, barium silicofluoride
Carbofuran
Cycloheximide
Dinitrocresols (DNOC); their compounds with a metal or a base
Dinoseb; its compounds with a metal or a base
Dinoterb
Drazoxolon; its salts
Endosulfan
Endothal; its salts
Endrin
Fentin, compounds of
Formaldehyde
Formic acid
Hydrochloric acid
Hydrofluoric acid, alkali metal bifluorides, ammonium bifluoride, alkali metal fluorides, ammonium fluoride, sodium silicofluoride
Mercuric chloride, mercuric iodide, organic compounds of mercury except compounds of mercury which contain a methyl (CH_3) group directly linked to the mercury atom
Metallic oxalates
Methomyl
Nicotine; its salts; its quaternary compounds
Nitric acid
Nitrobenzene
Oxamyl
Paraquat, salts of
Phenols (as defined in Part I of this List) in substances containing less than 60 per cent w/w of phenols; compounds of phenols with a metal in substances containing less than the equivalent of 60 per cent w/w of phenols
Phosphoric acid
Phosphorus compounds, the following: azinphos-methyl, chlorfenvinphos, demephion, demeton-S-methyl, demeton-S-methyl sulphone, dialifos, dichlorvos, dioxathion, disulfoton, fonofos, mecarbam, mephosfolan,

methidathion, mevinphos, omethoate, oxydemeton-methyl, parathion, phenkapton, phorate, phosphamidon, pirimiphos-ethyl, quinalphos, thiometon, thionazin, triazophos, vamidothion

Potassium hydroxide

Sodium hydroxide

Sodium nitrite

Sulphuric acid

Thiofanox

Zinc phosphide.

Appendix 7

The Poisons Rules 1982

The Poison Rules 1982 (SI 1982 No. 218, as amended), made under the Poisons Act 1972, are described in chapter 18. In this appendix are set out eight of the Schedules to the rules.

NB. Schedules 2, 3, 6 and 7 were deleted by the Poisons Rules (Amendment) Order 1985 (SI 1985 No. 1077).

Schedule 1 (Rules 5, 6, 7, 9, 10(1), 17(2) and 21(2))

Poisons included in the Poisons List to which special restrictions apply unless exempted by Rule 7 (chapter 18).

Aldicarb
Alpha-chloralose
Aluminium phosphide
Arsenic; its compounds, except substances containing less than the equivalent of 0.0075 per cent of arsenic (As)
Barium, salts of (other than barium sulphate)
Bromomethane
Carbofuran
Chloropicrin
Cycloheximide
Dinitrocresols (DNOC); their compounds with a metal or a base; except winter washes containing not more than the equivalent of 5 per cent of dinitrocresols
Dinoseb; its compounds with a metal or a base
Dinoterb
Drazoxolon; its salts
Endosulfan
Endothal: its salts
Endrin

Fentin, compounds of

Fluoroacetic acid; its salts, fluoroacetamide

Hydrogen cyanide except substances containing less than 0.15 per cent w/w
of hydrogen cyanide (HCN); metal cyanides, other than ferrocyanides
and ferricyanides, except substances containing less than the equivalent of
0.1 per cent w/w of hydrogen cyanide (HCN)

Lead, compounds of, with acids from fixed oils

Magnesium phosphide

Mercuric chloride, except substances containing less than 1 per cent of mercuric chloride; mercuric iodide except substances containing less than 2
per cent of mercuric iodide; mercury nitrates except substances containing
less than the equivalent of 3 per cent w/w of mercury; potassio-mercuric
iodides except substances containing less than the equivalent of 1 per cent
of mercuric iodide; organic compounds of mercury except substances, not
being aerosols, containing less than the equivalent of 0.2 per cent w/w of
mercury

Methomyl

Nicotine; its salts; its quaternary compounds

Oxamyl

Paraquat, salts of

Phosphorus compounds, the following:

    Azinphos-methyl

    Chlorfenvinphos

    Demephion

    Demeton-S-methyl

    Demeton-S-methyl sulphone

    Dialifos

    Dichlorvos

    Dioxathion

    Disulfoton

    Fonofos

    Mecarbam

    Mephosfolan

    Methidathion

    Mevinphos

    Omethoate

    Oxydemeton-methyl

    Parathion

    Phenkapton

    Phorate

Phosphamidon
Pirimiphos-ethyl
Quinalphos
Thiometon
Thionazin
Triazophos
Vamidothion

Strychnine, its salts, its quaternary compounds, except substances containing less than 0.2 per cent of strychnine

Thallium, salts of
Thiofanox
Zinc phosphide.

Schedule 4 (Rule 8)

Articles exempted from the provisions of the Act and Rules

Group I: general exemptions

Adhesives, anti-fouling compositions, builders' materials, ceramics, cosmetic products, distempers, electrical valves, enamels, explosives, fillers, fireworks, fluorescent lamps, flux in any form for use in soldering, glazes, glue, inks, lacquer solvents, loading materials, matches, medicated animal feeding stuffs, motor fuels and lubricants, paints, photographic paper, pigments, plastics, propellants, rubber, varnishes, vascular plants and their seeds.

Group II: special exemptions

In Group II in this Schedule, the expression *granular preparation* in relation to a poison means a preparation:

a which consists of absorbent mineral or synthetic solid particles impregnated with the poison, the size of the particles being such that not more than 4 per cent w/w of the preparation is capable of passing a sieve with a mesh of 250 microns [micrometres], and not more than 1 per cent w/w a sieve with a mesh of 150 microns [micrometres];
b which has an apparent density of not less than 0.4 g/mL if compacted without pressure; and
c that is not more than 12 per cent w/w consists of one or more poisons in respect of which an exemption is conferred by this Schedule in relation to granular preparations.

Table A7.1 Group II special exemptions

Poison	Substance or article in which exempted
Ammonia	Substances not being solutions of ammonia or preparations containing solutions of ammonia; substances containing less than 10% w/w ammonia (NH_3); refrigerators
Arsenic, its compounds	Pyrites ores or sulphuric acid containing arsenic or compounds of arsenic as natural impurities; in reagent kits or reagent devices supplied for medical or veterinary purposes, substances containing less than 0.1% w/w of arsanilic acid
Barium, salts of	Witherite other than finely ground witherite; barium carbonate bonded to charcoal for case hardening; fire extinguishers containing barium chloride; sealed smoke generators containing not more than 25% w/w of barium carbonate
Bromomethane	Fire extinguishers
Carbofuran	Granular preparations
Drazoxolon; its salts	Treatments on seeds
Formaldehyde	Substances containing less than 5% w/w of formaldehyde (HCHO); photographic glazing or hardening solutions
Formic acid	Substances containing less than 25% w/w of formic acid (HCOOH)
Hydrochloric acid	Substances containing less than 10% w/w of hydrochloric acid (HCl)
Hydrogen cyanide	Preparations of wild cherry; in reagent kits supplied for medical or veterinary purposes, substances containing less than the equivalent of 0.1% w/w of hydrogen cyanide
Lead acetate	Substances containing less than the equivalent of 2.5% w/w of elemental lead (Pb)
Mercuric chloride	Batteries, treatments on seeds or bulbs
Mercuric iodide	Treatments on seeds or bulbs
Mercury organic, compounds of	Treatments on seeds or bulbs
Mercury, oxides of	Canker and wound paints (for trees) containing not more than 3% w/w of yellow mercuric oxide
Methomyl	Solid substances containing not more than 1% w/w of methomyl

(continued overleaf)

Table A7.1 *(continued)*

Poison	Substance or article in which exempted
Nicotine, its salts, its quaternary compounds	Tobacco; in cigarettes, the paper of a cigarette (excluding any part of that paper forming part of or surrounding a filter), where that paper in each cigarette does not have more than the equivalent of 10 milligrams of nicotine; preparations in aerosol dispensers containing not more than 0.2% w/w of nicotine; other liquid preparations and solid preparations with a soap base containing not more than 7.5% w/w of nicotine
Nitric acid	Substances containing less than 20% w/w of nitric acid (HNO_3)
Nitrobenzene	Substances containing less than 0.1% of nitrobenzene; polishes
Oxalic acid; metallic	Laundry blue; polishes; cleaning powders or scouring products, containing the equivalent of not more than 10% of oxalic acid dihydrate
Oxamyl	Granular preparations
Paraquat, salts of	Preparations in pellet form containing not more than 5% of salts of paraquat calculated as paraquat ion
Phenols	Creosote obtained from coal tar; liquid disinfectants or antiseptics containing phenol less than 0.5% phenol and containing less than 5% of other phenols (as defined in the Poisons List); motor fuel treatments not containing phenol and containing less than 2.5% of other phenols; in reagent kits supplied for medical or veterinary purposes; solid substances containing less than 60% of phenols; tar (coal or wood), crude or refined; in tar oil distillation fractions containing not more than 5% of phenols; thymol
Phenylmercuric salts	Antiseptic dressings on toothbrushes; in textiles containing not more than 0. 01% of phenylmercuric salts as bacteriostat and fungicide
Phosphoric acid	Substances containing phosphoric acid, not being descaling preparations, containing more than 50% w/w of ortho-phosphoric acid
Phosphorus compounds, the following:	
Chlorfenvinphos	Treatments on seeds; granular preparations
Dichlorvos	Preparations in aerosol dispensers containing not more than 1% w/w of dichlorvos; materials impregnated with dichlorvos for slow release; granular preparations; ready for use liquid preparations containing not more than 1% w/v of dichlorvos

(continued overleaf)

Table A7.1 *(continued)*	
Poison	**Substance or article in which exempted**
Disulfoton	Granular preparations
Fonofos	Granular preparations
Oxydemeton-methyl	Aerosol dispensers containing not more than 0.25% w/w of oxydemeton-methyl
Parathion	Granular preparations
Phorate	Granular preparations
Pirimiphos-ethyl	Treatments on seeds
Thionazin	Granular preparations
Triazophos	Granular preparations
Potassium hydroxide	Substances containing the equivalent of less than 17% of total caustic alkalinity expressed as potassium hydroxide; accumulators; batteries
Sodium fluoride	Substances containing less than 3% of sodium fluoride as a preservative
Sodium hydroxide	Substances containing the equivalent of less than 12% of total caustic alkalinity expressed as sodium hydroxide
Sodium nitrite	Substances other than preparations containing more than 0.1% of sodium nitrite for the destruction of rats or mice
Sodium silicofluoride	Substances containing less than 3% of sodium silicofluoride as a preservative
Sulphuric acid	Substances containing less than 15% w/w of sulphuric acid (H_2SO_4); accumulators; batteries and sealed containers in which sulphuric acid is packed together with car batteries for use in those batteries; fire extinguishers
Thiofanox	Granular preparations

Schedule 5 (Rule 10(2))

Part A

Form to which the poisons specified are restricted when sold by listed sellers of Part II poisons (see p. 00).

Part B

Poisons which may be sold by listed sellers of Part II poisons only to persons engaged in the trade or business of agriculture, horticulture or forestry and for the purpose of that trade or business:

Aldicarb

Arsenic, compounds of: calcium arsenites, copper acetoarsenite, copper arsenates, copper arsenites, lead arsenates

Carbofuran

Cyclohexamide

Dinitrocresols (DNOC), their compounds with a metal or a base; except winter washes containing not more than the equivalent of 5 per cent of dinitrocresols

Dinoseb, its compounds with a metal or a base

Dinoterb

Drazoxolon, its salts

Endosulfan

Endothal, its salts

Endrin

Fentin, compounds of

Mercuric chloride, mercuric iodide, organic compounds of mercury, except solutions containing not more than 5 per cent w/v of phenyl mercuric acetate for use in swimming baths

Methomyl

Oxamyl

Paraquat, salts of

Phosphorus compounds, the following:

    Azinphos-methyl

    Chlorfenvinphos

    Demephion

    Demeton-S-methyl

    Demeton-S-methyl sulphone

    Dialifos

    Dichlorvos

    Dioxathion

    Disulfoton

    Fonofos

    Mecarbam

    Mephosfolan

    Methidathion

    Mevinphos

    Omethoate

    Oxydemeton-methyl

Table A7.2 Form to which the poisons specified are restricted

Poison	Form to which sale is restricted
Aldicarb	Preparations for use in agriculture, horticulture or forestry
Alpha-chloralose	Preparations intended for indoor use in the destruction of rats or mice and containing not more than 4% w/w of alpha-chloralose; preparations intended for indoor use in the destruction of rats or mice and containing not more than 8.5% w/w of alpha-chloralose, where the preparation is contained in a bag or sachet which is itself attached to the inside of a device in which the preparation is intended to be so used and the device contains not more than 3 g of the preparation
Arsenic compounds, the following: calcium arsenites, copper acetoarsenite, copper arsenates, copper arsenites, lead arsenates	Agricultural, horticultural and forestal insecticides or fungicides
Barium carbonate	Preparations for the destruction of rats or mice
Carbofuran	Preparations for use in agriculture, horticulture or forestry
Cycloheximide	Preparations for use in forestry
Dinitrocresols (DNOC), their compounds with a metal or a base	Preparations for use in agriculture, horticulture or forestry
Dinoseb, its compounds with a metal or a base	Preparations for use in agriculture, horticulture or forestry
Dinoterb	Preparations for use in agriculture, horticulture or forestry
Drazoxolon, its salts	Preparations for use in agriculture, horticulture or forestry
Endosulfan	Preparations for use in agriculture, horticulture or forestry
Endothal, its salts	Preparations for use in agriculture, horticulture or forestry
Endrin	Preparations for use in agriculture, horticulture or forestry
Fentin, compounds of	Preparations for use in agriculture, horticulture or forestry
Mercuric chloride	Agricultural, horticultural and forestal fungicides; treatments on seeds or bulbs; insecticides
Mercuric iodide	Agricultural, horticultural and forestal fungicides; treatments on seeds or bulbs

(continued overleaf)

Table A7.2 *(continued)*	
Poison	**Form to which sale is restricted**
Mercury, organic compounds of	Agricultural, horticultural and forestal fungicides; treatments on seeds or bulbs; solutions containing not more than 5% w/v of phenyl mercuric acetate for use in swimming baths
Metallic oxalates other than potassium quadroxalate	Photographic solutions or materials
Methomyl	Preparations for use in agriculture, horticulture or forestry
Nitrobenzene	Agricultural, horticultural and forestal insecticides
Oxamyl	Preparations for use in agriculture, horticulture or forestry
Paraquat, salts of	Preparations for use in agriculture, horticulture or forestry
Phosphorus compounds, the following: Azinphos-methyl, Chlorfenvinphos, Demephion, Demeton-S-methyl, Demeton-S-methylsulphone, Dialifos, Dichlorvos, Dioxathion, Disulfoton, Fonofos, Mecarbam, Mephosfolan, Methidathion, Mevinphos, Omethoate, Oxydemeton-methyl, Parathion, Phenkapton, Phorate, Phosphamidon, Pirimiphos-ethyl, Quinalphos, Thiometon, Thionazin, Triazophos, Vamidothion	Preparations for use in agriculture, horticulture or forestry
Thiofanox	Preparations for use in agriculture, horticulture or forestry
Zinc phosphide	Preparations for the destruction of rats or mice

Parathion
Phenkapton
Phorate
Phosphamidon
Pirimiphos-ethyl
Quinalphos
Thiometon
Thionazin
Triazophos
Vamidothion
Thiofanox.

Schedule 8 (Rule 24(1))

Form of application for entry in the list kept by a local authority under section 5 of the Act.

POISONS ACT 1972
(1972 c.66)

Form of application by a person to have his name entered in a local authority's list of persons entitled to sell non-medicinal poisons included in Part II of the Poisons List.

To the Chief Executive of...
I,..
being engaged in the business of ....
hereby apply to have my name entered in the list kept in pursuance of section 5 of the above Act in
respect of the following premises, namely, ...
....
....
as a person entitled to sell from those premises non-medicinal poisons included in Part II of the Poisons List.
I hereby nominate...
....
to act as my deputy (deputies) for the sale of non-medicinal poisons in accordance with Rule 10(1) of the Poisons Rules 1982
Signature of applicant...
Date...

Schedule 9 (Rule 24(2))

Format of the list to be kept by a local authority in pursuance of section 5(1) of the Act

POISONS ACT 1972
(1972 C3 66)
List of persons entitled to sell non-medicinal poisons in Part II of the Poisons List

Full name	Address of premises	Description of business carried on at the premises	Name of deputy (or deputies) permitted to sell

Schedule 10 (Rule 25)

Certificate for the purchase of non-medicinal poison (see pages 00 and 00–00).

For the purposes of section 3(2)(a)(i) of the Poisons Act 1972 I, the undersigned, a householder occupying (a) ....
hereby certify from my knowledge of (b) ....of
(a)...
that he is a person to whom (c)..may properly be supplied
I further certify that (d)...is the signature of the said
(b)...

....
Signature of the householder giving certificate
Date
(a) Insert full postal address
(b) Insert full name of intending purchaser.
(c) Insert name of poison.
(d) Intending purchaser to sign his name here.

Endorsement required by Rule 25 of the Poisons Rules 1982 to be made by a police officer in charge of a police station when, but only when, the householder giving the certificate is not known to the seller of the poison to be a responsible person of good character.

I hereby certify that in so far as is known to the police of the district in which * resides he is a responsible person of good character.

....Signature of Police Officer
....Rank
....In charge of Police Station at
Date

Office Stamp of

Police Station

*Insert full name of householder

giving the certificate.

Schedule 11 (Rule 26)

Form of entry to be made in a book to be kept by sellers of poisons in accordance with section 3(2)(b) of the Act (see p. 00).

Date of Sale	Name and quantity of poisons supplied	Purchaser's			Purpose for which the poison stated to be required	Date of certificate (if any)	Name and address of person giving certificate (if any)	Signature of purchaser or, where a signed order is permitted by the Poisons Rules 1982 the date of the signed order
		Name	Address	Business, trade or occupation				

Schedule 12 (Rule 12)

Restriction of sale and supply of strychnine and certain other poisons.

Part I

Cases of sale or supply to which provisions of Rule 12 do not apply:

1 The provisions of Rule 12 shall not apply in the case of the sale of substance to be exported to purchasers outside the UK;
2 The provisions of Rule 12 shall not apply in the case of the sale of a substance to a person or institution concerned with scientific education or research or chemical analysis, for the purposes of that education or research or analysis;
3 The provisions of Rule 12 shall not apply in the case of the sale of a substance by way of wholesale dealing;
4 Provisions relating to strychnine no longer applicable, see below;
5 The provisions of Rule 12 shall not apply in the case of the sale of strychnine, its salts or quaternary compounds to:
   a an officer of DEFRA who produces a written authority in the form set out in Part III of this Schedule issued by a person duly authorised by the Secretary of State for Environment, Food and Rural Affairs, or
   b an officer of the Department of Agriculture and Fisheries for Scotland or the Welsh Office who produces a written authority in the form set out in Part III of this Schedule issued by a person duly authorised by the Secretary of State, authorising the purchase by that officer of the substance for the purpose of killing foxes (other than foxes held in captivity) in an infected area within the meaning of the Rabies (Control) Order 1974; so, however, that the authority in question has been issued within the preceding 4 weeks and the quantity sold does not exceed the quantity specified therein;
6 The provisions of Rule 12 shall not apply in the case of the sale of fluoroacetic acid, it salts and fluoroacetamide:
   a to a person producing a certificate in form 'A' of the forms set out in Part IV of this Schedule issued by the proper officer of a local authority or port health authority certifying that the substance is required for use as a rodenticide by employees of that local authority or port health authority being such use,
      i in ships or sewers in such places as are identified in the certificate,
      ii in such drains as are identified in the certificate, being drains which are situated in restricted areas and wholly enclosed and to which all means of access are, when not in actual use, kept closed, or
      iii in such warehouses as are identified in the certificate, being warehouses which are situated in restricted dock areas and to which all means of access are, when not in actual use, kept securely locked or barred;

b to a person producing a certificate in form 'B' of the said forms issued by the proper officer of a local authority or port health authority certifying that the substance is required for use as a rodenticide by such person or by the employees of such body of persons, carrying on a business of pest control, as is named in the certificate, being such use as is mentioned in paragraph 1a(i) or 1a(ii) of this paragraph; or

c to a person producing a certificate in form 'B' of the said forms issued, in England, by a person duly authorised by the DEFRA or, in Scotland or Wales, by a person duly authorised by the Secretary of State certifying that the substance is required for use as a rodenticide by officers of DEFRA, of the Department of Agriculture and Fisheries for Scotland, or of the Welsh Office, being such use as is mentioned in sub-paragraph (1)(a)(i) or (ii) of this paragraph; so, however, that the certificate in question has been issued within the preceding three months and the quantity sold does not exceed the quantity specified therein;

7 Provisions relating to thallium no longer applicable, see below;

8 Provisions relating to zinc phosphide no longer applicable, see below.

In this list, the following meanings are used.

Dock area means an area in the vicinity of a dock as defined in section 57(1) of the Harbours Act 1964.

Drain and *sewer* have the meanings assigned to them by section 343(1) of the Public Health Act 1936.

Local authority in Greater London means the Common Council of the City of London or the council of a London borough, elsewhere in England or Wales means the council of a county or a district and, in Scotland, means an islands or district council.

Port health authority means, in England or Wales, the port health authority of the Port of London or a port health authority for the purposes of the Public Health Act 1936.

Restricted, in relation to any area, means controlled in such manner that access to the area by unauthorised persons is in normal circumstances prevented.

Paragraphs 4, 7 and 8 relate to exemptions for the sale or supply of strychnine for the control of moles (see p.00), for the sale of thallium salts and for the sale of zinc phosphide, respectively. Since these poisons no longer have Chemicals Regulation Directorate approval, these paragraphs cease to be relevant.

Part II

Strychnine is no longer approved for sale or supply for controlling moles so this part ceases to be relevant.

Part III

Form of authority for the purchase of strychnine or a salt or quaternary compound thereof for killing foxes.

For the purposes of Rule 12(1) of the Poisons Rules 1982 and of paragraph 5 of part I of Schedule 12 thereto I hereby authorise...
(an officer of [the Secretary of State for Environment, Food and Rural Affairs] [the Department of Agriculture and Fisheries for Scotland] [the Welsh Office]) to purchase within four weeks of the date hereof .... of............................ for the purpose of killing foxes (other than foxes held in captivity) in the following infected area (within the meaning of the Rabies (Control) Order 1974), namely the infected area in ....(locality).

....
A person authorised by [DEFRA]
[the Secretary of State for Scotland]
[the Secretary of State for Wales]

Date ....

Part IV

Forms of certificate authorising the purchase of fluoroacetic acid, a salt there of or fluoroacetamide as a rodenticide.

Form A

Certificate authorising the purchase of fluoroacetic acid, a salt thereof or fluoracetamide as a rodenticide for use by employees of a local authority or a port health authority (in Scotland, a port local authority or joint port authority)

For the purpose of Rule 12(2) of the Poisons Rules 1982 and of paragraph 6 of Part I Schedule 12 thereto, I hereby certify that ....
of.. is required for use by employees of ....
as a rodenticide in [ships][sewers] situated at ....
[the following warehouses] viz ....
situated in the restricted dock area at ....
being warehouses to which all means of access are, when not in actual use, kept securely locked or barred.
[the following warehouses] viz ....
situated in restricted dock area at..
being drains which are wholly enclosed and to which all means of access are, when not in actual use, kept closed.

....
The officer appointed for this purpose by
....

Date..

Part V

The sale or supply of salts of thallium for killing rats, mice or moles is no longer approved moles so this part ceases to be relevant (see p. 00).

Appendix 8

Classification and labelling of chemicals

The Chemical (Hazard Information and Packaging for Supply) Regulations 2009 (SI 2009 No. 716, as amended) are described in chapter 20. An Authorised and Approved List of Dangerous Substances is set out in *Approved Classification and Labelling Guide*, 6th edn (the CHIP Regulations).[1]

Many commonly used substances have already been classified and agreed at European level. These classifications must be used. These agreed, or 'harmonised' classifications used to be published in the Approved Supply List. However, because the law has changed, the Approved Supply List is no longer printed. A list of all harmonised classifications can now be found in Table 3.1 and Table 3.2 in Part 3 of Annex VI of the CLP Regulations.[2]

The classification of and symbols for substances dangerous for supply are set out in Schedule 1 to the CHIP Regulations (table A8.1).

It should be noted that under the CLP Regulations, the warning symbols will be changing, for example,

[1]Health and Safety Executive (2009). *Approved Classification and Labelling Guide*, 6th edn. London: HSE Books
[2]Classification, Labelling and Packaging Regulation EC 1272/2008

Table A8.1 Symbol, abbreviation/description of hazard

Symbol	Abbreviation	Hazard	Description of hazard
Physicochemical hazards			
	E	Explosive	Chemicals that explode
	O	Oxidising	Chemicals that react exothermically with other chemicals
	F+	Extremely flammable	Chemicals that have an extremely low flash point and boiling point, and gases that catch fire in contact with air
	F	Highly flammable	Chemicals that may catch fire in contact with air, only need brief contact with an ignition source, have a very low flash point or evolve highly flammable gases in contact with water
Health hazards			
	T+	Very toxic	Chemicals that at very low levels cause damage to health
	T	Toxic	Chemicals that at low levels cause damage to health
	Carc Cat 1	Category 1 carcinogens	Chemicals that may cause cancer or increase its incidence
	Carc Cat 2	Category 2 carcinogens	Chemicals that may cause cancer or increase its incidence
	Carc Cat 3	Category 3 carcinogens	Chemicals that may cause cancer or increase its incidence
	Muta Cat 1	Category 1 mutagens	Chemicals that induce heritable genetic defects or increase their incidence
	Muta Cat 2	Category 2 mutagens	Chemicals that induce heritable genetic defects or increase their incidence

(continued overleaf)

Table A8.1 (continued)

Symbol	Abbreviation	Hazard	Description of hazard
	Muta Cat 3	Category 3 mutagens	Chemicals that induce heritable genetic defects or increase their incidence
	Repr Cat 1	Category 1 reproductive toxins	Chemicals that produce or increase the incidence of non-heritable effects in progeny and/or an impairment in reproductive functions or capacity
	Repr Cat 2	Category 2 reproductive toxins	Chemicals that produce or increase the incidence of non-heritable effects in progeny and/or an impairment in reproductive functions or capacity
	Repr Cat 3	Category 3 reproductive toxins	Chemicals that produce or increase the incidence of non-heritable effects in progeny and/or an impairment in reproductive functions or capacity
	Xn	Harmful	Chemicals that may cause damage to health
	C	Corrosive	Chemicals that may destroy living tissue on contact
	Xi	Irritant	Chemicals that may cause inflammation to the skin or other mucous membranes
Environmental hazards			
	N	Dangerous for the environment	Chemicals that may present an immediate or delayed danger to one or more components of the environment

Indication of particular risks: R-phrase labelling

The R-phrase indicators are given in table A8.2.

Indication of safety precautions required: S-phrase labelling

The S-phrase indicators are given in table A8.3.

Table A8.2 The R-phrase indicators

R number	Indication
R1	Explosive when dry
R2	Risk of explosion by shock, friction, fire or other sources of ignition
R3	Extreme risk of explosion by shock, friction, fire or other sources of ignition
R4	Forms very sensitive explosive metallic compounds
R5	Heating may cause an explosion
R6	Explosive with or without contact with air
R7	May cause fire
R8	Contact with combustible material may cause fire
R9	Explosive when mixed with combustible material
R10	Flammable
R11	Highly flammable
R12	Extremely flammable
R14	Reacts violently with water
R14/15	Reacts violently with water, liberating extremely flammable gases
R15	Contact with water liberates extremely flammable gases
R15/29	Contact with water liberates toxic, extremely flammable gases
R16	Explosive when mixed with oxidising substances
R17	Spontaneously flammable in air
R18	In use, may form flammable/explosive vapour–air mixture
R19	May form explosive peroxides
R20	Harmful by inhalation
R20/21	Harmful by inhalation and in contact with skin
R20/21/22	Harmful by inhalation, in contact with skin and if swallowed
R20/22	Harmful by inhalation and if swallowed

(continued overleaf)

Table A8.2 (continued)

R number	Indication
R21	Harmful in contact with skin
R21/22	Harmful in contact with skin and if swallowed
R22	Harmful if swallowed
R23	Toxic by inhalation
R23/24	Toxic by inhalation and in contact with skin
R23/24/25	Toxic by inhalation, in contact with skin and if swallowed
R23/25	Toxic by inhalation and if swallowed
R24	Toxic in contact with skin
R24/25	Toxic in contact with skin and if swallowed
R25	Toxic if swallowed
R26	Very toxic by inhalation
R26/27	Very toxic by inhalation and in contact with skin
R26/27/28	Very toxic by inhalation, in contact with skin and if swallowed
R26/28	Very toxic by inhalation and if swallowed
R27	Very toxic in contact with skin
R27/28	Very toxic in contact with skin and if swallowed
R28	Very toxic if swallowed
R29	Contact with water liberates toxic gas
R30	Can become highly flammable in use
R31	Contact with acids liberates toxic gas
R32	Contact with acids liberates very toxic gas
R33	Danger of cumulative effects
R34	Causes burns
R35	Causes severe burns
R36	Irritating to eyes

(continued overleaf)

Table A8.2 *(continued)*

R number	Indication
R36/37	Irritating to eyes and respiratory system
R36/37/38	Irritating to eyes, respiratory system and skin
R36/38	Irritating to eyes and skin
R37	Irritating to respiratory system
R37/38	Irritating to respiratory system and skin
R38	Irritating to skin
R39	Danger of very serious irreversible effects
R39/23	Toxic: danger of very serious irreversible effects through inhalation
R39/23/24	Toxic: danger of very serious irreversible effects through inhalation and in contact with skin
R39/23/24/25	Toxic: danger of very serious irreversible effects through inhalation, in contact with skin and if swallowed
R39/23/25	Toxic: danger of very serious irreversible effects through inhalation and if swallowed
R39/24	Toxic: danger of very serious irreversible effects in contact with skin
R39/24/25	Toxic: danger of very serious irreversible effects in contact with skin and if swallowed
R39/25	Toxic: danger of very serious irreversible effects if swallowed
R39/26	Very toxic: danger of very serious irreversible effects through inhalation
R39/26/27	Very toxic: danger of very serious irreversible effects through inhalation and in contact with skin
R39/26/27/28	Very toxic: danger of very serious irreversible effects through inhalation, in contact with skin and if swallowed
R39/26/28	Very toxic: danger of very serious irreversible effects through inhalation and if swallowed
R39/27	Very toxic: danger of very serious irreversible effects in contact with skin
R37/38	Irritating to respiratory system and skin
R38	Irritating to skin

(continued overleaf)

Table A8.2 (continued)

R number	Indication
R39	Danger of very serious irreversible effects
R39/23	Toxic: danger of very serious irreversible effects through inhalation
R39/23/24	Toxic: danger of very serious irreversible effects through inhalation and in contact with skin
R39/23/24/25	Toxic: danger of very serious irreversible effects through inhalation, in contact with skin and if swallowed
R39/23/25	Toxic: danger of very serious irreversible effects through inhalation and if swallowed
R39/24	Toxic: danger of very serious irreversible effects in contact with skin
R39/24/25	Toxic: danger of very serious irreversible effects in contact with skin and if swallowed
R39/25	Toxic: danger of very serious irreversible effects if swallowed
R39/26	Very toxic: danger of very serious irreversible effects through inhalation
R39/26/27	Very toxic: danger of very serious irreversible effects through inhalation and in contact with skin
R39/26/27/28	Very toxic: danger of very serious irreversible effects through inhalation, in contact with skin and if swallowed
R39/26/28	Very toxic: danger of very serious irreversible effects through inhalation and if swallowed
R39/27	Very toxic: danger of very serious irreversible effects in contact with skin
R39/27/28	Very toxic: danger of very serious irreversible effects in contact with skin and if swallowed
R39/28	Very toxic: danger of very serious irreversible effects if swallowed
R40	Limited evidence of a carcinogenic effect
R41	Risk of serious damage to eyes
R42	May cause sensitisation by inhalation
R43	May cause sensitisation by skin contact
R42/43	May cause sensitisation by inhalation and skin contact
R44	Risk of explosion if heated under confinement

(continued overleaf)

Table A8.2 *(continued)*

R number	Indication
R45	May cause cancer
R46	May cause heritable genetic damage
R48	Danger of serious damage to health by prolonged exposure
R48/20	Harmful: danger of serious damage to health by prolonged exposure through inhalation
R48/20/21	Harmful: danger of serious damage to health by prolonged exposure through inhalation and in contact with skin
R48/20/21/22	Harmful: danger of serious damage to health by prolonged exposure through inhalation, in contact with skin and if swallowed
R48/20/22	Harmful: danger of serious damage to health by prolonged exposure through inhalation and if swallowed
R48/21	Harmful: danger of serious damage to health by prolonged exposure in contact with skin
R48/21/22	Harmful: danger of serious damage to health by prolonged exposure in contact with skin and if swallowed
R48/22	Harmful: danger of serious damage to health by prolonged exposure if swallowed
R48/23	Toxic: danger of serious damage to health by prolonged exposure through inhalation
R48/23/24	Toxic: danger of serious damage to health by prolonged exposure through inhalation and in contact with skin
R48/23/24/25	Toxic: danger of serious damage to health by prolonged exposure through inhalation, in contact with skin and if swallowed
R48/23/25	Toxic: danger of serious damage to health by prolonged exposure through inhalation and if swallowed
R48/24	Toxic: danger of serious damage to health by prolonged exposure in contact with skin
R48/24/25	Toxic: danger of serious damage to health by prolonged exposure in contact with skin and if swallowed
R48/25	Toxic: danger of serious damage to health by prolonged exposure if swallowed
R49	May cause cancer by inhalation

(continued overleaf)

Table A8.2 *(continued)*

R number	Indication
R50	Very toxic to aquatic organisms
R50/53	Very toxic to aquatic organisms, may cause long-term adverse effects in the aquatic environment
R51	Toxic to aquatic organisms
R51/53	Toxic to aquatic organisms, may cause long-term adverse effects in the aquatic environment
R52	Harmful to aquatic organisms
R52/53	Harmful to aquatic organisms, may cause long-term adverse effects in the aquatic environment
R53	May cause long-term adverse effects in the aquatic environment
R54	Toxic to flora
R55	Toxic to fauna
R56	Toxic to soil organisms
R57	Toxic to bees
R58	May cause long-term adverse effects in the environment
R59	Dangerous for the ozone layer
R60	May impair fertility
R61	May cause harm to the unborn child
R62	Possible risk of impaired fertility
R63	Possible risk of harm to the unborn child
R64	May cause harm to breast-fed babies
R65	Harmful: may cause lung damage if swallowed
R66	Repeated exposure may cause skin dryness or cracking
R67	Vapours may cause drowsiness and dizziness
R68	Possible risk of irreversible effects
R68/20	Harmful: possible risk of irreversible effects through inhalation

(continued overleaf)

Table A8.2 *(continued)*

R number	Indication
R68/20/21	Harmful: possible risk of irreversible effects through inhalation and in contact with skin
R68/20/21/22	Harmful: possible risk of irreversible effects through inhalation, in contact with skin and if swallowed
R68/20/22	Harmful: possible risk of irreversible effects through inhalation and if swallowed
R68/21	Harmful: possible risk of irreversible effects in contact with skin
R68/21/22	Harmful: possible risk of irreversible effects in contact with skin and if swallowed
R68/22	Harmful: possible risk of irreversible effects if swallowed

Table A8.3 The S-phrase indicators

S number	Indication
S1	Keep locked up
S(1/2)	Keep locked up and out of the reach of children
S2	Keep out of the reach of children
S3	Keep in a cool place
S3/7	Keep container tightly closed in a cool place
S3/7/9	Keep container tightly closed in a cool, well-ventilated place
S3/9/14	Keep in a cool, well-ventilated place away from .... (incompatible materials to be indicated by the manufacturer)
S3/9/14/49	Keep only in the original container in a cool, well-ventilated place away from ... (incompatible materials to be indicated by the manufacturer)
S3/9/49	Keep only in the original container in a cool, well-ventilated place
S3/14	Keep in a cool place away from ... (incompatible materials to be indicated by the manufacturer)
S4	Keep away from living quarters

(continued overleaf)

Table A8.3 *(continued)*	
S number	**Indication**
S5	Keep contents under … (appropriate liquid to be specified by the manufacturer)
S6	Keep under … (inert gas to be specified by the manufacturer)
S7	Keep container tightly closed
S7/8	Keep container tightly closed and dry
S7/9	Keep container tightly closed and in a well-ventilated place
S7/47	Keep container tightly closed and at temperature not exceeding … °C (to be specified by the manufacturer)
S8	Keep container dry
S9	Keep container in a well-ventilated place
S12	Do not keep the container sealed
S13	Keep away from food, drink and animal feeding stuffs
S14	Keep away from … (incompatible materials to be indicated by the manufacturer)
S15	Keep away from heat
S16	Keep away from sources of ignition – No smoking
S17	Keep away from combustible material
S18	Handle and open container with care
S20	When using do not eat or drink
S20/21	When using do not eat, drink or smoke
S21	When using do not smoke
S22	Do not breathe dust
S23	Do not breathe gas/fumes/vapour/spray (appropriate wording to be specified by the manufacturer)
S24	Avoid contact with skin
S24/25	Avoid contact with skin and eyes
S25	Avoid contact with eyes

(continued overleaf)

Table A8.3 *(continued)*

S number	Indication
S26	In case of contact with eyes, rinse immediately with plenty of water and seek medical advice
S27	Take off immediately all contaminated clothing
S27/28	After contact with skin, take off immediately all contaminated clothing, and wash immediately with plenty of ... (to be specified by the manufacturer)
S28	After contact with skin, wash immediately with plenty of ... (to be specified by the manufacturer)
S29	Do not empty into drains
S29/35	Do not empty into drains; dispose of this material and its container in a safe way
S29/56	Do not empty into drains, dispose of this material and its container at hazardous or special waste collection point
S30	Never add water to this product
S33	Take precautionary measures against static discharges
S35	This material and its container must be disposed of in a safe way
S36	Wear suitable protective clothing
S36/37	Wear suitable protective clothing and gloves
S36/37/39	Wear suitable protective clothing, gloves and eye/face protection
S36/39	Wear suitable protective clothing and eye/face protection
S37	Wear suitable gloves
S37/39	Wear suitable gloves and eye/face protection
S38	In case of insufficient ventilation wear suitable respiratory equipment
S39	Wear eye/face protection
S40	To clean the floor and all objects contaminated by this material use ... (to be specified by the manufacturer)
S41	In case of fire and/or explosion do not breathe fumes
S42	During fumigation/spraying wear suitable respiratory equipment (appropriate wording to be specified by the manufacturer)

(continued overleaf)

Table A8.3 *(continued)*

S number	Indication
S43	In case of fire use . . . (indicate in the space the precise type of fire-fighting equipment. If water increases the risk add - Never use water)
S45	In case of accident or if you feel unwell seek medical advice immediately (show the label where possible)
S46	If swallowed, seek medical advice immediately and show this container or label
S47	Keep at temperature not exceeding . . . $^{\circ}$C (to be specified by the manufacturer)
S47/49	Keep only in the original container at temperature not exceeding . . . $^{\circ}$C (to be specified by the manufacturer)
S48	Keep wet with . . . (appropriate material to be specified by the manufacturer)
S49	Keep only in the original container
S50	Do not mix with . . . (to be specified by the manufacturer)
S51	Use only in well-ventilated areas
S52	Not recommended for interior use on large surface areas
S53	Avoid exposure – obtain special instructions before use
S56	Dispose of this material and its container at hazardous or special waste collection point
S57	Use appropriate containment to avoid environmental contamination
S59	Refer to manufacturer/supplier for information on recovery/recycling
S60	This material and its container must be disposed of as hazardous waste
S61	Avoid release to the environment. Refer to special instructions/safety data sheet
S62	If swallowed, do not induce vomiting: seek medical advice immediately and show this container or label
S63	In case of accident by inhalation: remove casualty to fresh air and keep at rest
S64	If swallowed, rinse mouth with water (only if the person is conscious)

Appendix 9

Standards for registered pharmacies September 2012

The following extract is from the GPhC regarding standards at September 2012.

Introduction

The purpose of these standards is to create and maintain the right environment, both organisational and physical, for the safe and effective practice of pharmacy. The standards apply to all pharmacies registered with the GPhC.

We recognise that for anyone operating a registered pharmacy there will always be competing demands. These may be professional, managerial, legal or commercial. However, medicines are not ordinary items of commerce. Along with pharmacy services, the supply of medicines is a fundamental healthcare service. Pharmacy owners and superintendent pharmacists must take account of this when applying these standards.

Responsibility for meeting the standards lies with the pharmacy owner. If the registered pharmacy is owned by a 'body corporate' (for example a company or NHS organisation) the superintendent pharmacist also carries responsibility.

Pharmacy owners and superintendent pharmacists have the same set of responsibilities; a corporate owner does not avoid responsibility by employing a superintendent. Both are fully responsible for making sure that the standards are met. All those responsible need to take into account the nature of the pharmacy and the services provided and, most importantly, the needs of patients and the public. We also expect them to be familiar with all relevant guidance. As well as meeting our standards, the pharmacy owner and superintendent pharmacist must make sure they comply with all legal requirements including those covering medicines legislation, health and safety, employment, data protection and equalities legislation.

Pharmacy owners and superintendent pharmacists must make sure that all staff, including non-pharmacists, involved in the management of pharmacy services are familiar with the standards and understand the importance of their being met. All registered professionals working in a registered pharmacy should also be familiar with these standards; and pharmacists and pharmacy technicians must understand that they have a professional responsibility to raise concerns if they believe the standards are not being met.

The standards can also be used by patients and the public so that they know what they should expect when they receive pharmacy services from registered pharmacies.

Throughout this document we use the term 'pharmacy services'. This covers all pharmacy-related services provided by a registered pharmacy including the management of medicines, provision of advice and referral, clinical services such as vaccination services, and services provided to care homes.

Throughout this document we use the term 'staff'. This includes agency and contract workers, as well as employees and other people who are involved in the provision of pharmacy services by a registered pharmacy.

In this document we use the term 'you'. This means:

- a pharmacist who owns a pharmacy as a sole trader, and
- a pharmacist who owns a pharmacy as a partner in a partnership, and
- a pharmacist who is the appointed superintendent pharmacist for a body corporate, and
- the body corporate itself.

In some limited circumstances (for example following death or bankruptcy), a representative can take the role of the pharmacy owner. In these cases, the appointed representative will be responsible for making sure these standards are met.

Standards for registered pharmacies

We have grouped the standards under five principles. The principles are the backbone of our regulatory approach and are all equally important.

The principles

Principle 1. The governance arrangements safeguard the health, safety and wellbeing of patients and the public.

Principle 2. Staff are empowered and competent to safeguard the health, safety and wellbeing of patients and the public.

Principle 3. The environment and condition of the premises from which pharmacy services are provided, and any associated premises, safeguard the health, safety and wellbeing of patients and the public.

Principle 4. The way in which pharmacy services, including the management of medicines and medical devices, are delivered safeguards the health, safety and wellbeing of patients and the public.

Principle 5. The equipment and facilities used in the provision of pharmacy services safeguard the health, safety and wellbeing of patients and the public.

The standards under each principle are requirements that must be met when you operate a registered pharmacy. Responsibility for meeting the standards lies with the pharmacy owner. If the registered pharmacy is owned by a 'body corporate' (for example a company or NHS organisation) the superintendent pharmacist also carries responsibility. Pharmacy owners and superintendent pharmacists have the same set of responsibilities; a corporate owner does not avoid responsibility by employing a superintendent. Both are fully responsible for making sure that the standards are met.

If a registered pharmacy is owned by a body corporate, the superintendent must have the authority to:

- comply with their professional and legal obligations, and
- use their professional judgement in the best interests of patients and the public.

Applying the standards

The principles for registered pharmacies, and the standards that must be met, are all equally important. Therefore, you should read all the standards in their entirety. Pharmacy owners, superintendent pharmacists and other pharmacy professionals should also be familiar with the GPhC's Standards of Conduct, Ethics and Performance.

We know that a pharmacy owner and superintendent pharmacist may be accountable for one, a few or a large number of registered pharmacies. We expect the pharmacy owner and superintendent pharmacist to make sure that these standards are met whatever the number of pharmacies they are accountable for.

Principle 1

The governance arrangements safeguard the health, safety and wellbeing of patients and the public.

'Governance arrangements' includes having clear definitions of the roles and accountabilities of the people involved in providing and managing pharmacy services. It also includes the arrangements for managing risks, and the way the registered pharmacy is managed and operated.

Standards

1.1 The risks associated with providing pharmacy services are identified and managed.

1.2 The safety and quality of pharmacy services are reviewed and monitored.

1.3 Pharmacy services are provided by staff with clearly defined roles and clear lines of accountability.

1.4 Feedback and concerns about the pharmacy, services and staff can be raised by individuals and organisations, and these are taken into account and action taken where appropriate.

1.5 Appropriate indemnity or insurance arrangements are in place for the pharmacy services provided.

1.6 All necessary records for the safe provision of pharmacy services are kept and maintained.

1.7 Information is managed to protect the privacy, dignity and confidentiality of patients and the public who receive pharmacy services.

1.8 Children and vulnerable adults are safeguarded.

Principle 2

Staff are empowered and competent to safeguard the health, safety and wellbeing of patients and the public. The staff you employ and the people you work with are key to the safe and effective practice of pharmacy. Staff members, and anyone involved in providing pharmacy services, must be competent and empowered to safeguard the health, safety and wellbeing of patients and the public in all that they do.

Standards

2.1 There are enough staff, suitably qualified and skilled, for the safe and effective provision of the pharmacy services provided.

2.2 Staff have the appropriate skills, qualifications and competence for their role and the tasks they carry out, or are working under the supervision of another person while they are in training.

2.3 Staff can comply with their own professional and legal obligations and are empowered to exercise their professional judgement in the interests of patients and the public.

2.4 There is a culture of openness, honesty and learning.

2.5 Staff are empowered to provide feedback and raise concerns about meeting these standards and other aspects of pharmacy services.

2.6 Incentives or targets do not compromise the health, safety or wellbeing of patients and the public, or the professional judgement of staff.

Principle 3

The environment and condition of the premises from which pharmacy services are provided, and any associated premises, safeguard the health, safety and wellbeing of patients and the public. It is important that patients and the public receive pharmacy services from premises that are suitable for the services being provided and which protect and maintain their health, safety and wellbeing. To achieve this you must make sure that all premises where pharmacy services are provided are safe and suitable. Any associated premises, for example non-registered premises used to store medicines, must also comply with these standards where applicable.

Standards

3.1 Premises are safe, clean, properly maintained and suitable for the pharmacy services provided.

3.2 Premises protect the privacy, dignity and confidentiality of patients and the public who receive pharmacy services.

3.3 Premises are maintained to a level of hygiene appropriate to the pharmacy services provided.

3.4 Premises are secure and safeguarded from unauthorised access.

3.5 Pharmacy services are provided in an environment that is appropriate for the provision of healthcare.

Principle 4

The way in which pharmacy services, including the management of medicines and medical devices, are delivered safeguards the health, safety and wellbeing of patients and the public. 'Pharmacy services' covers all pharmacy-related services provided by a registered pharmacy including the management of medicines, advice and referral, and the wide range of clinical services pharmacies provide. The management of medicines includes arrangements for obtaining, keeping, handling, using and supplying medicinal products and medical devices, as well as security and waste management.

Medicines and medical devices are not ordinary commercial items. The way they are managed is fundamental to ensuring the health, safety and wellbeing of patients and the public who receive pharmacy services.

Standards

4.1 The pharmacy services provided are accessible to patients and the public.

4.2 Pharmacy services are managed and delivered safely and effectively.

4.3 Medicines and medical devices are:
- obtained from a reputable source
- safe and fit for purpose
- stored securely
- safeguarded from unauthorised access
- supplied to the patient safely
- disposed of safely and securely.

4.4 Concerns are raised when it is suspected that medicines or medical devices are not fit for purpose.

Principle 5

The equipment and facilities used in the provision of pharmacy services safeguard the health, safety and wellbeing of patients and the public. The availability of safe and suitable equipment and facilities is fundamental to the provision of pharmacy services and is essential if staff are to safeguard the health, safety and wellbeing of patients and the public when providing effective pharmacy services.

Standards

5.1 Equipment and facilities needed to provide pharmacy services are readily available.

5.2 Equipment and facilities are:
- obtained from a reputable source
- safe to use and fit for purpose
- stored securely
- safeguarded from unauthorised access
- appropriately maintained

5.3 Equipment and facilities are used in a way that protects the privacy and dignity of the patients and the public who receive pharmacy services.

Appendix 10

General Pharmaceutical Council referral criteria from the Investigating Committee

The following extract is from the GPhC regarding the Investigating Committee Referral Criteria in respect of an allegation capable of being referred, which came into effect 27 September 2010.

Here IC is the Investigating Committee and FtP is Fitness to Practice

Introduction

1.1 The objective of this guidance is to provide assistance and to set out the referral criteria that the Investigating Committee (IC) must have regard to before disposing of any allegation before it regarding the pharmacy professional or company/section 80 party where relevant (referred to throughout as 'the person concerned'). This guidance should be viewed as a 'living document' which may be updated and revised in line with case law and other developments in regulation and elsewhere.

1.2 The guidance has been developed in accordance with the General Pharmaceutical Council's (GPhC's) vision and strategy to be risk based and proportionate. Part 6 of the Pharmacy Order 2010 ('the 2010 Order'), supplemented by the General Pharmaceutical Council (Fitness to Practise and Disqualification etc. Rules) Order of Council 2010 ('the 2010 FtP Rules') makes provision for the fitness to practise procedures of the GPhC. One of the principal functions of the GPhC, as set out in Article 4 of the 2010 Order, is to ensure the continued fitness to practise of registrants. The Investigating Committee is a crucial element of the FtP Committee structure.

Article 53 of the 2010 Order provides that where a matter is referred to the IC by the Registrar, the Committee must decide whether the allegation ought to be considered by the FtP Committee. In addition, rule 9(3)(ii) of the 2010 FtP Rules requires the IC referral criteria to be 'published'. A copy of the IC referral criteria is available on the GPhC website.

Procedure

2.1 The GPhC's fitness to practise procedures recognise that an allegation of impairment requires an initial consideration to determine the most appropriate method of disposal.

2.1.2 The IC's role is to decide whether there is a real prospect of impairment of fitness to practise being established before the FtP Committee. The 'real prospect' test applies to both factual allegations and if proved, whether the facts would amount to impairment of fitness to practise. The IC meets in private and does not hear oral evidence. However, before disposing of any allegation the IC must consider all documents and recommendations placed before it by the Registrar and any written representations received from the person concerned.

2.1.3 The role of the IC is primarily that of a screening role. While the IC is entitled, as part of its function, to assess the materiality and weight of the evidence, it does not have the function of making judgments on nor should it seek to resolve substantial conflicts of evidence. It will not, therefore make findings of fact on the substantive issues arising in the allegation. Nonetheless, its practices and procedures are sufficiently rigorous to ensure that all allegations are thoroughly considered. The Committee is permitted to direct that further investigations are undertaken. The Committee is required to take into account all of the representations which have been made. It will be supported by legal advisers, and in appropriate cases, by clinical advisers.

The IC should give reasons for all of its decisions.

Referral criteria

3.1 In considering individual cases the IC should have regard to the seven principles set out in the Standards for Conduct, Ethics and Performance.

3.1.2 Regard should also be had to the fitness to practise criteria contained within rule 5 of the 2010 FtP rules. This states (paragraph (1)) that the FtP Committee:' ... must have regard to the criteria specified in paragraph (2) or, where appropriate, (3), or, where appropriate, paragraphs (2) and (3), when deciding, in the case of any registrant, whether or not the requirements as to fitness to practise are met in relation to that registrant.

(2) In relation to evidence about the conduct or behaviour of the registrant which might cast doubt on whether the requirements as to fitness to practise are met in relation to the registrant, the Committee must have regard to whether or not that conduct or behaviour

a   presents an actual or potential risk to patients or to the public,

b   has brought, or might bring, the profession of pharmacy into disrepute,

c   has breached one of the fundamental principles of the profession of pharmacy, or

d   shows that the integrity of the registrant can no longer be relied upon.

(3) In relation to evidence about the registrant's physical or mental health which might cast doubt on whether the requirements as to fitness to practise are met in relation to the registrant, the Committee must have regard to whether or not that evidence shows actual or potential

a   self-harm, or

b   harm to patients or to the public.

3.2   In addition to 3.1 and 3.1.2 above, regard should also be had to the following criteria listed below. It is important to bear in mind that this does not purport to be an exhaustive list and the IC may properly take into account all relevant factors relating to the particular circumstances of an individual case. The IC in performing its task should have regard to the following:

Conduct

Conduct which involves discrimination on grounds prohibited by law.

The extent of (or if relevant, the lack) of cooperation by the person concerned with any inquiries into their conduct.

How long ago the relevant conduct took place.

Whether the relevant conduct involves an abuse of trust or position.

Whether the person concerned has not complied with advice given by an Inspector.

The extent to which the conduct is characteristic of the person concerned or is indicative of a propensity to commit such conduct.

Any efforts (or if relevant, the lack) of rehabilitation by the person concerned since the conduct took place.

The person concerned's insight (or lack of insight, where relevant) in relation to their misconduct.

Any warnings, sanctions or advice relating to the same or similar conduct given by a pharmacy regulatory body in the 5 years preceding the conduct.

Whether there has been an attempt to impede/obstruct a relevant investigation into the alleged conduct.

Whether the person concerned put their own interests, or those of a third party, before those of their patients.

Whether there has been a failure to maintain appropriate professional boundaries in a relationship with patients and/or others.

Conduct which may indicate an intention to disregard provisions of the 2010 Order and legislation made under it.

Whether there may have been a deliberate or serious breach of the Standards of Conduct, Ethics and Performance and/or other supplementary guidance published by the GPhC.

Whether the person concerned damaged or put at significant risk the best interests of patients by failing to communicate appropriately with patients or others.

Physical or mental health

Whether the condition is episodic or recurrent.

Whether the condition has been sustained over a protracted period of time.

Whether the person concerned has sought help or has complied (or has not, where relevant) with treatment or support for their condition.

The person concerned's insight (or lack of insight, where relevant) in relation to their condition.

Any previous findings of misconduct in relation to the person concerned's physical or mental health.

Whether there has been a breach or failure to comply with any previous written undertakings.

Whether there has been an attempt to deliberately conceal the condition.

3.2.1 The IC should also take into account public interest considerations. This may include (but is not limited to) the maintenance of public confidence in the profession; declaring and upholding proper standards of conduct; and the protection of members of the public. These in turn will need to be balanced against the person concerned's own interests.

Equality and diversity statement

The GPhC is committed to promoting equality and valuing diversity and to operating procedures and processes which are fair, objective, transparent and free from unlawful discrimination.

Review

This Referral Criteria document shall be the subject of a regular review, to reflect developments and changes in the IC's practices and procedures. The first review took place after six months of the operation of the Investigating Committee and, thereafter, on a regular basis.

Appendix 11

General Pharmaceutical Council prosecution policy

The following extract is from the GPhC regarding the prosecution policy at September 2012.

Alternatives to prosecution

1.1 Consistent with the GPhC's values and regulatory principles, we always aim to select the most proportionate and cost-effective approach to addressing problems. In the case of criminal matters within our remit this usually means seeking alternatives to prosecution, including securing voluntary compliance and non-criminal regulatory interventions, for example fitness to practise proceedings where appropriate.

1.2 GPhC standards and regulatory proceedings are specifically designed as effective mechanisms for regulating the conduct and standards of pharmacy professionals. Where it appears that a relevant offence[1] may have been committed by a GPhC registrant, regulatory proceedings are more likely in most cases to provide an effective and proportionate mechanism for challenging that behaviour than criminal prosecution.

1.3 Exceptions to this general approach are possible and should be considered where a registrant's conduct demonstrates that in their particular case a regulatory intervention may not be an effective and adequate response (which could be the case, for example, if a registrant commits an offence by practising while suspended from the Register, thereby demonstrating a disregard for regulatory decisions).

1.4 In the case of a relevant offence which appears to have been committed by a non-GPhC registrant, then the institution of criminal proceedings may be the only enforcement tool available to the GPhC. By definition,

[1] An offence under the Pharmacy Order 2010 or an offence under the Medicines Act or the Poisons Act within the GPhC's enforcement remit

a person who is not registered with the GPhC is beyond the reach of GPhC regulation, including fitness to practise proceedings. This is equally true whether or not the person has ever been a registrant; a person who is removed from the Register and then commits an offence by continuing to practise is just as beyond the GPhC's reach as a person who masquerades as a registrant. In both cases the GPhC has a role in upholding the integrity of the Register by challenging this behaviour and seeking to stop it. A criminal prosecution may be the only option – and therefore the right and proportionate response – in such circumstances.

Deciding whether to prosecute

2.1 In cases in which it appears that a criminal prosecution may be an effective and proportionate response to alleged criminal behaviour, in England and Wales we apply the Code for Crown Prosecutors, which involves a two stage test examining firstly a review of all of the relevant evidence to decide whether there is a 'realistic prospect of conviction' and, if there is, a second stage to determine whether prosecution is in the public interest. In cases in which it appears that a criminal prosecution in Scotland may be an effective and proportionate response to alleged criminal behaviour we use the Scottish Prosecution Code to help us decide whether to refer a matter to the Crown Office and Procurator Fiscal Service, for them to consider whether to initiate a prosecution.

2.2 In cases in which a relevant offence appears to have been committed as part of a wider course or episode of criminality involving more serious offences, we liaise with the police and prosecution authorities to determine the best course of GPhC action in order to secure public and patient safety and to facilitate the prevention, investigation and detection of serious crime by the relevant authorities.

Sentencing

3.1 When acting as a prosecutor, the GPhC, has a duty to assist the court in relation to sentencing and in particular should, where possible, be in a position to provide the court will all relevant information relating to the facts of the case and the individual defendant's personal circumstances, including (but not limited to) the following:
- the defendant's age, background, present circumstances and previous convictions,
- all relevant aggravating and mitigating factors,

- any relevant statutory sentencing provisions and sentencing guidelines and/or guideline cases,
- ancillary orders, such as compensation,
- the views of any victim through the Victim Personal Statement, and
- the impact of the offending on a community.

3.2 This policy is reviewed at regular intervals.

Appendix 12

General Pharmaceutical Council Indicative Sanctions Guidance

The following extract is the Indicative Sanctions Guidance from the GPhC approved by the Fitness to Practise Committee on 13 May 2011.

Unless otherwise stated, references in the document below to Articles are to those contained in the Pharmacy Order 2010 and references to rules are to those in the General Pharmaceutical Council (Fitness to Practice and Disqualification etc.) Rules 2010. The Committee is the Fitness to Practise Committee.

Preamble

The Fitness to Practise Committee ('the Committee') is required under rule 5(d) of the GPhC (Statutory Committees and their Advisers) Rules 2010 to prepare, publish, review and amend from time to time its approach to decision making in the form of *Indicative Sanctions Guidance*. This guidance is also required to be published on the GPhC's website at www.pharmacyregulation.org.

Accordingly, the Committee has produced the following guidance, to which it refers when considering and determining the appropriate sanction in all cases that come before it under the Pharmacy Order 2010 ('the 2010 Order'). The guidance describes the options available to the Committee at the sanction stage of proceedings and sets out various factors that may make one sanction more or less appropriate in any particular case.

The Committee seeks to ensure that its procedures are open and transparent, compliant with human rights legislation and that they conform to models of good regulatory practice developed by other regulators and the Council for Healthcare Regulatory Excellence (CHRE).[1]

[1]Renamed in 2012, as the Professional Standards Authority for Health and Social Care

Agreement of undertakings

Registrants

Where the registrant admits that their fitness to practise is impaired the Committee may, if it thinks fit, dispose of the fitness to practise proceedings by agreeing undertakings with the registrant concerned.[2]

Where the Committee agrees undertakings with a registrant, the Registrar will record them in the Register.[3] Undertakings (that is, promises by the registrant to the Committee in respect of things they will or will not do in the future) may include restrictions on a registrant's practice or behaviour (but not amounting to a total suspension from practice) or the commitment to undergo supervision or retraining. Undertakings will only be appropriate where the Committee is satisfied that the registrant will comply with them, for example because s/he has shown genuine insight into his or her problems/deficiencies and potential for remediation.

Where the Registrar receives information that the registrant concerned has failed to comply with an undertaking or the registrant's health or performance has deteriorated or otherwise gives further cause for concern regarding their fitness to practise, the Registrar may refer the matter to the Committee for a review hearing.[4]

Corporate bodies

The Committee may, if it thinks fit, dispose of *disqualification proceedings* by agreeing appropriate undertakings with the 'section 80 party'[5] or by giving advice or a warning, instead of giving a direction under section 80 of the Medicines Act 1986.[6]

Where the Council becomes aware that a section 80 party has failed to comply with any undertakings agreed then the Committee must:[7]

- resume its consideration of the matter (the procedure at the hearing being for the Committee to determine); and
- reconsider the sanction imposed, and may instead issue a direction under section 80(1) or, as the case may be, section 80(4), of the Medicines Act 1968.

---

[2]Rule 26(1)
[3]Rule 5(5)
[4]Rule 45(3)
[5]Defined in rule 2 as 'an individual who, or a body corporate which, is subject to proceedings before the Committee in connection with the giving a direction under section 80(1) or (4) of the Medicines Act 1968 (or, where appropriate, their representatives)'
[6]Rule 26(2)
[7]Rule 32(18)

Sanctions available

The sanctions available to the Committee are as follows.[8]

(i) Registrants

a Where an allegation or matter is referred to the Committee and the Committee determines that the fitness to practise of the person in respect of whom the allegation is made is impaired, it may[9]:

- give a warning to the person concerned in connection with any matter arising out of, or related to, the allegation and give a direction that details of the warning be recorded in the Register,[10]
- give advice to any other person or other body involved in the investigation of the allegation on any issue arising out of, or related to, the allegation,
- impose conditions on the registrant's registration for a period not exceeding three years,
- suspend the registrant's registration for a period not exceeding twelve months,
- give a direction that the person concerned be removed from the Register.

If the person concerned is entered in more than one part of the Register, the Committee must make separate determinations in relation to each part of the Register. The Committee may impose one of the above sanctions in relation to only one part of the Register or different sanctions in relation to different parts of the Register.

Please note that the sanction of conditional registration and suspension may be subject to review, see below.

b If the Committee determines that the fitness to practise of the person concerned is not impaired the Committee[11] may give:

- a warning to the person concerned in connection with any matter that the Committee considers necessary or desirable taking into account the Committee's findings and give a direction that details of the warning be recorded in the Register),[12]

---

[8] Article 54
[9] Article 54(9)
[10] The Registrar must record any such warning in the Register in accordance with rule 5(5) of the GPhC (Registration Rules) 2010. Warnings remain on the Register for a period of 2 years. After 2 years the warning will cease to be published on the public facing register but shall form part of the registrant's previous history
[11] Article 54(5)
[12] Article 54(9)

- advice to the person concerned in connection with any such matter, and
- advice to any other person or other body involved in the investigation of the allegation on any issue arising out of, or related to, the allegation.

c Health cases; if the Committee determines that a person's fitness to practise is impaired solely by reason of adverse physical or mental health, it may not give a direction that the entry in the Register in respect of that person be removed.[13]

d Criminal proceedings, if, having considered the allegation, the Committee considers that the Council should consider exercising any of its powers to bring criminal proceedings under any enactment it must notify the Registrar accordingly.[14]

A person whose entry has been removed from one or more parts of the Register, in accordance with a direction by the Committee[15] may apply to the Registrar for restoration to the Register only after the expiration of five years from the date of the removal.[16]

(ii) Corporate bodies

In addition to the powers set out above the Committee also has the power,[17] under section 80 of the Medicines Act 1968, to deal with *'disqualification allegations'* made against a corporate body that carries on a retail pharmacy business. The Committee may direct that:

- a corporate body should be disqualified for the purposes of Part IV of the Medicines Act 1968;
- a 'representative' of the corporate body should be disqualified as being a representative for the purposes of Part IV of the Medicines Act 1968;
- the Registrar should remove from the Register of Premises some or all premises entered in that Register as being premises at which the corporate body carries on retail pharmacy; or
- the Registrar should remove from the Register of Premises some or all premises entered in that Register as being premises at which the corporate body carries on retail pharmacy, for a limited period.[18]

---

[13] Article 54(7)
[14] Article 54(9)
[15] Under Article 54(2)(c) or 54(3)(a)(i) or 54(3)(b)(iv)
[16] Article 57(1) and (2)
[17] Under section 80 Medicines Act 1968
[18] See s.80(3) of the Medicines Act 1968

Purpose of sanctions

In the context of fitness to practise proceedings before a professional regulatory body, the purpose of sanctions is threefold, namely:

- protection of the public
- the maintenance of public confidence in the profession
- the maintenance of proper standards of behaviour.

It matters not that a practitioner may already have paid a heavy price for his or her misconduct in prior criminal proceedings. In *Dey v General Medical Council* Privy Council Appeal No. 19 of 2001, it was said that the object of proceedings against a practitioner who had been convicted of a criminal offence was twofold. It was to protect members of the public who may use their services, and to maintain the high standards and reputation of the profession. The object was not to punish him or her a second time for the same offence. The important thing was not the facts themselves, but 'the perspective from which they are viewed'.

However, the fact that a sanction will have a punitive effect does not make such a sanction inappropriate where its purpose is one or more of the three listed above (see Laws LJ in *Rashid and Fatnani v GMC* [2007] 1 WLR 1460).

The Committee is entitled to give greater weight to the public interest and to the need to maintain public confidence in the profession than to the consequences of the appellant of the imposition of the penalty (see *Mairnovich v General Medical Council* [2002] UKPC 36).

General principles: fairness, proportionality and reasonableness

In considering the appropriate sanction the Committee has to exercise discretion and will have regard to the principles of fairness, proportionality and reasonableness. The Committee is required to weigh carefully the interests of the registrant against the public interest, which is made up of the three purposes set out above.

In making its decision, the Committee will have regard to the full range of sanctions available to it, and will seek to ensure that any sanction imposed is proportionate, fair and reasonable in all the circumstances of the case.

In determining the appropriate sanction to be imposed therefore the Committee may need to consider some or all of the following:

- any mitigating or aggravating features of the facts found proved;
- the personal circumstances of the registrant and any mitigation advanced;
- any testimonials and character references adduced in support of the registrant;

- any statement of views provided to the Committee by a patient or any individual affected by the conduct of the registrant; and
- any statement of views provided to the Committee by the Council.

In the context of proceedings before a professional regulatory body, the Privy Council said the following about the principle of proportionality: 'The application of the doctrine of proportionality is to ensure that a measure imposes no greater restriction upon a Convention right than is absolutely necessary to achieve its objectives' (*Chaudhury v General Medical Council* [2002] UKPC 41, at paragraph 21).

Thus, in order to ensure that proportionality is achieved, the Committee will usually consider sanctions in ascending order of severity.

Standards of Conduct, Ethics and Performance

In making its determination on the sanction, if any, to be imposed the Committee will have regard to the extent to which the registrant has breached the Standards of Conduct, Ethics and Performance published by the Council.

Aggravating features, general

The following aggravating factors may be present in a case before the Committee. Please note this is not an exhaustive list of all aggravating factors. Some of these factors may also be the actual subject of the allegation.

- Dishonesty
- Abuse of trust
- Taking advantage of a vulnerable person
- Sexual misconduct in relation to professional duties
- Misconduct/deficient professional performance sustained or repeated over a long period of time
- Previous convictions or findings of misconduct by the Committee or its predecessors, the Disciplinary Committee or the Statutory Committee of the previous regulatory body (RPSGB)
- Failure to comply with or disregard previous sanctions issued by the FtP Committee or previous committees of the RPSGB (whether statutory or non-statutory) charged with considering allegations of misconduct or impairment of fitness to practise, or warnings issued by any such Committee, etc.
- Failure to co-operate/comply with an assessment of professional performance
- Failure to co-operate with an investigation into an allegation(s)
- Breach of confidentiality
- Potential harm

- No/minimal steps taken to prevent actual harm
- Actions premeditated
- Abuse of position or dishonesty in the context of drug abuse
- Blatant disregard for the system of registration
- Blatant disregard for the Standards of Conduct, Ethics and Performance published by the Council or previously by the RPSGB
- Lack of insight
- Concealment of wrongdoing
- Failure to respond to complaint by patient
- Breach of any written undertaking(s) previously given to a fitness to practise committee or a statutory committee of the RPSGB
- Disregard of oral/written advice by a Professional Standards Inspector employed by the Council (or previously by the RPSGB)
- Misconduct/deficient professional performance committed by person in charge on pharmacy premises
- Conduct prior to and in the course of the hearing
- Breaches of statutory requirements[19] and
- Previous finding of impairment by the Committee and its predecessors.

Mitigating features, general

Note: The following list is illustrative but it is not an exhaustive list of all mitigating factors that the Committee may take into account.

- Repayment of any misappropriated funds
- No prior disciplinary history
- Ill health at the time of the misconduct/deficient professional performance
- Single isolated incident in a previous unblemished career
- Genuine insight (full/partial) into misconduct/deficient professional performance/ill health
- Open and frank admissions at an early stage, demonstrating insight
- No actual or potential harm to patients or the public
- Steps taken to prevent actual harm
- Genuine apology given to patient/genuine expression of remorse to Committee
- Steps taken to remedy, ameliorate or prevent recurrence of the misconduct or acts resulting in impairment and
- Lack of relevant support or training.

[19]The Committee will also be aware that the following is stated in *Balmoody v UKCC for Nurses, Midwives and Health Visitors* [1998] EWHC 521 that 'where a professional person had infringed important statutory requirements in the course of duties of a senior or supervisory kind so as to attract a criminal sanction, a professional body or court was bound to view those infringements with grave concern'.

Aggravating features, health

The following aggravating features may be present in a health related case before the Committee. The following is not an exhaustive list.

- Evidence of actual or potential danger to patients or to the public
- Evidence of actual or potential self-harm
- Lack of insight
- Episodic or recurrent condition
- Ill health or behaviour sustained over a long period of time
- Failure to seek help/treatment/support
- Failure to comply with conditions
- Failure to provide/comply with undertakings
- Failure to comply with/disregard of written/oral advice given by a Professional Standards Inspector employed by the Council (or formerly the RPSGB)
- Failure to comply with drug regime/treatment regime/medical supervision/support service recommendation
- Failure to co-operate with testing/investigations/medical assessment
- Inappropriate behaviour exhibited by a registrant in charge on pharmacy premises
- Previous findings of impairment by the Committee and its predecessors.

Mitigating features, health

The following mitigating features may be present in a health related case before the Committee. Please note the table [sic] is not an exhaustive list of all mitigating factors that may be present.

- Evidence of insight into ill-health
- Self reporting/full admission and full co-operation at and from an early stage
- No actual or potential harm to patients or public
- Compliance with medication/treatment range/support service recommendations
- Compliance with undertakings or conditions relating to health
- Evidence of voluntary attendance at addiction support services
- Evidence of regular attendance at medical supervisor
- Evidence of lengthy periods of abstinence from addictive substances.

Cases where a warning may be appropriate

Note: the following is not an exhaustive list of factors.

- No continued risk to patients or public

- Evidence of genuine insight
- Minor breaches of Standards of Conduct, Ethics and Performance published by the Council
- *Evidence of appropriate medical supervision*
- *Attendance at addiction support services*
- *Evidence of lengthy periods of abstinence from addictive substances.*

The factors italicised are usually only applicable in health cases.

Cases where conditions may be appropriate

Note: the following is not an exhaustive list of factors.

- Conditions will protect the public during the period they are in force
- Appropriate, real and verifiable conditions can be formulated
- Evidence that the registrant has insight and is likely to comply with conditions imposed
- Identifiable areas of registrant's practice in need of assessment or re-training
- Evidence of a minor breach or non-compliance with previous undertakings given
- Disregard of previous warnings
- Conduct or deficient professional performance is capable of being remedied and allowing the practitioner to continue to practise would not pose any risk to the public
- Practitioner would benefit from closer monitoring or medical supervision.

Cases where suspension from the Register may be appropriate

Note: the following list is not exhaustive.

- No conditions can adequately be framed to protect the public/conditions would be unworkable in practice
- Evidence of a serious breach or non-compliance with previous undertakings or conditions
- Deficient performance where there is a risk to patient safety if suspension not put in place – but where there is evidence of potential for remedy through retraining
- Evidence of disposition towards non-compliance
- Lack of sufficient insight on the part of the registrant
- Professionals performance is such as to call into question the continued ability of the registrant to practise safely but rehabilitation is considered possible

- Public confidence in the profession demands no lesser sanction
- Message needs to be sent to profession and public that conduct is unacceptable and unbefitting of person registered with the Council
- Conduct falls short of being fundamentally incompatible with continued registration.

Cases where removal from the Register may be appropriate

Note: the following is not an exhaustive list of factors.

- Continuing risk to patients or members of the public
- Serious potential harm
- Lack of insight on the part of the registrant
- Professional performance is such as to call into question the continued ability of the registrant to practise safely
- Dishonesty
- Violent or sexual misconduct
- Behaviour is fundamentally incompatible with registration
- Public confidence in the profession demands no lesser sanction
- Serious departure from/reckless disregard of the Standards of Conduct, Ethics and Performance published by the Council (or previously the RPSGB).

Reasons

The Committee will consider and announce its decision as to the appropriate course of action to be taken in respect of the registrant or corporate body and give its reasons for that decision.

The reasons will normally set out the matters that the Committee took into account when deciding whether or not to impose a sanction, and if so, what sanction to impose. The reasons will explain why the decision taken by the Committee is considered to be fair, proportionate and reasonable in all the circumstances of the case.

The Committee's reasons should also explain why the sanction chosen will protect the public (see *CHRE v GDC (Marshall)* [2006] EWHC 1870 (Admin)).

The Committee's reasons should be focused to the particulars in the allegation themselves and the proper ambit of the charges (see *Chauhan v GMC* [2010] EWHC 2093 (Admin)).

Interim Measures, Article 60 Pharmacy Order 2010

The power to impose 'interim measures' applies where the Committee gives a direction under Article 54 to remove a registrant's entry from one or more parts of the Register; or gives a direction for suspension.

If the Committee is satisfied that to do so is necessary for the protection of members of the public or is otherwise in the public interest or in the interests of the registrant it may order that the entry of the registrant who is the subject of the direction in the part or parts of the Register to which the direction relates be suspended forthwith, pending the coming into force of the direction.

Furthermore, if the Committee has given a direction for conditional registration (under Article 54) and the Committee is satisfied that to do so is necessary for the protection of members of the public or is otherwise in the public interest or in the interests of the registrant, it may order that the entry of the registrant who is the subject of the direction in the part or parts of the Register to which the direction relates, be conditional upon that registrant complying, pending the coming into force of the direction, with such requirements specified in the order as the Committee thinks fit to impose.

The effect of this is that interim measures will be in force during the period allowed for the bringing of an appeal and if an appeal is lodged, the interim measures remain in force until the appeal is finally disposed of.

Before making any such interim measures under Article 60, the Committee will invite representations from the parties before considering and announcing whether it is to impose such measures, together with its reasons for that decision.

A registrant who is aggrieved by a decision of the Committee to make an order under Article 60 may appeal against that decision to the relevant court.

Review of conditions/suspension

Review of suspension

Where the Committee has given a direction under Article 54 to suspend a registrant then, following a review, it may if it thinks fit give a direction under Article 54(3)(a) that:

- the entry be removed from the Register;
- the suspension of the entry be extended for such further period not exceeding 12 months as may be specified in the direction, starting from the time when the period of suspension would otherwise expire;
- the entry be suspended indefinitely, if the suspension has already been in force throughout a period of at least two years;[20]
- in the case of an indefinite suspension, the suspension be terminated; or
- on expiry or termination of the period of suspension (including a period of suspension that was expressed to be indefinite), the entry be conditional

[20]This direction must be reviewed if requested by the person concerned and at least two years have elapsed since the direction took effect or was reviewed: Article 54 (4)

upon that person complying, during such period not exceeding 3 years as may be specified in the direction, with such requirements specified in the direction as the Committee thinks fit to impose for the protection of the public or otherwise in the public interest or in the interests of the person concerned.

In some cases it may be self-evident that, following a short period of suspension, there will be no value in a review hearing. In most cases, however, where a period of suspension is imposed the Committee will need to be reassured that the registrant is fit to resume practice either unrestricted or with conditions or further conditions.

The Committee will also need to satisfy itself that the registrant has fully appreciated the seriousness of the relevant breach(es), has not committed any further breaches of the Council's Standards of Conduct, Ethics and Performance, has maintained his or her skills and knowledge up to date and that the public will not be placed at risk by resumption of practice or by the imposition of conditional registration.

Review of conditions

Where the entry in the Register of the person concerned is conditional upon that person complying with requirements specified in a direction given under Article 54, the Committee may give a direction under Article 54(3)(b) that:

- the period specified in the direction for complying with the requirements be extended for such further period not exceeding 3 years as may be specified in the direction, starting from the time when the earlier period would otherwise expire;
- the requirements be added to, removed or otherwise varied in such manner as may be specified in the direction;
- the entry instead be suspended (for example, where that person has failed, whether wholly or partly, to comply with the requirements), for such period not exceeding 12 months as may be specified in the direction; or
- the entry be removed from the Register, (for example, where that person has failed, whether wholly or partly, to comply with the requirements)

In most cases where conditions have been imposed, the Committee will need to be reassured that the registrant is fit to resume practice either unrestricted or with a variation of conditions or further conditions.

However, the Committee may request the Council to monitor any conditions imposed on registration. This may avoid the need for the Committee to ask for an early review of the case. Where monitoring has occurred, a review hearing should take place if there are any failures to adhere to the conditions imposed by the Committee.

Review hearings, general

Review hearings[21] should ordinarily take place towards the end of the relevant period unless there is good reason for the Committee to review the matter earlier, for example if the Council has evidence that the registrant has practised while suspended or has failed to comply with conditions imposed upon his practice etc.

Where, before a review hearing, the Council becomes aware of new evidence which it wishes to bring to the attention of the Committee,[22] for example evidence of a failure to comply with conditions etc.:

a   the Council may request case management directions; and
b   the chair may direct that the new evidence be considered at the review hearing, and that the fitness to practise rules are to apply as modified to take into account the particular circumstances of the case.

Entry on the Sex Offenders Register or the barred lists

Sexual misconduct seriously undermines public trust in the profession. The misconduct is particularly serious where there is an abuse of the special position of trust that a registrant occupies, or where the registrant has been required to register as a sex offender. The risk to the public is important. In such cases removal from the Register has therefore been judged the appropriate sanction. In *Dr Haikel v GMC* (Privy Council Appeal No. 69 of 2001) their Lordships stated the following:

> The public, and in particular female patients, must have confidence in the medical profession whatever their state of health might be. The conduct as found proved against Dr Haikel undoubtedly undermines such confidence and a severe sanction was inevitable. Their Lordships are satisfied that erasure was neither unreasonable, excessive nor disproportionate but necessary in the public interest.

The Committee is firmly of the view that no registrant that is registered on the Sex Offenders Register or has been included in a barred list (within the meaning of the Safeguarding Vulnerable Groups Act 2006 or the Safeguarding Vulnerable Groups (Northern Ireland) Order 2007) or the Children's List or the Adult's List (within the meaning of the Protection of Vulnerable Groups (Scotland) Act 2007) should have unrestricted registration.

The Committee may also need to consider whether registrants that are registered as sex offenders should be required to undergo an assessment, for example by a clinical psychologist, to assess the potential risk to patients before they may be permitted to resume any form of practice.

---

[21] See Rule 34 for the procedure to be followed at a review meeting
[22] Rule 30

Furthermore, when the Committee is dealing with a case where the registrant has completed the prescribed period of registration (which is dependent on the nature and gravity of the offence) and is no longer required to register as a sex offender the Committee will take into account:

- the seriousness of the original offence;
- evidence about a registrant's response to any treatment programme that s/he has undertaken;
- any insight shown by the registrant;
- the likelihood of the registrant re-offending if s/he was allowed to resume unrestricted practice; and
- the possible damage to the public's trust in the profession if the registrant was allowed to resume unrestricted practice etc.

Each case will be carefully considered on its merits and decisions taken in the light of the particular circumstances of the case.

Where the Committee has any doubt about whether a registrant who is no longer required to register as a sex offender should resume unrestricted practice, the registrant will not be granted unrestricted registration.

Index

Note: Page references in axx refer to appendices; bxx refer to boxes; fxx refer to Figures; and those in txx refer to Tables